A MIGHTY STRIVING

Maulana Muhammad Ali declared:

"… it is my firm conviction, which I acquired from that holy man (Hazrat Mirza Ghulam Ahmad) from whose company I benefited for a long time, that if we show the world the real picture of the truth of Islam, of the Holy Prophet Muhammad, and of the Quran, then undoubtedly people will bow their heads before it." — p. 372

"All of us must cherish but one desire, and only this must fill our hearts when we bow before God: that may the Divine religion, the Quran and Muhammad the Messenger of Allah be triumphant … Ask only of this, yearn only for this, shed tears only for this, seek that which has been destined to happen." — p. 318

A Mighty Striving

Biography of

Maulana Muhammad Ali

Renowned author, scholar and missionary of Islam
First Head of the Lahore Ahmadiyya Movement

Second Edition, Revised and Enlarged

From the Urdu book *Mujahid-i Kabir* by

Muhammad Ahmad

Mumtaz Ahmad Faruqui

Translated into English by

Mrs. Akhtar Jabeen Aziz

Revised and edited by

Dr. Zahid Aziz

Ahmadiyya Anjuman Lahore Publications, U.K.
2021

A LAHORE AHMADIYYA PUBLICATION

Original Urdu book first published, 1962
English Translation: First edition, 2004

Second edition (online only), revised and enlarged, 2011
Second edition, with minor revisions, 2020

Faruqui-Saleema Trust Printing, September 2021

Ahmadiyya Anjuman Lahore Publications, U.K.
15 Stanley Avenue, Wembley, U.K., HA0 4JQ

Available on the website www.ahmadiyya.org at the link:
www.ahmadiyya.org/bookspdf/muj-kabir-uk-online.pdf

This book has been published with the support of the

Faruqui-Salima Trust

Imbued with the love of the Holy Quran and community welfare, the late Mr Nasir Ahmad Faruqui (d. 1991, Lahore) is well-known to members of the Lahore Ahmadiyya *Jama'at* for his inspirational talks (*dars*) on the Quran conducted at home and the *Jama'at* centres. The dedication of his wife Begum Salima Faruqui (d. 2005) was no less and they both chose to leave behind a legacy which would continue to support the endeavours of the *Jama'at* to spread the light of Islam to the furthest corners of the world.

With this goal in mind, Mr Faruqui bequeathed his entire immovable property to found the Faruqui-Salima Trust. He placed the Trust under control of the Ahmadiyya Anjuman Lahore so that adequate funds are readily available for their charitable and religious works, particularly the printing and publishing of the Holy Quran and other religious books. May Almighty Allah recompense them for this noble deed and grant them an elevated place in heaven — *Aameen!*

This book is for Free Distribution. Not for Sale.

ISBN: 978-1-906109-12-7

Preface to the First Edition

Mujahid-i Kabir, the biography of Maulana Muhammad Ali, was written in Urdu by his son Muhammad Ahmad, with Mumtaz Ahmad Faruqui as co-author,[1] and published in 1962. It was soon recognised as an authoritative book not only on the life of the Maulana but also on the broad history of the Ahmadiyya Anjuman Isha'at Islam Lahore from 1914 to 1951 and the earlier history of the relationship between this body's founding stalwarts and the Founder of the Ahmadiyya Movement, Hazrat Mirza Ghulam Ahmad. It is also an invaluable book in laying out the mission and goal of the Lahore Ahmadiyya organisation and showing that it is true to the teachings of Hazrat Mirza both in its beliefs and its work. This book removes many misconceptions about Maulana Muhammad Ali and the Lahore Ahmadiyya body, particularly in connection with the reasons for the Split in 1914.

An abridged English translation of this book by Mumtaz Ahmad Faruqui, shortened to about one-fifth of the original, was published in 1966 under the title *Muhammad Ali, The Great Missionary of Islam.* In the Foreword it is stated that the condensed translation should satisfy the needs of the English-reading public abroad as the details in the Urdu account are only of local interest in Pakistan. However, circumstances have changed since that time in two respects: the name of Maulana Muhammad Ali has become more widespread due to the increasing distribution of his writings throughout the world, and there are now many more members of the Lahore Ahmadiyya community itself living in countries where the first language is not Urdu. Therefore an English translation of the whole book had become an urgent necessity.

---

1. For more about the authors, see Appendix 2 in this translation, p. 531.

i

The work of translation was undertaken by Mrs. Akhtar Aziz, M.A., M.Ed., who retired as a teacher of English in U.K. schools after 28 years of service, following an earlier teaching service of 13 years in Pakistan where she rose to Headmistress. She also obtained a certificate from the University of Texas at Austin, U.S.A., in teaching English as a Second Language. She has also been an experienced translator between English and Urdu/Punjabi for various bodies in the U.K. legal and justice system, receiving a Police award for her work. Besides these qualifications, Mrs. Aziz felt a personal, poignant association with the book *Mujahid-i Kabir* as she had observed and lived close to many of the leading figures featuring in this biography including Maulana Muhammad Ali. For about the first thirty years of her life, till the mid-1950s, she lived in the Muslim Town suburb of Lahore in the house of her father, Maulana Abdul Haq Vidyarthi, in close proximity to other leading Ahmadis including Maulana Muhammad Ali himself. She had also spent a summer in Dalhousie in 1939 with the Lahore Ahmadiyya members who used to repair there from the Punjab for the hot season as recounted in this book.

After Mrs. Aziz, who is my mother, had written out the entire translation by hand, painstakingly and meticulously, and the text had been typed into computer form by volunteers of the Lahore Ahmadiyya community, it fell to me to check and revise it and prepare it for final publication. The chief aspects of the work which I then carried out are listed below.

1. The translation was carefully compared with the original Urdu text and revised as necessary. It was formatted for printing in the shape and design of this book.
2. While going through the Urdu text, any details that seemed inaccurate, for example dates of events, were checked in external sources and corrected when required.
3. At some points, additional relevant material was inserted from external, original sources. In all such places in this translation, the sources of the additions are indicated in footnotes. Major examples of extra material are the reviews at the end of chapter 3.3, the obituaries at the end of chapter 3.8, and various additions within Part 4.

4. In the original book, several quotations and reviews are reproduced in Urdu translation that were originally in English. In almost every such case I succeeded in tracing the original English text, and that has been reproduced along with a footnote to indicate this.

5. The list of writings of Maulana Muhammad Ali given at the end of the Urdu book was checked thoroughly. Some omissions and minor inaccuracies in dates of publication and titles have been rectified. See Appendix 1.

6. It was considered indispensable to add brief information about the authors of *Mujahid-i Kabir*. This has been done in the form of Appendix 2.

7. *Mujahid-i Kabir* had no index. The English translation would have suffered from a serious handicap as a reference book if an index had not been provided. Despite this task being time-consuming, laborious and complex, I compiled an index which I hope will be found useful. It was difficult to strike the right balance between making the index too long and detailed, or leaving it inadequate.

The Urdu book contains several photographs, but unfortunately their reproduction quality is not sufficiently good to reprint from them. My sustained efforts to locate the original photographs through various contacts have so far not been successful. Similarly, issues of *The Light* and *Paigham Sulh* of the later years of Maulana Muhammad Ali's life contain some photographs, but again these cannot be reprinted from those magazines to an acceptable quality, and the originals cannot be found. Our efforts will be continued, and if successful the photographs will be included in a future edition of this translation. We regret that this visual treasure could not be published at this stage.

The title of the Urdu book, *Mujahid-i Kabir,* meaning 'The Great *Mujahid*' or the great one in striving in the way of God, is based on the verse of the Quran: "and strive against them a mighty striving (*jihad kabir*) with it",[2] where the words "with it" mean

2. Holy Quran, 25:52.

with the Quran. This is a command to every Muslim to undertake a great struggle, or great *jihad,* to spread the teachings of the Quran in the world by word and pen. As such a striving was at the heart of the work of Maulana Muhammad Ali, his Urdu biography was appropriately titled after this verse. In English we may represent the same title as *A Mighty Striving.*

Zahid Aziz, Dr.
October 2004

Preface to the Second Edition

In this second edition of *A Mighty Striving,* I have carefully checked through the book and made many revisions, corrections and additions as follows.

References to external sources, which are predominantly to the magazine *Paigham Sulh,* have been meticulously compared with the original publications. As a result, some minor inaccuracies that were found in dates of events and in dates of the issues of *Paigham Sulh,* as given in *Mujahid-i Kabir*, have been corrected. By consulting the original sources referred to by *Mujahid-i Kabir*, translations of extracts quoted in this book have been made more precise, where necessary. Some quotations were without reference to source, or without a full reference. I have been able to provide the full reference in all but three such cases.

Small, useful additions have been made within the body of the book as could be incorporated without disturbing the page divisions significantly. Some interesting additional material requiring more space has been compiled in the form of a Supplement placed after the Appendices. Photographs, and images of some original handwritings, have also been added in this edition.

Zahid Aziz, Dr.
November 2011

Contents

List of Photographs and Images

The front cover of this book shows a photograph of the *Kalima* on
the face of the mosque at Ahmadiyya Buildings, Lahore, where the
Ahmadiyya Anjuman Isha'at Islam Lahore was founded in 1914.

Maulana Muhammad Ali (1874–1951)

Part 1

The First Twenty-Five Years

From birth to May 1899

Family history

During the period of Moghul rule, a Hindu by the name of Hari Chand, who belonged to the *Janjū'a Rājpūt* community, migrated from Jhelum district and, arriving in the well-populated and fertile area of Doaba Bast Jalandhar, he settled in Kharla Kingra, a place two miles from Jalandhar city. As most of the population in that area were Muslims, Hari Chand too embraced Islam. In Kharla Kingra and surrounding places most of the inhabitants belonged to the *Arā'īn* ethnic community, so the descendants of Hari Chand also began to be counted amongst the *Arā'īn* people. Hari Chand was the progenitor of the family whose tree is given in the official records of Jalandhar District for 1860 as shown on top of the following page.

Doaba Bast Jalandhar and in particular Jalandhar District was very densely populated, and the farmers due to their small holdings were finding it difficult to make a living. Being industrious and hardworking, whenever they saw better economic opportunities elsewhere they did not allow love of the homeland to hold them back. So in the 19th century many of them emigrated to foreign lands. Facing the same dilemma and being mindful of good cultivation prospects, a man of this family by the name of

1

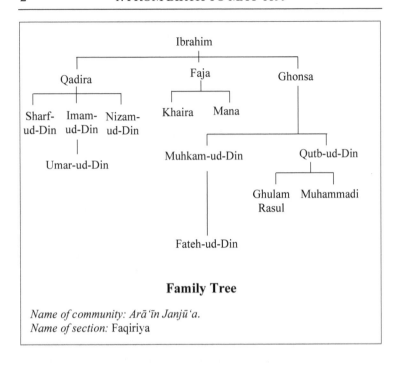

Family Tree

Name of community: Arā'īn Janjū'a.
Name of section: Faqiriya

Mian Muhkam-ud-Din and his brother Mian Qutb-ud-Din migrated from Kharla Kingra to the village of Murar in the state of
Kapurthala. At the time the chief minister of Kapurthala was a
Muslim who wanted to settle Muslims in the state. So he offered
large tracts of agricultural land to Muslims and called hard-
working farmers from the adjacent Jalandhar area to populate
untilled lands.

Around 1860 Mian Muhkam-ud-Din moved to Murar, and
Maharaja Nihal Singh of Kapurthala bestowed upon him all the
lands of the village. To populate that vast area, Mian Muhkam-ud-
Din brought his relatives and some other people of the neighbouring village to settle there. Such was his generosity that he
gave them equal shares in the lands that he received.

At that time, his only son Hafiz Fateh-ud-Din was about 30 to
35 years of age and well known in the area for his good morals,
honesty and integrity. He was made headman of the village by the

state government. Being just and fair-minded he was often asked to mediate in major disputes in the state, and the authorities used to appoint him to arbitrate in old, long-standing cases. His decisions were accepted because they were based on justice. Hafiz Fateh-ud-Din had not only committed the Holy Quran to memory, but he was also highly learned in Persian. So great was his love for the Holy Quran that he used to recite it during his daily activities. He had a mosque built next to his house where he led the prayers and children from the village were taught the Holy Quran.

Birth and early education

Hafiz Fateh-ud-Din had six sons and a daughter, as follows in order:

Khair-ud-Din
Amir-ud-Din
Aziz Bakhsh
Nabi Bakhsh
Muhammad Ali
Imam Begum
Ahmad Ali.

Muhammad Ali was the fifth son in order of birth and was born in December 1874.

There was no school in Murar, so for the purpose of elementary education Hafiz Fateh-ud-Din sent Maulvi Aziz Bakhsh, at the age of six or seven, to the Anglo-Vernacular school in the nearby town of Diyalpur. Muhammad Ali, who was only three and a half years old at that time, started to accompany his brother to school out of his own interest. The school teacher, Rahmatullah, was very impressed by the enthusiasm of such a young child who was walking two miles with his brother to come to school. Being the younger one, the teacher used to call him lovingly as "assistant sahib" and would teach him with the same affection. When the annual examination came, Muhammad Ali passed it too along with his older brother. After that both of them continued to study together for five years of primary education in the same class in this school.

In 1883, Hafiz Fateh-ud-Din sent both the brothers to Randhir High School, Kapurthala. At that time Maulana Muhammad Ali was nearly nine. Their father arranged for them to stay in Kapurthala in a room in the house of Nathoo Mal the *Patwari* (village registrar). For cooking their food, in the beginning he appointed a man by the name of Badr-ud-Din (whose younger brother Baba Nur-ud-Din was later on in Maulana Muhammad Ali's service for a long time). Later on, Maulvi Aziz Bakhsh mostly used to cook himself. He loved his younger brother very much and took care of all his needs.

Every Saturday evening Hafiz Fateh-ud-Din would ride on his horse the twenty miles from Murar to Kapurthala and fetch his children home on horseback; he would take them back similarly on Sunday evening. All along the way he would recite the Holy Quran and pray for the moral and material welfare of the children. As a result of his piety and devoutness, frequent recitation of the Holy Quran and prayers, Almighty God not only made all his children righteous and servants of the faith but chose one of them, Muhammad Ali, specially to serve Islam.

In the Kapurthala school both the brothers were noted for their good character and ability. They said the five daily prayers in the mosque regularly and carried on their studies quietly. In school sports, Maulana Muhammad Ali was interested in cricket and played it sometimes, but abstained from too much frivolous activity. In 1890 both brothers passed their matriculation examination. At school their good character and conduct was exemplary and their teachers had very high regard for them.

Education and employment in Lahore
After his sons had passed matriculation, Hafiz Fateh-ud-Din decided to send them for higher education. Despite his limited financial means he had them admitted in Government College Lahore, one of the best institutions not only in the Punjab but the whole of India. Consequently, they took up residence in Lahore, where they spent their student days leading a very simple, frugal life, mostly cooking their own meals. In 1892 both brothers passed the F.A. examination. For this examination Maulana Muhammad Ali took Arabic as an optional subject, but as he was very good in

mathematics he chose mathematics for his B.A. and passed this examination in 1894, standing first in the University. Once when he needed a reference from one of his professors, the professor wrote only this: "Muhammad Ali is the best mathematician of our college".

In 1894, after passing his B.A. examination, Maulvi Aziz Bakhsh got admission in the Central (Teacher) Training College, Lahore, where he passed his Senior Anglo-Vernacular examination and in 1897 he entered government service. However, Maulana Muhammad Ali, after passing B.A., continued his education in Government College Lahore, studying English for his M.A. At the same time he took a job in Islamia College Lahore as professor of mathematics. He taught mathematics in Islamia College for three years. In 1896 he passed his M.A. in English, being one of only five students who passed the examination out of a class of twenty-three.

After passing his B.A. when Maulana Muhammad Ali started teaching he was only nineteen. Chaudhry Muhammad Ismail (a retired Extra Assistant Commissioner) who himself was a student in Islamia College at that time said that most of Muhammad Ali's students were older than their teacher, and that his ability, good character and righteousness were so well established that the best compliment for any other student was that he was another Muhammad Ali. Many students of that era, who later on in life became famous and renowned in the fields of politics, law or business in the Punjab, could vouch for that. Chaudhry Sir Shahab-ud-Din, who was later Speaker of the Punjab Assembly for a long time, lived in the same house with Maulana Muhammad Ali. Khwaja Kamal-ud-Din also taught in Islamia College in those days and it was here that the two of them first met.

During his college days Maulana Muhammad Ali did not take part in any extra-curricular literary activities. He never wrote an article nor did he take part in debates or speeches. In sport he played soccer.

In 1896 after passing his M.A., while continuing to teach in Islamia College, he got admission in LL.B. (law) classes. In the three University examinations in law he secured second, first and third positions. In 1897 he left employment in Islamia College and took a job in Oriental College, Lahore, which in those days was outside Taxali Gate, and worked there as a professor of mathematics till May 1899.

Meeting Hazrat Mirza Ghulam Ahmad of Qadian

From the time when the two brothers were studying in Kapurthala they had heard the name of Mirza Ghulam Ahmad of Qadian. In 1890, after passing the entrance examination in Kapurthala, when they got admission in Government College Lahore, they came to learn about the claim of Hazrat Mirza sahib through their former fellow student Munshi Abdul Aziz, known as *Bhai Jan* (brother), who gave them a copy of *Izala Auham* by Hazrat Mirza sahib. After reading this book they became convinced of the truth of the Promised Messiah. Then in January 1892 when Hazrat Mirza sahib came to Lahore both brothers went to see him. Maulvi Aziz Bakhsh describes the occasion as follows:

> "We arrived in the field of debate.[1] There was a huge crowd and in the middle of it the Maulvis (religious leaders) were sitting with piles of books. By chance I looked towards the people who were standing in the veranda on one side and caught sight of a man whose face was radiant with inner light and his appearance dignified. He was wearing a long robe, and standing with his eyes cast down. It appeared as if he was a saint absorbed in contemplation whose sight was not towards this world. Immediately the thought came to my mind that if he was Mirza sahib who has claimed to be the Promised Messiah then he is really true because this cannot be the face of an imposter. I asked one of the people standing near me to tell me which one was Mirza sahib. He and his friends pointed towards the man with the radiant face. At that moment I felt such exhilaration in my heart that I cannot describe it."
>
> (*Paigham Sulh,* 7 November 1933)

---

1. This debate was with Maulvi Abdul Hakim of Kalanur. During this stay of Hazrat Mirza sahib in Lahore, Mirza Yaqub Baig, who was a medical student at the time, and his younger brother Mirza Ayub Baig took the *bai'at*.

In May 1893 when the two brothers were still doing their B.A. in Government College, a major debate took place between Hazrat Mirza sahib and Christians in Amritsar. The leader of the Christian side was Deputy Abdullah Atham. Full details of the debate are given in Hazrat Mirza sahib's book *Jang Muqaddas*. Reports of this debate were issued daily and the brothers would get them by post to read. Then from 1894 till 1897 when Maulana Muhammad Ali was still a professor in Islamia College Lahore, Khwaja Kamal-ud-Din was also teaching there and they used to discuss about Hazrat Mirza sahib and his claim. The Khwaja was already an Ahmadi. Maulana Muhammad Ali also wrote some articles in newspapers in support of Hazrat Mirza sahib; these were his first writings. However, he still had not taken the pledge (*bai'at*). At last in 1897 he went with Khwaja Kamal-ud-Din to Qadian for the first time and took the pledge of Hazrat Mirza sahib. Maulana Muhammad Ali has himself described in detail his acceptance of Ahmadiyyat as follows:

"I first came to know about the Promised Messiah from my dear friend and fellow student Munshi Abdul Aziz of Dehli. My elder brother and I were studying in Randhir College, Kapurthala, and this dear friend was also studying there, whom we used to call *Bhai Jan* (brother) out of affection.

"In 1890, after passing the entrance examination, both of us brothers joined Government College, Lahore, and it was here that we learnt about the Promised Messiah's claim. During the summer break of 1891 when we came home, we went to Kapurthala to see Bhai Jan and he gave us the book *Izala Auham* that had been published recently. On the way back we met a former teacher of ours, the late Maulvi Rahmatullah, who, seeing the book in our hands, showed much disapproval, saying that one can became *kafir* (unbeliever) by reading it. We explained that there was no harm in reading it and if we found in it anything against Islam we would not accept it.

"As soon as we got home, both of us and our father, the late Hafiz Fateh-ud-Din, read the book and we all agreed that whatever was written in it, was true: Jesus was dead and Hazrat Mirza sahib was right in his claim.

"Our late father had not only committed the Holy Quran to memory but had also mastered other Islamic books. So religious matters were always under discussion in our family. It was due to our father's influence that from an early age we became so zealous about prayers that during our school days in Kapurthala we said the five prayers regularly in congregation in the mosque.

"Our village Murar was not very far from Qadian, perhaps twenty miles, and Hazrat Mirza sahib was well known in these areas as a most holy man. People knew that in Qadian there was a very saintly man whose prayers were accepted by God and who was without equal in piety, worship and religious knowledge. My father knew all that, and it was the renown of the good name of Hazrat Mirza sahib that was the first reason in attracting us to accept him.

"Today the many people who are indifferent towards Ahmadiyyat are perhaps under the impression that before accepting it you have to engage in many complicated discussions and study many intricate religious issues, but the three of us at least never needed to go through that. The first deciding point for us was his righteous and blameless life. The Holy Quran itself has offered the same proof to establish the Holy Prophet Muhammad's truth: "I have lived among you a lifetime before this. Do you not then understand? " (10:16). When Allah wants to appoint someone to a high position, that is how the ground is prepared: first the hearts are captured by his saintliness, high moral character, truthfulness and service of humanity.

"The scholastic matters were not difficult either. Our father was well versed in religion, and though we two brothers were only students it was not difficult to understand the simple fact that the Holy Quran proves the death of Jesus. This belief is the foundation stone of accepting Ahmadiyyat. Even an illiterate person who is willing to accept the verdict of the Holy Quran can understand it without difficulty.

"The second stage of accepting Ahmadiyyat is the issue of the descent of Jesus. Even for this you do not need much knowledge. Everyone knows that the advent of the Messiah in the Muslim

Umma was foretold by the Holy Prophet Muhammad, and there are the most reliable Hadith reports speaking of this.

"If the foundation stone has been laid and you have accepted Jesus' death then the next step is also very easy. Who is this Messiah that had been mentioned in the Hadith reports? After admitting the death of Jesus, one of two views must be accepted: either that the Promised Messiah must be a *mujaddid* (Reformer) of this *Umma* or that all those Hadith reports are untrue. The second view cannot be accepted by any Muslim who has reverence for the Holy Prophet's Hadith because in that case the entire mass of Hadith reports will have to be rejected. So there is no choice but to accept the first view, that a *mujaddid* of this *Umma* will fulfil the prophecies of the descent of the Messiah.

"In resolving this issue some other points also come to mind. All Muslims agree that the Holy Prophet Muhammad was the Last Prophet. The Quran makes it clear that there will not be any prophet after him. A prophet can only come if there remains some work of prophethood to accomplish. If the doctrine of the finality of prophethood is true then no prophet can now come. It makes no difference whether he was raised to prophethood before the Holy Prophet or after him. After the Holy Prophet Muhammad the coming of any prophet in the world is prohibited, and after him only *mujaddids* are needed.

"The other point is that authentic Hadith reports give different physical descriptions of what Jesus and the coming Messiah look like. If the same Jesus was the coming Messiah, how could the physical appearance be different?

"The third question is that if it is true that Jesus has died and it is also true that the Promised Messiah must be a *mujaddid* of this *Umma,* then is Hazrat Mirza Ghulam Ahmad of Qadian that Messiah or do we wait for someone else? This step was also very clear because his claim to be *mujaddid* had been widely established. There was no one who could doubt his truthfulness and righteousness. A man who had never made a fabrication about a human being, could not make a fabrication about God, let alone that a *mujaddid* could do such a thing. Moreover, he was the man to whom such a great truth was disclosed, to whom Allah told the secret which had not been made known to other people for such a long time, and whom Allah had informed of the real meaning of the Holy Prophet Muhammad's prophecies. Who could be more deserving of fulfilling these prophecies than him? The truth is that when the time comes for the fulfilment of a prophecy it is only then that people are informed about its real meaning.

"I have mentioned these broad, basic points that helped my father, my brother and I to take our decision. These points were so clear that after studying *Izala Auham* all three of us reached the same decision simultaneously and were convinced of the truthfulness of the Promised Messiah's claim. However, none of us at that time entered into the pledge of Hazrat Mirza sahib. When in 1892 the Promised Messiah came to Lahore where he had a debate with Maulvi Abdul Hakim — which ended in his announcement that he was not claiming to be a prophet and that he used the word 'prophet' only in its linguistic sense as meaning *muhaddas,* and that even after this explanation if the Muslim brethren object to the use of this word then they may consider it deleted and replaced by the word *muhaddas* — it was on this occasion that we two brothers had a chance to see the Promised Messiah and our belief in his truth increased even further.

"After passing my B.A. examination in 1894, when I was studying for my Master of Arts, and Maulvi Aziz Bakhsh had gone to the teacher training college, I became a professor of mathematics in Islamia College and it was then that I met my dear friend Khwaja Kamal-ud-Din who was also doing his M.A. and was a professor at Islamia College. The Khwaja sahib had already taken the pledge, though I had not. Yet there was such affinity in our ideas that we soon became very close. In those days I used to write newspaper articles in favour of Hazrat Mirza sahib.

"About two years or so after I had befriended Khwaja sahib, he asked me to accompany him to Qadian and meet Hazrat Mirza sahib. So in March 1897 I went to Qadian with him (some other friends were also with us). Our stay of only a few days unfolded a new spiritual world before our eyes. Although the writings of Hazrat Mirza sahib showed his fervour and passion for the advancement of Islam, … but what we discovered in his company was that he had absolutely no other interest or occupation, day or night. After the *fajr* prayer he would sit and talk about the propagation of Islam. A little later when he would go for a walk, all the way the topic would be the same. On his return, while sitting and eating with his friends, the same thing would be under discussion; and similarly when he would sit in the mosque after the *maghrib* prayer till the *isha* prayer. The discussions would be about how no other religion can stand against the truth of Islam, how Islam can be propagated in the West, the need to meet the challenge of the Arya Samaj in India, how to create a connection with God, how to derive enjoyment from prayers, and the necessity to make the Holy Quran our guide. In short, this was the only pastime, which is not found in any worldly gatherings. ... I stayed there probably for seven or eight days, and in the end through Khwaja sahib I myself expressed the desire to take the pledge of this holy man and entered into his *bai'at*.

"After taking the pledge, I informed my elder brother Maulvi Aziz Bakhsh and my late father. Both of them immediately took the pledge. Later on, all my other brothers and various other relatives followed, so that today by the grace of Allah there is a very large group of these relations, all of whom are helping the cause of the faith according to their means." [2]

Letter from father on Muhammad Ali's *bai'at*

When Maulana Muhammad Ali informed his elder brother Maulvi Aziz Bakhsh that he had taken the pledge, the latter wrote to their father expressing his desire also to take the pledge. Hafiz Fateh-ud-Din replied as follows in a letter dated 2 April 1897:

"Praise be to Allah that you have asked for my permission regarding taking the pledge of Mirza sahib, the Promised Messiah. When I first heard about his claim, at the time of the census of 1891, I had little belief. Afterwards when I read books written by Hazrat sahib I turned away from the earlier belief. Since 1892 I have believed that in this age a special righteous man accepted by God,

---

2. *Paigham Sulh,* 7 November 1933.

the Promised Messiah, is undoubtedly preaching the truth of the Holy Prophet Muhammad and supporting the religion of God, and the claim of the Hazrat sahib is all correct and true. I have no doubt about his claim. Due to laxity I could not come to his presence, but I have taken the pledge truly in my heart. I am very pleased to learn that Maulvi Muhammad Ali has taken the pledge. I permit you also to do the same, and am happy at such a felicitous act. I too will come in a few days to the company of the Hazrat sahib to have the privilege of meeting him. Till I come to his presence I will remain anxious because there is no surety of life. I am there in my heart, as Allah knows best." [3]

Stay in Lahore after joining the Ahmadiyya Movement

After taking the pledge in 1897, Maulana Muhammad Ali stayed in Lahore for a further two years. This was the time when he was a professor in Oriental College and also taking his law examination. During that period the Promised Messiah used to send him some of his writings and submissions etc. to be translated into English. He used to go to Qadian almost every weekend and in other vacations, and used to spend all the summer vacations there. In those days it was not easy to travel to Qadian because there was no train service to it. Batala station was at a distance of twelve miles and there was an unpaved track from there to Qadian. Sometimes a horse-cart could be hired along that road but at other times you had to walk all the way. He himself once described the journey to Qadian in the following words:

"During our student life we often travelled to Qadian. The train from Lahore used to arrive at Batala at midnight and there would be no horse-cart or carriage to take us to Qadian. So we would set out on foot and after arriving in Qadian spend the night on the floor of the mosque and wake up for the *fajr* prayer. We used to go there just for one day, so much was our zeal and our longing to meet

---

3. This letter is not quoted in *Mujahid-i Kabir* and has been added from *Paigham Sulh,* 7 November 1933.

Hazrat Mirza sahib. We would go there on Saturday night and leave Sunday evening."

Correspondence with Hazrat Mirza sahib and arrangements for legal practice

Maulana Muhammad Ali passed his final law examination in 1899, and gave up his employment intending to set up a legal practice. At that stage he had been accepted as a candidate for the E.A.C. (Extra Assistant Commissioner) competitive examination and had a strong chance of qualifying. At that time this was the highest competitive examination that Indians could enter.

In these two years, from 1897 to 1899, Maulana Muhammad Ali and Hazrat Mirza sahib corresponded frequently. A large number of letters from Hazrat Mirza sahib are preserved in the papers of Maulana Muhammad Ali. Some of these are reproduced below by way of illustration. These letters are in connection with matters such as getting his writings translated into English, preparing his defence in some court cases, and various other topics. During that period Hazrat Mirza sahib sent many submissions to the government of India as well as the state government of the Punjab on topics such as reforming the ways in which religious debates and discussions were conducted so as to prevent offending any community's feelings, Muslims to be given time from work to attend Friday prayers, and facts about his own movement and its beliefs. In addition to translating these into English, Maulana Muhammad Ali also translated the defence statements for Hazrat Mirza sahib in court cases brought by his opponents, such as the cases involving Maulvi Muhammad Husain Batalvi and the income tax case.

Letter 1

My dear brother Maulvi Muhammad Ali sahib, M.A., *Assalamu alaikum wa rahmatullahi wa barakatuhu.*

I received your kind letter. I am praying for you whole heartedly all the time. May Allah the forgiving, the merciful, make you successful. It is hoped that, trusting in Allah, you will write the answers after careful consideration. You should also pray much.

May Allah be gracious to you. *Amen,* again *amen.* I have not received any letter from Doctor sahib. It is still awaited.

Humbly, Ghulam Ahmad from Qadian, 5 December 1898.

Letter 2

My dear brother Maulvi Muhammad Ali sahib, *Assalamu alaikum wa rahmatullahi wa barakatuhu.*

Looking at the hard work and amount of effort you are putting in purely in the way of Allah, the prayer comes out of my heart that may Allah give you good reward in this world and the hereafter. *Amen.*

At the moment I am sending you sixteen pages of the book. More will follow as they are printed. What you have asked is very appropriate. You may reduce or expand the biography as you like. I leave that entirely up to you.

Humbly, Mirza Ghulam Ahmad, 3 January 1899.

Letter 3

My dear brother Maulvi Muhammad Ali sahib, *Assalamu alaikum wa rahmatullahi wa barakatuhu.*

The defence paper that is to be printed today is being sent to you through brother Maulvi Sher Ali sahib. It is my firm opinion, which I consider absolutely essential, that you should translate it very carefully and get it printed as you translate it. For the costs a sum of money has been sent now. If the expenses exceed this then you may get them from Babu Taj-ud-Din. You must remember that in this defence in English it must be stated very clearly that the prophecy published in the announcement about the *Mubahila,* dated 21 November 1898, has come true, and references should be given to the announcements. If I have missed out any points in this paper, you should complete them. In the end I pray that Allah may grant you to pass, and reward you for these services. *Amen,* again *amen.*

Humbly, Mirza Ghulam Ahmad, 18 January 1899.

Letter 4

My dear brother Maulvi Muhammad Ali sahib, *Assalamu alaikum wa rahmatullahi wa barakatuhu.*

Congratulations on your success in the examination. In the days just before the result was announced I was very anxious and thinking about this. Praise be to Allah, that you passed it. In the defence that is to be published, if there is scope by the time you receive this letter then please mention at a suitable place the proceedings which took place at the meeting about the plague.

Humbly, Mirza Ghulam Ahmad, 8 February 1899.

Letter 5

My dear brother Maulvi Muhammad Ali sahib, *Assalamu alaikum wa rahmatullahi wa barakatuhu.*

Today, on 8 February 1899, your letter was received. The labour that you have undertaken out of sincere zeal, may Allah bestow upon you goodly reward for it. *Amen,* again *Amen.*

Humbly, Mirza Ghulam Ahmad, 8 February 1899.

Letter 6

My dear brother Maulvi Muhammad Ali sahib, *Assalamu alaikum wa rahmatullahi wa barakatuhu.*

I have received your kind letter and hope that, after spending a few days in your village, you will, according to your promise, come here for eight days. I have started to write the book which you are going to translate, and brother Shaikh Rahmatullah is ready to go to London so that it can be published in Europe. It would be best if you could arrange to come at the earliest possible convenient time so that you could say *Eid* prayers here. Many other friends are also expected. *Wassalam.*

Humbly, Mirza Ghulam Ahmad, 29 March 1899.

Letter 7

My dear brother Maulvi Muhammad Ali sahib, *Assalamu alaikum wa rahmatullahi wa barakatuhu.*

Your kind letter was received. I am very happy to know that Allah in His perfect wisdom has provided you an opportunity to stay in Qadian. It appears that Allah Almighty intends to shower much of His blessing and mercy upon you by this opportunity. I think it would be better if you spend the entire summer till October here in Qadian and devote yourself to religious work with youthful vigour. During this time you can learn the Holy Quran from Maulvi [Nur-ud-Din] sahib.

Then in October, which is the onset of winter, you will have the choice of starting your own career. This period will *inshallah* act as an elixir for you in the completion of religious tasks. I hold an extremely good opinion about you and believe that during this time you will make great progress. It has long been my intention to divide my community into two groups: one group consisting of those who are partly for this world and partly for religion, and are not able to withstand great trials, nor can they render any important services to religion; and the other group consisting of those who enter through this door with full sincerity and faithfulness and in reality sell themselves in this path. I wish that God would include you in the latter group. After 15 May 1899 you should come prepared for this long stay. I am sure God will reward you for this. During this period if you intend to take any other examination,[4] the solitude here will provide ample time to prepare. Anyhow I can see it will be a great blessing, but you must be determined to stay in Qadian in any case till October. Everything is fine. *Wassalam.*

Humbly, Mirza Ghulam Ahmad, 8 May 1899.

Images of all the original letters of Hazrat Mirza sahib translated above are reproduced in *Mujahid-i Kabir,* along with their text in printed form. The image of Letter 7 above is shown opposite.

---

4. His name had been accepted for the E.A.C. competitive examination.

This letter was received by Maulana Muhammad Ali at the time when he was about to give up his job at Oriental College and had decided to set up his legal practice. Accordingly, for this purpose he had already rented a house, bought books and furniture and hired a clerk. Before starting this legal practice he had expressed his wish to stay for some time with Hazrat Mirza sahib in Qadian, and intended to leave Lahore around 15 May 1899.

On this date the first phase of the life of Maulana Muhammad Ali, consisting of twenty five years, comes to an end.

Hazrat Mirza Ghulam Ahmad   *Hazrat Maulana Nur-ud-Din*

Part 2

Life at Qadian

from May 1899 to April 1914

Maulana Muhammad Ali in 1911

Image of letter by Hazrat Mirza Ghulam Ahmad to Maulana Muhammad Ali.

"I hold an extremely favourable opinion about you. This is why I have a special love for you. If your nature had not been pure in the sight of God, I could not possibly have thought so well of you, never. I love you fervently from the bottom of my heart…"

See page 37 for more of the translation.

2.1: The Promised Messiah's Time

Migration to Qadian and the early days

In 1899, after passing his law examination Maulana Muhammad Ali gave up his job at Oriental College and decided to set up his own legal practice. He was also accepted as a candidate for the competitive examination for the posts of Extra Assistant Commissioner. For his legal practice he chose Gurdaspur because it was near Qadian so that he could continue to visit Hazrat Mirza sahib and to translate his writings into English. He rented a house, bought furniture and books and employed a clerk. It appears from his constant correspondence with Hazrat Mirza sahib that he had expressed his wish to spend some time with the Promised Messiah before going to Gurdaspur and Hazrat Mirza sahib was very pleased with this. As the last letter of Hazrat Mirza sahib shows, he invited Maulana Muhammad Ali to stay in Qadian till October. At that time, after completing all the arrangements, Maulana Muhammad Ali was ready to leave Lahore. So on 18 May 1899 he arrived in Qadian and the news of his arrival was published in the Ahmadiyya community's newspaper *Al-Hakam* as follows:

> "Maulvi Muhammad Ali sahib, M.A., will stay in Qadian for a few months. He arrived in *Dar-ul-Aman* on 18 May 1899. As usual he is translating 'Jesus in India'."
> (*Al-Hakam,* 19 May 1899, p. 6, col. 3)

Because of his deep desire to stay in Hazrat Mirza sahib's company, and indeed according to the latter's instructions, Maulana Muhammad Ali soon vacated the house in Gurdaspur, after paying two months rent, so that he could stay in Qadian till October. During this period the proposal arose that a magazine in English should be started for the propagation of Islam. Hazrat Mirza sahib asked Maulana Muhammad Ali to carry out this religious service and Maulana Muhammad Ali accepted without hesitation. The publication of the magazine was delayed and his temporary stay in Qadian kept on being prolonged.

In March 1900 Maulana Muhammad Ali wrote the following note to Hazrat Mirza sahib:

> In the name of Allah, the Beneficent, the Merciful. We praise Him and invoke blessings upon His noble Prophet.
>
> My leader and mentor, *Assalamu alaikum wa rahmat-ullahi wa barakatuhu.*
>
> Yesterday at midday you directed that my humble self should stay here permanently. I want to say something about it. Last May when I came to your service, with the permission to stay here for an extended period, I had no other idea in my mind, and Allah is my witness to that, except that during this long stay a way might be found to enable me to give up all my worldly affairs and stay at your feet. This most cherished desire is still in my heart. Once or twice when I went back to my native town there was no other purpose but to please my parents, and it never occurred to me to settle there. I am at your service and am your servant, and it is you whom I request to pray that God may give me strength to adhere steadfastly to this promise throughout my life and make me die upon the same faith.
>
> I am ready to stay and to work whenever and in whatever way you command me to, sir. Though I am fearful of making this claim, as all guidance is only in Allah's hands, but I have dared to express this only because you, sir, also require this promise at the time of taking the pledge, that 'I will hold religion above worldly affairs'. These words mean that the one who takes the pledge must submit himself and all his faculties to the man sent by Allah.
>
> As for accommodation, my only desire is for a house where you are physically near, as is this place where you have allowed me to stay. If I start legal practice I am determined to visit you every week. I do not wish to live far away because distance makes the heart rusty. So wherever you order, I will have a house built there. I will now send for money from my home for this purpose.
>
> Humbly, Muhammad Ali, 23 March 1900.

On the back of this letter Hazrat Mirza sahib wrote:

My dear brother Maulvi sahib, *Assalamu alaikum wa rahmatullahi wa barakatuh!*

The arrival of your letter just now has given me so much pleasure that it is beyond description. May God grant your wishes both in this world and the hereafter! I am looking for accommodation for you all the time and hope that suitable houses can be found nearby. But for the time being the house in which you are living will suffice because I had it built only with you in mind. As the female section of the house needs to be bigger to meet all the requisites, so I am thinking about it. I hope that Allah will solve all problems and pave the way to achieve your goals, as He is all-powerful.

Wassalam. Humbly, Mirza Ghulam Ahmad, 23 March 1900.

In short, at the age of twenty five years when a bright worldly future was before him, Maulana Muhammad Ali set the most outstanding personal example of putting religion above worldly interests and, following the instruction of the Imam of the time, he left everything and went to join the Promised Messiah.

Residing in the Promised Messiah's house

When in May 1899 Maulana Muhammad Ali arrived in Qadian, the Promised Messiah gave him accommodation on the third storey of his own house. The ground floor was for guests, while he and his family occupied the middle storey. This storey was adjacent to the Masjid-i-Mubarak and there was a hatch from one room into this mosque through which Hazrat Mirza sahib used to enter the mosque. On one side of the same floor lived Maulana Nur-ud-Din. It was above his room, on the third storey, that Hazrat Mirza sahib made space for Maulana Muhammad Ali.

He had a room and a small courtyard. There was a stairway in the room which went down to the Promised Messiah's courtyard and the other door opened into the small courtyard. The door of the small courtyard opened on the roof of the Masjid-i-Mubarak.

This roof was used in the summer for *maghrib* and *isha* prayers, and it was here also that Hazrat Mirza sahib used to sit for his evening gatherings. Next to his room was Maulana Abdul Karim's room, and his courtyard was also adjacent to the roof of the Masjid-i-Mubarak. From the courtyard next to Maulana Muhammad Ali's room there was a little stairway going down into a tiny room, and this place served as his office. It was in there that he produced those invaluable English writings for the magazine the *Review of Religions,* whose language was so perfect that it was alleged by a Christian magazine that Mirza Ghulam Ahmad must be keeping an Englishman to do the writing! (See further pages 32 and 535.)

After going to stay in the Promised Messiah's company Maulana Muhammad Ali had no other worldly aspirations. Meals came twice daily from the community kitchen (*langar*) and he received a small subsistence for other living expenses. What was available all the time, however, was the company of the Promised Messiah and the priceless blessing of his spiritual grace and benevolence.

Hazrat Mirza sahib was very affectionate to him. He used to take personal care to have him sent his breakfast daily and would not be satisfied till he ascertained from the servant who took the breakfast that the Maulana had eaten it properly. At that time Qadian was a small village but because of the Promised Messiah's blessing it was turning into a place visited by all, both the famous and the ordinary. However, many necessities of life were not available. Whenever Hazrat Mirza sahib happened to receive a consignment of fresh fruit from outside Qadian, he would make it a special point to see that Maulana Muhammad Ali got his share. The Maulana related the following incident:

> "Once in summer someone brought ice. The Promised Messiah called me and he was sitting with blocks of ice and a large vessel containing milk in front of him. He poured out a glass of milk, added sugar and ice to it and gave it to me. I accepted it gratefully and drank it. Then he poured out another glass of milk with sugar and ice. I could not refuse as it was being offered by him, so I drank it. Then he poured out a glass a third time, which I declined.

The Promised Messiah smiled and said: You drank twice of your own accord, now drink a third time for my sake. So I drank the third one as well, and I felt no difficulty or burden while doing so." [1]

In short, Hazrat Mirza sahib cared for Maulana Muhammad Ali like a loving father. He found a suitable marriage partner for him as well and married him as if he were his own son. On 4 April 1901 he was married to Fatima, daughter of Nabi Bakhsh, at Gurdaspur, according to the wish of the Promised Messiah.

In addition to being close to and having the constant company of Hazrat Mirza sahib, Maulana Muhammad Ali also attended Maulana Nur-ud-Din's daily teaching of the Holy Quran. He has acknowledged on many occasions and in many ways that he received knowledge and understanding of the Quran from these two great saints. In the Preface of *Bayan-ul-Quran,* his Urdu translation of the Holy Quran with commentary, he wrote:

> "Finally, it is important to mention that, although in this humble service of the Holy Quran I have had much benefit from the work of the classical scholars, but the man who in my life inspired me with the love of the Holy Quran and the desire to serve it was the *Mujaddid* of this century, Hazrat Mirza Ghulam Ahmad sahib of Qadian. Then the man who enabled me to understand the Quran was my revered teacher Hazrat Maulvi Nur-ud-Din sahib. If anyone benefits from my work and prays for me, he must also include these two righteous men in his prayer. I am but dust; any fragrance anyone perceives in this work is the spirit breathed by these others."

---

1. This incident has also a symbolic meaning. Milk symbolizes knowledge. The Holy Prophet Muhammad related a dream in which he drank milk abundantly from a cup and then gave what was left to Hazrat Umar. The Holy Prophet interpreted the drinking of milk in this dream as being given knowledge (*Sahih Bukhari,* 3:22, hadith 82). In this incident the first two glasses which he drank signify Maulana Muhammad Ali being given knowledge of the Quran and of Islam, and the third glass, which he drank to please Hazrat Mirza sahib, signifies his knowledge of the claims of the Promised Messiah.

Similarly, in the Preface to his world-famous English translation of the Holy Quran with commentary he wrote:

> "And lastly, the greatest religious leader of the present time, Mirza Ghulam Ahmad of Qadian, has inspired me with all that is best in this work. I have drunk deep at the fountain of knowledge which this great Reformer — *Mujaddid* of the present century and founder of the Ahmadiyya Movement — has made to flow. There is one more person whose name I must mention in this connection, the late Maulawi Hakim Nur-ud-Din, who in his last long illness patiently went through much the greater part of the explanatory notes and made many valuable suggestions. To him, indeed, the Muslim world owes a deep debt of gratitude as the leader of the new turn given to the exposition of the Holy Quran. He has done his work and passed away silently, but it is a fact that he spent the whole of his life in studying the Holy Quran, and must be ranked with the greatest expositors of the Holy Book."

Right from the beginning Maulana Muhammad Ali liked to collect writings of Western thinkers and authors on religion and study them and read them out to Hazrat Mirza sahib. He would bear in mind their criticism of Islam while translating Hazrat Mirza sahib's writings into English or writing his own articles. He also managed to find time to teach a few classes in the Talim-ul-Islam School. As the secretary of the management committee of this school it was also his duty to deal with administrative matters and raise financial contributions. A glimpse of his engagements of those days can be seen in the following extract from the Ahmadiyya newspaper *Al-Hakam* of 30 November 1900:

> "The services to religion of Hazrat Maulana Muhammad Ali, M.A., LL.B., are enviable. For nearly two years he has been busy serving Islam in Qadian. During the last two or three years all the posters and books published in English are the outcome of the Maulvi sahib's efforts in the way of Allah. These days he is reading out an English book about the Anti-Christ to the Promised Messiah. ...

Despite his heavy schedule he has written many powerful articles in reply to Golarwi in the newspapers *'Am* and *Chaudveen Sadi,* and he is also writing English articles in a Christian newspaper of Calcutta. ... As the Middle annual examination is drawing nearer, he has set aside a part of his valuable time these days for the school, purely to serve the community, to earn the pleasure of Allah and for the satisfaction of the Imam of the time." (p. 6)

In *Al-Hakam* of 10 December 1900 it is reported:

"Hazrat Maulvi Muhammad Ali sahib is reading out the writings of some Western philosophers to the Hazrat sahib." (p. 6)

The early writings of the Promised Messiah about Maulana Muhammad Ali

From the very beginning that Maulana Muhammad Ali took up abode in Qadian, Hazrat Mirza sahib made a close and careful observation of his character and mode of life, and came to certain conclusions which he expressed as follows:

"Among the most sincere friends in our community is Maulvi Muhammad Ali, M.A., who, besides his other qualifications, has also just now passed his law examination. For the past few months, at much loss to his own work, he has been staying with me in Qadian to perform a service to religion by translating some of my writings into English. ...

During this period in which he has been with me, I have been observing him, both openly and discreetly, to assess his moral character, observance of religion and goodness of behaviour. So, thanks be to God, that I have found him to be a most excellent man as regards religion and good behaviour in all ways. He is unassuming, modest, of a righteous nature, and pious. He is to be envied for many qualities. ... It is obvious that such promising young men possessing these qualities, who are able and honourable, cannot be found by searching."

(Announcement dated 9 August 1899; *Majmu'a Ishtiha-rat,* 1986 edition, vol. 3, p. 137–138, number 206)

After that, in October 1899, he wrote on another occasion:

"I am very happy that another good young man, having found the grace of God, has joined our community, that is, Maulvi Muhammad Ali, M.A., Pleader. I have very good expectations of him. For a long time he has borne a worldly loss in order to stay in Qadian to serve the religion, and is learning the deep knowledge of the Holy Quran from Hazrat Maulvi Hakim Nur-ud-Din.

I am sure that my foresight will not go wrong in this, that this young man will make progress in the path of God, and I am sure that by the grace of God he will prove to be so firm in righteousness and love of religion that he will set an example worthy to be followed by his peers. O God, let it be so! *Amen,* again *amen.*"

(Announcement dated 4 October 1899; *Majmu'a Ishtiha-rat,* 1986 edition, vol. 3, p. 157–158, number 208)

Publication of the *Review of Religions*

As has already been mentioned, at first Maulana Muhammad Ali came to Qadian for a temporary stay but this stay kept on being extended. The object was that he should translate into English some of the submissions of Hazrat Mirza sahib addressed to the government and certain other writings, which included *Faryad-i Dard*. In the Announcement quoted above, Hazrat Mirza sahib also wrote in a footnote:

"All those books of mine which are published after translation into English are translated by Maulvi Muhammad Ali, M.A." (*ibid.,* p. 158)

Other reasons for prolonging his stay were that he would benefit from Hazrat Mirza sahib's company and take lessons in the Quran from Maulana Nur-ud-Din.

However, during this stay Hazrat Mirza sahib was to take

another important step in the fulfilment of his mission. He wrote:

> "It was always a matter of sadness and anxiety for me that all those truths, the spiritual knowledge, the sound arguments in support of the religion of Islam, and the teachings giving satisfaction to the human soul, which have been disclosed to me and are still being made known to me, have not yet benefited the English-educated people of this country or the seekers-after-truth of Europe. This pain was so intense that it was no longer bearable. But God Almighty intends that before I pass away from this temporary abode all my aims should be fulfilled so that my last journey is not one of disappointment. So to fulfil this object, which is the real purpose of my life, there is a suggestion that ... a magazine in English be published for the fulfillment of the objectives mentioned above."

> (Announcement dated 15 January 1901; *Majmu'a Ishtiharat,* 1986 edition, vol. 3, pages 393–394, number 234)

To edit this journal a very capable writer of English was needed. So Hazrat Mirza sahib asked Maulana Muhammad Ali to remain in Qadian to do this service to the cause of the faith. The Maulana considered it his good fortune and, as has been mentioned, cancelled all the arrangements to set up his legal practice. But the publication of the magazine was delayed. On 15 January 1901 Hazrat Mirza sahib had made his first declaration about this magazine in the announcement entitled 'An Important Proposal', from which we have quoted above. At that time there was no organisation nor any funds available for the publication of the magazine. At the invitation of Hazrat Mirza sahib some friends gathered in Qadian and decided that the magazine should be financed by subscriptions, and to collect the subscriptions and manage the magazine an organisation by the name of Anjuman-i Isha'at-i Islam be created. The office bearers of the Anjuman were declared to be the following:

1. Hazrat Mirza sahib   —   Patron
2. Maulana Nur-ud-Din   —   President
3. Maulana Abdul Karim   —   Vice President

4.	Khwaja Kamal-ud-Din	—	Secretary
5.	Maulana Muhammad Ali	—	Assistant Secretary

Maulana Muhammad Ali and Khwaja Kamal-ud-Din were to be the joint editors. Due to certain reasons the publication of the magazine was further delayed. During this period Maulana Muhammad Ali continued to prepare articles for the magazine and to translate Hazrat Mirza sahib's writings. In November 1901 it was decided that the office bearers of the Anjuman must be local residents, so Maulana Muhammad Ali was made Secretary and the magazine was to be published in Qadian.

From January 1902 this magazine started publication as a monthly under the editorship of Maulana Muhammad Ali, and its Urdu translation was also issued as a magazine.

Maulana Muhammad Ali was regularly employed as the editor from April 1901. His salary till 31 December 1901 was fixed at 60 Rupees a month, and from 1 January 1902 it was to be 100 Rupees a month, but the records of the Anjuman of Qadian show that for a long time Maulana Muhammad Ali decided to take only 20 Rupees a month for his needs. It is entered in the records in his own writing:

> From 1 April 1901, permanent salary of Editor *Review:* 20 Rupees.

Under *Comments* it is noted:

> The actual amount received has been entered. According to the decision, it was to be 60 Rupees till 31 December 1901 and 100 Rupees from 1 January 1902. (Signed) Muhammad Ali.

Because of taking this low salary he lived in financial stringency. He also had a wife to support. The result of drawing much less salary than his entitlement for some years was that he ran into debt. When Hazrat Mirza sahib became aware of this situation from some other source he gave the following instructions in writing:

> "I have discovered that Maulvi Muhammad Ali sahib, editor of the magazine, has run up a debt of nearly 1500

Rupees, the only reason for which is that in the first three years of the magazine's life he has been drawing only a paltry sum out of his appointed salary. It is clear from the accounts of the magazine that if he receives his full salary for the initial years he is at present entitled to a much larger sum than his debt. Therefore, as there is no surety of life, I instruct that 1500 Rupees be paid to him forthwith out of the magazine fund.

Mirza Ghulam Ahmad."

In the beginning most of the articles in the magazine were written by Hazrat Mirza sahib and translated into English by Maulana Muhammad Ali, though the Maulana himself also wrote some articles. Afterwards his own contribution increased and ultimately nearly the whole magazine consisted of the Maulana's writings. Many outstanding articles came from his pen which were well received by the Muslim as well as the non-Muslim readership, on topics such as heaven and hell, the seclusion of women, polygamy, slavery, Islamic wars, inheritance, usury, divorce, the collection and arrangement of Quranic verses, preservation of the Hadith reports of the Holy Prophet Muhammad etc.[2]

---

2. Regarding this last article, Dr. Basharat Ahmad notes the following incident in his book *Mujaddid-i Azam* (the biography of Hazrat Mirza sahib): "In the days when Maulana Muhammad Ali's article on the preservation of Hadith reports appeared in the *Review of Religions,* having read it it occurred to me that in order to write an article based on such thorough, detailed and deep research he must surely have had help from Maulana Nur-ud-Din or Maulana Muhammad Ahsan of Amroha as these two revered figures were the leading lights in the field of Hadith in those days. However, it so happened one day that I and Maulana Muhammad Ahsan were sitting on the top of the Masjid-i-Mubarak before *maghrib* prayers when Maulana Nur-ud-Din arrived, with a copy of the *Review of Religions* in hand. After greeting Maulana Ahsan he asked him if he had read the article on the preservation of Hadith. Maulana Ahsan replied in the affirmative. Maulana Nur-ud-Din said: 'We think that only people like us, the religious scholars, have deep knowledge of Hadith, but Maulvi Muhammad Ali has done such excellent research in this field also that I am astonished.' Maulana Ahsan also agreed with this. I then realized that these two scholars had no part in Maulana Muhammad Ali's research, and that it was all his own effort, labour and

In the same way, the writings of the Christian missionaries against Islam were refuted with such strong arguments in powerful series of articles that it shook the Christian world.

Apart from the high scholarly quality of the articles, the fluency and eloquence of the English language of the magazine was widely acknowledged. So much so that many readers thought that the editor must be an Englishman, kept concealed by the Mirza of Qadian, writing under the pseudonym Muhammad Ali. Hence in April 1902 the English Editor of the Christian periodical *Calcutta Review* wrote in a disparaging way that it was as plain as daylight that whatever was written in this magazine was from the pen of an Englishman, and it was exactly like when the Prophet Muhammad had a Syrian Christian as his helper whom they called the angel Gabriel. Then he warned this Englishman to give it up.[3]

In the Ahmadiyya newspaper *Al-Badr,* volume 1, number 2, dated 17 November 1902, it is reported from the talks of the Promised Messiah:

> "Maulvi Muhammad Ali sahib read out a letter from Mr. Khalid Snow [an English convert to Islam] in which the writer has expressed his surprise at the fact that the English used in the magazine was written by Maulana Muhammad Ali. ... Supporting Mir Nasir Nawab, Hazrat Mirza sahib said: 'Maulvi sahib's writing such excellent English is nothing but a miracle, so even the English people think that we have employed a European who writes for the magazine'. Maulvi Muhammad Ali sahib said: It is only a blessing of God because before this I have never published a single word."
>
> (22 October 1902; *Ruhani Khaza'in No. 2,* vol. 4, p. 114–115, edition used is 1984, 10-volume, edition)

Similarly, some years later in an issue of *Badr* dated 15 November 1906 it is reported in the talks of the Promised Messiah:

---

knowledge at which scholars of Hadith of this high stature were expressing amazement." (*Mujaddid-i Azam,* v. 2, p. 832–833)

3. See the Supplement, p. 535, for the exact quotation.

"The *Review of Religions* was being mentioned. A man praised it and said that its articles were of high standard. [Hazrat Mirza sahib] said: Its editor Maulvi Muhammad Ali sahib is an able and learned man. He has the M.A. degree, and along with it a religious bent of mind. He always passed with top marks and his name had gone forward for E.A.C. But leaving all this he has settled here. This is why God the Most High has blessed his writing."

(7 November 1906; *Ruhani Khaza'in No. 2,* vol. 9, p. 90)

The *Review of Religions* was the first journal which presented Islam in the English language with such vigour and eloquence, and proved its superiority over other religions with such incontestable arguments, that learned people among both the Muslims and the non-Muslims were spellbound. Hundreds of Western-educated young Muslims, who were under the influence of Christian missionaries or of irreligious Western thinkers, came back into the fold of Islam with their faith renewed. As Christianity was the main target of this magazine, it caused consternation in the Christian missionary camp. The triumph of Islam over other faiths by means of argument began to seem a real prospect.

The influence this journal had on Westerners can be illustrated by the following two examples. Chaudhry Hakim Ali, an Ahmadi land owner of the Sargoda district, had this magazine issued to Mr. Malcolm Hailey, incharge of settlements, Sargoda (who went on to be governor of the Punjab as Sir Malcolm Hailey). Sometime later when the Chaudhry sahib met him, Mr. Hailey told him that he had put him in a dilemma by getting this magazine issued to him because whenever he read it he was convinced that Islam was the only true religion and it worried him so much that he could not sleep. Another instance that Dr. Basharat Ahmad has noted in his book *Mujaddid-i Azam* was reported to him by Faqir Iftikhar-ud-Din of Rawalpindi about an English superior officer of his who used to receive this magazine free. He asked him to get it stopped because he could not refrain from reading it and when he read it he feared that by not accepting the true religion he might be judged guilty by God.

In September 1903 Hazrat Mirza sahib published an Announcement about this magazine, from which we quote an extract below because it throws light on the objectives of this Movement:

> "As our community would know, the real object for which I have been sent by God the Most High is that the errors and wrong beliefs spread by Christianity should be removed and the people of the world are drawn towards Islam, and this purpose mentioned above be fulfilled which has been referred to in the words of Hadith as 'breaking the cross'. For these purposes an English magazine has been launched and its publication has proved very effective in many parts of Europe and America, starting to win many hearts." (*Majmu'a Ishtiharat,* vol. 3, p. 496, number 253)

Urging the promotion of this plan he goes on to write:

> "Whoever will help me in my aims according to my wishes during my lifetime, I hope he will be with me on the day of Judgment also." (*ibid.,* p. 497)

In short, during his lifetime Hazrat Mirza sahib chose Maulana Muhammad Ali for the fulfilment of his mission. This magazine continued to be published very splendidly and magnificently, many highly valuable articles on Islam appeared in it, and it went on performing a glorious service to Islam. This was the first organ of the press which in those days was changing the views of the English speaking world about Islam. It was not only distributed to the Western educated people of India but also to the outside world in large numbers. Till March 1914 when Maulana Muhammad Ali was editor, it continued to flourish in its glory. But after the death of Maulana Nur-ud-Din, when Maulana Muhammad Ali had to leave everything behind in Qadian and come to Lahore, this magazine went into other hands and the quality of its articles deteriorated so that it became just another ordinary periodical.

Hazrat Mirza sahib's wishes regarding propagation of Islam

For the propagation of Islam, besides issuing a journal Hazrat Mirza sahib had also two other desires: to have the Quran translated into

English with commentary and sent to the West, and the writing and distribution of a comprehensive book in English on the doctrines of Islam.

After claiming to be Promised Messiah, he expressed his aspiration in his first book *Izala Auham* in the following words:

> "I would advise that, instead of these missionaries, writings of an excellent and high standard should be sent into these countries. If my people help me heart and soul I wish to prepare a commentary of the Quran which should be sent to them after it has been rendered into the English language. I cannot refrain from stating clearly that this is my work, and that definitely no one else can do it as I can, or as he can who is an offshoot of mine and thus is included in me." (p. 773; book published 1891)

Eight years later, in December 1899, he said in his talks:

> "I want to write a book on Islam and Maulvi Muhammad Ali sahib should translate it. It will consist of three parts: firstly, what are our duties to Allah, secondly what are our duties towards our own souls, and thirdly what are the rights of our fellow human beings upon us." (*Ruhani Khaza'in No. 2,* vol. 1, p. 392; from *Badr,* 19 March 1908)

On another occasion it is reported in the talks of the Promised Messiah:

> On 13 February 1907 Hazrat Mirza sahib sent for Maulvi Muhammad Ali sahib and said:
>
> "I want to fulfil the duty of the propagation of Islam to the Western people by having an English book written, and this is your work. The reason why Islam today is not spreading in those countries, and if someone does become a Muslim he is very weak, is that those people do not know the truth about Islam, nor has it been presented to them. It is their right that they should be shown the true Islam which God has made manifest to me. ... All those arguments that God has taught me to prove Islam to be true should be collected together in one place. If a comprehensive book

along these lines is compiled it is hoped that people would
benefit from it greatly."

(*Badr,* 21 February 1907; *Ruhani Khaza'in No. 2,* vol. 9,
pages 191–192)

Thus, just as after expressing the aims of his life Hazrat Mirza
sahib chose Maulana Muhammad Ali to be the editor of the magazine, it was also his wish for other writings that they too should be
produced by Maulana Muhammad Ali.

First photograph of Maulana Muhammad Ali

It once happened in those early days that a photographer was called
to Qadian and, apart from taking other photographs, he took a
photograph of Maulana Muhammad Ali as well. This was the first
photograph taken of the Maulana. He mentioned it in his Friday
khutba on 14 January 1944 as follows:

> "I want to tell you about an incident that occurred in the
> earliest days. I do not know how it happened. It was per-
> haps 1901 or 1902. I was living in Qadian and probably
> the *Review of Religions* had already started. The Promised
> Messiah called a photographer to have his photograph
> taken for inclusion in his books because there were
> people in the West, where those writings would go, who
> could form an opinion about the subject from his photo-
> graph. I cannot remember if any other group photo was
> taken but what I do recall is that by his bidding my photo-
> graph was also taken.

> "This is an ordinary event, but the strange thing, or what
> we can call God's work, is that in the photo on the right
> side there is a hand holding a book, upon which it is
> written: *Quran Sharif.* Where did it come from? At that
> time no one had in mind translating the Holy Quran.
> Hazrat Mirza sahib had entertained this desire for long
> but there were no resources available and in those early
> days no one could even imagine that I would translate the
> Holy Quran. However, it happened due to the working of
> God that there was a Quran in my very first photograph.
> Who was that man, why did he have a Quran in his hand,

how did he manage to stand on my right side so that the Quran could appear in the photograph, I cannot explain."

(*Paigham Sulh,* 16 February 1944)

The dreams, visions, revelations and writings of Hazrat Mirza sahib about Maulana Muhammad Ali

At that time it could not appear to the outward eye that this young man of twenty-five or twenty-six years of age would one day be a true successor of the 'Master of the Pen' (*Sultan-i Qalm*), the Promised Messiah, and would be the means through which his heartfelt desires and aspirations would be fulfilled. Hazrat Mirza sahib reviewed the character and qualities of Maulana Muhammad Ali and wrote, as quoted above, "I am sure that my foresight will not go wrong in this, that this young man will make progress in the path of God, and I am sure that by the grace of God he will prove to be so firm in righteousness and love of religion that he will set an example worthy to be followed by his peers." Then, mentioning his deeply-held wishes, he handed over to Maulana Muhammad Ali that practical work which he declared as the real aim of his coming. It was on the basis of his foresight that he gave the Maulana the responsibility for this work. According to Hadith, the foresight of a true believer is illuminated by the light of God, and the faith which Hazrat Mirza sahib had in his foresight could only have been created by Allah in his heart. The following letter proves this point, in which Hazrat Mirza sahib writes to Maulana Muhammad Ali:

> "I hold an extremely favourable opinion about you. This is why I have a special love for you. If your nature had not been pure in the sight of God, I could not possibly have thought so well of you, never. I love you fervently from the bottom of my heart, and often pray for you in the five daily prayers. I hope that at some future time these prayers will show their effect. ... I am busy praying, with heart-felt passion, for your welfare in this world and the hereafter, and for your body and soul, and I am awaiting the effects and results of the prayer."

As mentioned above, this opinion of the Promised Messiah was based not only on his foresight and his observation of Maulana

Muhammad Ali's character and qualities, but the Promised Messiah also had dreams, visions and Divine revelations indicating that it was ordained by Allah that Maulana Muhammad Ali would inherit the Promised Messiah's mantle of knowledge. Keeping in view the needs of the time, the Promised Messiah was to carry on *jihad* with the pen and not with the sword. So it was necessary that there should arise from among his companions a man who would be his successor in continuing this *jihad*. It was also natural that Hazrat Mirza sahib should see this man of letters in his visions. It appears from many dreams, visions and Divine revelations of his that he was shown beforehand that Maulana Muhammad Ali would accomplish the most tremendous service to the cause of religion.

The most important and foremost task was to produce a commentary of the Holy Quran which would prove the truth of Islam in this age. In his book *Izala Auham,* on page 773, the Promised Messiah had expressed his wish to write a commentary himself, as has been quoted earlier. But elsewhere he was shown in a clear vision that the commentary was written by 'Ali' and 'Ali' was presenting to him that commentary. Hazrat Mirza sahib referred to that vision in the following words:

> "I remember at this point a very clear vision."

The vision had two parts, the second part being related by him as follows:

> "After that a book was given to me, about which I was told that this was the commentary of the Holy Quran written by Ali and now Ali is handing that commentary to you. Allah be praised for this!"
>
> (*Tazkira,* p. 21; *Barahin Ahmadiyya,* p. 503, subnote 3 on footnote 11)

Though Hazrat Mirza sahib had expressed his intention to write the commentary himself, it was the will of Allah that this vision should be fulfilled and 'Ali' write a commentary and give it to him. Accordingly, in the preface of his English translation and commentary of the Quran, Maulana Muhammad Ali wrote the following words:

"... the greatest religious leader of the present time, Mirza Ghulam Ahmad of Qadian, has inspired me with all that is best in this work. I have drunk deep at the fountain of knowledge which this great Reformer — *Mujaddid* of the present century and founder of the Ahmadiyya Movement — has made to flow."

So the knowledge of the Maulana came from the Promised Messiah and the aspiration to produce the commentary was also of the Promised Messiah. This was indicated in the vision in the words that this was "the commentary of the Holy Quran written by Ali and now Ali is handing that commentary to you".

The selection of Maulana Muhammad Ali as the one to inherit the knowledge of the Promised Messiah and to carry out *jihad* by the pen is also elucidated in another vision, which was related by Hazrat Mirza sahib as follows:

"I saw in a dream that I was riding a horse and going somewhere. On the way it grew completely dark so I turned back. There were also some women accompanying me. On the return journey, due to dust in the air it became pitch dark. I was holding the reins by groping for them. After a few steps light appeared and in front of me I saw a large terrace. I dismounted on it. There were some boys there who cried out: 'Maulvi Abdul Karim has come'. Then I saw Maulvi Abdul Karim sahib approaching. I shook hands with him and said *assalamu alaikum*. The late Maulvi sahib took out something and gave it to me as a present, saying that the bishop, the senior officer of the Christian clerics, also uses it. This thing looked like a rabbit, brown in colour. Protruding from it was a long tube, with a pen at the front of the tube. That pen ran easily without effort. I said: 'I did not send for this pen.' Maulvi sahib said: 'Maulvi Muhammad Ali sahib must have sent for it'. I said: 'I will give it to him'."

(*Tazkira,* pages 675–676; *Al-Hakam,* 17 November 1906)

Hazrat Mirza sahib has himself added the interpretation of the vision as follows:

"The women may represent weak people. The pen seems to mean that Allah will give Maulvi Muhammad Ali sahib such power of intellect that he will write forceful articles to combat the opponents." (*Ibid.*)

There is another vision of Hazrat Mirza sahib which was narrated by Maulana Muhammad Ali as follows:

"Another of his dreams, which I have not seen in print anywhere, was told to me by the Promised Messiah himself. It was that the Promised Messiah and I were riding a horse, with me sitting behind him, and it was galloping at a great speed through the narrow streets of a city. At every corner there would be danger of a collision but the horse would clear it safely. In the end we reached an open ground where there was a man who pointed towards me and said: 'His name is *Majadd-ud-Din*'." (*Paigham Sulh,* 15 January 1935)

Maulana Muhammad Ali's riding a horse sitting behind Hazrat Mirza sahib indicated that it was destined that the Maulana would carry on Hazrat Mirza sahib's literary work after him and the name *Majadd-ud-Din* meant that the work would be for the glory of Islam (as *majad* means glory). By the grace of God, so did it happen. The literature produced by Maulana Muhammad Ali painted a beautiful, complete picture of the religion of Islam which resulted in the strengthening and glorification of Islam.[4]

It seems appropriate to mention here also that in the Hadith reports of the Holy Prophet Muhammad regarding the coming of the Mahdi there are three reports which Nawab Siddiq Hasan Khan has quoted in his book *Hujaj-ul-Kirama* on pages 442 to 443, which indicate that after the death of the Mahdi there would be a *khalifa* of his, but on the death of this *khalifa* people will desert the Quran and they will be involved in tribulation and dissension. Then they will

---

4. Maulana Muhammad Ali published this dream at the very beginning of the Split in the Ahmadiyya Movement, and also referred to it on two later occasions. After the Split, when the Qadiani community was making all kinds of allegations against him, this revealed name *Majadd-ud-Din* was printed appended to the Maulana's name in many issues of *Paigham Sulh* in 1914.

choose a *khalifa* from the household of the Mahdi, who would cause more harm than good. A man would arise against him who would have the title *Mansur*.

There is another Hadith report, in Abu Dawud, that the Promised Messiah has quoted along with one of his visions, in his book *Izala Auham* in a footnote on pages 95 to 99. He writes that a man shall come forth from *Ma wara'-un-nahr,* meaning that his country of origin will be Bokhara or Samarkand, and he shall be called by the name 'Harith', meaning that as regards the ancestral occupation of his family he will be a farmer. The words of the Hadith report are as follows:

> "It is related on the authority of Ali that the Messenger of Allah, may peace and the blessings of Allah be upon him, said: A man will come forth from *Ma wara'-un-nahr* who will be called 'Harith', a farmer. The commander of his army will be a man called 'Mansur'."

The Promised Messiah has applied the prophecy about Harith to himself, and so he writes:

> "Let it be clear that the prophecy contained in the authentic hadith of Abu Dawud, that a man called Harith, a farmer, will come forth from *Ma wara'-un-nahr*, which means Samarkand, who will strengthen the followers of the Holy Prophet ... this prophecy and the prophecy about the coming of the Messiah who would be an imam of the Muslims and be from among the Muslims, both of these are about the same subject, and they are both fulfilled by my humble self."

Then he explains the words of the hadith "the commander of his army will be a man called Mansur" as follows:

> "And the commander of his army, that is the head and leader of the followers of Harith, will be a man helped by God who will be known in heaven as Mansur because God Himself will be the helper of his aspirations to serve the faith. Although this Mansur is described as the commander of an army, what is really meant is not military war or fighting, but that this will be a spiritual army

which will be given to Harith. This is as I saw in a vision
that there are two men sitting in a house, one on the
ground and the other near the roof. Then I called to the
man who was on the ground, saying that I needed an army
of one hundred thousand. But he remained silent, giving
no answer. Then I turned towards the other man who was
near the roof and towards the sky and said to him that
I needed an army of one hundred thousand. He replied that
he could not give one hundred thousand, but five thousand soldiers would be given. Then I thought to myself
that although five thousand is not much, but if God so
wills, a few can triumph over a greater number, and I recited
the Quranic verse: 'How often has a small party vanquished a numerous host by Allah's permission!' [2:249].
Then I was shown that man Mansur in a vision, and I was
told that he would be successful and blessed. But due to
some hidden purpose of Divine wisdom, I was not allowed
to recognise him. However, I hope he will be shown to
me at some other time."

(*Izala Auham,* pages 95–99; *Tazkira,* pages 181–182)

It has been made very clear in this vision that the Promised
Messiah saw two men leading his community, one sitting on the
ground and the other near the roof towards the sky. The man on
the ground had so many people that he was asked to spare one
hundred thousand, but he remained silent. Then Hazrat Mirza
sahib addressed the man on the roof and repeated the same request.
He replied that he could only give five thousand men. In fact this
is the ratio between the Qadiani *Jama'at* and the Lahore Ahmadiyya *Jama'at*. The Lahore Ahmadiyya *Jama'at* is hardly one-
twentieth of the Qadiani *Jama'at*. The 'sitting on the ground' and
the 'sitting near the roof towards the sky' refer to the inclinations
of the leaders of the two *Jama'ats*. The Qadiani *Jama'at* has concentrated more on worldly gains while the other group focussed its
attention on those higher objectives which are those that fulfil the
mission of Hazrat Mirza sahib. Another point made clear from this
vision is that the leader of his spiritual army, Mansur, is the one
who is the leader of the smaller group whose *Jama'at,* in its work,

fulfils the Quranic verse: "How often has a small party vanquished a numerous host by Allah's permission!".

At the end of this vision, the Promised Messiah has mentioned another point. He says:

> "Then I was shown that man Mansur in a vision, and I was told that he would be successful and blessed. But due to some hidden purpose of Divine wisdom, I was not allowed to recognise him. However, I hope he will be shown to me at some other time."

His book *Izala Auham* in which this vision is written was published in 1891. At that time neither Hazrat Mirza sahib had seen Maulana Muhammad Ali nor had the Maulana seen Hazrat Mirza sahib. Later on, when Maulana Muhammad Ali settled in Qadian, the manner in which Hazrat Mirza sahib expressed his desires about his mission and handed over all the work relating to it to Maulana Muhammad Ali shows that Hazrat Mirza sahib himself appointed the leader of his army.

The Promised Messiah had another dream about Maulana Muhammad Ali in June 1904, which is perhaps in reply to what the leaders of the Qadiani *Jama'at* later on said about Maulana Muhammad Ali. He says:

> "I saw Maulvi Muhammad Ali sahib in a dream: You also were righteous and had noble intentions. Come and sit by me." (*Al-Badr,* 1 August 1904, p. 4; *Tazkira,* p. 518)

Two things have been said here: he was "righteous" and he had "noble intentions". The first quality really answers those Qadianis who accused Maulana Muhammad Ali of being impious (*fasiq*), for 'righteous' (*salih*) is the opposite of impious. The other accusation made against him was that he was a mischief (*fitna*) maker and the breaking away from Qadian was called 'the *Paighami fitna*' (the word *Paighami* was coined in reference to the Lahore Ahmadiyya periodical *Paigham Sulh*). But Hazrat Mirza sahib himself testified to the Maulana's pure and good intentions, and his asking Maulana Muhammad Ali to sit beside him in the hereafter indicates that the Maulana continued the work of the Promised Messiah.

In short, all these dreams, visions and other writings of the Promised Messiah show that it was willed by God the Most High that Maulana Muhammad Ali be chosen to carry on the mission of Hazrat Mirza sahib and to bring his aspirations to fulfilment, and that Hazrat Mirza sahib delegated this work in his lifetime to the Maulana. And as it turned out, it was Maulana Muhammad Ali who was enabled by Allah to produce the commentary of the Holy Quran and write other comprehensive and excellent books on Islam, and it was the Maulana through whom Allah brought to fulfilment all the wishes of Hazrat Mirza sahib. In this way the Maulana's life is a part and a continuation of the life of Hazrat Mirza sahib, for it was Hazrat Mirza sahib's heartfelt desire to do the work of the propagation of Islam but it was the will of Allah that he should do some of that work in his life and the rest be completed after him by one of his followers. This is just as the keys to the palaces of the Caesar and the Chosroes (Qaisar and Kasra) were given to the Holy Prophet Muhammad in a vision but both these kingdoms were conquered by Hazrat Umar and the keys came to his hands, so that the lives of Hazrat Abu Bakr and Umar proved to be part of the life of the Holy Prophet. Similarly, some of the aspirations of the Promised Messiah were granted by God during his own lifetime but others were fulfilled after his death through Maulana Muhammad Ali, proving that Maulana Muhammad Ali's life was part of Hazrat Mirza sahib's life.

Another interesting incident may be related in this connection. The epidemic of the plague started raging in the Punjab from 1902 onwards. In Qadian it never assumed a serious form even though it was causing havoc in the surrounding villages. At that time Hazrat Mirza sahib had a revelation from Allah as follows: "I will protect everyone in this house, except those who are disobedient with arrogance". As in this revelation God had promised protection for all those who lived in his house, Hazrat Mirza sahib invited many people to reside with him. Maulana Abdul Karim and Maulana Muhammad Ali were already living there. Then Maulana Nur-ud-Din, Maulana Muhammad Ahsan of Amroha with his family, and some other families also moved into his house, each family living in one room.

It so happened, on 4 May 1904, that Maulana Muhammad Ali

felt a high fever and he thought that, although he was living within the house, but as the revelation made an exception for the arrogantly disobedient ones he might have some spiritual weakness within him and as a result he may have got the plague. Overcome by this thought, he sent for Mufti Muhammad Sadiq and started making his last will before him. When the Promised Messiah heard of this, he immediately came to visit Maulana Muhammad Ali and enquired as to how he was. The Maulana said that he had got plague and pointed to his high fever. On this the Promised Messiah said with great emotion:

> "If you have got the plague then I am a liar and my claim to receive Divine revelation is wrong." [5]

Saying this, the Promised Messiah felt for the pulse of the Maulana with his hand. A strange manifestation of the power of God took place, that the body cooled down as soon as he touched it and there was no sign of any fever. Maulana Muhammad Ali sat up fully recovered.[6] Mufti Muhammad Sadiq has stated that he

---

5. Hazrat Mirza sahib has himself written of this incident in *Haqiqat-ul-Wahy,* p. 253, from where these words are quoted. See further our Supplement at the end of this book, p. 535–536, for more references.

6. On the one hand Hazrat Mirza sahib had such complete faith in Maulana Muhammad Ali's righteousness and God-fearing nature, and on the other the Maulana's faith and conviction had reached such perfection that in later years when there were outbreaks of the plague epidemic in the areas where the Maulana was living he continued to stay in those places and refused to be inoculated, saying that the Promised Messiah's command was enough for him. In March 1924 Lahore was struck by a severe epidemic of the plague. Large numbers of people were dying, schools and offices had to be closed down and many people left the city. Maulana Muhammad Ali and his family, accompanied by other friends, moved to tents in an open field in what is now Muslim Town. But every morning he would go to his house in Ahmadiyya Buildings in the centre of the city of Lahore, work there all day and return in the evening. When cases of the plague spread to the Ahmadiyya Buildings area as well, Dr. Mirza Yaqub Baig and Dr. Syed Muhammad Husain Shah who were also residing in tents tried to persuade him, in vain, either to get inoculated or to stop going to the city. But he refused. Then they asked Maulana Muhammad Ali's wife to persuade him of this, but he always evaded the issue though he had his family inoculated. One day a rat crawled out from under a bookshelf in his office and died. He simply sprinkled kerosene over it and burnt it, and carried on with his work.

had himself touched Maulana Muhammad Ali's body just previously to this and it was burning hot, but after Hazrat Mirza sahib arrived only a few minutes later, the fever just disappeared.

On another occasion, referring to the aims of the Talim-ul-Islam school, Hazrat Mirza sahib said:

> "Our aim in starting this school is only that it can enable people to give priority to religion over worldly matters. The general curriculum has been introduced alongside so that this knowledge can be made to serve religion. Our aim is not that the students after passing their F.A. and B.A. examinations should go in search of worldly jobs, but that they may devote their lives to serving their faith. This is why I feel such a school to be a necessity, that it could be a useful institution in the service of the religion. The problem is that whoever gets even a little education goes after material gains. I wish that such people could be produced who would do the kind of work that Maulvi Muhammad Ali sahib is doing. There is no certainty of life, and he is all alone. We cannot see anyone who can assist him or take his place." (*Al-Hakam,* 10 December 1905; *Ruhani Khaza'in No. 2,* vol. 8, p. 269–270)

The Promised Messiah had so much confidence in Maulana Muhammad Ali with regard to having a correct and true understanding of the Promised Messiah's teachings, beliefs and claims that he issued the following instructions:

> "Hazrat *Aqdas* [Mirza sahib] called in the editors of *Al-Hakam* and *Al-Badr* and emphasized to them that they must be very careful in writing down his speeches and articles, in case something got misreported by mistake, which would then be used by the critics in their support. … So [added Hazrat Mirza sahib] 'it is proper that before publishing such articles in your newspapers you should show them to Maulvi Muhammad Ali sahib, M.A. You will benefit by this, and also people will be saved from error'." (Diary for 2 November 1902; *Ruhani Khaza'in No. 2,* vol. 4, page 159)

Need for an English Translation of the Holy Quran

By 1907 the need for an English translation of the Holy Quran was being widely felt among the educated Muslims, and many Indian newspapers were alluding to it. At that time the editor of the Ahmadiyya community newspaper *Al-Hakam,* referring to the dire necessity for an English translation, wrote that for this work a person was needed who was not only an expert of the Arabic language but also had full command of English. Besides this, he should be a godly person, having great zeal and fervour for the propagation of Islam, and be fully acquainted with the needs of the modern times. As to who could be that saint, the editor wrote:

> "It is a fact, which, if people do not realise it now, they will do so at a future time, that this revered person is the worthy young man Maulvi Muhammad Ali, M.A. By writing in defence of Islam and expounding its truth through the *Review of Religions* he has established the reputation of his pen in Asia and Europe so firmly that figures like Russell Webb and philosophers like Tolstoy acknowledge that the concepts of Islam presented in this magazine give satisfaction to the soul. In Europe and America the articles of this magazine have been read with great interest. They are not ordinary articles but deal with such important topics as hell and heaven, slavery, polygamy, jihad, preservation of the Quran, and compilation of Hadith reports, etc., that not everyone can write about. Any truthful person can see from the issues of this magazine how magnificently the philosophy of Islam has been presented...
>
> I have not put forward Maulvi Muhammad Ali sahib's name so that Muslims of India may choose him for this purpose or send him subscriptions. He neither needs this nor desires it. He has been working for years, sincerely and enthusiastically, serving Islam under the man sent by God. He is neither motivated by any greed nor can any difficulty or problem stop him. If God allows, he will do this work quietly and the world will find out how zeal for the service of Islam is made manifest."

(*Al-Hakam,* 17 August 1907, p. 7)

Represents Hazrat Mirza sahib in court cases

In addition to the literary and other religious work which Maulana Muhammad Ali was doing in Qadian, he also assisted Khwaja Kamal-ud-Din in representing Hazrat Mirza sahib in some court cases in that period.

On 15 July 1901, Hazrat Mirza sahib had to go to Gurdaspur to testify in a court case instituted against one Mirza Nizam-ud-Din and others who had tried to block public access to the Masjid-i-Mubarak at Qadian. Maulana Muhammad Ali and many other friends accompanied him. In Gurdaspur, at the suggestion of Maulana Muhammad Ali, Hazrat Mirza sahib stayed at the house of Mian Nabi Bakhsh, Maulana Muhammad Ali's father-in-law, for two days. Both Khwaja Kamal-ud-Din, who came from Peshawar, and Maulana Muhammad Ali represented Hazrat Mirza sahib in court and eventually won the case.

From January 1903 to January 1905 there was a series of court cases between one Maulvi Karam Din and the Promised Messiah and certain of his companions. In these cases Khwaja Kamal-ud-Din was the senior advocate representing Hazrat Mirza sahib, but Maulana Muhammad Ali also appeared with him. These cases were eventually decided in favour of Hazrat Mirza sahib. On 15 January 1903 Hazrat Mirza sahib left Qadian to attend the first case, which was to be heard in Jhelum, and after spending the night in Lahore he arrived in Jhelum on 16 January. During this journey Khwaja Kamal-ud-Din and Maulana Muhammad Ali accompanied him, and also with them was Shaikh Nur Ahmad as a lawyer. They returned on 18 January.

After that there were several cases in court at Gurdaspur which were prolonged because of the bias of a Hindu magistrate. After a year Hazrat Mirza sahib tried to get the cases transferred but was unsuccessful. In February 1904 an appeal in this connection was lodged in the Chief Court in Lahore where Khwaja Kamal-ud-Din and Maulana Muhammad Ali appeared but were not successful. From April 1904 so many dates kept on being set for the court hearings that Khwaja Kamal-ud-Din gave up his own practice in Peshawar and came to stay in Gurdaspur. In August 1904 Hazrat Mirza sahib also took a house in Gurdaspur and stayed there with his family because it was very difficult to travel again and again between Qadian and Gurdaspur. Once, in July, it even happened that when Hazrat Mirza sahib and some of his companions were travelling from Qadian to Batala at night, some robbers surrounded their carriage. However, they did not have the courage to attack, and ran away when challenged by Maulana Muhammad Ali and his two companions who were following behind.

During Hazrat Mirza sahib's stay in Gurdaspur, Maulana Muhammad Ali used to keep on travelling between Qadian and Gurdaspur, as his presence in Qadian was essential due to the publication of the *Review of Religions* and his other administrative duties. The court cases were largely pursued by Khwaja Kamal-ud-Din. At last, in October 1904, Hazrat Mirza sahib came back to Qadian. The great services rendered by the Khwaja sahib and the sacrifices made by him during these court cases are unrivalled and unique. He left his flourishing legal practice and his family and home in Peshawar to stay in Gurdaspur and concentrate on these cases day and night. His family suffered financial privations and other troubles and tribulations, one small daughter fell ill and died, but the Khwaja sahib did not leave Gurdaspur. Hazrat Mirza sahib prayed for him much in those days, and on one occasion he told him that he had received the revelation about him, *husn-i-bayan* (meaning eloquence of expression), so God would endow him with the gift of eloquent speech and articulation. This was exactly what happened. The Khwaja sahib's oratory was not confined only to the court room, but his religious lectures, whether in English or in Urdu, in India or in Europe, used to hold his audience spellbound. Not only was the content rational and well reasoned, but his delivery was so engaging and attractive that he had complete command over the audience.

During the Karam Din cases, when Hazrat Mirza sahib decided to move with his family to Gurdaspur and fixed a date to travel, it was the rainy season and due to heavy rains Qadian had become like an island as all routes were closed and trains were not running. Shaikh Yaqub Ali had to attend the court case on the due date, so he made his way on foot through the flood water with great difficulty to reach Gurdaspur. Arriving there, he mentioned

the hardships of the journey to Maulana Muhammad Ali and
Khwaja Kamal-ud-Din. There were also problems in securing the
house which Hazrat Mirza sahib was to occupy. So all of them
were worried and it was agreed that a man be sent to Qadian to
stop Hazrat Mirza sahib from embarking on this journey. At that
point a remark made by Maulana Muhammad Ali, through his insight and faith, was greatly enjoyed by his friends. He said: "You
can certainly send someone if you like, explain all the difficulties,
but *these people*[7] can't be stopped from their plans because their
determination is also a miracle." And so did it happen. Hazrat
Mirza sahib came to Gurdaspur according to his plan and the
problem of accommodation was solved as well.

During these court cases in August 1904 the Promised
Messiah and his family went to Lahore from Gurdaspur for a few
days. Maulana Muhammad Ali, his wife, Maulana Nur-ud-Din,
Maulana Abdul Karim and Nawab Muhammad Ali Khan accompanied them. They all stayed at the house of Mian Charagh Din
known as 'Mubarak Manzil' and the house of Mian Miraj Din,
located outside Delhi Gate. During his stay, Hazrat Mirza sahib's
well known lecture 'Islam and other Religions in this Country'
was delivered at a meeting place behind the shrine of Data Ganj
Bakhsh and was attended by several thousands of people.

On 22 October 1905, Hazrat Mirza sahib left on a journey to
Delhi. He later on sent for Maulana Nur-ud-Din. Maulana Muhammad
Ali did not accompany Hazrat Mirza sahib on this journey, but
stayed behind in Qadian. On 4 November Hazrat Mirza sahib started the return journey and, stopping at Ludhiana and Amritsar,
arrived in Qadian on 10 November. What is notable is that for the
period of his absence Hazrat Mirza sahib placed Maulana Muhammad
Ali in charge of the affairs of the Guest House and its food service
which the Promised Messiah always used to keep under his personal supervision. Apart from this, in Maulana Muhammad Ali's
papers there are found many letters and notes, from the time of his
stay in Qadian, addressed to him by Hazrat Mirza sahib, showing
that on many occasions when Hazrat Mirza sahib had some other

---

7. By "these people" he meant persons who are sent by God.

engagement, such as going to meet the district administrative officials, he made Maulana Muhammad Ali as in charge in his absence. On some such occasions Maulana Muhammad Ali sent notes to Hazrat Mirza sahib suggesting other people for the job, but Hazrat Mirza sahib would return the notes with instructions in his own handwriting on the back of the paper reiterating that the Maulana should take charge of the matter.

Sadr Anjuman Ahmadiyya founded

In 1905, after the Promised Messiah learnt through some Divine revelations that his death was approaching, he wrote certain instructions entitled *Al-Wasiyyat* ('The Will') for his followers, as to the arrangements for the community after his death. This he published on 20 December 1905. In this 'Will' he did not appoint any successor, but enjoined on the entire community to work together and make decisions by mutual consultation. However, to enable new members to be admitted to the community, he laid down that such elders of the community on whom forty faithful agree, may take the pledge from the entrants in the Promised Messiah's name. He also proposed to establish a graveyard at Qadian for his community, which he named 'Bahishti Maqbara' (the graveyard of heavenly people).

On 6 January 1906, Hazrat Mirza sahib published an Appendix to his book *Al-Wasiyyat*, in which he gave in detail all the necessary instructions regarding his Will. For the administrative system after him he laid the foundations of an 'Anjuman' (association) and appointed that Anjuman as his successor. He framed some rules and regulations himself, and declared the main object of the Anjuman to be the propagation of Islam.

In Rule 13 he wrote:

> "As the Anjuman is the successor to the *Khalifa* appointed by God, this Anjuman must remain absolutely free of any taint of worldliness. All its affairs must be completely above board, and based on fairness."

He explained this in more detail as follows:

> "All members of the Anjuman must belong to the Ahmad-

iyya Movement, and must be virtuous and honest. And if, in future, it is felt that someone is not virtuous, or that he is not honest, or that he is cunning and tainted with worldly motives, it shall be the duty of the Anjuman to expel him from its ranks forthwith and to appoint another in his place." (Rule 10, Appendix, *Al-Wasiyyat*)

With the publication of *Al-Wasiyyat* and its Appendix, Hazrat Mirza sahib laid down the foundation of this Anjuman and named it Sadr Anjuman Ahmadiyya Qadian, and proposed establishing its branches in other places where the community existed. He appointed fourteen members as trustees of this Anjuman, with Maulana Nur-ud-Din as President and Maulana Muhammad Ali as Secretary. The following are the names of the fourteen members:

1.   Maulana Nur-ud-Din, *President*
2.   Maulana Muhammad Ali, *Secretary*
3.   Khwaja Kamal-ud-Din, *Legal Advisor*
4.   Maulana Syed Muhammad Ahsan of Amroha
5.   Mirza Bashir-ud-Din Mahmud Ahmad
6.   Nawab Muhammad Ali Khan of Malir Kotla
7.   Seth Abdur Rahman of Madras
8.   Maulana Ghulam Hasan Khan of Peshawar
9.   Mir Hamid Shah of Sailkot
10.   Shaikh Rahmatullah of Lahore
11.   Dr. Mirza Yaqub Baig of Lahore
12.   Dr. Syed Muhammad Husain Shah of Lahore
13.   Dr. Khalifa Rashid-ud-Din
14.   Dr. Mir Muhammad Ismail

For the remaining two and a half years of his life Hazrat Mirza sahib ran this Anjuman according to the system and rules laid down in *Al-Wasiyyat*. It so happened that in the winter of 1907, in connection with the extension of the Mubarak Mosque, Mir Nasir Nawab, father-in-law of the Promised Messiah, wanted to impose his own judgment as against that of the Anjuman. On a complaint about this made by the Anjuman, Hazrat Mirza sahib personally came to a meeting of the Anjuman and wrote a note, as reproduced below, which is preserved in Maulana Muhammad Ali's papers. Its English translation is as follows:

"My view is that when the Anjuman reaches a decision in
any matter, doing so by majority of opinion, that must be
considered as right, and as absolute and binding. I would,
however, like to add that in certain religious matters, which
are connected with the particular objects of my advent,
I should be kept informed. I am sure that this Anjuman
would never act against my wishes, but this is written only
by way of precaution, in case there is a matter in which
God the Most High has some special purpose. This proviso
applies only during my life. After that, the decision of the
Anjuman in any matter shall be final.

Was-salaam. Mirza Ghulam Ahmad, 27 October 1907."

The image of the original Urdu note is shown below:

It was decided by this document that after Hazrat Mirza sahib's death the Anjuman would have complete authority. There would be no individual ruling over the Anjuman, and all the administration would be in the hands of the Anjuman. This was a great achievement of his, that he eradicated both the system of putting absolute power in the hands of the religious leader and the tradition of having an inherited spiritual headship.

Some other events

On 28 December 1906, on the occasion of the annual gathering of the Ahmadiyya community, Maulana Muhammad Ali submitted and read out the first annual report on the working of the Anjuman, and presented its annual budget, which amounted to Rs. 30,000 excluding the free kitchen. He made an impassioned speech in which he mentioned the companions of the Holy Prophet and how they sacrificed their lives and money, and said that God had made things easier in our time as there was no need to sacrifice life, but sacrifice of money was still needed. Concluding his speech he advised members of the community to lead a religious life and do for the religion even more than what others do for the materialistic world. He also appealed for funds for constructing the school building. (*Badr,* 10 January 1907, p. 9)

In 1907, in addition to the other matters, Maulana Muhammad Ali paid special attention to two developments. First, establishing branches of the Sadr Anjuman Ahmadiyya Qadian in various towns and districts. So through the community's newspapers and his personal letters he started the work of establishing these branches, which came into existence in many places as a result of his efforts. The second important task was to raise funds for the extension of the Masjid-i-Mubarak and to supervise its construction. For this purpose Maulana Muhammad Ali issued special appeals starting in the months of May and June 1907 to raise funds. By the end of 1907 the construction work was completed under his personal supervision. His own office, as the secretary of the Sadr Anjuman, was on the lower storey of the mosque.

Talim-ul-Islam High School

One of the growing needs of the Ahmadiyya community was a

proper building for the Talim-ul-Islam school in Qadian. It was a high school but was housed in mud huts. It was proposed to cons-truct a large boarding house and a building for the school. So a plot of land was purchased from the community's funds, and appeals were made at the annual gatherings in 1906 and 1907. In January 1908 the executive committee of the Anjuman nominated Mau-lana Muhammad Ali to raise funds for the building. He took up this campaign with great vigour and started raising funds. Besides appeals at the annual gatherings which he made while presenting the Anjuman's report and budget, he also launched repeated appeals through both the community newspapers *Badr* and *Al-Hakam,* re-quiring between one-third to a half of the monthly income of each person as a single donation. In this connection he said:

> "I am prepared to say that what I have demanded is not much. Perhaps Allah knows that a time will come when even greater demands will be made upon you because spreading religion is not an easy task. But this small sacri-fice will prepare you for greater sacrifices."

(Badr, 13 February 1908, p. 12, col. 2)

In February 1908 he organised a delegation to go on tour to raise funds for the building of the school. Apart from himself this included: Khwaja Kamal-ud-Din, Dr. Mirza Yaqub Baig, Dr. Syed Muhammad Husain Shah, Mian Charagh Din and Mian Miraj Din. On 16 February 1908 Maulana Muhammad Ali went to Lahore in this connection, and then also visited Amritsar and Kapurthala. After that, as his other commitments would not permit him to stay away from Qadian for much longer, he returned and the delegation continued its tour. (*Al-Hakam,* 22 February 1908, front page)

Financial Commissioner's visit to Qadian

In March 1908, when the financial commissioner for the Punjab, Mr. Wilson, came on a tour of Qadian, elaborate arrangements were made for his reception and dinner was provided on behalf of Hazrat Mirza sahib and the Ahmadiyya community. The next day Mr. Wilson met Hazrat Mirza sahib, and a long conversation took place during which Maulana Muhammad Ali and Khwaja Kamal-ud-Din acted as interpreters. (*Al-Hakam,* 26 March 1908, p. 1–2)

Some domestic events

As has been mentioned, about a year after his arrival in Qadian Maulana Muhammad Ali married Fatima Begum, daughter of Mian Nabi Bakhsh of Gurdaspur, the match being arranged by Hazrat Mirza sahib himself. During 1908 Fatima Begum was not keeping good health, so in November 1908 Maulana Muhammad Ali took leave from his work as Secretary of Sadr Anjuman Ahmadiyya Qadian and Editor of the *Review of Religions* and went to Lahore with his wife for her medical treatment, staying with Shaikh Rahmatullah. However, on 20 November 1908 Fatima Begum died. In the December 1908 issue of the Urdu edition of the *Review of Religions* Maulana Muhammad Ali has mentioned his seven and a half years of married life while announcing the news of the death of his wife. He wrote as follows under the heading *About Myself:*

"With this page, seven years of the life of the *Review* and of my editorship are completed. Although every human being encounters some sad and some happy occasions in his life, I have never written anything about my life in this magazine as I consider this organ to be above any mention of personal circumstances. Even now I am hesitant to pen these few lines. However, I believe that over such a long period a rapport is built between an editor and his readers so that they can share his sorrows and happiness, especially where there is a religious bond between them strengthening that rapport.

"On the very day when the November issue was leaving this office, that is, Friday 20 November, my wife died in Lahore at about 4 a.m., at my revered friend Shaikh Rahmatullah's residence where we were staying for her treatment. *We belong to Allah and to Him do we return!*

"The deceased Fatima Begum was born on 17 March 1886 in Shakar Gharh in this district and was married to me on 4 April 1901 at Gurdaspur. On 20 November 1908, after three months of severe nausea, she returned to her Maker at the age of 22 years and 8 months in Lahore. She was buried in Maqbara-i Bahishti in

Qadian on 21 November.[8] During her 7 years and 7 months of married life she gave birth to two children who died at birth, and to a daughter Ruqayya Begum on 26 November 1906 who is left with me in her memory.

"This relationship was of special happiness for me because it was arranged by my leader and master, the Promised Messiah himself, who married me as if I were his own son. It was the result of his prayers that she proved to be such a sharer in my feelings that I myself was surprised. Another reason for my happiness was that when this union was arranged I had put everything together to start my legal practice in Gurdaspur and I had also been accepted as a candidate to take the E.A.C. examination, but when the marriage ceremony took place I was staying in Qadian having given up worldly ambitions. In spite of that, the deceased's father Munshi Nabi Bakhsh did not object to this, but what is more even my wife never alluded to it nor did she ever express any wish that I should leave Qadian and try to earn worldly wealth for her. In this way she helped me in my migration, and by sharing in my hardship she saved me from many trials and dilemmas.

"Women usually crave for material things but she did not find it difficult to give up any such hopes for the sake of her husband. This is not easy. I know of many instances in which some women who preferred worldly wealth hindered their husbands from carrying out their good intentions. The word of Allah also bears witness to this: 'Among your wives and children, there are those who are your enemies' [The Quran 64:14]. I cannot thank Allah enough for providing such a spouse for me who, far from being an opponent of my religious work, proved to be an aid and helper. So if I have done any service to the faith — and only God knows if I have, because He knows the intentions — I consider that my late wife too is a sharer in that work in the sight of God. That is why I have mentioned her death in these pages. She also had a great passion to help the poor and needy, so much so that sometimes she would help them even without my knowledge. When people were asked

8. On her gravestone Maulana Muhammad Ali also inscribed the words: *How well did you fulfil the covenant that was between us!*

to make wills [for the Movement], she was one of the first to do so, and made a will for one-third of her possessions.

"During her illness Hazrat Khalifat-ul-Masih [Maulana Nur-ud-Din] showed such sympathy that I cannot find the words to describe it. Similarly, the revered Khalifa Rashid-ud-Din made such exertions in providing treatment, purely for the sake of God, that there are very few examples of this kind of devotion on the basis of worldly ties. Then in Lahore the practical help provided by my honoured friends Shaikh Rahmatullah, Khwaja Kamal-ud-Din, Dr. Syed Muhammad Husain Shah, Dr. Mirza Yaqub Baig, Babu Ghulam Muhammad and Hakim Muhammad Husain Qureshi, was beyond all my expectations. I was taken aback because it is my misfortune that I have never had the chance to do anything for these people. Indeed, this passionate love which my elders and brothers show towards me, in the way of Allah, is living proof of the words: 'so by His favour you became brethren' [the Quran 3:103].

"Allah tries His servants with death of their near and dear ones. ... No matter how weak I proved in this test, due to my love for my late wife, there is no doubt that those who showed me love, for the sake of Allah, acquitted themselves successfully because in my hour of need they showed me sympathy beyond my expectations. May Allah reward them! However, all are not the same. If someone, despite being my benefactor, has instead of showing sympathy mentioned some past grievance at the time of this death, it was perhaps a lesson for me that it is a mistake to consider any worldly abode as your home."

Death of the Promised Messiah

On 27 April 1908 the Promised Messiah went to Lahore on his last journey. In his absence from Qadian, he put Maulana Muhammad Ali in charge of the Guest House, which used to be in the Promised Messiah's personal supervision, and of other matters. In Lahore, Hazrat Mirza sahib stayed first of all at the house of Khwaja Kamal-ud-Din. Some other friends including Maulana Nur-ud-Din and Maulana Muhammad Ahsan of Amroha also came to Lahore. After some time Hazrat Mirza sahib shifted to the residence of Dr. Syed Muhammad Husain Shah. In Ahmadiyya

Buildings the place where the mosque is now situated was then an open ground. By erecting marquees over it and spreading rolls of mats on the ground, it was used for holding Friday prayers and Maulana Nur-ud-Din gave daily talks on the Holy Quran.

On 26 May 1908 Hazrat Mirza Ghulam Ahmad, the Promised Messiah, breathed his last, and that night his coffin was taken by railway train to Batala and from there to Qadian. The whole of the Ahmadiyya community accepted Maulana Nur-ud-Din as successor to Hazrat Mirza sahib. It was a time of the utmost sorrow for the Ahmadiyya community on the one hand, and on the other at this very time its opponents had raised a storm of abuse and vilification. Thus the community faced a two-fold trial at that time.

During his stay in Lahore the Promised Messiah had composed his last writing, *Paigham-i Sulh* (Message of Peace). As after his death this was to be read out at a public meeting at University Hall, Lahore, on 21 June 1908, a large number of Ahmadis gathered in Lahore. On this occasion, in obedience to Maulana Nur-ud-Din's instructions, Maulana Muhammad Ali made a speech which was deeply effective, impassioned and moving. Mentioning Hazrat Mirza sahib he said:

"What a great and glorious objective is facing you. It is as if a gigantic mountain is standing in your way and you have to remove it to clear the way. It is easy to move a mountain but the mission that our Imam has entrusted to us is of even greater importance. It is to spread Islam in the world. Is it a small and easy task? What encourages us is that God Himself has promised that He will make Islam prevail through this community. So there is no reason to panic or lose heart. The holy Hazrat [Mirza sahib] has himself written: 'I do not know which impossible paths I will have to tread, which thorn-filled wildernesses and deserted jungles I will have to traverse, so if anyone has delicate feet he should take leave of me now.' Friends! that time has now come and those difficult-to-cross ravines, thorny jungles and frightful wildernesses are to come before us which we must cross to reach the destination pointed out by our pious Imam and true guide. Earlier we had a man among us who was taking care of our affairs splendidly with great skill. To tell you the truth, we used to sleep without a care while that pure hearted man, the chosen one of God, comforted us like a loving mother and protected us from every difficulty like a shield. We were untroubled and carefree. ... That era has now passed. That holy man who carried our loads on his own head, having done his work, has gone to meet his Creator in accordance with the Divine promises. Now you have to shoulder all the burden, and you are the people who have to accomplish that work and bring it to completion. ...

"Hazrat [Mirza] sahib's being was a cloud of mercy and a shade of benevolence sent over us from God. He turned us away from sins and established us upon goodness, he transformed our dead and dry belief in God into a fresh and living faith, and he filled our hearts with reverence and honour for God and His Prophet like solid steel. Our moral condition was unspeakable, but he made us drink such an elixir that we began to enjoy and get pleasure from our prayers and remembrance of God, and our hearts were filled with love for the Holy Quran. Everyone progressed in righteousness according to his power and aptitude. ... So we have to learn a lesson from his death. ... Blessed are those who can set an example of a pure transformation and steadfastness at this time. It is the sign of a believer that even at the time of a calamity he moves forward."

After this he refuted the objections being made by the opponents at the death of Hazrat Mirza sahib and said that, despite the severest opposition raging, he convinced hundreds of thousands of people of his views by his virtuous and noble life. He infused his spirit in his followers. If, filled with this spirit, we do this work the doors of spiritual victories will open for us. After the death of the Holy Prophet, great conquests were made by Hazrat Abu Bakr and Hazrat Umar, and many more after them. This was due to the Holy Prophet's spirit working in the companions. Likewise, after the Promised Messiah's death this Movement has not come to an end. God has not closed those doors to us that were open in his time. But it is our duty to continue the same work with hard labour and effort for this lofty objective, and to try to make Islam triumph over all other religions. (*Al-Hakam,* 18 July 1908)

2.2: The Times of Maulana Nur-ud-Din

May 1908 to March 1914

Overview

After the death of Hazrat Mirza Ghulam Ahmad, his successor Maulana Nur-ud-Din led the Ahmadiyya community from 1908 till 1914. During these six years, whereas on the one hand the Ahmadiyya Movement made tremendous progress and laid the foundations of many great and magnificent works, yet on the other hand there were some destructive activities undertaken by certain elements which not only brought about a split in the community but also did irreparable and lasting damage to the advancement and popularity of the Ahmadiyya Movement.

On the bright side, the annual budget of the Sadr Anjuman Ahmadiyya rose astonishingly from Rs. 30,000 to Rs. 200,000. This was largely due to Maulana Muhammad Ali's work because he was the General Secretary as well as the life and soul of the Sadr Anjuman Ahmadiyya. However, his success made certain people feel bitter and agitated. During this period a grand building was constructed for an educational establishment, whose physical structure is even today proclaiming that the man who played the central role in its construction, indeed under whose supervision and advice it was built, possessed a first-rate architectural mind. In the same period, under the guidance of Maulana Nur-ud-Din, Maulana Muhammad Ali laid down firm and permanent foundations for the propagation of Islam in the shape of the English and Urdu translations of the Holy Quran with commentaries. Again in those days, the Ahmadiyya Movement was gaining popularity among the general Muslim public. The *Review of Religions* edited by Maulana Muhammad Ali and the lectures given by Khwaja

Kamal-ud-Din in various parts of India raised the Ahmadiyya community to a prominent status among the educated Muslims of India. Later in the same period Khwaja Kamal-ud-Din went to England where he established the Woking mission in 1913.

On the dark side, some destructive activities also started during this period. Plots were made to sow the seeds of distrust in Maulana Nur-ud-Din's mind against Maulana Muhammad Ali and the members of the Anjuman. Efforts were made to deprive the Sadr Anjuman Ahmadiyya of its powers or to have some members from Lahore expelled from it. According to a conceived plan, a body known as 'Majlis Ansarullah' was created, while along with that the doctrine of calling other Muslims as unbelievers (*kafir*) was invented. In short, just as this was the period of progress for the community, at the same time all these activities were taking place behind the scenes whose devastating results became manifest upon the death of Maulana Nur-ud-Din in 1914. We will turn to the causes of the Split in the next chapter. First we look at the bright side of this period.

Early life of Maulana Nur-ud-Din

Maulana Nur-ud-Din came from a well respected family of Bhera, district Shahpur, Punjab, and was the pride of the family. He was widely renowned for his knowledge, scholarship, rectitude and virtuous character. Besides being a highly capable physician, he was an incomparable and illustrious scholar of all branches of religious knowledge and had a huge collection of books famed as being magnificent and comprehensive. He had travelled to many educational centres in India to learn the *Unani* system of medical treatment by the use of indigenous drugs, as well as the religion of Islam from the then famous teachers of theology. He was so widely-read and had such minute knowledge that on any topic under discussion he could quote from memory exact references to book and page from the works of scholars. He had a great love for the Holy Quran. During his youth he travelled to Delhi, Lucknow, Rampur and Bhopal etc. for purposes of education. He also went as far as Makkah and Madinah, and for some time there he joined Shah Abdul Ghani's students and disciples, gaining knowledge of both the exoteric and esoteric aspects of religion. On his return to

India he was appointed personal physician to the Maharaja of Jammu and served there for several years, earning a handsome salary. At the same time he kept up teaching and imparting the vast ocean of knowledge which he possessed. The events of his life can be read in more detail in the book *Mirqat-ul-Yaqin Fi Hayat Nur-ud-Din* by Maulvi Akbar Shah Khan of Najeebabad.

He happened to read Hazrat Mirza Ghulam Ahmad's book *Barahin Ahmadiyya* and came to know of Hazrat Mirza sahib's claim that today Islam is the only true and living religion by following which a person can find God, that Allah bestows revelation upon His chosen servants, and that Hazrat Mirza sahib himself had personal experience of this so that whoever so wished could come and stay with him and judge for himself. Having read this, Maulana Nur-ud-Din came to Qadian from Jammu to meet Hazrat Mirza sahib and stayed with him for some time. Here he realised that all the knowledge he had gained by travelling to different Islamic countries was inadequate. In 1888 Hazrat Mirza sahib received the Divine command to take the pledge (*bai'at*) from people and form a community (*jama'at*), and in March 1889 Maulana Nur-ud-Din became the first person to take the pledge. After some time he gave up his royal job and came to stay with Hazrat Mirza sahib, and in his obedience of the Promised Messiah and his sacrifices for the Movement he surpassed all others.

People of all faiths not only benefited by his medical practice but friend and foe alike acknowledged his scholarship, learning and godliness. The most prominent feature of his life was his love for the Holy Quran. God bestowed upon him the knowledge of His Book and he worked day and night to teach it to others. Till his death it was his daily routine to impart knowledge of the Holy Quran, and everyone benefited from his teaching to the extent of his or her ability. As has been mentioned before, he lived in a small part of Hazrat Mirza sahib's house, the same house where later on Maulana Abdul Karim and Maulana Muhammad Ali also occupied one or two rooms each.

When Hazrat Mirza sahib died, Maulana Nur-ud-Din was the man regarding whom the entire community was unanimous that only he could be his successor. However, he accepted this burden only with reluctance. When Khwaja Kamal-ud-Din and some other persons went to him with this request, he proposed one or two other names. When they insisted, he said that Mirza Mahmud Ahmad (eldest son of the Promised Messiah) and Mir Nasir Nawab (father-in-law of the Promised Messiah) did not agree with the proposal. So Mirza Mahmud Ahmad was questioned about it, and he replied that he would have to consult his mother. After that consultation, when both he and Mir Nasir Nawab expressed agreement, only then did Maulana Nur-ud-Din accept this responsibility. First he said two *raka'hs* of prayer, then he declared his beliefs and after that he took the pledge from people.

Commencement of the English Translation of the Holy Quran

For almost six years, from May 1908 to March 1914, Maulana Nur-ud-Din was the Head of the Ahmadiyya community. During this period, Maulana Muhammad Ali was every year elected as secretary of the Sadr Anjuman Ahmadiyya, he continued his duties as editor of the *Review of Religions,* he was in charge of the Anjuman's works relating to education, publication and buildings, and in addition he had to devote time to other affairs. However, the time had now come for that work to be started for which God the Most High had been preparing Maulana Muhammad Ali in Qadian. Maulana Nur-ud-Din, through his penetrating insight, selected his beloved student Maulana Muhammad Ali for the service and the spreading of the Holy Quran, and instructed him to start the work of writing the English translation and commentary of the Holy Quran. In 1909, at the age of 35 years, Maulana Muhammad Ali took up this great work which was completed in seven years. During this time, the Split took place in the Movement in 1914 after Maulana Nur-ud-Din's death; and even during his life, a faction of the community tried to cause problems for Maulana Muhammad Ali and created hindrances which, by the grace of God, were removed.

In 1909 Maulana Muhammad Ali, who was secretary of the Sadr Anjuman Ahmadiyya Qadian and editor of the *Review of Religions,* put the proposal for his English translation of the Holy Quran before the Anjuman in the following words:

"As far as I have considered the matter, before starting

the translation at least one year is required for a prepara-
tory study of different Urdu and English translations of
the Quran and lexicons of Arabic and English. After that,
the translation would take no less than two years to be
completed. So it will take at least three years to complete
the translation, and possibly four or five years. As it will
cost eight or nine thousand Rupees, and unlike the magazine there will be no immediately visible results, it is
possible that some well wishers of the community might
start to have misgivings. This is a very important and
delicate matter. The Ahmadiyya Anjumans must be consulted so that I am not blamed later on. This is a new
venture and I cannot say at the moment how good a translation I will be able to produce. It is all in Allah's hands.
... Of course if Allah's help and support comes to us then
this work can prove beneficial for the world. ... If the expenses cannot be borne then it is possible that Allah will
provide some other means for me and I might be able to
work in my spare time, little by little. In that way I would
hope to accomplish it in eight to ten years.
(Signed) Muhammad Ali. 30 May 1909."

The decision taken by the Anjuman was the following:

"Resolution 919 dated 6 June 1909 was put forward and it
was decided that the Holy Quran should be translated into
English and Maulvi Muhammad Ali sahib should be
appointed for this work."

Accordingly, Maulana Muhammad Ali still remained secretary of the Sadr Anjuman Ahmadiyya and editor of the *Review of
Religions*. He was also in charge of the Anjuman's educational,
construction and literary work. The magnificent building of the
Talim-ul-Islam High School and Boarding House was constructed
entirely by his efforts and under his supervision. Besides these he
also did various miscellaneous works.

On 27 December 1911 Maulana Muhammad Ali submitted
the following report to the executive committee of the Anjuman:

"Report of the Editor of the *Review of Religions:*

In the meeting of 26 June 1909 I presented a report to the effect that the English translation of the Holy Quran would take three years or somewhat more to complete. At this time, after two and a half years, 21 parts have been translated and it is hoped that the rest of the work will be finished in the next six months. But to publish only a translation is not very useful and the following additions are necessary:

1. A margin containing cross references from one place to other places in the Holy Quran.

2. In addition to the brief footnotes that will appear on each page below the translation, there should also be notes in the following places:

> *a.* At the beginning of each section (*rukū'*) its summary and the inter-relation of its verses should be given as a heading; *b.* At the beginning of each chapter (*sūrah*) its summary showing its connection with the previous chapter; *c.* At the end of each chapter a note on the important subjects dealt with in it.

3. A detailed introduction in the beginning of the translation.

To accomplish all these, it will take three or at least two years after the completion of the translation. In the two and a half years in which 21 parts have been translated much time was spent on other work, for example one month was spent on the debates in Rampur and Masuri. I have to travel here and there in connection with the work of the Anjuman. Here itself a great deal of time is taken up everyday in completing the work of different sections of the Anjuman. The book *The Teachings of Islam* was printed during this period. Revising its translation, proof-reading the typescript and re-reading the book took up much time. Then a lecture was prepared for the Convention of Religions in Allahabad. Another point which I have always borne in mind is that when I translate any word I should myself research its meaning, because it is not useful just to copy out the earlier translations. Mr. Macaulif spent fifteen years to translate and publish a few parts of the *Granth Sahib*. So in my opinion the translation can only be useful when the above mentioned features are incorporated.

(Signed) Muhammad Ali. 27 December 1911."

(From the report of the executive committee)

The records of the Sadr Anjuman Ahmadiyya Qadian do not show anywhere that Maulana Muhammad Ali was taken in paid employment to do the translation or that, as he was already emp-loyed by the Anjuman, his job was now being changed and his pay would be for different work. The Maulana continued to recei-ve his salary for the work he was already doing, which has been mentioned above, and he did the translation either in his spare time or when he was on leave.

It is necessary to make this clear because after the Split the Qadiani community raised the objection that the Sadr Anjuman Ahmadiyya was the owner of the translation. Many years later some members of the Lahore Ahmadiyya community, who had some other differences with Maulana Muhammad Ali, also tried to raise the same objection.

In the same connection it may be noted that on 14 July 1913 Maulana Muhammad Ali submitted the following report to the Sadr Anjuman:

"Resolution 335 dated 14 July 1913. Application from the Editor of the *Review of Religions:* 'As I am suffering from weakness after having been ill for a few days, and Hazrat *Khalifat-ul-Masih* has recommended that I should go to the mountains for a few days, so I have decided to go to Murree hills. I will take with me the work of trans-lating the Holy Quran which has been made my respon-sibility because I cannot remain idle there. If my absence from Qadian is considered as absence from my duties then I should be granted two months leave.'

> This having been presented, it was sanctioned that Maulvi Muhammad Ali sahib, Editor of the *Review of Religions,* should be granted two and a half months leave from 15 July 1913 to 30 September 1913."

If the work of translation had been assigned to him as a paid job then granting leave becomes meaningless. The Anjuman's granting him leave, during which he would continue the translation, makes it clear that he was not being paid to do this work though the Anjuman encouraged him to carry it on. Thus during his stay in Qadian the Maulana carried on this work in his own way and according to his own judgment. Sometimes at home, with piles of books on the table, he worked by candle light at night, and sometimes he continued on this work when on leave.

During his absence Khalifa Rashid-ud-Din performed the duties of secretary, and in those days Maulvi Sher Ali was the assistant editor of the *Review of Religions.*

Maulana Muhammad Ali later on repeated the same facts about this matter. Thus in *Paigham Sulh* of 6 February 1916 he said:

> "I put the proposal of translating the Quran before the Anjuman and also wrote in it that if the Anjuman cannot bear the expenses then Allah will provide some other means for me. ... I did not say to the Anjuman I am your employee so give me some work, but I said I want to translate the Quran and if the Anjuman cannot bear the expenses then God will provide some other means. Allah brought that about as well, that the Anjuman declined to pay the expenses and the generous Lord gave me other means."

Before this, in July 1914 after the Split, in his correspondence with the Sadr Anjuman Ahmadiyya Qadian he clearly wrote that the translation was his writing and his intellectual property.

Maulana Nur-ud-Din's interest in the English translation
As has been said above, Maulana Nur-ud-Din was a very great expositor of the Quran and Hadith, and a tremendous lover of the Quran. So Maulana Muhammad Ali used to read to him the

translation that he was doing and take guidance and amendments from him. Maulana Nur-ud-Din's love for the Quran and his interest in Maulana Muhammad Ali's translation had reached such a height that when in January 1914, following the annual gathering of 1913, he fell very ill and was so weak that even speaking exhausted him, so that on medical advice he discontinued his teaching of the Quran, even then, in a state of the most serious illness, he would still send for Maulana Muhammad Ali daily to listen to his translation and notes and give advice.

The last days of the life of Maulana Nur-ud-Din were chronicled by Dr. Mirza Yaqub Baig who was staying in Qadian in those days to treat him. This diary used to be published at that time, in February and March 1914, in every issue of the newspaper *Paigham Sulh.* It was again published in *Paigham Sulh* in 1935. Some extracts from it are given here. These relate to Maulana Muhammad Ali and his work on the English translation of the Quran and show a glimpse of Maulana Nur-ud-Din's love of the Quran. Maulana Muhammad Ali himself, once speaking of these last days of Maulana Nur-ud-Din's life, said:

> "It was my good fortune that I had the opportunity to learn the Quran from him even in those days when he was on his death bed. I used to read out to him notes from my English translation of the Holy Quran. He was seriously ill, but even in that state he used to be waiting for when Muhammad Ali would come. And when I came to his presence, that same critically ailing Nur-ud-Din would turn into a young man. The service of the Quran that I have done is just the result of his love for the Holy Quran." (*Paigham Sulh,* 28 April 1943, p. 3)

Here are some entries from the diary of Dr. Mirza Yaqub Baig:

"9 February 1914 — This evening we were feeding *Hazur* and he said to me: 'I have learnt something from you too'. I replied: 'But I have learnt much from you'. He said: 'I only know the Quran and I can only teach you that'. I said: 'May Allah grant you a long life so that we can learn the Holy Quran from you'. He said:

'Ask Maulvi Muhammad Ali sahib about my knowledge of the Quran. Having worked very hard Maulvi sahib comes with hundreds of pages and I abridge them. He sometimes says that my opinion is better than all research.'

Then he said: 'Maulvi sahib has pleased me very much, I am so happy. What wonderful research he has done on Gog and Magog, companions of the cave and Dhu-l-Qarnain! He has searched through encyclopaedias. How clearly he has solved this problem! Marvellous!"

(*Paigham Sulh,* 15 February 1914)

"**Qadian, 11 February 1914** — When Hazrat Maulvi Muhammad Ali sahib arrived to read to him the translation of the Holy Quran he said to him: Come that I may live!"

(*Paigham Sulh,* 26 February 1914)

"**15 February 1914** — Maulvi Sher Ali sahib, Nawab sahib, Maulvi Muhammad Ali sahib, Dr. Syed Muhammad Husain sahib, Marham Isa sahib and many other friends were present. He said:

'The issue of *kufr* and Islam is a very subtle matter, which many people have not understood'.

Mian Mahmud Ahmad sahib and Maulvi Muhammad Ali sahib were sitting near the Hazrat sahib. He pointed towards them and said: Our Mian has also not understood it."

(*Paigham Sulh,* 3 November 1935)

"**14 February 1914** — Hazrat sahib is still in a critical condition. His diarrhoea is better but he is getting weaker by the day. May Allah have mercy on him. He listens to Maulvi Muhammad Ali sahib's translation of the Quran daily. His courage and determination is very great and his love for the Quran is unequalled. He says: It is the Quran which is the source of my soul and life."

(*Paigham Sulh,* 17 February 1914)

"**16 February 1914** — Yesterday Hazrat sahib was relatively better though the weakness continues. He addressed me and Khalifa Rashid-ud-Din sahib, saying:

'For fifteen days I have completely obeyed your orders (that is, taken diet and medication according to your instructions). I used to teach seven classes daily (meaning, teaching the Quran and Hadith), but now I don't teach even one. Let me do something now.'

He wanted permission to teach classes in the Quran. I replied:

'Sir, at the moment you are teaching Maulvi Muhammad Ali sahib. When you are stronger then you can teach a class.'

… His love for the Quran is beyond description, so much that even in this state of extreme weakness all he can think of is giving classes in the Quran and his mind keeps working on the deep meanings of the Holy Quran.

When Maulvi Muhammad Ali sahib comes to read the notes of the Holy Quran to him, sometimes even before he begins Hazrat sahib gives a discourse about the topic of the translation of the day and says that throughout the night he had been consulting books and thinking about it. (He does not mean that he actually reads books; what he means is that he keeps running over in his mind what is written in commentaries of the Quran and books of Hadith.) Sometimes he quotes from books of Hadith or the Bible, and does it perfectly accurately. He says again and again that his mind is fully healthy and it never stops working on the Quran."

(*Paigham Sulh,* 19 February 1914)

"**18 February 1914** — While he was in a state of extreme weakness, showing few signs of life except pulse and breathing, and his body was cold, Maulvi Muhammad Ali sahib came as usual to read out notes from the Holy Quran. … [While instructing him regarding certain verses of the Quran] he spoke with pauses, sometimes of a minute or two. … Then he addressed Maulvi Muhammad Ali sahib and said:

'Seeing you every day is also food for my soul'.

Then he added: 'Maulvi sahib, you are very dear to me. I found one useful weapon (meaning Maulvi Muhammad Ali sahib), full of knowledge, it is God's grace to you'.

Maulvi Muhammad Ali sahib replied: 'It is my good fortune that I can expound your ideas'.

Hazrat sahib said: 'It is all the grace of God. What has happened is by His grace and what will happen will be by His grace'. ... Then he added: 'This translation will *inshallah* be beneficial in Europe, Africa, America, China, Japan and Australia'."

(*Paigham Sulh,* 3 November 1935)

"**21 February 1914** — Hazrat sahib called in Maulvi Muhammad Ali sahib for a discourse of the Quran. At that time Abdul Hayy's mother [wife of Maulana Nur-ud-Din] was also present. After the discourse Hazrat sahib got hold of Maulvi Muhammad Ali sahib's hand and slowly took it towards himself and kissed it."

(*Paigham Sulh,* 15 November 1935)

"**22 February 1914** — He was very cheerful today. ... When told that Maulvi Muhammad Ali sahib had come to read the [translation of the] Quran, he said: 'He is most welcome. Let him read it. Does my brain ever get tired of it?' Then he pointed towards his bed and said: 'Let Maulvi Muhammad Ali sahib come near me'. Then added: 'He is very dear to me'."

(*Paigham Sulh,* 15 November 1935)

One day Maulana Muhammad Ali was delayed. Maulana Nur-ud-Din was very weak but said in that state: "Send for my dear son, send for my dear son". People listening to him thought that he was asking for his son Abdul Hayy, but he said again: "Bring the food for my soul, bring the food for my soul". And he was much pleased when Maulana Muhammad Ali arrived.[1]

In short, these incidents show Maulana Nur-ud-Din's love for Maulana Muhammad Ali and his interest in the translation of the Quran. During the time when the English translation was in progress, once Mir Nasir Nawab, father-in-law of the Promised Messiah, wanted to get work started on an Urdu translation and commentary of the Holy Quran and even collected some funds for it. But Maulana Nur-ud-Din stopped him and said that the Urdu translation on behalf of the Movement would also be done by Maulana Muhammad Ali, after he had completed the English translation. Maulana Muhammad Ali stated that he was in Murree due to his ill health when Maulana Nur-ud-Din wrote to him saying that as he has also to translate the Quran in Urdu after completing his English translation, he should start doing it along with the English. Hence, according to these instructions, he started doing the Urdu translation as well, little by little, and almost six parts were seen by Maulana Nur-ud-Din.

An announcement dated 3 March 1914, that is, eleven days before the death of Maulana Nur-ud-Din, regarding the English translation of the Quran was published as an appendix to the *Review of Religions,* February 1914 issue. On the first page there is a statement by Maulana Nur-ud-Din in which he says:

> "I want to draw the attention of friends, by this announcement, towards raising funds for the English translation of the Holy Quran. Up to today I have listened to the notes of twenty-three parts, which is more than three-quarters of the work, and have also seen the Urdu translation of six parts. I hope by the grace of Allah that I will complete the rest. Even during my illness I have been listening to the notes and dictating as well. I have spent all my life, from childhood to old age, studying the Holy Quran and pondering over it, and Allah the Most High has given me the kind of understanding of His Holy Word that very few other people have. I have always adhered to the principles

---

1. This incident is not reported in Dr. Mirza Yaqub Baig's diary but was related to Maulana Muhammad Ali by one of those present.

of simplicity, avoidance of unfounded stories and following the obvious meaning of the Quran, and I have tried to
teach others on the same lines as well. In future times too,
servants of the Quran will continue to arise according to
the needs of the time.

Now I want to draw the attention of friends to the expenses of publishing the English translation, and after it the
Urdu translation. I hope for grace from Allah that He will
not let go to waste my efforts in the service of His Word.
I am also sure that those people who have a connection
with me and who love me have also been granted the zeal
to serve the Quran. ... This translation will *inshallah*
prove to be beneficial in Europe, Africa, America, China,
Japan, Australia, etc."

After this announcement there follows a statement by Maulana Muhammad Ali in which, among other things, he says:

"To translate the Holy Quran is a monumental work. The
way in which the meanings of the word of Allah have
been explained, in that respect I can say that this translation of the Holy Quran will not only remove numerous
misconceptions in the West and among the English speaking nations, but at the same time it will *inshallah* show
the resplendent picture of Islam in such a manner that at
least among fair minded people those adverse views about
Islam will be overturned which Westerners have been
holding till today. All this will happen only by the grace
of Allah. But my hopes rest on the fact that all the
important explanations given in this translation have come
from a man who has devoted his entire life, from childhood to the age of 80 years, to the study and service of
the Holy Quran, and has read thousands of books only to
gain insight into the meanings of some verse or other,
who is familiar with classical and modern thought and the
old and the new sciences, and has studied all these branches of knowledge to bring them into the service of the
Quran, who is not only the leader of the Ahmadiyya Movement but is one of those rare personalities who, because

of their vast study and extensive knowledge, are entitled to be leaders of communities. He is a unique individual as regards his knowledge, learning, uprightness and faith in Allah. ...

The real objective of our movement is the propagation of Islam, and in that work the propagation of the Holy Quran holds the foremost place. ... I end my appeal on a verse of the Quran which is the last one in my notes of today: 'Behold! you are those who are called upon to spend in Allah's way, but among you are those who are niggardly, and whoever is niggardly is niggardly against his own soul; and Allah is Self-sufficient and you have need (of Him), and if you turn back He will bring in your place another people, then they will not be like you' (47:38).

Humbly, Muhammad Ali, Qadian, 3 March 1914."

Underneath this announcement there are two notes as follows:

1. By the time this announcement was printed, the footnotes of 26 parts had been completed.

2. On 4 March Hazrat [Maulana Nur-ud-Din] said: 'Our English translation has been accepted by Allah. This good news has come by Divine revelation'.

The good news (*basharat*) mentioned in this quotation was revealed to a holy man of the Ahmadiyya community, Mir Abid Ali Shah, who had in a vision, while praying, heard this glad tiding. He told it to Maulana Nur-ud-Din during his last illness in the presence of Maulana Muhammad Ali and a large number of other Ahmadis. Hearing this, Maulana Nur-ud-Din, Maulana Muhammad Ali and everyone else who was present at once fell in prostration in thanksgiving (*sajda shukr*).

Calcutta Convention of Religions
In April 1909, a major, large scale Convention of Religions was held at Calcutta. When the announcement of this convention reached Qadian, then in compliance with Maulana Nur-ud-Din's instructions Maulana Muhammad Ali wrote a comprehensive paper in

English on Islam, and on 2 April he went to Lahore, from where on 6 April he went to Calcutta with Khwaja Kamal-ud-Din. The convention started on April 9 in the Town Hall. The first day was taken up by introductory speeches. On the second day, there were three speeches on Christianity and these were followed by three speeches on Islam: the first by Mirza Abul Fazal, the second by Maulvi Khuda Bakhsh and the third by Maulana Muhammad Ali. When the time came for the Maulana's speech, and Khwaja Kamal-ud-Din rose to deliver it, it was already afternoon and the audience were tired, so it was presumed that they would not pay attention. Maulana Muhammad Ali stated that he was sitting on a high stage, from where he could see all the audience. By some manifestation of Divine power it appeared as if the audience were captivated. They were listening in absolute silence with rapt attention, and cheering on occasions.

Witnessing this scene, those Ahmadis from Calcutta who were among the audience rose up from their seats and fell in prostration of thanksgiving there and then in the hall. As soon as the speech finished, all the delegates and many of the audience congratulated Maulana Muhammad Ali and Khwaja Kamal-ud-Din. The presiding officer of the meeting, Mr. Mitter, asked the Khwaja sahib if he would be available to deliver more speeches after the convention at some venue. As Maulana Muhammad Ali and the Khwaja sahib could not stay at that time, it was arranged that the Khwaja sahib would pay a visit later on. A European delegate remarked to him that the speech had dealt a death blow to Christianity. Thus God granted a distinctive victory. Maulana Muhammad Ali wrote about it as follows:

> "The success that Allah the Most High granted to the Movement in this convention was like the success at the Mahutasu conference.[2] Although the paper read at this

2. In December 1896 a conference of the great religions (*dharm mahutasu*) was held in Lahore. Representatives of different religions presented papers in support of their faiths. The Promised Messiah's paper on behalf of Islam was read by his respected follower Maulvi Abdul Karim, and was generally declared as the best paper, surpassing all others. It was later published in book form under the title *Islami Usul ki Philosophy,* and translated

convention was not the work of that saintly heart to whom Allah spoke, but rather a summary of some of his ideas compiled by a humble servant of his in his own words ... yet Allah still sent His aid and support."

(The full report appears in *Badr,* 22 April 1909.)

Debate in Rampur

In June 1909 the Nawab of Rampur arranged a major debate between Ahmadis and non-Ahmadis. The debator representing the non-Ahmadis was Maulvi Sanaullah of Amritsar. The Ahmadi delegation was led by Maulana Syed Muhammad Ahsan of Amroha, and included Maulana Muhammad Ali, Khwaja Kamal-ud-Din, Maulvi Sarwar Shah, Maulvi Mubarak Ali, Hafiz Roshan Ali and Shaikh Yaqub Ali. The debate took place from 15 June till 20 June. However, during the debate the Nawab sahib broke his promise and instead of remaining impartial he openly supported Maulvi Sanaullah. So the Ahmadi delegation had to discontinue the debate. A detailed report of the proceedings of this debate was written by Maulana Muhammad Ali and published in the Ahmadiyya community newspaper *Badr* dated 24 June 1909, and Maulana Muhammad Ahsan of Amroha wrote a book about it.

During the debate the Nawab sahib made a sarcastic remark saying: "Sir Syed Ahmad Khan also believed in the death of Jesus", alluding to the fact that Sir Syed's religious views were generally disparaged as being *naturi* or rationalistic. Khwaja Kamal-ud-Din instantly responded: "Indeed, which sensible person does not believe in the death of Jesus!"

Debate at Mansoori

In November 1909 another major religious debate was held at Mansoori between Ahmadis and non-Ahmadis. At that time some local events there had led to a rise in opposition to the Ahmadiyya Movement. So the people of the area organised the debate to decide what was the truth. The delegation sent to participate by Maulana Nur-ud-Din was headed by Maulana Muhammad Ali, with Maulvi Ghulam Rasul, Hafiz Roshan Ali and Mufti Muhammad

into English and published as the well-known book *The Teachings of Islam.*

Sadiq as the other members. From the non-Ahmadi side Maulvi Sanaullah of Amritsar did not come, and in his place Maulvi Muhammad Yaqub of Bihar and some other Maulvis represented the non-Ahmadis. On 15 November, the first day, the speeches were about the death of Jesus or his still being alive, and on the second day about the claims of Hazrat Mirza sahib. This debate created a very good impression of the Ahmadiyya Movement among the local Muslims and many came into the fold of the Movement. The speeches were all recorded in writing but the non-Ahmadi religious leaders refused to sign the record. A brief account of the proceedings of the debate was published in *Badr* dated 25 November 1909, in which Mufti Muhammad Sadiq made the following comments about Maulana Muhammad Ali:

> "The leader of the delegation was Maulvi Muhammad Ali M.A., whom everyone obeyed. However, despite being the leader, he served the delegation the most. He himself dealt with all the arrangements regarding the speeches and did not put his helpers to any hardship."

Religious convention at Allahabad

In January 1911 a religious convention was held at Allahabad. The organisers invited Maulana Muhammad Ali and Khwaja Kamal-ud-Din. The Maulana could not go himself because he was extremely busy with the English translation of the Quran and other duties but he sent a lecture in English. Khwaja Kamal-ud-Din went to participate. On 9 January, the first day of the convention, the Khwaja sahib gave a lecture which was as usual very successful and well-liked. On the second day, the lecture sent by Maulana Muhammad Ali was read out. It explained that Islam is the true religion which is in accordance with human nature, and it has brought the earlier religions to completion and perfection. This paper received the highest commendation of all the submissions and was considered to be the best one (*Badr,* 2 February 1911). It was published in 1912 in book form by the Sadr Anjuman Ahmadiyya Qadian under the title *Islam, The Natural Religion of Man* (in English), and its Urdu translation was published as *Usul-i Islam.*

Some domestic circumstances and trip to Murree

For some time after the death of the Promised Messiah, Maulana Muhammad Ali continued living in his house, and he lived there altogether for eight to nine years. Probably at the beginning of 1909 he moved to a house adjoining the Promised Messiah's house which was known as the old guest house. Here he stayed for four to five months. After that, he was given a new house by the Anjuman in the Dar-ul-Ulum area where the Anjuman's school, boarding house, the Nur mosque and a dispensary were under construction. This house consisted of three rooms, one of which was not of solid construction. Here he stayed till April 1914. Two of his nephews also lived with him, whom he had called to Qadian for their schooling. It was after moving to this house that he started the work on the English translation of the Quran, and he continued doing it for the last four years of his life in Qadian in addition to his other duties.

As mentioned before, Maulana Muhammad Ali's wife died in November 1908, leaving a little girl named Ruqayya. About one and a half years later, at the instigation of Maulana Nur-ud-Din, he married Mehrun Nisa, daughter of Dr. Basharat Ahmad. In September 1909, the doctor had written to Maulana Nur-ud-Din enquiring about a suitable match for his daughter. Another match was under consideration and the doctor had sought Maulana Nur-ud-Din's permission about it, but the latter wrote in reply saying that in his view there was not a better man for marriage than Muhammad Ali. In February 1910, Dr. Basharat Ahmad took a few days' leave to come to Qadian from Bhera, and the *nikah* of Maulana Muhammad Ali to his daughter took place. On 29 April 1910 Maulana Muhammad Ali went to Bhera and on 1st May he brought his wife to Qadian.

When his wife went to visit Maulana Nur-ud-Din, he was giving a discourse of the Quran to women. He patted her head with great affection and said a long prayer in which everyone joined in. Then he said: "I have seen the brightness of spiritual light on the face of Muhammad Ali and of his father, and also on the face of Basharat Ahmad and his wife. I am very pleased about this union." Then he said to her: "Your father and your husband are very dear to me, and so you are too." After that, on all occasions for the rest of his life he treated her with much affection.

This was the time when Maulana Muhammad Ali had started the English translation of the Quran. On the one hand, as secretary of the Sadr Anjuman Ahmadiyya Qadian he was performing all the administrative duties for the Anjuman, on the other hand he was supervising the construction of the building of the Taleem-ul-Islam school. In addition he was writing articles for the *Review of Religions* and also in some other journals. At night he would sit in his small house and work on the translation of the Quran. He had made a tiny room into his office, where a table was laden with piles of voluminous Arabic and English books in small print, dictionaries and commentaries of the Quran etc. In the solitude of the night he would be poring over one book, then another, holding a candle in his hand as the only source of light available.

At the beginning of June 1912 Maulana Muhammad Ali fell ill with high temperature which lasted for one week. He had not yet fully recovered when he resumed work, so his health deteriorated again and he started getting a high temperature every day. Maulana Nur-ud-Din, who was treating him, advised him to go for change of weather to some salubrious place with a healthy climate. During those days his wife's maternal grandfather Safdar Jang, former Police Inspector of Amritsar, had brought his daughter to Qadian to receive medical treatment from Maulana Nur-ud-Din. He owned a shop in Murree, the Punjab Drapery House, and he suggested that as the ground floor of the shop was vacant, Maulana Muhammad Ali could stay there. This place was on Mall Road near the post office. So Maulana Muhammad Ali went to Murree with his family. This house consisted of a large hall and two small rooms. He partitioned the large hall into two by a curtain, and used one part as his office and the other for holding congregational prayers and for receiving friends. The stay in Murree not only improved his health, but he was able to devote more concentration on the translation of the Holy Quran. During his two months' stay he felt that he had achieved much more than he could in Qadian. So again in 1913, with Maulana Nur-ud-Din's permission and taking leave from the Anjuman, he went to Murree and stayed in the same house for two and a half months, carrying on the work on the translation while there. This was the start of his practice of going to a cool, mountainous place every summer, which began under the advice and direction of Maulana Nur-ud-Din. Maulana Muhammad Ali often used to say that he had been able to do so much writing work only because of going to the hills. Later on, due to the strain of constant mental work and exertion, his health had suffered so that at the start of every summer he used to fall ill. Thus he was forced to retreat to a salubrious location in the mountains for the summer. Even there he used to take no rest, but in fact continue his scholarly work at twice the pace.

Maulana Muhammad Ali bought a plot of land adjacent to his residence in Qadian to have his own house built, and had his father send him some money for this purpose. Bricks had been bought and work on the garden had started when, due to the Split, he had to abandon all the plans and move to Lahore. He always had a great interest in planting fruit trees, flowers and vegetables, and wherever he lived later on he had a garden planted. While being heavily absorbed in his writing work, he would take a little time out for these activities, and this was his only hobby for recreation. Apart from this, he used to go for a long walk every morning after the *fajr* prayers without fail. The Promised Messiah also had the firm habit of going for a walk after *fajr* unless prevented by ill health.

Talim-ul-Islam school and construction of the boarding house

It has been mentioned earlier that during the Promised Messiah's life the decision had been taken to construct a building for the Talim-ul-Islam school and a boarding house, and land for this had been procured outside the old settlement of Qadian. In January 1908 the Sadr Anjuman Ahmadiyya appointed Maulana Muhammad Ali to raise funds for the construction of the school and the boarding house and to arrange for the work to start. After the Promised Messiah died in May 1908, Maulana Muhammad Ali started this project under the headship of Maulana Nur-ud-Din. To arrange for the materials for such huge buildings in a remote place like Qadian required much effort, and even a kiln had to be built for making bricks. Maulana Muhammad Ali carried out all these responsibilities with diligence and personally supervised the building of the kiln and the construction work.

One incident illustrative of his devotion to duty may be noted here. Once, on a very cold and dark winter night, there was a heavy storm of wind and rain and it was feared that water would enter the kiln and cause damage worth thousands of Rupees. Giving up his sleep, Maulana Muhammad Ali attended at the site during that heavy downpour in which even umbrellas were of no avail, in order to supervise the emergency arrangements in person. Seeing his example, all the workers continued working with great enthusiasm, and they managed to avert a substantial loss by timely intervention. The Maulana never hesitated to do the humblest manual labour by his own hand.

The construction of the boarding house was started first because there was inadequate accommodation for the increasing number of students, so much so that some of them had to live in the Nur mosque. The construction started in January 1909, and work also began on building the staff quarters. Besides the construction problems, the raising of funds also took much struggle and effort. So during 1909 and 1910 Maulana Muhammad Ali kept on impressing the need for this upon all branches of the community. He sent a delegation to visit various branches and issued repeated appeals in the newspapers *Al-Hakam* and *Badr*. In March 1910 he appealed for every Ahmadi to donate one month's income so that the boarding house could be finished and the school building constructed. Thus the fund raising and the building work were done in conjunction with each other. After the boarding house a grand building was built for the school, and in May 1913 it started to be used for holding classes though it was not complete till the end of that year.

Activities and health of Maulana Nur-ud-Din

The great works which began in the times of Maulana Nur-ud-Din have been mentioned above. Apart from these, from the year 1911 Khwaja Kamal-ud-Din started a series of lectures in the major cities of India. Due to his lectures and the journal the *Review of Religions,* the Ahmadiyya Movement acquired great fame and renown throughout the country. The Movement was becoming so popular that it seemed as if the whole of India would be won over to it. The educated sections of the population and important and leading figures became its admirers. Dr. Muhammad Iqbal, the famous Muslim poet and philosopher, remarked in one of his speeches in 1910, at the M.A.O. College, Aligarh, that if anyone wanted to see a glimpse of true and pure Islam he would find it in Qadian.[3] In important religious conferences and debates the Ahmadiyya representatives had the upper hand. Within Qadian, the head of the Movement laid stress on the Quran day and night. Maulana Nur-ud-Din used to give several discourses in the Quran everyday separately for different audiences, such as women, students, and people generally. He also gave discourses in Hadith. He made his living from his practice of medicine and treated all his patients from among the general public with great kindness and attention.

By the time he was head of the Movement, Maulana Nur-ud-Din was growing old. In November 1910, one day as he was coming from the residence of Nawab Muhammad Ali Khan on horseback he had a nasty fall from the horse and sustained serious injuries. Dr. Basharat Ahmad, who was in Qadian at the time, and Dr. Ilahi Bakhsh stitched his wounds and it was hoped that he would recover soon. However, after some time his health deteriorated and Dr. Mirza Yaqub Baig came from Lahore to treat him and stayed there. He remained confined to bed with one ailment or another for four to five months.

Publication of *The Teachings of Islam*

Maulana Muhammad Ali had translated several writings of the Promised Messiah into English for the magazine the *Review of Religions*. His translation of the famous, lengthy paper of Hazrat Mirza sahib entitled *Islami Usul Ki Philosophy* had appeared in the *Review of Religions* in 1902 and 1903. In 1910 he revised the translation and had it published as the book *The Teachings of Islam*.[4] The original Urdu paper had been presented in 1896 at the Congress of Religions held in Lahore and had achieved such glorious success that the triumph of Islam over all other religions by

---

3. This speech, *Millat Baiza Per Ayk 'Imrani Nazar*, was re-published by Aeenah Adab, Lahore, in 1970. These words are on p. 84.

4. This was published by Luzac & Co. in London.

means of knowledge, reason and arguments could be seen as a reality. This book is so powerful and effective that several editions were published in later years in quantities of thousands, large numbers were distributed free throughout the world by the Ahmadiyya Anjuman Isha'at Islam Lahore, and it was translated into numerous other languages of India as well as the outside world.

Beginning of the propagation of Islam in the U.K.

In the years 1912 and 1913, in order to fulfil another wish of the Promised Messiah, another important work was begun through Khwaja Kamal-ud-Din when he went to England in September 1912 on some legal business. Shortly after reaching England, he learnt about the existence of the Mosque at Woking in Surrey, about thirty miles from London. This mosque was built in 1889 by a Western orientalist by the name of Dr. Leitner, who was at one time Registrar of the University of the Punjab, at the expense of Her Highness Shah Jehan Begum, the Begum of Bhopal state, India. The mosque had been lying closed and unused for long. Khwaja Kamal-ud-Din had it opened up and went to court, with the help of some leading Muslims of India who were in England, to take possession of it from the heirs of Dr. Leitner and created a Trust to take charge of the mosque and the adjoining house. He himself became its first Imam and based his Woking Muslim Mission at these premises.

Gradually Khwaja Kamal-ud-Din began to succeed in his propagation work and soon an English Lord named Headley embraced Islam through him, and this brought even more fame to the Woking mission.

2.3: Events of the Split in the Movement and migration of Maulana Muhammad Ali to Lahore

The bright aspects of the time of Hazrat Maulana Nur-ud-Din have just been mentioned. Now we turn to the dark side of that same era, which led to the "Split" in the community after his death. Not only was the Movement ripped apart into two, the majority of it turning to extremism, but also the appeal and the progress of the Ahmadiyya Movement suffered a tremendous damage that was permanent and lasting. Though the foundations of the Split were laid during the life of Maulana Nur-ud-Din, but to understand it one has to go back to 1905 and 1906 when the Promised Messiah wrote the booklet *Al-Wasiyyat* and established the Sadr Anjuman Ahmadiyya, Qadian.

Al-Wasiyyat and the founding of the Sadr Anjuman Ahmadiyya, and its consequences

As mentioned before, in 1905 the Promised Messiah published his booklet entitled *Al-Wasiyyat* ('The Will') and established the administrative system of his community on the broad Islamic principles of democracy, thus putting before the world a magnificent achievement of the revival of true Islam. Then during his own lifetime he set that system into operation and ran the Movement according to those principles, by creating the Sadr Anjuman Ahmadiyya Qadian in 1906 and handing over to it all the management of the Movement. He declared that after his lifetime the decisions of this Anjuman would be final and binding.

Mirza Mahmud Ahmad, son of the Promised Messiah, inwardly resented this, and from that time he began to entertain feelings of

85

jealousy and animosity particularly towards Maulana Muhammad Ali and Khwaja Kamal-ud-Din. He devoted much time to devising ways of rendering the Anjuman powerless.

Near the end of the Promised Messiah's life, Mirza Mahmud Ahmad began to display his ill feeling, which he bore towards the men to whom the Promised Messiah had entrusted the funds of the Movement, in the form of open displeasure. Every year, according to the wishes of Hazrat Mirza sahib, Maulana Muhammad Ali used to be reappointed as secretary of the Sadr Anjuman. In the latter part of 1907, Maulana Muhammad Ali tried to allay the feelings of Mirza Mahmud Ahmad by taking leave for three months and making Mirza Mahmud Ahmad secretary in his place. When the time came for the next annual election of officers, the Maulana proposed to the Promised Messiah that Mirza Mahmud Ahmad should be made secretary for the coming year. However, Hazrat Mirza sahib ruled it out saying that Mirza Mahmud Ahmad's opinions were flawed or immature. So, once again, Maulana Muhammad Ali was made secretary.[1] This continued in the time of Maulana Nur-ud-Din, and by his advice Maulana Muhammad Ali was always reappointed secretary. During the period that he was secretary, from 1906 to 1913, the annual budget of the Anjuman increased from 30,000 Rupees to almost 200,000 Rupees, and a magnificent school building and boarding house worth 150,000 Rupees had been constructed.

Death of the Promised Messiah: Maulana Nur-ud-Din takes *bai'at* (pledge) from members

About a month before his death, when the Promised Messiah left Qadian to go to Lahore, he appointed Maulana Muhammad Ali to manage all affairs in his absence. After his death, when his body reached Qadian for burial, Khwaja Kamal-ud-Din said to Maulana Muhammad Ali in the cemetery garden that it had been proposed that Maulana Nur-ud-Din should succeed the Promised Messiah. He replied that he fully agreed with the proposal. Then the Khwaja

---

1. All these events have been narrated by Maulana Muhammad Ali in his book *Haqiqat-i Ikhtilaf,* published in 1922. This book was translated into English and published in 1966 as *True Facts about the Split.*

sahib added that it was also proposed that all Ahmadis should take the pledge (*bai'at*) on Maulana Nur-ud-Din's hand. Maulana Muhammad Ali replied that there was no need for that because only new entrants to the Movement need take the pledge and that this was the purport of *Al-Wasiyyat*. The Khwaja sahib said that it was a delicate time and any difference of opinion may cause division in the community, and there was no harm in Ahmadis taking the pledge again. Then Maulana Muhammad Ali agreed and the pledge was taken at Maulana Nur-ud-Din's hand.

Beginning of the discord and efforts to mislead Maulana Nur-ud-Din

Maulana Nur-ud-Din and Maulana Muhammad Ali were very close to one another. Maulana Nur-ud-Din consulted Maulana Muhammad Ali about all the matters in hand, and whatever announcement he had to issue he would get it drafted by Maulana Muhammad Ali. This close bond further intensified the jealousy that some others felt towards Maulana Muhammad Ali and they decided to undermine this relationship between the two. Now Maulana Muhammad Ali considered the *khilafat* after the Promised Messiah to be only in the sense of 'successorship', and he held that the Divinely-ordained *khilafat* whose establishment is mentioned in the *khilafat* verse of the Holy Quran (24:55) was promised to the Holy Prophet Muhammad only, and not to Hazrat Mirza sahib. The persons bearing a grudge against Maulana Muhammad Ali misrepresented this by telling Maulana Nur-ud-Din at every opportunity that Maulana Muhammad Ali did not accept him as *khalifa*. For some time they succeeded in misleading him.

In the annual report for 1908, prepared by Maulana Muhammad Ali and read out by him on 26 December 1908 at the annual gathering, the first such gathering since the death of the Promised Messiah, the creation of the Anjuman by Hazrat Mirza sahib was mentioned and it was stated that the running of the Movement after him had been placed by him in the hands of the Anjuman. The Maulana also read out the note by Hazrat Mirza sahib stipulating that after him the decisions of the Sadr Anjuman Ahmadiyya would be final. After the Maulana's speech, Khwaja Kamal-ud-Din also mentioned in his speech that Hazrat Mirza sahib had appointed the

Anjuman as his successor. (See *Badr,* 24–31 December 1908, p. 13.)

This gave an opportunity to the mischief makers, so that Mir Muhammad Ishaq, maternal uncle of Mirza Mahmud Ahmad, composed a set of seven questions: (1) Is the Anjuman subservient to the *Khalifa* (Maulana Nur-ud-Din) or vice versa? (2) Can the Anjuman dismiss the *Khalifa* or vice versa? (3) How far can the *Khalifa* interfere in the affairs of the Anjuman? There were four more questions of the same nature.

These they sent to Maulana Nur-ud-Din and told him that Maulana Muhammad Ali, Khwaja Kamal-ud-Din and their associates did not really accept him as *khalifa*. Maulana Nur-ud-Din sent those seven questions to Maulana Muhammad Ali to give a reply to. When he received his reply, he sent it to the questioner. But they did not rest at that, and sent further questions to Maulana Nur-ud-Din. The answers which Maulana Muhammad Ali gave are quoted in full by him in his book *Haqiqat-i Ikhtilaf*. In brief he repeated that Hazrat Mirza sahib had made the Anjuman as his successor but everyone unanimously accepted Maulana Nur-ud-Din as their leader. There was no dispute between him and the Anjuman so all these questions were hypothetical and premature, and an attempt to break up the Anjuman. He added that the Anjuman should answer these questions. On receiving this reply Maulana Nur-ud-Din directed that these questions be sent to forty people for their views, he should be informed of their opinions and they should all assemble in Qadian on 31 January 1909.

When these questions reached Lahore, Khwaja Kamal-ud-Din called a meeting of the members of the Anjuman's executive from Lahore (that is, the Khwaja sahib himself, Dr. Mirza Yaqub Baig, Dr. Syed Muhammad Husain Shah and Shaikh Rahmatullah) and sent their unanimous opinion, which was in agreement with what Maulana Muhammad Ali had already said. They agreed that Hazrat Mirza sahib's real successor was the Anjuman and the Anjuman had unanimously accepted Maulana Nur-ud-Din as leader, this acceptance being an act of the Anjuman, and they were all united upon his person as leader. On the other side in Qadian, Shaikh Yaqub Ali had a meeting at his house, which fuelled the controversy.

At the gathering on 31 January, Maulana Nur-ud-Din expressed his views. Though he did state that a *khalifa* had other
duties and functions than merely to lead the prayers, he did not
clarify any further and in the end he repeated what Maulana
Muhammad Ali had already said, that these questions were irrele-
vant at that stage and it was wrong to dwell on them. His final
decision was that, as both the parties had confidence in him, these
questions must not be raised in his lifetime. After his speech he
made Mirza Mahmud Ahmad and Mir Nasir Nawab to promise
that they would obey him, and then he took the pledge from Maulana Muhammad Ali and Khwaja Kamal-ud-Din on one side and
from Shaikh Yaqub Ali and Mir Muhammad Ishaq on the other.
The purpose of this was to affirm that they would obey him during
his life, as both sides had already acknowledged that they obeyed
him.

This was all that happened, but afterwards this incident was
misrepresented with embellishments by Mirza Mahmud Ahmad
and his followers. In practice too, Maulana Nur-ud-Din never
made people acknowledge him as the kind of autocratic *khalifa*
with absolute and dictatorial powers that Mirza Mahmud Ahmad
became later on, nor did he ever override any decision of the
Anjuman. Above all, the rules and regulations of the Anjuman
remained the same during his period of headship as they had been
framed by the Promised Messiah, but Mirza Mahmud Ahmad started altering them as soon as he became *khalifa*.

Efforts to get Maulana Muhammad Ali and his friends expelled from the Ahmadiyya community

This mischief-making should have ceased at this point, but as
Mirza Mahmud Ahmad and his supporters did not succeed in
achieving their real aim they continued trying to revive the
dissension. They tried their level best to impress again and again
upon Maulana Nur-ud-Din that these people were inwardly
opposed to him. Mirza Mahmud Ahmad was the main instigator
of this, as is proved by a letter he wrote to Maulana Nur-ud-Din
which was published later on by Maulana Muhammad Ali in his
book *Haqiqat-i Ikhtilaf*. In this long letter, he related a dream of
his and then did his best to provoke Maulana Nur-ud-Din to expel

Maulana Muhammad Ali and his associates from the community. In that letter he tried to poison Maulana Nur-ud-Din's mind against them by going as far as to insinuate that these people had been plotting even during the Promised Messiah's time and had wanted to hold him to account for the income of the Movement. He made a false allegation against Maulana Muhammad Ali and Khwaja Kamal-ud-Din that, just before the Promised Messiah's death, they used to say that he had been misappropriating the funds of the community. Then Mirza Mahmud Ahmad writes:

> "A boil full of pus gets worse the longer it is left. Till now my opinion was that this matter should be suppressed as far as possible ... but now, after prayer, my feeling and view has changed completely and I have come to the conclusion that now is the time that this ill condition should be remedied."

This letter ends as follows:

> "So my view is that God may open your heart, sir, to this course of action and this matter must be brought to an end, no matter how. There is bound to be trial and tribulation, but it is best to nip it in the bud before it becomes a firm tree.
>
> Humbly, Mahmud."

At the same time an incident involving the sale of the house of Hakim Fazl Din occurred, in which the decision taken by the Sadr Anjuman Ahmadiyya did not quite tally with the opinion of Maulana Nur-ud-Din. Mirza Mahmud Ahmad and his party used this to raise a storm of propaganda. Letters were sent to Maulana Nur-ud-Din even from Lahore alleging that certain remarks were being made by Dr. Syed Muhammad Husain Shah, and certain remarks by Dr. Mirza Yaqub Baig, against the *Khalifa*. Maulana Nur-ud-Din, being after all human, was somewhat angered and said that he was going to make an announcement on the coming *Eid* day. It was not clear what the announcement was to be about. Some people thought that he might take away power from the Anjuman, which would foment trouble in the Movement. (Later events showed that he intended to announce that he would have no more to do with the financial decisions of the Anjuman, though such an announcement too would have been harmful for the Movement.)

A day before the *Eid* day, Shaikh Rahmatullah came from Lahore as usual, and he and Maulana Muhammad Ali went to see Maulana Nur-ud-Din and assured him that the two doctors were obedient to him. Maulana Nur-ud-Din brought out a bag full of letters that he had received against them. Both of them told him that all those allegations were completely false and that they all were obedient to him. Maulana Nur-ud-Din was satisfied by their statements and did not make any announcement on *Eid* day. So the day of *Eid,* on which the mischief makers had pinned their hopes, turned out to be a day, not of joy, but of disappointment for them.

During the course of his *Eid khutba,* on 16 October 1909, Maulana Nur-ud-Din reiterated the position and the powers given to the Anjuman by the Promised Messiah. Referring to the booklet *Al-Wasiyyat* (The Will) he said:

> "In the writing of Hazrat sahib [i.e. *Al-Wasiyyat* by the Promised Messiah] there is a point of deep knowledge which I will explain to you fully. He left it up to God as to who was going to be the *khalifa.* On the other hand, he said to fourteen men: You are collectively the *Khalifat-ul-Masih,* your decisions are final and binding, and the government authorities too consider them as absolute. Then all those fourteen men became united in taking the *bai'at* at the hand of one man, accepting him as their *khalifa,* and thus you were united. And then not only fourteen, but the whole community agreed upon my *khilafat.* ...
>
> I have read *Al-Wasiyyat* very thoroughly. It is indeed true that he has made fourteen men the *Khalifat-ul-Masih,* and written that their decision arrived at by majority opinion is final and binding. Now observe that these God-fearing men, whom Hazrat sahib chose for his *khilafat,* have by their righteous opinion, by their unanimous opinion, appointed one man as their *Khalifa* and *Amir.* And then

not only themselves, but they made thousands upon thousands of people to embark in the same boat in which they had themselves embarked."

(*Badr,* 21 October 1909, p. 11, col. 1)

In the same issue of *Badr,* immediately after the above *khutba,* a statement by the members from Lahore is published as follows:

"When on the auspicious occasion of *Eid-ul-Fitr* we went to Qadian as usual, we learnt that some people had written letters to Hazrat *Khalifat-ul-Masih* stating that some members of the *Majlis-i-Mu'timiddin* (executive committee) of the Sadr Anjuman Ahmadiyya are against him. We were very grieved by these letters and think that Hazrat *Khalifat-ul-Masih* must have been hurt as well. We do not harbour ill thoughts against our brethren, and we pray that they too think well of us, as is very strongly commanded in the Quran and Hadith. We cannot rip open our hearts and show anyone what thoughts are within them, but with this announcement we assure all friends that the pledge we took of Hazrat *Khalifat-ul-Masih* was not due to any pressure or compulsion but willingly from the bottom of our hearts, and we still stand firm on that pledge and obey Hazrat *Khalifat-ul-Masih*. It is clear that the unity of this Movement is not a unity on pain of punishment but a voluntary unity. It is on the principle of that voluntary unity that all of us took the pledge of Hazrat *Khalifat-ul-Masih,* and as regards the future we pray to Allah to keep us steadfast on this covenant as Noah prayed: 'I seek refuge in Thee from asking Thee about that of which I have no knowledge', for the granting of all capability and strength is only in Allah's hands.

— Humbly: Mirza Yaqub Baig, signed by his own hand; Rahmatullah, signed by his own hand; members of the executive committee, Sadr Anjuman Ahmadiyya Qadian, 17 October 1909.

I agree with each and every word of the above announcement and I am proud of obeying Hazrat *Khalifat-ul-Masih*
— Humbly, Muhammad Ali from Qadian."

(*Badr,* 21 October 1909)

The anxiety of Mirza Mahmud Ahmad to have Maulana
Muhammad Ali and some other persons expelled from the
community can be glimpsed in his account of one of his dreams
which he had published in *Badr* dated 23 February 1911. He
wrote:

> "Near to morning time I saw a large palace, one part of
> which was being demolished, and near the palace there
> was an open ground where thousands of men were doing
> stonework. ... I asked them what building it was and who
> were those people and why were they demolishing it. One
> of them replied that it was the Ahmadiyya community
> and one part of it was being demolished in order that old
> bricks be removed (may Allah have mercy) and some
> hollow bricks be replaced by solid ones."

More efforts to create suspicion in Maulana Nur-ud-Din's mind

Many other incidents like these carried on happening, in which
Mirza Mahmud Ahmad continued his most strenuous efforts to create
in Maulana Nur-ud-Din's mind as much mistrust as possible
against Maulana Muhammad Ali, Khwaja Kamal-ud-Din,
Dr. Syed Muhammad Husain Shah and Dr. Mirza Yaqub Baig.
The details of these can be found in the book *Haqiqat-i Ikhtilaf.*
As the Ansarullah party of Mirza Mahmud Ahmad continued their
false propaganda especially against Maulana Muhammad
Ali and Khwaja Kamal-ud-Din, Maulana Muhammad Ali wrote a
letter to Maulana Nur-ud-Din in November 1913 protesting
about this. Some extracts from the letter are given below which
illustrate the atmosphere prevailing at the time:

> "Yesterday you, honourable sir, mentioned that people accuse
> me and the Khwaja sahib, but you did not say in what matter. If it
> has been brought to your notice, sir, that we two disobey you or

that we had anything to do with the anonymous tracts,[2] or that either one of us wants to be a claimant to *khilafat,* then I state on oath in the name of Allah, on my behalf with full certainty and on behalf of the Khwaja sahib with the absolute confidence which is tantamount to full belief because of several years of close friendship, that these three allegations are absolutely false. If anyone alleges that we have ever said any such thing to him then he must at least be made to take an oath in front of me. More than this, I myself can produce sworn statements from all persons who have relations with me that I have never said anything like it. ...

"I assure you, sir, that we have obeyed you even to the extent of accepting blame upon ourselves when in certain matters you said something but we refrained from speaking in our defence in case it displeased you. ... This position of secretary I never accepted out of personal desire, nor did I perform the duties for selfish ends. During the time of the Promised Messiah I requested him many times to relieve me of my duties but my request was not granted. Every year, until he placed this burden upon me by writing my name with his own hand, I was never keen to shoulder the responsibility. ...

"My name and the name of the Khwaja sahib are indeed today mentioned, and that is in order to label us as hypocrites and unfaithful. This disease has spread so much that when certain missionaries travel to any place they believe it to be a meritorious deed to use these terms about us and to convey this to their audiences. In Qadian this has gone beyond all bounds. As regards what is the purpose of this propaganda and who are the people at the root of spreading it, these are matters about which I will not say anything because I do not wish to cause you any anguish. This is a trial which has come upon us. The Khwaja sahib, even having gone out of India, is still the victim of these reproachful attacks, and despite the fact that you on two occasions in your sermons exonerated him that propaganda is still going on. I am here so far,

---

2. Two anonymous tracts had appeared from Lahore containing some criticisms against Maulana Nur-ud-Din and some against Mirza Mahmud Ahmad.

but after five to seven months at most I too will go to England, if I am still alive. ...

"In the name of Allah, please, you yourself, sir, tell us where can we go to, in order to be safe from these accusations and false allegations? God, the One, knows that we never conspired any plot, nor is it our practice to do so, nor is it in our nature. It was to be away from such things that I took abode in a secluded corner to serve the religion. What can we do if some people do not like this? I swear on oath in the name of God that we are not conspirators. We are rather the victims of a conspiracy. ... It would not have mattered if we had been called hypocrites and unfaithful only before the ordinary people, but this has gone much further and efforts are now being made to portray us like that in your eyes.

Wassalam. Humbly, Muhammad Ali. 23 November 1913."

Maulana Nur-ud-Din's true feelings

Maulana Nur-ud-Din sent this letter to Mirza Mahmud Ahmad and he wrote back in reply that he would instruct the Ansar (meaning his party Ansarullah) not to say such things, and he also wrote that he himself had never heard Maulana Muhammad Ali say the things he was accused of saying. Maulana Nur-ud-Din sent this reply to Maulana Muhammad Ali and added the following words in his own hand:

> "By Allah, besides Whom there is no god, and Who holds my life in His hand, it never came to my mind even for an instant that you or the Khwaja sahib hold such ideas. It is my belief that neither of you entertain such thoughts. ..."

This was written on 23 November 1913 when his last illness had commenced. Prior to this, when Maulana Nur-ud-Din came to Lahore in June 1912 he made a speech in Ahmadiyya Buildings during which he said:

> "The third thing is that some persons, who are known as my friends and are my friends, hold the view and say that the people from Lahore are an obstacle in the affairs of the *khilafat*. ... Allah has given the teaching to refrain

from thinking ill of others, as it will turn you into evil doers. The Holy Prophet has said that he who indulges in thinking ill of others is a great liar, so keep away from this. Even now I have a slip of paper in my hand on which someone writes that the Lahore *Jama'at* is an obstacle in the way of the *khilafat*. I say to such critics, you are thinking ill of others, give it up. You should first of all try to make yourself sincere as they are. The people from Lahore are sincere. They love Hazrat [Mirza Ghulam Ahmad] sahib. Human beings make mistakes and they too can make mistakes, but the works which they have performed, you should also try to do the same.

I say at the top of my voice that whoever thinks ill of the people from Lahore, saying that they are an obstacle in the way of the *khilafat,* he should remember that the Holy Prophet has referred to those who indulge in ill-thinking by calling it 'the biggest lie', and Allah says: 'Avoid much of suspicion, surely suspicion is in many cases a sin', so it is called a sin by Allah. ... You mistrust the sincere ones and hurt me. Fear God. ...

If you say that the people from Lahore are an obstacle in the *khilafat,* this is to think ill about my sincere friends. Give it up. ...

Remember what I have said and give up thinking ill of others and causing discord. ... Give up the notion that the people from Lahore are an obstacle in the affairs of the *khilafat.* If you do not, then God will make your case like that of Musailima."

(*Badr,* 11 July 1912, pages 4, 5)

As is obvious from these statements of Maulana Nur-ud-Din, it had become fully clear to him that this was just mischief created by certain persons, and there were no grounds for the allegations against Maulana Muhammad Ali and his associates (see further the Supplement, pages 536–539). He got so exasperated with the insidious propaganda that he wrote a letter to Khwaja Kamal-ud-Din, dated 13 May 1913, who was then in England, expressing his heartfelt feelings, one sentence of which is translated below:

"Nawab,[3] Mir Nasir and Mahmud are useless people, fanatical for no good reason. This trouble is still afflicting us. O Allah, deliver us from it. *Amen!*"

A facsimile of this letter was published in *Paigham Sulh,* dated 26 November 1937.

In addition to this, the love that Maulana Nur-ud-Din felt for Maulana Muhammad Ali was clearly expressed in those events from his last illness which have been quoted above from the daily diary reports published by Dr. Mirza Yaqub Baig.

Maulana Muhammad Ali's announcement about the disunity and mistrust

With regard to the atmosphere of disunity and mistrust created in Qadian by a certain group, Maulana Muhammad Ali wrote a letter in the Ahmadiyya community newspaper *Badr* a few days before the annual gathering of December 1913, three months before Maulana Nur-ud-Din's death, in which he addressed all the members of the community. This letter shows the kind of circumstances that had been created in Qadian, and his deep concern about them. This letter was as follows:

"Brothers, *assalamu alaikum wa rahmatullahi wa barakatuhu.*

"I consider it to be a great favour of Allah that after the death of the Promised Messiah He united the whole community under one man, and it was also the grace of Allah by which all hearts were inclined to the obedience of this man, and at a time of such sorrow Allah sent tranquillity by His grace. I request all of you to be grateful for this favour of Allah, and you can do that by avoiding mischievous activities that lead to disunity in the community. Have favourable opinions about your brethren and leave the matter of their inner faith to be judged by Allah. Everyone of you should try to avoid bad mouthing another brother, and if you hear about someone that he speaks ill of you, do not try to get even with him because sometimes a news, when reaching somewhere, becomes completely distorted and very different from reality. If you observe

---

3. Nawab Muhammad Ali of Malerkotla is meant.

any mischief being created, then instead of vying to take part in it, keep your silence. The path of righteousness is in fact the path of caution, and at times of discord no path of caution is better than keeping silent.

"In the Quran Allah admonishes those who spread discord. It says that 'if any news of security or fear comes to them they spread it all over' (4:83), and it instructs that instead of spreading it they should refer it to the Messenger or those in authority. Keep in mind that to create disunity is not gallantry of any kind, but unity cannot be achieved without Allah's favour: 'If you had spent all that is in the earth, you could not have united their hearts, but Allah united them' (8:63). Once you lose the gift of unity you will not acquire it again even by spending all that you can, and all your works will remain incomplete and unfulfilled. Instead of malice and spite, create love and compassion for your brethren in your hearts, and if you cannot go that far then at least remove the malice and spite from within you. If someone is working for your Movement or serving religion, and you also notice some flaw in him, think of his service and his work in contrast with his flaw. Instead of trying to expel your brothers from within you, try to bring others to join you. If you expend all your energies in reject- ing your brothers, then you will not have any strength left to do the opposite work.

"I implore you again, it is not too late, do not discard the strength of unity. Take in the favours of God. Keep in view the pledge that you first took at the hand of the Promised Messiah and then at the hand of Hazrat *Khalifat-ul-Masih,* to give religion priori- ty over worldly interests. Fight your egotism. If something is not to your liking, bear with it. The Promised Messiah has gone so far as to say in *Kishti-i Nuh* that even if you are in the right, be like one who considers himself to be in the wrong. For God's sake, think. Are you trying to be like one considers himself in the right while being in the wrong, or vice versa? If this teaching was not meant for you, for which other community was it meant?

"I say it again, that Allah by His grace has raised a man among you who has brought together the entire community, and Allah made all hearts inclined to that man's obedience. Do not lose that grace by your own hands. Forgetting your disagreements, turn to matters which unite you. Incline not to worldly gain, but give preference to religion. You were brought into existence in this world to propagate and strengthen the religion. If you are set upon weakening the power of the religion, how can Allah the Most High come to your help?

Wassalam, Humbly, Muhammad Ali,
Editor, *Review of Religions,* Qadian, 1 December 1913."

(*Badr,* 4 December 1913)

The second tactic

What has been mentioned above was one tactic used by Mirza Mahmud Ahmad and his party to get Maulana Muhammad Ali and his co-thinkers expelled from the community or to disillusion Maulana Nur-ud-Din with them. Another tactic used to establish the foundation for Mirza Mahmud Ahmad's succession was to spread propaganda to impress upon the community his scholarship and righteousness, so that after Maulana Nur-ud-Din the community would not consider anybody else for the position. To achieve this goal, Mirza Mahmud Ahmad's maternal grandfather Mir Nasir Nawab toured towns and cities, on the pretext of raising funds for *Dar-uz-Zu'afa,* and carried out propaganda against Maulana Muhammad Ali and Khwaja Kamal-ud-Din. Similarly, missionaries sent by Mirza Mahmud Ahmad also carried out the same propaganda.

That was the age when the evil custom of rendering blind obedience to spiritual leaders prevailed among the Muslims of India and they followed rituals and superstitions unquestioningly. It was a great achievement of the Promised Messiah that he eradicated this wrong system of absolute, autocratic rule by spiritual leaders over their followers, and after him Maulana Nur-ud-Din continued the same example. This was a distinction of the Ahmadiyya community which greatly impressed other Muslims. But the succession that was being planned for Mirza Mahmud Ahmad was of a different nature altogether. A proof of it is provided by the testimony of an impartial outsider. Muhammad Aslam of Amritsar, who was not an Ahmadi, came to Qadian and wrote of his impressions of his visit. Regarding Maulana Nur-ud-Din he wrote:

> "Having attended his spiritual guidance gatherings and his teaching of the Quran for two days, as far as I reflected upon his work it appeared to me to be of the highest purity and based solely on serving Allah. His behaviour is above pretence, show and hypocrisy. He has a strong passion for the truth of Islam which is reflected from his heart. ... If true Islam is what is contained in the Holy Quran, then I have not come across anyone who loves the Quran as truly as the Maulvi sahib does. It is not that he is compelled to do it just out of force of conformity; rather, he is a great thinker and has fallen in love with the Quran as a result of his critical scholarly evaluation. ... What amazed me was to see an eighty years old man working from dawn to dusk. ... All his actions and movements reflect the dignified simplicity and informality of the companions of the Holy Prophet."

Then he goes on to say that he has not seen the evil of spiritual leader worship prevailing anywhere in the company of Maulana Nur-ud-Din.

Now look at the other side of the picture reported by the same observer:

> "I did notice something which could, to some extent, lead to spiritual leader worship being established in Qadian in the future. This was the published poster from the editor of *Al-Hakam* displayed at many places in Qadian congratulating Mirza Mahmud Ahmad sahib on his safe return from his pilgrimage to Makka. ... Its language reveals the tendency towards spiritual leader worship and I regret to see such a poster so widely published that for several days it is sticking upon the walls of the God worshipping Qadian. ... Seeing that made me fearful, lest this quiet spark of spiritual leader worship, which probably is awaiting the demise of Maulana Nur-ud-Din, might spread as a fire and completely engulf Qadian."

(*Badr,* 13 March 1913, pages 8 and 9)

Thus, even an impartial observer could envisage the pedestal to which Mirza Mahmud Ahmad was to be raised.

The scandal of calling Muslims as *kafir* and the establishment of the Ansarullah party

In those days Khwaja Kamal-ud-Din used to lecture in different cities of the Punjab as well as India generally and his fame had spread throughout the land. When, during a public meeting in Jhang, he declared that Ahmadis consider all those who profess the *Kalima* of Islam ('There is no God but Allah, Muhammad is the Messenger of Allah') as Muslims, Mirza Mahmud Ahmad contradicted this in an article published in his magazine *Tashhiz-ul-Azhan* for April 1911 and declared that each and every Muslim in the whole world who has not formally taken the *bai'at* (pledge) of the Promised Messiah is a *kafir* and outside the pale of Islam, even if that person has never heard of the Promised Messiah or even if he believes the Promised Messiah to be true. It was this article that struck at the very foundations of the Ahmadiyya Movement and split it into two. However, to acquire the successorship it was not enough just to write an article. Mirza Mahmud Ahmad at the same time founded a party called the Ansarullah, with himself as its leader. Its members actively propagated his viewpoints as well as canvassed for him to succeed Maulana Nur-ud-Din as the next *khalifa,* while the Maulana was on his death bed. The propagation of the wrong belief that other Muslims are *kafir* went so far that Maulana Nur-ud-Din, from his sickbed, on 15 February 1914, said in the presence of a large number of people that Mirza Mahmud Ahmad failed to comprehend the doctrine of *Kufr* (unbelief) and Islam, and he asked Maulana Muhammad Ali to clarify this issue (see *Paigham Sulh,* 3 March 1914, p. 4, col. 3). This made Mirza Mahmud Ahmad furious and he wrote an article saying that the *fatwa* (a ruling on a religious matter) of a *khalifa* has no value and that anyone wanting a *fatwa* need only send him a postcard of one penny and he would provide a *fatwa* from the Promised Messiah's books (*Al-Fazl,* 25 February 1914, p. 3, col. 3).

This Ansarullah was the party that had been brought into Qadian just before the death of Maulana Nur-ud-Din to help in taking over the succession after him. Thus one of the letters written by Hafiz

Roshan Ali to the Ansarullah party in various towns and cities, which was reproduced in *Paigham Sulh* dated 17 March 1914 (p. 1), stated that Maulana Nur-ud-Din's life was now only a matter of hours, not of days, so they must immediately assemble in Qadian.

A tract on calling Muslims as *kafir* and one on *khilafat*

As has been mentioned above, Maulana Nur-ud-Din openly stated from his sickbed that Mirza Mahmud Ahmad did not understand the doctrine of unbelief and Islam, and he had asked Maulana Muhammad Ali to expound this doctrine properly. Accordingly, Maulana Muhammad Ali wrote a tract which was published in Qadian on 13 March 1914, in which he refuted Mirza Mahmud Ahmad's wrong belief. The Maulana writes in it:

> "After writing this article I read it to Hazrat *Khilafat-ul-Masih*. As he was ill in those days, his son Abdul Hayy, thinking that he perhaps could not listen with full attention, asked him: Sir, are you listening? He replied: I am well able to listen to it, if I disagreed with anything I would say so. When the article ended, he directed that a hadith report from Sahih Muslim be added at the close. That has been done."

> (Urdu pamphlet entitled: Issue of Unbelief and Islam according to the directions of Hazrat *Khalifat-ul-Masih*)

At the same time he also wrote and issued a tract entitled *Ayk Nihayat Zaroori I'lan* ('A Very Important Announcement') in which he impressed the following five points upon the Ahmadiyya community:

1. It is not the case that an Ahmadi upon whom forty members have agreed becomes *khalifa*. Rather, what the Promised Messiah has instructed is that such a man can take the *bai'at* (pledge) from new entrants to admit them into the Movement.

2. The Promised Messiah has not given any instruction that existing Ahmadis have to renew their *bai'at* upon another person's hand.

3. The executive committee of the Sadr Anjuman Ahmadiyya Qadian is the real and true successor of the Promised Messiah.

4. Be very careful and fearful of God in the matter of 'unbelief and Islam', and follow the belief of the Promised Messiah who never declared as *kafir* those Muslims who did not accept his claims.

5. Settle the successorship to Maulana Nur-ud-Din with thought and deliberation by consulting the entire community.

This tract explained clearly and in detail all the points above as well as explaining the true powers and position of the Anjuman. But it arrived in Qadian, after being printed in Lahore, when Hazrat Maulana Nur-ud-Din had already died and the state of affairs in Qadian had worsened.

Maulana Nur-ud-Din's death and subsequent events
On 13 March 1914, while saying his Friday prayers despite great weakness, Maulana Nur-ud-Din breathed his last (may his soul rest in peace). What happened afterwards is described by Maulana Muhammad Ali in his book *Haqiqat-i Ikhtilaf* as follows:

"The same day, after *Asr* prayer, we five went to Nawab [Muhammad Ali Khan] sahib's house to discuss the future. Before our arrival there, the Mian sahib [Mirza Mahmud Ahmad] had already gone for a walk on his own in the direction of the village of Khara. I told my friends that it would be better if I spoke to him alone. So I went after him, and said to him that as the community is openly split into two on the question of unbelief and Islam, so we have to think about the future and devise some way of keeping the community united. The Mian sahib's answer was that we should elect a *khalifa* at whose hand both parties should take the *bai'at,* and obey him; only thus could we remain united. I replied that the very problem was that both parties could not take the pledge of the same man. At least I could not accept a man as spiritual guide who calls Muslims as *kafir,* and by the same token how can the other party take *bai'at* on the hand of a man who according to them is in error on such an important issue. I suggested two possible solutions to the Mian sahib. One was to choose a leader now and not make the *bai'at* obligatory: whoever wished could take the *bai'at* but those who did not so wish need not do it. Then after some time had passed over this, each side should put forward its arguments on the question of unbelief and Islam. This would make it possible that, seeing which side had the stronger case, the entire community would unite upon that as its creed. To this the Mian sahib answered that anyone who does not take the *bai'at* of the *khalifa* cannot remain in the community, so this cannot work. My other suggestion was that no leader be elected at this time for at least fourteen days, and in this interim a representative gathering of the community be called to find a solution to the problem. But the Mian sahib's answer was that there could not be such a wait because unless the next *khalifa* was elected, the previous *khalifa* could not be buried.[4] The result was that no solution could be achieved.

"The next day the five of us, i.e. Shaikh Rahmatullah, Maulvi Sadr-ud-Din, the two doctors and I, again went to the house of the Nawab sahib and tried to discuss the matter, but it was in vain. At last, after the *Asr* prayer a meeting took place. The Nawab sahib read out the will of Maulana Nur-ud-Din. Maulana Muhammad Ahsan of Amroha proposed the name of Mirza Mahmud Ahmad for *khilafat*. I rose up to mention the discussion that had taken place between me and the Mian sahib but some men began to shout that they would not listen, and there arose cries of: *Takht-i khilafat mubarak* (congratulations on the throne of *khilafat*)! The Mian sahib listened to all this silently and did not even ask the people to let me speak. So we left from there."

This gathering which Maulana Muhammad Ali has mentioned was held in the Nur mosque. When Maulana Muhammad Ali tried to speak, Hafiz Roshan Ali, secretary of the Ansarullah party, and Shaikh Yaqub Ali Turab, who were waiting for this point, started

---

4. This standpoint does not accord with what happened when Hazrat Umar died. After being wounded, he appointed a board of six leading Companions and instructed them to elect a *khalifa* from among themselves. Then Hazrat Umar died and his funeral prayers were led by Hazrat Suhaib. The next *khalifa,* Hazrat Usman, was chosen afterwards.

shouting that they did not want to hear. This was a prearranged signal at which the whole of the Ansarullah party at once stood up, raising the cry that they would not listen, and they all surged towards Mirza Mahmud Ahmad, jostling to take the *bai'at* on his hand. A great uproar and tumult was created, and cries went up: *Takht-i khilafat mubarak* and *Iwaan-i khilafat mubarak* (Congratulations on the throne of *khilafat!* Congratulations on the palace of *khilafat!*) Maulana Muhammad Ali and his friends could not prevail upon this coarse element and left.

Afterwards telegrams were sent to the government and to all branches of the Anjuman, wrongly informing them that Mirza Mahmud Ahmad had been elected unanimously. Men were sent in all directions who got written pledges signed and returned by Ahmadis unaware of the situation, living in distant places. How a false propaganda was carried out to mislead the community to bring it under Mirza Mahmud Ahmad is a long story.

When Maulana Muhammad Ali and some other people with him left the Nur mosque and came back to the Maulana's house, Dr. Basharat Ahmad was among them. He related that, while they could still hear the chanting from the mosque, Mirza Sultan Ahmad, the eldest son of the Promised Messiah from his first wife, who was not a regular member of the Ahmadiyya community, and also had happened to be present in the mosque, came to them and immediately addressed Maulana Muhammad Ali saying:

> "I have come to seek forgiveness for the rude treatment that my brother [Mirza Mahmud Ahmad] has meted out to the old friends of his father [the Promised Messiah]. When I saw the discourtesy that was allowed to prevail in the mosque just now I sank to the ground in shame."

(*Paigham Sulh,* 27 April 1937, p. 6)

In the *Paigham Sulh* of 10 March 1914, an article by Maulana Muhammad Ali entitled *Hazrat Mirza Sahib's claim to prophethood* was published, refuting the wrong beliefs falsely attributed to Hazrat Mirza sahib by Mirza Mahmud Ahmad. The article about 'Islam and Unbelief' that was written "according to the directions of Maulana Nur-ud-Din" was published in the issue of the paper

dated 17 March 1914. In the same issue a letter by Dr. Syed
Muhammad Husain Shah written from Qadian was published
which throws further light on the events. Some extracts from it are
given below:

> "I and some friends from Lahore arrived in Qadian on the
> morning of 14 March. Here we found that the dangerous
> circumstances to which Maulana Muhammad Ali had
> alerted the community beforehand by his foresight were
> prevailing exactly as he had warned. Everywhere, stud-
> ents from the Ahmadiyya school, zealous members of the
> Ansarullah, and Shaikh Yaqub Ali, Mufti Fazl-ur-Rahman
> etc., etc., were running around trying to incite the igno-
> rant people and rouse them to support Mirza Mahmud
> Ahmad for *khalifa*. ... Mistry Musa was stationed on the
> canal bridge on the way to Qadian, where he was obtain-
> ing signatures from newly arriving members by asking
> them if they wanted a *khalifa* to be appointed or not, but
> the paper on which their signatures were obtained said: a
> *khalifa* should be appointed and have the power to keep
> or disband the Anjuman and to expel any member as he
> wishes. ...
>
> Midday came while all this was going on, but no one
> asked the consultative representatives who had come from
> other areas. In the Nur mosque Mirza Mahmud Ahmad
> made a speech and after that Maulana Muhammad Ali
> advised that whatever was to be done should be decided
> after consultation, as haste would make matters go wrong.
> At midday we sent Khalifa Rajab-ud-Din and Dr. Mirza
> Yaqub Baig to impress that the matters should be decided
> by consulting the whole community, there was no need to
> rush as this was not the administration of a country which
> would stop working; the funeral and burial should take
> place first and then the representatives of the community
> should be called for discussion within ten to fifteen days;
> because when Hazrat *Khalifat-ul-Masih* [Maulana Nur-
> ud-Din] was chosen there was no disagreement among us
> but today there is a grave and serious difference; one party
> considers that all those Muslims who do not believe in

Hazrat Mirza sahib are *kafir,* the other party considers that every person professing the *Kalima* is a Muslim, except those who declare us as *kafir.* ... However, they responded that they could not wait; whatever was to be done must be decided today, and a *khalifa* had to be appointed before the burial."

As to what happened after the *Asr* prayers in the Nur mosque, he writes:

"... the Nawab sahib stood up and read the will of Hazrat *Khalifat-ul-Masih,* and then said that a successor should be chosen. ... As had been prearranged, voices were raised from different directions calling out 'Mian sahib' [Mirza Mahmud Ahmad]. After that Maulvi Muhammad Ahsan also proposed the Mian sahib, but when Maulana Muhammad Ali stood up to say something, Shaikh Yaqub Ali, Hafiz Roshan Ali and some others shouted 'sit down, sit down' and did not let him speak. ... The Mian sahib himself also instructed that, after Maulvi Muhammad Ahsan, no one should be allowed to speak. Thus the instruction in the will of Hazrat *Khalifat-ul-Masih,* that his successor should treat the older members with tolerance, forbearance and kindness, was violated and it was ignored in the euphoria of acquiring the *khilafat.*

After this, although the body of Hazrat *Khalifat-ul-Masih* lay unburied, yet slogans of congratulations to Mirza Mahmud Ahmad on becoming *khalifa* were being raised and loud shouting broke out like that of a common mob. ... After that, some supporters of the *khilafat* took up position at the arrival port in the town while others started roaming around the town, forcing people to sign."

The regrettable treatment which Maulana Muhammad Ali received in the Nur mosque was deplored by a newspaper of Qadian itself, the *Nur,* as follows:

"A painful matter —
Though some friends will be upset by what I have to declare, but tell me, my friends, the man who forsook such

close relatives as his own parents for the sake of the cause
of truth, what could prevent him from speaking the truth
now? After the speech of Hazrat Syed Muhammad Ahsan,
Maulvi Muhammad Ali sahib expressed his wish to say a
few words, but regrettably some irresponsible people forcibly prevented him. It is our belief that it would not have
altered the result, so why was Maulvi Muhammad Ali sahib
not given the chance to speak? It could have happened
that Allah might have caused him to say something at that
time which was to our advantage. We should be generous
towards our friends. But alas, these days a child who does
not even know the manners for speaking is not reluctant
to abuse others. We do not deny that Maulvi Muhammad
Ali sahib has a strong zeal, passion and fervour in his
heart for the propagation of Islam and service of the religion. For serving the religion he has not cared even for
his life and health. People living in Qadian are aware that
the cause of myself, the editor of *Nur,* having to depart from
the school, was brought about solely by Maulvi Muhammad
Ali sahib. But it would be the height of meanness on my
part if, due to a personal grudge, I deny an honourable
brother's abilities. The love and affection with which the
Promised Messiah and then Hazrat *Khalifat-ul-Masih*
treated Maulvi Muhammad Ali sahib is no secret."

(From the newspaper *Nur* dated 17 March 1914)

In addition to this, many members of the community who were
present in the mosque on this occasion wrote letters at that time
expressing regret and dismay about what had happened. Many of
these letters were published in *Paigham Sulh*. What they deeply
regretted above all was that, in the very presence of Mirza Mahmud
Ahmad, people who had no stature or standing as compared to
Maulana Muhammad Ali told the Maulana insolently to sit down
and keep quiet, but Mirza Mahmud Ahmad watched all this in
silence even though the will of Maulana Nur-ud-Din had just been
read out exhorting that his successor must treat all the old and new
friends of the Promised Messiah with kindness. All these letters were

written in the month of March when Maulana Muhammad Ali was still in Qadian.

Further stay in Qadian and migration from there

After these events Maulana Muhammad Ali continued to stay in Qadian for a while. On 17 March he made an announcement in *Paigham Sulh* (pages 3–4) to the following effect. In matters of faith and religion, decisions must not be made in haste. However, our Movement cannot unite on regarding other Muslims as unbelievers. Hazrat Mirza sahib had never declared that those who did not accept him were *kafir* because of denying his claims. Maulana Nur-ud-Din held the same belief and in his last days he had plainly told Mirza Mahmud Ahmad that he did not correctly understand this issue and had appointed him (Maulana Muhammad Ali) to publish a clarification of this matter. So we cannot take the *bai'at* at the hands of a man who calls Muslims as *kafir*, although we do wish to stay together for the sake of the work of the Movement.

In the issue for 19 March he again repeated some of the events and stressed the same points, and also wrote:

"The actions that have been taken I would call regrettable to say the least. ... If our community's basic principle is merely that we stick together in a partisan way, then I am definitely in the wrong. But if truth and right have some value, and to support one another in any wrong doing is a sin according to the Quran, no matter how closely you may be related to one another, then I have always done my duty of speaking out the truth and I will continue to do so whatever ruling may be issued against me.[5] If I am seeking and desiring any personal gain, creating discord under the guise of upholding the truth, then I am the most accursed person. But I have an urge in my heart that compels me to speak out even if I have to accept all manner of tribulation. Calling the followers of the *Qibla* as being *kafir* is the crime which Hazrat Mirza sahib bitterly accused his opponent Maulvis of committing. But alas!

---

5. At that time the Maulana was being called a *fāsiq* (wrong-doer) on account of not entering into the *bai'at* of Mirza Mahmud Ahmad.

Today we ourselves are doing what we accused others of. I shudder at the thought of calling those who recite the *Kalima*, 'There is no God but Allah, Muhammad is the Messenger of Allah', as being *kafirs* and excluded from the fold of Islam. ...

"If it is true that all those who profess the *Kalima* are *kafirs* until they accept the Promised Messiah then our efforts to propagate Islam are futile, and to get a Hindu or Christian to proclaim the *Kalima* is purposeless. ...

"In these circumstances the question of electing a leader or a *khalifa* becomes very difficult. To solve this problem the community needed, and still needs, much deliberation, consultation and prayers. Such important affairs cannot be decided in minutes. ...

"I am prepared to face whatever consequences I may have to bear, and I pray to Allah to give me the strength to be steadfast upon the truth and grant me patience in adversity. In the end I beg to say that even in these conditions we must remain united in carrying on our mission as before and not let anything detract from performing the tasks the Promised Messiah assigned to us. ... Among these tasks I include the work that my honourable friend Khwaja Kamal-ud-Din is doing. ... Anyone who tries to weaken it will be sowing the seed of discord." [6]

After Maulana Nur-ud-Din's death while Maulana Muhammad Ali was still in Qadian, his life was being made intolerable by people shouting abusive slogans and hurling insults at him. When conditions deteriorated from bad to worse he left Qadian for Lahore (*Paigham Sulh,* 12 April 1914). What followed after this date will be related in the next chapter.

The world of Islam and the event of 1914

Apart from the Ahmadiyya community, the rest of the Islamic world in India also took note of this dissension and the fact that the strength of faith of a few men had saved a section of the

---

6. At that time the first action of Mirza Mahmud Ahmad and his supporters was to stop Maulvi Sher Ali being sent to Woking to assist Khwaja Kamal-ud-Din and to cut off connection with the Woking Mission.

Ahmadiyya community from the curse of extreme sectarianism and of labelling other Muslims as *kafir*. Maulana Abul Kalam Azad commented on this in his newspaper *Al-Hilal,* dated 25 March 1914, as follows:

> "For some time, there had been two parties in this Movement over the question of *takfir*. One party believed that non-Ahmadis are Muslims even though they may not believe in Mirza sahib's claims. The other party, however, declared openly and clearly that those people who do not believe in Mirza sahib are *kafir* absolutely — *innā li-llāhi wa innā ilai-hi rāji'ūn.*[7] The head of the latter party is Mirza Bashir-ud-Din Mahmud Ahmad, and this faction has now made him *khalifa* but the first group does not accept this. The writing published in this connection by Maulana Muhammad Ali, and the wonderful and admirable courage he has shown in expressing these views while staying in Qadian, where the heads of the other party live, is truly an event which shall always be regarded as a memorable event of this year."

End of second phase of Maulana Muhammad Ali's life

With this event the second phase of the life of Maulana Muhammad Ali, consisting of fifteen years in Qadian, comes to a close in April 1914. This phase had begun with his great sacrifice, at the age of 25 years, when he gave up his worldly future to sit at the feet of Hazrat Mirza sahib, and he spent the best of his youth in Qadian till the age of 40. In the first eight out of these fifteen years he had such close company of, and nearness to, the Promised Messiah as was attained by very few. Hazrat Mirza sahib not only provided him with accommodation in his own house, giving him physical nearness to him, but the Maulana also acquired spiritual affinity to Hazrat Mirza sahib and absorbed from him zeal and passion for the propagation of Islam, love for the Holy Quran and the urge to spread it in the world. Hazrat Mirza sahib himself

---

7. Meaning "Surely we are Allah's and to Him do we return". This is the expression uttered by Muslims to express grief at a sad event such as a death.

entrusted to him all those tasks which he had declared as being his mission from Allah. The Maulana also acquired knowledge and scholarship of the Holy Quran from Hazrat Mirza sahib and Maulana Nur-ud-Din.

In the latter six years of this phase of his life, according to the wishes of Maulana Nur-ud-Din, Maulana Muhammad Ali began work on the English and Urdu translations of the Quran, which the Promised Messiah had declared was his own task or it would be done by a man "who is an offshoot of mine and thus is included in me." For thirteen out of these fifteen years he was the Editor of the *Review of Religions,* a work he did so magnificently that in those days the fame of this magazine spread in India and then in the outside world. Friend and foe all had to admit that no one had presented such a captivating picture of Islam as the Promised Messiah had done through this periodical.

After Hazrat Mirza sahib established the Sadr Anjuman Ahmadiyya, Qadian, as his successor, Maulana Muhammad Ali remained its secretary and its moving force for eight years. Branches of the community were set up and organised in many places. The Anjuman's budget reached to the value of two hundred thousand Rupees of those days. Its property increased substantially and included a building and a boarding house for the Talim-ul-Islam school worth 150,000 Rupees, which were constructed under the Maulana's personal supervision.

However, in 1914, for the sake of a matter of principle he left behind all these achievements and the fully-functioning organisation which he had played a major role in building up; and he departed from the beloved place where he had been blessed with the company of the Imam of the Age, where he had received that spiritual benefit from him and from other elders of the Movement which had transformed his life. He left for Lahore empty handed, but he had with him one thing, and that was the English translation of the Holy Quran which he brought with him from Qadian to Lahore.

Part 3

Life at Lahore

April 1914 to October 1951

3.1: Founding of the Ahmadiyya Anjuman Isha'at Islam Lahore

Brief history of Ahmadiyya Buildings

After migrating from Qadian, Maulana Muhammad Ali settled in Ahmadiyya Buildings, Brandreth Road, Lahore, where Khwaja Kamal-ud-Din, Dr. Mirza Yaqub Baig and Dr. Syed Muhammad Husain Shah, who were members of the Sadr Anjuman's executive from Lahore, lived and had their houses. Here the Ahmadiyya Anjuman Isha'at Islam was founded. The nearly fifty years of the Anjuman's life till today, first during Maulana Muhammad Ali's life up to 1951 and after that till now, is connected with this place,[1] and so it seems appropriate to relate a brief history of Ahmadiyya Buildings.

The foundations of the Ahmadiyya Buildings were laid in 1906. The land on which it is situated was owned by Chaudhry Allah Yar, who was the father of the respected elder of the Movement Chaudhry Zahur Ahmad. At the beginning, it was taken on a very long lease from him by Dr. Syed Muhmmad Husain Shah, Dr. Mirza Yaqub Baig and Khwaja Kamal-ud-Din. First the Shah sahib and the Khwaja sahib had their houses built by the main road side, and sometime after that Dr. Mirza sahib and Babu Manzur Ilahi had their houses built as well. At that time the whole of the area was not densely populated, though Islamia College had already been built on the other side of the road. In 1908 the Promised Messiah first stayed at Khwaja Kamal-ud-Din's house and

---

1. This was written in 1962. In the early 1970s the Anjuman's headquarters moved from Ahmadiyya Buildings in the centre of Lahore to a purpose-built colony, *Darus Salaam,* in the New Garden Town suburb about six miles away. Ahmadiyya Buildings is still maintained by the Anjuman.

after a few days went to stay with Dr. Syed Muhammad Husain Shah. On 22 May 1908 Friday prayers (*Jumu'a*) were held for the first time at Ahmadiyya Buildings. Before that, the Friday prayers were held at Mian Chirag-ud-Din's house outside Delhi Gate. After Friday prayers on 22 May, Hazrat Mirza sahib made a speech which was published afterwards under the title of *Hujjat-ullah.* Hazrat Mirza sahib also produced his last writing, *Paigham-i Sulh,* while staying at Ahmadiyya Buildings. On 26 May 1908, the Promised Messiah breathed his last in the house of Dr. Syed Muhammad Husain Shah.

At that time the present mosque in Ahmadiyya Buildings had not been built. Some time later a terrace was built, upon which the daytime prayers were held, and sometimes lectures and classes were given. The Friday prayers were held in a large room in the house of Khwaja Kamal-ud-Din. Hazrat Maulana Nur-ud-Din visited Lahore two or three times while he was head of the Movement and stayed in Ahmadiyya Buildings. Once he addressed a large gathering on this terrace, where the mosque stands today. Later on Khwaja Kamal-ud-Din started a series of lectures every Sunday from the same spot. His delivery of speech was so attractive that the general public, members of the nobility, learned people and government officers used to come from far and wide to attend. After a short while, a mosque was built upon this terrace, though in the beginning it was very small.

After the death of Hazrat Maulana Nur-ud-Din, Maulana Muhammad Ali came to Lahore and settled in Ahmadiyya Buildings, as will be explained in full detail later. The first consultative council (*Majlis-i Shura*) was held on 22 March 1914 on the courtyard of the upper storey of the house of Dr. Syed Muhammad Husain Shah; and when there remained no hope of a reconciliation with Mirza Mahmud Ahmad, as he violated the Will of the Promised Messiah by reducing the Sadr Anjuman Ahmadiyya to a powerless body, the foundation of the Ahmadiyya Anjuman Isha'at Islam was laid here on 3 May 1914.

Though the Anjuman had been founded in name, the position was that it had no funds, offices or assets. Missionaries and workers were all in the opposite camp. The founders of this Anjuman had used up their life earnings in Qadian by spending them on having buildings and property built for the Anjuman of Qadian and had come to Lahore empty handed. Here there were very few houses. The offices of the Anjuman and the guest house were set up in the houses of various members. The construction of the house adjacent to the mosque, which was later Maulana Muhammad Ali's residence for a long time, was started at that time by Dr. Syed Muhammad Husain Shah for the offices of the Anjuman. Later, however, the offices were moved to the house which is to the west of the present offices. After that the offices were shifted to the houses of Dr. Mirza Yaqub Baig, and that is where they have been located till today.[2] Later on, at the annual gathering of 1920, when Maulana Muhammad Ali appealed for donations of one hundred thousand Rupees, the Shah sahib and the Mirza sahib, who were always among the major contributors on such occasions, donated these properties to the Anjuman. In the same way another respected elder, Babu Ahmad Din, gave the Anjuman his house which was in the western part of the present Muslim High school. In the beginning the guest house was located in it, but later on it was demolished and incorporated into the school building.

This is a brief history of the houses at Ahmadiyya Buildings, but the most important house is the one which became the House of God, from where sounds of *Allahu Akbar* rose and echoed as far as Europe and most parts of Asia, and which illuminated countless hearts with the light of faith. For 37 years Maulana Muhammad Ali delivered his spiritually uplifting sermons in this mosque, exhorting and urging the community to spread the name of God, the message of Islam, in the world. For years he taught here the meanings of the Holy Quran, and after him other elders continued this work. The Maulana lived for 22 years in the house adjacent to it and here he penned those renowned books which were published in large numbers, translated into many languages and spread throughout the world. Thus, not only was a wealth of invaluable knowledge created here for the Movement but also the name Ahmadiyya Buildings became famous all over the world.

---

2. See footnote on p. 115 about the move in the early 1970s.

Newspaper and journal *Paigham Sulh*

The newspaper *Paigham Sulh*[3] had been started before Maulana Muhammad Ali came to Lahore. In July 1913, by when much friction and disagreement had arisen within the Movement, and Mirza Mahmud Ahmad and his faction were spreading false propaganda against the members from Lahore, trying to turn Maulana Nur-ud-Din against Maulana Muhammad Ali, Khwaja Kamal-ud-Din and the Lahore members, at that time the Ahmadiyya community newspapers *Al-Hakam* and *Badr* in Qadian were largely under the influence of Mirza Mahmud Ahmad. There was an urgent need to counter this propaganda. Also, Khwaja Kamal-ud-Din had gone to England a year earlier and issued from there a monthly magazine entitled *Islamic Review and Muslim India,* and there was a great need to publish in Urdu selected material from this English magazine for the benefit of Indian readership, as well as inform people in India about the activities of the Woking Muslim Mission founded by the Khwaja sahib.

In view of these needs, Dr. Syed Muhammad Husain Shah floated a company by the name of the *Paigham Sulh* Society, and under its auspices the paper *Paigham Sulh* was started in July 1913. Maulana Nur-ud-Din approved of its publication and purchased a five Rupee share as a token of his blessing. Its first editor was one Ahmad Husain of Faridabad, who was secretly connected with Mirza Mahmud Ahmad's Ansarullah party. In its first few issues he tried to use *Paigham Sulh* for expressing the views of that faction. So he was dismissed in November 1913 after he published some statements fabricated by himself, and Maulvi Dost Muhammad was appointed editor. In those early days the persons who played a special role in the development of this newspaper were, firstly, Dr. Syed Muhammad Husain Shah himself, secondly Babu Manzur Ilahi, and thirdly Maulana Abdul Haq Vidyarthi.

When, following the death of Maulana Nur-ud-Din, the *khilafat* was taken over by Mirza Mahmud Ahmad, with prearranged help from his supporters, who became an autocratic head by altering

---

3. The word *Sulh* is spelt here according to its Arabic form. Its common pronunciation in Urdu is like *Sulah* or *Sula.*

the regulations of the Sadr Anjuman Ahmadiyya, and it became necessary to set up the Ahmadiyya Anjuman Isha'at Islam, then the *Paigham Sulh* became the property and the organ of this Anjuman and the *Paigham Sulh* Society ceased to exist.

Establishment of Ahmadiyya Anjuman Isha'at Islam, Lahore

After the deplorable events in Qadian which have been mentioned earlier, Maulana Muhammad Ali called a meeting of Ahmadis at Lahore on 22 March 1914. A few members attended this at the house of Dr. Syed Muhammad Husain Shah and after giving careful consideration to the prevailing state of affairs some resolutions were passed the gist of which is as follows:

1. According to the Will (*Al-Wasiyyat*) of the Promised Messiah the decisions of the Sadr Anjuman Ahmadiyya, Qadian, should be regarded as final and binding, and no individual should have the power to revoke them.

2. It should not be obligatory for people who have previously taken the *bai'at* to renew their pledge at the hand of the new head of the Movement.

3. As forty persons or more have already taken the *bai'at* at the hand of Mirza Mahmud Ahmad, he is entitled to take the *bai'at* from new entrants to admit them into the Ahmadiyya Movement.

4. If Mirza Mahmud Ahmad accepts the decisions of the Anjuman as being final and binding, and does not consider it obligatory for existing Ahmadis to renew their *bai'at* at his hand, then he should be accepted as the President of the Sadr Anjuman Ahmadiyya and Head of the entire community (*jama'at*).

These resolutions were exactly according to the following directions of the Promised Messiah — that "you must all work together after me", that after him the decisions of the Anjuman were to be final and no individual would have the power to alter them, that the Anjuman was to be his successor, and that to admit new entrants into the Movement, any elders upon whom forty members agree would be entitled to administer the *bai'at* in the name of the Promised Messiah.

Although all those who attended this meeting disagreed in principle with Mirza Mahmud Ahmad's doctrine of calling other Muslims as *kafir*, they were prepared in order to preserve the unity of the community to accept him as head if he worked according to the conditions of *Al-Wasiyyat*. They intended to put the issue of *takfir* before the entire community and believed that the *Jama'at* would accept the right belief.

Copies of these resolutions were sent to Mirza Mahmud Ahmad in Qadian and also published in *Paigham Sulh,* dated 24 and 26 March 1914. A deputation of fifteen men was proposed to go and meet Mirza Mahmud Ahmad on 28 March in order to seek his acceptance of these terms. However, Mirza Mahmud Ahmad, in his response, refused to talk to the deputation about these proposals. As a result, on 28 March once again a meeting was held in Lahore and Maulana Muhammad Ali put to it the question as to how to proceed. He made a very well reasoned, detailed speech to the effect that the question was whether we should give priority to Hazrat Mirza sahib's writings or not. He placed before the meeting the hand-written note of Hazrat Mirza sahib dated 27 October 1907 which stated in plain words that the Anjuman was to be his successor and all its decisions were to be final. He also proved that Hazrat Mirza sahib never envisaged a *khalifa* as his successor who would rule over the Anjuman.

He also related all the past events when during Maulana Nur-ud-Din's time efforts were made to expel him and the Lahore members from the Sadr Anjuman, and how these efforts had failed. After his speech, others gave expression to their views. Dr. Syed Muhammad Husain Shah described the conditions in Qadian, explaining that it had now become impossible for Maulana Muhammad Ali to continue working in Qadian.

Accordingly, the following decisions were taken:

1. As Mirza Mahmud Ahmad has refused to meet the deputation to discuss the proposals of 22 March, the delegation need not now go to Qadian.

2. The resolutions passed previously still remain in force (i.e., the door for reconciliation with Mirza Mahmud Ahmad would remain open).

3. According to the Will of the Promised Messiah, the propagation of Islam is the real aim of the Movement and it is obligatory to carry out this service so far as it is within our power. As, due to the dissension, it would be troublesome to do this work from Qadian, so it is appropriate as a matter of necessity that an Anjuman be created by the name of *Isha'at-i Islam* which should have its head office in Lahore.

4. There shall be at least forty trustees of this Anjuman. The following office holders were agreed upon:

   President: Maulana Muhammad Ali, editor *Review of Religions.*

   Vice-Presidents: Maulvi Ghulam Hasan Khan of Peshawar, Shaikh Niaz Ahmad of Wazirabad, Khan Ajab Khan of North-West Frontier Province.

   Secretary: Dr. Mirza Yaqub Baig.

   Assistant Secretary: Hakim Muhammad Husain ('Marham-i Isa').

   Treasurer: Shaikh Rahmatullah.

To draft the rules and regulations a committee was set up having the following as its members: Maulana Muhammad Ali, Maulvi Alam Din *Wakeel,* Dr. Mirza Yaqub Baig, Dr. Syed Muhammad Husain Shah, Shaikh Rahmatullah, Chishti Abdur Rahman and Khalifa Rajab Din. An appeal for funds was made there and then and a sum of 325 Rupees was collected.

Twenty-nine members were present in this meeting. The names of some of them are: Maulana Muhammad Ali, Dr. Syed Muhammad Husain Shah, Dr. Mirza Yaqub Baig, Shaikh Rahmatullah, Shaikh Niaz Ahmad (Wazirabad), Shaikh Muhammad Jan (Wazirabad), Syed Hamid Shah, Hakim Muhammad Husain ('Marham-i Isa'), Chaudhry Muhammad Sarfraz (Baddomalhi), Maulvi Alam Din *Wakeel* (Shaikhupura), Chishti Abdur Rahman, Master Ghulam Muhammad (Sialkot), Shaikh Faiz-ur-Rahman

(Amritsar), Sufi Ahmad Din, Abdul Hanan Khan (Peshawar) and Mirza Abdul Ghani. (See *Paigham Sulh,* 31 March 1914.)

The position at that time was that all these people had not severed their ties with the Sadr Anjuman Ahmadiyya, Qadian. However, as it had become impossible for Maulana Muhammad Ali and his associates to work and serve religion in Qadian, this was why they wanted to continue their work from Lahore through an Anjuman. To divide the community in two was a step they were forced to take after very careful consideration, but their first offer was still open, namely, that within the limits specified by the Promised Messiah in his *Al-Wasiyyat* and in his other rules, Mirza Mahmud Ahmad could be the head of the community.

Mirza Mahmud Ahmad strictly forbade his followers to read any writing from Lahore. Members in Lahore had no other means to express their views except *Paigham Sulh,* and even this did not reach all members. Anyhow Maulana Muhammad Ali started to put the facts before the community through this paper. A long article by him entitled *Chand Khuli Khuli Baten* ('Some Plain Truths') was published as an appendix in the issue of *Paigham Sulh* for 2 April 1914, in which Hazrat Mirza sahib's writing dated 27 October 1907 was printed and practical examples from the time of Maulana Nur-ud-Din were put forward. Then after mentioning the proposals of the consultative meeting of 22 March and Mirza Mahmud Ahmad's rejection of them, Maulana Muhammad Ali wrote:

> "Having in mind that the energies of the community should be channelled towards its real objective, ... and consider-ing that the doctrine of calling other Muslims as *kafir* poses a danger to the work of the propagation of Islam and the progress of the Movement, and in order to prevent damage to the work of spreading Islam in Europe that has just now been started,[4] it has been deemed advisable that in addition to the work that members of the Movement are carrying on under the Sadr Anjuman Ahmadiyya, an

---

4. The reference is to the Woking Mission and the work of Khwaja Kamal-ud-Din in England.

Anjuman be created in Lahore for the purpose of the propagation of Islam whose main aim should be to strengthen the real objective of this Movement, which is the propagation of Islam. A firm foundation should be laid for this work and all friends who do not call the general Muslims, the *ahl-i Qibla* and the reciters of the *Kalima* as being *kafir* should join it with renewed fervour. ... Accordingly, it is on this basis that the foundation of an Anjuman has been laid, with trust in Allah. ...

The real objective of our Movement, as the Promised Messiah has stated again and again, is the propagation of Islam. ... Therefore, however much effort we devote to it, and however much of our own possessions and lives we give for this work, it would still be insufficient. My friends, Islam is in greatly troubled waters. Its propagation ... is such a grand and mighty task that whatever you have done so far in this way is really only the first step. ... If you are firm in your belief of giving preference to the cause of religion over worldly ambitions then come and support this cause with all your strength. ... Worry not that you are small in numbers. It is determination that matters and not numbers: 'How often has a small party vanquished a numerous host by Allah's permission!' [the Quran, 2:249] But Allah's permission will only come when you spare no effort on your part. ... Make all practical efforts, and also spiritual efforts, in other words, by prayer. ... 'Our Lord, accept our prayer. You are the Hearer and the Knower'."

On 10 April 1914 was held the first meeting of the Sadr Anjuman Ahmadiyya, Qadian, after the death of Maulana Nur-ud-Din, and was attended by Maulana Muhammad Ali, Dr. Mirza Yaqub Baig, Dr. Syed Muhammad Husain Shah and Shaikh Rahmatullah. However, they soon found that dictatorship prevailed in the meeting and matters that were not on the agenda were being approved. When those members who disagreed with the motions insisted that their dissenting views should be noted in writing, this was rejected. Besides other matters, it was also decided by the casting vote of the president of the meeting, Mirza Mahmud Ahmad, that Maulvi Sher Ali should not be sent to England to help Khwaja Kamal-ud-Din even though in Maulana Nur-ud-Din's time a firm decision had been taken to this effect. After this, these four members left the meeting: Maulana Muhammad Ali, Shaikh Rahmatullah, Dr. Mirza Yaqub Baig and Dr. Syed Muhammad Husain Shah (*Paigham Sulh,* 12 April, p. 2).

Two days after this, on 12 April 1914, Mirza Mahmud Ahmad called a meeting of a few select persons and made an attack on the powers of the Sadr Anjuman Ahmadiyya which destroyed its very foundations. Regarding Rule number 18 of the Sadr Anjuman Ahmadiyya which read:

> "In every matter, for the *Majlis-i Mu'timidin* [Council of Trustees] and its subordinate branches if any, and for the Sadr Anjuman and all its branches, the order of the Promised Messiah shall be absolute and final"

it was proposed that it should be amended by replacing the words "the Promised Messiah" by the words: "Hazrat Khalifat-ul-Masih Mirza Bashir-ud-Din Mahmud Ahmad the second Khalifa", so that Mirza Mahmud Ahmad would gain absolute power over the Anjuman. When the news of this proposal reached Maulana Muhammad Ali he published an announcement in *Paigham Sulh* of 21 April entitled:

> Sadr Anjuman Ahmadiyya Qadian,
> *Innā li-llāhi wa innā ilai-hi rāji'ūn.*[5]

He warned that if this amendment were made, the Sadr Anjuman as founded by Hazrat Mirza sahib would in effect cease to exist. However, Mirza Mahmud Ahmad was undeterred and got this motion passed in a meeting of the Council of Trustees on 26 April due to the majority of the members having taken the *bai'at* at his hand. When this happened, an announcement was published in *Paigham Sulh* of 5 May 1914 from Maulana Muhammad Ali, Dr. Mirza Yaqub Baig, Dr. Syed Muhammad Husain Shah and others,

---

5. Meaning "Surely we are Allah's and to Him do we return". This is the expression uttered by Muslims to express grief at a sad event such as a death.

in which they clarified again the whole matter and announced:

> "We declare with the deepest regret that Sahibzada sahib [Mirza Mahmud Ahmad] and his pledged followers, by removing the name of the Promised Messiah from the Rules, have not only given to a man who is not appointed by God the status of one sent by God, but have shown disrespect for the name of the Promised Messiah. ... Moreover, after destroying the foundations of the Anjuman and dismantling it in practice, ... two important funds, i.e. the zakat fund and the fund for the propagation of Islam, which during the life of the Promised Messiah and the *Khalifat-ul-Masih* [Maulana Nur-ud-Din] were in the control of the Anjuman, have been removed from the Anjuman's treasury and placed in his complete charge.[6] ... If legal action were taken, all this could be declared invalid and the Anjuman restored to its original status. But since we do not wish to waste the Movement's energy and money on litigation, we issue this declaration to absolve ourselves from these moves. ... By this declaration we discharge our duty and clear ourselves of responsibility in the eyes of God, for it appears that taking legal action will do more harm than good."

It was under these circumstances that the Ahmadiyya Anjuman Isha'at Islam Lahore came into existence formally on 3 May 1914, and on the same day the first meeting of its Council of Trustees was held. Dr. Mirza Yaqub Baig presented the rules and regulations of the Anjuman, which were approved. Maulana Muhammad Ali was elected as the Head (*amir*) of the community and President, and the other office bearers retained their positions as mentioned earlier except that in Shaikh Rahmatullah's place Dr. Syed Muhammad Husain Shah became Financial Secretary. In all 59 members were elected as trustees, of whom fourteen were permanent life members. The names of these 59 members are as follows:

---

6. Mirza Mahmud Ahmad had directed that donations for the propagation of Islam as well as all other donations should be sent to him and would be spent only as determined by him.

1. Maulana Muhammad Ali.
2. Khwaja Kamal-ud-Din.
3. Dr. Mirza Yaqub Baig.
4. Dr. Syed Muhammad Husain Shah.
5. Shaikh Rahmatullah.
6. Shaikh Niaz Ahmad (Wazirabad).
7. Shaikh Muhammad Jan (Wazirabad).
8. Dr. Basharat Ahmad.
9. Maulvi Ghulam Hasan Khan (Peshawar).
10. Maulana Aziz Bakhsh.
11. Babu Manzur Ilahi.
12. Maulvi Sadr-ud-Din.
13. Malik Ghulam Muhammad.
14. Shaikh Faiz-ur-Rahman (Amritsar).
15. Chaudhry Muhammad Sarfraz Khan (Baddomalhi).
16. Maulvi Alam Din (Shaikhupura).
17. Master Ghulam Muhammad (Sialkot).
18. Babu Ali Bakhsh (Gujranwala).
19. Syed Amir Ali Shah (Sialkot).
20. Sufi Ahmad Din (Lahore).
21. Khan Ajab Khan (Frontier).
22. Shaikh Abdur Rahman (Sialkot).
23. Hafiz Ghulam Rasul (Wazirabad).
24. Khwaja Jamal-ud-Din (Jammu).
25. Mirza Hakim Baig (Sialkot).
26. Khalifa Rajab-ud-Din (Lahore).
27. Dr. Muhammad Umar (Lucknow).
28. Babu Muhammad Isa (Jhelum).
29. Shaikh Nur Ahmad (Abbottabad).
30. Shaikh Shah Nawaz (Rawalpindi).
31. Babu Ata Ilahi (Wazirabad).
32. Shaikh Maula Bakhsh (Sialkot).
33. Shaikh Abdur Razak (Gujranwala).
34. Babu Muhammad (Ludhiana).
35. Maulvi Nazar Ali (Peshawar).
36. Malik Sher Ali Khan (Kashmir).
37. Mir Hayat Ali Shah (Hazara).
38 Dr. Muhammad Sharif (Muzaffargarh).
39. Dr. Ghulam Muhammad, Assitant Surgeon (Peshawar).
40. Dr. Ataullah.
41. Babu Muhammad Ilahi (Haripur).
42. Babu Ali Gohar (Sialkot).
43. Dr. Hasan Ali (Gujranwala).
44. Maulvi Rukan Din (Gujranwala).
45. Babu Muhammad Husain (Lahore Cantonment).
46. Qazi Muhammad Yusuf (Peshawar).
47. Maulvi Mustafa Khan (Patiala).
48. Mr. M.A. Maulvi (Shikarpur).
49. Dr. Nabi Bakhsh (Lahore).
50. Shaikh Muzaffar-ud-Din (Abbottabad).
51. Maulvi Mubarak Ali (Sialkot).
52. Muhammad Wilayatullah Khan (Ajmer).
53. Dr. Khaliq Dad (Hungo).
54. Chaudhry Muhammad Bakhsh (Sialkot).
55. Babu Ghulam Rasul (Peshawar).
56. Babu Imam Din (Jhelum).
57. Shaikh Nizam Din (Mianwali).
58. Shaikh Mian Muhammad Ismail (Lyallpur).
59. Shaikh Maula Bakhsh (Lyallpur).

It will have become clear from all these events that for one and a half months after the dispute Maulana Muhammad Ali and his associates kept on trying to maintain the unity of the community if at all possible. They even offered to accept Mirza Mahmud Ahmad as Head on condition that he would not become an autocratic leader in violation of the directions of the Promised Messiah because, firstly, this was against *Al-Wasiyyat* and, secondly, Mirza Mahmud Ahmad had invented the dangerous belief of calling all other Muslims as *kafir*. However, when Mirza Mahmud Ahmad went ahead to change the regulations of the Anjuman and assume all power himself, then it became unavoidable to separate from the Sadr Anjuman Ahmadiyya and create the Ahmadiyya Anjuman Isha'at Islam. A question remains that, as Hazrat Mirza sahib had declared the decisions of the Sadr Anjuman Ahmadiyya to be final, so if that Anjuman made Mirza Mahmud Ahmad an autocratic *khalifa,* then was it not binding to accept him? The answer to this has been given very clearly in the announcement dated 5 May 1914 and it has been proved that Hazrat Mirza sahib had created the Sadr Anjuman Ahmadiyya with the limitation that no individual would be his successor. Therefore the Anjuman according to its own regulations did not have the power to violate the decision of the Promised Messiah and break the limitations imposed by him.

Expulsion of Maulana Muhammad Ali and his comrades from the Sadr Anjuman Ahmadiyya Qadian

On 12 May 1916 a resolution was presented in the Sadr Anjuman Ahmadiyya, Qadian, to expel Maulana Muhammad Ali and five other members. Then, by Resolution 213 dated 22 June 1916, the following six members were served notice as to why they should not be expelled from the Sadr Anjuman Ahmadiyya:

1.   Maulana Muhammad Ali
2.   Dr. Mirza Yaqub Baig
3.   Dr. Syed Muhammad Husain Shah
4.   Shaikh Rahmatullah
5.   Khwaja Kamal-ud-Din
6.   Maulana Ghulam Hasan Khan.

Quoted below are some extracts from the reply to this notice given by these six members in *Paigham Sulh,* 17 August 1916:

"1. The basis of the Sadr Anjuman Ahmadiyya, Qadian, founded 1906 is *Al-Wasiyyat* of the Promised Messiah. Its regulations were formulated during Hazrat Mirza sahib's life and published with his permission and approval, and the Anjuman operated according to them. Hazrat Mirza sahib wrote a codicil to this Will in 1907 as a warning when Mir Nasir Nawab went against the Anjuman, in which he gave the clear verdict that the decisions of the Anjuman taken by majority of opinion were to be final, and after him no individual would have the power to issue or to annul its decisions.

"2. You people have forsaken this basic principle, and in Rule 18 formulated by the Promised Messiah you have deleted his name and replaced it by the name of Mirza Mahmud Ahmad, and against the wishes of Hazrat Mirza sahib you have made one man, Mirza Mahmud Ahmad, supreme over the Anjuman. So after this action of yours, this does not remain the Anjuman based on Hazrat Mirza sahib's *Al-Wasiyyat* and his codicil added to it. ... We being Ahmadis, and regarding it as our duty to honour the words of Hazrat Mirza sahib, consider it an insult to the Ahmadiyya Movement to participate in the activities of this Anjuman.

"3. It is a misconception that this authority has been given to Mirza Mahmud Ahmad by majority vote in a meeting of the Sadr Anjuman and so the conditions laid by Hazrat Mirza sahib have been fulfilled. In the first place the whole procedure is riddled with legal flaws ... which render all the proceedings null and void. Moreover, ... no executor can violate the aims and principles of a will. In a will in which its aims are implemented by the executors by majority, they cannot by majority nullify its objectives. ... The majority cannot make a valid decision that in future all matters concerning the propagation of Islam shall not be decided by majority but imposed by a single person. ... As the Founder of the Anjuman, the Promised Messiah, has handed his conclusive writing to the Anjuman, penned in his own hand, that after him no individual has the right to overturn the decisions of the Anjuman taken by majority of opinion, then for you to give this authority to one person among you constitutes nullifying the terms of the Will."

The concluding part of this reply is as follows:

"So we waited for a long time, hoping that you might find a way to rectify the situation, but when it became apparent that the income of the Sadr Anjuman and its duties are gradually being transferred to another body and matters are deteriorating day by day, we did not wish to leave the enforcement of our wills in your hands. So we cancelled the wills, and to fulfil the objective for which Hazrat Mirza sahib created the Sadr Anjuman we formed an Anjuman by the name of Ahmadiyya Anjuman Isha'at Islam and made our wills in its favour."

The original document is signed as follows:

Ghulam Hasan, Sub-Registrar, Peshawar.
Khwaja Kamal-ud-Din.
Syed Muhammad Husain.
Rahmatullah. 30 July 1916.
Mirza Yaqub Baig, 3 August 1916
Muhammad Ali, 3 August 1916.

In this concluding part, the mention of the income of the Sadr Anjuman being transferred to another Anjuman refers to the fact that Mirza Mahmud Ahmad had formed a new Anjuman by the name of *Taraqqi-i Islam* ('Progress of Islam') and was receiving donations in its name. This was probably done under legal advice so that the Lahore members would not be able to take legal action over the funds of the Sadr Anjuman Ahmadiyya.

Anyhow the Qadian Anjuman was not concerned with the merits of this reply and the arguments put forward in it. They did what they intended to all along, and after a short while these six members were expelled from the Qadian Anjuman. It should be made clear that at this time the Qadian Anjuman was no longer the Sadr Anjuman Ahmadiyya because from the day this Anjuman amended a basic regulation, in breach of the limits imposed by the Promised Messiah, the Sadr Anjuman Ahmadiyya Qadian ceased to exist.

It is also noteworthy that out of the original fourteen members appointed by the Promised Messiah to the Sadr Anjuman

Ahmadiyya Qadian, seven were with the Lahore side after the Split. As Maulana Nur-ud-Din had died, there remained six other members who were in Qadian. One was Mirza Mahmud Ahmad himself and three others were his close relations: Dr. Mir Muhammad Ismail, (maternal uncle), Dr. Khalifa Rashid-ud-Din (father-in-law) and Nawab Muhammad Ali Khan (brother-in-law). The only two members who were not related were Mir Hamid Shah and Seth Abdur Rahman of Madras. This means that in practice too the true successor of the Promised Messiah's Sadr Anjuman Ahmadiyya Qadian was the Ahmadiyya Anjuman Isha'at Islam Lahore whose leader and *Amir* was Maulana Muhammad Ali.

A writing of that occasion, from August 1916, penned in the hand of Maulana Muhammad Ali and signed by eleven elders, is as follows:

> "We, the undersigned, seeking the pleasure of Allah, solemnly affirm that:
>
> 1. We are, and shall remain, bound to the ten conditions of the *bai'at* laid down by the Promised Messiah.
>
> 2. We affirm that we will completely obey the injunctions of the Holy Quran and remain bound by the commands of Allah and the Holy Prophet Muhammad in all matters.
>
> 3. We affirm that we will make all efforts to read and teach the Holy Quran and to act upon it and urge others to do the same.
>
> 4. We affirm that we shall consider our wealth and property as belonging to Allah, and shall donate at least one-tenth of our income for the propagation of Islam to the Ahmadiyya Anjuman Isha'at Islam.
>
> 5. We affirm that we shall treat our time as being devoted to the propagation of Islam, and whenever required we will aid the work of the preaching of Islam in all ways. 'There is no granting of strength except from Allah. O Allah, Thee do we serve, and Thee do we ask for help."

It bears the following signatures: Muhammad Ali, Khwaja Kamal-ud-Din, Rahmatullah, Syed Muhammad Husain Shah, Mirza

Yaqub Baig, Nur Ahmad, Basharat Ahmad, Hayat Ali Shah, Abdur Rahim, Asmatullah, and Muhammad Ajab.

When was the Qadiani doctrine of the prophethood of Hazrat Mirza Ghulam Ahmad invented?

It seems appropriate to explain here briefly as to when the Qadiani belief in the prophethood of Hazrat Mirza Ghulam Ahmad was invented. Detailed discussions have been published on this issue, the most comprehensive book on this topic being written by Maulana Muhammad Ali under the title *An-Nubuwwat fil-Islam* ('Prophethood in Islam'), to which the Qadian community has not produced any response. As in this account of the life of Maulana Muhammad Ali there will be mention, later on, of arguments with the Qadiani community and calls to debate with them, so a brief treatment of this topic is given here for those who cannot read the books on this question.

In 1891 when the Founder of the Ahmadiyya Movement claimed to be the Promised Messiah, along with that claim he also denied that he was claiming prophethood. He went so far as to declare:

"We also curse the person who claims prophethood."

(*Majmu'a Ishtiharat,* 1986 edition, vol. 2, p. 297–298)

In his writings, certain words had occurred which were misinterpreted by the opponent Muslim religious leaders as a claim to prophethood, and on that basis they had declared him a *kafir*. In reply, Hazrat Mirza Ghulam Ahmad gave very clear and repeated answers to their accusations, some examples of which are as follows:

1. "There is no claim of prophethood. On the contrary, the claim is of sainthood (*muhaddasiyyat*) which has been advanced by the command of God."

    (*Izala Auham,* p. 421–422; *Ruhani Khaza'in,* vol. 3, p. 320)

2. "Those people have fabricated a lie against me who say that this man claims to be a prophet."

    (*Hamamat-ul-Bushra,* p. 8; *Ruhani Khaza'in,* vol. 7, p. 184)

3. "I make no claim to prophethood. This is your mistake."
    (*Jang Muqaddas*, p. 67; *Ruhani Khaza'in*, vol. 6, p. 156)

4. "If the objection is that I have made a claim to pro-
    phethood, and such a thing is heresy, what else can I say
    except that may the curse of Allah be upon liars and fabri-
    cators."
    (*Anwar-ul-Islam*, p. 34; *Ruhani Khaza'in*, vol. 9, p. 35)

5. "By way of a fabrication, they slander me by saying that
    I have made a claim to prophethood. But it should be
    remembered that all this is a fabrication."
    (*Kitab-ul-Bariyya*, p. 182, footnote; *Ruhani Khaza'in*, vol. 13, p.
    215)

So why did the opponents fall into the misconception that he
claimed to be a prophet? The answer to it will be found in the
writings of leading Qadianis themselves from the time before the
Split, as quoted below. These writings also show that until Mirza
Mahmud Ahmad, for his own ends, coined the doctrine that other
Muslims are *kafir,* no member of the Ahmadiyya community even
entertained the idea that Hazrat Mirza sahib claimed to be a
prophet. They believed that the word *nabi* ('prophet') used on
occasion in Hazrat Mirza sahib's writings about himself was,
according to Hazrat Mirza sahib's own explanation, meant in its
literal sense of 'one with whom God speaks', and that Hazrat
Mirza sahib himself made it clear that it meant a *muhaddas,* not a
prophet.

Here are some testimonies of leading figures of the Qadiani
community, made before the Split in 1914.

1. Mufti Muhammad Sadiq, editor newspaper *Badr,* Qadian,
who after the Split become one of Mirza Mahmud Ahmad's
topmost disciples, wrote an account of a tour of various cities of
India that he undertook, in which he was accompanied by Maulvi
Sarwar Shah (another topmost disciple of Mirza Mahmud
Ahmad). In this account, published in *Badr* dated 27 October
1910, he mentions their meeting with the famous Muslim historian
and scholar Maulana Shibli and writes in this connection on page
9 of this issue of the newspaper:

"Shibli asked if we believe the late Mirza sahib to be a prophet. I replied that our belief in this respect was the same as that of other Muslims, namely, that the Holy Prophet Muhammad is the *Khatam-un-nabiyyin.* After him, no other prophet can come, neither new nor old. However, the phenomenon of Divine revelation still continues, but even that is through the agency of the Holy Prophet. By receiving spiritual benefit from him, there have been men among the Muslims who had the privilege of Divine revelation, and in future too there shall be such. As Hazrat Mirza sahib was also privileged with Divine revelation, and in his revelations God gave him many news of the future as prophecies, which were fulfilled, for this reason Mirza sahib was one who made prophecies. Such a one is called *nabi* in Arabic lexicology, and in Hadith too the coming Promised Messiah is called *nabi.*

To this, Shibli replied that certainly, according to the dictionary meanings, this can be so, and in the Arabic language this word does have this meaning, but the ordinary people become perturbed because they do not know this significance, and they raise objections. I responded that, with us, the question of Mirza sahib's prophethood is not such that it is included in the conditions of the pledge (*bai'at*), nor is it required to be acknowledged when taking the pledge, nor do we go about preaching it. Our belief is what we have explained above."

Mufti Muhammad Sadiq then goes on to write:

"It seems appropriate at this point that I should include in this newspaper a recent letter by Hazrat *Khalifat-ul-Masih* [Maulana Nur-ud-Din] which he has written in reply to Sardar Muhammad Ajab Khan, and made it a sworn statement. The Sardar sahib had had a discussion with someone on this topic. The answer which the Sardar sahib gave to that man, he also sent it in writing to Hazrat [Maulana Nur-ud-Din] sahib, enquiring if his answer was correct or not. Hazrat sahib agreed with his answer and wrote a further clarification in his own hand which is reproduced below."

So Mufti Muhammad Sadiq then quotes the letter by Maulana Nur-ud-Din, which is as follows:

> "*Assalamu alaikum wa rahmatullahi wa barakatuhu.* To cut open the heart and look into it, or make others look into it, is beyond human power. If one relies on oaths, I see no oath equal to: *By Allah, the Great.* Neither you nor anyone else will accompany me after my death, except my faith and deeds. As this matter will be presented before Allah the Most High, I swear *by Allah, the Great, by Whose leave heaven and earth exist,* I believe Mirza sahib to be the *Mujaddid* of this century. I believe him to be righteous. I believe him to be a slave of Hazrat Muhammad, Messenger of Allah, the Arabian Prophet, of Makkah and Madinah, the *Khatam-un-nabiyyin,* and to be a sincere servant of his *Shari'ah.* And Mirza too considered himself to be a life-sacrificing slave of the Arabian Prophet, Muhammad ibn Abdullah.

> The dictionary meaning of the word *nabi,* we believe, is one who gives news, having received knowledge before-hand from Allah the Most High, not one who brings a *shari'ah.* Both Mirza sahib and I consider any person who rejects even an iota of the Holy Quran or the *Shari'ah* of the Holy Prophet Muhammad to be a *kafir* and an accursed one. This is my belief, and this was also I consider the belief of Mirza Ghulam Ahmad sahib. If anyone rejects this, refuses to accept it, or calls us hypocrites, his affair is with God. — *Nur-ud-Din, by own hand,* 22 October 1910."

Note: This letter is preserved in the papers of Maulana Muhammad Ali.

2. Mirza Mahmud Ahmad's teacher, Syed Sarwar Shah, writes:

> "The word *nabi,* according to its origins, has two meanings: firstly, one who receives news of matters unseen

from God; secondly, a man of a high status, to whom God grants the distinction of abundant revelation, and informs him of news of the unseen, he is a *nabi.* In this sense I believe that all the previous *mujaddids* were prophets of various grades."

(*Badr*, 16 February 1911, p. 3)

Here it is clearly acknowledged that any of the previous *mujaddids* may have the word 'prophet' applied to him in its literal sense. They do not become prophets thereby.

3. Mirza Mahmud Ahmad himself states:

"Allah the Most High, by granting him [the Holy Prophet Muhammad] the status of *Khatam-un-nabiyyin,* ended with him every kind of prophethood."

(*Al-Hakam*, 14 March 1911, p. 10; *Badr,* 23 March, p. 6)

"Thus God has said that the Holy Prophet Muhammad's prophethood was meant not only for his times, but that in future too no prophet would come. ...

The fact is that the Holy Prophet's being the *Khatam-un-nabiyyin* contains a prophecy. This is that before the Holy Prophet Muhammad there arose hundreds of prophets in the world who had great success. ... But thirteen hundred years have now passed since the Holy Prophet's claim, and no one has ever attained success by claiming prophethood. After all, prior to his time people used to claim prophethood, and many of them were successful, whom we believe to be true. But why has this arrangement stopped with his advent? Obviously because of the prophecy that he is the *Khatam-un-nabiyyin.* Now we ask the opponents of Islam, what greater sign can there be than the fact that, after the Holy Prophet, no person who claimed prophethood was successful."

(*Tashhiz-ul-Azhan,* April 1910, vol. v, no. 4, p. 151–152)

4. Mir Muhammad Saeed, leader of the Ahmadiyya community in Hyderabad Deccan, wrote in a book published in 1914:

"To sum up, Hazrat Mirza sahib has only claimed to be a
muhaddas — and not an actual prophet which negatives
the *Khatam-un-nabiyyin,* and is against [the hadith report]
'There is no prophet after me'."

(*Anwar-ullah*, p. 269)

So it is obvious that neither did Hazrat Mirza Ghulam Ahmad
claim to be a prophet nor did this notion ever occur to any member
of his Movement for many years after his death. All his followers
clearly understood that the word *nabi* which occurred occasionally
in his revelations or writings was used in a metaphorical and figu-
rative sense according to its literal meaning.

After the death of Hazrat Mirza sahib, when Maulana Nur-ud-
Din was known as *Khalifat-ul-Masih* and the *bai'at* was taken at
his hand, it was not in compliance with any Divine commandment
because he was not a *khalifa* in terms of the *istikhlaf* verse of the
Quran (ch. 24, v. 55). That verse was revealed as a promise to the
Holy Prophet Muhammad, may peace and the blessings of Allah
be upon him, so after him there began a series of *khalifas,* the
Promised Messiah being one of them. Secondly, this *bai'at* with
Maulana Nur-ud-Din was not taken in compliance with any
instruction of the Promised Messiah because according to his *Al-
Wasiyyat* existing Ahmadis were not obliged to take the *bai'at* at
anyone's hand after him. So the taking of the *bai'at* at the hand of
Maulana Nur-ud-Din was people's own choice and it was a pledge
of obedience. Maulana Muhammad Ali had raised the objection at
that very time, that there was no need for Ahmadis to take the
bai'at again with Maulana Nur-ud-Din. But Khwaja Kamal-ud-
Din said that there was no harm in renewing the pledge as at that
critical moment it would unite the community. Maulana Nur-ud-
Din was called *khalifa* in the literal sense of this word, meaning a
successor, not as being *khalifa* in terms of the promise given in the
istikhlaf verse of the Quran. It is conclusively proved from the
events of his time and his practice that he never overrode any
decision of the Anjuman, nor did he amend any of its regulations
to assume all power himself, as Mirza Mahmud Ahmad did.

When Mirza Mahmud Ahmad was making preparations and plans to become *khalifa,* he realized that as everyone was aware of the views of Maulana Muhammad Ali and his associates about *khilafat,* the question would arise that, as the Promised Messiah himself was a *khalifa* of the Holy Prophet Muhammad, how could there be a *khalifa* of a *khalifa*? So, to get over this objection, what he did first was to invent the doctrine of *takfir,* that every Muslim who had not taken the *bai'at* of the Promised Messiah was a *kafir* and outside the pale of Islam. Then he alleged that in the year 1901 the Promised Messiah, by altering his previous definition of prophethood, had changed his claim to that of being a prophet. Thus Mirza Mahmud Ahmad declared the Promised Messiah's writings before the year 1901 to be abrogated in the matter of prophethood, and by ascribing to him the claim of prophethood he laid the basis for his own *khilafat.*

This allegation, that the Promised Messiah made a change in his claim in 1901, announcing it through his pamphlet *Ayk Ghalati Ka Izala* published in November 1901, was such a dangerous accusation that Maulana Muhammad Ali and other elders challenged it at once. We will see later how the Maulana repeatedly addressed Mirza Mahmud Ahmad on this issue, but the Qadiani head did not have the courage to face him. Here we reproduce the sworn statement, issued again and again in 1915, signed by seventy members of the community who had taken the *bai'at* before November 1901, that neither did Hazrat Mirza sahib make a claim of prophethood at the start in 1891 nor did he change his claim in 1901 to that of prophethood:

> "We, the undersigned, declare on oath that when Hazrat Mirza Ghulam Ahmad of Qadian, the Founder of the Ahmadiyya Movement, announced in 1891, that the prophet Jesus was dead according to the Holy Quran, and that the 'son of Mary' whose advent among the Muslims was spoken of in Hadith was he [Hazrat Mirza] himself, he did not lay claim to prophethood. However, the Maulvis misled the public, and issued a *fatwa* of *kufr* against him by alleging that he claimed prophethood. After this, the Promised Messiah declared time after time

in plain words, as his writings show, that to ascribe to him
a claim of prophethood was a fabrication against him, that
he considered prophethood to have come to a close with
the Holy Prophet Muhammad, and that he looked upon a
claimant to prophethood, after the Holy Prophet, as a liar
and a *kafir*. And that the words *mursal, rasul,* and *nabi*
which had occurred in some of his revelations, or the word
nabi which had been used about the coming Messiah in
Hadith, do not denote a prophet in actual fact, but rather a
metaphorical, partial or *zilli* prophet who is known as a
muhaddas. After the *Khatam-un-nabiyyin* the Holy Prophet Muhammad, no prophet can come, neither new nor
old.

We also declare on oath that we entered into the
bai'at of the Promised Messiah before November 1901,
and that the statements of Mirza Mahmud Ahmad, the
head of the Qadian section, that though in the beginning
Hazrat Mirza Sahib did not claim prophethood, but that
he changed his claim in November 1901, and laid claim
to prophethood on that date, and that his previous
writings of ten or eleven years denying prophethood are
abrogated — all this is entirely wrong and absolutely
opposed to facts. We do swear by Allah that the idea
never even entered our minds that the Promised Messiah
made a change in his claim in 1901 or that his previous
writings, which are full of denials of a claim to prophethood, were ever abrogated; nor, to our knowledge, did we
ever hear such words from the mouth of even a single
person until Mirza Mahmud Ahmad made these statements.
And Allah is witness to what we have said."

The original document, bearing the signatures of seventy
members including that of Maulana Muhammad Ali, is preserved
in the papers of the Maulana.

Along with the publication of this sworn statement, Khwaja
Kamal-ud-Din and Maulana Muhammad Ali issued vigorous and
repeated challenges to Mirza Mahmud Ahmad to produce a similar sworn declaration from companions of Hazrat Mirza sahib who

had taken the *bai'at* before 1901 to the effect that while before 1901 they believed Hazrat Mirza sahib to be a *mujaddid,* in 1901 they came to know that he changed his belief about prophethood so that from then on they believed him to be a prophet. When Mirza Mahmud Ahmad failed to respond to this demand, they challenged him to produce even one single witness to testify to this effect, but he never had the courage to accept the challenge. The only response was an announcement in the Qadiani news-paper *Al-Fazl,* dated 20 July 1915, which stated:

> "As regards the sworn testimonies demanded by the Khwaja sahib from Ahmadi brethren and leaders, there is no need to send them individually and separately. One single reply on behalf of all from the centre of the Move-ment and the seat of the *khilafat* will be sufficient and satisfactory. It is hoped to publish it soon." (p. 1)

Some forty years passed after this announcement, but despite Mau-lana Muhammad Ali's repeated demands, not even one such sworn testimony came out of Qadian.

This, then, was the background to the development of the Qadiani belief that Hazrat Mirza Ghulam Ahmad was a prophet and that non-Ahmadi Muslims are *kafir.* The history of the rela-tions between the Lahore Ahmadiyya community and the Qadiani community during the life of Maulana Muhammad Ali will be recounted at appropriate places in this book later on. Here it must be added that immediately after the Split Mirza Mahmud Ahmad started giving vent to his boiling rage and fury against the Lahore Ahmadis, and this always remained his technique. Derogatory and scornful epithets were applied to Maulana Muhammad Ali and his associates, and they were called "the living fire of hell", "like rotten, decaying skins of vegetables" and "a worse people than them have never existed in the history of the world".

Besides applying these abusive epithets, Mirza Mahmud Ahmad also claimed to receive revelation that the Lahore Ahmadis would be "shattered into pieces" and he prophesied accordingly. Then whenever any internal disagreement arose among Lahore Ahmadis this was pointed out as fulfilment of the prophecy. However, history itself proclaimed the great progress made by the Lahore Ahmadiyya community under the leadership of Maulana Muhammad Ali and testified to the achievements of his time.

On one occasion Maulana Muhammad Ali mentioned a revelation of his in this connection as follows:

> "When we separated I also had a revelation: *wa lal-akhiratu khair-un la-ka min al-ula* ('The latter state is better for you than the former') and events have proved today that this revelation has been fulfilled and how God has made this community to progress and enabled it to do the most magnificent work for the victory of His religion which the Qadiani community could not do." [1]

> (Friday *khutba,* 5 January 1945; *Paigham Sulh,* 17 January 1945, p. 2)

---

1. Maulana Muhammad Ali never publicly referred to any of his revelations, and this is probably the only instance that he directly mentioned a revelation of his in a publication. Privately too, he scarcely used to talk about his revelations even to his near relations. Towards the end of his life, however, and particularly during his critical illness, he made mention of certain of his dreams in the paper *Paigham Sulh.*

3.2: From 1914 to 1917

Completion and publication of the English translation of the Holy Quran

Early stay in Lahore

Following the death of Maulana Nur-ud-Din when conditions had deteriorated in Qadian, Maulana Muhammad Ali had sent his wife and children to her father Dr. Basharat Ahmad who lived in Rawalpindi at that time. In mid-April 1914 Maulana Muhammad Ali migrated to Lahore all by himself. It was decided that he would live in a house adjacent to the mosque in Ahmadiyya Buildings belonging to Dr. Syed Muhammad Husain Shah which was still under construction. Two rooms had already been built on the ground storey but still needed plastering and laying of the floor. In one of these rooms he had a door fixed and made it his office, and the other room was for receiving guests. On the second storey there were two rooms for his family; these did not yet have doors so they managed by hanging sack cloth curtains in place of doors. A hearth in the courtyard was used for cooking. He sent for his family to stay in this house and they managed to live there under these difficult conditions.

Two initial tasks

Though the Lahore Anjuman had been formed in name but it was in a state of the utmost destitution. There was no office, no funds and no missionaries. Under those circumstances, in addition to building a community, they faced two principal tasks of the propagation of Islam. One was to support the Woking Mission in England and the other was the completion and publication of the English translation of the Holy Quran. The translation of 26 parts of the Quran and their commentary had already been read to

Maulana Nur-ud-Din; four more parts remained to be completed. There was revision of the manuscript, getting it typed, writing the introduction, and other aspects of the work still to be done which Maulana Muhammad Ali had mentioned to the Sadr Anjuman Qadian in the beginning in June 1909. Consequently he buried himself in this work day and night.

On the other side in England Khwaja Kamal-ud-Din was working with great energy and the Woking Mission was progressing daily. The Khwaja sahib was sending letters stressing that the English translation of the Holy Quran should be completed as soon as possible because there was an urgent demand for it among converts to Islam as well as Christians and there was no translation available to present the true picture of Islam. For Maulana Muhammad Ali this was the most urgent task, in addition to organisational matters. For the next four years he spent three or four months in the summer in Abbottabad where he could work undisturbed, devoting as much attention as possible to this task.

Before the Split, the Sadr Anjuman Ahmadiyya, Qadian, had decided to send Maulvi Sher Ali, assistant editor of the *Review of Religions,* to help the Khwaja sahib in Woking, but when Mirza Mahmud Ahmad became *khalifa* one of his first actions was to cancel this decision. So when the Lahore Anjuman was formed it was decided to send Maulana Sadr-ud-Din to Woking, and he left in August 1914. After his arrival Khwaja Kamal-ud-Din came back to India temporarily in November 1914 and stayed here till August 1916.

To organise the Lahore Ahmadiyya community, Shaikh Rahmatullah, Dr. Mirza Yaqub Baig and Dr. Syed Muhammad Husain Shah toured districts of the Punjab and Maulana Muhammad Ali himself visited many places. Due to their efforts branches of the Anjuman were set up, regular monthly subscriptions began to be received and the Anjuman's budget steadily increased.

Teaching meanings of the Quran (*Dars-i Quran*)

As soon as he came to Lahore in April 1914, Maulana Muhammad Ali started daily classes at Ahmadiyya Buildings in which he explained meanings of the Quran, the first *dars* being held on 27 April. When he lived in Qadian, the Maulana had for many years attended Maulana Nur-ud-Din's teaching of the Quran and gained knowledge of the Holy Book from it. Then he had also read out to Maulana Nur-ud-Din his own English translation and commentary of the Quran. Now the time had come for him to impart this knowledge so that others could benefit by it. Therefore, he made it a rule for himself to give regular classes in the Quran. His teaching had such an attraction that a large number of educated people of Lahore, both Ahmadis and other Muslims, used to attend. Maulana Zafar Ali Khan, editor of the newspaper *Zamindar*, who used to attend these meetings, wrote on one occasion:

> "Respected Maulvi Muhammad Ali sahib, M.A., is one of those esteemed persons who devote every single moment of their scholarly lives, without exception, in serving Islam. Daily he holds classes in the Quran, and in explaining each and every verse he lets flow rivers of knowledge and fine and deep points. Recently he himself has written and published the most important extracts from his teaching. This commentary (*tafsir*) is of such high merit that one may not be able to find similar precious gems anywhere within the treasure of Urdu literature even after making the hardest search."

> (*Zamindar*, 15 April 1915; *Paigham Sulh,* 20 April 1915)

Afterwards circumstances changed and Maulana Zafar Ali Khan found it expedient to turn against the Ahmadiyya Movement. But his tribute of that time is even now an evidence of the grandeur of those classes.

In addition to non-Ahmadi Muslims, people who had taken the *bai'at* of Mirza Mahmud Ahmad or those who had not yet decided which side was right, used to attend his classes in great number. This was very worrying for Mirza Mahmud Ahmad because he feared that Maulana Muhammad Ali's teaching as well as his arguments about the Split were so strongly effective that it would damage his *khilafat*. So he issued announcements from Qadian again and again declaring that Maulana Muhammad Ali and others who had not taken the *bai'at* at his hand were transgressors (*fāsiq*) and that Maulana Muhammad Ali was not capable of translating or teaching the Quran. In connection with these announcements, Maulana Muhammad Ali wrote an article addressing Mirza Mahmud Ahmad, published in *Paigham Sulh* in December 1914, in which he said:

> "Did not your whole community, your council of trustees, and that unique commentator of the Quran the late Hazrat Maulana Nur-ud-Din, finding me capable not only of translating the Quran into English but also into Urdu, entrust me with this work? So much so that when the Quran was being translated in English and Mir Nasir Nawab tried to get work started on an Urdu translation, the late Hazrat *Khalifat-ul-Masih* said very clearly that the Urdu translation would also be done by me. So why are those Ahmadis who have taken the *bai'at* with Mirza Mahmud Ahmad being forbidden from listening to my teaching of the Quran? I am not saying this because I am worried about the publication of my translation. In that matter Maulvi Sher Ali has already been raising hue and cry in all the Muslim newspapers. You people's writings have also appeared in the *Paisa Akhbar*. Do as much as you possibly can, so that you don't have any regrets that you did not try your hardest. According to you, we are only a few men and no one else is on our side. We left all the funds and property with you. Be patient and wait; if you are right then we will fail by ourselves and all the activities we have started will come to nothing. But if the help of Allah is with us then He Himself will solve our lack of men and means…"

(*Paigham Sulh,* 29 December 1914)

In addition to the Holy Quran classes, Maulana Muhammad Ali had also started teaching *Sahih Bukhari* in Lahore three times a week, and continued it in subsequent years from time to time. In the summer months when he went to Abbottabad he held the Holy Quran classes daily there and these were attended by both Ahmadis and non-Ahmadis of Abbottabad. Then during every month of Ramadan he would teach one part (*para*) of the Quran everyday so as to finish it in the month, and many members of the Lahore Ahmadiyya community who could take leave used to spend Ramadan in Abbottabad. In short, teaching the Quran held a prominent place in his life. For many years in Ahmadiyya Buildings Lahore and wherever he went in the summer to a mountainous place, he gave these classes himself. Later on, Dr. Basharat Ahmad and other elders of the Movement continued this institution at Lahore. Teaching the meanings of the Quran was a distinctive feature of the Ahmadiyya community, and it continued in Lahore just as it existed during the time of the Promised Messiah and Maulana Nur-ud-Din in Qadian.

Completion and publication of the English Translation of the Holy Quran

At last, after a labour of about seven years, in April 1916 Maulana Muhammad Ali completed work on the English translation and commentary of the Holy Quran. In his Friday *khutba* on 28 April he gave the good news to the community. After reading *Sura Al-Fatiha, Sura Al-Falaq* and *Sura An-Nas,* he said:

> "A human being can only take on a task by Allah's help and it is only with Allah's help that he can complete it…. Today is a day of happiness for me. For years I have been busy in the work of translating the Holy Quran into English. By the grace of Allah I have completed it today. I am not happy like a student who, at the end of his examination, feels that now he will have free time and can rest for a few days. I am happy because all the time that I was involved in this work I was worried that life is so fickle and it may be that this work would be left incomplete. Of course, Allah is not short of men and it was His work which would have been completed somehow; if He has given strength to a weak person like me to start this work, there is no reason why He could not get it done by someone else. But it gives great pleasure to a person to complete by his own hand in his own life the work that he had started." (*Paigham Sulh,* 28 May 1916, p. 6)

After this he explained the meanings of *Sura Al-Falaq* and *Al-Nas,* as to how a person can seek God's protection and the purpose of every work of a human being should be to seek that Divine protection. He then said that God caused all the stages of this work to be completed, lifted all darkness and as to those who were trying to lay obstacles in the way, God brought them to failure.

It was decided to have the English translation printed in England because the printing machines that were required for the high quality, fine paper that was to be used were not available in India. So Maulana Sadr-ud-Din at Woking was entrusted with the arrangements for its printing, a task which he fulfilled extremely well. Later on, Mian Ghulam Rasul's son Mian Ghulam Abbas also went to Woking for the same work. The instructions that Maulana Muhammad Ali gave to Maulana Sadr-ud-Din in connection with this work can be seen in the following letter which he wrote to him at the end of 1915 when the translation itself was ready but some other work remained to be done:

> Respected Maulvi Sadr-ud-Din sahib, Imam Woking Mosque. *Assalamu alaikum wa rahmatullahi wa barakatuhu.*
>
> As your letters show that the English translation of the Quran is urgently needed for your mission of the propagation of Islam, and without it you as well as the new converts are facing great problems, and as the translation part of my work is ready, while some work remains to be done on the footnotes, and because of difficulties with Arabic type there could be a further delay, so I give you authority to get the first edition printed consisting of the translation only, to arrange for the finance as you think fit and to publish it as you wish. However, no change, alteration or amendment whatsoever should be made in the translation except for corrections required during proof reading. You do not even have to send me the proofs.
>
> *Wassalam*. Humbly, Muhammad Ali, 29 October 1915.

But this translation without Arabic text was not printed at that time. Later on, in 1928, a smaller edition consisting of the translation without Arabic text and with brief footnotes was published by Maulana Muhammad Ali for the first time.

He spent the whole of the year 1916 preparing the index and the preface for the English translation, and at the same time going through the first proofs which came printed from England. These proofs were initially read by Maulana Sadr-ud-Din in England, and then read and corrected by Maulana Muhammad Ali in his own hand here. After that stage, the reading of the second proofs, the correction of the Arabic text, and all the other tasks in connection with the printing were done by Maulana Sadr-ud-Din. As mentioned above, Khwaja Kamal-ud-Din returned from England to India in November 1914, and then on 25 August 1916 he left again for England. After his arrival in England at the end of September, Maulana Sadr-ud-Din came back to Lahore in January 1917.

By the end of 1917 the printing had been completed and the publication of the book had started in England. Its first copies reached India at the end of November 1917. Thus was this great work accomplished which he had undertaken according to the wishes of the Promised Messiah and begun during Maulana Nur-ud-Din's time, on which he had laboured hard, day and night, for seven years, in spite of his other religious work and engagements. So was fulfilled the vision of Hazrat Mirza sahib which he had recorded as follows:

> "After that a book was given to me, about which I was told that this was the commentary of the Holy Quran written by Ali and now Ali is handing that commentary to you. Allah be praised for this!"
>
> (*Tazkira,* p. 21; *Barahin Ahmadiyya,* p. 503, subnote 3 on footnote 11)

After its publication, this translation became exceedingly popular. All its reviews in Indian and British journals were highly favourable and appreciative. Besides the English and Christian world, it spread among the educated classes of India in abundance, and brought to the right path many well known, Western-educated Muslims who had come under the misguiding influence of Christianity or modern godlessness. The glad tidings mentioned by Hazrat Maulana Nur-ud-Din, that 'our translation has been accepted by Allah', can be seen to be fulfilled by reading the newspapers of the time and those countless letters received about this translation which were then published.

This translation is resplendent with the light of the truth of Islam as it contains that unique religious thought and knowledge which was produced by the Promised Messiah and which Maulana Muhammad Ali gained from him and from Maulana Nur-ud-Din. It also has the following chief features. The translation is in plain, fluent and idiomatic English, containing very few extra explanatory words and these are given within parenthesis. The footnotes have been written keeping in view the objections raised against Islam by the Christian and other religions. These notes contain an invaluable treasure of information from dictionaries, commentaries of the Holy Quran, collections of Hadith and works of history, with full references. All the chapters (*sūrah*), sections (*rukū'*) and verses (*āyāt*) are numbered, and there are plenty of cross references given so that the meaning of a passage in the Quran can be explained in the light of other places in the Holy Book. Every chapter carries an introductory note in which the subject matter of its sections is summarised and the connection between its sections and between that chapter and its neighbouring chapters is indicated. The introduction is so comprehensive as to be a book in itself, and throws light on the essentials of Islam, the compilation and collection of the Quran, and other questions. The introduction in the first edition (and its reprint editions) also presented details of the Muslim prayers, the words of prayers being given in Arabic text, Roman transliteration and English translation. In short, this work has many unique features.

Its popularity can be judged by the fact that its first three editions (the 1917 original edition and its two reprint editions of 1920 and 1935) and the various printings of the version without Arabic text totalled forty-two thousand copies. The fourth edition, which was thoroughly revised by Maulana Muhammad Ali with many changes, was first published in 1951 in a quantity of twenty thousand. As that has been exhausted, the fifth edition with many print corrections is being produced in a quantity of ten thousand.[1]

---

1. Up to the fifth edition mentioned here, published in 1963, the printing was done in England. From the sixth reprint edition onwards in 1973, the

Another distinction of this translation is that Maulana Muhammad Ali did not have before him any previous example of such a translation. The translations done by Christians reflected their deep hostility and prejudice against Islam. So he had to embark upon very difficult and laborious research from scratch, like having to dig a well to find water. For this translation and commentary the Maulana went through the previous commentaries of the Quran, works of Hadith and dictionaries, and having extracted the gist of their knowledge and opinions he provided thousands of references to them in his explanatory notes. The translations of the Quran done by Muslims after this, for example Hafiz Ghulam Sarwar, Abdullah Yusuf Ali and Marmaduke Pickthall, derived much benefit from Maulana Muhammad Ali's work.

English translation of the Quran and the Qadian community

After the migration of Maulana Muhammad Ali to Lahore, the Qadian community carried out much false propaganda about many matters including the English translation of the Quran. Announcements were made by Maulvi Sher Ali that this English translation was the property of the Qadiani *Jama'at,* so no one must help the Ahmadiyya Anjuman Isha'at Islam Lahore in its printing or publication. When this translation was ready Maulana Muhammad Ali wrote a letter to the Anjuman at Qadian, dated 28 October 1915, which began as follows:

> "To the Secretary, Sadr Anjuman Ahmadiyya, Qadian, *Assalamu alaikum wa rahmatullahi wa barakatuhu.*
>
> When I took leave at the beginning of April 1914 the work of the English translation of the Holy Quran was far from complete. Since then I have been completing it and now, purely by the grace of Allah, thanks to Allah, it has reached the finishing stage and within a month it will be ready to give to the press for printing. Last year your deputation which came, refused to discuss the translation. So I had to remain silent till its completion.

publication has been done from the U.S.A. From 1985 onwards, reprints have been published frequently in large numbers. A newly typeset edition incorporating many misprint corrections, with an improved layout and a much-expanded index, was published in 2002.

> You are aware that it was from my own proposal that this translation was started, and at that time whether the Anjuman had encouraged me or not, I was going to do this work in any event. However, the Anjuman of that time not only approved of my idea but encouraged me to succeed in what was my own objective. So now may I enquire of you whether you would undertake to publish the first edition of my translation? If you are agreeable then you may participate in this noble venture subject to the following conditions."

Among the conditions, the first one is:

> "No alteration or amendment whatsoever shall be made to my translation. What I have written shall be printed exactly word for word. The final printed proofs shall be approved by me and it is those which will be printed."

The rest of the conditions were in relation to the expenses. The printing costs were to be shared by the two Anjumans and each would take a number of printed copies in proportion to its share of the costs. It was also proposed that as the estimated cost was 30,000 Rupees, each Anjuman should deposit 15,000 Rupees in the bank. However, the response from Qadian was a flat rejection of the proposal. A month earlier, Mirza Mahmud Ahmad in a Friday sermon on 24 September 1915 had used highly offensive language about Maulana Muhammad Ali and his translation. He not only charged the Maulana with dishonesty but declared that he was unfit to do this work, and went so far as to say:

> "Why should we take this paper trash just to set fire to it? Tell them: keep this translation yourselves." [2]

Regarding these bitter comments, Maulana Muhammad Ali said in an article in *Paigham Sulh* of 6 February 1916:

---

2. *Al-Fazl,* 30 September 1915, p. 8, col. 2. See *Ahmadi Jama'at main muqadmat* by Khwaja Kamal-ud-Din, pp. 3–11, in which the letter by Maulana Muhammad Ali to the Qadian Anjuman is quoted in full. See also this matter dealt with in *Mir'at-ul-Ikhtilaf* by Dr. Basharat Ahmad, pp. 56–61.

"This is what is called being blinded by rage. He has not even seen my translation, and without seeing it has branded it as trash, fit to be burnt. Strangely, along with that he has called me dishonest. Can a person be dishonest who has only taken worthless trash? Those people can be called dishonest who knew that I was unfamiliar with Arabic grammar and utterly devoid of the knowledge of the Quran, and yet they remained silent. ... Was it not his duty to put it before the Anjuman, or inform the community through his newspapers, that I was unfit for the task of translation? ... Ask your *khalifa* when did he come to know that Muhammad Ali was not capable of translating. Did he not know this after reading articles in the *Review of Religions* for years? ... Did he not know this when Hazrat Maulvi sahib [Maulana Nur-ud-Din] was getting the Urdu translation of the first few parts also done by me and when he told Mir Nasir Nawab that only Muhammad Ali's Urdu translation will be published, and not that by anyone else? ... Did he not know this when I had left Qadian and he used to get the Anjuman to pass resolutions whose aim was that I should continue the translation? ... Some eight or ten days before the death of Hazrat Maulvi Nur-ud-Din when he said that glad tidings had come from God that 'this translation has been accepted' all the community present there with me went into *sajda* (prostration). ...

What is my dishonesty in this? I put the proposal of translating the Quran before the Anjuman and also wrote in it that if the Anjuman cannot bear the expenses then Allah will provide some other means for me. ... I did not say to the Anjuman I am your employee so give me some work, but I said I want to translate the Quran and if the Anjuman cannot bear the expenses then God will provide some other means. Allah brought that about as well, that the Anjuman declined to pay the expenses and the generous Lord gave me other means." (p. 7)

In these circumstances the Qadian community was deprived of this important service of the Quran. They proclaimed boldly and arrogantly that this translation was useless and that they were starting their own English translation and would publish one part every month, completing the entire work in thirty months. A little later the first part was even published. Then God knows what happened, that for the next thirty years nothing more was done.

To cover up this weakness they even said that this was not an important service to the religion and that translating the Quran was not the duty of an Imam sent by God, otherwise Hazrat Mirza sahib would himself have done it. Referring to this many years later, Maulana Muhammad Ali said:

> "Someone should ask them that if it was not an important service then why did Hazrat Mirza sahib, when making his claim [to be Promised Messiah], express this wish in these words:
>
>> 'I would advise that, instead of these missionaries, writings of an excellent and high standard should be sent into these countries. If my people help me heart and soul I wish to prepare a commentary of the Quran which should be sent to them after it has been rendered into the English language. I cannot refrain from stating clearly that this is my work, and that no one else can do it as well as I or he who is an off-shoot of mine and thus is included in me.'
>
> If this [spreading the Quran in the world] was not Hazrat Mirza sahib's mission then for what other purpose did he come? To propagate the Quran in the world is the duty of every Muslim and Hazrat Mirza sahib specifically came so that this light could be spread to all the nations of the world, especially the Western nations. ... They say that if it had been an important task Hazrat Mirza sahib would have done it himself. I say that this translation that has been done, it is the work of the Promised Messiah and has been done by his spiritual power. ... The Holy Prophet Muhammad, may peace and the blessings of Allah be upon him, had prophesied that the keys to the treasures of the Caesar and the Chosroes had been handed to him, but those keys were handed during the time of Hazrat Umar.

So the truth is that the works that are done by a follower are included in the works of the Imam. This is his work, the man who infused into our hearts the urge to translate the Quran into English and who induced us to take up this work. Remember it well that this work has not been done by our *Jama'at* nor by me. It is surely the work of Hazrat Mirza sahib. We are only the means and the tools."

(Friday *khutba,* 23 December 1938, on the occasion of the silver jubilee of the Lahore Anjuman. *Paigham Sulh,* 17 January 1939, p. 6)

Other writings of the Maulana during 1914 to 1917

In March 1915 the Urdu translation and commentary of the first part (*para*) of the Holy Quran was published under the title *Nukat-ul-Quran,* Volume 1. Many newspapers of the time published appreciative reviews of it, including Maulana Zafar Ali Khan's newspaper *Zamindar.* In the educated circles, this translation and notes became immensely popular.

Among smaller writings, the first book is *Hudoos-i Madah* ('Creation of Matter') in which is reproduced the debate between Maulana Muhammad Ali and a follower of Swami Dayanand, which took place in September 1913 at Murree. In 1914 he wrote a booklet *Al-Muslih al-Mau'ud* ('The Promised Reformer') after a Qadiani wrote an article in May 1914 in the magazine *Tashhiz-ul-Azhan,* published from Qadian, trying to prove that Mirza Mahmud Ahmad was the Reformer whose coming had been prophesied by the Promised Messiah. In this booklet Maulana Muhammad Ali proved that none of the then living sons of Hazrat Mirza sahib fulfilled the prophecy of being *Muslih Mau'ud.* In 1915 his book *Ayatullah* was published, in which the events of the fleeing of Maulvi Sanaullah of Amritsar from a *mubahila* with the Promised Messiah are described. At the end of the year 1915, two booklets *'Asmat-i Anbiya* ('Sinlessness of the Prophets') and *Ghulami* ('Slavery') were published.

In December 1915, the Urdu translation of *Sūra Al-Baqara* with explanatory notes was completed and published as *Nukat-ul-Quran,* Volume 2. As with the first volume, this turned out to be very popular.

Also in December 1915 there appeared one of his most monumental works, *An-Nubuwwat fil-Islam* ('Prophethood in Islam').
Mirza Mahmud Ahmad, having established his *khilafat* and having
branded as *kafir* all those Muslims who did not believe in the
Promised Messiah, had alleged that the Promised Messiah claimed
to be a prophet and wrote a book on this subject entitled *Haqiqat-
un-Nubuwwat*. Although Maulana Muhammad Ali and other
leaders of the community had from time to time written articles in
Paigham Sulh to refute this allegation of Mirza Mahmud Ahmad,
there was no permanent, comprehensive book dealing with this.
An-Nubuwwat fil-Islam was not only a shattering reply to Mirza
Mahmud Ahmad's book *Haqiqat-un-Nubuwwat* but it also throws
full light on issues such as the aim and purpose of the institution
of prophethood, the distinctive attributes of *wahy nubuwwat* (the
type of revelation which only comes to prophets and distinguishes
prophets from saints), reasons for the ending of prophethood with
the Holy Prophet Muhammad, the true position of visions and
revelations of saints, and the status of the Promised Messiah. This
book consists of about 575 pages, out of which about 200 pages
are an appendix containing all the extracts and references from the
writings of Hazrat Mirza Ghulam Ahmad on the issue of prophethood.

In May 1916 he published the pamphlet *Jihad-i Kabir* ('The
Greatest Jihad'), in which the need and importance of the propagation of Islam was highlighted, and Muslims in general who were
completely neglectful of this obligation were reminded of their
duty.

At the end of 1916, *Nukat-ul-Quran* Volumes 3 and 4 were
published, being the Urdu translation and notes on *Sura Al-i
Imran* and *Sura Al-Nisa*, and became as popular as the previous
volumes.

In July 1917, his book *Jama'-ul-Quran* ('Collection of the
Quran') was published in which the history of the revelation of the
Holy Quran, its preservation, writing down, collection and arrangement etc. are discussed and the objections of the critics of Islam
are answered.

In September 1917, his book *Ahmad Mujtaba* was published, in which it is proved from the Quran, Hadith reports and the writings of the Promised Messiah that 'Ahmad' was the name of the Holy Prophet Muhammad and the prophecy referred to in the words *ismu-hu Ahmad*, "his name being Ahmad", in the Quran (chapter 61, verse 6) referred to him. This book was written to refute Mirza Mahmud Ahmad's wrong belief that this prophecy applied to Hazrat Mirza Ghulam Ahmad. To counter this erroneous belief Maulana Muhammad Ali and other scholars of the community had already written many articles in *Paigham Sulh,* and the Maulana had invited Mirza Mahmud Ahmad several times to a decisive debate on the matter, but he did not accept the invitation.

Some other events from 1914 to 1917

The first annual gathering (*jalsa*) of the Ahmadiyya Anjuman Isha'at Islam Lahore was held from 25 to 27 December 1914 at Ahmadiyya Buildings, Lahore. The institution of the annual gathering was founded by the Promised Messiah for his Movement and he used strongly to urge members to attend this occasion so that they could get together at least once a year, strengthen their ties of love and brotherhood, review the past year's work, plan for the coming year and consider new proposals for the propagation of Islam. So from 1914 onwards such a gathering of the Lahore Ahmadiyya community was held every December at Ahmadiyya Buildings. The community was very small at the time of this first gathering and donations of Rupees 3,846 were collected on appeal for the propagation of Islam. After a few years God made this *Jama'at* to progress so much, and He infused in it such a strong spirit of sacrifice, that on appeals by Maulana Muhammad Ali for different plans that he put forward, not only thousands but hundreds of thousands of Rupees were raised.

At the end of 1914 a college by the name of the Isha'at-i-Islam ('Propagation of Islam') College was opened in Lahore to train missionaries and impart education to those who intended to do research. This was located in a house on Mcleod Road, and from the beginning of December 1914 Maulana Muhammad Ali took up his residence in the same building. The official opening ceremony of this college was performed on 28 December 1914 by Khwaja Kamal-ud-Din who had returned from England in November. Maulana Muhammad Ali was its honorary principal and used to teach in the college as well as hold his Quran classes there. The Khwaja sahib also lectured there during his stay in Lahore (from January 1915 to August 1916). Maulvi Fazl Ilahi, a convert from Christianity, delivered lectures on the Christian religion and Maulvi Mubarak Ali of Sialkot taught Arabic. The students lived in a part of the college building and one of those students was Maulana Abdul Haq Vidyarthi who had started learning Sanskrit at that time.

In July 1915 Maulana Muhammad Ali went to Abbottabad for the second time for three months. In Lahore he had so many commitments that it was only during his stay in Abbottabad that he had available sufficient time to devote to the English transla- tion of the Quran and other writing work. That year Khwaja Kamal-ud-Din had arranged to stay in the residence of Shahzada Bukhara and he invited Maulana Muhammad Ali to join him in the same house. The Maulana took two rooms while the Khwaja sahib occupied the rest of the residence. In Abbottabad the Mau- lana continued giving daily classes in the Quran, as he did on his previous visit, and in the month of Ramadan he taught one part (*para*) of the Quran every day. Many members of the *Jama'at* used to take leave from their work to go to Abbottabad for a month to attend these classes.

In November 1915 Abdul Hayy, son of the late Maulana Nur- ud-Din, died in his youth. So on 14 November Maulana Muhammad Ali along with some friends went to Qadian, but they stayed there for a few hours only and after paying their condolences to Mau- lana Nur-ud-Din's wife and visiting the grave of the Promised Messiah to offer prayers they returned to Lahore.

In December 1915, the second annual gathering of the Anju- man was held. The annual budget had now risen to 22,000 Rupees. Before and after the annual gatherings Maulana Muhammad Ali, apart from his other engagements, used also to tour the *Jama'at* in various towns and cities of the Punjab.

He again spent the summer of 1916 in Abbottabad. During his stay the previous year, Shaikh Nur Ahmad, a lawyer and a highly respected member of the Lahore Ahmadiyya community, who was also a relation of the Maulana's wife, and many other members made him promise to come again the following year. As the accommodation where he was staying was too small, so Deputy Muzaffar-ud-Din offered a room in his residence to be used as office. Consequently, the Maulana would go to this office immediately after breakfast and return home after the *zuhr* prayer, and then he would go back before the *asr* prayer and return home at night after the *isha* prayer. At the residence of Deputy Muzaffar-ud-Din the Quran classes were held and congregational prayers were said. Then when it was proposed that during Ramadan the Quran classes would cover one part (*para*) of the Quran everyday, two more residences were taken and Dr. Mirza Yaqub Baig, Dr. Basharat Ahmad and many other members spent Ramadan there. At that time proofs of the English translation of the Quran were coming and the Maulana was busy in reading them and in doing other writing work. In August of that year Khwaja Kamal-ud-Din left for England for the second time and Maulana Muhammad Ali came to Lahore for two days from Abbottabad to keep him company. At Lahore railway station a large crowd consisting of both Ahmadis and non-Ahmadis was present to bid him farewell. Among them was Mian Muhammad Shafi, who afterwards became Sir Muhammad Shafi.

From 27 to 30 October 1916 Maulana Muhammad Ali along with Dr. Mirza Yaqub Baig and Shaikh Rahmatullah went to visit Syed Muhammad Ahsan in Amroha as he was ailing. After the third annual gathering the Maulana toured different branches of the *Jama'at* for organizational purposes and attended the annual meetings of local branches in many places.

At the beginning of 1916, the Isha'at-i-Islam College was shifted from Mcleod Road to Ahmadiyya Buildings, and Maulana Muhammad Ali also shifted his residence to the house at Ahmadiyya Buildings. In April 1917 the Muslim High School was inaugurated in a house on Mcleod Road and Maulana Sadr-ud-Din was appointed its Headmaster.

The first three and a half years of the Anjuman's life

These, then, were the first three and a half years of this Anjuman and of the life of Maulana Muhammad Ali in Lahore. During this period the *Jama'at* began its life, took shape, and its branches were established in different towns and cities. Right from the beginning the history of the Anjuman opened with great achievements in the field of the propagation of Islam. In the annual reports presented at the annual gatherings of 1916 and 1917 by Dr. Mirza Yaqub Baig as secretary of the Anjuman, he described the events and impressions of that time as follows:

> "Many members of our *Jama'at* were confused and bewildered about what would be the fate of the community. But it is the favour of Allah that the efforts of the head of the community Maulana Muhammad Ali over two and a half years have been made to prosper by the Almighty. The community has been organised anew and raised to the stage of being devout and God fearing. A new life and freshness has been infused into the *Jama'at*.
>
> The world is a witness to the service Hazrat Maulana Muhammad Ali has rendered to Islam and Ahmadiyyat at this time through his powerful writings and speeches, and by his personal example and dedication. Nobody could imagine that a reclusive and quiet man like Hazrat Maulana sahib will perform such magnificent service to defeat this heresy and false innovation and keep the community established on the path of worship of one God."

(From the Annual Report for 1915–16)

In the next annual report in 1917, when the English translation of the Holy Quran had been published, he writes:

> "As long as the world remains, it is hoped that this service to the Holy Quran will be remembered, a large part of which was the contribution of Maulana Nur-ud-Din, namely that he listened to the notes of the translation of almost 28 parts from Maulana Muhammad Ali and gave the benefit of his guidance and improvement. Most of all,

he prayed with whole-hearted feeling and urge for this translation to be popular and useful for mankind. This was his last service to the Holy Word, which he performed during his fatal illness.

No one is a better witness than my humble self to how during this most painful ailment he taught Maulana Muhammad Ali the Holy Quran when he could not even turn in bed or feed himself, and yet that spiritual being fed his spiritual son with the spiritual diet of the Holy Quran through his own pure nature. Nearly four years ago Allah gave the glad tidings to Hazrat Maulana sahib that this translation had been approved in the court of Allah, and this was the happiest news which he received a few days before his departing from this world. So he straight-away called for Maulvi Muhammad Ali sahib and related this good news to him and to the entire community which he had received through Mir Abid Ali Shah, and he went into prostration of thanksgiving along with Hazrat Maulvi Muhammad Ali sahib, myself and others present. He said: 'It is the benevolence of Allah that He has bestowed this favour upon a dying man like me, and given this good news; all thanks be to Allah that He kept me alive till this moment'."

(Annual Report of the Anjuman, 1916–17)

Opinions and reviews about the English translation of the Holy Quran

The special features of the English translation have already been mentioned. Some of the opinions expressed about this work from time to time are given below.

The famous Indian Muslim leader Maulana Muhammad Ali Jauhar, editor of *Comrade,* wrote in his autobiography:

"It was about this time [December 1918] that a kind friend sent to us a gift than which nothing could be more acceptable, a copy of the Quran for my brother and one for myself ... with an austerely faithful translation in English and copious footnotes based on a close study of commentaries of the Quran and of such Biblical literature as could throw light upon the latest Holy Writ. This was the work of my learned namesake, Maulvi Muhammad Ali of Lahore, leader of a fairly numerous religious community, some of whose members were doing missionary work in England. ... The translation and the notes which supplied the antidote so greatly needed for the poison squirted in the footnotes of English translators of the Quran like Sale, Rodwell and Palmer, the fine printing, both English and Arabic, the India paper and the exquisite binding in green limp Morocco with characteristic Oriental Tughra or ornamental calligraphy in gold, all demonstrated the labour of love and devoted zeal that so many willing workers had obviously contributed. This beautiful book acted like the maddening music of the Sarod, according to the Persian proverb, on the mentally deranged, and in the frame of mind in which I then was I wrote back to my friend who had sent these copies of the Quran that nothing would please me better than to go to Europe as soon as I could get out of the 'bounds' prescribed by my internment and preach to these war maniacs from every park and at every street corner, if not within the dubious precincts of every public house, about a faith that was meant to silence all this clamour of warring nations in the one unifying peace of Islam." [1]

The same Maulana Muhammad Ali Jauhar once met Maulana Muhammad Ali before going to England and said by way of joke: "Please allow me to tell one lie, that when I go to England I can say there that I am the author of this translation". On this Maulana Muhammad Ali, the author, smiled and remarked: "No doubt it is Muhammad Ali who has translated it."

Maulana Abdul Majid Daryabadi wrote:

"To deny the excellence of Maulana Muhammad Ali's translation, the influence it has exercised and its prosely-

---

1. *My Life — A Fragment,* edited by Afzal Iqbal, published by Muhammad Ashraf, Lahore, 1966 reprint, p. 115.

tising utility, would be to deny the light of the sun. The translation certainly helped in bringing thousands of non-Muslims to the Muslim fold and hundreds of thousands of unbelievers much nearer Islam. Speaking of my own self, I gladly admit that this translation was one of the few books which brought me towards Islam fifteen or sixteen years ago when I was groping in darkness, atheism and scepticism. Even Maulana Mohamed Ali of the *Comrade* was greatly enthralled by this translation and had nothing but praise for it." [2]

Hafiz Ghulam Sarwar, who later himself translated the Quran into English, wrote:

> "The English translation of the Holy Quran is not the only book he has written, but it is the one by which he will perhaps become an immortal amongst those who have written about the Holy Quran. ... The English of the Preface and the notes is unimpeachable, and Maulvi Muhammad Ali has corrected the mistakes of the previous translators in scores of passages; and wherever he differs from them his rendering is either the correct and most authoritative one or has at the back of it full support to be found in the standard dictionaries of Arabic. ... There is no other translation or commentary of the Holy Quran in the English language to compete with Maulvi Muhammad Ali's masterpiece. ... It was reprinted in 1920, and both editions have had phenomenal success and popularity amongst all classes of Muslims." [3]

S. H. Leeder, a well-known author of England, wrote:

> "I have received the copy of the Holy Quran, and hasten to congratulate you on the appearance your Scripture, in such a truly beautiful and chaste form. It is pure delight to

2. Newspaper *Such,* Lucknow, 25 June 1943.

3. *Translation of the Holy Quran,* by Hafiz Ghulam Sarwar, second edition, National Book Foundation, Pakistan, 1973, pp. xxxvi – xxxvii.

handle such a book, but when one turns to its treasures of light and learning, one is filled with thankfulness and gratitude for all the labour ... I rejoice to see the Holy Quran in my own language and explained by a deeply learned and pious Muslim, and I believe that the work will be found to mark a new epoch in the religious life of the world."

The reviews of some newspapers and periodicals over the years are now given.

1. *The Quest,* London:

"It is certainly a work, of which any scholar might legitimately be proud."

2. *The Madras Mail,* 15 October 1929:

"Maulvi Muhammad Ali's name is a guarantee that the translation is as accurate as it could be ... few translations into English have reached such a high standard."

3. *The Hindu,* Madras, 15 October 1929:

"As a translator, he always had the reputation of being accurate and reliable ... The wealth of material put into the introduction and explanatory footnotes is impressive."

4. *United India and Indian States,* Delhi, 21 December 1929:

"Among human productions of literary masterpieces, the English translation of the Holy Book by Maulvi Muhammad Ali undoubtedly claims a position of distinction and pre-eminence."

5. *The Advocate, Lucknow*, 24 October 1935:

"Maulana Muhammad Ali, M.A., Ll.B., is a well-known personality, a great scholar, and as a translator he has the good reputation of being accurate and reliable, and his translation in English is of high standard ... We congratulate Maulana Muhammad Ali for this production which has surpassed other English translations."

6. *The Hindustan Times,* Delhi, 6 May 1935:

> "Maulana Muhammad Ali's name is known to every lover of the holy literature of Islam. ... Very illuminating notes are provided by the translator which will be of great use to students. Maulana Muhammad Ali's language is restrained and eminently suitable for the purpose." [4]

Two opinions from recent years may also be added here.

1. In the *Atlas of the Islamic World since 1500* by Francis Robinson (Time-Life Books, 1991 reprint), it is stated in the bibliography about translations of the Quran:

> "Notable for its precision is that of Muhammad Ali of Lahore, the version used with one exception throughout this book." (page 229, column 2)

2. In the Urdu monthly *Islami Digest* of Karachi, Pakistan, March 1996, in its series *Tashrih-ul-Quran,* the following comment appears:

> "This commentary of Maulana Muhammad Ali appeared in 1917, seventeen years before the commentary of Allama Abdullah Yusuf Ali. This is why the Allama, in the Preface of his commentary, besides mentioning other English commentaries, has also appreciated this commentary and written as follows:
>
>> 'Its Lahore Anjuman has published Maulvi Muhammad Ali's translation (first edition in 1917), which has passed through more than one edition. It is a scholarly work, and is equipped with adequate explanatory matter in the notes and the Preface, and a fairly full Index'."

---

4. Quotations given from p. 159 up to here, except the one from Abdul Majid Daryabadi, were originally in English, and appear only in Urdu translation in *Mujahid-i Kabir.* We have obtained and reproduced here the original English wording of these quotations, thereby avoiding the inaccuracy that would result from retranslating the Urdu translation back into English.

In the well-known Christian missionary magazine *The Moslem World,* edited by Rev. S.M. Zwemer, an article appeared in the July 1931 issue, comparing the translations of the Quran by Maulana Muhammad Ali, Marmaduke Pickthall and Hafiz Ghulam Sarwar.[5] It is plainly stated in that review that "both Mr. Sarwar and Mr. Pickthall have followed Muhammad Ali very closely" and that: "In the passages which we have examined carefully ... the translation of Mr. Pickthall follows Muhammad Ali so closely that one finds very few evidences of original work".[6]

The reason for this is that Maulana Muhammad Ali's translation and footnotes are based on an extensive study of sources and deep research work. In this sense the later translations cannot be called original works.

There are many other instances of such opinions expressed from time to time, most of which have been published in the Anjuman's journals *Paigham Sulh* and *The Light.* In addition to these, numerous letters have been received from many countries of the world in which English speaking people have acknowledged the merits and qualities of this translation and admitted receiving guidance from it.

---

5. *Can a Moslem translate the Koran* by W.G. Shellabear, in *The Moslem World,* July 1931, pp. 287–303.

6. See p. 294 and p. 297 of this review. These and further quotations from this article are given by Maulana Muhammad Ali in the Preface to his revised edition of the translation of the Holy Quran, first published 1951, and in current circulation.

3.3: From 1918 to 1923

Completion and publication of *Bayan-ul-Quran,* Urdu translation of the Holy Quran

Urdu translation and commentary

Immediately after the publication of the English translation and commentary of the Holy Quran, Maulana Muhammad Ali started the Urdu translation and commentary on a regular basis. The years from 1918 to 1923 is the period during which he produced his magnificent Urdu commentary of the Holy Quran which was published in three volumes under the title *Bayan-ul-Quran.* In Qadian at the time when he was reading his English translation of the Quran and footnotes to Maulana Nur-ud-Din, Mir Nasir Nawab[1] tried to get work started on an Urdu translation of the Holy Quran but Hazrat Maulana Nur-ud-Din stopped him and said that the Urdu translation would also be done by Muhammad Ali. He instructed Maulana Muhammad Ali to make a start on the Urdu translation alongside doing the English version. Accordingly Maulana Muhammad Ali translated six or seven parts which he read out to him for approval.

After the death of Maulana Nur-ud-Din a great transformation, namely the Split, occurred in the Ahmadiyya Movement. Maulana Muhammad Ali, having moved to Lahore, was busy in the formation of a new community, starting from scratch in a state of the utmost destitution. On top of that, due to increasing and urgent demand for the English translation of the Holy Quran he had to stop work on the Urdu translation and commentary. During this time the notes of his daily Quran classes were published in

---

1. Father-in-law of the Promised Messiah.

newspapers, and the translation and commentary up to chapter 4, *Al-Nisa,* was published in four volumes under the title *Nukat-ul-Quran.* From May 1921 the publication of *Bayan-ul-Quran* began one part (*para*) at a time, the first six or seven parts being published in this series. Afterwards the entire work was published in the form of volumes, with the third and final volume appearing in November 1923.

In April 1923, on the completion of *Bayan-ul-Quran,* Maulana Muhammad Ali wrote about it in *Paigham Sulh,* dated 7 April, as follows:

Completion of the Quran

'The favour of your Lord, do proclaim'

"Monday, 2 April 1923 was a very auspicious day for me as on this day Allah the Most High enabled me to reach the completion of the Urdu translation of the Holy Quran, and it was merely by the grace of the Almighty that, after the English translation, the Urdu translation and commentary was finished. All praise is due to Allah Who has enabled a helpless man of limited knowledge like me to do work of this enormous magnitude. Praising Allah for this achievement fills my heart with a delight that cannot be described in words.

"It was in 1913, when much of the work on the English translation still remained to be done, that Mir Nasir Nawab proposed the plan to publish an Urdu translation of the Holy Quran and even got as far as collecting funds from many members. Then he sought permission from Hazrat Maulana Nur-ud-Din to embark on this project but Hazrat Maulvi sahib replied that in our Movement there would be only one translation and that would be done by Muhammad Ali after the completion of his English translation. At the same time he instructed me to start the Urdu translation and show it to him little by little. So I translated six or seven parts and showed them to him — such a great lover of the Holy Quran like Hazrat Maulvi sahib having so much confidence in a weak man like me. Then in the last days of his life he told a large gathering that the English translation had been accepted by Allah.

"The English translation took some three more years to complete and due to some other important commitments the Urdu translation remained in abeyance. On the other side, in 1914 the Qadiani
Jama'at vigorously launched a plan on a grand scale for a body of
ten or twelve men jointly to produce an Urdu and an English
translation of the Quran. I started work on the Urdu translation in
1918 but after completing *Sura Al-Baqarah* it was realized that the
manuscript for this one *sura* alone was five hundred pages. So the
work was started again with brevity. Finally, ten years after it was
first proposed, and after four to five years of hard labour on the
Urdu translation, this work is complete merely by the grace of
Allah. The foresight of Hazrat Maulvi sahib proved to fulfil the
hadith that a true believer sees the future with the light of Allah.

"I am sure it is not only numerous friends of mine who feel
the same spiritual pleasure today as I do, but the departed souls of
Hazrat Maulvi Nur-ud-Din and also of that holy man who, by
writing that the English translation and commentary would be
done by him or by one 'who is an offshoot of mine and thus is
included in me', plainly declared me as his son — their souls
today will surely be happy at this work. May Allah shower His
greatest blessings on these two who set me on this path and made
me capable of doing this work.

"It was the benevolence of Allah the Most High that He
enabled me to perform this great service. I was not capable of
doing it but it was by His grace that such a high goal was accomplished, for He granted me to live for fourteen years after starting
this work during which the holy word of God was the source of
nourishment for my soul day and night....

"I have tried my best to be faithful to the word of Allah but
I know I have made errors. So today, after completing this task, if
on the one hand I am happy because of Allah's blessings bestowed
upon me in the form of the service to the Quran, at the same time
I am afraid in case any errors I may have made, due to human
fallibility or because of lacking knowledge, may cause others to
stumble. Every single word of the Quran is a guiding light and a
conclusive argument for every Muslim. In my translation and
commentary I have tried, according to the best of my understanding,

to subject my views to the word of God, the hadith of the Holy Prophet, and rules of the Arabic language. But still it is my interpretation and not binding upon anyone else unless it conforms with the word of God and the authentic hadith reports of the Messenger of Allah. My attempt is only to make people study the knowledge contained in the Quran and to turn their minds to its service."

In the preface of *Bayan-ul-Quran* Maulana Muhammad Ali has referred to the Promised Messiah and Maulana Nur-ud-Din in the following words:

> "Finally, it is important to mention that, although in this humble service of the Holy Quran I have had much benefit from the work of the classical scholars, but the man who in my life inspired me with the love of the Holy Quran and the desire to serve it was the *Mujaddid* of this century, Hazrat Mirza Ghulam Ahmad sahib of Qadian. Then the man who enabled me to understand the Quran was my revered teacher Hazrat Maulvi Nur-ud-Din sahib. If anyone benefits from my work and prays for me, he must also include these two righteous men in his prayer. I am but dust; any fragrance anyone perceives in this work is the spirit breathed by these others."

As compared to the footnotes in the English translation, there is much more detail and elucidation in the Urdu commentary. In addition to a more detailed analysis of the meaning of Arabic words based on lexicons, there are many more notes in exposition of the meaning of the text. There are many special features of the translation. It is usually restricted to following the original text closely, but still adhering to Urdu idiom. Wherever additional words could not be avoided they are inserted within parentheses. Within the commentary, one part consists of explaining the dictionary meanings of Arabic words, giving numerous references to comprehensive and authentic works such as the *Mufradat* of Imam Raghib, *Taj-ul-'Urus* and *Lisan-ul-'Arab,* and wherever required other reliable lexicons are also referred to. As words of the Arabic language have a vast range of meanings, he lists all the meanings of a word as given by the past commentators and lexicographers, and then explains his reasons for adopting a particular meaning.

This enables the reader to see all the different viewpoints, and makes available a summary of these voluminous books for the benefit of future investigators. The chief principle followed in the commentary is that the meaning of any place in the Holy Quran should be sought by reference to other places in the Quran itself; this being the principle laid down in this scripture itself. At whichever point the meaning is not clear, explanation is sought from another place in the Quran. The other principle kept in mind is that authentic Hadith reports should be given preference over other sources, and for this reason Imam Bukhari's chapter on the commentary of the Quran, and the commentaries of Ibn Jarir and Ibn Kathir are kept in view. However, reports which relate stories and tales are only accepted with caution, and anything conflicting with a clear statement in the Holy Quran or with the principles of Islam is rejected. Another point much stressed is the arrangement and sequence of the Holy Quran, and attention is drawn to three types of arrangement: firstly, the connection between successive verses, which he has clarified in the footnotes whenever necessary; secondly, the connection between the sections (*ruku‘*) of each chapter (*sura*); and thirdly the connection between successive chapters. The summary of each section is given in the footnotes below it, and the introductory note to each chapter shows the link between its sections as well as explaining in detail the inter-connection between successive chapters. In addition, many classical commentaries are kept in view and referred to extensively, for example *Bahr-ul-Muhit, Tafsir Kabir* of Imam Razi, *Badawi, Ghara'ib-ul-Quran, Fath-ul-Bayan* and *Kashshaf* of Zamakhshari, etc.

To sum up, it contains on the one hand the gist of the monumental commentaries and lexicons of the classical scholars, and on the other it is written with reference to the needs of the modern times and in accordance with the knowledge he gained in the company of the Promised Messiah and Hazrat Maulana Nur-ud-Din. It keeps in view the objections against Islam raised by other religions, especially by the Christian critics of Islam, and by Western nations generally. He has thus rendered a unique service in the field of exegesis of the Quran that will serve as a guiding light for the world for years to come.

An idea of the tremendous labour that he devoted to writing the *Bayan-ul-Quran* can be obtained by seeing his handwritten manuscripts which are still preserved. For the whole book, there are three voluminous manuscripts consisting of thousands of pages hand written by him. After completing the first draft the explanatory notes were amended so thoroughly that all the space on the pages and their margins is full of writing. Then from this he wrote out a neat second draft, copying each and every word of these thousands of pages. To this again he made several changes to give it better shape, and wrote it out afresh a third time for giving to the printer. Today the outcome of this arduous labour exists in the form of the monumental commentary *Bayan-ul-Quran* in three volumes of two and a half thousand pages.[2]

The popularity, appeal and utility of this commentary can be judged by the fact that many prominent non-Ahmadi scholars of Islam, including opponents of the Ahmadiyya Movement, have been using it in their Quran teaching.[3] Many friends have even seen this commentary being used in teaching the Quran in Makkah and Madinah, and some parts of it have been translated into Arabic. It has also been observed that some maulvis who, for some reason of their own, feel it necessary to call Ahmadis as *kafir* keep this commentary in front of them while teaching the Quran, having removed the cover and the title page as it bears the name of Maulana Muhammad Ali and the Ahmadiyya Anjuman Isha'at Islam.

Other publications from 1918 to 1923

During these years when Maulana Muhammad Ali was busy producing this magnificient translation and commentary, he also wrote many other books according to need. These are listed below chronologically.

---

2. A recalligraphed edition of *Bayan-ul-Quran* with a modern page format was produced around the year 1970. It was first published all in one volume. In later printings it was split into a two-volume edition, as available today.

3. For some modern reviews of *Bayan-ul-Quran* by Pakistani scholars, see the Addendum to this chapter.

In January 1918 his Urdu book *Masih Mau'ud* (the Promised Messiah) was published, in which the so-called second coming of Jesus is explained in the light of the Quran and Hadith, and the claims of Hazrat Mirza Ghulam Ahmad are set forth. Besides this, four booklets in English were published in a series entitled *The Ahmadiyya Movement* between June 1917 and January 1918:

The Ahmadiyya Movement — I. The Founder
The Ahmadiyya Movement — II. The Doctrine
The Ahmadiyya Movement — III. Prophecy
The Ahmadiyya Movement — IV. The Split

In January 1919 his book *Mir'at-ul-Haqiqat* was published in reply to Mirza Mahmud Ahmad's book *Haqiqat-ul-Amr*.

In March 1919 the book *Shanakhat-i Mamurin* (Identifying those appointed by God) was published, which discusses in detail the criteria for determining the truth of those who claim to be sent by God.

During his stay in Simla in 1919 two other important books were written: *Sirat Khair-ul-Bashar,* biography of the Holy Prophet Muhammad in which the criticism of the opponents of Islam is also answered, and *Jam'a Hadith,* published in 1920, which throws detailed light on the subject of the collection of Hadith.

In summer of 1920, during his stay in Simla, he wrote two pamphlets: *Zarurat-i Mujaddidiyya* (Need of the Institution of Reformership) and *'Isawiyyat ka Akhari Sahara* (The Last Refuge of Christianity). Another writing was *Khilafat-i Islamia bi-ru'i Quran wa Hadith* (Islamic *Khilafat* according to the Quran and Hadith).

In October 1921 an important English book *Muhammad and Christ* was published, in which the Holy Prophet Muhammad and Jesus have been compared according to the Quran as well as the life of Jesus from the Bible. This book became very popular in various countries and was subsequently translated in fifteen languages of the West and Asia. It refuted the arguments of a tract, *Haqa'iq-i-Quran,* originally written in Urdu, which sought to prove the superiority of Jesus over the Prophet Muhammad on the basis of the Quran itself. Its English translation appeared within an article by

Rev. E.M. Wherry in the Christian missionary journal *The Moslem World* (July 1919, pp. 252–264). He wrote that its clear arguments establish "that Christ is in every possible aspect of the case a thousandfold superior and more exalted than Mohammed" and that this tract "has fallen as a bomb in the Moslem camp" (p. 255).

Some twenty years later, another Christian missionary in India, Rev. Lewis Bevan Jones, wrote an article in *The Moslem World,* entitled *How not to use the Quran* (July 1940, pp. 280–291), in which he listed the arguments put forward in *Haqa'iq-i-Quran* and the response to these by Maulana Muhammad Ali in *Muhammad and Christ.* Bevan Jones wrote that Christians in the past have tried to use the Quran to provide evidence in favour of the Christian claims about Jesus. *Haqa'iq-i-Quran,* he says, had by 1919 run into four editions, published in a quantity of nineteen thousand. In 1928 the sixth edition of one hundred thousand copies was published by the Bible Society in Lahore. He writes: "Quite clearly the original pamphlet has had far-reaching influence ... the Arya Samajists make use of it in their propaganda against the Muslims" (p. 285). After listing Maulana Muhammad Ali's arguments in *Muhammad and Christ,* Bevan Jones writes: "Surely there is enough in the above record to give the Christian evangelist reason to reflect carefully on the ways in which he may make use of the Quran" (p. 291). In other words, Christian missionaries should change their style of preaching and argumentation.

This shows how bold and audacious Christian missionaries had become, that ignoring their own scriptures they claimed to have proved "the infinite superiority of Christ over Mohammed" (E.M. Wherry in article cited above, p. 263) on the basis of the Quran. At this critical juncture this writing of Maulana Muhammad Ali showed that this approach was a complete failure.

Also in 1921 the second edition of the English translation of the Quran was published in England in a quantity of 10,750.

In June 1922 his book *Haqiqat-i Ikhtilaf* was published, in reply to Mirza Mahmud Ahmad's book *A'inah-i Sadaqat,* published in December 1921. These books were in connection with the split in the Ahmadiyya Movement. Mirza Mahmud Ahmad in his book had presented the events in a highly distorted form and alleged that Khwaja Kamal-ud-Din and Maulana Muhammad Ali were both hypocrites from the very beginning and had been giving trouble even to Hazrat Mirza sahib himself. In *Haqiqat-i Ikhtilaf* Maulana Muhammad Ali has not only refuted these false allegations but also explained the real causes of the split and the events of that time (which have been mentioned earlier in this biography in Chapter 2.3).[4]

In the summer of 1922 the third edition of his booklet *Radd-i Takfir Ahl-i Qiblah* was published, which refutes the dangerous Qadiani doctrine that those Muslims who do not believe in Hazrat Mirza sahib are *kafir* and excluded from the fold of Islam. To this day the Qadian community has not been able to answer this booklet in which it has been proved from the Holy Quran, Hadith and the writings of the Promised Messiah as well as his practice that all those who profess the *Kalima* are Muslims. The issue of the holding of funeral prayers for deceased non-Ahmadis by Ahmadis has also been clarified, this being the topic that Mirza Mahmud Ahmad always avoided to discuss as it most plainly showed the falsity of his belief that all other Muslims are *kafir*.

In 1923 two English tracts, *Back to Islam* and *Back to the Quran,* and an Urdu tract *Mazhab Ki Gharaz* (Aim of Religion) were published.

Quran teaching classes (*Dars-i Quran*)

During all these years Maulana Muhammad Ali continued with his daily classes in teaching the meanings of the Holy Quran. In December 1917 one phase of this teaching ended, and following that he started another phase in January 1918. This time he taught a quarter of one part (*para*) everyday in order to cover the entire Quran in four months. In this phase many members from outside Lahore came and stayed in Lahore to benefit from the teaching. This phase ended in April 1918.

---

4. Mirza Mahmud Ahmad's book *A'inah-i Sadaqat* was translated and published in English by the Qadiani *Jama'at* in 1924 under the title *The Truth about the Split.* The Maulana's reply, *Haqiqat-i Ikhtilaf,* was also later published in English as *True Facts about the Split* in 1966.

In the summer of 1918 these classes were held in Simla during his stay there, continuing again at Ahmadiyya Buildings after his return to Lahore. Along with these he also started classes in Hadith. This became his practice every year. In the winter of 1921–22, in addition to his regular Quran teaching after the *maghrib* prayer, he also started a new series of classes in the Holy Quran and Hadith specifically for school teachers and missionaries who were to be sent abroad.

In Lahore in 1922 and 1923 he adopted a new style of delivering the Quran teaching. In addition to the translation he would give only the essential commentary and explanation, without going too deeply into the finer points, so that people from every background would be able to understand. He also set a written examination for those who attended regularly.

He thus made it a part of his life to conduct these classes, using a variety of methods and approaches. In his Friday sermons and through other means, while he would stress upon the need for spreading the Holy Quran and propagating Islam, he also made clear that it is absolutely essential for the members of a Movement which seeks to spread the Quran that they themselves study the Quran and act upon its teachings.

Touring branches and other trips

The importance Maulana Muhammad Ali gave to the organization of the *Jama'at* is clear from the fact that, despite all his literary commitments of producing such monumental books and his other multifarious duties, he would always find time to visit the various branches of the Movement and stay with them for a day or two, and frequently attend their annual meetings. Thus every year he would visit in person some ten or twelve branches, and in addition to other matters he would stress in particular the importance of paying the monthly subscriptions, holding Holy Quran study classes and gathering for the Friday congregational service.

Accordingly, in these five or six years he continued this practice. His tours were usually to places in the Punjab and the North West Frontier, that is to say, ranging from Peshawar to Delhi.

In 1920 he embarked upon his first long journey and went to Bombay and Madras in the company of Khwaja Kamal-ud-Din. In the middle of February they went first to Bombay and after a few days' stay there, during which they delivered speeches, they reached Madras where the Muslim public gave them a grand welcome. They stayed at the house of Seth Malang Ahmad Badshah. No sooner had they arrived in Madras that Maulana Muhammad Ali was taken ill and could not make any public speeches. However, the Khwaja sahib delivered many speeches. During this tour of Bombay and Madras they addressed the Muslim public and emphasised upon them the importance and need of the propagation of Islam and appealed for donations for the Anjuman. During this tour not only were reasonable funds raised for the Anjuman and the Woking Mission but many supporters were also gained who appreciated the work done by this Movement.

At that time, due to the publication of the English translation of the Holy Quran and other literature and the work of the propagation of Islam in Europe, the educated Muslims of India, leaving aside the bigoted Maulvis, were beginning to value the services of the Lahore Ahmadiyya *Jama'at* and of Maulana Muhammad Ali. He always used to be invited to meetings of the Anjuman Islamia of Punjab which were held in different cities, and he attended many meetings of such outside bodies. In addition to that, in April 1920 he made a speech at the annual meeting of the Anjuman Himayat-i Islam Lahore entitled 'Our problems and their solution' and put before all the Muslims the work of the propagation of Islam and invited them to help his *Jama'at*.

Stay in Simla, 1918–1921

As has been mentioned before, till 1917 Maulana Muhammad Ali used to go to Abbottabad in summer. At that time Simla was the summer capital of the British Government of India and quite a few members of the Lahore Ahmadiyya *Jama'at* used to be there. In 1918 they invited him to spend summer in Simla. So on 31 May that year he and his family went to Simla for four months and stayed in a residence named Eva Lodge. As during his stay in the hilly regions he used to be joined by many other senior figures of the *Jama'at*, especially to attend the Quran classes in the month of Ramadan, so he allocated half of his residence for the guests and also had to rent a small cottage nearby. Master Faqirullah, a melodious reciter of the Holy Quran, was there with him and everyday he would recite one part of the Holy Quran before the gathering and the Maulana would explain its meanings. They would all come together to offer *tahajjud* prayers in Ramadan. The fame of his daily Quran classes had spread in Simla and a large number of Muslims who were not Ahmadis also used to attend them.

The same year, in September 1918, at the close of the First World War, the virulent epidemic of influenza raging in the outside world broke out in India as well. Thousands of people were dying daily, big cities like Lahore being particularly affected.[5] Some friends tried to stop the Maulana from returning to Lahore but he left his family in Khanpur with Dr. Basharat Ahmad, who was on medical duty there, and came to Lahore by himself.

At the end of May 1919 he again went to Simla and occupied the residence known as Hari Villa in Chhota Simla. This year Khwaja Kamal-ud-Din, who had returned from England in May 1919, also came to Simla with him and stayed in a cottage known as Hari cottage which was next to Hari Villa. Shaikh Maula Bakhsh of Lyallpur also stayed in Hari Villa that summer. Another house was acquired that year in Simla where Maulana Muhammad Ali started a missionary class for certain educated men of the *Jama'at*. He gave lectures to the class for two hours everyday. This class continued to be held in Simla for two years during the summer. In addition to that, Quran teaching (*dars*) was conducted daily as usual.

---

5. Khwaja Kamal-ud-Din was in Woking, England, at the time when his eldest son Bashir Ahmad died tragically in Lahore. Maulana Muhammad Ali sent the Khwaja sahib a telegraphic message in the following English words: "Beloved Bashir called back. Sorrowfully we submit." It is difficult to find more appropriate, brief words in which to express sympathy, shock and resignation to the will of God as well as the aim of human life. The Khwaja sahib himself said that this message, while conveying news of this unexpected, terrible tragedy, also urged patience and acceptance of the Divine will.

He thus spent the summer during four years in Simla in this way. This was the time when he was busy working on *Bayan-ul Quran*. He also wrote the books *Sirat Khair-ul-Bashar* (Biography of the Holy Prophet Muhammad), *Jam'a Hadith* (Collection of the Hadith reports of the Holy Prophet), and *Muhammad and Christ*, and several pamphlets and tracts which have been mentioned earlier.

Other events, 1918–1923

In 1918 Maulana Yaqub Khan relinquished his prestigious post to dedicate his life to the service of Islam and settled in Lahore.

Khwaja Kamal-ud-Din returned from England in May 1919. In his place Maulana Sadr-ud-Din was sent again to Woking in July 1919 and he stayed there till April 1920. The Khwaja sahib left in October 1921 for his third visit to Woking. Earlier, in September 1921, Maulana Yaqub Khan was sent to Woking because the work had increased.

The *Jama'at* did not have any journal in English so far and the need for it was very keenly felt. So in January 1922 *The Light* was launched. This magazine gradually made good progress, especially when Maulana Yaqub Khan returned from Woking and became its editor. During his editorship *The Light* not only came to be appreciated by the English-reading public within India but it also acquired international fame and began to be sent abroad in large numbers.

Stay in Dalhousie, 1922–23

In April 1922, sometime before Ramadan, Maulana Muhammad Ali went to Dalhousie, a town in the mountains, to seek solitude for the spiritual devotion of worship and prayer. This hill station was not as busy and full of activity as Abbottabad, Murree or Simla, but was a very peaceful and quiet place. He liked its serenity and tranquillity so much that he decided to spend the next summer there. In this connection he wrote the following statement for members of the *Jama'at* in the organ *Paigham Sulh*:

My absence and our work

Brothers of the *Jama'at*,

Assalamu alaikum wa rahmatullahi wa barakatuhu.

Two years even before coming to Lahore I used to go to
the hills for my literary activities. After the establishment
of the Anjuman in Lahore it has become even more important because in Lahore there are so many other responsibilities of my office that keep interfering in my writing
work. ... Literary composition, especially that which demands
much mental exertion such as the commentary of the Holy
Quran, ... needs undisturbed attention which cannot be
found in Lahore. This year in seven months in Lahore
I could not translate more than three quarters of one part
(*para*) of the Holy Quran, ... even though by the grace of
Allah I still have the habit of working as hard as I did when
I was a student preparing for examinations — and in reality
the most important test is still to be taken. Because of my
stay in Simla a *Jama'at* has been well established there.
But this time I have turned away even from there and taken
up residence in Dalhousie in order to devote my whole
time to the translation work.

(*Paigham Sulh*, 10 May 1922, p. 3)

In the first year he occupied the residence 'Mall House' in
lower Dalhousie. However, he was soon followed by his admirers,
longing to be with the one who was their light, and so Shaikh
Rahmatullah, Mian Ghulam Rasul, Dr. Mirza Yaqub Baig and
some other friends also joined him in Dalhousie. Though Mall
House was spacious and half of it was used to accommodate the
guests but another residence next to it, Mall Cottage, was also
acquired for this purpose. So the quiet, lush green, beautiful
mountains of Dalhousie echoed with the call to prayer, recitation
of the Holy Quran and the sounds of *tahajjud* prayers. From then
on, the Maulana spent every summer there and other friends also
went to join him there most times.

German Mission

During these years another foundation was laid for the propagation
of Islam in Europe. The Anjuman founded a mission in Germany.

The first person to call for the opening of a mission in Germany was one Abdul Jabbar Khairi, who wrote to the Woking Mission in 1921 urging that a similar Islamic mission be established there. This proposal was referred to the Anjuman in Lahore which decided the same year to open a mission in Berlin. In June 1922, Maulvi Abdul Majid (who later on became editor of *The Islamic Review,* Woking) was sent there and a mission was formally opened in July 1922. Khwaja Kamal-ud-Din also reached Berlin from Woking in July, and after studying the situation there, advised the Anjuman of the necessity of building a mosque there in order to do propagation work.

After this beginning, arrangements were gradually made to buy land in Berlin and construct the mosque, as will be discussed later, and during this time Maulana Muhammad Ali started to make special appeals for funds for the Berlin mosque. The Anjuman decided to send Maulana Sadr-ud-Din there, who left Lahore at the end of December 1922 for Germany.

Royalty and how it began

Since April 1914, when he came to Lahore, Maulana Muhammad Ali had faced much personal financial hardship. For a period of more than five years he had no means of income. During this time many of his books were published, including the first edition of the English Translation of the Holy Quran which then spread in the world. However, the Maulana did not accept any income from the Anjuman nor was he given any royalty for his books. During that time he bore many difficulties upon his shoulders for subsistence. At one stage he had to sell part of his furniture and copper utensils to meet the household expenses. During the first year neither the Anjuman nor any of its members gave a thought to the matter. After a year some members made a proposal to him on their own that he should accept a monthly stipend from the Anjuman but he refused. Then in 1917 and again in 1918 this matter was put before the Anjuman. Those proposals were as follows:

Resolution No. 59/61, dated 29 April 1917, proposed by Dr. Syed Muhammad Husain Shah: The Head of the Community, Hazrat Maulana Muhammad Ali, did the English translation of the Holy Quran after a constant labour of eight years, then he served the

Movement with great devotion during the tribulation of the Split, all this adversely affecting his health. Even now, despite his weak health, he is serving the Movement. He has to write articles, give daily classes in the Holy Quran, go out of Lahore to deliver lectures, carry on correspondence, meet people daily, take part in debates, and on top of that since breaking away from Qadian he has to worry about how to make his living. He has not taken any remuneration from the Anjuman. If this situation continues the danger is that his health will be badly damaged. As he is devoting all his time for the work of the Anjuman, so to lighten his burden I put forward the following proposal before the Anjuman for consideration:

First: He should be relieved of the burden of earning a livelihood.
Second: He should be provided with assistants to help him.

Report of Secretary: I agree entirely with the proposal of the Shah sahib. In my opinion the Anjuman should offer him at least Rs. 200 per month for his maintenance.

Decision: The following members should consider the matter and report back: Shaikh Rahmatullah, Dr. Muhammad Husain Shah, Maulvi Sadr-ud-Din, Mian Ghulam Rasul — Secretary (Yaqub Baig).

Another proposal was as follows:

Resolution No. 277 of the Executive Committee, dated 13 January 1918, proposed by Hazrat Maulvi Sadr-ud-Din: The Head of the Community has for the past four years somehow managed to survive, but this sort of existence cuts life short. Such valued and precious men, as he is, do not appear in the world very often. So the Anjuman should give some thought to it and request the Head of the Community to accept Anjuman's offer. The Holy Prophet Muhammad and the righteous *Khalifas* accepted a stipend for religious duties. He should not discard this *Sunna*. It is not possible for him to write books on Islam, lead the Movement and at the same time worry about earning a living. ... We wish we possessed the means to offer him much more, but for the time being he should accept 200 Rupees per month.

This proposal was again put forward by Resolution No. 19, dated 3 February 1918, and the following decision was taken:

Members of the Anjuman unanimously request the Head of the Community to accept the offer, although it is meagre. However, as he does not want to accept any monetary help, so for the time being this proposal should be postponed.

Regarding his reasons for declining this financial support, Maulana Muhammad Ali gave the following explanation in a writing which he penned a few days before his death:

> "I also want to make it clear that the reason why from the beginning I did not like to accept any remuneration from the Anjuman, even though I had no source of income, was that I did not wish to burden the Anjuman as it had been newly founded just then and I was afraid that this extra strain on it may cause it to falter. The second reason was to belie a senior Qadiani who had declared, on my departure from Qadian, that without getting any salary for six months I would go back and bow my head before the *khalifa* of Qadian."

Besides this, in a letter dated 2 December 1930 addressed to Maulana Ghulam Hasan Khan he wrote:

> "The Anjuman came into being on 3 May 1914 and I was elected its *Amir* (Head) but for one whole year neither the Anjuman nor any of its members even discussed the matter of the *Amir's* subsistence nor was I asked by anyone about how I made a living. After one year some members of the Anjuman, on their own behalf, put to me a proposal according to which the Anjuman would pay me some stipend. I did not accept the proposal, for which there were many reasons. One was that the financial position of the Anjuman was so precarious that this extra burden would have caused it severe difficulties. Another was that I could see that just as on one side [in the Qadiani *Jama'at*] blind obedience to the head was in vogue, on our side there was excessive freedom. So in my view by accepting the stipend the prestige of the *Amir* would be further lowered. There were some other reasons as well. But these two were the main considerations in my mind. During this time all my writings were published by the Anjuman and it made a profit on them. In 1918 I started working on *Bayan-ul-Quran* and in 1919 I proposed to some members that I would get it printed myself. After discussing the matter among themselves, they proposed to me that the Anjuman should

continue to print all my books and pay me a part of the sale
price as royalty. Among these friends were certainly the
Khwaja [Kamal-ud-Din] sahib, [Syed Muhammad Husain]
Shah sahib and Mirza [Yaqub Baig] sahib. Any one of
them could be asked even today to vouch under oath that
I never indicated to anyone, even indirectly, that the Anjuman should pay me any royalty. However, when this
proposal was put to me I approved it as the Anjuman was
to pay me a part of what it was earning itself. After settling
this with me, the matter was put formally before the Anjuman."

This proposal, which was the beginning of royalty being paid
to Maulana Muhammad Ali, was put before the Anjuman on 30
July 1919 by Dr. Mirza Yaqub Baig, who was General Secretary
of the Anjuman at that time, as follows:

No. 191, 30 July 1919, Report of Secretary: Hazrat Amir Maulana
Muhammad Ali is busy in the work of the Anjuman day and night
but he does not wish to accept any remuneration for it from the
Anjuman. It had been tried several times that either the Anjuman or
some members should do something for him financially but he has
always refused to accept any help. As the cost of living has risen in
present times, so some members being mindful of these difficulties,
which he himself being a godly and selfless person does not care
about, requested him to accept for his needs a part of the profits
from the writings which he does for the Anjuman. After much insistence he has agreed that in future the sale price of his books will
be set as follows. If, for example, the cost of publishing a book is
4 Rupees, then 1 Rupee shall be added as administrative expenses,
4 Rupees as profit and 3 Rupees as the author's royalty. Royalty
will be paid to *Hazrat Amir* on every copy sold, an account being
prepared monthly. Accordingly, this proposal is put before the
meeting for approval.

Decision: To pay royalty for the books written by *Hazrat Amir*
Maulana Muhammad Ali the following system shall be adopted.
New books written in future shall be priced at three times their cost
and one fourth of the sale price per copy shall be paid to *Hazrat
Amir* Maulvi Muhammad Ali. As to the books that are already in
existence, including the translation of the Holy Quran, one sixth of

the sale price per copy shall be paid to *Hazrat Amir* from today. An account shall be prepared monthly and the calculated amount paid to *Hazrat Amir* as royalty.

Accordingly, this began to be acted upon from August 1919 and continued in the same way subsequently: the Anjuman printed, published and sold his books and a share of the profits, according to the set rate, was paid to him from time to time in the form of royalty, as is the generally recognised and standard practice of compensating authors. This was a most appropriate and proper means by which he made his living. He never burdened the Anjuman with having to pay him a salary, nor did he, like the common practice of religious leaders, take offerings and donations from followers. He only took his rightful due for his labour and even that was from the income earned by the Anjuman by publishing his books.

Relations with the Qadian community

Ever since the Split in 1914 Maulana Muhammad Ali continued to address the Qadiani community on the issues under dispute by writing extensively in *Paigham Sulh*. Again and again he wrote in refutation of the wrong beliefs of Mirza Mahmud Ahmad, i.e., ascribing a claim of prophethood to the Promised Messiah, considering him as the one who fulfilled the prophecy about the coming Ahmad given in the Holy Quran, and declaring all non-Ahmadi Muslims to be outside the fold of Islam. The Maulana always tried to get a written, decisive debate held between himself and Mirza Mahmud Ahmad which would then be printed and circulated among both the communities to enable every one to decide for himself. But for some reason or other Mirza Mahmud Ahmad never agreed to it. It has been mentioned before that seventy Ahmadis from the Lahore *Jama'at*, who had taken the *bai'at* before November 1901 at the Promised Messiah's hand, had issued sworn testimony that the Promised Messiah did not make any change whatsoever in his claim in 1901. But Mirza Mahmud Ahmad could not produce a single witness to testify to the opposite effect.

During this period Maulana Muhammad Ali produced the following tracts[6] addressing the Qadian *Jama'at:*

1. Invitation to Mirza Mahmud Ahmad for exchange of views at the Annual Gathering (*Jalsa*).
2. Prophet or *Muhaddas*.
3. Claim to Prophethood.
4. Denial of Prophethood and the year 1901.
5. The Last Prophet.
6. The Promised Messiah's sworn statement.

Addendum by the Translator

Reviews of *Bayan-ul-Quran* by modern Pakistani scholars

1. In the Urdu book *Quran aur Insan*, which quotes verses of the Holy Quran dealing with various problems and aspects of human life, the author Safdar Hasan Siddiqi writes in the Preface:

> "I have taken the translation of the verses of the Holy Quran mostly from the translation by the late Maulana Muhammad Ali because it is, to a great extent, a translation of the words and not his own interpretation, and for this reason it expresses the Divine will in the Urdu language in a better way."
>
> (*Quran aur Insan* by Safdar Hasan Siddiqi, published 1995 by Ferozsons, Lahore, page 29)

2. The Urdu monthly *Islami Digest* of Karachi (editor: Syed Qasim Mahmud) in its March 1996 issue opened a series entitled *Tashrih-ul-Quran.* Its review of Maulana Muhammad Ali's English translation has already been quoted in the last chapter. Regarding *Bayan-ul-Quran* it says:

---

6. These tracts were all in Urdu. Their titles have been translated into English here. For their Urdu titles, see Appendix 1, List II, p. 527.

"Five years after his English translation and commentary the Urdu translation and commentary was published, having the title *Bayan-ul-Quran*. ... Expressing her view about this work Dr. Saliha writes:

'The translation, while being simple, has literary weight. The language is eloquent and chaste. As to the meaning, some people have objections against his translation and commentary because of his beliefs and views. The fact is that he was the head of the Lahore Ahmadiyya *Jama'at*. Despite this, we consider that his translation and commentary is almost free of 'wrong beliefs'. He has done the translation very cautiously, with great sincerity, and having kept before him the generally prevailing views. Despite closely following the text and the order of the original words, the translation has continuity and flow.' "

3. Professor Dr. Muhammad Nasim Usmani in his book *Urdu Main Tafsiri Adab: Aik Tarikhi aur Tajziyati Ja'iza* ('Quranic Commentaries in Urdu: A Historical and Critical Analysis', published Karachi, 1994) writes on pages 416 to 418:

"This translation and commentary is different from the famous commentary *Bayan-ul-Quran* by Maulana Ashraf Ali Thanvi. Its author is the Head of the Lahore Ahmadiyya *Jama'at,* Maulana Muhammad Ali of Lahore, and it was published by the Ahmadiyya Anjuman Isha'at Islam Lahore. Maulana Muhammad Ali first produced a translation and commentary of the Holy Quran in English, and then, to make it more widely available, he rendered it into Urdu. As the commentary in Urdu is more comprehensive, the size of the book increased considerably. So for convenience it was first published in three volumes, around the year 1922. Since Pakistan came into being, three editions have been published which were in one volume, in 1969, 1972 and 1980."

He then gives two quotations from the Maulana's Preface, in the first of which the Maulana has stressed the need for Muslims to understand the Quran, and in the second the Maulana has refuted the notion that the Quran does not have a systematic arrangement of subject matter. After citing these quotations, the reviewer makes the following comment:

> "The views that the translator has expressed in these lines are not very different from what the vast majority of Muslims believe. In fact, this commentary is clearly different from the *Tafsir Saghir* of Mirza Bashir-ud-Din Mahmud Ahmad. To see this difference, look at the translation and commentary of the following verses."

He quotes as his example the translation and explanation of the 'finality of prophethood' verse (33:40) from *Bayan-ul-Quran*.

3.4: From 1924 to 1937

Publication of *Fazl-ul-Bari*
and *The Religion of Islam*

By 1923 Maulana Muhammad Ali had completed the English and Urdu translations of the Holy Quran with commentary. During this period he also wrote a life of the Holy Prophet Muhammad (may peace and the blessings of Allah be upon him) in Urdu under the title *Sirat Khair-ul-Bashar*. Then comes the fourteen year period 1924 to 1937 during which, in addition to other writings, two of his monumental books were published: *Fazl-ul-Bari,* being an Urdu translation of *Sahih Bukhari* with explanatory notes, and the English work *The Religion of Islam*. During this period the Ahmadiyya Anjuman Isha'at Islam made tremendous progress under his leadership and performed many major services in the cause of the propagation of Islam. The annual budget of the Anjuman increased to Rs. 200,000 and its branches were opened all over India and in several foreign countries. The Anjuman acquired property worth several millions of Rupees. New editions of the English translation of the Holy Quran were published, the literature produced by Maulana Muhammad Ali spread in other countries in large numbers and it was translated into foreign languages. A building for the Muslim High School at Ahmadiyya Buildings, Lahore was constructed. The Mosque in Berlin was built and work on the German translation of the Holy Quran was started. A mission was established in Java (East Indies) and the Dutch translation of the Holy Quran was published. Maulana Muhammad Ali went on several tours to other parts of India.

While, on the one hand, the literature produced by Maulana Muhammad Ali and the achievements of the Ahmadiyya Anjuman

Isha'at Islam gained widespread popularity, the community had to endure a severe storm of opposition from some Muslim leaders in its home country. However, even then it remained on the path of progress. During this period, while the Anjuman's budget increased so much and valuable properties were acquired, at the same time it faced many financial difficulties due to the scale of its worldwide work of the propagation of Islam. However, its work did not suffer because it had a leader who never wavered in the least in the path of the propagation of Islam. There was overwhelming fervour, devotion and sincerity of purpose in his heart which, on the one hand, created in him an iron determination and unflagging energy, and on the other hand it made him rise in the middle of the night to pray to Allah and cry before the Almighty for the success of the *Jama'at* and the victory of Islam. This was why Allah placed such convincing power in his speech that even though he would appeal tirelessly for regular donations and for funds for special projects, the *Jama'at* for its part never tired of making donations and offering its money in response to his appeals. The financial sacrifices made by Ahmadis were proverbial even among other Muslims.

Publications from 1924–1937: *Fazl-ul-Bari*

After producing the English and Urdu translations of the Holy Quran with commentaries, Maulana Muhammad Ali began work on translating *Sahih Bukhari* into Urdu with explanatory notes. Hazrat Maulana Nur-ud-Din, during his last days, while listening to the commentary of the last portions of the English translation of the Holy Quran, had said to Maulana Muhammad Ali:

> "Maulvi sahib, the Quran has been done but Bukhari still remains."

Maulana Muhammad Ali has stated that Maulana Nur-ud-Din wanted him to do this work as well. So after finishing the *Bayan-ul-Quran* and then writing *Tarikh Khilafat-i Rashidah* (History of the Early Caliphs), he immediately took this work in hand. From 1926 onwards this translation and explanatory notes began to be published in parts under the title of *Fazl-ul-Bari* and were as much appreciated by the educated classes as was the translation of the Holy Quran. For example, Maulana Abdul Majid Daryabadi wrote in his newspaper *Such* of 13 September 1926 as follows:

> "[Despite existing Urdu translations] there still remained a
> dire need of a good translation of Sahih Bukhari. By the
> grace of God, the time has come for the fulfilment of this
> vital necessity, and for this service God chose a man who is
> considered, not only by the 'mischief-making Ulama' but by
> many well-intentioned Ulama as well, perhaps not to be a
> Muslim at all. The head of the Lahore Ahmadiyya *Jama'at*,
> Maulana Muhammad Ali, M.A., is one of those few entirely
> sincere sons of Islam who has been quietly engaged for years
> in rendering the most valuable services to the cause of Islam.
> His English translation of the Quran has till now succeeded
> in showing the right path to God knows how many mis-
> guided people. A fresh addition to these glorious services is
> his Urdu translation of *Sahih Bukhari* which he has started
> publishing under the title *Fazl-ul-Bari*, the first part of which
> has just come out of the press."
>
> (*Paigham Sulh,* v. 14, no. 46. Reviews in Muslim organs
> *Zamindar* and *Amristar* were published in *Paigham Sulh,* v.
> 14, no. 47 and 49, October 1926.)

The complete work was published by the end of 1937. He had
written and published its introduction as a separate book under the
title *Maqam-i Hadith*, containing a detailed discussion on the
rightful status of Hadith and how its reports were collected. The
biggest obstacle in the translation of *Sahih Bukhari* is its huge volume which is due to the repetition of reports in different chapters.
If the repeated reported are omitted, the reader is deprived of
Imam Bukhari's insight and judgment, and the useful conclusions
which can sometimes be drawn from the variation in the wording
of the same report cannot be seen. Imam Bukhari repeats a report
under different headings in order to show its bearing on different
subjects and his method of thus drawing inferences holds an important position in jurisprudence.

Maulana Muhammad Ali has solved this difficulty very skil-
fully. The chapters are arranged exactly as in *Sahih Bukhari*.
Every hadith report, when occurring the first time, is allocated a
serial number. If that report occurs again later on, then just the
reference to its serial number is given in the translation, and if

there is any variation, addition or omission of wording in that version of the report then that is indicated in a footnote. His foot-notes are a work of the most arduous labour. He has followed the principles enunciated by the Promised Messiah, which he has dealt with in detail in his book *Maqam-i Hadith,* viz., that if he found a hadith report to conflict with the Quran he has tried to give it an interpretation which makes it conform to the Quran, and if that is not possible the report is rejected as unauthentic. In the notes he has taken account of the criticism of Islam by non-Muslims. The translation is in simple language, and while being faithful to the original it is also idiomatic.

Publications from 1924–1937: *The Religion of Islam*

During the time that *Fazl-ul-Bari* was being published, Maulana Muhammad Ali wrote his famous English book *The Religion of Islam* in 1934 and 1935. He had in fact been working on it gra-dually since 1928. That year, a book of the same title written by a Christian clergyman, the Rev. F. A. Klein, was given to Maulana Muhammad Ali by Chaudhry Sir Shahab-ud-Din who was Presi-dent of the Punjab Legislative Council. This book presented a grievously distorted picture of Islam, and after going through it the Maulana decided to write a comprehensive book on Islam in English. On one occasion the Promised Messiah had also bidden him to write such a book in English. However, due to other wri-ting work and various engagements he could not complete this task. In March 1935 he was taken ill and his condition become serious enough that he had to be moved to Dalhousie on 11 April for a change of climate and recuperation. When he recovered a little, he first completed this task. In December 1935, at the annual gathering, he mentioned this in the following words:

> "Not long before his death the Promised Messiah had expressed a wish in 1907, and he expressed it to me by telling me that a book about the teachings of Islam should be written in English. In 1908 I got involved in the Eng-lish translation of the Holy Quran and in fact I forgot all about this work.
>
> In 1928 a friend gave me a book written by a Chris-tian clergyman in which the teachings of Islam were

presented in a highly distorted form. So I embarked upon the task of writing a book about Islam and kept working on it gradually in addition to my other commitments.

Last March I was suddenly taken ill and it took such a serious turn that the doctors had me confined to bed and disallowed me to do any work. At that time I kept wondering whether I would be able to finish this book in my life.

By the grace of Allah I recovered, and getting out of my sick bed I started to complete this book, working as hard as a student preparing for his examinations. Sometimes I even had to give up my morning walk and work on it constantly from morning till nine at night. By the grace of Allah the printing of the book is now entirely complete. All the proofs have been checked. Its name is *The Religion of Islam*."

(*Paigham Sulh,* 7 February 1936)

This monumental work of almost 800 pages is divided into three parts, containing all essential knowledge about Islam necessary for a Muslim or non-Muslim. The first part deals with the sources of Islam, that is, the Holy Quran, the Hadith and *Ijtihad* (inference and exercise of judgment). In the second part the principles of Islam are discussed: Faith, Existence of God, Angels, Divine Revelation, Prophets, Life after death and *Taqdir* (Predestination), etc. The third part deals with practical religious obligations and Islamic Law and commandments, that is, Prayer, *Zakat,* Fasting, *Hajj,* Jihad, Marriage and Divorce, Property and Inheritance, Loan and Interest, Directions about Food and Drink, and other laws. On every issue discussed, references are copiously given from the Holy Quran, Hadith, books of Islamic jurisprudence and other works, there being altogether more than 2500 references in the entire book. The following are some examples of the tributes it received from learned Muslims:[1]

---

1. In the reviews marked with an asterisk * at the end, the quotation is reproduced in the original English in which the review was written. Other quotations have been translated from the Urdu text given in *Mujahid-i Kabir*.

Chief Justice S.M. Suleman, High Court, Allahabad, 6 February 1936:

> "...a great and comprehensive work, embodying Islamic philosophy and jurisprudence and embracing Muslim theology as well as the cardinal points of Muslim Law. This exhaustive work contains a vast store of information as to the Islamic tenets and doctrines, much of which is not available in English. It is the product of great learning, deep scholarship and enormous labour." *

Sir Shafa'at Ahmad Khan:

> "This book has been written in a highly scholarly manner and is proof of the learned author's high ability and ingenuity. In it the learned author has thrown sufficient light on the important Islamic issues and in explaining them he has displayed the highest capability. I hope this will prove to be an authentic and unequalled book on Islam."

Dr. Sir Muhammad Iqbal, letter dated 6 February 1936:

> "I have glanced through parts of it, and find it an extremely useful work almost indispensable to the students of Islam. You have already written a number of books; one cannot but admire your energy and power of sustained work." *

Chaudhry Sir Shahab-ud-Din, Speaker, Punjab Legislative Assembly, 20 January 1936:

> "The 'Religion of Islam' is the latest masterpiece from the pen of Maulana Muhammad Ali. ... It is a mine of very useful information on the principles, doctrines and laws of the Muslim religion. It is a monumental collection of exceptional merit. It contains very full, detailed and reliable information on all questions dealt with in it." *

Mr. Justice Abdur Rashid, 5 January 1936:

> "It reveals great learning, deep research and a thorough mastery of the subject. ... The conclusions of the learned

author are amply supported by authority, and every controversial doctrine has been critically examined." *

Eastern Times, Lahore, 28 February 1936:

"For a long time a need has been felt for an authentic book on Islam which could properly explain its meanings and its mission. Such a book was needed all the more because the literature produced by missionaries of other religions about Islam usually portrayed a distorted picture. Realising this need Maulana Muhammad Ali has written this book after years of experience and study. From beginning to end the author has taken extraordinary pains to include references from the Holy Quran, Hadith and other authoritative books and in this way this book is like an encyclopaedia of Islam."

Nawab Bahadur Yar Jang, Hyderabad, Deccan:

"No one can be unaware of the service rendered to Islam and the Holy Quran by the Head of the Lahore *Jama'at* Maulana Muhammad Ali. Most of all I have been impressed by his English book *The Religion of Islam.* Its greatest merit is that it is written keeping in view modern trends and ways of thinking. I consider this book as the Maulana's best gift to the Islamic world and a highly effective message for those who are ignorant of the religion of Islam."

Muhammad Marmaduke Pickthall, translator of the Quran into English:

"Probably no man living has done longer or more valuable service for the cause of Islamic revival than Maulana Muhammad Ali of Lahore. His literary works, with those of the late Khwaja Kamal-ud-Din, have given fame and distinction to the Ahmadiyya Movement. In our opinion the present volume is his finest work. ... It is a description of Al-Islam by one well-versed in the Sunna who has on his mind the shame of the Muslim decadence of the past five centuries and in his heart the hope of the revival, of which signs can now be seen on every side.

"Such a book is greatly needed at the present day when in
many Muslim countries we see persons eager for the reformation and revival of Islam making mistakes through
lack of just this knowledge. ...

"We do not always agree with Maulana Muhammad Ali's
conclusions upon minor points — sometimes they appear
to us eccentric — but his premises are always sound, we
are always conscious of his deep sincerity; and his reverence for the holy Quran is sufficient in itself to guarantee
his work in all essentials. There are some, no doubt, who
will disagree with his general findings, but they will not
be those from whom Al-Islam has anything to hope in the
future." *

(*Islamic Culture,* quarterly review published from Hyderabad Deccan, India, October 1936, pp. 659–660)

Publications from 1924–1937: other writings

Besides *Fazl-ul-Bari* and *The Religion of Islam,* Maulana Muhammad
Ali wrote many other books during the period 1924 to 1937, as
well as producing tracts and pamphlets on the need for the propagation of Islam and on the message of the Ahmadiyya Movement
which were distributed free in thousands within India and particularly abroad. Details of these publications are given below in
chronological order.

In 1924 the English pamphlet *The Call of Islam* was written,
explaining the duties and responsibilities of a Muslim in regard to
the propagation of Islam and how these are fulfilled through the
Ahmadiyya Movement. Up to the present, ten editions of this
booklet consisting of more than 30 thousand copies have been
published, and in other countries it has been translated into several
languages of those countries. He wrote a similar tract in Urdu
entitled *Da'wat-i 'Amal* ('Call to Action').

In January 1924 the English translation of *Sirat Khair-ul-
Bashar* was published as *Muhammad the Prophet*. This translation
was done by Maulana Muhammad Yaqub Khan.

In November 1924 *Tarikh Khilafat-i Rashidah* was published,
recording the history of the four Righteous Caliphs.

In 1928 he wrote two English pamphlets: *Islam the Religion of Humanity* and *The Prophet of Islam*. These two pamphlets have proved invaluable in presenting the religion of Islam and its Holy Prophet to non-Muslims. Numerous editions of these pamphlets, consisting of as many as thirty thousand copies, were printed from Lahore and distributed free. They were also translated into thirty languages of India and other countries.

During 1927 and 1928 Maulana Muhammad Ali prepared a smaller edition of the English translation of the Holy Quran for publication, in which the explanatory footnotes were much condensed and the Arabic text was not included, so that it could be distributed on an even larger scale in the English-speaking world. Its first edition, printed in England, reached India in May 1929 and further editions were published later. In total, twenty-one thousand copies have been printed and distributed up to now, a large quantity being disseminated free in foreign countries.

In March 1929, a brief booklet in English, *The Islamic Institution of Prayer* was published, throwing light on the manner, necessity and value of prayer in Islam.

In August 1929 a short biography of the Holy Prophet Muhammad was published in Urdu, entitled *Muhammad Mustafa,* being a briefer version of the book *Sirat Khair-ul-Bashar.*

In December 1929 the Urdu *Hama'il-i Sharif* was published, consisting of the translation and the text of the Holy Quran, with notes much condensed from *Bayan-ul-Quran* particularly by omitting the discussion on the lexicology of Arabic words, so that more people would be able to afford this less costly version.

During the same period four booklets *Abu Bakr*, *Umar*, *Uthman* and *Ali* were issued, giving brief biographies of these Righteous Caliphs.

In the beginning of 1930 a new writing, *Hasti Bari Ta'ala* ('Existence of God'), was published.

In May 1930 he started writing his famous Urdu book *Tahrik-i Ahmadiyyat* ('The Ahmadiyya Movement') which was published in December 1931. In the first chapter of this book are discussed a brief history of the Movement, the early life of the Promised Messiah, his claim to be *Mujaddid* and his services to Islam. The second chapter deals fully with his claims. In the third chapter there is a study of the arising of the Antichrist and Gog and Magog and other signs fulfilled in our times. The fourth chapter sheds light on the real significance of the Ahmadiyya Movement and its distinctive features. The fifth chapter records its practical work and achievements in the field of the propagation of Islam.

In December 1931, a separate Urdu book on the Antichrist and Gog and Magog was published under the title *Al-Masih ad-Dajjal wa Yajuj wa Majuj,* in which it was proved by interpreting Hadith reports in the light of modern history that the present Western powers in their political aspect are Gog and Magog, and the Christian nations in their religious characteristics symbolise the Antichrist.

In 1932 the English translation of *Tarikh Khilafat-i Rashidah,* rendered by Maulana Yaqub Khan, was published as *The Early Caliphat*e.

In 1932, when the first edition of *Muhammad the Prophet* had been exhausted, before publishing the second edition Maulana Muhammad Ali revised it and added two chapters, namely, 'Islamic wars' and 'Alleged Atrocities of the Prophet Muhammad'. The same year he revised *Maqam-i Hadith* and its new edition came out. That year also he wrote the English book *Introduction to the study of Hadith.*

In December 1932 his English booklet *World-Wide Religious Revolution* was published, in which the beliefs and achievements of the Ahmadiyya Movement were presented. The same year another pamphlet in English, entitled *Pre-destination,* came out.

In 1933 he published an English book about Bahaism entitled *History and Doctrines of the Babi Movement.*

In 1933 the English book *Selections from the Holy Quran* was published, in which verses from the Holy Quran have been arranged under nearly one hundred and twenty-five subject headings. The second book in this series, entitled *Collection and Arrange-*

ment of the Holy Quran, was published in 1934, dealing with the collection, order and subject arrangement of the Holy Quran.

In April 1935 the *Jama'at* in Java published the Dutch translation of the Holy Quran, which was done from the English translation. Earlier they had translated *The Teachings of Islam, Muhammad the Prophet* and many other pamphlets and books into Dutch.

In November 1934 an Urdu booklet was published entitled *Maghrib main Tabligh Islam ya Islam ka Daur-i Jadid* ('Propagation of Islam in the West or the new era of Islam'), in which the need and importance of the propagation of Islam in the West was stressed and it was explained that Hazrat Mirza Ghulam Ahmad was the first to think of this and it was being done practically by the Lahore Ahmadiyya *Jama'at.* The Promised Messiah's claim and the beliefs and works of the *Jama'at* are also discussed in it.

In 1934 and 1935 some Urdu tracts were written addressing the general body of the Muslims such as *Ek Dardmandana Guzarish* ('A heart-felt plea'), *Taswir ka Doosra Rukh* ('The other side of the picture') and *Hamaray Aqa'id aur Hamaray Kam* ('Our beliefs and our works').

In 1936 the English book *Introduction to the Study of the Holy Quran* was published, discussing the arrangement of the Holy Quran, its essential teachings, histories of the prophets as related in the Quran, and answering some criticism about the Holy Quran.

In 1937 the English book *Founder of the Ahmadiyya Movement* was published. This is a brief biography of Hazrat Mirza Ghulam Ahmad, dealing with his life, claims, beliefs and achievements.

In 1937 a small English booklet entitled *The Ahmadiyya Movement as the West Sees It* was published, being a compilation of the views of Western orientalists and Christian writers about the Lahore Ahmadiyya *Jama'at* as expressed in their books and journals, with some comments upon these views.

In addition to the books and booklets mentioned above, Mau-lana Muhammad Ali also wrote many other pamphlets dealing with the then-current issues. In 1924 two tracts were published on the question of Apostasy in Urdu whose titles mean 'Punishment for an apostate according to Islamic Shariah' and 'Is there any punishment for reverting to unbelief after accepting Islam?' In 1925 he wrote *Jihad, Saltanat-i Afghanistan aur Ahmadi Musal-man* ('Jihad, the government of Afghanistan and Ahmadi Mus-lims'). Two more pamphlets on the Finality of Prophethood were published, one in Urdu in 1926 entitled *Masih Mau'ud aur Khatm-i Nubuwwat* ('The Promised Messiah and the finality of prophethood') and one in English in 1930 entitled *The Finality of Prophethood*. Another tract in English entitled *The Prophet's Message* was also published in 1930. The same year the English pamphlet *The Alleged Atrocities of the Prophet* was published refu-ting accusations of alleged cruelties by the Holy Prophet. In 1932, in answer to *Muwaddat Nama* by Maulana Sanaullah of Amritsar, *Jawab Mawaddat Nama* was published.

During these years the leaders of the Untouchables of India announced their growing disillusionment with the Hindu religion. This was a golden opportunity for the Muslims to convert some eighty million Untouchables to Islam. As will be mentioned later, the Ahmadiyya Anjuman Isha'at Islam undertook this work within its limited resources and achieved much success. But regrettably the large, main Muslim organizations and their leaders paid no attention to this work, and this most valuable opportunity was lost to the Muslims of India. In this connection Maulana Muhammad Ali wrote the following pamphlets to draw the attention of the Muslims towards this issue (the first is in Urdu and the remaining three in English):

1. *Achhutun ki Mushkilat ka Hal Sirf Islam main hai* ('Solution of the problems of the Untouchables is only in Islam').
2. Islam's Great Opportunity.
3. Islamic Brotherhood and the Harigans.
4. Depressed Classes and the Poona Mission.

Various other pamphlets he wrote during these years are as follows. (Except for those indicated as English, all are in Urdu.)

1. *Jama'at Qadian ki Tabdili 'Aqida* ('Change in belief of the Qadiani *Jama'at* ').
2. *Kya Hazrat Mirza sahib nay Nubuwwat ka Da'wa Kiya?* ('Did Hazrat Mirza sahib claim prophethood?').
3. *Ahmadiyya Jama'at Lahore kay 'Aqa'id* ('Beliefs of the Lahore Ahmadiyya *Jama'at*').
4. *Sir Muhammad Iqbal's Statement re the Qadianis* (English).
5. *Maulana Abul Kalam Azad and the Ahmadiyya Movement* (English).
6. *Mr. Pickthall on the Revival of Islam* (English).
7. *Jama'at ko Mujahida ki Da'wat* ('Our *Jama'at* exhorted to undertake spiritual struggle').
8. *Qadiani Jama'at aur Kalima Go'un ki Takfir* ('The Qadiani *Jama'at* and declaring Muslims as *kafir*').
9. *Musulmanun ki Takfir ka Nateeja* ('Consequences of declaring Muslims as *kafir*').
10. *Anjuman Himayat-i Islam ka I'lan* ('Announcement by the Anjuman Himayat-i Islam').
11. *Jama'at Ahmadiyya Lahore aur Jama'at Qadian per Ayk Nazar* ('Brief comparison of the Lahore Ahmadiyya *Jama'at* and the Qadiani *Jama'at*').
12. *Mian Mahmud Ahmad per un kay Murideen kay Ilzamat aur Bariyyat ka Nirala Tareeq* ('Allegations against Mirza Mahmud Ahmad by his followers and his novel technique of exoneration').
13. *Ahbab Qadian say Ayk Appeal* ('An appeal to Qadiani friends').

Quran teaching (*Dars-i Quran*)

In 1914, immediately upon his arrival in Lahore, Maulana Muhammad Ali had instituted the daily teaching of the Holy Quran. He continued this till 1930. While on the one hand he was anxious about the propagation of the Quran in the whole world, on the other he wanted to infuse the desire to study and learn the Quran in the members of the *Jama'at*. Accordingly, his writings and sermons, from the beginning to the end, show his fervour and heart-felt desire for this.

As has been mentioned before, not only did he give daily teaching in the Holy Quran himself, but he also adopted different ways of doing it. During 1924–1925 the teaching was delivered by holding a *Ta'lim-ul-Quran* class in which the whole Quran was covered in six months. In 1925 and 1926 during the month of Ramadan (March and April) he covered one part of the Holy Quran daily, and for this *dars* he especially invited those people from the outside branches who could stay in Lahore for the entire month and attend the classes. In 1930 he added a new style of teaching, twice a week, by selecting various subjects and discussing all the verses of the Quran bearing upon each such topic. This was in addition to the daily *dars* of the Holy Quran. From 1930 onwards Dr. Basharat Ahmad was in Lahore and took over the daily sessions at the Ahmadiyya Buildings mosque. He was a unique lover of the Holy Quran; expounding the meanings of the Quran was such a distinctive feature of his life that wherever he was stationed in the course of his employment he always instituted *dars* of the Quran. God had bestowed upon him a profound understanding of the Holy Quran and his style of delivery was so appealing that people felt drawn to attend. Many young people not particularly interested in religion, as well as other persons, were captivated after attending just one session.

In March 1932, in order to infuse enthusiasm among the younger generation for the study of Islam, Maulana Muhammad Ali started quarterly examinations. The curriculum was based on the Quran, Hadith and books of the Promised Messiah. These examinations were held from time to time and continued till 1947.

Stay in Dalhousie

As has been mentioned before, from 1922 Maulana Muhammad Ali started going to Dalhousie for the summer, where he found solitude and was able to concentrate. In the beginning he used to stay in the residence known as 'Mall House' in the lower part of Dalhousie near the post office. From 1925 he started to reside in a house called 'Peterborough' on Bakrota Hill, which was situated at a secluded spot reached after much climbing. Bakrota was very sparsely populated but had the advantage that there was a level, circular road going around it which was two and a half miles long. Maulana Muhammad Ali was always in the habit of taking a morning walk, and here in the hills he went for a walk before *maghrib* prayer also. This road around Bakrota became the walk for him and the other members who went to stay in Dalhousie.

In 1930 he bought a plot of land a little further along in upper Bakrota at a very low price. At that time this was a deserted place with only one or two houses nearby. That year he sold some of his ancestral land in the village of Murar to his nephews and built his own residence in Dalhousie which he named *Darus Salam*. From 1931 to 1947 he spent every summer in this house and completed many of his books here.

In 1930 his father-in-law Dr. Basharat Ahmad retired and moved to Lahore in order to devote the rest of his life to the service of the religion. In the summer he too used to go to Dalhousie. On the advice of Maulana Muhammad Ali, he bought a plot of land adjacent to the Maulana's with his pension fund and built a small house there in 1932. That year, on 4 June 1932, Dr. Basharat Ahmad's wife, the mother-in-law of Maulana Muhammad Ali, died of pneumonia in Dalhousie. For her burial they both went to Lahore for two or three days. As Maulana Muhammad Ali had a great interest in, as well as experience of, having buildings constructed, he had the house built for the Doctor sahib under his own supervision with special attention. From then on, the Doctor sahib spent every summer in that house and that is where he wrote his well-known books *Anwar-ul-Quran*, parts one and two, and *Mujaddid-i Azam*. In Dalhousie Dr. Basharat Ahmad started giving daily talks on the Holy Quran which were attended by members of his family and some neighbours. Later on when Shaikh Maula Bakhsh of Lyallpur also had a residence built in upper Bakrota, the *dars* of the Holy Quran was conducted at his house in the evening.

During his stay in Dalhousie the *azan* was called out for the five daily prayers and the prayers held in congregation. Any members of the *Jama'at* or other guests staying, and the whole family, used to join in the prayers. Even if no one else was present, just Maulana Muhammad Ali and Maulvi Abdul Wahhab (who was for a long time his personal assistant) prayed together as a congregation. There was always a bigger gathering for Friday prayers because many friends who resided some distance away would also attend. As mentioned earlier, the Dalhousie hill resort was not busy and crowded like Simla or Murree Hills; and Bakrota, where Maulana Muhammad Ali and Dr. Basharat Ahmad had their residences, was sparsely populated and located quite far from and at a greater height than main Dalhousie, so the distances to be travelled were greater.

From Dalhousie Maulana Muhammad Ali regularly wrote articles in a series under the title *Baradaran-i Jama'at kay Naam Khatut* (Letters to the brethren of the *Jama'at*), which acted as a substitute for his Friday sermons in Lahore. These articles contained that same strong passion for the propagation of Islam and spreading the Quran in the world which was generally the topic for his Friday sermons. Some of these letters were specially addressed to certain persons who had become discontented with the *Jama'at* due to personal grievances and disputes.

Muslim High School buildings at Lahore and Baddomalhi

It was decided in 1924 that the Muslim High School, which was located in a rented house in McLeod Road, Lahore, should have its own premises built in Ahmadiyya Buildings. The construction was started in December 1924. At that time the Berlin Mosque was also being built, so Maulana Muhammad Ali made special appeals and toured different places to raise funds for both constructions. Appeals were made particularly during the annual gathering of 1924, in which he asked members to donate five days' earnings for this purpose. During the construction of this building Maulana Muhammad Ali and some of his friends personally supervised the work. On 15 February 1925 Maulana Muhammad Ali laid the commemorative stone and in June 1925 the school was moved into this new building. Earlier, in 1918, the Anjuman had also inaugurated a school in Baddomalhi, the building for which was erected by the determination and efforts of Chaudhry Ghulam Haidar and Chaudhry Sarfraz Khan.

Death of Shaikh Rahmatullah

In March 1924 the death took place of Shaikh Rahmatullah, a pillar of the Ahmadiyya Community since the early days of the Promised Messiah (*The Islamic Review,* April-May 1924, p. 130; see also *Paigham Sulh,* 12 March 1924, p. 5). When Hazrat Mirza sahib established the Sadr Anjuman Ahmadiyya Qadian, he was appointed as one of its fourteen members, and was a most devoted, sincere and active member. He had a business in Lahore and had been bestowed by Almighty God with much wealth which he spent profusely for the service of Islam. He frequently visited Qadian to be in the company of the Promised Messiah and later Maulana Nur-ud-Din. After the Split, he became one of the founders of the Ahmadiyya Anjuman Isha'at Islam Lahore. These five senior figures, namely, Maulana Muhammad Ali, Khwaja Kamal-ud-Din, Shaikh Rahmatullah, Dr. Mirza Yaqub Baig and Dr. Syed Muhammad Husain Shah were bound together by the closest ties of deep love and friendship. In Qadian Maulana Muhammad Ali was the moving spirit behind the Sadr Anjuman Ahmadiyya while these four were his best helpers and counsellors. After the establishment of the Anjuman in Lahore these five were the mainstay of the *Jama'at*. Shaikh Rahmatullah was the first of them to meet his Maker, having faithfully discharged his compact and duty.

Death of Syed Muhammad Ahsan of Amroha

On 15 July 1926, another very senior figure in the Movement, Syed Muhammad Ahsan of Amroha, died. He was among the earliest followers of the Promised Messiah and was highly respected by Hazrat Mirza sahib. He was a recognised, leading authority on the Holy Quran and Hadith, and was the right hand man of the ruler of Bhopal, the Nawab Siddiq Hasan Khan. After accepting the Promised Messiah he left his high post and came to live in Qadian in a small room near Hazrat Mirza sahib merely for the sake of the Divine cause. Hazrat Mirza sahib received the following Divine revelation about his sincerity and sacrifice:

> *In praise of Muhammad Ahsan, I see him giving up his livelihood for my sake.*

After the death of the Promised Messiah, he went back to live in his native place Amroha. Right from the beginning he had a very high opinion of Maulana Muhammad Ali. In a letter to him dated 5 February 1910 he writes:

> "No one else in the *Jama'at* has the virtues that you possess. I do not say this out of flattery but out of my faith and belief. I regard a flatterer as a hypocrite, in fact as a cursed one." (*Paigham Sulh*, 7 April 1914)

He was in Qadian at the time of the death of Maulana Nur-ud-Din and it was he who proposed the name of Mirza Mahmud Ahmad as the new head at the gathering in the Nur Mosque. However, as he later explained, he was unaware that Mirza Mahmud Ahmad held such dangerous beliefs as he was out of touch with the situation in Qadian, living in Amroha. In his announcement of 24 December 1916 he writes:

> "All of you are aware that at the beginning of 1914, upon the death of Hazrat Maulana Nur-ud-Din sahib, a difference arose in our community. So at that time, in order to preserve unity, I considered it advisable that all of us should take the pledge at the hand of Mirza Mahmud Ahmad sahib. I did not know then that his beliefs had undergone corruption."

Later on, the Lahore members drew his attention to the wrong doctrines being promulgated by Mirza Mahmud Ahmad, and they quoted from Syed Muhammad Ahsan's own writings to show that his beliefs on prophethood accorded with the Lahore *Jama'at* and not with the views of Mirza Mahmud Ahmad. Upon this, the Qadiani *Jama'at* leadership wrote to Syed Muhammad Ahsan asking him to change his beliefs. He then undertook a visit to Qadian to try personally to bring about reform but was disillusioned. As a result he made the announcement referred to above in which he declared:

> "Bearing in mind that I have to please Allah the Most High, and fearing that I am answerable to Him, I declare that *sahibzada* Mirza Mahmud Ahmad, because of his insistence on his wrong beliefs, is no longer considered by me to be fit to be the *khalifa* or head of the *Jama'at* of the Promised Messiah. Therefore I remove him from this *khilafat,* which is not a political office but an optional one, and thereby absolve myself before Allah and the people of the responsibility which was upon my shoulders.
>
> "I inform the Ahmadiyya *Jama'at* that the beliefs of Mirza Mahmud Ahmad, namely, that:

1. All other Muslims, even though they face the *Qibla* and recite the *Kalima,* are *kafir* and excluded from Islam;

2. The Promised Messiah is a full and real prophet, not a partial prophet which is a *muhaddas;*

3. The prophecy in the words of the Quran "his name being Ahmad" applies to Hazrat Mirza sahib and not to the Holy Prophet Muhammad;

   — these doctrines are a source of a dangerous disruption in Islam, and it is the prime duty of every Ahmadi to stand up to refute them."

At the same time he wrote two comprehensive books entitled *Ismu-hu Ahmad* ('His name being Ahmad') and *Khatam-un-nabiyyin* ('Last of the Prophets'). Due to old age and ill health he remained in Amroha but attended the annual gatherings of the Anjuman in Lahore. He breathed his last at the age of more than ninety years.

Missionary work in India

Although the main object of the *Jama'at* was the propagation of Islam to the West, yet it also paid attention to preaching in the Indian subcontinent itself. When in 1920 or thereabouts the Arya Samaj Hindus launched a vigorous campaign of *shuddi* or returning Muslims back to the Hindu faith, the Anjuman did an enormous amount of work in combating this anti-Islamic movement. Missionaries were sent everywhere as required and branches were set up in many places to continue this work. Later on when the Hindu campaign petered out and also the Anjuman was facing financial problems, these activities were reduced. In 1926 the Anjuman decided to propagate the message of Islam among the Untouchable communities of India. Accordingly this work was started in many districts and hundreds of Untouchables were converted to Islam. Maulana Muhammad Ali appealed to the *Jama'at* for all members to donate one-sixth of their monthly incomes for this cause. Thus for years missionaries of the Anjuman gave lectures before huge gatherings in refutation of the Ayra Samaj and put them to rout in momentous public debates. There were in particular two such prominent missionaries of the Anjuman whose fame spread far and wide in India: Maulana Abdul Haq Vidyarthi and Maulana Ismatullah. In addition, Shaikh Muhammad Yusuf Garanthi and Mirza Muzaffar Baig also rendered very valuable services. These Ahmadi missionaries were so triumphant in argument that the Arya Samajists began to dread holding debates with them. Similarly, the missionaries of this *Jama'at* battled with conspicuous success against Christian missionaries for many years until the latter stopped holding debates with them after receiving confidential instructions from their superior officials that they must cease debating with the Ahmadis or preaching to them.

Organizational tours and other travels, 1924 to 1937

Taking time out from his literary activities, Maulana Muhammad Ali used to visit various branches of the *Jama'at* every year, as far as possible. He would visit many of the branches on the occasion of their annual meetings. This practice he continued all during these years. He would also be invited to meetings of the Anjuman Islamia (a general Muslim body) in many places, which he would attend and in his speeches draw the attention of non-Ahmadi Muslims towards the magnificent work that was the goal of the Ahmadiyya Movement and his own goal, namely, the propagation of Islam and dissemination of the Holy Quran in the whole world, especially among the Western nations.

In November 1924, accompanied by Khwaja Kamal-ud-Din and Dr. Mirza Yaqub Baig, he went to Aligarh, travelling through Delhi, and reached there on 21 November. There he and the Khwaja sahib gave several lectures in the Muslim University. In those days the solid work done by this *Jama'at* and the invaluable writings of Maulana Muhammad Ali had created a highly favourable impression among the educated sections of the general Muslim public. Sahibzada Aftab Ahmad Khan, who was then the Vice-Chancellor of the University, expressed great appreciation of these achievements during the course of these lectures, especially the English translation of the Holy Quran. In his speech introducing the speakers he mentioned that during his stay in England he once had occasion to meet some Egyptian Muslim dignitaries who told him that although Arabic was their mother tongue but it was through the English translation of Maulana Muhammad Ali that they had learnt the meanings of the Quran. He also mentioned some other famous public figures who had benefitted from this translation.

In 1929 Maulana Muhammad Ali undertook a major trip to Mangrol, a small state in Kathiawar. He went there on 20 February, accompanied by Maulvi Ismatullah, Maulvi Sadr-ud-Din and Shaikh Muhammad Yusuf Garanthi. The Nawab of this state, Shaikh Muhammad Jahangir Mian, was a great admirer of Maulana Muhammad Ali and the work of the Anjuman, and from time to time he made financial donations to the Anjuman. Maulana Muhammad Ali stayed in Mangrol till 1st March. He delivered a lecture in a public meeting, and spent much of the time in discussion with the Nawab and his officials.

During the winters of 1931 and 1932, Maulana Muhammad Ali could not go out much to visit other branches in person due to ill health. So he deputed Dr. Basharat Ahmad and Mian Ghulam Rasul who made tours of different branches for organisational purposes. In 1933 also he was indisposed for a long time, suffering from eczema.

In 1934 Maulana Muhammad Ali was again able to tour several cities in the Punjab, and he also went to Peshawar where he delivered a speech to the students of Islamia College, Peshawar.

From 1935 onwards he reduced his tours of the branches of the *Jama'at,* both due to a decline in his health and a great increase in his writing work and other engagements.

In December 1937 he had occasion to go to Qadian. He had been called to Batala as a defence witness in connection with a court case against a Qadiani, Shaikh Abdur Rahman, which had been brought because he had written in a pamphlet that Guru Nanak was a Muslim. Maulana Muhammad Ali went to Batala by car, accompanied by Dr. Syed Muhammad Husain Shah and Babu Manzur Ilahi. After he had testified in court, they went to Qadian and offered a prayer at the grave of the Promised Messiah, returning in the evening.

Arrival of Lord Headley in India, December 1927

Among the British people who had accepted Islam within a short period after the establishment of the Woking Muslim Mission by Khwaja Kamal-ud-Din, the most prominent man was Lord Headley. His conversion became much talked about both in Britain and India and proved a great help to the cause of propagation of Islam, bringing further successes to Khwaja Kamal-ud-Din's mission. In December 1927, Khwaja Kamal-ud-Din and Lord Headley came together on a tour of India from England. The annual gathering of the Lahore Ahmadiyya *Jama'at* that year was delayed by a few days and held from 28th to 30th December to enable Lord Headley to attend it. He presided over the first session. On 28 December 1927 when Lord Headley and the Khwaja sahib arrived in Lahore, they were given a grand recaption at the railway station where not only Maulana Muhammad Ali and members of the Lahore Ahmadiyya Community but also thousands of other Muslims of Lahore were present. Lord Headley, the Khwaja sahib and Maulana Muhammad Ali were driven in a car around the city in a huge procession. On the way the procession halted at various places and Lord Headley addressed the crowds briefly. The first session was held at the grounds of Islamia College where Maulana Muhammad Ali presented an address to Lord Headley. Also present in that session, and delivering speeches during it, were Sir Muhammad Shafi, Dr. Sir Muhammad Iqbal and Maulana Zafar Ali Khan. After staying in Lahore for a few more days Lord Headley, in the company of Khwaja Kamal-ud-Din, toured other cities of the Punjab as well as India generally before he returned to England.

Construction of the Berlin Mosque and translation of the Holy Quran into German

As mentioned before, the construction of the mosque in Berlin had started. The original estimate of the cost was between Rs. 50,000 and 60,000 but due to certain circumstances this subsequently increased to almost Rs. 100,000. When, by the end of 1924, the minarets of the mosque had not been constructed, Maulana Muhammad Ali wrote to Maulana Sadr-ud-Din to postpone the construction of the minarets. Raising of funds for the Berlin Mosque had been going on for quite sometime at the special appeals of Maulana Muhammad Ali. During the annual gathering of 1924 also, funds were raised for this purpose. On 27 December, the third day of the gathering, Maulana Muhammad Ali made a speech to the ladies section, mentioning that work on construction of the minarets had been halted (see *Paigham Sulh,* 31 December 1924, p. 4). He appealed to the women in the following words:

> "Perhaps many of the sisters in our *Jama'at* may think that because their husbands, fathers or elders take part in services to the religion, this is enough for them as well. But this view is not right. Just as the virtuous deeds of the husband are not credited by Allah to the wife, similarly his giving to charitable causes would not be considered as that of the wife. Where the Holy Quran mentions men who spend in the way of Allah, it also mentions *muta-saddiqat* or women who spend in the way of Allah. So just as Allah has made it a duty for men to serve the faith, He has also imposed this duty on women. The women of our *Jama'at* must bear in mind that no matter how much their husbands serve the religion if they themselves do not take part in service of the faith then they are as deprived of participating in that noble work as any other woman..." (*Paigham Sulh,* 18 January 1925)

In response to this appeal a most inspiring scene was beheld: the women responded so generously that they took off their jewellery and donated it for the propagation of Islam. At the main gathering the men provided enough further funds to reach the required amount for the completion of the construction. The opening ceremony of the mosque took place on *Eid* day in April 1925, and in May Maulana Sadr-ud-Din returned from Germany.

In 1928, at the suggestion of a member of the *Jama'at* Malik Ghulam Muhammad, it was proposed that the Holy Quran be translated into the German language. On 13 March 1928 the following appeal for funds by Maulana Muhammad Ali appeared in *Paigham Sulh*:

> "I am fully aware that this small *Jama'at* is already bearing a heavy burden. But I believe that the help of

Allah comes only to those who work in His way. So I am pleased that, after a suggestion from an honourable friend of ours, the plan for the German translation of the Holy Quran has been put forward. The opening of the mission in Germany, the starting of a quarterly magazine, and then the completion of the mosque at a cost of a hundred thousand Rupees, were all achieved by the grace of Allah. Our *Jama'at* took the first step and Allah opened many doors of His help. But it is obvious that whatever has been achieved is incomplete until we put before those people the translation of the Holy Quran in their own language."

With this appeal he started the fund-raising through his sermons and newspaper articles. The first announcement from the Anjuman about this translation appeared in *Paigham Sulh* in March 1928 in the following words:

> *German Translation of the Holy Quran*:
>
> The Ahmadiyya Anjuman Isha'at Islam Lahore has decided to translate the Holy Quran into the German language. The work will be done by two German converts to Islam, who know the German, English and Arabic languages, under the supervision of Maulana Sadr-ud-Din. It is a great opportunity for those Muslims who feel passionately about Islam to participate in this noble task. ...
>
> Muhammad Din Jan, Assistant Secretary, Ahmadiyya Anjuman Isha'at Islam Lahore.
>
> (*Paigham Sulh,* 30 March 1928)

But due to some unavoidable circumstances this translation could not be started. Then in February 1932 a Doctor Mansur who had lived in Germany for a long time came to Lahore and the work of translation started under the supervision of Maulana Sadr-ud-Din.

From May 1925, after the return of Maulana Sadr-ud-Din from Germany, one Fazal Karim Khan Durrani was in charge of the mission for three years. Previously he had been sent to Trinidad as missionary by the Anjuman, but as his attitude there was not satisfactory he had been dismissed. Afterwards, at his own request, the Anjuman employed him again as missionary and sent him to Berlin. During his stay there he again acted inappropriately, spending large sums of money on the construction of the mosque without the Anjuman's permission and running the mosque into debt. So in March 1928 the Anjuman sent Dr. Muhammad Abdullah to Berlin to take charge from him. At that time the Anjuman was faced with many financial problems. The debt of the Berlin mosque and its expenses amounted to twenty thousand Marks. Maulana Muhammad Ali made repeated appeals for this and finally the money owed was cleared in November 1932, releasing the mosque from debt.

Coming of Baron Umar Ehrenfels to India

On the occasion of the annual gathering of the Anjuman in December 1932, an Austrian convert to Islam, belonging to the aristocracy, Baron Umar Rolf Ehrenfels, came to India from Berlin in the company of Dr. Abdullah. He was given a grand reception at the Lahore Railway station on 24 December. Besides Maulana Muhammad Ali and other prominent Ahmadis, a large number of leading Muslims from outside the Movement were present at the station, including Sir Abdul Qadir, Nawab Mamdot and Maulana Ghulam Muhy-ud-Din Qasoori. From the station the Baron was brought in a procession to Ahmadiyya Buildings where Nawab Mamdot presided over the first session of the annual gathering of the Anjuman. After the recitation of the Holy Quran the session was inaugurated by Abul Asar Hafiz Jalandhary by reciting his poem which he had written upon the acceptance of Islam by Baron Umar (*Paigham Sulh,* 7 January 1933). During his stay in Lahore, Baron Umar was invited by various associations, societies and dignitaries of Lahore and he made many speeches. Later on both he and Dr. Abdullah toured the country. In May 1933 Baron Umar went back to Vienna (Austria), and for a time he was in charge of a mission which the Anjuman opened there.

Java mission

This mission was opened in 1924. At that time Java, Sumatra, etc. were being ruled by Holland and were known as the Dutch East Indies. The Muslims there were in a state of the utmost destitution and backwardness. The Anjuman sent three men, Maulana Ahmad, Hafiz Muhammad Hasan Cheema and Mirza Wali Ahmad Baig, to that country. Due to certain reasons the Hafiz sahib stopped in Singapore. Maulana Ahmad was taken ill after arriving in Java and had to return to India after four months. This left Mirza Wali Ahmad Baig there by himself, facing many problems such as being a stranger in the country and not knowing its language. However, he persevered in his activities and over a period of fourteen years he brought about a transformation in the religious situation. Muslims rose out of their slump and despondency and were able to counter the attacks of the Christian missionaries. The Ahmadiyya Movement expanded in large numbers, the Holy Quran and other essential literature was translated into Dutch, and a strong, magnificent *Jama'at* was established.

Mirza Wali Ahmad Baig returned to Lahore from Java after fourteen years, on 16 December 1937. Maulana Muhammad Ali paid him the following tribute in his Friday *khutba* on 17 December, published in *Paigham Sulh,* 22 December 1937:

> "It is by the grace of God that even in this day the spiritual power of the Promised Messiah has produced such persons who follow the path of the Companions of the Holy Prophet in their exertions and in their humbleness. ... If I had to give an example of hard work and humbleness from our *Jama'at* I would name the man who arrived here last evening — Mirza Wali Ahmad Baig."

He then went on to mention Mirza Wali Ahmad Baig's achievements, how in a vast country of fifty-five million people, an awakening took place creating a defence to counteract the Christian missionary activity against Islam. Fourteen years earlier when Mirza Wali Ahmad Baig was leaving along with another missionary he was asked in his farewell meeting to make a speech. He only said: "What can I say at this time? If I am able to achieve something then I will speak about it on my return". In those fourteen years he had done unparalleled work. A strong *Jama'at* had been created, Islamic literature had been spread in the country, all our important books had been translated in Dutch, and now this embodiment of humility and modesty had returned. He had gone in his youth and returned aged and ill, but still he had no complaint or grumble.

Then Maulana Muhammad Ali urged the missionaries and the *Jama'at* to produce such exemplary workers who can go on working tirelessly and still think that they had done little. He added:

> "How many of us are working for our cause? A part of the *Jama'at* is idle, not realising that there is so much work yet to be done. How many of us realise the importance of this work, and the greatness of our goal, that we have to spread Islam in the world. To spread Islam is no easy task. It is to continue the work of the Holy Prophet Muhammad as his successors. When you join this *Jama'at,* do not keep on thinking of worldly allure, thinking of how you could have achieved much success in the world if you had not come here, because there is no way here of achieving worldly gains."

Purchase of land in Okara

In 1930 an important addition was made to the properties of the Anjuman by purchasing forty one 'squares' (1025 acres) of canal-irrigated land near Okara. Maulana Muhammad Ali was always considering ways to improve the Anjuman's financial position and create permanent sources of income. It was due to his personal efforts and relations with government officials that the Anjuman was able to acquire such valuable land. A few years later land was also purchased in the Sindh and Karachi. History bears witness that these lands were a source of the greatest financial strength for the Anjuman. In the annual gathering of December 1930 Maulana Muhammad Ali appealed for funds to meet the expenses of these lands and asked every member to contribute ten days' income. He had lists of names of members prepared and assigned contributions to the names. The members contributed the amounts assigned to them and thus was this task accomplished.

Maulana Aziz Bakhsh

It has been mentioned that Maulana Aziz Bakhsh and Maulana Muhammad Ali went to school together and till 1897 they lived together in Lahore. Afterwards Maulana Muhammad Ali went to Qadian and Maulana Aziz Bakhsh joined government service and went to Dera Ghazi Khan, Jhang and Amritsar in the course of his employment. In 1930 Maulana Aziz Bakhsh retired and took a half of his pension fund as a lump sum with the intention of developing his land in his ancestral village of Murar and settling there. However, when Maulana Muhammad Ali drew his attention to doing religious work, he agreed without hesitation and came to settle in Ahmadiyya Buildings, Lahore. From then on he worked in various capacities in the Anjuman and had the distinction of regularly leading the five daily congregational prayers in the Ahmadiya Buildings mosque.

Founding of the Woking Muslim Mission and Literary Trust

Up to the end of 1929, the affairs of the Woking Muslim Mission had been under the control of the Ahmadiyya Anjuman Isha'at Islam Lahore. After that the mission began to operate as an independent Trust. A summary of these circumstances was publi-shed by Maulana Muhammad Ali in the issue of *Paigham Sulh* for 27 January 1931 under the title *Woking Mission aur Anjuman kay Ta'allaqat* ('The relationship between the Woking Mission and the Anjuman'), some extracts from which are given below:

> "At the end of 1929 the connection between the Woking Mission and the Anjuman was severed. The view of the Khwaja [Kamal-ud-Din] sahib was that the mission should be managed by an independent committee having no connection with the Anjuman but the Anjuman believed that some connection must be maintained because the Anjuman, acting as a body, had made such great financial sacrifices for the mission which no other organisation could possibly have done. For more or less ten years the affairs of the mission were in the hands of the Anjuman, and although during this period there had been differ-ences of opinion on some matters between the Khwaja sahib and the Anjuman it did not harm the work in any way. Finally, in December 1928, to settle the differences the Khwaja sahib gave it in writing to the Anjuman that in future he would abide by all the decisions of the

Anjuman. For these reasons the Anjuman did not want to sever its link with the mission, though it agreed that other people interested in the propagation of Islam can be included in the administration of the mission. When the affairs of the mission were in the hands of the Anjuman, the Khwaja sahib toured Africa and collected about Rs. 40,000, with which he set up a separate Literary Trust. In April 1929, he thought of amalgamating the Woking Muslim Mission and the Literary Trust, creating a body having eight trustees from the Anjuman and four non-Ahmadi trustees. He believed that by including non-Ahmadis the prospects of continued monetary help from various Muslim states in India would be better. I supported this proposal but it had to be approved by the General Council of the Anjuman. In October the General Council decided not to approve it, but after some discussion it imposed the condition that the eight Ahmadi trustees would be appointed by the Anjuman and regarded as its representatives, and the rest of the proposal would be accepted as it was. The Khwaja sahib did not agree with this. During the annual gathering of 1929 the matter was again put forward twice. The first time the General Council insisted that they would abide by the Khwaja sahib's writing of December 1928 according to which the mission was to be handed back to the Anjuman. But on further urging by the Khwaja sahib, and after reading his statement published in the *Madinah* newspaper, it was decided that the Khwaja sahib would be given freedom to proceed as he wishes. The decision was as follows:

> 'As the Khwaja sahib has not accepted this Council's decision of 28 October 1929, and has written that if his own proposals are not accepted he will arrange to run the mission on his own responsibility, and the Council cannot accept his proposals as this will lead to further disagreements, therefore to put an end to all such disputes this Council allows the Khwaja sahib to manage the affairs of the mission as he thinks fit.' ..."

On this the Khwaja sahib amalgamated the Mission and the Literary Trust and appointed some trustees including some

Ahmadis among them but they were not representatives of the Anjuman.

This did not mean that relations between the Woking Mission and the Anjuman were severed. Even after this, the Anjuman continued to supply the Woking Muslim Mission with missionaries to run the work of the mission, and the literature published by the Anjuman kept on being distributed from the mission. Also, at times of financial difficulty for the mission the Anjuman raised funds for it through special appeals. As will be seen later, the mission was again brought under the charge of the Anjuman in 1948.

Death of Khwaja Kamal-ud-Din

On 28 December 1932 Khwaja Kamal-ud-Din died in Lahore. The Khwaja sahib was born in 1870. He passed his law examination in 1897 and practised as a lawyer in Peshawar till 1903. He had already taken the *bai'at* at the hand of the Promised Messiah in 1893, and had met Maulana Muhammad Ali while serving in Islamia College, Lahore. It has been mentioned before that the Khwaja sahib represented Hazrat Mirza Ghulam Ahmad in several of his court cases, so much so that on one occasion he gave up his flourishing practice and left his family in circumstances of much hardship in Peshawar to go and serve the Promised Messiah. It was due to the spiritual nurture he received from Hazrat Mirza sahib that he was charged with the passion and zeal to propagate Islam in Europe. In 1903 he came to live in Lahore where Dr. Mirza Yaqub Baig, Dr. Syed Muhammad Husain Shah and Shaikh Rahmatullah also resided. These four servants of the Promised Messiah were among the fourteen members of the Sadr Anjuman Ahmadiyya, Qadian. From 1904 to 1911 the Khwaja sahib toured various cities in India giving lectures whose fame spread all over the country. According to a revelation of the Promised Messiah, God had blessed him with *husn-i bayan* or eloquence. His lectures used to be so captivating that the audience, whether Muslims or non-Muslims, would be entranced. In 1912 he went to England for the first time for the propagation of Islam where he founded the Woking Muslim Mission in 1913 and issued the magazine originally entitled *Muslim India and Islamic Review*. During the next few years he toured parts of Africa, Europe and India. He performed the pilgrimage to Makkah twice, first in October 1914 and the second time along with Lord Headley in July 1923.

Since 1928 he had not been keeping good health, and after four years of illness he died in Lahore in 1932. To do full justice to his services and achievements requires a book itself. He was, in fact, the founder of the propagation of Islam in England. Through him many native inhabitants of Britain accepted Islam including dignitaries such as Lord Headley, Sir Abdullah Archibald Hamilton, Sir Umar Hubert Rankin and Mr. Muhammad Marmaduke Pickthall etc.

In his Friday *khutba* on 30 December 1932 speaking of the Khwaja sahib's death, Maulana Muhammad Ali dwelt in detail on his magnificent services and the tremendous strength of his faith. Regarding his personal connection and friendship with Khwaja Kamal-ud-Din he said:

> "Those men whose names shine in heaven do not lose their radiance when they are buried under the earth. My personal connection with him went back a long way. I met him for the first time in 1894 when both of us were teaching at Islamia College, though he had taken his B.A. examination a year before me. He was the cause of my taking the *bai'at,* though I had known about Hazrat Mirza sahib previously and had loved him since that time and also used to affirm his claim. Right from the beginning when I read his book *Izala Auham,* I became convinced of the truth of the Promised Messiah. Both my brother Maulvi Aziz Bakhsh and I are witness to it because both of us were fellow students and shared the same thinking. The third witness was our revered father. However, it was this honoured friend of mine, of whom I am speaking now, who led me to take the *bai'at* of Hazrat Mirza sahib. He had already taken the *bai'at* and in 1897 it was he who took me to Qadian where I entered into the *bai'at.* I wish to declare the fact that the *bai'at* brought a great inner transformation in me. No doubt I used to say my prayers

regularly from childhood, and due to my father I was much under the influence of religion, but when I took the *bai'at* of the Promised Messiah I noticed a tremendous change within me from what I was like before. "He who does not thank people does not thank Allah": The Khwaja sahib was my guide in this respect. Had I remained as I was before, I would not have had the opportunity to serve the faith and would have been deprived of the light I received. So I think that my honoured friend played a major part in my receiving the spiritual good that I was blessed with. This happened in 1897. Since then we became even closer and by the grace of God this relationship was maintained till the end."

(*Paigham Sulh*, 27 January 1933, p. 2)

Conversion of Mr. Gauba to Islam

On 1 March 1933, Kanahya Lal Gauba, a barrister and eldest son of a prominent Hindu banker and businessman, Lala Harkishan Lal Gauba, accepted Islam along with his wife at the hand of Maulana Muhammad Ali and was given the Islamic name Khalid Latif Gauba. This ceremony, held at K.L. Gauba's residence, was also attended by leading non-Ahmadi Muslim figures of Lahore including Abdullah Yusuf Ali, Sir Muhammad Iqbal, Nawab Mamdot, Malik Feroz Khan Noon and Maulana Syed Mumtaz Ali (*Paigham Sulh,* 3 March 1933). In those days Baron Umar was also in Lahore during his tour of India. A group photograph was taken showing Mr. Khalid Latif Gauba and Baron Umar with senior members of the *Jama'at* (see page 240).

Opening of the Fiji Islands Muslim Mission

In April 1934 at the request of the Muslim inhabitants of these Islands the Anjuman opened a Muslim Mission in Fiji and Mirza Muzaffar Baig Sati was sent there. In these Islands both the Hindu Arya Samaj and the Christian missionaries were vigorously active and the Muslims were facing defeat and degradation in the religious arena. After the arrival of Mirza Muzaffar Baig Sati there was an entire transformation within a short time and everywhere both the Arya Samaj and the Christian missionaries began to be vanquished and defeated. Besides this, the Mirza sahib's efforts led to the formation of a very strong and active branch of this *Jama'at* and the educated Muslims of Fiji welcomed this Movement. The books written by Maulana Muhammad Ali spread there abundantly and were translated into the local languages.

Opposition to the Ahmadiyya Community in its homeland

Due to the influence of the narrow-minded and bigoted *Mullas,* some Muslims were always opposed to the Lahore Ahmadiyya *Jama'at,* and in particular there was much prejudice against it among the general Muslim public of the Punjab. Nonetheless the educated, reasonable and moderate people in the Punjab, as well as in India as a whole, viewed this *Jama'at* very favourably because of the services to the cause of Islam rendered by Maulana Muhammad Ali and the *Jama'at.* Maulana Muhammad Ali also had personal friendly relations with some high government officers, public figures and intellectuals among the Muslims of the Punjab, and these good relations never changed. These people often attended the meetings and special functions of the Anjuman and made financial donations for various projects. From time to time Maulana Muhammad Ali also participated in meetings of the Anjuman Himayat-i Islam and the Anjuman Islamia, delivering speeches in which he put forward to the general Muslim community the goal of the propagation of Islam. Besides Maulana Muhammad Ali, other leading figures of the *Jama'at,* such as Dr. Mirza Yaqub Baig and Dr. Syed Muhammad Husain Shah, were also greatly respected by the enlightened sections of the Muslim community for their high moral qualities and services to Islam.

In the beginning of 1932 some *Mullahs* along with some political and semi-religious political leaders started a campaign against the Ahmadiyya Movement. This campaign gained strength and a storm of abuse, false allegations and declarations of being *kafir* was raised against the Ahmadis. The malicious *Ahrar* political party came into being, and the strategy began to be employed of gaining popularity among the Muslim masses by opposing the Ahmadiyya Movement and denouncing Ahmadis as *kafir.* Most of the Lahore Muslim press also jumped on this bandwagon. Syed

Habib, editor of *Siyasat,* wrote a long series of articles against Hazrat Mirza sahib and the Ahmadiyya Movement.[2]

To counteract this hostile propaganda, Maulana Muhammad Ali wrote many pamphlets in Lahore and Dalhousie during 1932 and 1933, in which he clarified the beliefs of the *Jama'at* in detail for the benefit of the general Muslim public and drew their attention towards its works. However, where the motive is to win political popularity and the means used are to incite the religious passions of the uninformed public, no one listens to reason or uses their sense. Thus this storm of opposition continued and later on fizzled out in its own time. Its instigators, who strutted and swaggered arrogantly on the political and religious stage in the Punjab, met with extinction by themselves but they could do no harm to the Ahmadiyya *Jama'at* whose work continued to progress. There is no doubt that if Mirza Mahmud Ahmad and his community had let the Promised Messiah remain at his real and true status and not exaggerated his position, this wave of opposition would never have gained any strength and Ahmadiyyat would have made progress by leaps and bounds. However, it was Divinely ordained that a resemblance between the Israelite Messiah and the Promised Muslim Messiah be fulfilled in this respect also, that just as the extreme followers of Jesus raised him from the position of prophet to the status of the Son of God, so did the extreme followers of the Promised Messiah raise him from the position of *mujaddid* to the status of a prophet. It is obvious that both the groups went astray.

Death of Dr. Mirza Yaqub Baig

On 11 February 1936, Dr. Mirza Yaqub Baig died. He was born in 1872, and when he was just twenty years old and a student of the Medical College, Lahore, he took the *bai'at* of the Promised Messiah in 1892. He and his younger brother Ayub Baig were the first among young people to take the *bai'at* and they were deeply loved by the Promised Messiah because of their devoutness and

---

2. A comprehensive reply to those articles was written in *Paigham Sulh* by Maulana Dost Muhammad under the title *A'inah Ahmadiyyat,* and this was subsequently published in book form at the end of 1932.

religious virtues. When the Promised Messiah established the Sadr Anjuman Ahmadiyya Qadian in 1906 he appointed Dr. Mirza Yaqub Baig as one of its members. From 1897 he was in government service, first in Lahore and then elsewhere. In 1914 or 1915 when he was teaching in the Medical College, Lahore, he received orders transferring him away from Lahore to a very prestigious post. He resigned his job to remain in Lahore for the sake of the Anjuman and went into private medical practice. The Ahmadiyya Anjuman Isha'at Islam was created in a state of the utmost lack of means and the Doctor sahib was its first General Secretary. The offices of the Anjuman were in the beginning located in his property. Not only due to his medical skills but also because of his uprightness, saintliness, integrity, philanthropy and service of humanity he was a highly respected and distinguished public figure. The general non-Ahmadi Muslim associations, societies and bodies considered it a matter of honour and pride to have him as their member. Having been the first General Secretary of the Ahmadiyya Anjuman Isha'at Islam he later became its Vice-President. He was always in the forefront in participating in the work of the *Jama'at,* making the greatest financial sacrifices for the Anjuman. In 1920 when Maulana Muhammad Ali appealed to raise Rs. 100,000 for the Anjuman, Dr. Mirza Yaqub Baig donated those of his properties in which the Anjuman's offices were housed.

In Lahore, in addition to the work of the propagation of Islam, he took upon himself the duty of serving the elders of the *Jama'at.* Prior to this, he had served and treated the Promised Messiah devotedly during his final illness in Ahmadiyya Buildings, and that Divine elect breathed his last in his hands. When Maulana Nur-ud-Din, during his period of leadership of the Movement, had a fall while riding his horse Dr. Mirza Yaqub Baig kept on going to Qadian again and again to treat him, and when his final illness became prolonged he stayed in Qadian looking after him day and night. Likewise when Maulvi Abdul Karim, during the life of the Promised Messiah, developed a carbuncle, Dr. Mirza Yaqub Baig took leave from his job and came to stay in Qadian for his treatment. This devotion made a deep impression on the Promised Messiah. His sympathy and attention was, however, not only for great men but his kindness extended to the most ordinary and the poorest of people and patients, belonging to every creed, race and community.

His death was an incalculable loss to the *Jama'at* and a great shock to everyone. On that occasion Maulana Muhammad Ali, paying tribute to his qualities and services, said in his Friday *khutba* on 14 February:

> "Our connection went back a very long way. In the Anjuman of Qadian these five of us had a unique closeness. Three of us have already passed away: Shaikh Rahmatullah sahib, Khwaja Kamal-ud-Din sahib and Dr. Mirza sahib have faithfully completed their obligations. Two remain, who are waiting.[3] Allah will deal with them as He wills."

> (*Paigham Sulh,* 24 February 1936)

In an article in *Paigham Sulh* of 11 March 1936, he wrote:

> "A handful of men laid the foundations of a *Jama'at* in Lahore. But we had no building, no missionary, no office, and no money. ... The sacrifices that the late Hazrat Mirza [Yaqub Baig] sahib made in those days, it is entirely beyond my power to describe them; only Allah knows them, and we pray that He rewards him for them. ... The *Jama'at* was newly formed when he was transferred away from Lahore to be civil surgeon. ... He resigned from his job and fulfilled his pledge of giving priority to religion over worldly gain. The promise he had given at the hand of the man sent by God, he abided by that at the time of need. ... He donated his newly-built, valuable house for the offices of the Anjuman, and till today the offices are located in that building."

Appeal to make Wills

Among the major plans that Maulana Muhammad Ali put before the *Jama'at* to carry into action, one was the making of wills

---

3. Meaning Dr. Syed Muhammad Husain Shah and Maulana Muhammad Ali himself.

which he initiated at the annual gathering of 1936. He said that while we had embraced the Promised Messiah's *Al-Wasiyyat* in the ideological sense, we had paid little attention to putting it into practice. One objective of *Al-Wasiyyat* was that just as we spend some of our money in the service of the faith during our lifetime, similarly after our death some of our property and money should go to the same cause. The Promised Messiah's exhortation for making wills was not for the purpose of getting a plot in the *Bahishti Maqbara* of Qadian. To think in that way would be just to take his words literally. God's paradise is very extensive, and the Promised Messiah instructed in *Al-Wasiyyat* that to inherit that Garden one must continue the striving to serve the faith even after death. Maulana Muhammad Ali further said that the Holy Quran has made it obligatory for everyone leaving behind any money or property to make a bequest, and what is meant is a bequest for charitable and religious endowments, and not for near and dear ones. According to the Shariah, a maximum of one-third of one's wealth can be willed for such purposes. The Promised Messiah instructed that at least one tenth should be willed, and he expressed his desire that the funds so collected should be spent on the propagation of Islam and spreading translations of the Holy Quran in different languages of the world.

From 1936 onwards the campaign to urge the making of wills continued every year and members of the *Jama'at* took part in it. On the occasion of the silver jubilee of the Anjuman, a large part of the jubilee fund was raised by this means.

Some other events

On 10 February 1937 a deputation of the *Ulama* of Al-Azhar University of Cairo, Egypt, then touring India, was invited to Ahmadiyya Buildings by Maulana Muhammad Ali. He discussed with them in detail the claims of Hazrat Mirza Ghulam Ahmad, the death of Jesus, the teaching that a Muslim cannot be dubbed as a *kafir,* the concept of *jihad* etc., and answered their objections. He also explained in full the work being done by the Anjuman and presented to them some of the literature published. In March 1937, the Mufti of Islam of Poland also came to see Maulana Muhammad Ali.

Payment of royalty, 1924–1937

It has been mentioned before that Maulana Muhammad Ali, for five years after his migration from Qadian and the establishment of the Ahmadiyya Anjuman Isha'at Islam, in 1914, had taken no stipend or salary from the Anjuman nor any share of the sale price of his books. It was from July 1919 that it was decided by the Anjuman to pay him royalty on his books. Further events that took place in this connection until 1937 are as follows.

In May 1925 Khwaja Kamal-ud-Din, considering the rate of the royalty to be inadequate, presented the following proposal to the Anjuman about royalty and copyright:

> No. 115, dated 16 May 1925. The Khwaja sahib has made the following submission, arguing that the rate of royalty paid to Hazrat Amir (Head of the community) is far from adequate and should be increased. It is presented for the consideration of the meeting:
>
> To Mr. Secretary,
>
> *Assalamu alaikum wa rahmatullah*
>
> While going through the accounts of the Holy Quran I have discovered that Hazrat Amir is paid, as author's royalty, one-sixth of the sale price of the Holy Quran and other books written by him. I cannot understand on what basis this sum was approved. If I were to take royalty for my own writings I would not be satisfied even with one-third, despite the fact that my scholarship bears no comparison with that of Hazrat Amir. Also considering that the Anjuman is making such large profits on his books, I believe that he should be paid at least one-third, and the loss he has suffered throughout this period should be compensated at least for the last two years. Kindly place this proposal on the agenda as soon as possible for the approval of the Management Committee. I also suggest that when this matter is submitted to the Management Committee, Hazrat Amir should not express any opinion and the Committee should be presided over by the Vice-President.
>
> (Signed) Khwaja Kamal-ud-Din, 7 May 1925.

Decision: From 1st October 1924 royalty on all books by Hazrat Amir should be paid at one-quarter, that is 25%. (Secretary, Muhammad Husain Shah).

Consequently, this decision was put into practice. Later on, at the occasion of the annual gathering in 1928, Maulana Ghulam Hasan of Peshawar put the proposal to the General Council of the Anjuman, on 25 December, that Maulana Muhammad Ali should be paid an appointed sum periodically as salary and the paying of royalty be discontinued. But it was unanimously decided that the previous arrangement of paying royalty should continue. Then in 1937 Maulana Ghulam Hasan wrote a long letter full of objections which he insisted on presenting before the General Council. It was mentioned in the letter that for Maulana Muhammad Ali to take royalty on the English translation of the Holy Quran was un-ethical. At the meeting of the General Council held on 30 October 1937, his following statement was presented:

> "The English translation of the Holy Quran by Maulana Muhammad Ali, which he did on payment as a paid employee of the Anjuman, has been made his property by the irregular action of a few persons, which was not justi-fied in any way. ... For the Maulana to accept royalty is contrary to morality."

Upon this the decision taken was as follows:

> "The previous decisions of the Management Committee and the 1928 decision of the General Council according to Resolution No. 130, dated 25 December 1928, which was passed unanimously in Maulana Ghulam Hasan's presence, that the arrangement of paying royalty should be main-tained, were put before the General Council. It is clear from these decisions that the Management Committee of the Anjuman placed this matter on the agenda in a regular way and used its valid authority to decide about the royalty and the General Council unanimously accepted the deci-sion as being right. So Maulvi Ghulam Hasan's objection that this was done by a few persons who had no authority is not correct. Irrespective of the previous decisions, this meeting of the General Council has again considered the

matter and after detailed discussion reached the unanimous conclusion that the previous decisions were right and that the Maulvi sahib's attack on the integrity of Hazrat Amir is regrettable."

It seems appropriate to include here some extracts from a letter by Maulana Muhammad Ali which he wrote to Maulana Ghulam Hasan in answer to his objections, because they clarify his own views about the royalty. This letter was published in *Paigham Sulh* dated 13 April 1940 when Maulvi Ghulam Hasan had gone to Qadian and taken the pledge there and Maulana Muhammad Ali was writing a series of articles in this connection. Maulana Muhammad Ali writes:

> "If the objection is regarding my receiving royalty then I am proud that for my sustenance I am not robbing people by taking their money in the form of gifts and offerings. I earn by my own work to provide for my family. Hazrat Maulana Nur-ud-Din earned his living by practising medicine and I earn it by writing. My mentor and master the Promised Messiah used to write as well, and an ignorant group is still complaining that he took thousands of Rupees for the printing of *Barahin Ahmadiyya* and used it himself. If another group is destined to object to my right to royalty then it is not my fault.
>
> What is royalty? It is remuneration for my labour which provides my livelihood. The community would have had to provide it one way or another. I never asked for it myself. I worked for five years without taking any pay from the Anjuman. There was no royalty at that time. Then the Anjuman itself made this proposal. After ten or eleven years, when you or one or two other people raised objections to it, the General Council of the Anjuman approved it not once but three times, and the last time on your objection unanimously declared it to be right and the objection to be wrong."

Then he writes about the English translation of the Holy Quran:

"Your view that I was paid by the Qadian Anjuman to do this work is also not correct because:

Firstly, I cleared this matter at the very time when I left Qadian and the people in Qadian also took legal advice of their own about this matter.

Secondly, in Qadian I worked on it only for four years, from 1910 to February 1914. After that I worked on it from 1914 to 1917, about another four years, when I was not receiving any pay from them.

Thirdly, when the translation was completed, before printing it I sent a registered letter to the Qadian people asking them, if they so wished, to share in the cost of printing and thus receive a return for the money they had spent in the first four years and take a number of copies according to their share. However, as I am the author they would not be entitled to make any changes in the work. But they rejected the offer and themselves discarded any moral entitlement they may have had.

Fourthly, the first edition of the translation of the Holy Quran was sold out in four years, and for the first two years, when much more than a half of the total copies were sold, I did not take any royalty on the sale. Even if half of the translation work was done by receiving salary when I worked for the Qadian Anjuman, I did not get any royalty on a half of the copies sold. All those proceeds, and much more, went to the Lahore Anjuman's funds, so even that objection does not stand that for a part of the time when I was translating I received remuneration.

Fifthly, from 1919 till 1925 the Anjuman paid royalty at a different rate for the translation of the Holy Quran from the rate for other books, being one sixth for the former and one fourth for the latter."

In this same article, which he wrote addressing Maulana Ghulam Hasan Khan, he included some extracts from a letter by Maulana Ghulam Hasan Khan which he had written him in September 1930. In this letter, after considering the above facts, Maulana Ghulam Hasan Khan had written:

"I had only mentioned the English translation of the Holy Quran to the Mirza sahib [Dr. Mirza Yaqub Baig], not any other book. I had also pointed out that I was not raising it as an objection myself but only wanted clarification of the objection raised by some other people. I have never had any objection to your right to royalty on books written by you. ... I could only see an objection about one thing, and that is the English translation of the Holy Quran. The explanation you have now offered and the events that you have described show that your position in this matter also is somewhat reasonable. I was not aware of these events and there may also be many others who do not know about them."

The readers can judge how, after having written such a letter in 1930, it can be right to repeat the same criticism later.

In any case, as has been mentioned, Maulana Ghulam Hasan Khan assumed silence after the General Council's repeated unanimous decisions. However, some other people took up the same objections. It is regrettable that, despite the Anjuman's clear decisions, this straight forward matter was used as an easy means to attack Maulana Muhammad Ali through underhand propaganda and constant rumour. It was presented as if Maulana Muhammad Ali had wrongfully appropriated money from the Anjuman. The whole issue was clear and simple. Maulana Muhammad Ali did not agree to accept any salary or stipend from the Anjuman but as an author who was giving his writings to the Anjuman for publication and sale he received a certain share of the sale proceeds according to the law of the country. This was also entirely unobjectionable ethically, morally or in religious terms. Nor did the Anjuman suffer any loss by this arrangement; in fact it made large profits. However, no reply can satisfy those who criticise just for the sake of raising objections. So in 1939 this issue was raised in another form, it being claimed that the Anjuman was making huge financial losses because of the Book Depot. This will be mentioned at a later stage.

Some internal conflicts

Till 1930 the Lahore Ahmadiyya *Jama'at* was working with great unity and harmony, but after that grievances began to arise in the minds of some people on small matters and these kept on surfacing from time to time.

For example, in 1929 when the Anjuman decided to close the Isha'at-i-Islam College due to increased expenses and shortage of funds, some people blamed Maulana Muhammad Ali for it and became highly displeased, so much so that one person stopped coming to the mosque and praying behind him. During that same time Shaikh Ghulam Muhammad, a member of the Lahore Ahmadiyya *Jama'at,* made several announcements, levelling certain charges against Maulana Muhammad Ali and some other people. All this had an influence on some members of the *Jama'at,* one of whom was Maulana Ghulam Hasan Khan who openly aired his views from time to time. As stated above, some of his writings were presented before the General Council which unanimously declared him to be in error and asked him to refrain from raising those objections, after which he assumed silence but some others took up his views.

As regards Shaikh Ghulam Muhammad's writings and notices, the General Council according to Resolution No. 220, dated 25 April 1931, made the following decision:

> "Shaikh Ghulam Muhammad's writings and notices were reviewed. On that basis, in the opinion of this meeting, Shaikh Ghulam Muhammad is no longer a member of the Ahmadiyya Anjuman and is removed from his membership of the General Council. Having deliberated upon the accusations he has levelled in his writings and notices against the Anjuman, its President and other workers, the General Council has arrived at the conclusion that some of the accusations are clear fabrications, with facts having been mis-stated, while others are based on exaggeration. The aim of all this propaganda is to create misunderstandings and doubts to weaken the *Jama'at*."

Regarding the accusations levelled by some other persons against Maulana Muhammad Ali, the Management Committee of the Anjuman issued the following statement dated 22 December 1933:

> "Leaving aside those people who, because of some unfortunate mental disturbance, are excusable and not answerable for their actions, some other people due to selfish motives have started a propaganda to bring the Anjuman into disrepute by levelling false accusations against Maulana Muhammad Ali. Those who have for a long time been involved in the Anjuman's affairs and have had dealings with Maulana Muhammad Ali himself are aware of the reasons behind these allegations. We, the members of the Anjuman, announce that all these accusations are entirely groundless and Maulana Muhammad Ali is personally absolutely clear of them by far. His selflessness, integrity and dedication are unparalleled. Such accusations were also levelled in 1931 and were satisfactorily replied to at that time."
>
> (*Paigham Sulh*, 3 January 1934, front page)

On this occasion this matter was also put before the Anjuman's General Council and an announcement about it appeared in *Paigham Sulh* on 7 January 1934 as follows:

> "*An Important Announcement: Refutation of a false report.*
>
> Hazrat Amir [Maulana Muhammad Ali] announced in the meeting of the General Council which was held during the annual gathering that as propaganda was being carried out against him which is not only affecting him personally but damaging the whole community, so until he is completely cleared by a full enquiry he resigns from the Presidency of the Anjuman and nominates Dr. Mirza Yaqub Baig, the Vice-President, as President. Accordingly, the General Council under the Presidency of Dr. Mirza Yaqub Baig examined all aspects of these matters thoroughly, and after a full investigation reached the

conclusion that the propaganda against Hazrat Amir is entirely baseless and false and is contradicted by facts, and the General Council has full confidence in him. ...

After the Council's decision Hazrat Amir has withdrawn his resignation. This announcement is being made because some gossip-mongers are spreading the rumour that Hazrat Amir has severed his ties with the Anjuman. This is a false and slanderous accusation. In this General Council forty members were present as listed below, and this is their unanimous decision."

However, as has been mentioned before, some people were not sincere and their personal grudges kept on coming to the surface in one form or another. The easiest means that these people had for spreading rumour and misgivings was the issue of royalty. This matter came up again and again before the Anjuman and on every occasion the Anjuman decided that it was the right and proper way and was not causing any loss to the Anjuman, but the gossip-mongers did not stop.

On the one hand this man of God was completely absorbed by his concern for spreading Islam in the world, disseminating the Holy Quran and making this *Jama'at* progress, while on the other hand from among Muslims themselves a storm of opposition was raging against this *Jama'at*. In view of this, the damage that was being done by these internal disputes and false rumours was a source of great distress and pain to Maulana Muhammad Ali. A glimpse of his feelings can be seen in one of his letters he wrote from Dalhousie which was published in the *Paigham Sulh* on 23 September 1933. This was a letter in a series entitled 'Letters to the brethren of the *Jama'at*'. The feelings that are expressed in this letter still serve as a beacon of light to the *Jama'at*. He wrote:

Need to work with total harmony

In the last letter I pointed out to you that we must not let small internal conflicts or personal disputes make us negligent in our efforts to promote the cause of the religion of God. This slackness in reality creeps in when a man loses the sense of importance of service for the Divine cause. Though he may make a hundred excuses to console his heart, the fact is that by giving undue priority to his personal disputes and views he makes them the object of worship, and his own wishes become a barrier preventing him from serving the religion.

We would not have separated from Qadian if it had not been resolved to establish a prophethood after the *Khatam-un-nabiyyin* and declare some 400 million Muslims as being *kafir*. Our demand was that we should be given freedom of opinion on the issue of *takfir* so that we could put forward our views before the entire *Jama'at* but this was rejected on the grounds that no one was to express views contrary to *khalifa's* views. After the Split from there, we followed the same objectives that the Promised Messiah had put before us; in fact, we redoubled our efforts when we began this work in Lahore. A few scattered individuals united under one banner to lay a new foundation for the whole work and built such a magnificent building that its high minarets are visible today in the most distant countries. Our small *Jama'at,* which in terms of size is of no account, appears as a great nation in terms of its work.

After this, he advises his comrades as follows:

If our friends cannot dispel their personal grievances, they should at least keep them in proportion. ... Just consider how hard it was tried first of all from Qadian to wipe out our small *Jama'at*. ... To avoid conflict we left behind an established organization and a running operation and laid a new foundation of this work in Lahore. Then look at your Muslim brothers and you see that they are not expending one-tenth of the energy refuting Christianity and the Arya Samaj that they are spending on destroying the Ahmadiyya *Jama'at* ... then look beyond this, as to how the world is bent upon effacing Islam itself. Realize how essential it is that in the face of so many forces bent on our destruction we work in complete unity.

On the other hand, look at the magnificent work that has been done and the lofty building that has been raised, and who has laid the basis for that work. The real mission is that of defending and propagating the faith of the Holy Prophet Muhammad, may peace and the blessings of Allah be upon him, whose foundation has been laid by the Promised Messiah sent by Allah. ... Till today hundreds of worthy men have spent their lives on constructing this building. Millions, nay tens of millions, of Rupees have been spent on it. There are many prominent men of this *Jama'at* each of whom has spent hundreds of thousands of Rupees on it, and those people are countless who sacrificed their daily bread, deprived their wives and children of essentials, or sold their possessions to spend on this construction. As to the earnest pleas before the Almighty that have come from the hearts, supplicating for the progress of the Divine faith, if there was any record of them, and God definitely has one, it would raise the loudest clamour in the silence of the night. The tears that have been shed with this urge during prayers, if they were to be collected, they would fill a river. Should a building raised with such hard labour be destroyed in pursuance of a few personal desires?

Hands luminous with Divine light laid the foundation, builders possessing the highest skills and ability carried out the construction, and honest, sincere labourers working purely for Allah's pleasure helped to build it. So today when this minaret has reached such towering heights that its light is reaching thousands of miles, who would be more foolish than one who, instead of continuing to build it, tries to demolish it merely because of some minor complaint and disagreement with his brother. I say 'demolish' because although he may not realise it but in fact his neglect of his real work or his separation or his dispute is tantamount to him demolishing this building. "Dispute not one with another lest you get weak-hearted and your power depart" [Holy Quran, 8:46]. Internal disputes always destroy the strength of a nation. You are the people who constructed this building, whose power and energy was used to build it, whose money created this organization. Will you destroy it with your own hands? "Be not like the mad woman who unravels her yarn, disintegrating it into pieces, after she has spun it strongly" [Holy Quran, 16:92].

Remember well that this magnificent edifice, whose foundations were laid by one sent by God Himself, and for whose construction an entire community has been toiling whole-heartedly with its man-power, strength and money for the last 45 years, is not something insignificant that you can destroy today and rebuild tomorrow. So if you are going to do anything, then devote your energy and power to strengthen it, so that when the time comes to meet your Lord you will be happy with Him and He with you. Just as we all came together to start this work, only seeking God's pleasure, let us remain together to complete it purely for His pleasure. All this has, of course, been achieved by the grace of Allah, but remember that it was your energy and your money that was spent on it, so do not destroy your own creation by your own hands."

Relations with the Qadian *Jama'at,* 1924 to 1937

During this entire period, much continued to be written by both sides about the issues under dispute, and a large part of the columns of *Al-Fazl* of Qadian and *Paigham Sulh* of Lahore was devoted to discussion of these questions. It has been made clear that the disagreement between the two *Jama'ats* was caused by the doctrine of *takfir* advanced by Mirza Mahmud Ahmad, that anyone who does not believe in Hazrat Mirza Ghulam Ahmad's claims is an unbeliever (*kafir*), excluded from the fold of Islam. Then Mirza Mahmud Ahmad attributed a claim of prophethood to the Promised Messiah and tried to prove that he was the 'Ahmad' spoken of in the Holy Quran, 61:6. All these inventions had been refuted by Maulana Muhammad Ali in his various writings nume- rous times, and other senior figures in the Lahore *Jama'at* had also clarified these issues. But the Qadian *Jama'at* by this time had become so steeped in blind, unquestioning obedience to its leader that it was impossible to bring about its reform and correc- tion.

Maulana Muhammad Ali was always very concerned that a part of the time and attention of his *Jama'at* was being expended in these arguments, to the detriment of the work of the propa- gation of Islam. So, as mentioned earlier, he addressed Mirza Mahmud Ahmad again and again, in his *khutbas* and by open letters to him published in *Paigham Sulh,* inviting and challenging him to a decisive and final written debate between the heads of the two groups which would be published and circulated in the two *Jama'ats* to inform every member of the arguments of both sides. Then every person could judge for himself which *Jama'at* he wished to belong to, and after that there would be no further writings by both sides on these issues, each *Jama'at* concentrating solely on the work of the propagation of Islam. However, Mirza Mahmud Ahmad always evaded a written debate under one pretext or another.

In 1926 when Maulana Muhammad Ali was in Dalhousie, Mirza Mahmud Ahmad also happened to go there, and the two of them met for the first time since the Split in 1914. In September the Maulana invited Mirza Mahmud Ahmad and his companions to a meal, and Mirza Mahmud Ahmad reciprocated by inviting the Maulana and some of his friends to a meal. During their talks Mirza Mahmud Ahmad agreed to Maulana Muhammad Ali's suggestion that, in the writings of one side against the other, personal attacks and offensive language should be avoided. At that time the two Qadiani organs *Al-Fazl* and *Al-Faruq* were full of such attacks. Accordingly, Maulana Muhammad Ali also sent an instruction in writing to the editor of *Paigham Sulh* to be cautious as to what he published. For a time both sides observed this pact. However, in 1928 there arose a storm of opposition and personal allegations from the Qadian *Jama'at* which began with an article in *Al-Fazl* levelling certain charges against Maulana Muhammad Ali and Maulana Yaqub Khan. These were published in *Al-Fazl* with the preposterous claim that these accusations were being levied by a member of the Lahore *Jama'at* itself. In response to this article of *Al-Fazl*, the members of the Management Committee of the Lahore *Jama'at* issued a statement from which an extract is given below:

> "The purpose of these slanderous accusations is to impugn the honesty and integrity of Hazrat Maulana Muhammad Ali. We think it sufficient to announce that, after knowing him personally and working with him for several years, we testify that Hazrat Amir follows such a high standard of righteousness, in the most minute detail, that it is a unique example for Muslims in this age. To say that the Hazrat Maulana derives illicit benefit from the funds of this Anjuman for himself is a dastardly attack. The fact is that he has not only been serving this Anjuman with great hard work and energy for many years without receiving any remuneration but, on the contrary, his valuable writings, which have brought acclaim to Islam in the Muslim and non-Muslim worlds, are the best source of the Anjuman's income. The Anjuman is indebted to him in that, in return for a reasonable royalty, he gave the Anjuman the right to publish his writings, from which the Anjuman derives thousands of Rupees every year.
>
> The third matter in which it has been sought to gravely mislead the public is the charge that the Hazrat Maulana disregards the Anjuman as if it does not exist, and although the Anjuman exists in name, it is only a tool in his hands. We declare that this accusation also is entirely groundless. The Hazrat Maulana has a high regard for difference of opinion, and all the business of the Anjuman is decided by majority of opinion, and many a time decisions have gone against his views."

(Paigham Sulh, 8 September 1928)

In accordance with the directions of the General Council of the Anjuman, Maulana Muhammad Ali and Maulana Yaqub Khan had a legal notice served on the editor of *Al-Fazl* and instituted law suits. Ultimately, a settlement was agreed on 6 July 1929, under which an apology was published in *Al-Fazl* (15 October 1929, p. 8), retracting the accusations and the cases were withdrawn.

After that, articles kept on appearing in the newspapers of both sides from time to time on various aspects of the disputed issues and certain other affairs. Maulana Muhammad Ali and the Lahore *Jama'at* tried several times to find ways of ending these controversies. In April 1935 some prominent members of the Lahore *Jama'at* appealed to Mirza Mahmud Ahmad to have a decisive debate between the heads of the two groups in the presence of a selected audience, which should then be published along with the comments of the audience, and after that all disputations should end. But the Qadian *Jama'at* did not agree to it. Maulana Muhammad Ali himself tried many times to arrange a decisive discussion in one format or another and put forward many proposals. One was to select three moderators from each side. Another was that the written submissions in the debate between the heads of the two groups should be published together in one place. Then in December 1936 another proposal was put before Mirza Mahmud Ahmad, that there was no need for the two heads to come together in one location for discussion. Mirza Mahmud Ahmad should write his submission and send it to Maulana Muhammad Ali who would send him back a written reply of the same length within seven days. These two submissions should be published both in *Paigham Sulh* and in *Al-Fazl*. There would be six such submissions on each side, the first one being on the issue of *takfir* (whether a Muslim who does not accept Hazrat Mirza Ghulam Ahmad still remains a Muslim) and then on the question of prophethood (whether Hazrat Mirza Ghulam Ahmad claimed to be a prophet). Mirza Mahmud Ahmad always rejected these suggestions saying that he was not willing to discuss the question of declaring other Muslims as unbelievers, and that the question of prophethood should be discussed.

In 1936 Maulana Muhammad Ali again and again drew the attention of Mirza Mahmud Ahmad to the fact that the real difference between the two *Jama'ats* arose on the issue of *takfir,* and stemmed from Mirza Mahmud Ahmad's well-known article 'A Muslim is one who believes in all those appointed by Allah'. During Maulana Nur-ud-Din's illness the issue of *takfir* was the topic of controversy, and upon his death the pamphlet issued by Maulana Muhammad Ali stated the reason for the disagreement to be this very question. All the writings from our side in that period close to the Split state this as the reason for not taking the *bai'at* at Mirza Mahmud Ahmad's hand, that he had invented the doctrine of dubbing all other Muslims as *kafirs*. This belief of his was expressed by him a little later in his book *A'inah-i Sadaqat* in the following words:

> "…all those so-called Muslims who have not entered into his [Hazrat Mirza Ghulam Ahmad's] *bai'at* formally, wherever they may be, are *Kafirs* and outside the pale of Islam, even though they may not have heard the name of the Promised Messiah." (p. 35) [4]

So the main reason for the Split was the issue of *takfir* and it was in support of this doctrine that a claim to prophethood was attributed to Hazrat Mirza Ghulam Ahmad. But not one person from the Qadian *Jama'at* dared to come forward for debate.

On 1st January 1937 in his Friday *khutba* Maulana Muhammad Ali, while mentioning the *jihad* for the propagation of Islam, noted that there were certain activities that seem harmless but the devil brings them to the fore and diverts people's attention to them in order to hinder the work of the propagation of Islam. In this context he mentioned that the Qadian *Jama'at* had turned its attention to the field of politics and other worldly activities, and added that the knowledge that the Promised Messiah brought was not ordinary. That knowledge is what this Movement is based upon. The source of that knowledge was not something in this world but it came from God Himself. Our real work is to broadcast that knowledge and to propagate Islam according to it. Maulana Muhammad Ali expressed regret that the Qadian *Jama'at* was devoting more attention to other affairs and moving away from the real objective of this Movement which was to spread the word of God in the world. After the publication of this *khutba*, abusive

---

4. The extract quoted here is taken from the Qadiani *Jama'at* English translation of *A'inah-i Sadaqat*, published under the title *The Truth about the Split*, p. 55 of the 3rd edition, 1965. In the 2007 edition, see p. 56.

articles against Maulana Muhammad Ali were published from Qadian, and among other criticism it was also written in *Al-Fazl*:

> "As to what the Maulvi Sahib is so proud of, neither the Promised Messiah nor Hazrat *Khalifa-tul-Masih* (Maulana Nur-ud-Din) translated the Quran.... So how can he, by merely publishing the translation of the Quran, claim that he and his community are the sole standard bearers of the propagation and the defence of Islam. ... If Rodwell, being a Christian, can translate the Quran into English and publish it, then what is so special about the Maulvi sahib's achievement."

(*Al-Fazl,* 5 February 1937, p. 2)

As some members of the Lahore Ahmadiyya community were raising a similar objection regarding the work of the translation of the Holy Quran, an extract is quoted below from the article which Maulana Muhammad Ali wrote in answer to Mirza Mahmud Ahmad which was published in *Paigham Sulh,* 27 February 1937:

> "Remember that Rodwell's translation was already in existence when the Promised Messiah expressed his longing in the following words:
>
> > 'I wish to prepare a commentary of the Quran which should be sent to them after it has been rendered into the English language. I cannot refrain from stating clearly that this is my work, and that no one else can do it as well as I or he who is an offshoot of mine and thus is included in me.'
>
> This was the work of the Promised Messiah's offshoot or branch, to fulfil this wish of his."

Then, mentioning in detail the diversion of attention of the Qadian *Jama'at* towards other goals, he writes:

> "They ought to remember that they have strayed very far from the right path that the Promised Messiah had set us upon. What was the Promised Messiah's real mission? He wrote:
>
> > 'There could be no any greater tribulation than that ... Islam is under attack from all sides. At this critical juncture a man has been raised by God who wants to make known the beauty of

Islam to the whole world and open ways for it to reach the Western countries but his community is refraining from helping him' (*Izala Auham*, p. 769).

'As far as is possible for me, I should spread this knowledge in Asian and European countries through my writings. ... I would advise that, instead of these missionaries, **writings of an excellent and high standard should be sent into these countries.**' (*Izala Auham*, pp. 771–773).

The words of the last line are written in bold letters like this in the original book."

In short, this was the aim always stressed by Maulana Muhammad Ali, and it was only because of this faith and firm belief of his that he kept the attention of the Lahore *Jama'at* ever focussed on this real mission. While the Qadian *Jama'at* went in a different direction, it is regrettable that there were some members of the Lahore *Jama'at* who had not imbibed that same zeal and fervour from the benefit of the company of the Promised Messiah as had Maulana Muhammad Ali, and they tried to divert the attention of the Lahore *Jama'at* to activities which did not lead to the fulfilment of its real objective. Even so, it was as a result of the strong personality and spiritual power of Maulana Muhammad Ali that during his life the *Jama'at* as a whole kept only one purpose before it.

In 1937, certain circumstances arose in the Qadian *Jama'at* which led to one of their senior figures Shaikh Abdur Rahman Misri and some other persons separating themselves from the Qadian *Jama'at* as a result of allegations surrounding some aspects of the life of Mirza Mahmud Ahmad. One of the people who separated, Fakhr-ud-Din Multani, was even stabbed to death by a fanatic follower of the Qadiani *khalifa*. After this, anonymous letters containing death threats were sent to Maulana Muhammad Ali, Dr. Syed Muhammad Husain Shah and Dr. Basharat Ahmad. During this period, from June to September 1937, Maulana Muhammad Ali addressed the Qadian *Jama'at* through articles in *Paigham Sulh*, the substance of his message being that we should all be concerned about the attacks on the Holy Prophet Muhammad and Islam by other religions, and create an urge within our hearts to dispel that criticism.

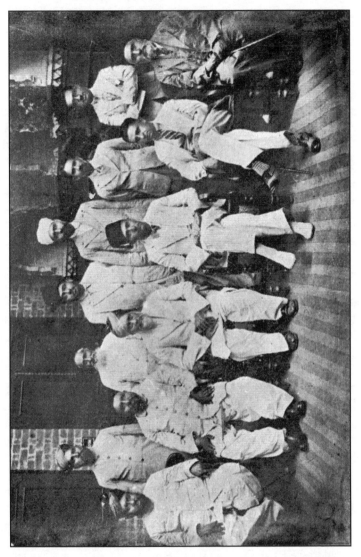

For the occasion of this photograph in March 1933, see page 218

Seated: Dr. Basharat Ahmad, Dr. Syed Muhammad Husain Shah, Maulana Muhammad Ali, Baron Umar Ehrenfels, K.L. Gauba, Dr. Mirza Yaqub Baig.

Standing: Ch. Manzur Ilahi, Maulana Aziz Bakhsh, Syed Ghulam Mustafa Shah, Syed Amjad Ali Shah, Dr. Ghulam Muhammad, Sh. Ezad Bakhsh.

3.5: The Anjuman's Silver Jubilee 1938 and recovery from a critical illness

Initial move to mark Silver Jubilee

The Ahmadiyya Anjuman Isha'at Islam Lahore was founded in May 1914 and its first annual gathering was held in December of that year. By 1938 the Anjuman had been working for almost twenty-five years. In February 1938 Maulana Muhammad Ali referred to this in a Friday *khutba* and advised that to mark this occasion something special should be done to glorify the Holy Quran. Our *Jama'at* had gained a distinction because of its service to the Holy Quran. While there are plenty of Muslims making verbal claims, but practical service of the Quran, out of love for this Book, is nowhere to be found except in our *Jama'at*. The Maulana added that he could not yet say what proposal he would put forward as to how to mark the Silver Jubilee but we must remember that if that work would not reveal the greatness of the Holy Quran then we would have drifted away from the right path. In April he called a meeting of the General Council of the Anjuman. Before that, by means of his articles and Friday *khutbas,* he made a heart-felt appeal to all members to pray to God the Most High for forty days, asking Him to make us continue on the path shown by the *Mujaddid* of the Age, the goal of which is to proclaim the name of Allah in the world and spread His Book, and to grant us to conceive the best possible plan for this occasion.

While the passionate zeal and fervour in the heart of Maulana Muhammad Ali, to raise the banner of God and spread the Holy Quran in the world, is always apparent in his writings and speeches, but on this occasion he specially expressed his feelings in numerous articles and almost every *khutba*. Thus in his Friday *khutba* on 1st April 1938 he said:

"Up to now we have been working in bit fashion: we finish one project and then need to be prompted to take a step for the next one. On this occasion I specially want to draw attention that we must establish permanent, long-term foundations to act like a perpetual endowment so that our activities should keep on running in continuity by themselves.... We must set the basis for a long-lasting endowment to enable our work of the publication of the Holy Quran and the propagation of Islam to continue under its own momentum and be expanded by its helpers."

(*Paigham Sulh,* 9 April 1938)

Earlier, in his Friday *khutba* on 18 February 1938, explaining the Quranic command "So flee to Allah" (51:50), he said that the real aim of the life of a human being is to run towards Allah as if madly in love with Him, to give this love an exclusive place in his heart, and not let anything else stand in its way. He said:

"The great aim of our *Jama'at* is to spread the Divine teachings and the religion of Islam in the world. So we must pay the fullest attention towards it. Our greatest need above all is to study the Holy Quran, to try to understand it, to organise classes for imparting its knowledge, to teach it to others, to make it a practice to ponder upon its verses, to learn the various branches of human knowledge and sciences and use them in the study and service of the Holy Quran.

The greatness of the Holy Quran is of the highest order, just as the glory of Allah is so high as to be even beyond our comprehension and conception. If we reflect upon the Holy Quran we can find out some of its pro-found knowledge, while its wonders and deep truths, being infinite, will not be exhausted till the Day of Judgment. ... The real purpose of the coming of the Promised Messiah was to spread the Holy Quran in the world, to propagate it and to publish its translations. ...

At present the Holy Quran is in a state of the utmost helplessness. Even though it is most highly revered by six hundred million people yet it is helpless because the aim of its revelation is not being fulfilled. The six hundred million Muslims who most certainly adore it are entirely negligent about taking it to the world. If our *Jama'at* has taken upon itself this responsibility then we must not forget it under any circumstances and always keep on trying to fulfil it. What is meant by spreading the Holy Quran is that its meanings should be made available to people and they should be provided with the translation of the Holy Quran in their own languages. ... At every opportunity and at every campaign that is put before you, you must keep your objective in view all the time as to how you can spread the glory of the Holy Quran. All other work that you do is in support of this objective. The task of strengthening and consolidating the *Jama'at,* without which we cannot fulfil this objective, is itself a part of this great goal. In this work there is no such thing as over-indulgence or excess, as there is in other works, because to propagate the word of God is an indication of your love for God and love for God can never be excessive. The stronger this passion becomes the better.

We require the greatest strength in order to spread the Holy Quran, and we cannot find that strength without having love for God and a close connection with Him. When you are overwhelmed by love for something, you are attracted towards it unstintingly, sacrificing every-thing in its way. If you develop love for God then you will go on making sacrifices in His way without hesi-tation. ... A *Jama'at* which is custodian of the Holy Quran must realise this well, as this is the secret of its success. Numbers do not matter. The size of the *Jama'at* is in fact a means to achieve the end, but to consider the means as the real objective, or to rely on it excessively, constitutes nothing but *shirk* (worship of others than God). It is only in trust in God that *shirk* does not exist. To rely too much on anything else is *shirk.* So you must create so much love for God and closeness to Him as if you are running towards Him. Only this is the means to your success and triumph." (*Paigham Sulh,* 4 March 1938)

This, then, was the glorious objective for which Maulana Muhammad Ali wanted to lay a permanent foundation on the occasion of this Silver Jubilee. However, the decision made by the meetings of the consultative council and the General Council held on 15 April 1938 was that a sum of one hundred thousand Rupees should be raised at the Jubilee for the reserve fund. To raise this money, the movement for making wills should be completed and special collections be made, and all this should be spent on the consolidation of the *Jama'at.*

Ill health

After 1931–1932 Maulana Muhammad Ali was not keeping good health. He was then over fifty-seven years of age. He had reduced his previously extensive visits to branches of the *Jama'at* outside Lahore. Once or twice he was taken ill while travelling. His ailment used to increase as the summer began and he used to get high temperature. Because of this it had become even more necessary for him to go to a mountain resort. His doctors advised him to rest but it made no difference to his habit, since his youth, of working from morning to night and rising shortly after midnight to supplicate and plead before God the Most High for hours. Although he found quietude when he went to Dalhousie, he used this opportunity to do even more writing work. At the beginning of July 1937 and again in September the same year, he was confined to bed while in Dalhousie. He published the following report about his health in *Paigham Sulh* dated 12 October 1937:

> *The State of my health:*
>
> I do not want to keep my friends unaware that for the last, about ten, months I have been suffering from an illness for which I might need an operation but it is not confirmed yet. It is almost certainly tubercular trouble, and during the last four or five months I have lost 8 pounds in weight. … In these circumstances it is imperative for me to refrain from overwork and rest more. So I request my friends to bear in mind my disability. Also I entreat those friends who, despite being aware of my faults nonetheless have sympathy for me, to pray for me, but on condition that they first pray for Islam, for its strength, stability and

triumph, and pray for this *Jama'at* which is engaged in the propagation of Islam and dissemination of the Quran. This prayer must arise from the depth of their hearts, their souls must fall at the threshold of Allah with the utmost humility, and their hearts must melt and flow like water at seeing the state of helplessness of Islam and the Quran. If at that moment they find some feeling for me in their hearts, then that is the kind of prayer I want. Whenever I have prayed for my friends I have generally prayed in a way like this, and if my friends pray for me then I want them to pray in the same manner so that the real object is achieved.

O Allah! help those who help the religion of Muhammad, peace be upon him, and make us from among them.

Humbly, Muhammad Ali.

From the middle of April 1938 he became unwell. For the first few days he had fever and a cold. Then he started getting a high temperature every evening. At the end of May the illness was exacerbated, with an increase in temperature as well as weakness. The doctors advised that he should be taken to Dalhousie at once because the heat of the summer was making the fever worse. Accordingly, he was moved to Dalhousie in this state of illness, where he improved temporarily but on 15 June his temperature suddenly escalated and weakness increased so much that it became difficult for him even to speak. He was under the treatment of the Civil Surgeon of Dalhousie. Dr. Ghulam Muhammad also went from Lahore for a day, and Dr. Basharat Ahmad was already residing there in his own house. Nonetheless, the illness could not be diagnosed. A stage came when even the doctors gave up hope and he remained in this serious condition for about ten days. At the end of June, however, he began to improve gradually and at the beginning of July the fever subsided. Throughout July he could not leave his bed due to weakness and temperature. At the end of July he was strong enough to be able to write a few words from his sick bed by his own hand. So he sent the following letter to *Paigham Sulh* which was published in its issue for 27 July:

Thanks to Friends:

It is difficult for me to thank every friend individually who has prayed for my health from the bottom of his heart. May Allah reward all of them well. It does suggest to my mind that these prayers proved so effective in attracting the mercy of Allah that a weak and helpless man, who was not only himself feeling that he was on his way to the next world but his doctors were also of the same opinion, was granted a new lease of life. I still need these heart-felt prayers in order that I can become able to serve religion. But an even greater need is that even more heart-felt prayers be said for this small *Jama'at* that Allah fill the hearts of its members with such fervent feelings for the faith that they become utterly devoted to the propagation of the Divine Word, and holding the needs of the faith higher than their personal needs they rescue their *Jama'at* from its financial problems. To spend your wealth in the path of spreading the Divine religion is a practical proof of your love for Allah, otherwise all our verbal claims are worthless. I am sure that God Who listened to the prayers of my *Jama'at* for me will also listen to their prayers to infuse new life in the *Jama'at*. The need is to kneel at His door.

Wassalam, Muhammad Ali

Darus-Salam, Dalhousie, 23 July 1938.

After this, for about one month he had various problems due to weakness but his health kept on improving and in September he was on his feet as usual.

Silver Jubilee

At the end of July 1938, when Maulana Muhammad Ali had launched the plan for the Jubilee while on his sick bed, the circumstances were highly unfavourable. The Anjuman faced serious financial problems, his own health was very poor, the doctors advising him complete rest, and there remained only a little time. Prominent members of the *Jama'at* themselves held out no hope for it, believing that the plans would fail and the *Jama'at*

would be disgraced. But Maulana Muhammad Ali did not lose
heart and started the work while on his sick bed. Some years later
he described these events in the following words:

> "It was probably April 1938 or the start of May when the
> General Council approved the Jubilee plan. After that
> I became ill and my illness became serious and prolonged.
> Even my doctors lost hope and during my illness the Jubi-
> lee campaign also died. When Allah granted me health
> I tried to revive the Jubilee plan but all the friends were
> against it. The Anjuman was in debt by about a hundred
> thousand Rupees, and as the *Jama'at* could not meet the
> regular expenses, the debt was continuing to increase. At
> that time Syed Tasaddaq Husain Qadari of Baghdad was
> the one who strengthened my resolve. When I recovered,
> I received his letter from Baghdad informing me that he
> had raised a reasonable sum for the Jubilee. Upon this,
> I recited the prayer 'In the name of Allah be its sailing and
> its anchoring' [the Quran, 11:41] and restarted the Jubilee
> campaign despite the opposition of friends, and Allah
> blessed it so much so that within two to three months the
> promised donations reached 175,000 Rupees. I consider
> Syed Tasaddaq Husain Qadari to be the real initiator."

(*Paigham Sulh*, 18 August 1943, p. 1)

So at the end of July 1938 he began directing his efforts
towards this plan, and from 1 August till the end of November
1938 he published six forceful, fervent appeals in *Paigham Sulh*.
In the first appeal, on 8 August 1938, under the title *Man ansari
ila-Allah* ('Who are my helpers in the cause of Allah'— Holy
Quran, 61:14), he asked for names of volunteers from the *Jama'at*
who would help him at every step in this campaign. In the second
appeal, in *Paigham Sulh,* 17 August (p. 2), he asked the *Jama'at*
to undertake spiritual exertions in *tahajjud* or other prayers, individually and in congregation, and repeat this prayer again and again:

> "O God, infuse in our hearts such love for our religion
> that while spending in Your way we feel no reluctance
> within us but joy and happiness. When any opportunity
> arises to serve Your religion, let our hearts open generously

and let them not be constricted. O God, damp down our love for worldly goods and ignite in its place such a fire of love for You and Your Messenger in our hearts that it may burn all the greed and desires of this world like trash. O God, let our personal adversities seem trivial to us compared to the calamity faced by our religion. Let us feel pleasure in our pains by seeing the affliction faced by Your religion. O God, we have fallen short of doing our rightful duty of serving Your faith; whatever little we have done, may You accept it."

Because of the overwhelming urge in his heart to place the work of the propagation of Islam above all else, he referred in a Friday *khutba* in Dalhousie on 12 August to a misconception of some members who thought that the Promised Messiah was the first *Mujaddid* to form a *Jama'at* and therefore his main purpose was to create a *Jama'at*. He said:

"Some people ask whether any previous *Mujaddid* formed a *Jama'at* as the Promised Messiah did? This question arises out of ignorance. In every age work is done according to the needs of the time. The urgent need of today was to bring together a group of people who passionately wish to serve the cause of the faith, because Muslims had lost all feeling for the service of Islam.

One of our dear members is mistaken in questioning whether the objective of the Promised Messiah was the propagation of Islam or the formation of a *Jama'at*. In his opinion the work of the Promised Messiah was to form a *Jama'at* and this takes precedence over the work of propagation. In fact these are two separate issues. The real object is propagation but for that work a *Jama'at* was required, ... otherwise his mission would have come to an end at his death.

In the statement of the Promised Messiah that is adduced in support of this idea, he says that the *Jama'at* has not reached the high stage of spiritual purity which is needed for the work of propagation. And it is true that the work of preaching is not like a business. You must first have the strongest belief in the truth of what you are preaching and then the urge to take to others the faith you have yourself. This is what he wanted, as he says:

> 'The real object of my coming is to form a *Jama'at* of true believers who have real faith in God and a true connection with Him, and who make Islam their sign of identity and adhere to the example of the Holy Prophet ... so that the world can then find guidance through such a *Jama'at*.'

The last words above make it clear that the aim of forming the *Jama'at* was to bring guidance to the world by its work and preaching, and it was this guiding of the world and spreading the message of Islam that was the objective of the Promised Messiah." (*Paigham Sulh,* 22 August 1938, p. 6)

In his third appeal, in *Paigham Sulh,* 13 September 1938, he stressed upon making wills. Everyone should make a will, and contribute at least one-fifth of it by the time of the Jubilee in cash or property. Those who do not make a will, or whose will amounts to less than one month's income, should donate at least one month's income to the Jubilee fund. Women should donate at least one-tenth of the value of their jewellery to the Jubilee fund.

In his fourth appeal, in *Paigham Sulh,* 8 October, he made a heart-felt plea especially to the wealthy members, calling upon them to realise the importance of the *Jama'at* and its work for twenty-five years. He drew their attention to the fact that when Islam had become completely subjugated and defeated, both politically and spiritually, that was the time of the Promised Messiah who then heard in that dark age this voice from on High:

> *Rejoice that you shall see that time very soon, when the Muslims have been firmly established on a lofty minaret.*

The words 'lofty minaret' are worth pondering. This was the path of spiritual conquests, which far excel political or territorial victory. Then all the knowledge, which is the weaponry for these spiritual conquests, was disclosed by Allah to the Promised Messiah, and today this small *Jama'at* holds this inheritance from him.

The fifth appeal that he made in this connection contains exhortations which were significant not only on the occasion of the Jubilee but are of great importance for this *Jama'at* at all times because this small community has the same magnificent task before it all the time. It was published under the heading:

> "You will remember what I say to you, and I entrust my affair to Allah." [Holy Quran, 40:44]

A heart-felt plea

In it he wrote as follows:

> "… O men of wealth, where can I find words to appeal to you? … Your indifference towards my appeals has straitened my heart. Your silence has halted my tongue. So, O Allah, again I bow down before You and ask: 'My Lord, expand my breast for me, and ease my affair for me, and loose the knot from my tongue' [Holy Quran, 20:25–27].

Should I appeal in the words of the Promised Messiah:

> 'O Muslims, are these the signs of being Muslims, that the religion is in a ruined state and you are holding fast to the dead world? Is the citadel of the world impregnable in your opinion, or perhaps the memory of the passing away of the earlier people has left your hearts?'

Or should I appeal in the words of the Leader of mankind, Muhammad, may peace and the blessings of Allah be upon him:

> 'I swear by Allah that the one who gives wealth in the way of Allah does not suffer any loss.'

Or should I convey to your ears the voice of the Lord of the worlds:

> 'Surely Allah has bought from the believers their persons and their property — theirs in return is the Garden' [Holy Quran, 9:111]. This wealth is not yours; if you are believers then Allah has bought it from you.

'Only those are believers who, having believed in Allah and His Messenger, ... struggle hard with their wealth and their lives in the way of Allah' [Holy Quran, 49:15]

'Spend of that whereof He has made you heirs ... Who is he that will offer to Allah a good gift, so He will double it for him and he will have a generous reward' [Holy Quran, 57:7,11]. You are not the owner of your wealth. You are appointed as custodian by your Maker. When an order comes from the King, the custodian cannot set it aside. Give something out of your wealth for Allah and He will return it many times over.

You hesitate in spending in the way of Allah. There could be only two reasons for this. Either it may be because of some shortcoming that you perceive in me or in the Anjuman, or it could be because of your love for the wealth of this world. If it is the first one, then by giving your wealth your reward will not be reduced; ... and if it is the second one, then it will cause great loss to you and we might be like those people about whom Allah says:

'On the day (of judgment) when the hypocrites, men and women, will say to those who believe: Wait for us, that we may borrow from your light. It will be said: Turn back (to the world and spend in it in the way of Allah) and seek a light. ... Then they will cry out to them (the believers): Were we not with you? They will say: Yes (on the face of it you were), but you caused yourselves to fall into temptation and you waited (to do it tomorrow or the day after that) and doubted, and vain desires deceived you till the threatened punishment of Allah came (leaving you with no control over your wealth)' [Holy Quran, 57:13,14]."

Then the Maulana writes that the purification of the self which we all deeply desire, and the light we want to receive by worshipping God, can only be achieved when we cleanse our hearts of the love of wealth. The biggest idol that is worshipped is love of wealth, so it must be guarded against. The Divine religion should be treated as a son. If you have two sons, let it be the third one, or if you have three let it be the fourth one, to share your wealth with the other sons. (See *Paigham Sulh,* 22 October 1938.)

The sixth appeal which he made on 30 November was to raise funds from the non-Ahmadis as well. Also members of the *Jama'at* were asked to sacrifice their time along with their money.

In addition to these appeals that Maulana Muhammad Ali made to the *Jama'at* through his writings, he also visited in person branches outside Lahore on a large scale in November and December in spite of his weak health, and went to see many prominent leaders of the general Muslim community. Above all these efforts, were his prayers and tearful pleadings before God the Most High, and falling before the Almighty in his *tahajjud* prayers, for the strengthening of the *Jama'at*, for the spread of the Divine teachings and the Word of God in the world, for the diminution of the love of wealth from the hearts of the members of the *Jama'at,* and for the infusion in them of the same spirit and zeal to work for the Divine cause that he himself had inherited from the Promised Messiah.

All these efforts and prayers were accepted by God. The *Jama'at* that had been making sacrifices incessantly showed another incomparable example of sacrifice and selflessness. By the time of the annual gathering of 1938 a sum of 182,000 Rupees was raised in the Jubilee fund and later it increased to 200,000 Rupees, a half of which was in cash and the remaining in the form of property.

The sacrifice this small *Jama'at* made on this occasion was quite unparalleled. Nothing like it could be witnessed in any other Muslim organization. A famous newspaper of Lahore, the *Inqilab,* wrote about it as follows in its issue of 4 January 1939:

> "The Anjuman *Himayat-i Islam* [famous association of the general Muslim community] held its Golden Jubilee, at which more than 150,000 Rupees was raised, including a

donation of 25,000 Rupees from the Government of the Punjab. Muslims are very pleased at this success. ...

But at exactly the same time, opposite to the grounds of Islamia College [where this Golden Jubilee was held], in the mosque in Ahmadiyya Buildings, the Anjuman Isha'at Islam of the Lahore Ahmadis celebrated its Silver Jubilee where there was gathering of hardly one thousand people. But do Muslims know that this handful of Muslims, who are dubbed as *kafir,* misguided and all other bad things, by the general Muslim community, raised 182,000 Rupees for the propagation of Islam on this occasion and this sum did not include any donations from the Government or any ruler of a state, but this large sum was raised by merely three or four hundred people? ... Have the non-Ahmadi Muslims ever pondered why it is that the tens of millions of them, trying their hardest to raise funds for their national objectives, can never raise as much money as this handful of people? It is very easy to call any *Jama'at* as *kafir* and misguided, but it is extremely hard for the general Muslim community to provide a practical proof that, as compared with this, they themselves are the true believers. ..."
(*Paigham Sulh,* 4 January 1939, quoting *Inqilab*)

The annual gathering and 25 year work of the Anjuman

From 25 to 27 December 1938 was held the 25th annual gathering of the Anjuman. It was like previous annual gatherings. There was no trumpet, fanfare or ceremony of celebration, but the hearts of those present were filled with thanks-giving and praise of God at the fact that the small plant sown by Maulana Muhammad Ali and his few comrades in 1914, in the face of the most adverse circum-stances, had by the grace of Allah grown into a strong tree in 25 years, doing such magnificent work of the propagation of Islam which none of the other Muslim associations had even paid any attention to, and the many times bigger Qadian *Jama'at* had not done even a small fraction of that work.

It seems appropriate at this point to give a summary of the achievements of the Anjuman over this 25 year period. In his presidential address on this occasion Maulana Muhammad Ali described the state of destitution in which the foundation of the Anjuman was laid in 1914, and then he gave a brief account of its 25 years work. Extracts from this are given below from *Paigham Sulh,* 9 January 1939:

> At the end of the first year our total income was 7,333 Rupees, which today after 25 years has grown 25 fold to almost 200,000 Rupees, and the Anjuman owns assets worth about one million Rupees. All praise is due to Allah, the Lord of the worlds. But the worth of a community cannot be judged by its numbers or by its income and assets. Rather, what counts is the service it has rendered. So praise be to Allah that the service to Islam this *Jama'at* has carried out cannot be matched by any other Muslim community.

A. First Category of Practical Work

1. Propagation of the Holy Quran

The most valuable asset of the Muslims is the Word of God, but to this they have paid the least attention. Service to the Holy Quran holds the highest place in the works of the Anjuman. In 1914 the Anjuman was founded, and at the beginning of 1918 the English translation of the Holy Quran was published. ... The first edition consisting of five thousand copies was exhausted in two years. The second edition of eleven thousand copies was printed in 1920, and now it is into the third edition. During this period the Urdu translation and commentary, *Bayan-ul-Quran,* was published in three volumes in 1923, and an edition of the English translation without Arabic text was first published in 1928 consisting of five thousand copies, followed by another printing in 1934 of eleven thousand copies.

Around 1930, on the one hand the Central *Jama'at* took in hand the work of translating the Quran in German, and on the other hand the Java branch started to translate the Quran in Dutch. The Dutch translation was published in 1936 and its five thousand copies have almost been exhausted. The German translation went to press in 1937 and three thousand copies are under print.

2. Writings on the life of the Holy Prophet

After the translation of the Holy Quran the Anjuman has turned its attention to biography of the Holy Prophet Muhammad. The Muslims possess these two strong weapons to win the world: the Holy Quran which inspires love for itself in the hearts of its readers, and the virtues of the Holy Prophet which win the respect of people. *Sirat Khair-ul-Bashar* in Urdu was first published in 1917. Its English translation, *Muhammad the Prophet*, was published in 1924.

A short life-story in English (*The Prophet of Islam*) was published in 1928 for wider circulation among non-Muslims. Both of these have so far been translated into sixteen languages.

3. Valuable literature on the teachings of Islam

Many valuable pamphlets were written on the teachings of Islam, the best of which is *The Teachings of Islam*. This has also been translated into many languages. *Islam the Religion of Humanity* and some other pamphlets have been translated into thirty languages. The most comprehensive book on Islam is *The Religion of Islam,* published in 1936. It consists of almost 900 pages dealing in full detail with all chief Islamic issues, whether related to belief and doctrine or to practice and actions. This book has been highly appreciated by prominent Muslim leaders, so much so that the late Marmaduke Pickthall opened his review of it in *Islamic Culture*, Hyderabad Deccan, with these words: "Probably no man living has done longer or more valuable service for the cause of Islamic revival than Maulana Muhammad Ali of Lahore."

4. Service to Hadith literature

The Anjuman did not lag behind in doing service to Hadith. A book was written about the status of Hadith reports (*Maqam Hadith*). *Sahih Bukhari* was translated into Urdu with explanatory notes and published in two volumes under the title *Fazl-ul-Bari.*

5. Research about other religions

In this connection the Urdu translation of one part of the Vedas has been done and published. In the book *Misaq-un-nabiyyin,* written by Maulana Abdul Haq Vidyarthi, prophecies about the Holy Prophet Muhammad from the scriptures of various religions have been compiled and reproduced in the original text along with their translations. Many books and pamphlets have been written on Christianity and have been published in large numbers in different languages. A book has also been written on the Babi religion.

6. Pamphlets

In addition to these treasures of knowledge, an extensive series of pamphlets continues to be published in which all kinds of criticism of Islam has been refuted as well as right guidance provided to Muslims both for their religious and worldly needs.

7. Free distribution of Islamic literature

A large number of books has been distributed free, reaching the most remote parts of the world. Ten thousand copies of the English translation of the Quran, fifteen thousand copies of the life of the Holy Prophet, and other pamphlets in even larger numbers have been distributed free. The literature that has been translated into other languages has mostly been distributed free. The tracts distributed free amount to a total of about ten million pages.

B. Second Category of Practical Work

1. The Woking Mission

... When the Anjuman came into existence, while its first task was the completion and publication of the English translation of the Holy Quran, its second was to manage the Woking Mission. Till 1930 the Woking Mission worked under the Anjuman. Now there is a separate Trust for it. The Islamic and the Christian worlds today are well aware of the useful work this mission has done. ...

2. Berlin Mosque

The second mission was established in Berlin in 1922 where a magnificent mosque was built at a cost of 150,000 Rupees. A quarterly magazine in the German language is issued from there. A number of European intellectuals and scholars have embraced Islam through this mission....

3. Vienna Mission

Four years ago a mission was established in Vienna, Austria, under the supervision of Baron Umar Ehrenfels, but due to political problems he had to flee his country and the work of the mission is in abeyance. ...

5. Java Mission, Indonesia

The Java Mission was established in 1924. The majority of the population here is Muslim but Christian missionary activity is very strong. This mission has not only succeeded conspicuously in infusing a new spirit in the Muslims but has also translated a large amount of our literature into the Javi language. Its Dutch translation of the Quran has also conveyed the message of Islam to the people of Holland. ...

7. Other countries

In many countries the work of the propagation of Islam continues by distributing literature through local organizations, for example Nigeria, Congo, Southern and Eastern Africa, Algeria, Egypt, Iraq, North and South America and China. ...

9. Educational work

In twenty-five years the Anjuman has founded two high schools, and constructed buildings for both of these along with boarding houses.

For a long time the Anjuman managed a Muslim Hostel where college students resided.

In this period of twenty-five years, the name that this *Jama'at* earned for itself in the world can be seen from the excerpts given below. It is especially worthy of note that the particular quality of the Ahmadiyya community pointed out in these excerpts, namely that it is the only Muslim group whose attention is focussed wholly on the propagation of Islam and on nothing else, was exactly what Maulana Muhammad Ali always emphasised. He never allowed the attention of the *Jama'at* to be diverted from this objective despite some instances when certain people within the *Jama'at* tried to initiate activities which had no direct bearing on the propagation of Islam. Here are the views of some Christian and Western writers about the *Jama'at:* [1]

1. "The Ahmadiyya Movement ... has become essentially a Moslem propagandist Society, though still looked upon with suspicion by the orthodox Ulama." (Prof. H.A.R. Gibb, *Whither Islam,* p. 353)

2. "The Ahmadis are at present the most active propagandists of Islam in the world." (Dr. Murray Titus, *Indian Islam,* p. 217)

3. "Here we find the newest and most aggressive forms of propaganda against Christianity which have ever originated, and from here a world-wide programme of Muslim Foreign Missions is being maintained and financed." (*Ibid.,* p. 239)

4. "The Ahmadiyya split into two camps ... The Lahore branch, being the more active, resolved to see what might be achieved in the direction of commending Islam to the western world ... The English translation [of the Quran], published in 1916, is the work of a modernist ...the editor takes great pains to demonstrate the surpassing excellence

---

1. These excerpts have been reproduced in their original English words.

of Islam ... he tries to show the inferiority of the religion of Christ." (E.J. Bolus, *The Influence of Islam,* p. 109)

5. "The Lahore group, who have seceded from the original community on the ground that they venerate the founder as a *mujaddid* (renewer of religion) and not as a *nabi,* are therefore more acceptable to public opinion in Islam ... their activity is more exclusively concentrated on the proclamation of Islam as the only religion that is in conformity with reason and nature ... Their influence is far wider than the number of their adherents would suggest. Their vindication and defence of Islam is accepted by many educated Muslims as the form in which they can remain intellectually loyal to Islam." (Rev. H. Kraemer, under *Islam in India Today* in *The Moslem World* edited by Dr. Zwemer, vol. 21, no. 11, April 1931, pages 170–171)

6. "The Ahmadiyya are an interesting exception to the generally prevailing communal spirit of Islam. They concentrate on religious propaganda and abstain from all politics, ... In this respect they are a very remarkable group in modern Islam, the only group that has purely missionary aims." (*Ibid.*)

7. "After the death of Mirza, his followers were divided into two camps. Whereas the one group led by the eldest son of the Messiah ... the other group which is the real and proper 'Ahmadiyya' made progress and extended itself within India as well as outside it. ... A very valuable literature has been produced by its members. To this belong the various translations of the Holy Quran in English, Dutch, etc." (*Der Orient,* edited by Paul Fleischmann, May-June 1937, under 'The Vital Power and Missionary Capacity of Islam')

Details of many such articles written by Christians about the Ahmadiyya Movement are given in the English booklet *The Ahmadiyya Movement as the West Sees it* compiled by Maulana Muhammad Ali.

Residence in Muslim Town, Lahore, and other events of 1938

At the end of 1937 and beginning of 1938, Maulana Muhammad Ali started construction of a house in Muslim Town, a development located outside the urban area of Lahore, on a plot of land he had earlier bought from Dr. Syed Muhammad Husain Shah. To build this new house he sold all his land in Qadian and some of his land in his ancestral village Murar. In May 1938 he was taken ill and went to Dalhousie. When he returned from Dalhousie in October after his recovery, he took up residence in his new house. He had lived nearly 23 years in the house at Ahmadiyya Buildings. On moving from there, he published the following letter in *Paigham Sulh* addressed to all members:

> "As friends know through this newspaper, on my return from Dalhousie this year I have taken up residence in Muslim Town, Ichhra. This settlement, which was founded many years ago by Dr. Syed Muhammad Husain Shah, is on Ferozpur Road by the side of the canal, and is approximately five miles from Ahmadiyya Buildings.
>
> One part of this settlement was named *Ahmadiyya Basti* (Ahmadiyya township), where many Ahmadi friends purchased plots to build houses. Now the Anjuman has itself acquired a large tract of land at a distance of about half a mile from there, and many other members have also bought lands there. I am sure that in the near future these will be populated and become a means of progress for the community. The purpose of founding this *Ahmadiyya Basti* was that in Ahmadiyya Buildings there was not enough space to meet the growing needs of the Movement and many members also felt that having our own settlement at one place is a way of consolidating the *Jama'at*. However, that stage has not yet been reached where that purpose can be fulfilled, though some members of the *Jama'at* have gathered here and the Shah sahib has built a mosque where congregational prayers are now held regularly.
>
> Though that stage had not yet been reached that I should move from Ahmadiyya Buildings to this new settlement, but last year, at the beginning of 1937, a few

days after the annual gathering, an illness came upon me which I took initially to be an ordinary ailment. However, by June, when I was ready to go to Dalhousie, the illness had progressed and in the opinion of the doctors it was tuberculosis. It was thought that by going to Dalhousie there would be remission from it; however, against expectation my condition deteriorated there and I was confined to bed for nearly two months. Then there was some improvement but all my doctors concurred that the cause was tuberculosis and under these circumstances I was forced to arrange for residence in an open area. After this, when the fever started again last May and continued till July, our friend Dr. Ghulam Muhammad also was of the firm opinion that it is tuberculosis. It was Allah's favour that He helped me just at that time of complete disappointment and granted me a new lease of life. Keeping in view the causes of these circumstances, I had no choice but to take up residence in an area of open air.

It was not easy for me either to leave the house where I had spent more than twenty years of my life and on which I had spent much money to make it suitable for living and to provide the necessities of the house. But to disregard treatment and ignore precautionary measures would have been against the Divine law. So I was forced by circumstances to move. I cannot yet say whether this move of house will be beneficial for me or not. This is in Allah's hands but it was my duty to try so that if Allah wills I could serve the religion a little longer. There is no doubt that here I would not be able to do the service that I could do by living in Ahmadiyya Buildings. Besides other facilities, I used to be able to meet friends and visitors at any time, but that is not possible here. However, I also want to say that, due to the attacks of illnesses during the past two years as well as on account of age, I cannot now work as hard as I used to be able to. By living away, I will also be more free from office work as well as being able to rest more. So I hope that friends will excuse this move of house as being beyond my control.

It is true that my convenience will cause difficulty for those who want to meet me. But I hope that in view of my illness and disability they will be prepared to accept it for my sake. I assure them that my heart is still in Ahmadiyya Buildings, and it is my wish to spend the rest of my life in the company of those friends to whom I have become close during my stay of twenty-two years in Ahmadiyya Buildings, and that I die in their hands. In fact, it has always been my heart-felt desire that upon my death my funeral service should be conducted in the mosque of this same Ahmadiyya Buildings, my body being placed at the very spot where I have stood over the years drawing the attention of my friends to the service of Islam, and where I have spent the best time of my life after Qadian.

Under these circumstances I certainly request friends that whenever they take the trouble to come to Lahore they should take a little more trouble to accord me the privilege of a visit because meeting such sincere friends, who gather only to please Allah, comforts and strengthens my heart. Though it has become more difficult for my friends to visit me here, their reward has also increased by the same measure, and my separation has become a means of greater reward for them. Perhaps it is also a trial for them because when they have been coming to Lahore their visit has often involved some worldly purpose, but now that they will have to extend their journey it will be purely in the way of Allah and marked by more sincerity. It was my desire to come to Ahmadiyya Buildings every day regularly at a fixed time and spend one or two hours there, but in the present circumstances my friends do not agree."

Passing away of Syed Ghulam Mustafa Shah and Babu Manzur Ilahi

In 1938 two valuable souls of the Lahore Ahmadiyya *Jama'at* departed to meet their Creator. In the middle of May the death took place of Syed Ghulam Mustafa Shah, headmaster of the Muslim High School. He was distinguished by his high moral virtues, love for Islam and Ahmadiyyat and zeal to serve the *Jama'at*. He had a natural aptitude for teaching and education, and the high renown of the Muslim High School was due to his hard work.

The other venerable figure was Babu Manzur Ilahi who died on 8 October 1938. Although he had been a zealous Ahmadi since during his employment in the railways, on retirement he devoted himself entirely to service of the religion and came to live in Ahmadiyya Buildings. The duty that he took up particularly, which he performed most excellently, was to disseminate information about Islam and the *Jama'at* all over the world by means of correspondence and letter. It was as a result of his efforts that the valuable literature of this *Jama'at* reached many countries of the world where it was translated into the local languages and branches of the *Jama'at* were created in several countries. He did his work so quietly, unassumingly and selflessly that most people in the *Jama'at* were not even aware of his valuable contribution and ceaseless efforts. The single-handed achievements of this one man are a golden chapter in the history of the *Jama'at,* a glimpse of which can be seen in the obituary that Maulana Muhammad Ali wrote upon his death from Dalhousie:

> "The news of the death of Chaudhry Manzur Ilahi reached me yesterday at about ten o'clock — *'We belong to Allah and to Him do we return'*. A few days ago I was delighted to hear that he had recovered and was on his way back from Batut. When we parted in Lahore, both of us were ill. By the grace of Allah I recovered and I received the good news of his recovery as well. I thought that we had been given further opportunity to work together. But alas, with the Chaudhry sahib's death, I have lost my arm.
>
> This is an irreplaceable loss for our *Jama'at.* We cannot see anyone else to take his place, but of course God has power over everything.
>
> Most members of the *Jama'at* will probably be unaware of the tremendous service to the religion done by the Chaudhry sahib because he worked so quietly that no one knew about it. I have never seen anyone working with so much sincerity, dedication, commitment and diligence.

When he was in employment he performed his official duties most ably and diligently. Alongside that, he carried on with his missionary work not only during his tours of branches of the *Jama'at,* but when he would return from a trip or from his office, tired and exhausted, instead of resting at home he would head straight for the Anjuman's office and busy himself in his extensive correspondence work till midnight. He kept in touch with news from Islamic countries so that if there was any useful information [from the propagation point of view] it would find a permanent place in his mind. He would search through newspapers and magazines to find out where in the world the work of propagation of Islam was required and to which corners of the world the message of Islam could be taken.

During the last two or three years, when his health deteriorated, even then he did not give up this hard labour and despite the repeated advice of his friends to take rest and reduce his workload he continued as before. Allah made his hard work and devotion bear great fruit. He made the Holy Quran and other Islamic literature reach such places in the world that were not even known to most Muslims. He spread the light of Islam to libraries of America and Japan, libraries on board ships, and to countries of Europe, Asia and Africa. By searching information about various islands and countries he tracked down Muslim communities whose existence was unknown to the outside world. His work in the field of propagation of Islam is unequalled by any other individual in this age. In outward appearance he was sitting at home, but his spirit used to travel over all the countries, spreading the message of Islam everywhere. The translation of our literature in different languages of the world and its distribution in those countries was due to his resolve and determination.

In the spread of the Ahmadiyya Movement also, no one else did as much as the late Chaudhry Manzur Ilahi. He set up branches of the Ahmadiyya *Jama'at* in more than fifty countries. If the Ahmadiyya *Jama'at* had spent hundreds of thousands of Rupees to send its missionaries to all those countries, all of them together could perhaps not have achieved as much as this man of God did single-handedly staying at home. There are many who call out for the extension of the *Jama'at* but no one did as much practical work of *Jama'at* building as the late Chaudhry sahib. What is painful is that there does not appear to be anyone to continue his magnificent work; but 'you know not that Allah, after that, may bring about a new event' [the Quran, 65:1]. He showed by his example that if a person is sincere and full of zeal he can achieve by working from home what others cannot do even by travelling all over.

The desire expressed by the Promised Messiah that we should propagate Islam by sending literature all over the world, and that it is not necessary to send missionaries to every place, was fulfilled by the late Chaudhry sahib. His name will remain forever as a guiding star in every country in the field of the service of Islam.

O God! shower Your countless blessings and mercies on his soul and produce in this *Jama'at* such young people who would follow in his footsteps and grant them to work with the same dedication and diligence, quietly and unassumingly. *Amen!*

Muhammad Ali,

Dalhousie, 9 October 1938."

Deepest desire of a true devotee of Islam

The zeal in Maulana Muhammad Ali's heart for the service and propagation of Islam, and his fervent desire for its triumph, can be glimpsed from a prayer he sent in writing to Shaikh Muhammad Ismail of Lyallpur (now Faisalabad) when the latter was going for the Hajj to Makkah. He wrote:

"The place you are going to is the abode of all the grace and help of Allah the Most High. The days you will be spending there are the special days of the bestowal of the gifts of the Almighty. It will be a time when all veils between God and man will have been lifted. It will be the time when prayers are granted. Hearts will be melting, eyes will be full of tears, and thoughts will run towards God uncontrollably. In such an atmosphere, whether you are passing by the walls of the House of God, or standing in the gathering at Arafat, or are alone at night, and of course when you go to Madinah and are at the Holy Prophet's mausoleum, say the following prayer, in any form as God guides you."

That prayer was as follows:

"O God, Your religion is in a state of the utmost destitution. The world is full of your bounties; there are mountains of gold and silver in the world. Yet, O Master, means cannot be found to spread the religion sent by You, the very religion that You promised to make triumphant over all other religions, and about which You commanded that it should be taken to all corners of the world. O God, money is being spent like water to spread the teachings of Trinity and Atonement, with the backing of worldly power, but the true religion sent by You is so helpless that even the hearts of the Muslims do not melt for it. Many are the lovers of Your Holy Prophet but none to sacrifice themselves for that love's sake.

O God, Your Promised Messiah created a community to spread Your religion in the world and to show Your promises being fulfilled, but sadly that community too has gone after the field of politics, leaving only a small group which the world looks down upon with contempt. But, O God, it is weak and unable to fulfil the duty You have entrusted to it. O God, create in their hearts the same passion for the cause of Your religion as You created in the heart of Your Holy Prophet. Create in them the same feeling of anguish for their religion as You created in Your Holy Prophet, as indicated in the words: 'Perhaps you will kill yourself with grief because they believe not' [Holy Quran, 26:3].

O God, cool down their love for this world and ignite such a fire of love for You in their hearts that it burns all trash and its heat inspires dead hearts with new life.

O God, send the winds of Your succour over this *Jama'at,* pour down the rains of Your blessings upon them and open the doors of Your mercies for them. O God, grant this group to spread Your Word to the corners of the world. O God, make us witness in our life-time that in the lands of the *Dajjal* the sounds of *Allahu Akbar* arise loudly, mosques are built and Your name echoes in the air. O God, show us the same sight that You showed to Your Messenger and his true followers, of people entering into Islam through them in groups upon groups. *Amen,* again *amen!*"

(*Paigham Sulh*, 26 January 1938, p. 2)

Address to young people

On *Eid-ul-Fitr,* 24 November 1938, he addressed the young people of the *Jama'at* in the following words:

"At the end I want to say something to my young friends, particularly those studying in colleges — that is that you must keep alive the traditions of the Ahmadiyya comm-unity. The Ahmadiyya *Jama'at* stands for spreading Islam in the world and taking the Holy Quran to people. Do not let this tradition of yours go into decline. Some may perhaps think, what honour will they achieve if they propagate Islam? I assure you that there is no other work in this world worthy of greater respect. This is the mission for which God has been raising the prophets and the righteous. There are countless other tasks in the world but God did not send prophets for any of those. So it is a matter of pride for us that in this age, when the Muslims have entirely neglected the propagation of Islam, Allah the Most High has chosen our *Jama'at* to spread Islam. While it is a matter of pride, it is also a position in which we must humbly plead before Allah, as the task for which Allah had raised such great people in the past has now been given to unworthy and incapable people like us to have the opportunity to carry out. So pray to God for strength to enable you to live up to this standard.

I will say again to my young friends, and say it again and again: keep alive the traditions of your community. Adhere to the Islamic code of morals and behaviour, read the Quran, listen to it, ponder over it and act upon it. Make it a your mark of identity that you respect the commandments of Islam.

The day will come, for each and every one of your elders, when you will bury their bodies in the ground with your own hands, and your descendants will do the same to your bodies. My young friends, I stress upon you with the greatest emphasis and advise you not to bury your traditions along with the bodies of your elders. Keep them alive and take them forward lest people say that this community is dying away."

(*Paigham Sulh*, 30 November 1938, p. 4)

3.6: From 1939 to June 1947

Publication of *A Manual of Hadith, Living Thoughts* and *The New World Order.* Three campaigns for Quran publication

The eight years 1939 to 1947 are the period during which Maulana Muhammad Ali, besides other writings, made some extremely valuable additions to Islamic literature in English by writing the books *The New World Order*, *A Manual of Hadith* and *Living Thoughts of the Prophet Muhammad*. He also started three very important campaigns: Translations of the Quran, Propagation of the Quran through missionary centres, and the proposal to establish an *Idara Talim-ul-Quran* (Institute for the study and teaching of the Quran). Through these campaigns he showed the *Jama'at* the path by following which it could succeed in attaining its real objective. To make these campaigns successful he not only appealed to the *Jama'at* again and again for donations and raised funds but he also went to Hyderabad Deccan twice and paid a visit to Bombay, raising a large amount of money from non-Ahmadi Muslims as well. He kept striving for these campaigns continuously. His zeal and fervour for the Quran can be gauged by reading his writings and *khutbas* of that period which are full of a particularly strong passion.

During this period, due to the Second World War, direct communications between the Anjuman and some foreign countries and missions were interrupted but the work of the propagation of Islam continued despite this, and as soon as the war ended new ventures were initiated. During this period the Anjuman's financial problems were reduced and its budget continued to make progress as usual. Also in these years Maulana Muhammad Ali used all possible ways to prove his case conclusively and irrefutably to the Qadiani *Jama'at* and its head. In this period, two more of the greatest stalwarts of this *Jama'at,* Dr. Syed Muhammad Husain Shah and Dr. Basharat Ahmad, passed away. The details of all these events are given below.

Writings from 1939 to 1947

These eight years included six years of the Second World War. During this period Maulana Muhammad Ali in his *khutbas* and writings very often drew the attention of the *Jama'at* towards the fact that as this terrible war was the conflict between Gog and Magog, which testified to the truth of Islam, the only solution for these problems of the world was to be found in Islamic teachings and therefore it was a heavy responsibility of our *Jama'at* to present Islam on an even larger scale to the Western nations. In this connection he first wrote two pamphlets: *Islam and the Present War* in both Urdu and English in 1940. Then in December 1942 a booklet *Niya Nizam 'alam* was published, in which it was argued that Islam is the only system that can establish lasting peace and security in the world. It was absolutely essential to present this treatise in English. When Maulana Muhammad Ali rendered it into English he expanded it to greater detail and produced it in the form of a new book *The New World Order,* which was published in February 1944. It especially addresses the Western nations, and offers the Islamic solution to their spiritual, economic, social and political ailments. It consists of four chapters:

1. Foundations of the New World Order
2. The Economic Problem
3. Home and Social Problems
4. The State.

Summaries of the teachings of Islam on these subjects are given in appendixes to the chapters. This book proved so popular that in 1945 a special plan was undertaken to publish it on a wide scale all over the world. It was also translated into several languages of Europe and Asia. Its first translation was in Arabic, into which Syed Tasaddaq Husain Qadari of Baghdad had it rendered. Such was the demand for it that all the twenty-five thousand copies of the first edition were sold in the first month, and a second printing was needed straightaway. This Arabic translation was widely distributed in Iraq, Syria, Palestine, Egypt, Tunisia, Morocco etc. and newspapers in all these countries wrote glowing reviews of the book, going so far as to recommend it as a text book for the Arab youth. These reviews and opinions of some renowned persons about this book were printed in *Paigham Sulh* from time to time. Another edition has been published in Beirut. In addition to German, Dutch, Turkish, French, Italian and various languages of India, it was also translated into the Siamese and Indonesian languages.

Around the time of the publication of the above book, another essential and valuable addition to Islamic literature in English was made when Maulana Muhammad Ali wrote the book *A Manual of Hadith*. This contains about 690 selected sayings and traditions of the Holy Prophet Muhammad on all aspects of life (out of which 523 are from *Sahih al-Bukhari*), given in the original Arabic text along with English translation and explanatory notes. There are some distinctive features that have greatly enhanced its usefulness. One is that at the beginning of each chapter he has quoted verses of the Holy Quran which deal with the subject-matter in hand, enabling the reader to realise that all the principles of Islam are set forth in the Quran and that the Hadith is the explanation of these principles as given by the Holy Prophet by his words and his practice. Then after quoting the verses of the Quran, he has summarised in a note the teachings contained in these verses and how that guidance is further elaborated in the Hadith reports that have been compiled in that particular chapter. There are altogether 31 chapters: for example, Faith, Divine Revelation, Knowledge, Purification, Ablution, Prayer, Mosque, Charity, Fasting, Pilgrimage, Jihad, Marriage, Divorce, Trade, Agriculture, Wills and Bequests, Inheritance, Regulations relating to Food and Drink, Dress and Adornment, and Morals and Manners. This book was printed beautifully as well. Its first edition, consisting of two thousand copies, was exhausted in two years. This book too became very popular among English-reading people all over the world. In May 1948 its Urdu translation was published under the title of *Ahadith-ul-'Amal*.

In the summer of 1945, when Maulana Muhammad Ali was in Dalhousie, the famous publishing firm of the United Kingdom, Cassell and Company, approached him through the Imam of the Woking Mosque to write a book on the life and teachings of the Holy Prophet Muhammad for their series of books entitled 'Living Thoughts' covering in brief the lives of famous teachers and thinkers in world history. The Maulana started to write this book while still in Dalhousie and sent the complete typescript to England at the beginning of 1946. This book was printed in 1947 but, due to problems in binding, its publication in Britain was delayed till March 1948. During this period the manuscript was read in detail by the publishers and it was liked so much that the company director Sir Newman Flower, himself an author, wrote to the Imam of the Woking Mosque saying that he had read the book from beginning to end and while he found the whole book to be excellent, the first chapter in particular, which gives the life of the Holy Prophet in brief, was "a masterly piece of work".

In this chapter, in addition to summarising the life of the Holy Prophet, the criticism levelled against him regarding the plurality of his marriages and the wars fought by him is also refuted. The rest of the book gives a summary of the teachings of the Holy Quran on various points. Though it is brief, still it is in a sense a comprehensive book on the life of the Holy Prophet and the teachings of the Quran, throwing light on all aspects of human life from the viewpoint of the Holy Quran and the practical life of the Holy Prophet Muhammad.

In the summer of 1946 Maulana Muhammad Ali translated this book into Urdu himself, in Dalhousie, which, after some delay, was published in the beginning of 1948. He named the Urdu translation not as 'The Living Thoughts' (*Zinda Afkar*) but as 'The Living Teaching' (*Zinda Ta'lim*). Several editions of this book under the title *Zinda Nabi Ki Zinda Ta'lim* have been published in Urdu.

When the English version of this book reached various countries, it was translated and published in the local languages. Foreign newspapers, especially English newspapers, wrote many glowing reviews of this book. Some reviews were quoted by the Maulana in his *khutba* of 11 March 1949 (*Paigham Sulh,* 23 March 1949).

Besides the important books mentioned above, he produced
many other writings during these eight years. In 1939 *The Muslim
Prayer Book* was published. In 1944 he revised his booklet *Al-Muslih
al-Mau'ud* ('The Promised Reformer'), which he had written in
1914. Now he published it again after revision and adding a new
preface because in January and February 1944 Mirza Mahmud
Ahmad had announced his claim to be the Promised Reformer on
the basis of a dream. In 1946 *History of the Prophets* was published, and another short book, *Prayers of the Holy Quran,* written
during that period was published in 1948, its Urdu translation,
Ad'iyat-ul-Quran, coming out later.

During these eight years he wrote many pamphlets, most of
these being about the Qadian *Jama'at,* as will be mentioned later.
In this period Maulana Muhammad Ali conclusively established
the argument over the leader of the Qadian *Jama'at* in particular.
He wrote and published the following pamphlets for distribution
in the Qadian *Jama'at* in this connection:

1. *Ahbab Qadian say appeal* ('An appeal to Qadiani friends').
2. *Maulvi Ghulam Hasan Sahib say ayk mukhlisana guzarish*
    ('Sincere Request to Maulvi Ghulam Hasan').
3. *Qadiani Yaum Tabligh* ('Qadiani Day of Preaching').
4. *Qadiani ahbab kay leeay ayk qabal-i ghaur mawazina* ('A
    comparison to ponder for Qadiani friends').
5. *Khalifa Qadian ka 1914 say pehlay mazhab* ('Beliefs of Khalifa of
    Qadian before 1914').
6. *Qadian aur Lahore kay jalson main donon fariqon kay rahnamaon
    key taqreeron key zaroorat* ('Need for the Heads of the two parties
    to make speeches at both the annual gatherings at Qadian and
    Lahore').
7. *Ahmadiyya Jama'at Lahore aur Qadiani Jama'at ka ikhtilaf*
    ('Difference of belief between the Lahore Ahmadiyya *Jama'at* and
    the Qadiani *Jama'at*').
8. *Mian Mahmud Ahmad Sahib ko half uthanay kay leeay muqabilay
    ki da'wat* ('Mirza Mahmud Ahmad called to compete in making a
    sworn statement').
9. *Mian Mahmud Ahmad Sahib ki da'wat-i mubahila* ('The call by
    Mirza Mahmud Ahmad to a *Mubahila*').
10. *Mian Mahmud Ahmad Sahib kay naam khuli chithi* ('Open letter to
    Mirza Mahmud Ahmad').
11. *Hazrat Nabi Karim ka maqam* ('Status of the Holy Prophet
    Muhammad').

12. *Faisla ka sahih tareeq* ('Right way to make judgment').
13. *Silsila Ahmadiyya kay do fareeq* ('Two Sections of the Ahmadiyya Movement').

Besides these, the other booklets he wrote are the following:

1. *Maujuda waqt main hamara faraz* ('Our duty at the present time'), 1940.
2. *Takfir of Fellow Muslims* (English), 1944.
3. *Wafat-i Masih, Nuzul-i Masih* ('The death of Jesus and his descent'), 1947.
4. *Islam ki musibat-i 'azma, iskay wujuh aur iska i'laj* ('The great tribulation faced by Islam, its causes and remedy'), 1947.

In 1948 the third, revised edition of the English translation of the Holy Quran without Arabic text was published.

Founding of the Holland Mission

In the beginning of 1939 Mirza Wali Ahmad Baig went to Holland and established a mission there. Maulana Muhammad Ali had issued an appeal for funds to meet the expenses of the mission. Dr. Syed Muhammad Husain Shah took it on himself to meet these expenses. In September 1939, however, the Second World War broke out and Holland having been occupied by the Nazis, not only was this mission closed but Mirza Wali Ahmad Baig was interned by the Germans and remained a prisoner of war till the end of the war. In 1948-49 there was a move to re-open this mission, which will be covered later.

The German translation of the Holy Quran and the Berlin Mosque

The German translation of the Quran has been mentioned before. Its printing was completed in Berlin in June 1939 and after binding it was published in August. However, the Second World War broke out shortly afterwards on 3rd September, and due to the bombardment of Berlin during the war the entire stock of this translation was destroyed except for a few copies.

Before the start of the war, Dr. Muhammad Abdullah, the missionary in Berlin, had returned to Lahore via Copenhagen (Denmark), entrusting the management of the Mission to the hands of the German converts. Till the end of the war, the Anjuman was out of communication with Berlin. First Germany occupied most of Europe but gradually she began to be defeated. British and American air forces carried out intense bombing of Berlin, destroying most of this city. In August 1945 the first news came through Reuters news agency that the Berlin mosque was safe. On receiving this news Maulana Muhammad Ali wrote the following in *Paigham Sulh*:

> "Berlin has been destroyed. ... Fire from the skies rained down upon it day and night. Thousands of tons of bombs were dropped on it. ... In the end a nation bent on revenge entered it and reduced the buildings of the city to rubble. But a correspondent of Reuter from this ruined city informs us today that the mosque is still standing.
>
> A poor *Jama'at* built a house of God in this city. The *Jama'at* did not do it for purposes of show and display. ... This *Jama'at* donated its money towards building the House of God and prayed humbly: 'Our Lord, accept it from us'.
>
> I remember that scene when there was a handful of women present at the annual gathering and the appeal came from our missionary in Berlin that there were no funds left to erect the minarets. I appealed to the small group of women and Allah opened their hearts so much so that many thousands of Rupees were raised by a few women of a small *Jama'at*. So today I congratulate my *Jama'at,* that Allah the Most High has shown the manifest sign that He has accepted their sacrifice ... and today He has shown the world that whatever He wishes to protect, He can keep it safe even in the raging fire."
>
> *(Paigham Sulh*, 22 August 1945, p. 4)

Death of Dr. Syed Muhammad Husain Shah

On 26 April 1939 there occurred the death of Dr. Syed Muhammad Husain Shah. He had fallen ill a few days earlier, and on 26 April he had a fatal stroke which he did not survive. The Doctor sahib has been mentioned earlier from time to time. He was a member of the original Sadr Anjuman Ahmadiyya, Qadian, appointed by the

Promised Messiah. It was in his house at Ahmadiyya Buildings, Lahore, that the Promised Messiah passed the last few days of his life and breathed his last. He was not only a God-fearing and righteous Ahmadi, but was a great philanthropist and spender in the way of Allah. With his death a pillar of the *Jama'at* was lost. Just at the time when he suffered the stroke, Maulana Muhammad Ali while praying in the small hours of the morning heard a voice saying again and again: "Carry him on your shoulders towards Allah". Maulana Muhammad Ali's thoughts turned to his elder brother Maulana Aziz Bakhsh who was ill at that time, but soon he received the news of the Shah sahib's illness.

At this great loss, Maulana Muhammad Ali issued a message to the *Jama'at* in *Paigham Sulh,* and in his Friday *khutba* while mentioning the unique personality of the Shah sahib and the services he rendered to the religion he said that, notwithstanding his previous financial sacrifices, the Shah sahib had just now donated property worth 52 thousand Rupees to the Jubilee fund and after that he agreed to give 200 Rupees per month permanently to support the Dutch mission. Maulana Muhammad Ali wrote:

> "This high rank of excellence was in fact in fulfilment of the trust that the Promised Messiah had reposed in the late Shah sahib. When the Promised Messiah was informed by Allah of his own approaching death he made an Anjuman as his successor, and while selecting fourteen members for it he picked four from Lahore. These four were: the late Shaikh Rahmatullah, Khwaja Kamal-ud-Din, Dr. Mirza Yaqub Baig and the Shah sahib. The excellence and sincerity with which these four carried out the task entrusted to them by Hazrat Mirza sahib seems to be indicated in this Divine revelation: 'In Lahore are our virtuous members'. These four friends had such passion to serve the Divine religion that they would travel from Lahore to attend every meeting of the Anjuman in Qadian and were always in the forefront in providing financial help. ... I held the position of Secretary of the Anjuman. The advice of these four revered friends was a source of strength for me, and their sincerity made a deep impression on me.

This was how, at the beginning of 1906, there began that friendship between the five of us which developed to the stage that we five became, as it were, one mind and heart. Now four of these friends, one by one, have gone to meet their Lord, and even though I see all around me true, sincere and faithful friends in our *Jama'at* but after the departure of these four I feel somewhat alone. But 'Allah is my Friend in this world and the hereafter'.

These four friends have set such a unique example of faithfulness, and of constancy and sincerity in the service of the religion, that it has few parallels today. The Messiah sent by God identified certain virtuous men to carry on his mission after him, and after Maulana Nur-ud-Din these four were the most prominent in this regard who bore the burden of work in practice. They discharged the trust placed upon them by the Promised Messiah so faithfully that they ever kept on making progress in the way of Allah." (*Paigham Sulh,* 4 May 1939, p. 3)

Other events of 1939

From 4 June till 1st October 1939, Maulana Muhammad Ali stayed in Dalhousie as usual. The series of articles he used to write from Dalhousie, in the form of letters to the members of the *Jama'at*, were that year published from August to October under the title: 'Who are we and what are our duties'. In these articles he kept reminding the *Jama'at* of its real position and work. He stressed that each one of us must always feel that firstly he has been prepared for a battle, and secondly that our *jihad* is the *jihad* with the Holy Quran as his weapon and each one of us is a soldier in this field. You must do your worldly work but the thought must always dominate your minds as to which means you can use to spread the message of truth to others and what service you can render to the Holy Quran. Among the means for doing this work stressed by him in these letters, the first and foremost is prayer. Falling before God to pray for the victory of the religion is a distinctive feature of our *Jama'at*. He specially stressed the importance of the *tahajjud* prayer. The second means is sacrifice, which is a constant, collective *jihad* through your property and possessions.

From October till the annual gathering of December 1939 Maulana Muhammad Ali continuously toured the outside branches of the *Jama'at,* visiting in addition to other cities Delhi and Quetta. A particular purpose he had in view in these visits was to organise the monthly subscriptions, so that every member should pay his dues according to the rate fixed by the Anjuman. He kept stressing this point in his Friday *khutbas* also during this entire period.

Events of 1940

After his illness in 1938 Maulana Muhammad Ali did not remain in good health. Following the annual gathering of December 1939 he fell ill again. During January 1940 he suffered from influenza and was unable to lead the Friday and the *Eid* prayers. Throughout February he was bed ridden. However, even during these periods of illness he did not give up his writing work and the management of the affairs of the *Jama'at.* The increasingly hot weather at the end of the month of May again caused him to get high temperature, so on 2nd June he went to Dalhousie, returning to Lahore on 30 September.

During all this time, while on the one hand he wrote numerous articles comprehensively refuting the wrong beliefs of Mirza Mahmud Ahmad, on the other he also expressed again and again his overwhelming zeal and fervour for the service of the Holy Quran in his *khutbas* and writings. In his Friday *khutba* on 11 October 1940, while dealing with the topic of the importance of making the Holy Quran an integral part of one's life, he pointed out the negligence shown by the general Muslim community to the Quran, that in their religious institutions subjects like Philosophy, Hadith and Logic are taught but no teaching of the meanings of the Holy Quran (*dars*) is given. He referred to the revolution brought about by the Promised Messiah in this respect, that he infused love of the Holy Quran into the hearts of his followers. Then he laid stress on the importance of instituting teaching of the Holy Quran (*dars*) in the *Jama'at* as a special characteristic of the *Jama'at,* and said:

> "Read the Quran by yourself and ponder and reflect over it. ... Study of the Holy Quran should become an essential

part of every Ahmadi's life. Teach your children to read the Holy Quran, along with meaning and significance; ... not much at a time, but a little, perhaps only a few verses, but make it a regular part of your life. ... No one can say which of you God will enable to understand the Holy Quran in such a way that he can thereby benefit the world. ... Develop such an urge in your hearts which creates a link between you and the Holy Prophet. This is his urge as portrayed in the words: 'Maybe you will kill yourself with grief, sorrowing after them, if they believe not in this announcement' [Holy Quran, 18:6]. Whoever will create such a zeal within himself will establish a connection for himself with the Holy Prophet. Both a transformation will take place within him and he will be a cause of producing a transformation in the world. ...

Allah the Most High does not let go to waste anyone's labour on the Holy Quran, however lowly he may be. I am an ordinary person; it is merely that a man who had spiritual power created a zeal and passion within my heart and as a result Allah enabled me to do some service to the Holy Quran. ... When I look at myself, I think, O Allah, how could a weak and worthless person like me do service of the Holy Quran? Yet Allah bestowed upon me so much blessing for the sake of His Holy Word. Today the man who would have set up his legal practice after passing his law examinations, or who would have passed the competitive civil service examination and at most become a judge of the High Court, then retiring into obscurity, ... he has by the grace of Allah been granted such a position of honour due to service of the Quran that even opponents are forced to acknowledge it....

There was a time when the renowned English convert to Islam Mr. Pickthall came here [to India]. He had been indoctrinated so much against us [Ahmadis] that he could not even bear to mention our name in any gathering. He stayed in Hyderabad Deccan for a long time. When he was leaving, he somehow came across my book *The Religion of Islam,* and [shortly] before his death he wrote such a glowing review of it that any book could hardly have ever received. He wrote: 'Probably no man living has done longer or more valuable service for the cause of Islamic revival than Maulana Muhammad Ali of Lahore.'

I am not mentioning this to claim that it is my achievement or an honour conferred upon me. I am mentioning it because it is the achievement of my Master, and an acknowledgment of his services to Islam ... because whatever knowledge there is in the book *The Religion of Islam* I acquired it from him or because of him....

I have come across a writing by an American author W. J. Milburn. He has recently written a book on different religions. To gather information about Islam he communicated with Muslim scholars from different Islamic countries. ... Ultimately he wrote to me and I sent him the English Translation of the Holy Quran, *The Religion of Islam* and *Islam the Religion of Humanity*. ... In his book he has copied almost the whole of the last-mentioned pamphlet and included many excerpts from *The Religion of Islam*. Along with that he writes:

'Perhaps no Muslim, living or dead, has done more than Maulana Muhammad Ali to lead people to see the good side of Islam [*orig:* Mohammadanism]. ... With these books no student of world religions would find any excuse for failing to understand Islam.'

... It is all due to the grace of Allah, the blessing of the Holy Quran, and the spirit infused by the Promised Messiah and benefit of his companionship; otherwise I am nothing: *'The beauty of my companion has produced this effect in me, otherwise I am but dust.'* ...

When I fall before God during the nightly prayers, my supplication to Him is that He bestow upon each and every member of our *Jama'at* love for the Holy Quran, passion for its service and propagation, and its understanding. ...

These days there is much clamour about organization — it is said that the *Jama'at* should be well organised and

> large, as this is the way to uphold the high repute of the
> Ahmadiyya Movement. There is no doubt that organiza-
> tion is commendable but it is not the real means of attain-
> ment of honour for this Movement. Other movements are
> also well organised. ... Our honour is not connected with
> strong organization but with the service of Islam and the
> Quran." (*Paigham Sulh,* 4 November 1940)

To certain persons in the *Jama'at* who, due to some grievance
with him personally or with the Anjuman, would become withdrawn and uncooperative, he always emphasised that they must
realise the importance of the work of upholding the glory of the
Holy Quran and the Holy Prophet, and not forget the greatness of
this work on account of personal reasons. He says:

> "If someone, seeing a fault in me, says that he does not
> care about the *Jama'at* ... why does it happen? It is when
> we ignore the greatness of the magnificent work for which
> we have come together and made our pledge. Such people
> in reality sacrifice the glory of God, the glory of Islam
> and the glory of the Holy Prophet for the sake of their
> personal desires, because on account of personal grievan-
> ces and the most minor wishes of their own they are pre-
> pared to cut their ties with the *Jama'at* whose only aim is
> to establish the glory of God, Islam and the Holy Pro-
> phet."

(Friday *khutba,* 8 March; *Paigham Sulh,* 17 March 1940)

Similarly in another *khutba* on 3 May 1940 he said:

> "Some matters seem trivial but in fact are very serious
> due to their consequences and are like a trial. The test of
> your faith is when you are hurt by a brother of yours but it
> does not make you lose faith in the cause. Some people
> claim to love God and His religion but when they are hurt
> in the least by a brother they give up service of God and
> the Divine religion. Their claim to love God and His
> religion is worthless. Those who are offended by me or
> by the Anjuman or by another prominent member of the
> Anjuman, should they be saying: we care not about this

work, we will not take part in it, we will not say our prayers behind such and such a man, we will not come to the mosque? No, instead of this, our feelings should be as has been expressed by the Promised Messiah in the following couplet [addressing Allah] :

> *Whether You forsake me in anger or show Yourself to me as a sign of pleasure,*
> *Whether You punish me or let me be, I can never stop clinging to You.*

Having accepted that man and having started the service of Islam because of accepting him, then unless the passion he had within him also rules in our hearts how can we carry on his mission successfully? What a great contrast between this noble and virtuous zeal, on the one hand, and on the other giving up the service of Islam by becoming offended on petty matters? There are also cases where a person, because of discontentment with a brother, has gone to Qadian and taken the pledge there."

(*Paigham Sulh*, 8 May 1940, p. 5)

In the Friday *khutba* of 5 April 1940 (*Paigham Sulh*, 18 April), he pointed out that the greatest mistake of the Qadiani *Jama'at* was to become so obsessed with forming and organizing the *Jama'at* that they neglected the propagation of Islam. He said:

"Some people from outside write to me saying that this *Jama'at* is small and will not survive after me. I consider myself so powerless and unworthy of being accorded such a status that God knows it best. The desire repeatedly arises in my heart that people who are more worthy should arise from the *Jama'at* and bear this responsibility. Along with that, I also firmly believe that, no matter what happens, if there is even one person in this *Jama'at* who truly loves God, then this *Jama'at* will remain alive.

No doubt you must expand, organise and strengthen the *Jama'at,* but for God's sake don't make organization an object of worship. If God is with you, you will succeed. But if, instead of relying on God, you place your reliance on the *Jama'at* and its strength, then you can never succeed in spreading the name of God. … Certainly you must rectify the weaknesses you see in the *Jama'at,* but let not that task hinder the work of propagation."

From time to time he especially used to address young people through letters in *Paigham Sulh,* impressing upon them the need to acquire knowledge of the Holy Quran, to do service of the Holy Quran and to achieve closeness to God. Hence he writes in a letter from Dalhousie:

"Knowledge of the Quran is a great inheritance from the Promised Messiah, with which the triumph of Islam in the world is bound up. Learn all the branches of knowledge but use them to serve the Holy Quran. … But you cannot bring them into its service unless you yourselves understand the Quran. You cannot take the Quran to the world unless you have the following three acquirements: firstly, learning the Holy Quran yourself; secondly, learning other branches of knowledge and bringing them into the service of the Quran; … and thirdly, learning other languages, and spreading the teachings of the Holy Quran in the world by translating them into those languages. Every young person should have these three objectives before him. … Along with that, you must remember that this is God's work; … the strength to do it can only be obtained by falling before God in prayer and beseeching Him for help. So just as it is the object of your life to acquire the knowledge of the Holy Quran for the purpose of spreading it in the world for its guidance, likewise praying to God to ask for help and for strength to do this work should also be considered as the purpose of your life. Allah has made the regular prayer (*salat* or *namaz*) the means for this. … Prayer is the foundation of Islamic culture and the Holy Prophet Muhammad has given it the prime place as the means for training the Muslims. … Adopt the habit of prayer firmly like a discipline. First get used to prayer as a formal regulation, then gradually you will develop joy and interest in it which will make it the means to gain strength from the Divine Power." (*Paigham Sulh,* 26 July 1940, p. 6)

Events of 1941

At the annual gathering in December 1940, Maulana Muhammad Ali put forward two important proposals to the community. One was in connection with his book *The Religion of Islam*, which had fulfilled the wish of the Promised Messiah he had expressed in 1892, at the time of making his claim, that a comprehensive book on Islam should be written in the English language to show the beautiful face of Islam. On this occasion Maulana Muhammad Ali proposed that copies of this book should be presented to persons whose views are influential in forming public opinion, such as authors. Accordingly this proposal was acted upon in 1941. The second proposal was that, to strengthen the foundations of the propagation of Islam in the West, a group of people should be prepared who, on the one hand, gain proficiency in different languages, and on the other hand study Islamic knowledge. So in 1941, and after that as well, he kept on stressing upon young people, from time to time, the need to learn foreign languages. Funds were also raised at this annual gathering to present the famous book *Muhammad in World Scriptures* by Maulana Abdul Haq Vidyarthi to different libraries, and also to help the Woking Mission.

In his Friday *khutba* on the third day of the annual gathering, Maulana Muhammad Ali addressed young people as follows:

> "Young people who are just at the start of their lives ought firstly to have a purpose before them, and it should be a grand objective. It is in accordance with the high or low nature of the aim before us that the good or evil powers within us develop and progress. ... The Holy Quran has pointed out that high purpose of life in the following words: 'And thus have We made you an exalted nation that you may be bearer of witness to humanity' [2:143], meaning that just as the Holy Prophet is your guide and model, so you must also become guides and models for the nations of the world. This is exactly the lofty purpose towards which the Imam of the Age has called us, that we become guides who show the right path. ...
>
> Secondly, not only has a grand objective been put before you but the path towards it has been made clear to you;

moreover some stages of the journey have already been covered, which encourages us. ...

Thirdly, I wish to say in this connection that no aim can be achieved unless you identify yourself with it and devote yourself to it entirely and whole-heartedly, and have the greatest passion for it.

Fourthly, to achieve the goal you must work hard, so hard as never to tire of it.... All of you, young or otherwise, are like soldiers of an army....

No night passes when I do not fall before God in prayer in the latter part of the night, feeling in my heart that I am in the presence of God along with my *Jama'at*. At that time, during prayer, the face of each and every member of the *Jama'at* appears in my view and I pray for all of them that Allah may increase their strength and courage and enable them to make ever greater sacrifices for the religion.

As I have just stated, we are in the last stages of our lives. In future all this burden is to fall upon you. I have reached such an age that every extra year that is granted to me I regard as only the grace of God. ... My beloved companions, Khwaja Kamal-ud-Din, Dr. Syed Muhammad Husain Shah and Dr. Mirza Yaqub Baig have gone to meet their Creator at the ages of sixty-two or sixty-three. When in 1938, at the age of sixty-three, I fell seriously ill, it seemed that my time had come, but God in His wisdom granted me some further opportunity to serve Islam."

(*Paigham Sulh*, 27 January 1941, p. 5 and 6)

After this he gave important advice to the young people. First of all he exhorted them to study the Quran, by making it a part of their daily routine to read it with understanding. Then he drew their attention towards other Islamic literature and the books of the Promised Messiah. Thirdly, he stressed the regular prayer, especially the *tahajjud* prayer. He added that we need both such young persons who earn income in the world, earning plenty of it, but spend a part of their income in the way of God, as well as such young ones who devote their lives to acquiring knowledge of the

Quran and spreading it. In many further Friday *khutbas* he kept on urging that young persons should each select one language and master it so thoroughly that they can translate the Holy Quran in it, and for this purpose they must study Arabic as well.

Maulana Muhammad Ali wanted to see such zeal and fervour in the hearts of Ahmadis for the religion of Islam and the propagation of the Quran that it would wake them in the middle of the night to rise and bow before God in prayer. This was exactly the kind of enthusiasm ruling his own heart. During 1941 he expressed these feelings in several Friday *khutbas*. He said:

> "The Holy Prophet has taught by his own example of rising at night and praying to Allah for long in solitude. ... What an anxiety there was in the heart of the Holy Prophet that kept him so restless! Until you develop that same anxiety within your hearts, prayers do not acquire their real sense. So rise up in the night, shed tears before God and seek His assistance by praying from the depth of your heart that He make His religion succeed. Remember it well that ultimately the religion of Islam will succeed. And whose greatness shall remain? The greatness of Allah, the Quran and Muhammad the Messenger of Allah. The religion of Islam will most surely be victorious but your hearts should overflow with the urge and deep desire to make it happen.
>
> Remember that no one can find enjoyment in prayer without getting up during the night. There should be such restlessness in your hearts that it wakes you up during the night: 'They forsake their beds, calling upon their Lord in fear and in hope, and spend out of what We have given them' [Holy Quran, 32:16]. Your warm and soft beds should not lull you to such sleep that you cannot wake. If at this time when the religion of Islam is crying for help, your heart is not so moved that you are restless to get up and cry before God, then you have achieved nothing. This is the only way you can make it victorious. ... Arise and cry for God's help to bring about the days of the victory and success of Islam soon. The day when the condition of

the entire *Jama'at* is that it rises in the night and falls before God with the prayer: O God, You sent this Quran for the spiritual nurture of the world and its reform, and for establishing peace; O God, this world is going astray and moving further off from peace; O God, it was Your promise to make the religion of Islam prevail in the world, so bring that time and establish peace in the world through this religion — that is the day success will lie at our feet."

(Friday *khutba,* 16 May. *Paigham Sulh,* 26 June 1941)

"You have before you the mighty aim of making Islam to prevail in the world. Set yourselves to this work. No doubt you are making financial sacrifices, self-sacrifices, but still one thing is required and that is to develop the same overwhelming urge that was in the Holy Prophet's heart ... 'Maybe you will kill yourself with grief, sorrowing after them, if they believe not in this announcement' [The Holy Quran, 18:6]. ...This was the pain that would not let him sleep. He would get up at night and fall in prostration before God. It is such an inner state that leads to a manifestation of the power of God, and it is for such a person that the aid and help of Allah comes. Make your hearts the abode of such feelings. Rise up at night and pray: O God, You Who promised Your Holy Prophet the triumph of the religion to take place in this age, help us to become the means of fulfilling that promise of Yours. Grant us to witness the victory of Islam in the world so that the purpose of the coming of the Promised Messiah, Your appointed one, is achieved."

(Friday *khutba,* 3 October. *Paigham Sulh,* 17 October 1941)

"As strongly as I believe that no opposition, however formidable, can shake Hazrat Mirza sahib, I also believe just as firmly that no one can destroy this *Jama'at* as long as there are people in it who shed tears at night. ... And I want to tell the doubters, whether they are within the *Jama'at* or outside it, that as long as there is a group in this *Jama'at* who cry in prayer at night, as described in the words [about the Holy Prophet and his companions]

'a party of those with you' [the Quran, 73:20], this
Jama'at will go on conquering the world with its spiritual
strength." (Friday *khutba,* 28 November 1941. *Paigham
Sulh,* 24 February 1942, p. 6)

From the beginning of June 1941 till the end of September
Maulana Muhammad Ali stayed in Dalhousie as usual. During this
time he went to Srinagar in Kashmir in June where he laid the
foundation stone for the mosque of the Srinagar *Jama'at* on 11
June. He stayed there for ten or eleven days, and dealt with organising the *Jama'at* as well as delivering public lectures. During
August 1941 he became quite ill with cough and cold. Also after
his return to Lahore in September he developed a temperature and
remained ill during October.

Campaign for charitable loan, December 1941
At the annual gathering in December 1941, Maulana Muhammad
Ali launched a scheme by the name of 'charitable loan'. At that
time the Second World War had entered a very critical stage and it
seemed that it would spread to India. On one side, the enemy was
at the eastern door of India and on the other, Europe and North
Africa were under German occupation and there was a possibility
that the Germans might reach India. At that time Maulana
Muhammad Ali launched a plan for the Ahmadiyya community to
make charitable donations to pay off the Anjuman's foreign debt
which amounted to fifty-five thousand Rupees. He appealed to
everyone to donate ten days' income and, after estimating the
income of various members, he prepared a list of names and
assigned contributions to them. He read out the list at the annual
gathering, and as he read each name people responded by shouting
labbaik (meaning, 'here I am to do thy bidding'). Thus in a few
minutes a sum of 25 thousand Rupees was collected from a small
Jama'at. Later on during the year, as a result of further appeals by
him, the Anjuman was relieved of foreign debt by the annual gathering of 1942.

First trip to Hyderabad, Deccan, 1942
For propagation purposes and at the invitation of some dignitaries
of Hyderabad Deccan, Maulana Muhammad Ali left on a tour of
Hyderabad on 20 February 1942. On the way he stayed in Delhi

for two days, and departing from there on the 23rd by the Grand Trunk Express he arrived at Hyderabad on the morning of 25 February. Maulana Abdul Haq Vidyarthi and Syed Akhtar Husain accompanied him. The news of his coming was already well-known in the intellectual and religious circles of Hyderabad and had also been published in the local newspapers. So at Sikanderabad railway station he was welcomed by Abdul Karim Babu Khan the *Ra'is* (Chief) of Sikanderabad and a large crowd of people. At Nampali railway station, where he alighted, there was a huge crowd of Muslims of all classes and religious denominations. He stayed at the residence of Abdul Karim Babu Khan.

His stay in Hyderabad was for seven days, till 3 March 1942. During this period three large public meetings were addressed by him. The first meeting was on 27 February at Sikanderabad under the chairmanship of Nawab Mazar Yar Jang Bahadur. In this meeting the topic of Maulana Muhammad Ali's speech was 'The Greatest Benefactor of the Human Race', in which he stressed the importance and imperative need of spreading the message of the Holy Prophet Muhammad in the world. In this connection he also removed some misconceptions about the Ahmadiyya Movement and acquainted the Hyderabad public with the work of the Lahore Ahmadiyya *Jama'at*.

The second meeting was also held in Sikanderabad on 28 February under the chairmanship of Dr. Khalifa Abdul Hakim, and the third meeting was in Hyderabad on 2 March under the chairmanship of Nawab Bahadur Yar Jang. In all these speeches the work of the propagation of Islam was highlighted, the attention of the general Muslim community was drawn towards the task of spreading the Holy Quran in the world, and some wrong impressions about the Lahore Ahmadiya *Jama'at* were corrected.

On Friday 27 February he led the Friday prayers at the library of the Hyderabad *Jama'at* and properly organised the *Jama'at*. At that time Shaikh Muhammad Inam-ul-Haq was the missionary from the Anjuman stationed in Hyderabad and head of the mission.

In addition to the public speeches, Maulana Muhammad Ali also delivered many speeches at various functions. Many dignitaries of Hyderabad and Sikanderabad invited him to dinners and on all occasions he made speeches. Besides this, from morning to evening people came to see him at Abdul Karim Babu Khan's residence.

This stay in Hyderabad made a very favourable impression: not only did the Anjuman benefit financially but the *Jama'at* there was strengthened and many dignitaries became admirers of the Anjuman. Thereafter they kept on insisting that he come again to Hyderabad. So in 1946 he paid another visit, which will be mentioned later.

On the evening of 3rd March he started his return journey via Bombay. Till 6 March he stayed with Mr. Naseer Ahmad Faruqui at Thana, a suburb of Bombay. Here too he had occasion to make speeches at various functions and meet some prominent people of Bombay. On his return from there, he stayed in Delhi for one day and arrived back in Lahore on 9 March.

Visit of Mr. Usman Woo

In September 1942, Mr. Usman Woo, a prominent Chinese Muslim leader who was touring India, came to Lahore. He was keen to meet Maulana Muhammad Ali who at that time was in Dalhousie. As Mr. Woo did not have much time, a telegram was sent to Maulana Muhammad Ali who came to Lahore on 28 September and met Mr. Woo in the evening. Mr. Woo told him that Chinese Muslims were well acquainted with the Maulana's name and work. He said that they knew two persons by the name of 'Muhammad Ali': the Muhammad Ali of politics (that is, Maulana Muhammad Ali Jauhar, editor *Comrade*) and the Muhammad Ali of religion. He said that he considered himself most fortunate to meet such a great author of Islam. On the morning of the 29th, Mr. Woo again came to Ahmadiyya Buildings and spoke at length with Maulana Muhammad Ali and other prominent members of the *Jama'at*. He informed them that many of the writings of Maulana Muhammad Ali had been translated into Chinese, mentioning in particular *Introduction to the Study of the Holy Quran*, *The Call of Islam*, *Muhammad The Prophet* and *Islam the Religion of Humanity*. This literature had reached China due to the efforts of Babu Manzur Ilahi through his work of propagation by means of postal correspondence.[1] Mr. Woo also said that this was such a *Jama'at* that has no parallel in the whole world and if Maulana Muhammad Ali ever visited China the Muslims there would treat him with the greatest reverence.

Passing away of Dr. Basharat Ahmad

In April 1943, Maulana Muhammad Ali and his family in particular, and the *Jama'at* in general, suffered a terrible loss when Dr. Basharat Ahmad died on 21 April. At that time he was staying with his younger son Mr. Naseer Ahmad Faruqui in Bombay. On 23 April his body arrived in Lahore by train and he was buried the same day. A few months before this, in January 1943, the Doctor sahib had completed the third volume of his monumental book *Mujaddid-i Azam.* After that he remained ill and had gone to Bombay.

Dr. Basharat Ahmad was born in October 1876 in Dharamsala. He received his early education in Sialkot, after which he got admission in the Medical College Lahore. In 1894 he married Halima Begum, daughter of Babu Safdar Jang, who was a police inspector. After completing his medical education he went to Africa for his first post, remaining there for eighteen months. After that he was stationed in different areas of the Punjab. He took the *bai'at* in 1902 and, like other notable Ahmadis, he became so attracted to Qadian that he would avail every possible opportunity to visit it. In 1910 his eldest daughter was married to Maulana Muhammad Ali so that, in addition to other shared attributes which will be mentioned later, a family relationship was also established between them, forging a close connection between these two elders of the *Jama'at.*

In 1931, when the Doctor sahib retired from his post in Ludhiana, a very lucrative employment was offered to him on behalf of a state. He wrote to Maulana Muhammad Ali, asking for his advice. In reply the Maulana wrote back the following couplet:

---

1. It was reported some years later that the books *The Teachings of Islam, A Manual of Hadith, The Religion of Islam, The Early Caliphate* and *Living Thoughts of the Prophet Muhammad* had also been translated into Chinese (Annual Report of the Anjuman, 1960–61).

"Life has been spent, there remains nothing except a few days.

Better it is that I should spend whole nights in the remembrance of Someone [i.e. God]."

The Doctor sahib was so moved by this poetic verse[2] that he decided to settle in Lahore, and the tremendous work he then performed in the service of the Holy Quran and the strengthening of the *Jama'at* will be remembered forever. A glimpse of his incomparable personality and his love for the Holy Quran can be gleaned from Maulana Muhammad Ali's Friday *khutba* and his article about the Doctor sahib's life which were published in *Paigham Sulh* upon his death. He was buried on Friday, and in his Friday *khutba* on the same day Maulana Muhammad Ali said that although he did not feel able to deliver the *khutba* due to his shock and grief, he considered it important to tell the *Jama'at* the lessons we can learn from the late Doctor sahib's life. He said in this connection:

"Dr. Basharat Ahmad was not an ordinary person. He was in fact a saint of Allah whose life was a model for others. Just now at the railway station, a young man said to me: the Doctor sahib was a lover of the Holy Quran and we young ones were lovers of his Quran teaching (*dars*). ... Hazrat Mirza sahib was commissioned by God, so no one can equal his love for the Holy Quran. After him Maulana Nur-ud-Din was the one in whom love for the Holy Quran had reached the highest stage. ... And after him the late Dr. Basharat Ahmad showed the greatest love for the Holy Quran. By profession he was a medical practitioner in government service, but wherever he was posted in connection with his employment he started regular Quran teaching sessions there. His exposition had such great power of attraction that... even non-Ahmadis also who once attended his *dars* would come again and again. ...

2. Dr. Basharat Ahmad had this verse framed and installed it in his room. After his death, in his memory Maulana Muhammad Ali took it and affixed it in his own office.

He served people in two ways: he treated their physical illnesses and their spiritual ailments....

In 1936 he fell critically ill but Allah restored him to health because He had ordained a task for him which no one else in either of the two *Jama'ats* was capable of doing. After this illness he wrote *Mujaddid-i Azam,* which will make his name live forever. Two volumes had already been printed during his life and he had completed the manuscript of the third despite ill-health. ... It was when this work was accomplished that God called him back.

His whole life was spent in performing the noblest deeds. He helped orphans and the poor and led them to better positions in life. ... His offspring that he has left behind are also very morally upright. ... Though by his death we have lost a pillar of our *Jama'at,* yet he has left two strong pillars he created in the form of his two sons."

(*Paigham Sulh,* 28 April 1943)

Maulana Muhammad Ali finished his *khutba* with the following words:

"Come, let us spend all our energies and strength to propagate the religion of Allah. Very few days remain of our lives. I am two years older than the Doctor sahib. I take everyday as a God-sent boon. Come and devote your life to the way of God. If you revive God's name in the world, God will keep your names alive."

Then Maulana Muhammad Ali wrote an article under the title *Doguna Qabil-i Rashk Zindagi* ('A doubly enviable life') in *Paigham Sulh* dated 23 June 1943. Some excerpts from it are given below:

"It is mentioned in Hadith that there are two persons whose lives are enviable: one on whom Allah bestows wealth and grants him the moral strength to spend this wealth in the path of truth, and the other on whom Allah bestows knowledge and he uses it to give judgment and teaches it to others. How enviable is that person's life who is enabled to do both of these: that is, he spends

wealth in the way of God and benefits the world with his knowledge as well!

"Hazrat Dr. Basharat Ahmad was not a very wealthy person.
He could have been if he had so wished, but this selfless man
never entertained the desire to amass wealth. ... He was a reflec-
tion of the Holy Prophet's attributes of helping poor relatives and
being a support for all. Right from the beginning, a considerable
number of his relatives who, due to misfortunes of life, were
unable to support themselves, became part of his immediate
family just like his own children. ... Ever since the Doctor sahib
joined the Ahmadiyya Movement, he gave the appointed proportion of his income in the way of Allah as if it did not belong to
him. ... He considered the regular subscription to be a trust which
he separated from his money, and he was always in the forefront
in contributing to various appeals. ... He placed reliance on Allah
to the utmost degree. ... He possessed many of the qualities of
Maulana Nur-ud-Din; in addition to love and understanding of the
Holy Quran, trust in God was one of these. When he retired he did
not wish to take a half of his pension fund as a lump sum, saying
that he did not need it. I suggested that he could use the money to
build a house in Dalhousie where he could then spend summer
months comfortably and serve the religion. He agreed to this
somewhat reluctantly. I had this residence, named 'Parveen', built
for him myself, putting much effort into it and supervising all the
work personally. Then for the next ten years, without a break,
I heard the recital of the remembrance of Allah from that house.
... In fact it was my selfishness because I wanted him to be near
me and me to be near him 'so that we may glorify You much
(O Allah), and much remember You' [Holy Quran, 20:33–34, on
Moses and Aaron]. ...

"He left one-third of his estate to the Anjuman. More than
one-third is not allowed by Islamic law, so whoever gives one-
third actually leaves everything in the way of Allah. ... The whole
of his life, from beginning to end, shows a shining example of
spending in the way of Allah. In an age when the hell of worldly
gain is calling out for more and more people to enter into it, and
the small belly of a man, which one day will be filled with a handful of earth in his grave, is not satisfied even by heaps upon heaps

of gold and silver, and the fire of greed for material wealth is burning the heart and mind of every person — at such a time if there is a man in whose heart there is not even one corner touched by love of material things, then he is most definitely a saint. ... Love of mammon and love of God cannot co-exist in one heart. ... Until a man's heart is cleansed of the dirt of the love of wealth he cannot attain spiritual purity. ...

"When some virtue reaches the utmost height in a person, it then radiates out from him like a beam of light, illuminating the hearts of others. I have witnessed that the closer people were to Dr. Basharat Ahmad the less love of worldly wealth they had. Closest to a man are his offspring, but a person is powerless, no matter how deeply he wishes, to create the same qualities in his progeny as are in him. However, I have witnessed this particular virtue in all the sons and daughters of the late Doctor sahib. He had two sons, to both of whom God has granted positions of high worldly rank and given them much wealth, but the passion with which they serve the religion and the sacrifices they make in the cause of the faith are very rarely met with in people who reach such high positions. ... Material wealth has no attraction for these two. ... I have also noticed the same traits in his daughters according to their status. His eldest daughter is my wife. I have had some very difficult times in my life, including the long period of five and a half years when I had no means of livelihood. But neither in that period nor afterwards, whether in prosperity or poverty, did she make any burdensome demands on me. In fact, during the period of prosperity, in response to various appeals over time she donated all her jewellery, by and by, which was never replaced. ...

"Another quality that the late Doctor sahib possessed, which our Holy Prophet has declared as the second enviable one, was that Allah bestowed upon him knowledge and understanding of His Holy Book to the highest degree and, along with that, He enabled him to impart this knowledge to others. ... And he imparted it in such a wonderful way that he infused into those people who listened to his teaching or read his explanations of the Quran the same love for this Holy Book as he himself entertained. A feature I noticed in his comprehension of the Holy Quran was that it overflowed with spirituality, which made your heart firmly convinced of the truth of his explanation. ... His manner of expression was also highly effective, in writing as well as speaking. His own overwhelming conviction that everything in the Holy Quran is resplendent with truth, he filled the hearts of others with the same faith as well. I had little opportunity to listen to his teaching, and that only on three or four occasions surreptitiously, because due to his generous opinion about me he thought that whenever I was present I should teach the Holy Quran. ... Those three or four occasions were during the annual gatherings. Usually I used to leave the mosque after the *fajr* prayers and then the Doctor sahib would start his teaching. However, on those occasions I purposely remained in the last row so that he would not be aware of my presence. The last such occasion was during that annual gathering when on the last day he gave explanation of the two chapters *The Elephant* and *The Quraish* combined. It put the whole gathering in a state of ecstasy and it furthered my own faith in the word of God so much as to make a lasting impact on my heart. So on the same day in my concluding speech I said that when I was listening to his explanation I was wishing that the author of *Bayan-ul-Quran* should have been the Doctor sahib.

"Along with love of God and of His Holy Prophet and of His Holy Book, the Doctor sahib also entertained another love in his heart, and that was love for the man who had endeared the Holy Quran to him, in other words the Imam of the Age. After retirement, ... having reached the age of sixty years, he performed that monumental task which will not only make his name live forever but testify to the tremendous power that love can create in one's heart. This work was the writing of *Mujaddid-i Azam*. In 1936 at the age of sixty, at a time when he was laid low with illness ...he had an urge in his heart as he has mentioned in the Preface to *Mujaddid-i Azam* ... He had still to take care of two daughters following the death of his wife. At that age, in those circumstances, what was it that moved him to undertake the writing of a magnificent book of two thousand pages for which he had to study and research through some twenty or twenty-five thousand printed pages. It was love for the Promised Messiah. ... By writing this book he has vastly excelled and surpassed all other biographers of the Promised Messiah. Only one man was worthy of such a task, and after his first serious illness Allah granted him a new life as if to enable him to write *Mujaddid-i Azam*. Just when the third volume was completed, the author was recalled by Allah. ...

"Love of wealth makes a person miserly while love of Allah makes him generous and enhances his moral character. Love of Allah is a light which bursts out from the heart and illumines the face. When such a person meets others it seems as if his face is radiant with light. ... A man's character is really tested inside his home. ... The late Doctor sahib's children loved him as dearly as it is possible for believers in One God to love someone while remaining within the limit of not worshipping anyone other than God. ... They were convinced of his closeness to Allah and the acceptance of his prayers by Allah. Whenever they faced any problem they would forthwith turn to him to pray for them. A true saint is he who is accepted as such by his close family. Many can appear to be saints to the outside world, but to be a saint at home is not easy. The late Doctor sahib was a saint in the home as well as outside. ... For me he was always such a friend by merely meeting whom any sorrows I may have had were lifted from my heart regardless of whether I mentioned my troubles to him or not — and usually I was not in the habit of mentioning them. But the One Who really relieves us of our troubles is Everlasting: 'And Allah is Best and ever Abiding' [Holy Quran, 20:73]."

Three ways for service of the Holy Quran

During the three years 1943, 1944 and 1945, Maulana Muhammad Ali laid the foundations of three grand schemes for the service of the Holy Quran, and he began work on these schemes during the remaining six or seven years of his life. He thus showed the *Jama'at* the path to follow in order to fulfil the role of being heirs of the Promised Messiah and carry out the tasks entrusted to him by Allah. After this there was another large-scale scheme, that of distributing literature, which he promoted in the last two years of his life. He raised funds for it himself and went much of the way towards accomplishing this scheme in his own lifetime. During these last years of his life, he devoted all his efforts to establishing some permanent basis for the service of the Holy Quran, and to achieve this, his first proposal was to set up a 'Quran Publication Trust' which later on took the form of the 'Quran Translations Fund'.

Proposal for 'Quran Publication Trust'

In September 1943, before the last ten days of Ramadan, Maulana Muhammad Ali made an appeal to the *Jama'at* in the paper *Paigham Sulh* for a special prayer. He wrote as follows:

> "It was the 14th or 15th of the month of Sha'ban that about half an hour before my usual waking time, a state of half drowsiness descended upon me and in that state the following words were on my lips which I kept on re-peating: *Rabbi qarrib-nī ilai-ka, qarrib nuṣrata-ka illaya,* 'O my Lord, draw me towards You and bring Your help near me', till it was time for me to rise. I feel that the time of help from Allah the Most High is drawing nearer, whether it comes in my lifetime or comes to the *Jama'at* after me. I want to appeal to you for a special prayer. ...
>
> The dearest wish in the heart of the Promised Messiah was to have the Holy Quran translated into different languages and sent to non-Muslims. Exactly this has been the highest goal of our *Jama'at*, and what God has enabled our small *Jama'at* to do in this respect no Islamic state or other Muslim organization has been able to do. ... However, so far we have not laid a permanent foundation for this work. Now on the 13th and 14th of Ramadan a proposal has come from afar which gives a strong hope of placing this work on a permanent basis. It is suggested to establish a Trust for the publication of the Quran with a capital of 100,000 Rupees to translate the Holy Quran into various languages and distribute it among non-Muslims. By the grace of God signs of success of this scheme have immediately appeared, and instead of 100,000 Rupees perhaps funds of 200,000 Rupees may be raised by December. So it occurred to me that we should lay the foundation of this task during the blessed month of Ramadan, the month that is specially associated with the revelation of the Quran. ... While on the one hand I am taking

some practical steps to establish this scheme, on the other hand I would like to request members of the *Jama'at,* in *tahajjud* prayers during these last ten days of Ramadan which include the night *Lailat-ul-Qadr*, to pray specially for success in this mission. Our work is to spread the Quran in the world, and that can only be done by translating it into other languages and making it reach the people. To win the hearts of the people is the Quran's own work, and that will happen for sure because it is the promise of Allah Himself: 'We have not revealed to you the Quran that you may be unsuccessful' [the Quran, 20:2]. Neither did he fail to whom the Quran was revealed nor will those fail who spread the Quran in the world."

(*Paigham Sulh*, 22 September 1943)

It has been mentioned before that on the occasion of the Silver Jubilee Maulana Muhammad Ali had tried to place the work of the propagation of the Quran on a firm footing so that it would continue to be done into the future by the help of a permanent fund dedicated for this purpose. On that earlier occasion also he had requested the *Jama'at* to pray for 40 days; as this work was ordained by God, so only by praying to Him could the resources be found to establish a permanent basis for it and to develop it further. However, at that time also the General Council of the Anjuman did not agree to allocate the Jubilee Fund to the propagation of the Quran but decided to spend it on consolidation of the *Jama'at*. No notable consolidation of the *Jama'at* was achieved, only an opportunity was lost for the propagation of the Quran. Now he put this suggestion again before the *Jama'at,* and laid stress on prayer because by falling before God the same zeal and passion for the propagation of the Quran that dominated his own heart could perhaps be fired up in other hearts as well. In his Friday *khutba* on 15 October 1943 he further explained his proposal in the following words:

"The suggestion to establish a Quran Publication Trust has come from a place much afar, but it is the work of this *Jama'at* and if it please Allah this *Jama'at* will do it. What does the 'Quran Publication Trust' mean? Some funds will be donated by the Anjuman for the propagation of Islam and for some we will ask our friends to donate individually. This 100,000 to 200,000 Rupees could be invested in some business, and the resulting income be used to translate the Holy Quran into different languages of the world.

... I mentioned this for the first time in my Friday *khutba* in Dalhousie, and after the prayers Shaikh Mian Muhammad was the first one to agree, offering to give ten thousand Rupees. It is a matter of being convinced. I hope that, for the sake of the Quran, our *Jama'at* will make financial sacrifices, and every one will feel the urge to keep his name remembered forever after him by means of this perpetual endowment. The Holy Quran will be translated into different languages and made available to people, whether free or at a low price or at full price, in languages whether of India or of Europe.

There is no organization at present that has this as its objective. Just think, you cannot find any power or state in the world whose aim is what this *Jama'at* is doing, or who has been as successful as this *Jama'at*. Keep it in your mind that there is no other task more virtuous than this. Try to support it. This proposal will be launched very soon. I wish to be able to announce at the annual gathering that this trust has started functioning with some funds. Then it will be strengthened as more and more people come to join this effort."

(*Paigham Sulh,* 20 October 1943)

Calling a meeting of the General Council on 31 October, he presented this proposal to it, but the meeting could not reach a decision. Then at the time of the annual gathering the General Council decided that the Anjuman should start a 'Quran Translations Fund', which would be used for producing translations of the Quran. However, later events proved that the proposal to create a separate trust to safeguard the funds was more sound because the Anjuman, whenever facing financial problems, transferred money from the Quran Translations Fund to other expenditure. Though this work commenced on the right lines and translations of the

Holy Quran were started in four languages, but after a while the Anjuman's resolve weakened, and after Maulana Muhammad Ali's death there was no one to repeatedly emphasise the importance of this work, so the translations started during his life were not completed. Anyhow, at that time it was the General Council's decision which was acted upon.

The first proposal — Quran Translations Fund

Accordingly, at the annual gathering in December 1943 Maulana Muhammad Ali launched this fund and made an appeal for it. Before the appeal he made a very moving, comprehensive speech (*Paigham Sulh,* 5 January 1944). Reciting the verses "And if there could be a Quran with which the mountains were made to pass away…" from chapter *Al-Ra'd* (13:31), he said that the Holy Quran intrinsically possesses a tremendous power that clears all obstructions in its way. According to this verse calamities will continue to befall the dwellings of those who deny the Holy Quran, until Allah's promise to make Islam triumphant is fulfilled. Then, regarding the words "or the earth were cloven asunder" which can also signify "the earth will be travelled over", he said that this Quran will cover the distances of the earth and reach its ends. It is a historical fact that it happened in the past. Thirdly, it is said here: "or the dead were made to speak". Thus the work of raising the spiritually dead to life was done by the Quran at the time of its revelation and will be done by it again.

Following these words God says: Have the believers lost hope that if Allah please He would certainly guide the whole world? It too will come about as it happened in the past, that tribulations will continue to befall the deniers until the promise of Allah is fulfilled. He mentioned the two phases of opposition to Islam: one which occurred at its beginning and the other by the nations of Gog and Magog. These nations first tried by means of the Crusades to wipe out Islam with the sword, but failing in that they tried more subtle means. It is promised that, after the success of Gog and Magog, Islam will be triumphant.

After this he made an appeal for starting the 'Quran Translations Fund', upon which approximately 100,000 Rupees were raised in the form of cash and promises.

At the opening of the annual gathering in 1943, in his Friday *khutba* on 24 December (*Paigham Sulh,* 12 January 1944), he drew the attention of the *Jama'at* to the point that each one of its members was a spiritual soldier. He said:

> "Firstly, I want to tell you who we are and what are our objectives. Forty three years ago, with some thoughts of a worldly career, having made some arrangements to start my law practice, and after making preparations for my future, I arrived in Qadian. After I had been staying there for two or three months, when I had rented a property in Gurdaspur and put all the resources together for practising law, Hazrat Mirza sahib told me one day that he intended to start a magazine in English to convey conclusive arguments to Christianity and other religions, and that he wanted me to do this work. I had never, even during my college days, gained experience of speaking or writing in English. If I had given a reply in view of my lack of ability, I would have confessed my handicap and told him that I was not capable of doing that work. Instead I bowed to his command. The Promised Messiah himself wrote the objectives of this magazine and published them in the first issue, writing that in this age there was a great spiritual war going on in the world, ... and when progress in worldly affairs reaches its peak, that is exactly the time of the progress of religion. I have told you this because our *Jama'at* has been formed to wage a spiritual war against the satanic forces. You must all understand this objective well. You are gathered here because the man whose coming was promised 1300 years ago put this objective before you, and you are engaged in a spiritual battle according to his command."

During 1944 Maulana Muhammad Ali kept on making appeals for the Quran Translations Fund. In addition to his Friday *khutbas,* he kept writing letters to members personally as well as collectively through *Paigham Sulh*. On one occasion he said:

> "I am in the last phase of my life. I cannot say how much longer I will be granted, but this is your task and you have to do it."

In his *khutba* on 28 April, he said:

> "During the Promised Messiah's time, those people who lived there were struck by the fact that, when people from outside came to see him daily, he would go over the same issue of the death of Jesus every time. Those who lived there wondered why the same point was being stressed again and again. But, glory be to God, as a result of one man emphasising this issue so much, people today have generally accepted it, or there are others who recognise the truth within their hearts but dare not discuss it openly.
>
> Repeating certain points is because of their importance and in order to firmly establish them in the world. In the case of the issue of the death of Jesus, it was the foundation of the Promised Messiah's claim, but in practical matters what Hazrat Mirza sahib has drawn people's attention to is to make the Holy Quran uppermost in their lives and to propagate it in the world. This was his real aim, and he felt deeply pained in his heart to see that Muslims were no longer concerned about the propagation of the Quran. ...
>
> I too wish to stress repeatedly — in fact it should be the duty of all of us — the necessity of making the Holy Quran uppermost and propagating it, until the same effect is achieved as in the case of the issue of Jesus' death, and it becomes firmly established in the minds of the Muslims that without propagating the Holy Quran and making it uppermost, there is no salvation for them."

(*Paigham Sulh*, 4 May 1944)

In the Friday *khutba* on 14 April 1944, published in *Paigham Sulh* dated 19 April 1944, he said:

> "The propagation of the Quran is such a magnificent work that it cannot be done by any community except those people who have the most strongly-felt faith in Allah in their hearts. ... Hazrat Mirza sahib had tremendous love for the Quran ... but when we people read his writings we pay little attention to the need for creating the same passion within us as that which ruled over his heart.

In many of his poems Hazrat Mirza sahib has expressed his love for the Quran. In particular there is a short Persian poem in which he has expressed his deep desire for the propagation of the Quran. He begins it as follows:

Alas, that the beauty of the face of the Quran is not manifest anymore; the fact is, it manifests its own beauty but to recognise it there is no one left.

This poem shows how deeply he felt that the Holy Quran should reach the whole world....

I see everyone engrossed in his own sorrows, there is no room left in anyone's heart to sorrow over the propagation of the Quran.

'Own sorrows' include all the matters related to our worldly interests....

My soul is burning in grief because of this Holy Book, so consumed by fire am I that there is left no hope for my survival.

O head of all created beings! ask for help, this is the time help is required; for there is no gardener left to take care of your orchard.

Here he addresses the Holy Prophet, asking him also to seek help as there was no gardener left in his orchard.

I would dance with joy a hundred times, if I see that the captivating beauty of the Quran is no longer hidden.

Such was his passion that the beauty of the Holy Quran should be known to the world....

The last couplet of this poem is as follows:

O you indifferent, unaware one! gird up your loins to serve the Quran, before the call is sounded that your life is over."

In his Friday *khutba* on 12 May 1944, while mentioning the Promised Messiah's passion for spreading the Quran in the world, he said:

> "Praising the Holy Quran and its scribes and those who spread it, Allah says: 'Nay, surely it is a Reminder. So let him, who will, mind it. In honoured books, exalted, purified, in the hands of scribes, noble, virtuous.' [80:11–16]. That is, the Holy Quran is a means of eminence, whoever wishes let him remember it; it is in honoured scriptures, in the hands of scribes (*safara*) who are noble and virtuous. The word *safara* is plural of *musafir,* derived from *safr* which has both the meanings of spreading and opening. It bears both the significances of writing the Quran and spreading it. Who are *safara?* Those who spread the Quran with translation and commentary.
>
> There have been many eminent scribes of the Holy Quran. ... Allah the Most High raised them and their helpers to the rank of 'noble, virtuous', showing how He exalts those who serve the Holy Quran. ... Besides these, some great Muslim monarchs earned their livelihood by copying out the Holy Quran ... You may wonder whether it is allowed for a person to make his living by writing out copies of the Holy Quran. In a hadith in Bukhari the Holy Prophet says: 'The most worthy thing for which you take remuneration is the Book of Allah'. It means that just as it is allowed to take recompense for every kind of work, so if you do service to the Quran, teach the Quran, write the Quran and take recompense it is lawful. It is very noble work and a highly moral way of making a living."
>
> (*Paigham Sulh,* 24 May 1944)

To sum up, this was how intensely and how frequently he stressed to the *Jama'at* the work of the publication of the Quran. When an elder of the *Jama'at* once made the comment about him "our *Hazrat Amir* has pinned all hopes on the Quran", this truly portrayed the inner feelings of Maulana Muhammad Ali.

The second proposal for the propagation of the Quran — opening of missionary centres

The second major plan for the service of the Quran was launched by Maulana Muhammad Ali in December 1944 at the annual gathering. This was to open further Islamic propagation centres in other countries after the Second World War would be over. The Anjuman already had some missions outside India, although their activities were now hampered due to the war. In many countries where the Anjuman's missionaries were stationed, sizeable branches of the *Jama'at* had been created. Maulana Muhammad Ali proposed that one million Rupees should be raised to expand the work of the missions after the war. Accordingly, funds were collected for this scheme when it was inaugurated at this annual gathering.

Trip to Bombay

To take practical steps to raise funds, Maulana Muhammad Ali undertook first a journey to Bombay and Delhi to put this plan before the general Muslim community and seek their help. On 22 January 1945 he left for Bombay for two weeks, accompanied by Chaudhry Fazal Haq. There he stayed at Malabar Hill at the residence of Mr. Naseer Ahmad Faruqui, who held the post of Collector of Bombay. During this stay he spent most of his time in meeting prominent local Muslims and raising subscriptions from them. Sir Rahmatullah Chana'i and other Muslim leaders, government officials and businessmen gave dinners in his honour, where on every such occasion Maulana Muhammad Ali made speeches putting forward the plan of the Ahmadiyya *Jama'at* for the propagation of Islam and appealed for funds. Besides these meetings he also gave classes in the Holy Quran every day at the residence of Mr. Faruqui, attended by large numbers of Ahmadis as well as other Muslims. Due to the erroneous beliefs of the Qadiani *Jama'at,* a section of the Muslims expressed strong opposition to the Ahmadiyya Movement during his visit. In this connection he used the newspapers as a means to disseminate true information about the Movement to the public, and many articles by him were published in the Urdu newspapers of Bombay. Apart from other gatherings, he also made speeches at special functions held at the Taj Mahal Hotel and the Radio Club. He also delivered a speech at the Government College Bombay on the topic of 'The rising of the Sun from the West'.

During this stay in Bombay a total of 44,000 Rupees was collected for the publication of the Quran.

The third proposal — *Idara Talim-ul-Quran*

The third year, at the annual gathering in December 1945, he announced the third major proposal in this series. This was for the establishment of an institute, the *Idara Talim-ul-Quran* (Institute for the study and teaching of the Quran), for those doing research on the Quran, where there would also be residential facilities for young people of the *Jama'at* to acquire knowledge of the Quran so that scholars and missionaries could be produced to continue the research work. On 26 December 1945 Maulana Muhammad Ali made a very comprehensive and compelling speech at the annual gathering in which he illustrated the greatness and eminence of the Quran, and its triumph in the world, by referring to verses of the Quran itself. Then he went over Hazrat Mirza sahib's passion for the Holy Quran and his heart-felt longing and fervour in this respect, and mentioned the achievements so far of the *Jama'at* in this connection. He also made reference to the first two proposals, that is, translating the Holy Quran and its propagation. Then in connection with the work of teaching the Quran and preparing missionaries he said:

> "Who would be the people and where would they come from who would spread these translations of the Holy Quran in the world from our missionary centres? ... Unless our children and young people become knowledgeable in the Quran the task of its propagation cannot be fulfilled properly. As to those men who are commissioned by God, for them God Himself makes human resources available so that workers come and offer them their services spontaneously. But after the time of these men commissioned by God, their followers have to make their own plans and preparations as to how to continue this work. The problem to be solved today is to create a system whereby the mission of the service of Islam and the Quran can continue into the future, and this can only be achieved if there are

permanent arrangements for training the workers. ... If you do not start making arrangements now for teaching the Quran to your younger generation then this *Jama'at* will perish by its own hands and you will fall from your exalted position. Remember that God does not care to rely upon anyone, He does not depend on anyone, the mission of His religion will not stop. If one community becomes neglectful of the service of religion, He will raise another to take its place."

(*Paigham Sulh*, 20 February 1946, p. 5)

With that he put forward the proposal to establish an institution where, besides general education, there would be arrangements to provide teaching in the Quran to young people from an early age. They would be taught the Holy Quran, the Hadith and the history of Islam, and be so trained that they would love the work of the service of the Holy Quran. Missionaries could also be trained in this institute as well as scholars who would do research on the Quran and find solutions to modern problems from this Holy Book in order to provide guidance to the world. A part of the work of this institute would be to cater for the education of the poor of the *Jama'at*.

On this new proposal being put, members of the *Jama'at* gave promises of almost 100,000 Rupees at once, immediately following his speech. After the annual gathering he repeated this proposal to the entire community by a letter written on 16 January. At that time the intention was to build the institute on land of almost 200 *kanals*[3] outside Muslim Town, Lahore, which he had bought for the Anjuman with funds from the *Irshad-i Ilahi* scheme, because the new campus of the Punjab University was also later to be built adjacent to this land. However, the plan for the institute could not be put into practice during his lifetime because the Improvement Trust did not make any decision about this land for a long time. Anyhow, the first step in this direction that was taken was to establish a hostel in the Muslim High School number 2 where

---

3. A *kanal* is a unit of measurement of land area and is equivalent to 605 square yards or one-eighth of an acre.

accommodation and arrangements for religious education were provided for pupils studying in Lahore.

Emphasising service of the Quran

Besides laying down the foundations of these three schemes for the service of the Quran and its propagation in the world, Maulana Muhammad Ali used to urge the importance of this work over and over again, as has been mentioned earlier. His *khutbas* and writings of these years are so thoroughly imbued with this passion that no biography of his could be complete without giving the fullest expression to these feelings. This love for the Quran manifests itself in his *khutbas* in many different ways and forms.

In the Friday *khutba* of 11 January 1946, explaining the verses "Surely it is a bounteous Quran, in a book that is protected, which none touches save the purified ones" (56:77–79) as testifying that this Quran is 'bounteous', that is, its benefits are open to all, and these are attainable by those whose hearts have been purified, he said:

> "It is a remarkable fact of Islamic history that those who brought about a transformation in the world through the Quran were only those people who had a very strong connection with God, the ones whose hearts were pure. ... Our work is also to spread the Quran in the world. So I want to draw your attention to the fact that we can only make the world benefit from the Quran if our own hearts are pure and we establish a close relationship with God.
>
> ... You must remember it well that the heart is pure only when it is cleansed of love of everything except the love of God. The strongest love is love for wealth. There is no bigger idol than mammon before which people bow down. To remove love for this false god from the heart and replace it with love of God is actually the first step towards purification of the heart.... The Holy Prophet Muhammad was told very plainly: 'Take charity out of their property — you would cleanse them and purify them thereby' [the Quran, 9:103]....
>
> This is the teaching we have inherited from the Imam of the Age. ... This is what purifies the hearts.... Reduce

love for wealth so that you may establish a close bond with God the Most High and the wonders of the Quran may be revealed to the world." (*Paigham Sulh,* 30 January 1946)

In his *khutbas* of 25 January and 1 February 1946, explaining the meaning of the verse of *Sura Fatiha* "Thee do we serve and Thee do we beseech for help", he said that the true concept of worship is to render perfect obedience and submission with humility. A person can only achieve the true meaning of obedience in its fullest sense when he is absorbed every moment in concern for doing the work commanded by his master. The work commanded by God is work for His religion. When we say *iyyā-ka na'budu* ("You do we serve") then this worship will reach its perfection only when we entirely dedicate ourselves to the service of the religion of God, and by *iyyā-ka nasta'īn* ("You do we beseech for help") the Holy Prophet Muhammad showed the help of God as a great reality because he took worship to its perfection in the true sense. We too today, by using this weapon, can recreate the miracle shown by Islam in the world. Whoever will help the cause of the religion of God, God will most surely help him, provided that we prove ourselves true to the words *iyyā-ka na'budu.*

Similarly on another occasion, in his Friday *khutba* on 16 August 1946, he explained the verse "when My servants ask you about Me, (say) I am near" (the Quran, 2:186) as follows. In this verse it is taught that God is very near to His servants, indicating that it is not difficult to attain closeness to Him. However, most people, even while believing in Him, cannot get close to Him, and men of spiritual knowledge have also declared that it is very difficult to attain nearness to God. In fact, the secret underlying this closeness and remoteness is disclosed by the word 'My servants' (*'ibādī*). Whoever will become a servant (*'abd*) of God, he will draw near to God and God will draw near to him. And who is an *'abd*? It is the one who always looks to observing the commandments of God, and who reaches perfection in serving God. To bring human beings near to God was the magnificent task entrusted to the most perfect *'abd* — the Holy Prophet Muhammad. Exalting the name of God in the world is the work which brings a person closest to God. By deciding to do just that one work we

can, in one step, bridge the gap that exists between us and God.
Then, after mentioning that it was just this work which the Promised Messiah entrusted to us, he said:

> "From the powerful inner sentiments of the Promised
> Messiah, different people who sat in his company absor-
> bed different aspects. My dead heart was raised to life by
> his passion for the propagation of Islam. It is one of the
> rays of the light emanating from his heart that has left an
> impression on my heart and infused a fervent desire in me
> to try to spread the Quran in the world. This is my heart's
> desire, more than that, it is my obsession. Although some
> people are irritated by this obsession, so much so that one
> elder feels the need to vent his anger by writing me an
> abusive letter after almost every *khutba* of mine, yet I feel
> that my passion is still not strong enough. Although in
> each one of my *khutbas* I draw people's attention to the
> propagation of the Quran or its translation or its teachings
> or acting upon the Quran, my words have not much effect
> because I am a weak person myself. … I am sure that the
> day this entire *Jama'at* becomes infused with this passion,
> the whole Muslim nation that day would be raised to a
> new life, and when the same deep anxiety for the propa-
> gation of the Quran which made the Promised Messiah's
> heart restless is infused in the hearts of the whole Muslim
> community, that will be the day of the triumph of Islam."

(*Paigham Sulh,* 28 August 1946)

Second journey to Hyderabad

To make these three schemes successful, Maulana Muhammad Ali
visited many branches of the *Jama'at* outside Lahore and toured
various cities in his efforts to get assistance for these plans. In
March 1946 he visited Hyderabad Deccan a second time. His first
visit in 1942 had made a tremendous impact there and had been of
much advantage to the cause of Islam and its propagation. The
Ahmadis of Deccan and other supporters of the *Jama'at* there
wanted him to pay another visit. So on 7 March he left Lahore,
with Maulana Abdul Haq Vidyarthi and Maulana Sadr-ud-Din also
accompanying him. He arrived in Delhi on the morning of 8 March

and led the Friday prayer there. The same day he left for Hyder-abad by the Grand Trunk Express train service. On the morning of 10 March, they were received by Ahmadis as well as non-Ahmadi friends at Sikanderabad station. He stayed at the residence of Abdul Karim Babu Khan. During his stay, which was till 20 March, he had extensive meetings and talks with people from different walks of life and of diverse outlook, and the leaders and *Ulama* of the state. Receptions were given in his honour by dignitaries such as Mir Laiq Ali, Khan Bahadur Ishfaq Ahmad, Maulvi Abdul Latif and Nawab Ali Nawaz Jang, where he made speeches. In addition to this, on 12 March a public meeting was held under the chair-manship of Nawab Maqsud Jang in Sikanderabad where Maulana Muhammad Ali made a speech entitled *Quran Karim Umm-ul-Kitab Aur Jami'a Hai* ('The Holy Quran is Chief of all Scriptures and a comprehensive Book'). On 14 March he addressed a public meeting in Hyderabad, held under the chairmanship of Nawab Nazar Yar Jang, on the topic of the magnificent transformation brought about by the Quran in the world.

On 19 March he visited Osmania University, especially going to see its department of translation, *Da'irat-ul-Ma'arif*. The same day he went to the residence of the late Nawab Bahadur Yar Jang, who had been one of his admirers, to pay his condolences. During the Maulana's first visit to Hyderabad the late Nawab had given him a most heart-felt and warm welcome and also chaired a public meeting.

On 20 March he left Hyderabad and arrived in Delhi on 22 March. After leading the Friday prayers in Delhi he left for Lahore, arriving on 23 March.

From 1946 to June 1947

At the annual gathering in December 1946, Maulana Muhammad Ali reiterated before the *Jama'at* the same three campaigns which had been going on previously. In his speech on 26 December, expounding the verse "all praise be to Allah, the Lord of the worlds", he said that while God the Most High does provide phy-sical sustenance for all human beings these words refer also to the nourishment of the soul. Those persons in the world who are con-cerned about improving the material condition of mankind excel the ordinary human beings, but surpassing them are those persons who are concerned also with the spiritual welfare of humanity. The first forty years of the Holy Prophet's life were spent in caring for the livelihood and physical needs of people, and as everyone knows he provided support and refuge to fatherless children and widows. However, that great man had another anxiety in his heart, and after reaching the age of forty years he was elevated to that most exalted position. That must also be the real aim of his followers. The Maulana then recounted in detail the current state of affairs in the world and the need for the propagation of the Quran. He mentioned in this connection the Promised Messiah's heartfelt desire, and urged the *Jama'at* to keep the three campaigns always in the forefront of their minds.

During this annual gathering, and after that in his Friday *khutbas,* apart from these proposals he also made appeals for funds to repair the Berlin Mosque. Although God the Most High had protected the Berlin Mosque from destruction, its dome and one of its minarets were damaged. So in 1947 arrangements were made for repair. Dr. Shaikh Muhammad Abdullah had gone to Berlin at the end of the war and the Mission had been re-opened.

In 1946 there was another increase in the property of the Anjuman when almost 1400 acres of land were acquired in the province of Sindh at a low price from the government. For this purchase Maulana Muhammad Ali himself went to Karachi and with the efforts of some other members of the *Jama'at* the transaction was completed.

This land was bought with money from the Quran Translations Fund and the *Idara Talim-ul-Quran* Fund in order to provide a permanent source of income for these projects. Similarly, some 225 acres of land were purchased at Malir near Karachi from these funds at low prices, which later became very valuable property for the Anjuman and was sold for hundreds of thousands of Rupees.

Founding of the American Mission
In April 1946 a mission was established in the U.S.A. and Bashir Ahmad Minto left for San Francisco for this purpose. Maulana Muhammad Ali and all other leading figures of the *Jama'at* went

to Lahore railway station to bid him farewell. This was the first mission established under the second scheme mentioned above to open propagation centres.

Translation of the Quran in Javanese language

In April 1946 news came from Batavia (Indonesia) that the translation of the Holy Quran into the Javanese language had been completed. This was done by the *Jama'at* which was founded there by Mirza Wali Ahmad Baig. Like the Dutch translation this was also translated from Maulana Muhammad Ali's English translation and commentary.

Last trip to Dalhousie

At the end of May 1947 Maulana Muhammad Ali started getting fever again. In that state he left for Dalhousie, where he recovered. From June 1947 begins that phase when he took in hand the work of revising the English translation and commentary of the Holy Quran. At that time there erupted a monumental upheaval in the country as Pakistan came into existence amidst horrific communal riots. Maulana Muhammad Ali, his family and some other members of the *Jama'at* had to leave Dalhousie under the most dangerous life threatening conditions for Lahore in Pakistan. This will be covered in the next chapter.

Special spiritual exertions in the month of Ramadan

Throughout these years there was a distinctive feature in Maulana Muhammad Ali's *khutbas* and writings, that every year in the month of Ramadan he exhorted the *Jama'at* to undertake a spiritual exertion (*mujahida*) in two forms. One was to fall in prayer before God and beseech Him tearfully in *tahajjud* prayers to enable us to carry out the work of the propagation of Islam and the Quran, and the other was to make financial sacrifices. In this connection he has written many heart-felt, moving prayers in his letters published in *Paigham Sulh* and entreated every member of the *Jama'at* that at least in the month of Ramadan they should treat the *tahajjud* prayer as obligatory for them. For instance, in September 1939 he suggested three types of supplications which were published in several issues of *Paigham Sulh* in the form of a block. These prayers were as follows:

1. Prayer for spiritual fostering by Allah:

'All praise is for Allah, the Lord of the worlds.' O God, Your providence comprehends every iota of the universe. You have provided the very best means for the physical development of human beings. Now provide for Your creation, who have moved far off from You and are lost in darkness racing towards destruction, spiritual nourishment through the Quran. Acquaint their hearts with the bliss that is attained by bowing at Your threshold.

O God, Who granted the Holy Prophet Muhammad and his Companions unique success enabling them to transform the destinies of the entire countries and nations, foster and nourish us and our *Jama'at* today to make it reach the pinnacle of success in spreading the Quran and propagating Islam in the world. Let the foundations for the propagation of Your religion be laid by our hands, upon which an edifice continues to be raised till the Day of Judgment.

2. Prayer for triumph over unbelief:

'Forgive us, grant us protection, have mercy on us. You are our Patron, grant us victory over the disbelieving people!' O God, unbelief is dominant over the world. Love of worldly things and wealth have taken hold of human hearts. Human beings are being led astray by possession of physical power, material resources and outward adornments. But, O God, it is Your promise that You shall make Islam triumph in the world. It is Your promise that after falling into the greatest deviation and wrongdoing people will again turn to You. Fulfil this promise of Yours today and let the truth overcome falsehood and let Islam triumph over unbelief.

O God, the armies of unbelief and misguidance are attacking with full force. Your strength in the past too has been manifested through weak human beings. Let it be manifest today through this small *Jama'at*. We are weak, humble and sinners but we have a strong zeal to see Islam prevail over unbelief. Forgive us our faults, grant us protection, save us from stumbling, and be our helper and make this weak *Jama'at* of Islam overcome the vast strength of unbelief. O God, make the Quran and Muhammad *Rasulullah* and Islam triumphant in the world, and wipe off the forces of unbelief and misguidance.

3. Prayer for help from Allah:

'Thee do we serve and Thee do we beseech for help.' O God, we do as much as it is in our power to obey You and to spread Your name and Your Word in the world, but we are weak and cannot fully discharge our duty of obeying You. Help us and produce within us the greatest strength to obey You.

O God, spreading Your name in the world is the exalted mission for which You had been appointing Your chosen ones, and it was only with Your help that they succeeded in achieving this magnificent goal. One such chosen man of Yours has entrusted us with this task, but we are small in numbers, weak, and lacking in means. We are opposed not only by outsiders but also by our own who hamper our way. Guide us through Your graciousness and infuse in us the same strength with which You have ever filled Your chosen ones, and create in our hearts the same light with which You have been illuminating the hearts of Your chosen ones.

O God, spreading Your message in the world is the most difficult of tasks in the world. Whenever such a reformation came about, it was not because of the strength of any man or army but it was from Your aid and succour. So we seek from You that help and aid which You have been bestowing upon Your chosen ones.

Similarly, in September 1940, in a letter entitled *Mujahida ka Mahina* ('A month of spiritual exertion'), while explaining the Quranic verse, "And those who strive hard for Us, We shall certainly guide them in Our ways" (29:69), he wrote that success or otherwise is in God's hands. Our duty is to seek and struggle. To strive hard is the condition. Death is inevitable, but if it comes

when we are searching for the means to spread His religion then
there could be no more successful and happier end to one's life
than that. If we do not succeed, then those who would continue the
work after us shall find success. In this world there are people who
are playing with blood and fire for the sake of material gains. Can
we not shed a few tears for the propagation of the Divine religion
which would enrich humanity in a spiritual sense? Then he added:

> "We must pray for only one objective, and that is for the
> triumph of Islam. When we recite *Sura Fatiha* the same
> purpose should be before our minds.
>
> *Al-ḥamdu li-llāhi Rabb il-'ālamīn* ('All praise is for
> Allah, the Lord of the worlds'). O God, You are the
> nourisher unto perfection of all the worlds. Now nourish
> those by means of the Quran who are deprived of this
> blessing of Yours. Nourish us as well and provide for us
> the means by which we can spread Your Quran and Your
> name in the world. Yes, nourish the *Jama'at* whose sole
> aim is to take this spiritual sustenance of Yours to the
> world.
>
> *Ar-Raḥmān-ir-Raḥīm* ('The Beneficent, the Merciful').
> Your mercy is so boundless that it is aroused even with-
> out humans asking for it. It is by Your mercy that the
> efforts of human beings come to fruition. By Your benefi-
> cence, provide guidance through the Quran to those who
> are engulfed in darkness.... Make successful our insigni-
> ficant efforts, that we may take Your holy message to
> these people.
>
> *Māliki yaum-id-dīn* ('Master of the day of Judg-
> ment'). O God, we are Your humble, unworthy servants.
> There are shortcomings in us, in myself, in my *Jama'at*.
> Sometimes Your orders are even disobeyed. By means of
> Your authority of judgment, forgive our faults and infrin-
> gements, and let them not be obstacles to the success of
> our efforts.
>
> *Iyyā-ka na'budu wa iyyā-ka nasta'īn* ('You do we
> serve and You do we beseech for help'). We serve You
> and wish to exalt Your name in the world. This is the sole

aim of our lives. But we are small in numbers and weak while the task is mammoth.... We who are exhausted, weak, humble and sinful, beg only You for help.... Grant this *Jama'at* the success which You bestow on people who spread Your name in the world.

Ihdi-naṣ-ṣirāṭ al-mustaqīm, ṣirāṭ-alladhīna an'amta 'alai-him ('Guide us on the right path, the path of those upon whom You bestowed favours'). You have been showering Your servants with the greatest favours. You have never let those fail who made it their aim in life to exalt Your name.... Guiding us on the straight path, confer on us the same favour which You granted to those before us.... Blow the breeze of Your help upon us as You made it flow for them and open the doors of Your bounty upon us in the same way.

Ghair-il-maghḍūbi 'alaihim wa la-ḍḍāllīn ('Not those upon whom wrath is brought down, nor those who go astray'). O Master, let it not be that we make worldly gain to be our objective and give up spreading religion, like the Jews, as is the state of the Muslims today, or that we make exaggerations in religion like the Christians and destroy our powers for the sake of establishing a wrong belief, as our Qadiani friends are doing today."

In the same way, taking the powerful prayer which is at the end of *Sura Al-Baqarah,* he expressed his feelings and passion with each sentence of this prayer and ended with its final prayer, "so grant us victory over the unbelieving people", as follows:

"O God, Your Holy Word which was revealed for the guidance of the world ... is not being spread even by its believers. But it is Your promise that You will make it prevail in the world.... We too heard the voice of one sent by You to say that the time of the triumph of Islam had arrived, and our feeble hands came forward to take this great burden. It was this voice which revived our dead hearts.... But our *Jama'at* is like an ant facing the mountain of unbelief. It is Your promise that has strengthened our hearts. We need Your help above all.... We know we are unworthy and not fit to receive Your help, but, O God, Your religion, Your Quran and Your Prophet are deserving of Your help.... Let help for them be today manifested through our hands, may Your light illuminate our dark hearts, and may we witness with our own eyes the fulfilment of Your promise."

(*Paigham Sulh*, 26 September 1940)

In *Paigham Sulh,* 10 September 1942, explaining that fasting in Ramadan is not merely an effort to endure hunger and thirst but it is a struggle of three more kinds, he said:

"Man can perform great feats using his God-given powers. He can bring into his service winds, waters and electricity,... and he can conquer countries and overthrow governments. However, he is unable to change the state of human hearts by his own power. For this purpose another power is needed which is obtained by bowing before God in prayer. Gaining strength by praying to God is not merely a claim: it is the greatest reality, the highest truth. The best-known fact in the world is that whoever bows before God the world bows before him.... So the first condition for the *Jama'at* which is engaged in inviting people to God is that it must bow before God and seek strength from that fountain of power." (p. 5)

After this he has given some deeply moving prayers which he has urged to be repeated again and again, and said:

"All of us must cherish but one desire... and only this must fill our hearts when we bow before God: that may the Divine religion, the Quran and Muhammad the Messenger of Allah be triumphant ... Ask only of this, yearn only for this, shed tears only for this, seek that which has been destined to happen. ... It is these prayers that will take you to that height of closeness to God where every prayer of a human being is answered." (p. 5)

Then in the next letter he wrote that in the spiritual exertions of Ramadan the fourth and the most difficult struggle is the purification of one's heart, and this is achieved by giving your money in the way of God. God the Most High has declared in many places spending money in the way of Allah to be the means for man to attain spiritual cleansing and purification. The one who has not learnt to give money, is unaware of the significance of prayer also.

In the same way, the issues of *Paigham Sulh* of every year are full of such writings by him. In 1945, in connection with the spiritual exertions made in the month of Ramadan, he mentioned the relationship between Ramadan and the Quran and explained that there are three types of struggle (*jihad*) to do with the Holy Quran: academic, practical and missionary. The first step is to acquire knowledge of the Quran, above that is to act upon it, and then even more difficult than that is the struggle of propagation. He then went over in detail all the things this *Jama'at,* as bearer of the Quran, could do in order to perform these types of *jihad* in the most effective way (*Paigham Sulh,* 8 August 1945).

The royalty issue

It has been mentioned earlier how, according to the decisions of the Anjuman, the arrangements for paying royalty were first instituted and continued to be followed. However, there were some persons in the *Jama'at* who, to gain importance for themselves and to find some fault with Maulana Muhammad Ali, made this issue into a basis for accusation. It is true that in a democratic system everyone has a right to criticise and the leader of the community must be blameless of all allegations. However, democracy also requires that the majority decisions must be accepted by all and given precedence by each person over his personal opinion. This matter was brought before the Anjuman probably more frequently than any other, and there were more clear-cut decisions of the Anjuman approving royalty than its decisions probably on any other subject. But some persons, who did not have the moral courage to ask for their dissenting views to be recorded whenever the General Council was making its decision, were always spreading rumours behind the back. For years they tried to put misgivings into the minds of the members of the *Jama'at,* by suggesting that this arrangement was causing a financial loss to the Anjuman. In fact Maulana Muhammad Ali was not a burden for the Anjuman, rather the Anjuman was deriving much financial benefit from this arrangement.

Events up to 1938 have already been mentioned. In 1939, after Maulana Muhammad Ali's illness, this question was raised again, this time in the form of the allegation that the Anjuman was making a loss in running the Book Depot (through which Maulana Muhammad Ali's books were sold). So at the end of 1939 a sub-committee was appointed to investigate the matter, with Maulana Sadr-ud-Din, Dr. Ghulam Muhammad, Shaikh Muhammad Din Jan and Master Faqirullah as its members. (Resolution No. 117 of the General Council, dated 29 October 1939).

Regarding the report submitted by this committee to the Anjuman, Maulana Muhammad Ali later wrote as follows:[4]

"On the basis of many false assumptions, mistaken notions and wrong figures the conclusion has been drawn that the Book Depot is running at a heavy loss and in the past twenty years it has lost 33,000 Rupees. A most glaring error in the report is that when the Book Depot came into being with the publication of the English Translation of the Quran the Anjuman's initial expenditure on it is shown as 54,000 Rupees whereas the true figure was 34,000 Rupees. Then 54,000 Rupees are added as interest. The fact is that if the expenses were incurred starting in 1917 then by its sale, which began a year later, not only was the 34,000 Rupees recouped but by the end of 1921 a sum of 91,500 Rupees had been received into Anjuman's funds from the sale of the Holy Quran. Perhaps not even the proverbial Hindu or Jewish money lender ever dared charge such high interest.

"But the matter does not end there. Besides this, the sub-committee assumed a fictitious sum of 40,000 Rupees spent on

---

4. This extract is taken from the last writing of Maulana Muhammad Ali which bears his signature and is dated 13 August 1951, two months before his death. At this time too, that is in 1940, Maulana Muhammad Ali submitted a detailed statement to the Anjuman on this committee's report which is in the records of the Anjuman. He proved from confirmed facts and figures that the report of the committee was totally flawed.

free distribution and added to it 20,000 Rupees as interest. The fact is that funds for free distribution came from external donations. Just one such sum of 7,500 Rupees was donated by Seth Muhammad Ali Habib, and similarly from time to time other friends donated considerable sums for free distribution of literature, so it would not be surprising if in twenty years these amounted to 40,000 Rupees. But it is quite incomprehensible how a committee which is involved in the propagation of Islam could think of adding 20,000 Rupees to this as interest. So with one stroke of the pen this sub-committee turned the expenditure of 34,000 Rupees into 54,000 Rupees, added a further 54,000 Rupees of interest to it, assumed a fictitious sum of 40,000 Rupees for free distribution of publications, and added 20,000 Rupees to it as interest, making the real figure of 34,000 Rupees into 168,000 Rupees. Thus 34,000 Rupees was increased by an imaginary figure of 134,000 Rupees. This is a miracle indeed. On the other hand, in its zeal to show a lower income from sales the sub-committee even left out the names of some books which were sold for 20,000 Rupees. In some cases only the second and third editions were shown, not mentioning at all the first editions whose price amounts to 26,800 Rupees. The sales of some books were shown lower than the actual. On the one hand the original capital invested of 34,000 Rupees was inflated to 168,000 Rupees, and on the other hand the income from the sale of books was reduced by an amount of 137,800 Rupees to show that the Book Depot was running at a loss.

"The story does not end here. When the committee assessed the existing stock they calculated that the total number of my books in stock was 25,000 and stated that their sale would take from ten to twenty years, from which the income would be 20,000 Rupees. I there and then offered to buy the stock for 20,000 Rupees, which I would pay over ten years in annual instalments of 2,000 Rupees. But all these were fictitious figures and myths. After sometime the late Malik Sher Muhammad assessed the stock and it was found to be worth more than 150,000 Rupees. At this time,[5] by the grace of God, it must be worth probably more than

5. Close to the time of his death in 1951.

600,000 Rupees. It is only due to the grace of God that a small investment of 34,000 Rupees has been blessed so much that today there is not only a stock worth 600,000 Rupees but also a great number of people have benefitted from this treasure of knowledge."

On the report of this sub-committee, the Anjuman asked Maulana Muhammad Ali for details as well. So he presented a document of several pages containing confirmed facts and figures, which is worth reading. The Anjuman did not question the sub-committee but gave the following decision:

> "Resolution No. 19, dated 28 April 1940. The report of the sub-committee was presented. The details submitted by *Hazrat Amir* [Maulana Muhammad Ali] were also presented. In the Anjuman's view the figures of the sub-committee are not correct. The Anjuman considers that it did not suffer any loss because of Maulana Muhammad Ali's books, rather it made a profit. (2) From 1st November 1938 the rate of royalty is approved at 33½%, and as before 350 Rupees per month will be paid and any additional amount will be considered as an honorarium."

However, the Anjuman never took up the matter with the sub-committee. If Maulana Muhammad Ali had not put forward the real facts, this report would probably have been accepted without question.

In 1938, at the suggestion of Malik Sher Muhammad, a civil agency was established to improve arrangements for the sale of books. From 1941 till 1945 this issue was the target of attack. In this connection in May 1945 this matter was raised in a regrettable manner in the absence of Maulana Muhammad Ali. Some claims were circulated in public without investigation and before the Anjuman had reached any decision, so much so that these stories were published word for word in the Qadiani newspaper *Al-Fazl*. In the end all these reports proved to be wrong, but the campaign against the civil agency continued and eventually the agency was closed down in 1946. What happened afterwards is clear from the written statement of Mian Ghulam Rasul which was put before the Management Committee of the Anjuman by Resolution No. 624, dated 19 March 1948, in which he wrote that all this happened because of "the emotions of some members".

It seems appropriate to include here the last decision taken about royalty, which was in 1948. According to Resolution No. 5 of the General Council, dated 27/28 May 1948, and on Khwaja Nazir Ahmad's proposal, the Anjuman decided that royalty should be paid at the rate of 33^1/$_3$% subject to a minimum of 800 Rupees per month. This remained in force till Maulana Muhammad Ali's death.

Relations with the Qadian *Jama'at*, 1939 to 1947

It has been mentioned before that Maulana Muhammad Ali was always concerned that if the *Jama'at* devoted too much attention to the issues of the differences between the two parties, this might detract from its task of the propagation of Islam. Accordingly, on many occasions he would ignore attacks from the Qadian *Jama'at* and its paper *Al-Fazl*. However, at times some events would happen, making it unavoidable to engage in argument. The greatest problem was that, due to the publicising and propagation of those beliefs of Mirza Mahmud Ahmad that were contrary to the beliefs of the Promised Messiah, misconceptions arose among the general Muslim community regarding the Promised Messiah's own position and views. The exaggerations of the Qadiani *Jama'at* were becoming a hindrance in the path of the propagation of Islam because they made other Muslims hesitant to join or assist the Lahore Ahmadiyya Movement as they could not be sure that the Founder of the Movement held the beliefs that the Lahore *Jama'at* was presenting.

In December 1939 Maulana Ghulam Hasan took the *bai'at* (pledge) at the hand of Mirza Mahmud Ahmad, and with that the Qadian *Jama'at* launched an aggressive campaign against the Lahore *Jama'at*. Mirza Mahmud Ahmad instructed his *Jama'at* to make special efforts to preach to the "*Paighamis*".[6] It became imperative to take steps to counteract this assault. So, during 1941 and 1942, much of Maulana Muhammad Ali's attention was taken up in presenting conclusive arguments to Mirza Mahmud Ahmad and trying to bring about rectification in this matter.

Maulana Ghulam Hasan was the man who had refused to take the *bai'at* at the hand of Maulana Nur-ud-Din after the Promised Messiah's death because he believed that the Anjuman was the Promised Messiah's successor and that it was an error to re-take the *bai'at* at the hand of another individual. Maulana Ghulam Hasan was one of the fourteen members of the Sadr Anjuman Ahmadiyya and despite having family connections in Qadian he was one of six members who, at the time of the Split, rose to oppose openly the *khilafat* of Mirza Mahmud Ahmad and his reducing the Sadr Anjuman Ahmadiyya to a subservient body. As to why, after adhering strictly to this standpoint for almost 32 years, he took the *bai'at* at Mirza Mahmud Ahmad's hand, there is no need to go into the details of that. Anyhow, after he had taken this step Maulana Muhammad Ali, through *Paigham Sulh,* drew his attention to his previous beliefs and writings and asked him repeatedly on what basis he had taken the *bai'at*, which he had been opposing for 32 years, and on what grounds he had joined the *Jama'at* which he had labelled in his Quran commentary *Husn-i Bayan* as "a group of extremists" and "followers of falsehood". However, in the answers that Maulana Ghulam Hasan published, he nowhere gave the arguments that had made him change his standpoint. In this connection Maulana Muhammad Ali wrote many articles in *Paigham Sulh* from March to June 1940, addressed to Maulana Ghulam Hasan, in which he compared the beliefs and the practical work of the two groups and clarified the issues of *khilafat* and of 'unbelief and Islam'.

Appeal to Qadian *Jama'at,* 1939
Along with that, Maulana Muhammad Ali repeatedly addressed Mirza Mahmud Ahmad in an effort to settle these differences.

---

6. This was a term they used for members of the Lahore *Jama'at,* coining it from the name of the Anjuman's Urdu organ *Paigham Sulh.*

At the annual gathering of 1939, he addressed the Qadiani *Jama'at* by means of a pamphlet entitled *Ahbab-i Qadian say appeal* ('An Appeal to Friends of Qadian'). In this pamphlet he did not elaborate upon the issues of disagreement, which had been discussed exhaustively on many previous occasions, but only dealt with the heart-felt wishes of the Promised Messiah and the work of the Lahore Ahmadiyya *Jama'at* over the past twenty-five years, and drew the attention of the Qadian *Jama'at* to facts about what the Promised Messiah had wanted his followers to accomplish, and what we had achieved in the twenty-five years of our existence starting from scratch, as contrasted with what the much larger *Jama'at* of Qadian had done in the same period.

Invitation and challenge to debate, 1940

In his Friday *Khutba* on 5 April 1940 (*P.S.,* 18 April 1940), Maulana Muhammad Ali issued a challenge to Mirza Mahmud Ahmad to enter into a debate on the following three issues, whether with or without judges as he wished, as to which party was holding beliefs contrary to the beliefs of the Promised Messiah:

1. Unbelief and Islam (whether a person must believe in the Promised Messiah in order to be a Muslim).
2. Prophethood (whether the Promised Messiah claimed to be a prophet).
3. *Khilafat* (whether the kind of headship instituted in the Qadiani *Jama'at* is in conformity with, or contrary to, the teachings of Islam and the Promised Messiah).

The condition was that the debate must be in writing. On our side Maulana Muhammad Ali alone would write, while Mirza Mahmud Ahmad would be free to write by himself or with as many supporters as he wished. In his *khutba* on 26 April Maulana Muhammad Ali repeated this proposal and in this connection he announced:

> "Remember it well that it is on the issue of *kufr* and Islam that the Qadianis will flounder. Their position on this issue is entirely weak and unsound, beyond all limits. The ground has been cut away from under their feet. No Qadiani knows what is his belief about this. They say by word of

mouth: 'There is no god but Allah and Muhammad is the Messenger of Allah', but in practice they have cancelled this *Kalima*. It is obvious that if the *Kalima* is not abrogated, then those who proclaim and profess it cannot be called *kafir* and outside the pale of Islam. And if those who do not accept Hazrat Mirza Ghulam Ahmad, while professing the *Kalima,* are *kafir* then this *Kalima* is abrogated. But the Qadianis do not take either of these positions clearly, or declare it plainly and boldly. The reason is that they have no belief on this question. Whenever they have occasion to discuss this issue with anyone, they express a belief depending on the views and thinking of that person. I say again, on this question, and also on the question of *khilafat,* the Qadianis cannot at all make a stand.

Remember, we will not let them get away. Either they have to enter the field of combat and prove that, except the Qadiani *Jama'at,* all others on earth who profess the *Kalima* are *kafir* and expelled from Islam, or they have to admit defeat, and acknowledge that according to the Quran, Hadith, and the teachings of the Promised Messiah every person professing the *Kalima* is a Muslim — and this latter is what we want because our aim is reform. The root of the difference between us is, in fact, this issue of *kufr* and Islam. Once that is settled, the issue of prophethood [the belief that Hazrat Mirza sahib claimed to be a prophet] can be solved in one instant."

(*Paigham Sulh,* 3 May 1940, p. 5)

Still in May 1940 Maulana Muhammad Ali put forth another proposal before Mirza Mahmud Ahmad, in a letter published in *Paigham Sulh* in its issue of 12 May, that both sides would specify a certain number of questions or objections to be answered, to which the answers would be published in the newspapers of both the parties. After that every person could draw his own conclusions. No further debates would take place, and the energy and time saved thereby would be spent on doing constructive work. He also proposed that if Mirza Mahmud Ahmad was prepared to have a written debate in the presence of judges, then Maulana Muhammad Ali would appoint five such judges from the Qadiani *Jama'at* itself. However, Mirza Mahmud Ahmad was not willing even to have judges from among his own followers. When there was no response to all his proposals and challenges, Maulana Muhammad Ali wrote an open letter addressed to Mirza Mahmud Ahmad, dated 10 June 1940, in which, after repeating those proposals, he wrote:

> "I implore you for the sake of the Holy Quran, for whose propagation in the world we have been established, for the sake of the Holy Prophet, to make whose religion triumphant in the world our *Jama'at* was created, and lastly for the sake of the Promised Messiah, who in this age assigned this magnificent task to us, that you accept any one of these three proposals that you wish to, and take a step towards ending these disputes. If you pay a little attention, the two communities, instead of indulging in mud-slinging against one another, can be instrumental in acquiring and spreading the knowledge of the Holy Quran in the world, for which the way was paved by the Imam of the Age." (*Paigham Sulh,* 17 June 1940)

There was still no response whatsoever from Mirza Mahmud Ahmad, except that in his *khutba* published in *Al-Fazl* on 12 July 1940, he said that first Maulana Muhammad Ali should point out proof of acceptance of his prayers in comparison with the Qadian *Jama'at*. He referred to a bizarre sign to prove acceptance of his own prayers. He said that the suffering Britain was undergoing at that time in the Second World War was the result of the heart-felt crying of the Qadian *Jama'at* before Allah during 1934 to 1936, after two local British officials had created some difficulties for Mirza Mahmud Ahmad (see *Al-Fazl,* 4 June 1940, p. 2, col. 4). According to his claim, it would appear that his *Jama'at* lost all sense of balance and they cried before Allah with so much pain, forgetting that their vociferous pleas were entirely out of proportion with the severity of the injustice they had suffered. The result according to them was that God struck all the British Empire with a terrible calamity, but in order to remove these dreadful effects of the heart-felt cries of the Qadiani *Jama'at* if the British government were to officially request Mirza Mahmud Ahmad for prayer then Hitler's forces would be repulsed.[7]

In reply to this, Maulana Muhammad Ali wrote that we also believe in the acceptance of prayers but we do not want to turn prayer into a childish antic as Mirza Mahmud Ahmad has done. The greatest proof of the acceptance of our prayers is that our *Jama'at,* which was created by a few men lacking all resources, and whose disintegration was prophesied by Mirza Mahmud Ahmad, has in 25 years made such tremendous progress that the outside world admits it. The service to His religion that God has enabled us to render is the result of His acceptance of our prayers, for our principal prayer with which we have been constantly imploring the Almighty over the years is just that Allah may choose us for the service of His religion (*Paigham Sulh,* 30 July 1940).

What Mirza Mahmud Ahmad said about the actual point under discussion, in his Friday *khutba* published in *Al-Fazl,* 24 July 1940 (see p. 1, and *Paigham Sulh,* 17 August, p. 6), was as follows:

> "As far as I remember, he [Maulana Muhammad Ali] has been putting forward this method since probably 1915, and thus not three months but 23 years have elapsed over his proposal. During all this time I have not accepted it."

And he gave the following reason for it:

> "In the matter of religious beliefs, I am not even prepared to accept the verdict of my wife, my sons or my brothers. … My beliefs are a matter for me. Why should I accept someone else's decision about them?"

The fact is that Mirza Mahmud Ahmad was not at all being asked to adopt the judges' decision as his personal beliefs. But as he had determined the beliefs of an entire community in his capacity as its Head, and had misled it, he was being asked to produce

---

7. It appears that while the fault was of two local British officials of the Punjab Government, yet destruction was wrought not only upon Britain but also upon countless innocent men, women and children of Poland, Belgium, Holland, Denmark, Norway, and other European countries!

arguments to support his beliefs. The demand was for a written discussion before some judges, who would then simply decide whose arguments were stronger. After that an end would be put to all such discussions, and henceforth both communities would be able to concentrate entirely on the propagation of Islam.

Finding Mirza Mahmud Ahmad avoiding the real issues, Maulana Muhammad Ali again addressed him in August by means of a direct letter, stressing his demand as to why he was unwilling to debate the beliefs of the Promised Messiah and the question whether other Muslims were to be regarded as unbelievers (*Paigham Sulh,* 12 August 1940). Similarly on various other occasions, through his Friday *khutbas* and the newspaper *Paigham Sulh,* Maulana Muhammad Ali did everything possible to convey the most conclusive arguments to prove his standpoint to the Qadiani leader. At the annual gathering in 1940, he published a leaflet entitled *Jama'at Qadian kay aik aik adami ko salis ban nay ki da'wat* ('Each and Every member of the Qadiani *Jama'at* invited to be judge'), clarifying the standpoint of the Promised Messiah that he allowed his followers to say the funeral prayers of other Muslims, and did so himself as well, thus showing that he regarded them as Muslims.

Efforts in 1941

Again during 1941, on many occasions, he addressed the Qadian *Jama'at* and Mirza Mahmud Ahmad. In *Paigham Sulh* dated 21 April 1941 he clarified the misconception spread about him from Qadian that in his early writings he had regarded the Promised Messiah as a prophet. Maulana Muhammad Ali explained that he had never even imagined at any time that the Founder of the Movement was claiming to be a prophet. However, sometimes following the style of the Promised Messiah, he too had used the word 'prophet' about him metaphorically and figuratively, or in its linguistic sense of meaning a person who makes prophecies. Moreover, this style of writing was not exclusive to the Promised Messiah or to him, but is found in the writings of many renowned Muslim saints in history. He repeated his challenge to Mirza Mahmud Ahmad that he would never be able to provide any quotation from his writings in which he had declared other Muslims as being *kafirs*. In the *Review of Religions* itself, from which Mirza Mahmud Ahmad had put forward some quotations in which Maulana Muhammad Ali had used the word 'prophet' about the Promised Messiah, the explanation of the use of this word can be found several times. After giving some examples of such explanation from the *Review of Religions,* Maulana Muhammad Ali writes in his above statement:

> "The above examples are from 1904. Then in 1914 there was an occasion where a misunderstanding could arise, when there appeared an article in the *Review of Religions* entitled 'Ahmad as a Prophet', which was not written by me. I added to it the following note:
>
> 'The word *prophet* is used here not in the strict terminology of the Muslim Law, the holy Prophet Muhammad, may peace and the blessings of God be upon him, being the last of the prophets in that sense, but in the broad sense of one endowed with the gift of prophecy by Divine inspiration, a gift which is promised to every true Muslim by the holy Quran, and one which was possessed in an eminent degree by the late Mirza Ghulam Ahmad of Qadian.' " [8]

After this, he writes in this same reply:

> "This interpretation was not an invention of mine. At that time the Qadiani religious scholars were assuring all people that they were not using the word *nabi* according to its meaning in the terminology of the *Shari'ah* but taking it only in its linguistic sense of one who makes prophecies."

Accordingly, he gave quotations from the early writings of Mirza Mahmud Ahmad and the Qadiani religious scholars Maulvi Sarwar Shah and Mufti Muhammad Sadiq.[9]

---

8. We have reproduced here the original English wording of this note as it appeared in the *Review of Religions,* February 1914 issue, first page.

9. These have been quoted earlier in this book in the closing section of Chapter 3.1 (see pages 132–136).

Similarly, Maulana Muhammad Ali made other efforts of the same kind repeatedly, which we do not fully detail here for the sake of brevity. Anyone who wants further information can consult the archives of *Paigham Sulh* for those years. However, all these efforts proved fruitless. Prior to the annual gathering of 1941, Maulana Muhammad Ali invited Mirza Mahmud Ahmad to come to Lahore for a day and make a speech to the gathering of the Lahore *Jama'at,* and reciprocate by allowing Maulana Muhammad Ali to address the gathering in Qadian on the last day of their annual gathering, giving each party the opportunity at least to hear the arguments of the other side. Mirza Mahmud Ahmad first responded by saying that Maulana Muhammad Ali could come to Qadian for two days after the annual gathering on the condition that he paid Rs. 3000 per day to meet the expenses of the other people present there. Maulana Muhammad Ali wrote in reply that to ask a guest to pay not only his own expenses but also the host's expenses was entirely against Islamic etiquette. Secondly, after the annual gathering people attending from outside Qadian would have departed, so who would the Maulana be addressing? Therefore he insisted that he should be given time to speak during the annual gathering itself. However, Mirza Mahmud Ahmad did not accept it. Then Maulana Muhammad Ali offered that even if he was not to be allowed to make a speech to the *Jama'at* in Qadian, his own invitation to Mirza Mahmud Ahmad was still open. He should come to Lahore and make a speech on the first day of our annual gathering; all his expenses would be paid by us. There was no response to this.

Challenge to take oath on beliefs, 1944

When these sustained efforts of two years failed to achieve any result, Maulana Muhammad Ali put before Mirza Mahmud Ahmad in 1944 another easy mode of reaching a decision. In his Friday *khutba* of 5 May 1944, he said:

> "They believe that before the year 1901 Hazrat Mirza sahib denied claiming prophethood and believed other Muslims to be Muslims, but that in 1901 he made a change by acknowledging his prophethood and calling those who professed the *Kalima* as *kafir....* This can be decided by

sworn evidence. We had suggested an easy method, that just one man from the whole of the Qadiani *Jama'at* should make a statement on oath as follows:

> *In the year 1901 my belief regarding the prophethood of Hazrat Mirza sahib changed.*

From our side, seventy men made a statement on oath [in 1915] that in the year 1901 the idea never even entered their minds that Hazrat Mirza sahib had changed his claim. ... Now I say that if they cannot find anyone else, let Mirza Mahmud Ahmad himself make this statement under oath." (*Paigham Sulh,* 17 May 1944, p. 3)

In this *khutba* the Maulana went one step further and invited Mirza Mahmud Ahmad to make the statement under oath that his beliefs, as expressed on page 35 of his book *A'inah-i Sadaqat,* were the beliefs held by Hazrat Mirza sahib. The Maulana himself would state under oath that those beliefs of Mirza Mahmud Ahmad were contrary to the beliefs of Hazrat Mirza sahib. The Maulana added that if Mirza Mahmud Ahmad took an oath in which he invoked God's punishment upon himself in case of making a false statement, the Maulana would also take a similar oath, invoking God's punishment upon his own self.

Those beliefs of Mirza Mahmud Ahmad are as follows:

1. The belief that Hazrat Mirza Ghulam Ahmad was actually a *Nabi;*
2. The belief that he was 'the Ahmad' spoken of in the prophecy of Jesus referred to in the Holy Quran in 61:6;
3. The belief that all those so-called Muslims who have not entered into his [Hazrat Mirza Ghulam Ahmad's] *bai'at* formally, wherever they may be, are *Kafirs* and outside the pale of Islam, even though they may not have heard the name of the Promised Messiah.[10]

---

10. We have quoted the wording of these three beliefs from the Qadiani group's own English translation of Mirza Mahmud Ahmad's book *A'inah-i Sadaqat,* entitled *The Truth About the Split,* p. 55, 3rd edition, 1965.

On none of these points did Mirza Mahmud Ahmad dare come forward to meet the challenge. However, when Maulana Muhammad Ali, in his Friday *khutba* of 26 May 1944 (*Paigham Sulh,* 31 May 1944), stated that Mirza Mahmud Ahmad had made the *Kalima* null and void, and that this was a pollution with which he had contaminated the teachings of the Promised Messiah, there was a furious and wrathful response by Mirza Mahmud Ahmad in an article published in *Al-Fazl* of 7 July 1944 which ended with the following words:

> "Maulana Muhammad Ali is both a coward and a liar ... but if he does not desist from his calumnies ... then a day will come when he will be overtaken by God's noose and the curse of God will strangle him as it chokes liars. ... He will see the curse of his fabrications descend in front of his residence and will die the death of a liar." (p. 4)

Maulana Muhammad Ali published a lengthy reply to this in *Paigham Sulh,* 26 July 1944. He asked Mirza Mahmud Ahmad what fabrication he had committed against him which led to this incensed outburst? All this wrath and fury erupted because the belief was ascribed to him that he does not consider that a person can now become a Muslim by professing the *Kalima,* although Mirza Mahmud Ahmad had himself been expressing this belief for the past thirty years and the Maulana had been denouncing it also during all this period, refuting it by arguments and calling upon Mirza Mahmud Ahmad to repent from this pollution in belief. He had written in his book *A'inah-i Sadaqat* on page 35 that:

> "... all those so-called Muslims who have not entered into his [Hazrat Mirza Ghulam Ahmad's] *bai'at* formally, wherever they may be, are *Kafirs* and outside the pale of Islam, even though they may not have heard the name of the Promised Messiah."

As to his desire for the destruction of our *Jama'at,* Mirza Mahmud Ahmad had been making predictions about it since 1914.

Maulana Muhammad Ali, once again in this article, fully exposed those wrong beliefs which Mirza Mahmud Ahmad had attributed to the Promised Messiah.

Open publication of charge of falsehood

After the publication of this article, Maulana Muhammad Ali made the following demands upon Mirza Mahmud Ahmad which were published in the form of a highlighted block, starting in the issue of *Paigham Sulh* for 2 August 1944:

Let Mirza Mahmud Ahmad answer

The fabrications that Mirza Mahmud Ahmad has committed against the Promised Messiah, I call them nothing but fabrications and will continue to do so. If he considers me to be a liar, then he must accept my invitation to make a statement on oath invoking Divine punishment upon himself in case of being false, and I will also take a similar oath invoking Divine punishment upon myself in case of being false. Otherwise, my allegations against him will prove to be established facts.

I again repeat my allegations in clear words:

1. Mirza Mahmud Ahmad has made a false statement and committed a fabrication against the Promised Messiah that in 1901 he changed his claim in this way that, while previously denying a claim to prophethood and sending curses upon anyone who would claim to be a prophet, he now made a claim to prophethood himself, and cancelled his former writings of several years containing denials of a claim to prophethood.

2. Mirza Mahmud Ahmad has made a false statement and committed a fabrication against the Promised Messiah that he (Hazrat Mirza Ghulam Ahmad sahib) himself used to say that prior to 1901 he was misinterpreting the word 'prophet'.

3. Mirza Mahmud Ahmad has made a false statement and committed a fabrication against the Promised Messiah that around the year 1901 it used to be said in the gatherings of the Promised Messiah that his previous interpretation of prophethood was not correct.

If Mirza Mahmud Ahmad has the courage, he can hold a debate with me about these allegations. I will appoint persons from among his own followers as the judges. If he wishes, he can hold a *mubahila* after the debate, that is to say, he would take an oath, invoking Divine punishment upon himself in case of making a false statement, testifying that his beliefs as given on page 35 of *A'inah-i Sadaqat* are in agreement with the beliefs of the Promised Messiah; and I will take a similar oath, invoking Divine punishment upon myself in case of making a false statement, testifying that these beliefs of his are entirely opposed to the beliefs of the Promised Messiah. However, a debate will be necessary before the *mubahila*.

If Mirza Mahmud Ahmad remains silent even now, I will continue to repeat these accusations until his followers are impelled by their faith to ask him to clear himself of these charges.

———————————

This statement was printed in the form of a block in *Paigham Sulh* in several issues from 2 August till October 1944, but Mirza Mahmud Ahmad could not pluck up the courage to reply. During this time Maulana Muhammad Ali suggested Sir Muhammad Zafrullah Khan as judge and demanded of Mirza Mahmud Ahmad to show Zafrullah Khan the references from the Promised Messiah on the basis of which he had imputed those beliefs to the Promised Messiah. If Zafrullah Khan wrote in judgment that those beliefs have been established from the records of the time of the Promised Messiah then Maulana Muhammad Ali would admit his own error and make a public apology to Mirza Mahmud Ahmad.

However, Mirza Mahmud Ahmad's lips were sealed. In the Friday *khutba* on 20 October, published in *Paigham Sulh* for 25 October 1944, Maulana Muhammad Ali summed up the whole matter and informed the *Jama'at* that God had now shown us the sign during our lives that the wrong beliefs and the falsehood attributed to the Promised Messiah had been proved to be lies. He asked the *Jama'at* to keep up these demands and continue asking the Qadianis for proof of their wrong beliefs.

After this, at the annual gathering in Qadian in 1944, Mirza Mahmud Ahmad in a speech appeared to express his willingness to participate in a debate. So Maulana Muhammad Ali, in his

Friday *khutba* on 5 January 1945, again invited Mirza Mahmud Ahmad to a debate on the three points of contention, which have been mentioned above, whether with judges or without judges as he wished (*Paigham Sulh,* 17 January 1945). But after this there was again complete and utter silence from Qadian.

Challenge to debate and *mubahila,* 1945

In his Friday *khutba* on 9 March 1945 (*Paigham Sulh,* 21 March 1945) Maulana Muhammad Ali invited Mirza Mahmud Ahmad to a *mubahila* on the question whether the Promised Messiah ever said that before 1901 he was misinterpreting the word *nabi.* The *mubahila* would have to be preceded by a debate on this issue. After almost six months had elapsed upon this invitation, Maulana Muhammad Ali reminded Mirza Mahmud Ahmad of it, in *Paigham Sulh,* 8 August 1945, and asked if he was prepared to hold the *mubahila.* He drew his attention to the statements he had been publishing for the past year, and his repeated announcements that "Mirza Mahmud Ahmad has made a false statement and committed a fabrication against the Promised Messiah", and asked him why he was not showing his proofs to Sir Muhammad Zafrullah Khan, whom the Maulana had suggested as judge. If he could not agree to have Zafrullah Khan as judge, then Mirza Mahmud Ahmad can himself choose someone else from his *Jama'at* as judge. Otherwise, he should take legal action against Maulana Muhammad Ali for falsely accusing him of fabrication and defaming his name.

In this article Maulana Muhammad Ali wrote that he had already declared under oath that Mirza Mahmud Ahmad had made this fabrication and he invited Mirza Mahmud Ahmad also to take an oath. He said:

> "I have no wish whatsoever to humiliate Mirza Mahmud Ahmad, nor am I at all seeking to ruin him. But I cannot tolerate the humiliation of the religion of Islam or the ruination of the true teachings of the Promised Messiah. So I am compelled to say this. My demand is not a difficult one. It is that Mirza Mahmud Ahmad make a sworn state-ment that in the year 1901 he changed his own belief as to whether or not the Promised Messiah was a prophet, or else

he should desist from this fabrication against the Promised
Messiah that he changed his belief in 1901."

Summary of efforts

However, matters continued in the same vein. Then in *Paigham Sulh*
on 21 August 1946, in boldly printed words, Maulana Muhammad
Ali again repeated his demand for a debate and *mubahila.* The
heading of this article was as follows:

> "I am prepared to hold with the leader of the Qadian
> *Jama'at:* (1) a debate, (2) a *mubahila,* on the question:
> Did the Promised Messiah change his belief in the year
> 1901 about whether he himself claimed prophethood or
> about prophethood having ended with the Holy Prophet
> Muhammad."

As the accompanying announcement issued by him was a
summary of all the preceding events, it is reproduced below:

" **1.** We and the Qadian *Jama'at* both agree that when Hazrat
Mirza Ghulam Ahmad claimed to be the Promised Messiah in 1891,
he denied claiming to be a prophet. He announced his claim as that of
being a *muhaddas,* declared prophethood as having ended with the
Holy Prophet Muhammad, and denounced as an imposter and liar
anyone claiming prophethood after the Holy Prophet Muhammad. The
disagreement between us and the head of the Qadian *Jama'at* is that
we hold that the Promised Messiah adhered to this position for the rest
of his life, but the head of the Qadian *Jama'at* writes that the Promised Messiah changed his belief in 1901 by laying claim to be a
prophet himself and opening the door of prophethood after the Holy
Prophet Muhammad.

2. It is obvious that the burden of proof regarding the change in
claim in 1901 lies upon the Qadiani leader. If he cannot prove it, it
would show that to ascribe a claim of prophethood to Hazrat Mirza
sahib is a mere fabrication.

3. I have invited Mirza Mahmud Ahmad, again and again, to a
debate on this issue. I went so far as to say that I would nominate
some five or seven judges all from among his own followers. But he
does not respond.

4. Seventy men from among us, including myself, made a sworn declaration [in 1915] that we had taken the *bai'at* of Hazrat Mirza sahib before 1901, and the belief which we held at the time of our pledge, that prophethood ended with the Holy Prophet Muhammad, was the belief we held unchangingly for the rest of his life. He did not change his belief about prophethood in 1901.

5. Today more than thirty years have elapsed that we have been demanding that seventy members of the Qadian *Jama'at* make the sworn statement that they took the *bai'at* before 1901 believing that Hazrat Mirza sahib claimed to be a *muhaddas* and that prophethood ended with the Holy Prophet Muhammad, but that in 1901 they changed their belief, no longer considering prophethood as closed, and started to believe that Hazrat Mirza sahib was a prophet because in that year they came to know that he had changed his belief. We also demanded the same statement from Mirza Mahmud Ahmad. But the entire Qadian *Jama'at* has been silent upon this demand for thirty years, and so has he.

6. I then had recourse to the last resort allowed in Islam, namely, that Mirza Mahmud Ahmad should undertake a *mubahila* with me, on the question whether the Promised Messiah changed his belief in 1901 about claiming prophethood and the ending of prophethood. But he still remained silent.

7. However, some followers of Mirza Mahmud Ahmad keep on demanding from me if I am prepared to enter into a *mubahila* with Mirza Mahmud Ahmad, and on what issues. To dispel all doubts, I announce again the following.

8. On the question whether the Promised Messiah changed his belief in 1901 ... I am prepared to hold a debate with Mirza Mahmud Ahmad, and I am willing to appoint as judges only persons from among his own followers, one of whom would be Sir Zafrullah Khan.

9. By having judges, it does not imply that Mirza Mahmud Ahmad must personally accept their verdict and change his own beliefs. But the misconception in people's minds will be cleared. If he considers it beneath his dignity to have judges, I will withdraw this condition, and hold an unconditional debate with him, whether it is in a public gathering or in writing. He can set any other conditions as he wishes. My only proviso is that the topic of the debate will be restricted to the question whether Hazrat Mirza sahib changed his belief in 1901 or not.

10. I am prepared to hold a *mubahila* on this issue with Mirza Mahmud Ahmad, if he so wishes. The *mubahila* can be between just himself and me, or other people from both sides can be included who joined the Movement before 1901. If Mirza Mahmud Ahmad does not now regard 1901 as the date of change of claim, as it appears from the writings of some of his followers, then whatever other date he proposes for this change I am prepared to hold a debate and *mubahila* with reference to that date. I ask Mirza Mahmud Ahmad himself to reply to this announcement."

Challenge by a Qadiani for oath

However, there was no response from Mirza Mahmud Ahmad himself to this announcement and demand, but one of his followers, Seth Abdullah Allahdin of Sikanderabad, Deccan, who had been spreading misconceptions earlier by announcing challenges with offers of great rewards, made the following announcement in *Al-Fazl*, dated 26 October 1946:

> "Maulvi Muhammad Ali sahib believes that Hazrat Mirza sahib was a *mujaddid* and the Promised Messiah but not a prophet, nor can any person become a *kafir* by denying him, and this was also the belief of Hazrat Mirza sahib. We challenged him that if he announces his belief in a public meeting under oath, then we will pay him Rs. 5000 in cash in the same meeting, and if some examplary wrath from God, in which human hands play no part, does not befall him within a year for this wrong belief and false oath, then a sum of Rs. 50,000 will be paid in addition. But he has been avoiding this challenge for years. Anyone who can persuade him to accept this challenge will also receive Rs. 5000 in cash." (p. 6)

Following this, the Anjuman's missionary in Hyderabad, Deccan, Shaikh Muhammad Inam-ul-Haq, wrote to Seth Allahdin informing him that "on my request, Hazrat Maulana Muhammad Ali has agreed to take the oath" and asking him to deposit the total sum of Rs. 60,000 with Abdul Karim Babu Khan of Sikanderabad,

to be paid out when the conditions were fulfilled as promised
(*Paigham Sulh,* 4 December 1946). Seth Allahdin agreed to this, on
condition that the oath must include a prayer for punishment and it
must be published in *Paigham Sulh.* So Maulana Muhammad Ali
published the required oath in *Paigham Sulh* of 11 December 1946,
which he would take during the forthcoming annual gathering. But
Seth Allahdin never fulfilled his promise to deposit the money with
Abdul Karim Babu Khan.

M. Muhammad Ali takes oath in speech, December 1946

On 25 December 1946, the first day of the annual gathering, Maulana Muhammad Ali delivered a speech on the topic 'The demand
for oath by the *Jama'at* of Qadian'. In this speech he fully exp-
ounded the denial of a claim to prophethood by Hazrat Mirza
Ghulam Ahmad and the differences between the Lahore and Qadian
Jama'ats on this issue. He said that when he invited Mirza Mahmud
Ahmad for the last time in August 1946 to hold a debate or a
mubahila, Mirza Mahmud Ahmad gave no reply directly, but his
private secretary wrote letters to some of Mirza Mahmud Ahmad's
followers in which it was said:

> "Let him quote any writing in which I have said that the
> Promised Messiah had changed his **belief** (*'aqīda*) about
> prophethood. I only wrote that the Promised Messiah
> changed the **definition** (*ta'rīf*) of prophethood."

At this, Maulana Muhammad Ali had immediately published
in *Paigham Sulh* examples of quotations from Mirza Mahmud
Ahmad in which he had written many times that the Promised
Messiah, either in 1901 or in 1902, had changed his **belief** about
prophethood.[11] But there was no answer from Mirza Mahmud
Ahmad which made any sense. Then, turning to the demand of

11. For example, Mirza Mahmud Ahmad wrote: "…as regards his belief
(*'aqīda*) about prophethood which he expressed in *Tiryaq-ul-Qulub,* later
revelation made him change it" (*Al-Qaul-ul-Fasl,* p. 24), and "…the issue of
prophethood became clear to him in 1900 or 1901, and as *Ayk Ghalati Ka
Izala* was published in 1901, in which he has proclaimed his prophethood
most forcefully, this shows that he made a change in his belief (*'aqīda*) in
1901" (*Haqiqat-un-Nubuwwat,* p. 121).

Seth Abdullah Allahdin and other members of the Qadiani *Jama'at,* Maulana Muhammad Ali related the following history.

He said that he had already declared under oath in 1915, as one of a group of seventy members of the Lahore Ahmadiyya *Jama'at,* that the Promised Messiah did not change his belief in 1901. In response, not even one member of the Qadian *Jama'at* had dared take an oath stating the contrary to this. The second time, in 1944, when the Lahore and Qadian communities of the village of Data (District Hazara) came to an agreement that each would ask its head to take an oath about his beliefs, he had again taken the oath, with wording formulated by them, as follows:

> "I, Muhammad Ali, head of the Lahore Ahmadiyya *Jama'at,* knowing Allah the Most High to be witness to this, Who holds my life in His hands, do swear that to my knowledge the belief of the Promised Messiah from 1901 to 1908 was that a person not believing in him *is still a Muslim and within the fold of Islam, and his denier is not a kafir or excluded from the fold of Islam.* The same has also been my belief, from 1901 till this day, on the basis of the belief of the Promised Messiah." [12]

But Mirza Mahmud Ahmad had not responded to the same demand upon him by that branch of his *Jama'at* to take a corresponding oath about his beliefs. Then his follower Seth Abdullah Allahdin started publishing, again and again, demands for an oath with offer of financial reward. Now that Maulana Muhammad Ali had published in the paper that he was prepared to accept the challenge to take the oath, Seth Allahdin became silent and did not deposit the reward-money as he had promised to do. In short, concluded Maulana Muhammad Ali, as Mirza Mahmud Ahmad was not willing to take part in a debate or a *mubahila*, it must have become clear to everyone that those who attribute this change of claim to the Promised Messiah are absolutely wrong.

During this speech Maulana Muhammad Ali took the oath in the words demanded by Seth Allahdin as follows:

---

12. This oath was published in *Paigham Sulh,* 21 September 1944, p. 5.

"I, Muhammad Ali, head of the Lahore Ahmadiyya *Jama'at,* do swear that my belief is that Hazrat Mirza [Ghulam Ahmad] sahib of Qadian is a *mujaddid* and the Promised Messiah, but not a prophet, nor can any person become a *kafir* or excluded from the fold of Islam by denying him. This was also the belief of Hazrat Mirza sahib.

O God, if I have uttered falsehood in this oath taken in Thy name, then send upon me from Thyself such exemplary punishment as has no human hand in it, and from which the world would learn how stern and terrible is God's retribution for one who deceives His creatures by swearing falsely in His name."

This speech was published in *Paigham Sulh,* dated 15 January 1947.

These events have been recorded here in some detail to make it abundantly clear that Maulana Muhammad Ali, within his life-time, established his arguments comprehensively, conclusively and irrefutably upon the leader of the Qadian *Jama'at,* proving the utter falsity of the Qadiani beliefs, but the other side never had the courage to confront him.

Epilogue 1954: Mirza Mahmud Ahmad retracts his extremist beliefs in court

Before closing this section it is also essential to refer to Maulana Muhammad Ali's prophetic-like statement which has been publi-shed many times before:

"They (the Qadianis) would either, at last, give up the belief in the prophethood of the Promised Messiah or formulate a separate *kalima* and a separate religion for themselves." [13]

This prediction, which Maulana Muhammad Ali made, based

---

13. See Maulana Muhammad Ali's Urdu book *Tahrik-i Ahmadiyyat,* chapter 4, pages 165–166, and the English translation of this chapter pub-lished as *True Conception of the Ahmadiyya Movement.*

on his complete trust in Allah's support and full faith in the truth of his beliefs, was fulfilled after his death in a most remarkable manner which is now a part of history. In March and April 1953 there erupted a strong wave of opposition against the Ahmadiyya community in Pakistan, leading to serious disturbances and rioting. By the middle of April the situation had became so dangerous that the Central Government imposed martial law in Lahore. After that, not only did the Provincial Government of the Punjab fall but a group of anti-Ahmadiyya religious leaders was arrested and put behind bars. To investigate the causes of these disturbances, Chief Justice Muhammad Munir was appointed to head a Court of Inquiry. The report of this court was published, and is commonly known as the Munir Report.[14]

To change one's beliefs while testifying in court is a matter of much disgrace and humiliation, as the Promised Messiah has written about his opponent Maulvi Muhammad Husain Batalvi in his book *Tiryaq-ul-Qulub*. It was the plan of Allah the Most High that Mirza Mahmud Ahmad's extremist beliefs be exposed in court. Previously he used to claim that:

> "all those so-called Muslims who have not entered into his [Hazrat Mirza Ghulam Ahmad's] *bai'at* formally, wherever they may be, are *Kafirs* and outside the pale of Islam, even though they may not have heard the name of the Promised Messiah." (See his books: *A'inah-i Sadaqat,* p. 35; *The Truth About the Split,* pages 55–56).

But now in court he stated:

> "No one who does not believe in Mirza Ghulam Ahmad sahib can be taken as out of the pale of Islam." [15]

---

14. Its full title is: *Report of the Court of Inquiry constituted under Punjab Act II of 1954 to enquire into the Punjab Disturbances of 1953,* published in Lahore by the Superintendent, Government Printing, Punjab, 1954.

15. Statement of Mirza Mahmud Ahmad before the Court of Inquiry, 14 January 1954. It is reproduced in Urdu in the Qadiani publication *Tahqiqati 'adalat main Hazrat Imam Jama'at Ahmadiyya ka Bayan* ('Testimony of the Head of the Ahmadiyya Community at the Court of Inquiry'), published by Dar-ut-Tajleed, Lahore, page 28.

The conclusions of the Court of Inquiry on this matter are given in its Report in the following words:

> "The question, therefore, is reduced to this whether Mirza Ghulam Ahmad ever claimed to be the receiver of such *wahi* as amounted to *wahi-i-nubuwwat.* ... whether he claimed for his *wahi* the status of *wahi-i-nubuwwat,* omission to believe in which involves certain spiritual and ultramundane consequences. Before us the Ahmadis and their present head[16] have, after careful consideration, taken the stand that he did not ... and that an omission to believe in Mirza Sahib's *wahi* does not take a person outside the pale of Islam." (Pages 188, 189)

> "On the question whether the Ahmadis consider the other Musalmans to be *kafirs* in the sense of their being outside the pale of Islam, the position taken before us is that such persons are not *kafirs* and that the word *kufr,* when used in the literature of the Ahmadis in respect of such persons, is used in the sense of minor heresy and that it was never intended to convey that such persons were outside the pale of Islam." (Page 199)

Similarly, regarding the question of saying funeral prayers for non-Ahmadi Muslims the Report says:

> "The position finally adopted by the Ahmadis before us on the question of funeral prayers is that an opinion of Mirza Ghulam Ahmad has now been discovered which permits the Ahmadis to join the funeral prayers of the other Muslims who are not *mukazzibs* and *mukaffirs* of Mirza Sahib." (Page 199)

As regards the statement of Mirza Mahmud Ahmad before the Inquiry mentioned in the above extract, that "an opinion of Mirza Ghulam Ahmad has now been discovered which permits the Ahmadis to join the funeral prayers of the other Muslims", it must be pointed out that Maulana Muhammad Ali had been putting forward this opinion of the Promised Messiah, and many similar

---

16. The Qadiani *Jama'at* and Mirza Mahmud Ahmad are meant.

references, to Mirza Mahmud Ahmad ever since the Split took place in 1914, but he had never given any satisfactory response.

When he was asked in the Court of Inquiry if the differences between Ahmadis and non-Ahmadis are "fundamental" (*bunyadi*), Mirza Mahmud Ahmad replied: "If the word 'fundamental' is taken in the sense in which the Holy Prophet Muhammad has taken it, then these differences are not fundamental." He was then asked: "What if the word 'fundamental' is taken in its ordinary sense?" He replied: "In the ordinary sense it means 'important' (*ahm*). According to this sense also, the differences are not fundamental but secondary (*farau'i*)." [17]

However, some forty years earlier he had declared the following in a speech in a section headed *Differences in religious issues between Ahmadis and non-Ahmadis:*

> "The Promised Messiah has said: Their Islam and our Islam are different. Their God and our God are different. Our *Hajj* and their *Hajj* are different. Similarly, we differ from them in every matter." [18]

When this statement of his from *Al-Fazl* was put to him in the Court of Inquiry and he was asked "Is this true?", he replied:

> "When this was published, I did not have a diarist to copy it down. Therefore, I cannot be certain whether my words were correctly reported or not." [19]

To conclude, Maulana Muhammad Ali's pronouncement that the Qadianis will either have to create a different religion and separate themselves from the Muslim community, or they will have to change their beliefs, was fulfilled word for word, just over two years after his death.

---

17. The Qadiani publication *Tahqiqati 'adalat main Hazrat Imam Jama'at Ahmadiyya ka Bayan,* p. 15–16.

18. *Al-Fazl,* 21 August 1917, p. 8, col. 1.

19. *Tahqiqati 'adalat main Hazrat Imam Jama'at Ahmadiyya ka Bayan,* p. 16, last answer on page.

3.7: From June 1947 to 1950

Revision of the English Translation of the Holy Quran and campaign for distribution of literature

As already mentioned, at the end of May 1947 Maulana Muhammad Ali along with his family went to Dalhousie as usual. During the month of May, due to intensity of heat in Lahore, he used to suffer from fever and some other ailments. That year also in May he was in a very poor state of health, but after reaching Dalhousie the fever stopped. On 25 June 1947 he embarked upon his last monumental literary project, the revision of the English translation and commentary of the Holy Quran. Thirty years had elapsed since this translation and commentary was first published and during these years, starting with *Bayan-ul-Quran,* the Urdu translation of the Quran with exhaustive commentary, he had produced many substantial writings in Urdu and English on the Holy Quran, Hadith, life of the Holy Prophet Muhammad and the religion of Islam. As a result, he felt the need for revision of the English translation. In these circumstances, at the age of 71 years this man of God took this revision work in hand. It was not a minor revision that he undertook: he made a great many changes in the translation, almost entirely rewrote most footnotes, and made other substantial amendments. However, two months had not yet passed upon starting this work when the country was overtaken by the cataclysmic events of the partition of India, and Maulana Muhammad Ali had to leave for Lahore in the most dangerous conditions, leaving his books and other belongings behind in his residence in Dalhousie.

Partition of India and journey from Dalhousie to Lahore

In 1947 India was in a state of turmoil and uncertainty. The British government was on the verge of quitting India, but no one knew who would take over power after that withdrawal. The most serious communal riots had broken out all over the country. In Lahore itself there had been terrible disturbances during the months of March and April, so much so that on two Fridays it was impossible for Maulana Muhammad Ali to go to Ahmadiyya Buildings from Muslim Town. On 3 June 1947, the Viceroy of India announced in principle the partitioning of the country into India and Pakistan, and on 14 August 1947 the state of Pakistan came into being after a provisional award of areas. Dalhousie was in Gurdaspur district, and in the provisional award the status of this and some other districts had not been finally determined, but as Gurdaspur had a Muslim majority it was assumed that it would be included in Pakistan. Consequently, on 14 August the Muslim postmaster of Dalhousie hoisted the Pakistan flag on the post office. At that time, due to riots, carnage and massacres having erupted in the plains of the Punjab, communication with Dalhousie by post and telegram was cut off and radio was the only source of receiving news there. After two or three days when the final award of partition was announced, the whole of the Gurdaspur district was given to India.

Dalhousie's town population largely consisted of people who had come from the plains, the majority of them being Hindus. The local population consisted of Hindu mountain folk who worked as labourers, and among other such tasks they carried the luggage of the tourists from and to the bus station. When Dalhousie became a part of the new India, the Hindus there also went on the rampage, looting and burning Muslim shops and houses. Bakrota, where the residence of Maulana Muhammad Ali was located, was in an isolated place at a high position some distance away from the town. Now Hindu mobs started roaming this area, though still they did not have the courage to turn to violence.

Conditions were deteriorating rapidly. It is well known what happened to Muslims in East Punjab. Millions of Muslim men, women and children were abandoning their homes and fleeing to Pakistan. Thousands of them were brutally massacred on the way. Neither rail nor road travel remained a safe means of transport. At that time Mian Ghulam Rasul and Shaikh Mian Muhammad were also in Dalhousie with Maulana Muhammad Ali. On 21 or 22 August they learnt that a military convoy had arrived to escort them to Lahore. Maulana Muhammad Ali and his family quickly left home to meet the convey, but due to the long distance involved they discovered midway that the convoy had already gone. After that, it rained heavily for three or four days, and this saved their lives because Hindu mobs could not set fire to their homes.

On 26 August another military convoy was sent from Lahore to rescue them. They left their homes early on the morning of 27 August. No porters could be found to carry their luggage. With difficulty a few men were procured, and only the most essential belongings were given to them to carry, while Maulana Muhammad Ali and his family, and Mian Ghulam Rasul, Shaikh Mian Muhammad and Mian Afzal Husain made their way to the bus station. However, when they arrived there they discovered, after waiting for some time, that the Hindu porters had absconded with the luggage. So, almost empty-handed, they left for Pakistan. Men were in one truck and women in the other, and the military escorting party accompanied them. Even this did not guarantee safety because road transport was being looted even in the presence of the army. All through the journey they met crowds of distressed Muslims trying to make it to Pakistan, but who were being cruelly slaughtered on the way. As many of these as could be fitted into these trucks were taken on board. At last this convoy entered Pakistan on 27 August at about sunset time.

In Dalhousie, Maulana Muhammad Ali's residence 'Darus Salaam', with his valuable books and other belongings, was burnt to the ground by the rioting mobs. He could only bring with him his bag containing the manuscript of his writing, which he was carrying in his hand. Similarly, his brothers and other relatives who lived in the village of Murar managed, with much difficulty, to escape to Pakistan with their lives.

Refugees Relief Fund

To help the Muslim refugees who had come to Pakistan having lost everything, Maulana Muhammad Ali opened the Refugees Relief Fund and appealed to members of the *Jama'at* for each to donate one month's pay to it. About Rs. 40,000 were raised to help refugees.

The annual gathering for 1947

In 1947, due to the devastating communal riots, the partition of the country and the influx of hundreds of thousands of refugees into Pakistan, the annual gathering could not be held in December according to the usual practice. It was postponed and held on 26–28 March 1948. It was inaugurated by Maulana Muhammad Ali's Friday *khutba* in which he referred to the twin treasures of faith and knowledge which enabled Muslims of the first generations to advance and bring the world out of the darkness of ignorance into the light of knowledge. He said that in the present age the spirit of Islam had been lost, and it was revived by Hazrat Mirza sahib. Today it is only knowledge that can build the state of Pakistan, and that is what Hazrat Mirza sahib has bequeathed to us. Let us not squander that inheritance like the prodigal son who wastes his father's wealth. We should rise and revive the dying world with the spirit of faith and knowledge, without caring whether our name receives renown for doing this work. The world would be alive and Pakistan would be strengthened.

The next day he made a very moving speech, full of deep truths and knowledge, on the topic: 'No one will overpower Allah's Religion, but Allah's Religion will overcome all'. He said that these were not his own words but were based on the Holy Quran's claims. He cited the testimony of historical events, statements of the Holy Quran and prophetic visions of the Holy Prophet Muhammad to prove that, just as at its beginning Islam emerged from a state of oppression to become victorious, it is again now emerging from its latter-day downfall, which came upon it according to Allah's plan, and is at the start of its path of triumph in the world. It will achieve complete triumph, if Allah please. He said that we should keep it firmly in our minds and hearts that this is what the history of Islam was to be, it is God's

promise: Islam was under persecution first, then it became victorious, then it met with downfall and defeat, and now the time is
again coming for it to be triumphant. It is now our mission to show
the world the right path. Then in this connection he added:

> "Two points are important. Firstly, you should have the
> same faith in the sure triumph of Islam as did the Holy
> Prophet Muhammad. If we have not acquired that faith
> from the Holy Prophet, then what did we gain? Secondly,
> we gave an undertaking at the hand of the *Mujaddid* that
> we will hold aloft the name of God. If, after making that
> confirmation, we do nothing, then what did we gain from
> that *Mujaddid*? Nothing is achieved by making these
> formal distinctions that we are Muslims and we are
> Ahmadis. Create real distinctions, and that cannot happen
> unless we have that fervour raging in our hearts. God also
> will not fulfil His promises with us until we create that
> zeal within us." (*Paigham Sulh,* 14 April 1948, p. 7)

Then he appealed for donations of Rs. 50,000 for the Woking
Mission and Rs. 50,000 for buying a property for a mission in San
Francisco, U.S.A. In the end, he called upon the *Jama'at* as
follows:

> "Prepare your hearts. Pray to God, falling before Him in
> helplessness. When I found out that my residence in Dal-
> housie had been burnt down, I prayed: 'O God, I used to
> pray for the victory of Your religion in that house. Now
> that house itself is lying before You, extending its hands
> in prayer'. Make it your habit that whatever you are doing,
> whether walking around, sitting or rising, whether in
> comfort or in distress, prayers are emanating from your
> hearts for the triumph of the Divine religion."

Affiliation of the Woking Mission

It has been mentioned before that at the beginning of its life the
Woking Mission was affliated to the Anjuman but from 1929 it
functioned as a separate Trust. From 1 April 1948 this Mission
was again affiliated to the Anjuman because it had been facing

financial difficulties. From then on, the Anjuman took over both the expenditure and the administrative responsibility of this Mission and its magazine *The Islamic Review*.

Stay in Quetta

As Dalhousie was now a part of the newly independent India, it was not possible for Maulana Muhammad Ali to spend summer there. So in 1948 he decided to spend summer in the city of Quetta (on the Western border of Pakistan), where his elder son Muhammad Ahmad was stationed in the course of his employment. On 8 June 1948 Maulana Muhammad Ali along with his family went to Quetta. At that time the most important task before him was the revision of the English translation of the Holy Quran, on which he was busily engaged day and night. Regular gatherings of the local *Jama'at* also started to take place at his residence, and in the evenings he gave teaching in the Holy Quran. At the age of 73 years he was working so hard on the English translation of the Quran that, after the *fajr* prayer and then going for his morning walk, he would immediately have breakfast and then set to work. He would work ceaselessly till it was time for the *zuhr* prayer. In the afternoon he would take a rest for an hour and then resume work till night, except for that time in the evening when he met visitors or gave teaching in the Holy Quran. Although the weather in Quetta was very pleasant and salubrious, nonetheless this constant mental exertion weighed upon his health, as will be mentioned later.

Instructions for spiritual exertions in Ramadan

During his stay in Quetta, the topic of his Friday *khutbas* was always the service and propagation of the Holy Quran and prayer to God to help achieve these ends. That year during the month of Ramadan he specially emphasized all this in his addresses and writings. He had the following announcement printed in bold letters in the paper *Paigham Sulh*, 7 July 1948, every word of which expresses his passion for this cause:

About Ramadan and its blessings

Allah says: O My servants I am very near to you, whoever calls on Me I accept his prayers. Our Holy Prophet says: When Ramadan comes, the doors of Allah's mercy open.

This was a fact to which the lives of our Guide, his companions and his true followers bear witness. But today it is a mere story. Why? Because our hearts do not have the same fervour for God, our bodies prostrate before God but not our hearts. Real prayer means only the rising of an urge within the heart.

Let us, during this Ramadan, shed tears not on the wrongs that others have done to us but on the wrongs we have done to ourselves, saying: O God, we have failed to value You, we have failed to value Your message, we have concealed Your message. We wish not to dedicate our lives to spread Your message in the world, we wish not to spend our money to take Your message to the world. We do things for which You have plainly threatened punishment. 'Those who conceal the clear proofs and the guidance that We have revealed' [the Quran, 2:159], the punishment for which is: 'these it is whom Allah curses, and those who curse, curse them too ... these it is on whom is the curse of Allah and the angels and men, of all of them' [the Quran, 2:159, 161].

Even then we expect that the doors of Your blessings will open for us. With our mouths we say that You are near us, but our hearts are so distant from You that nothing could be any further.

Our foreheads are placed at Your threshold where we should find paradise, but in our hearts we are like the one who 'amasses wealth and counts it, he thinks that his wealth will make him abide' [104:2, 3]. With our tongues we say: O God, we are Your slaves, our wealth belongs not to us but to You. But our hearts are such that when we have to spend a few pennies to exalt Your name in the world, it feels to us like a huge hurdle, and we make false pretexts to try every possible way of avoiding parting with our wealth. O God, deliver us from this false existence. When, in the quietness of the night, we place our foreheads on the ground in prayer, we hear the ground saying in reply:

'You have desecrated me with your hypocritical pros-trations'.

O God, enable us to prostrate truly at Your threshold. Make us Your slaves that we would have no other anxiety but to raise high Your name. Be our Lord that You may turn to exalting the Muslim *Umma* in the world.

— Muhammad Ali.

A letter of advice

While Maulana Muhammad Ali was in Quetta, he bid farewell to his younger son Hamid Farooq who was leaving for England to pursue higher studies. At Quetta railway station, as the train was about to depart for Karachi, he gave his son a sealed envelope, instructing him to open it on reaching England. The letter in the envelope, published after the Maulana's death, read as follows:

" 2 Colvin Road, Quetta, 1 August 1948, 24 *Ramadan.*

My dear Hamid,
May Allah keep you safe and sound. *Assalamu alaikum wa rah-matullahi wa barakatuhu.*

I have reached an age where I am not sure if I will ever meet you again in this world's life. I am writing some words of advice which may guide you in your long journey.

1. Never forget that we have an Almighty God, Who helps us in our troubles and difficulties, and opens such ways for us as we could never imagine.

2. Do not forget that each and every deed of ours is noted in God's record. If it is good, it leaves a beneficial effect upon us, if bad then a detrimental effect upon us. We may hide our shortcomings from people but never from God.

3. Alcohol is the root of all evils. Never go near it, never, never. Do not join in a gathering where alcohol is par-taken.

4. Keep up your daily prayers. Every morning make sure that you rise and say your prayers, and also recite a few verses of the Quran. Make it such a firm habit that it is the one thing that you never omit to do.

5. Work hard and live a simple life. If you stick to these two habits, they will keep you happy all your life.

6. Work very hard on your studies, but always keep in mind that you also do some work of service of your religion and good to humanity. Without this, there can be no bliss in life.

7. Never hide this fact that, by the grace of God, we are Muslims, and we accept the *Mujaddid* of this century as our *Imam* — we are **Ahmadis** who do not accept the coming of any prophet after the Holy Prophet Muhammad, nor do we call as *kafir* anyone who professes the *Kalima*.

If you try to live up to this advice, God will be pleased with you, your parents will also be pleased with you, and you yourself will be pleased as well. When I am gone, be very good to your mother.

Wassalam, Muhammad Ali. "

(This letter was later published in *Paigham Sulh,* 2 April 1952, about six months after the death of Maulana Muhammad Ali.)

Another serious illness

At the beginning of September 1948, Maulana Muhammad Ali again fell somewhat ill. There was bronchial and lung trouble and persistent fever. The fever was always present mildly, and would at times increase. By the end of September the fever had become very serious and there was swelling on various parts of the body, probably because of the spread of toxins due to the throat infection. His debility worsened so much that his condition gave cause for grave concern. So on 5 October the renowned Lahore doctor Colonel Ilahi Bakhsh was sent to Quetta. He was accompanied by Dr. Allah Bakhsh, and Dr. Saeed Ahmad also went from Dadar. After a thorough examination, Colonel Ilahi Bakhsh said that the effects of pus had spread throughout the body. The basal parts of both lungs, the pericardium, and the front of the chest were also affected. In addition, the kidney function was defective. The infection was thus affecting all the major organs. Colonel Ilahi Bakhsh started treatment, and by the grace of God, there was a significant improvement within two days. The power of God the Most High was clearly seen behind this recovery, in that the right medical assistance was received just in time, while before this the treatment by the doctors in Quetta was not having any effect. Slowly and gradually the illness subsided, although weakness and infirmity persisted for a long time.

Being nearly the end of October, he left Quetta on the 23rd and arrived in Lahore on 24 October 1948. Before leaving, while being bed-ridden he gathered members of the Quetta *Jama'at* around him and gave them instructions and advice for a long time. After this, on his directions each person individually promised under oath that as far as possible he would try to join the Friday congregational prayers. What Maulana Muhammad Ali was aiming at was that if all members met regularly even just once a week for Friday prayers, this would lead to the creation of an organised *Jama'at*.

On 24 October a large number of members received him at Lahore railway station. He was still so weak that he was carried on a chair out of the station. After returning to Muslim Town his health improved day by day, although according to medical advice he had to spend another month in bed. Even in that state he continued his work and literary activities, and remained engaged in the revision of the English translation of the Quran.

Exhortations to the *Jama'at*

It was a source of continuing distress for Maulana Muhammad Ali that some people in the *Jama'at* were indulging in destructive criticism and carping at others, as such behaviour was damaging to the work of the propagation of Islam. To remedy this misbehaviour, he would address the *Jama'at* from time to time in his *khutbas*. In his Friday *khutba* on 5 March 1948, reciting the verse from the Holy Quran "O you who believe, take care of your own souls — he who errs cannot harm you when you are on the right way" (5:105), he said that although this verse means that you must pay attention to your own selves and think first of mending your own ways, but in fact the words "take care of your own souls" are the foundation-stone of creating a community:

> "These words draw attention to the fact that no person can make progress for himself by fault-finding in others and dragging them down, nor can a community be built in this way. Rather, everyone must first be concerned with his own reform, his own development. ... Construction is difficult and people do not readily take a step to do such difficult work. As compared with this, destructive activity and running others down is very easy. ... To destroy and ruin another person is very easy, but to become something yourself is very difficult....
>
> Today you are established as the heirs of a Reformer. You have undertaken the responsibility of spreading the message of God in the world. Have we all reached the stage that is required by the words: 'O you who believe, take care of your own souls'? Have we given up carping at others, fault-finding and trying to knock them down, and instead are devoting all our energies to make ourselves more useful? Have we reached the stage of setting good examples for others to follow? Sadly, even here there are many who pay little attention to doing constructive works. Their minds are less on their own reform and more on showing up faults in others. I say to my friends, this is not the way to build a *Jama'at*. To create a *Jama'at* you must ignore the weaknesses and shortcomings of others, and focus instead on the correction of your own faults and failings."
>
> (*Paigham Sulh*, 17 March 1948)

He gave another Friday *khutba,* on 16 April 1948, on the topic that if we want God to forgive us our sins we must forgive the faults of others. He said:

> "If anyone seeks forgiveness from Allah, his desire to be forgiven is false if he does not forgive other human beings. ... This is the teaching given in the words: 'Imbue yourselves with Divine morals'. ... God is the Forgiver, but for those who are forgivers of others. ... He forgives even

without repentance on your part, ... so you should do the same. ... The Imam of the Age has also stressed this point and said that even if you are right, be humble as if you are in the wrong. It does not mean that you call yourself wrong unreasonably, but that while you are in the right you should also exercise your power of forgiveness. Expect not that the person who is in the wrong should come to you and apologise. ...

Some people take offence over trivial matters and think that unless the other person apologises they will not have anything to do with him. This way is not right. The Holy Quran prohibits it, and the Promised Messiah forbade it. Only by forgiving our brothers can the organisation of the *Jama'at* continue to function. ... Save your power of fighting to confront the enemy, and use your power of submission on your brethren. ... I see that we feel no concern for our own ghastly faults but criticise those who are doing great and important works at the slightest error on their part. This is not right. When judging others, give precedence to their virtues and ignore their shortcomings." (*Paigham Sulh,* 5 May 1948)

Press conference

On 23 December 1948, prior to the annual gathering, Maulana Muhammad Ali called a press conference at the hotel Stiffles in Lahore. In a short speech he told newspaper reporters that for the development of Pakistan, while there were many other issues, a crucially important problem was that the image of Islam and the Muslims in the eyes of the developed nations of the world was highly unfavourable, and this was why they were hostile to Islamic governments. Generally the European and American newspapers gave more importance to India and the views of its Congress Party, showing less respect for us. It was needed to show the world the real picture of Islam and the Holy Prophet Muhammad. Muslims should be urged to take this work in hand. Wrong impressions of Islam can be changed, and our experience had shown that our efforts had brought about some change in thinking in the West. This, he said, was the responsibility of the Pakistani press. While they stress upon other issues and try to influence public opinion, they should also motivate Muslims to present a good example and true picture of Islam to the world.

At this press conference he showed the audience translations of the Holy Quran as well as other books, and expressed his belief that if the Western nations were shown the picture of Islam as presented in this literature they would surely be impressed. He added that this literature had gained universal acceptance and some of the books had been translated into different languages of the world by the people of those countries themselves. He declared that the honour of Pakistan was linked with Islam and if the newspapers could create this spirit among the public, of presenting the true picture of Islam, it would be a great service. Every Muslim should be a born missionary, and if he understands this point and becomes determined to spread Islam then a transformation can be brought about all over the world.

The annual gathering 1948 and campaign for distribution of literature

The annual gathering of 1948 took place on the usual dates of 25, 26 and 27 December. Maulana Muhammad Ali made speeches on all the three days. One speech was entitled 'Prayer and the three ways to success', in which he explained how prayer is the means of progress of three kinds for the human race. This speech was later on published in the form of a booklet. Its Arabic translation was published in Baghdad by Syed Tassadaq Husain Qadari under the title *As-Salat wa taraq-ut-taqaddam ath-thalath,* which became very popular in Arab countries and soon this booklet was translated in many other languages in various countries.

His other two speeches related to the propagation of Islam. Following up on the fact that the Anjuman had in the past spent more than 100,000 Rupees on the free distribution of literature, the particular plan he proposed to the *Jama'at* in these speeches was that this work should be expanded and 100,000 Rupees should be spent for this purpose during 1949. After his three earlier campaigns for translations of the Quran, establishment of missionary centres, and creation of an institute of study and research of the Quran, this was his fourth and last great campaign.

The subsequent work of the distribution of sets of books was also a part of this same fourth plan.

His own view was that 50,000 Rupees should be spent on sending literature to non-Muslims, mainly those in Europe and America, and the other half spent on distributing literature to Muslims, largely in Asian countries, paying special attention to making this literature available through libraries. He asked for advice of members of the *Jama'at* about this and made an appeal to them for funds which was repeated after the annual gathering from time to time through *Paigham Sulh* and Friday *khutbas*. At the annual gathering itself he had appealed for 50,000 Rupees, in consequence of which 35,000 Rupees were raised in cash and the form of promises.

Another proposal was to organise the regular monthly subscription paid by members, as there was some laxity in this regard in the *Jama'at*. After the annual gathering, in the Friday *khutba* on 31 December 1948, he requested Maulana Sadr-ud-Din to attend to this important task, explaining that his own health was now so weak that after delivering a *khutba* he could not do any work. Just after the annual gathering when he was examined again by Dr. Saeed Ahmad and X-rayed, he was advised to have complete rest for a further two to three months and to abstain even from his regular morning walk. So, he said in his *khutba,* he was unable to travel and was requesting Maulana Sadr-ud-Din to undertake this task (*Paigham Sulh,* 12 January 1949).

Emphasis on publishing literature

During 1949 he put forward proposals of several different forms in connection with distribution of literature. In his Friday *khutba* on 21 January, referring to the command of God the Most High not to break trust, he said:

> "We are also the holders of a trust. ... As a *Jama'at* we have been made responsible for a trust assigned to us by the *Mujaddid* of the time. What is that? His first book, after his claim to be Promised Messiah was *Fath-i Islam*, in which he has explained that the purpose of his advent was to spread the word of Allah and the light of the Holy

Prophet Muhammad in the world and to come to the aid of the Muslims. After this, he writes that for the attainment of this purpose his work is divided into five kinds. Out of the five kinds that he enumerated, the fundamental ones are the first one and the last one. The first is the writing and producing of literature and the last is forming the *Jama'at*. The ones in between these are encompassed by these two, so that booklets and notices come under the production of literature, and maintaining the guest house is connected with the formation of the *Jama'at*.

In reality, therefore, he has given us two main tasks: one is to spread the Divine religion by means of writings and literature, and the other one is to form a *Jama'at*. The *Jama'at* is like an army and the literature is its weapon. These are the two means whose real purpose is the revival of the faith." (*Paigham Sulh,* 2 February 1949)

Then he mentioned the impact that this literature had made and said that we need to produce such people in our *Jama'at* who maintain the heritage we received from Hazrat Mirza sahib and set themselves to do the work that he entrusted to us.

The reason that he laid stress again and again on the work of the propagation of Islam was that there were some members of the *Jama'at* who did not give it the importance that was due to it. They believed that it was more important to build a school and a college. One such member, in a Friday *khutba,* launched the proposal to build a college before any decision had been made by the Anjuman about it. In this connection Maulana Muhammad Ali, in his Friday *khutba* on 28 January 1949, drawing attention to the Quranic verses "There should be a party from among you who invite to good" (3:104) and "Who is better in speech than one who invites to Allah" (41:33), said that the first verse deals with the necessary arrangements for the advancement and progress of Islam, while the second verse tells us that the best work a person can do is to invite people towards the religion of Allah. This was the purpose for which Hazrat Mirza sahib had formed the *Jama'at*. This work requires zeal, fervour and enthusiasm. On the one hand, you must be selfless, giving precedence to this work over all else.

On the other hand, after dedicating yourself to the work of inviting towards Allah, you must not create disunity nor have mixed motives. He said:

> "Unity and harmony are great blessings. Bear that in mind. Whichever path you take, move together as one. If you think that inviting people to Allah is not a worthwhile objective, or there is some other goal better than that, then unite and start working towards it all together. The worthwhile purpose is only one: inviting to Allah. By the grace of God, we have a system that depends on the consensus of the *Jama'at,* and this system was established by the Imam of the Age. So whatever other work you want to do, place it before that system, and when the *Jama'at* as a whole agrees on a course of action, then unite upon it. At that time ignore a man of limited thinking like me, and let him sit in a corner by himself.
>
> Let me make it clear. A scheme has been put before you (i.e., publication and distribution of literature). Last Friday another proposal, for a college, was put before you. I want to make it clear that this was not the decision of your *Jama'at*. So far your community has not decided to do it. The last General Council set up a committee to prepare a detailed plan to put before the Anjuman. The Anjuman has not decided anything as yet. When details are put before the Anjuman, it will be up to it to accept or reject the proposal. I have my own personal view but the decision will be taken by majority opinion. I have been told that I want to stop the creation of a college. I am not stopping it, but I do say that this proposal causes disunity and division. Do not let that happen. This proposal for a college is not new. It has been coming before the Anjuman previously, but the Anjuman did not approve it. Till the Anjuman gives its approval, concentrate on one task, that of spreading the word of Allah.
>
> The Promised Messiah has well said that our concern is not whether we succeed or fail in our efforts. We have to do the work in any case. As he wrote:

Whether You forsake me in anger or show Yourself to me as a sign of pleasure,

Whether You punish me or let me be, I can never stop clinging to You.

He says: O God, I have taken firm hold of You. If You wish You can separate me out of anger or allow me to see Your countenance out of pleasure; if You wish You can destroy me or grant me respite, but I will never let go of holding on to You."

(*Paigham Sulh*, 9 Febuary 1949)

Along with this, Maulana Muhammad Ali also had a great passion for the welfare and betterment of the fatherless children and poor members of the *Jama'at*. In his very next Friday *khutba* after the one quoted above, he stressed upon the need to take care of the poor, the orphans and the indigent, which he believed to be very important for the progress of the *Jama'at*. He explained that when he put forward the proposal for an institute for the study and teaching of the Quran (*Idara Talim-ul-Quran*), one idea behind it was that it would be an institution where boys from poor and rich families would live in the same conditions, with no distinction being made on the basis of wealth. If we set up English public schools, how many people would be able to bear the expenses of sending their children there? We should have an institute where all students live together as well as acquire knowledge of the Quran. He said that he was particularly hurt when, at a meeting of the General Council, the proposals for founding a college and a public school were being discussed, but the members forgot that one of the needs of the *Jama'at* is to bear the burden of the fatherless children and the poor (*Paigham Sulh*, 16 Febuary 1949).

Due to the doubts being spread in the *Jama'at* by some members, the plan for the distribution of literature was not proceeding at a satisfactory pace, and Maulana Muhammad Ali had to make appeals again and again for this scheme. In his Friday *khutba* on 11 March 1949 (*Paigham Sulh*, 23 March 1949) he said:

"Is it not a matter of wonder that your literature, which has been acknowledged at home and abroad as presenting the best picture of Islam, when I made an appeal for its distribution, very little attention was paid to it. It is saddening for me. I have no right to ask you to avoid causing me distress, but you should at least make some allowance for my age. ... Try to present what is admitted to be the best picture of Islam to people who have not seen it so far. I know I have weaknesses and shortcomings, but I appeal to friends that if I am punished for my faults in this way then the damage that is done is to the religion of Muhammad the Holy Prophet.

I also say that service that is attributed to me is only fortuitous. The real service has been rendered by the *Jama'at,* whose financial sacrifices enabled this literature to reach the world. ... You are the people who published this literature, and it is your responsibility to spread it in the world. I entreat you again: look, service of the religion of God is a trust handed to you by the Imam of the Age. You have taken great care of it and performed your duty to it. Rise and do your duty to it again today."

Idara Talim-ul-Quran

In April 1949 Maulana Muhammad Ali again presented his proposals to establish the *Idara Talim-ul-Quran* (Institute for the study and teaching of the Quran) by re-publishing his speech delivered at the annual gathering of December 1945 about this institute in *Paigham Sulh* of 6 April. He invited members to send their views to him. His own suggestion was that until a proper building for this institute is constructed on the land in Muslim Town, the work could be started on a small scale as follows:

"Five to ten students, having the ability to learn the Quran, should be selected and accommodated by us, and alongside their college education they should also acquire knowledge of the Quran. They should live here together and, if necessary, some of their expenses should be met by us. ... Then we would be able to find such people from among them who would be prepared to dedicate their lives for this work and become our missionaries."

(Friday *Khutba,* 29 April; *Paigham Sulh*, 11 May 1949)

Some time later this institution was founded in a limited form, in that a hostel for Ahmadi students who were studying in colleges was established in the building of Muslim High School No. 2 where they could live. Arrangements were made for their regular prayers, teaching of the Quran and weekly gatherings. In 1950 he proposed that a house be acquired in a better location, to which this institute would be moved. However, at that same time he fell dangerously ill in Karachi due to an attack of coronary thrombosis and this proposal could not be put into practice.

Passion for the propagation of the Holy Quran

During this entire period, each and every Friday *khutba* that he delivered was imbued with a distinctive spirituality. He urged repeatedly, and in different forms, the importance of studying the Quran, propagating it in the world, and beseeching God in prayers, particularly during *tahajjud,* for help. Extracts from these *khutbas* cannot be reproduced here, as it would be excessively lengthy to do so. He emphasised again and again that the Holy Quran inherently possesses the power to win the world over to it; the need is only to spread it. He considered all other work to be secondary. He never favoured any other plan on which the limited income of this *Jama'at* should be spent.

All-Pakistan Economic Conference

In April 1949 the Pakistan Economic Conference was held in Lahore. The meetings were held in University Hall for three days. On 28 April Maulana Muhammad Ali invited to tea the conference delegates who had assembled from different parts of Pakistan. In a short speech he introduced the Ahmadiyya Anjuman Isha'at Islam, informed them of its past achievements and explained in detail its future plans. In reply Mr. Zahid Husain, who was at that time Governor of the State Bank of Pakistan, thanked him and highly praised the work of the *Jama'at*. The same evening Mirza Masud Baig read out an English speech by Maulana Muhammad Ali to the delegates in University Hall.

Stay in Karachi in 1949

In view of his old age and frail health, and under medical advice, Maulana Muhammad Ali decided this year not to repair to any hill resort for the summer but instead go to Karachi. It was also in mind that during his stay there he would raise funds for the distribution of literature. So he left for Karachi on 23 May 1949 and stayed with Mr. Naseer Ahmad Faruqui for about four and a half months, a stay that proved to be of immense advantage. His health improved greatly by the grace of God despite the fact that the revision of the English translation of the Holy Quran still demanded much work, and in Karachi there were many other commitments also to keep him busy. But what pleased him most was that during this stay he was able to do what he could not have done at any hill resort, that God opened new ways and means for the plans he was pursuing which he could not have envisaged. The work he used to concentrate on single-mindedly in his stays at hill resorts in the summer was that of writing books. However, during his stay in Karachi, this year and the next, many opportunities arose which enabled, in addition, many arrangements to be made for the propagation of Islam, and the foundations laid for the free distribution of literature. Besides this, he held many meetings with prominent Muslims from outside the Ahmadiyya Movement, Pakistani government officials and ambassadors from other Muslim countries.[1] He had also the opportunity to clarify the real beliefs and work of the Ahmadiyya Movement at various functions. He made one speech to students of the Sindh Madrassa College.

Some letters to members of the *Jama'at*

From Karachi Maulana Muhammad Ali wrote some letters addressed to members of the *Jama'at* through the paper *Paigham Sulh*. The first letter was published under the title 'An Appeal to Senior Members of the *Jama'at* ' (*Paigham Sulh,* 15 June 1949). He wrote in it that while there are many people in the *Jama'at* deserving to be called senior figures, on the principle that "the best of you is he who is the most dutiful", who are quietly carrying on the *jihad* that the Imam of the Age set them upon, and due to their efforts the *Jama'at* has attained great achievements, but here he was particularly addressing those people whom the

---

1. Karachi was the capital of Pakistan at that time.

Jama'at had appointed to administer its affairs, such as members of the executive committee and of the General Council and office holders in branches of the *Jama'at*. He drew their attention to the fact that religious work could not be carried out without adopting humility and lowliness. Our aim is not to exalt ourselves. He said:

> "I appeal from the depth of my heart to the senior people, who are involved in administration and management of affairs, that in leading the *Jama'at* they should present a good example for other Muslims. First and foremost, they must not hanker after positions or make demands that certain work be made their responsibility. People want these positions believing the work to be easy or wishing to elevate themselves. They do not realise what enormous responsibility they are taking on. ... In religious work, which is done only for God, the person to whom responsibility is given should, instead of rejoicing, greatly fear that a burden has been placed upon him which is so difficult to discharge. ... Our Holy Prophet Muhammad has taught us the golden rule that ... we must not appoint such people to duties who are yearning for appointment."

Then he appealed to these senior men of responsibility that if, at the time of election, a position is offered to someone else rather than to them, they must not be offended, but develop the quality of selflessness. Secondly, when there is difference of opinion, it is not right that some people are prepared to resign because the decision has not gone their way. Our principle should be: *qiyām fī mā aqāma-llāh,* so that when a duty is assigned to us we must not refuse to accept it nor must we contemplate resigning, and if a duty is taken away from us, we must relinquish it without ill-feeling. This is the way of attaining the high station of the pleasure of God.

Then Maulana Muhammad Ali made some points about appointments, and said that only those people should be selected who set an example of righteousness and virtue for the *Jama'at* and who use their powers as a trust that they have been given. As our *Jama'at* has been formed to carry out a struggle (*jihad*) in the way of Allah, our leading persons must themselves be those who struggle. This *jihad* of ours is a struggle by means of one's life as well as possessions. The person who does not make financial contributions according to his means is not, according to the instructions of the Promised Messiah, to be regarded as a member of the *Jama'at,* let alone that such persons be elected to leading positions. In the end, he drew the attention of these senior members of the *Jama'at* to refrain from criticising each other's work or the work of the Anjuman in common gatherings as it is damaging. Proper ways should be used in order to correct faults and weaknesses, instead of publicising them everywhere.

Apart from the above, the other letters he addressed to members of the *Jama'at* were in relation to *jihad* in the month of Ramadan, which that time was to consist of procuring subscribers for the magazine *The Islamic Review* and setting up a mission in Holland. Dr. Shaikh Muhammad Abdullah, Imam at the Woking Mosque, had again urged the setting up of a mission in Holland, as our Movement had an extensive amount of literature in the Dutch language. When Maulana Muhammad Ali received Dr. Abdullah's letter in Karachi, Shaikh Mian Muhammad, who was visiting Karachi on some business, immediately took it upon himself to bear the entire cost of the Dutch Mission. Later on he established this Mission as a Trust.

Completion of the revision of the English translation of the Holy Quran

It was on Friday 19 August 1949 that Maulana Muhammad Ali, after a labour of more than two years, completed in Karachi the revision of the English translation of the Holy Quran. Given below are some extracts from the Friday *khutba* he delivered that day. This *khutba* was published with the following titles:

> *The second important occasion of happiness in my life —*
> *Completion of the Revision of the English Translation of*
> *the Quran.*

> *We acquired knowledge of the Quran by sitting at the feet*
> *of the Promised Messiah.*

> *Take advantage of this inheritance of knowledge and try*
> *to take the Quran to the world.*

He announced:

> "The verse I have recited today, 'Praise be to Allah, the
> Lord of the worlds', I have recited on a specially joyous
> occasion. In my life there have been many other happy
> moments but this is the second occasion of special happi-
> ness. The first occasion was when I completed the English
> translation of the Holy Quran, and today it is the second
> when I have completed the revision of the translation. ...
> Starting such a monumental task and taking it to comple-
> tion depended entirely on the grace and favour of God.
> Many friends had been asking me for several years for
> this revision, but at my age I could not muster the strength
> required for this stupendous hard work. It was a task both
> huge and difficult. My earlier experience was there, when
> I had worked day and night for seven years. But those
> days were different. Then I had much more physical
> strength than I have now. I used to work for twelve to
> fourteen hours daily. When I got tired sitting down, I would
> work standing up. Now, firstly due to my age, and second-
> ly the magnitude of the task, I felt I had no strength to
> take on this work. But Allah's grace and mercy knows no
> bounds, and with His help this work has been completed
> today.
>
> By coincidence when I wrote *Living Thoughts of the
> Prophet Muhammad*, the gist of the teachings of the Quran
> on several subjects appeared in this book, and many points
> were included in it which had not occurred to me when
> I was writing the translation and commentary of the Holy
> Quran. This new light that thus illuminated my mind
> created a renewed strength within me. ... How much
> change I have made in this revision, you can find out from
> my three friends who are at this time doing the typing as
> honorary work only to please Allah, namely, Chaudhry
> Khushi Muhammad, Muhammad Hasan Khan and Chau-
> dhry Ghulam Rasul, or after the translation is published
> then you will know.
>
> I started this work in Dalhousie on 25 June 1947. Hardly
> had I worked for a month and a half when calamity befell.

... Three or four of us were living three miles away from the centre of Dalhousie. Our safe escape was only by the special grace of God. ... The jealous opponents of the Muslims had us marked as targets, so much so that their first action after we left was to burn down the residences of myself, Mian Muhammad and Mian Maula Bakhsh. ... So this work was discontinued for a long time. Then I took up this work again and continued on it in Quetta last year. There I went through another ordeal but I was granted a new lease of life by the grace of God. Having passed through these two difficult phases, completing the revision of the translation of the Quran is a source of tremendous joy for me. ...

Reading the Quran illuminates your heart, but this depends on the concentration with which you read this word of God. ... The boundless treasures of knowledge contained in the Quran will continue to be unfolded till the Day of Judgment. It is an ocean that no one is denied access to, but to get the valuable pearls from it is dependent on how much effort we put in for their acquisition.

I advise my friends to try to find solutions to the problems of the world from the Holy Quran. Apply thought to these problems and then ponder over the Quran. Remember this principle that the solution of the problems of the world lies in developing faith in God, and nothing else can create as much faith in God as can the Holy Quran. ...

The true knowledge of the Holy Quran has in this age been disclosed distinctively to your *Jama'at,* and this blessing is in reality due to that man at whose feet we gained this knowledge. He set us on the right path. To gain true knowledge, a balanced mind is required, and it is the blessing of God that this *Jama'at* has maintained its mental equilibrium. This is why Hazrat Mirza sahib's intellectual heritage continues in this small *Jama'at.* There is another larger *Jama'at* but it could not share in this because it became extremist in belief, and due to its system of blind obedience by the followers to the leader it lost its mental balance. Its own leader complains that his *Jama'at* has lost its mental equilibrium. ...

You must read the Quran, and read it with thought and concentration. Only God knows to whom He will grant knowledge, for the benefit of His creatures. ... The other task is to spread the Holy Quran, in which everyone of you can participate, whether you are great or small. You can do whatever work you wish to, but make this task the aim of your life." (*Paigham Sulh,* 7 September 1949)

Meetings with ambassadors of Muslim countries

Apart from his meetings and talks in Karachi with prominent Muslims from outside the *Jama'at,* Maulana Muhammad Ali established contact in particular with ambassadors from different Muslim countries based in Karachi, and provided them with essential information about the beliefs and achievements of the Ahmadiyya Movement. When he began to arrange to meet the ambassadors of Egypt, Iraq and Turkey, it was discovered that they had not only heard of his name but held his services in deep respect, and considered it a great honour to visit him. Only the ambassador of Saudi Arabia was reluctant, and twice after promising to come and see him he cancelled his visit. So Maulana Muhammad Ali made an appointment see him and went to the Saudi Arabian Embassy accompanied by Mr. N. A. Faruqui and Shaikh Muhammad Tufail. There he spoke at length with Syed Abdul Hamid al-Khateeb, the ambassador. Maulana Muhammad Ali shed light on the Ahmadiyya Movement, the claims of Hazrat Mirza Ghulam Ahmad, and the false allegation that he claimed to be a prophet. The ambassador said that he was previously unaware of the fact that this *Jama'at* from among the followers of Hazrat Mirza Ghulam Ahmad believed him to be a *mujaddid.* This, he said, was analogous to what happened in case of the followers of Jesus, and now his mind was clear about the actual facts. Maulana Muhammad Ali presented him with some of his own writings as well as a copy of the Arabic book *Hamamat-ul-Bushra* by Hazrat Mirza Ghulam Ahmad, which he gratefully accepted. Before they parted he embraced Maulana Muhammad Ali, telling him that he had great regard for him, and urged him to make efforts to remove these misunderstandings about

the Ahmadiyya Movement from the Arab world and send literature
to these countries in Arabic

Later on the ambassador, accompanied by his son, visited Maulana Muhammad Ali at his residence and invited him to a sump-
tuous dinner. Then again, before departing for the *Hajj,* he invited
the Maulana to another meal. It was Maulana Muhammad Ali's
wish that his book *Tahrik-i Ahmadiyyat* be translated into Arabic,
and Hazrat Mirza sahib's Arabic books, along with this translation,
sent to Arab countries. However, due to his illness and certain other
circumstances later on, he could not get this work started.

Distribution of free sets of books

Earlier, during the annual gathering of 1948, the plan to distribute
literature free had been inaugurated, and work had started on it
after some funds were raised. In Karachi Maulana Muhammad Ali
was devoting special attention to this project. In August 1949 he
reshaped this plan into that of distributing the literature in the
form of complete sets of books to be sent to different countries. In
his Friday *khutba* in Karachi on 5 August 1949 (*Paigham Sulh,* 24
August 1949), Maulana Muhammad Ali declared that the complete picture of Islam is today available only from the followers of
the *Mujaddid* of the Age, and by the grace of God all aspects of
this picture have been covered in the following literature:

1. Translation of the Holy Quran with commentary.
2. Life of the Holy Prophet Muhammad.
3. History of the Early Caliphate.
4. Books on authentic Hadith, in particular Bukhari.
5. The book *The Religion of Islam.*
6. The book *Living Thoughts of the Prophet Muhammad.*
7. The book *The New World Order.*

All this was available in English and had been translated into
other languages. We would be rendering a glorious service to the
religion of Islam and its propagation if we disseminate sets of
these books in the world.

After this, in many other *khutbas* he kept putting forward the
argument that, as Islam possesses such an intrinsic power of truth

and beauty, if its true and complete picture is made to reach the world, then people will by themselves yield to it. He said:

> "What will be the resources that will turn the vision that we have in our minds into reality? What those means will be, God alone knows. However, it is my firm conviction, which I acquired from that holy man from whose company I benefited for a long time, that if we show the world the real picture of the truth of Islam, of the Holy Prophet Muhammad, and of the Quran, then undoubtedly people will bow their heads before it. Today we possess that picture. There is only the question of propagating it."
>
> (*Paigham Sulh,* 31 August 1949, p. 6)

Before returning from Karachi, in his Friday *khutba* on 23 September 1949, after reading the verse "Perhaps you (O Prophet) will kill yourself with grief because they believe not" (the Quran, 26:3), Maulana Muhammad Ali referred to the Holy Prophet Muhammad's deep zeal to guide humanity and also the great transformation that ensued from that urge. Then he went on to explain that those who partake of that zeal and urge achieve success of the same kind, in accordance with their level of passion. He then spoke of the fervour of the Companions of the Holy Prophet and other eminent religious elders in Islamic history and their work of reforming the world. After this he dwelt at length upon the heart-felt desire of the Promised Messiah which resulted in practical work being done, on the one side, and an increased demand for knowledge of Islam in the world generally, on the other. He added:

> "Every human being has a mission, and I have now completed my mission to an extent. Man has only a limited capacity, but due to the grace of God such Islamic literature has been produced which is needed by the world today, by both Muslims and non-Muslims. Allah the Most High, by providing me the opportunity of sitting at the feet of Hazrat Mirza sahib, enabled me to render this service to Islam. If we now keep this prepared literature locked up at home, then there is no difference between us and the other Muslims. The real work is to make this

literature reach the world. There is a very large English-speaking world, and then there are other languages to be considered as well.

We have not yet built up the determination to spread this literature in the world. Even one individual's resolve has great power, so if the whole *Jama'at* shows the determination to do it, then nothing can stand in its way. But we are not yet fully resolute. ... This literature in fact constitutes the weapons given to us by God the Most High. ... Literature even in hundreds of languages is still not enough. The literature in English was not produced in a day; it took forty years. It has facilitated producing literature in other languages. but it needs immense effort and hard labour." (*Paigham Sulh,* 12 October 1949)

Proposal to send free sets to five thousand libraries

On 10 October 1949 Maulana Muhammad Ali returned from Karachi, and in the Friday *khutba* on 14 October, while speaking in detail about his stay in Karachi, he put forward the proposal of free distribution of sets of books (*Paigham Sulh,* 19 October 1949). A set consisting of the following eight books should be sent to each of five thousand libraries throughout the world:

1. English translation of the Holy Quran with commentary.
2. *Muhammad The Prophet,* the English translation of *Sirat Khair-ul-Bashar.*
3. *The Early Caliphate,* the English translation of *Tarikh Khilafat Rashida.*
4. *The Religion of Islam,* a book dealing comprehensively with all the doctrines and practices of Islam.
5. *A Manual of Hadith,* English translation, with footnotes, of Hadith reports dealing with the practical side of human life.
6. *Living Thoughts of Prophet Muhammad,* consisting of a summary of the life of the Holy Prophet and a gist of the teachings of the Holy Quran on various aspects of human life.
7. *The New World Order,* in which it is shown that the only

acceptable order for the affairs of the world is one based on Islamic principles.

8. *The Teachings of Islam,* English translation of the speech written by Hazrat Mirza Ghulam Ahmad, presented at the multi-religious conference in Lahore in 1896, which contains the essence of the moral and spiritual teachings of Islam.

For the accomplishment of this plan, after the meeting of the General Council on 6 November Maulana Muhammad Ali went again to Karachi on 8 November and stayed there for over a month. During this stay he approached selected members of the general Muslim community outside the Ahmadiyya Movement, explaining to them the need and importance of this task and asking for monetary assistance. Before taking this practical step, he requested and urged the *Jama'at* to say special prayers for its success. In the Friday *khutba* of 4 November he drew attention to two specific points. Firstly, we should make a special effort to improve our prayers, since at an earlier time in history also it had been the humble prayers of a community before God that had brought about a transformation in the world. Secondly, he requested that for the next forty to fifty days up to the annual gathering of December 1949 every member of the *Jama'at* should take it upon himself to say *tahajjud* prayers.

On 5 November he wrote an article entitled *Du'a, Du'a, Du'a* ('Prayer, Prayer, Prayer') which was published in *Paigham Sulh* of 16 November. In it he urged the *Jama'at,* in most sincere, heartfelt and powerful words, to pray to God for its own improvement and for success, and also for God to send him succour during the mission for which he was going to Karachi again. He also appealed to those people who harboured objections against him and had doubts about the plan for the distribution of literature, saying that they would not find any faultless human being to follow and obey, and that in any case taking part in this spiritual endeavour by means of prayer would not do them any harm but could only bring them closer to God. Then in the same article he has explicated the *Sura Fatiha,* the glorifications uttered during bowing and prostration, and every phrase of *At-tahiyyat* recited in the sitting posture, in such a way that as we utter these expressions during prayers an urge and zeal is sparked within us to carry the message of God to the world, and we pray for this mission from the very depths of our hearts. The entire article is worth reading and makes a powerful impact.

Charged with this passion and zeal, and accompanied by humble prayers beseeching God the Most High for help, Maulana Muhammad Ali in his second brief stay in Karachi promoted his proposal for the free distribution of five thousand sets of books before government officials, businessmen, industrialists and other affluent persons belonging to the general Muslim community. The Almighty answered his prayers, and those of a large number of members of the *Jama'at,* and as a result of these efforts arrangements were completed during his stay to enable the distribution of 3500 sets whose total cost was 250,000 Rupees.

An objection and answer to it

While on the one hand there was all this fervour and passion, accompanied by hard work and prayers, to strengthen the ways of presenting the true picture of Islam to the world, on the other hand there were some persons who were reluctant to accept the importance of this work because they harboured some objections against Maulana Muhammad Ali on a subjective basis. They claimed that the classical, monumental and voluminous works including commentaries of the Quran written by the illustrious Muslim scholars of earlier times, for instance, Ghazali, Ibn Taimiyya, Razi the author of *Tafsir-i Kabir,* Ibn Jarir etc., could not be equalled by anyone, and that as compared to these great works we had not produced anything to be proud of. According to them, spending money to spread the literature produced by our Movement was not as useful work as to establish a college or run an orphanage. They held that the general Muslims had, in every age and time, enriched people by writing valuable books, so our literary work was nothing special.

It is necessary to clarify the position in response to these objections. No one can deny that the great scholars of previous times have written magnificent books on Islam and commentaries of the Holy Quran, from which everyone has been drawing benefit even till this day. Accordingly, Maulana Muhammad Ali writes in the Preface of his English Translation of the Holy Quran:

> "Among the commentators, I have made the greatest use of the voluminous commentaries of Ibn Jarir, Imam Fakhr al-Din Razi, Imam Athir al-Din Abu Hayyan and the shorter but by no means less valuable commentaries of *Zamakhshari, Baidawi* and *Jami' al-Bayan* of Ibn Kathir. Among the lexicons, *Taj al-'Arus* and the *Lisan al-'Arab* are voluminous standard works and have been freely consulted, but the smaller work of Imam Raghib Isfahani, known as *Mufradat fi Gharib al-Quran,* has afforded immense help, and it undoubtedly occupies the first place among the standard works in Arabic Lexicology so far as the Quran is concerned. The valuable dictionaries of Hadith, the *Nihayah,* of Ibn Athir and the *Majma' al-Bihar* have also proved very serviceable in explaining many a moot point. ... Besides commentaries and lexicons, historical and other works have also been consulted. ... And lastly, the greatest religious leader of the present time, Mirza Ghulam Ahmad of Qadian, has inspired me with all that is best in this work. ... There is one more person whose name I must mention in this connection, the late Maulawi Hakim Nur al-Din, who in his last long illness patiently went through much the greater part of the explanatory notes and made many valuable suggestions."

The question is whether the *Mujaddid* of this Age produced any religious knowledge, and whether the mission he set before us can be accomplished by publishing the classical commentaries and dictionaries of the Holy Quran and of Hadith, such as the works of Imam Ghazali and Ibn Jarir, or should we do something else?

This was answered by Maulana Muhammad Ali, after his return from Karachi in December, in the following words:

> "What I said was not that we have written huge, voluminous books, but that if anyone has fulfilled the wishes of the Promised Messiah and carried out his mission it is only the Lahore Ahmadiyya *Jama'at.* ... From among

these wishes relating to the propagation of Islam, deep in the heart of the Promised Messiah, ... the first one was expressed by him in *Izala Auham*:

> 'If my people help me heart and soul I wish to prepare a commentary of the Quran which should be sent to them [the Western nations] after it has been rendered into the English language. I cannot refrain from stating clearly that this is my work, and that definitely no one else can do it as I can, or as he can who is an offshoot of mine and thus is included in me.' (p. 773)

... This is not something insignificant. It was the Promised Messiah's wish to do it himself. As it happened, he died and the work remained undone. But in fact his wish had been granted by God. So God enabled it to be done after his death, by very feeble hands. ...

Now I come to a second wish of the Promised Messiah which is mentioned in *Malfuzat* [book of his reported talks]. He says:

> 'I want to write a book on Islam and Maulvi Muhammad Ali sahib should translate it. It will consist of three parts: firstly, what are our duties to Allah, secondly what are our duties towards our own souls, and thirdly what are the rights of our fellow human beings upon us.' (*Manzur Ilahi,* p. 188) [2]

Now think about how the book *The Religion of Islam*, which I wrote and which is highly popular, is fulfilling this longing of the Promised Messiah. In this book the foundation of jurisprudence has been laid which has been accepted as the basis for developing a new Islamic jurisprudence. All the issues on which the world today needs guidance have been discussed so comprehensively that many eminent men have described this book as an encyclopaedia of Islamic teachings. I met a Justice of the Chief Court who told me that he keeps my book in his library and when the need arises he consults it. As regards my

---

2. See *Ruhani Khaza'in No. 2,* 1984, 10-volume, edition, vol. 1, p. 392.

commentary of the Quran, it is not one person but scores of people who have said, not to me privately but in public, that after reading this translation their faith in the Holy Quran has been strengthened and they are highly indebted to it. I am not saying this as a boast. All this has been granted by God. ...

Hazrat Mirza sahib had also a third wish, which it was granted to this *Jama'at* to fulfil. He writes in *Izala Auham* [right before the above extract]*:*

> "I would advise that, instead of these missionaries, writings of an excellent and high standard should be sent into these countries."

... Ponder over why the Imam of the Age expressed his wish to send excellent literature all over the world instead of missionaries. It happens sometimes that missionaries, instead of bringing about reform, cause people to fall into a trial, and such trials have actually befallen. ...

Think about how this wish of the Imam of the Age has also been fulfilled at the hands of this small *Jama'at,* that high quality literature should be disseminated in the world. This *Jama'at* has produced monumental literature in support of the truth of Islam and of the Holy Prophet, containing facts showing the shining example of his life. It was the help of God the Most High sent down to this *Jama'at* that enabled such glorious work to be done. But there is an even higher cause for which Allah has recently provided the resources..."

(Friday *Khutba,* 16 December 1949. *Paigham Sulh,* 21 December 1949)

The above explanation is contained in his Friday *khutba* which he delivered after returning from Karachi. In it, mentioning the scheme of the free distribution of 5000 sets of books and his efforts in that connection during his stay in Karachi, he explained how God had created resources to accomplish this plan, so that Hazrat Mirza sahib's wish to produce literature of a high standard and distribute it in the world was being fulfilled by this *Jama'at.*

His last address to the Qadian *Jama'at*

In September 1949 Maulana Muhammad Ali wrote a pamphlet while he was in Karachi which was published under the title *Jama'at Qadian aur har Musalman ke liye lamha-i fikria* ('A pause for thought for the Qadian *Jama'at* and for every Muslim'). The Qadian *Jama'at* is specially addressed in this pamphlet, and it was his last address to this *Jama'at*. It does not contain any discussion of beliefs but mentions only the deeply-held wishes of Hazrat Mirza Ghulam Ahmad and explains how these were fulfilled through the work of Lahore *Jama'at* and his (the Maulana's) writings. Attention is also drawn to various dreams, visions and writings of Hazrat Mirza sahib relating to Maulana Muhammad Ali and it is proved that they were fulfilled in him. He has invited the Qadian *Jama'at* to ponder over this and come to the place where they will find the heritage of the Promised Messiah's knowledge and where the work which fulfils the Promised Messiah's wishes has been done.

Then, addressing the general Muslim community outside the Ahmadiyya Movement, he asks how can that man, the *Mujaddid,* have been an impostor who infused the love of God and a passion for the propagation of Islam in the hearts of those who joined him and who created a community whose members devoted their lives and possessions for spreading Islam in the world. Has there ever been in the world an impostor who filled the hearts of his companions with such zeal and fervour to propagate Islam?

Death of Mian Ghulam Rasul

On 23 December 1949 Maulana Muhammd Ali and the whole *Jama'at* received a tremendous shock when the death occurred of Mian Ghulam Rasul Tamim. On that day Maulana Muhammd Ali in his Friday *khutba* dwelt only upon the late Mian Ghulam Rasul. He said that although he was a police officer but the company of Hazrat Mirza Ghulam Ahmad had illumined his heart with the light of God, as a result of which he led a life of high moral virtue that was an example to all. Wherever he was based, his moral behaviour won love and admiration from people. His heart was full of sympathy for humanity, and a large number of people bene-fitted from his kindness. He was a tower of strength for this *Jama'at*.

God had given him much wealth and he spent it generously in the way of God. Hardly anyone excelled him in the work of propagation of this Movement and extension of this *Jama'at*. His qualities of sound opinion, experience and forthrightness occupied a special place in the affairs of the community (*Paigham Sulh,* 4 January 1950).

The entire *Jama'at* was deeply shocked at the death of Mian Ghulam Rasul. On 24 December, when the annual gathering opened, the first session was cancelled in his memory, and after the *zuhr* prayers the *Jama'at* held his funeral prayers in absentia.

The late Mian Ghulam Rasul was one of Maulana Muhammad Ali's closest and most long-standing friends. The Maulana had the greatest love and regard for him due to his virtues mentioned above. He was with Maulana Muhammad Ali not only in connection with the affairs of the Anjuman when he came to Lahore, but he also often used to go to Dalhousie when the Maulana went there. These two saintly men were very close friends.

The annual gathering, 1949

On the second day of the annual gathering of December 1949 Maulana Muhammad Ali made a speech on the topic 'Remembrance of Allah — the sole means of achieving tranquillity of mind' (*Paigham Sulh,* 18 January 1950). He said that peace and salvation for humanity can only be achieved by establishing the rule of Allah. The Promised Messiah set us on this path and his wishes had been fulfilled through us. He referred to the universal popularity of the English translation and commentary of the Holy Quran. Some 40,000 copies had been spread in the world and many persons had admitted learning about Islam from it. He also mentioned the various countries where, upon some of our literature reaching there, it had led to the creation of branches of our *Jama'at* and had changed people's views. Then he put forward the plan of sending sets of books to 5000 libraries and informed that he had already made arrangements for almost 4000 sets to be sent. He wanted the *Jama'at* to make arrangements to send the remaining 1000 sets. Upon this appeal, members began to respond and displayed a wonderful spirit of sacrifice. Depending on their means, some agreed to fund 100 sets each, some 50, some 25, and some members one or two sets each. They thus fulfilled his wish and supported this plan to completion. After this, ending his speech, Maulana Muhammad Ali said:

> "The renaissance of Islam has begun. Outsiders are also now admitting it. Let not your eyes be closed to this work. The task that the Promised Messiah has entrusted to you is no small work. Keep its importance in view all the time and struggle whole-heartedly to make it successful."

Events of 1950

Due to exertion during the annual gathering, weak health and the shock of the death of a dear and close friend Mian Ghulam Rasul, Maulana Muhammad Ali fell ill after the Gathering and was confined to bed for several days. By the middle of January 1950, he was comparatively better, began to move about and became busy in his work as usual. However, in the beginning of May, as the weather grew hotter, he started having high temperature in the afternoons. Almost every year he used to suffer from this problem due to weak health and other medical conditions. On 30 May he again went to Karachi to spend the summer there. During all this period he rewrote the Preface and Introduction to the English translation of the Holy Quran and revised the manuscript of the translation. By the end of July, the proofs of the translation started arriving from England, and he read and revised them himself. He continued this work even after his serious heart attacks, which will be mentioned later, and completed the task before his death.

Khutbas of 1950

A particular characteristic of the *khutbas* and writings of Maulana Muhammad Ali throughout his life was the emphasis he placed on praying, and especially the saying of the *tahajjud* prayer, acquiring knowledge of the Holy Quran, the need and importance of spreading the Quran and other Islamic literature in the world, and making financial sacrifices for this end. In his last days, his *khutbas* and writings became even more than ever before marked by spirituality and by passion and zeal for these objectives, and they

will always serve as a beacon of light for the *Jama'at*. As sometimes the focus of the *Jama'at* is distracted away from its real
goal, and some members place more emphasis on secondary
matters, it seems important to include here some extracts from his
khutbas and writings. These would make clear to the *Jama'at* what
was the real aim and substance of the work of his entire life, on
which path he led the *Jama'at* himself, to which path he wanted to
lead it, and what was the yearning and passion in his heart in his
last days. This was the man who, in the prime of his youth, gave
up worldly entanglements to join the company of the *Mujaddid* of
the Age. Then having illuminated his heart with the light he
received from his Mentor he served the religion of Islam day and
night for fifty years, fulfilling the wishes of the *Mujaddid* and producing unique literature on Islam including commentaries of the
Holy Quran.

From February to April 1950 he delivered a series of *khutbas*
in this connection. First he devoted several *khutbas* to the verse of
the Quran which begins: "And when My servants ask you about
Me, I am near…" (2:186), and explained that to attain the nearness
to God spoken of here, two means have to be adopted: to develop
a strong passion in your heart to spread the message of God in the
world, and to bow before Him for this objective and pray for it.

In his first *khutba*, on 3 February 1950, he explained that
prayer is the means of attaining nearness to God. He said:

> "I want to draw the attention of friends to the fact that our
> work is the very monumental task of spreading Islam in
> the world and removing darkness in the world by means
> of the light of the Holy Quran and of the Holy Prophet
> Muhammad. This glorious task demands from us that we
> spend our wealth for its attainment. … But there is some-
> thing more we need, without which even our money and
> our efforts are of no avail … that is falling before God in
> prayer and endeavouring to attain nearness to Him. …
> People find it difficult to follow this path, but you must
> remember that prayer is the simple means by which man
> can achieve sure and definite success. The best time for

prayer, as you will see by reading the whole of the Quran or studying the life of the Holy Prophet Muhammad, is none other than the later part of the night. Although in the early days of the mission of the Holy Prophet only a small portion of the Holy Quran would have been revealed, but read *Sura Muzammil* (ch. 73) and you will find that the Holy Prophet Muhammad and that hallowed group, his Companions, used to rise at night and remain in prayer before God. ... God the Most High says that rising at night creates tremendous power and strength in one's heart. ...

Getting up at night to pray before God is the recipe for doing more work, which everyone can experience. We saw the Imam of the Age, Hazrat Mirza sahib. He used to spend the greater part of the night in *tahajjud* prayer. Look at his work, how magnificent it is! Even till the last moments of his life he continued to write books upon books. He was not merely an author, but one who had created a connection with God and used to write through the Divine light that he thus received. ... Many great saints and men of God have tried this path and found it the right one. So two aspects are clearly seen in their lives: an excess of worship of God and an excessive amount of work. ...

Rise up at night and pray. To be enabled to serve the Quran is a great blessing. ... Implore God to grant you the spiritual strength by which you can carry the light of the Quran to others. ... I appeal to all members of the *Jama'at* that if they want to succeed in achieving their magnificent goal, there is only one way — prayer. As much as possible they must cry before God and keep their stress on prayer, so much so that prayer must be uppermost in their minds during all activities. ... While prayers in congregation are a means of attaining a high goal, you must also say some of your prayers in solitude, ... in some corner of the house where there is no one to see you but God. Develop the kind of prayer in which, when you

> are in prostration before God and the time comes to rise
> from it, you feel unable to lift your head."

(Paigham Sulh, 8 February 1950)

In his next *khutba,* on 10 February, he made it clear as to
which prayer can take a human being closer to God in actual fact.
There are some aims which also coincide with the will of God.
While Hazrat Mirza sahib has set us upon an arduous task, he has
also given us the good news that it is the Divine will that it shall
be accomplished. What is required is that by praying we instil this
Divine intent within ourselves. That Divine will is what was destined to happen with the coming of the Imam of the Age, namely,
the triumph of Islam over all other faiths and the spread of the
light of the Quran over all the world. So our prayer should also be
for the triumph of Islam in the world and the spread of the light of
the Quran. This is the prayer about the acceptance of which there
is no doubt. He added:

> "I ask of you only one thing: that is zeal in your hearts.
> Develop a passion in your hearts for the propagation of
> the Quran. Bow before God and implore Him, saying:
> O God, this holy word of Yours, which contains a price-
> less treasure, … it is today in a state of neglect. … Create
> some means, by Your grace, for its propagation and gene-
> rate in our hearts the desire to serve it.
>
> Each and every one of you should get up and cry
> before God. … If you cannot leave your warm beds at
> night then find time at least during the day to bow before
> God in solitude and pray, … as to why we are so power-
> less to take the Holy Quran to the world. We had made an
> affirmation and pledge with the Imam of the Age. Why,
> then, have we lost the power and strength to fulfil our
> promise." *(Paigham Sulh,* 15 February 1950)

In his third Friday *khutba* in this series, on 17 February 1950,
he said that in his first two *khutbas* he had drawn attention to
prayer, that what is needed most by an organization which is
bearer of the Quran is not abundance of assets and funds but the
power of spirituality. The second principle that he now wished to
explain was the study and teaching of the Quran. He then went

over, in detail, the great qualities of the Holy Quran and explained what state a believer ought to be in when reciting the Holy Quran. It is "a Book ... at which do shudder the skins of those who fear their Lord" (39:23), that is, the awe of Divine greatness must cast its influence on the body of the reciter as well. And continuing this verse: "Then their skins and their hearts soften at Allah's remembrance", that is, the body and heart should soften to receive the influence of the Divine word, and the heart should be so moved that the eyes shed tears spontaneously. When a person sheds tears because he is overwhelmed by the greatness of Allah or he cries because of feeling sympathy for another human being, it creates within him a power and energy.

Then Maulana Muhammad Ali spoke of the Holy Prophet Muhammad reciting the Quran, having it read out to him, and shedding tears upon hearing it. He described in detail the Promised Messiah's love for the Quran and said:

> "I would request friends to develop true, heartfelt love and adoration for the Holy Quran and to read it over and over again. ... What a great love and devotion for the Holy Quran was shown in this age by the Imam of the time! If you are really the followers of this Imam then create such a love in your hearts, the example of which was set before us by the Imam of the Age in his life."

Then he advised that, firstly, every man and woman should read some portion of the Holy Quran daily, the best time for this being *fajr* (early morning). Secondly, asking others to read the Holy Quran to you is also *Sunna*. Thirdly, the Holy Quran should be taught to those who do not know it. Fourthly, some portions of the Quran should be committed to memory. Fifthly, there should be an institute for doing research in knowledge of the Quran. (*Paigham Sulh,* 22 February 1950).

In his fourth *khutba* in this series, on 24 February 1950, he said that as regards the great task before us, he had already drawn attention to two basic points for carrying it out. One is prayer and the other is reciting the Holy Quran, acting upon it, and studying and teaching it. Now he wanted to refer to a third basic point, and that is that the Ahmadiyya Movement demands sacrifice from its members.

This is the kind of sacrifice that is spoken of in the Quran in the words: "Perhaps you will kill yourself with grief because they believe not" (26:3). Although this is addressed primarily to the Holy Prophet Muhammad, it also addresses every person who professes *La ilaha ill-allah Muhammad-ur Rasul- ullah*. The religion of Islam was established and spread through sacrifices and in future too it will be spread only by sacrifices.

He then said that the highest sacrifice is to devote one's life for the mission of spreading the message of God, but a person can still make sacrifice while engaged in worldly business. Both of these are necessary. The community cannot survive unless it has both kinds of people. Then he referred to monetary sacrifice and explained the importance and necessity of the regular monthly subscription, and said that those who do not pay this subscription are harming the Divine cause. (*Paigham Sulh,* 1 March 1950).

In his fifth *khutba,* on 3 March 1950, he spoke about spending in the way of Allah, that the Quran from the earliest period of its revelation to the last days has presented this concept as a trans-action between God and a human being, and in other places it has used the word 'trade' for it. It is made clear in many places that love of wealth is hell itself or it brings hell, and spending in the way of Allah is the garden of heaven, and this garden is attained not only in the next world but it begins in this very life. (*Paigham Sulh,* 8 March 1950).

In the five *khutbas* after this, he stressed upon the need and importance of prayer, explaining how it creates outward and inward virtues in a person, acts as a means of spiritual and physical train-ing, and instils discipline and organization. If you want to produce a state of humility in your prayers, then make the propagation of the word of Allah as your objective. Make your regular prayer (*salat* or *namaz*) entirely into a supplication and stand in the presence of God like a petitioner.

He ended this series of *khutbas* on 28 April 1950 on his start-ing note, that in order to achieve success in propagating the word of Allah, we must shed tears before God and humbly implore Him, and do our work only for the sake of Allah. (*Paigham Sulh,* 3 May 1950).

Stay in Karachi in 1950 and illness

Maulana Muhammad Ali was in a weak state of health now. From the beginning of May, as summer started, he began to get high temperature every day in the afternoons. By the middle of May there was some improvement and on 30 May he went to Karachi, as before, to spend summer there.

In Karachi, where he stayed at the residence of Mr. Naseer Ahmad Faruqui, he was busy with the same engagements as in the previous year. The work of the distribution of sets of books was continuing under his personal direction. Since August he had been slowly and steadily reading the proofs of the revised, fourth edition of the English translation of the Holy Quran, when in September he fell seriously ill due to severe heart attacks. For fifteen to twenty days previously he had been feeling a light pain in his heart and the doctors had recommended rest even then, but resting was not in his nature. As was usual with him, after getting up for *tahajjud* prayers at 2 a.m. in the night, he would continue to be absorbed in work or in prayer till sunset time, resting only for an hour and a half to two hours in the afternoon.

During the night of 17–18 September from midnight to 3 a.m. he had a severe attack of coronary thrombosis. However, such was his courage and perseverance that he did not even wake anyone in the house, not wanting to disturb their sleep. When the pain subsided at 3 a.m. he fell asleep, and woke again at 4 a.m. and said his *tahajjud* prayer. It was only at breakfast that he mentioned his illness. The doctor was called who immediately ordered him to bed. But while lying in bed, he still went through his mail and other papers with the help of his personal assistant Maulvi Abdul Wahhab.

In the afternoon he had another most serious attack. Morphine injections were administered. Then he had four further attacks one after another and was put on oxygen. He could not now even turn in bed and was in grave danger. Although the pain stopped on 19 September, but other problems began. Anyhow he was gradually regaining strength when on the night of 28 September he had another heart attack, and the following day, Friday, all hope was given up. Mr. Faruqui reported the events of that day as follows:

"The time for Friday prayer came. It was impossible for
me to leave the house, but the women folk insisted that
I go and join the congregation and pray. Accordingly, I went
and gave the *Jama'at* the news. Under those circumstances it was impossible to deliver the *khutba* or even to
listen to one. I said to the *Jama'at* that the time for talking
was over; now it was time only for prayer. So during the
khutba of fifteen to twenty minutes, nothing else was said
except heartfelt prayers. The Friday prayer service afterwards was nothing other than praying for him. The whole
congregation prayed so earnestly and fervently that it was
perhaps answered by the Almighty and at about 3.30 p.m.
he started to improve. ... What will happen next, only
God the Most High knows. When there is heart disease,
weakness after years of illness, and the age is between 75
and 80, what can one predict in these circumstances? But
the present condition has, by the grace of God, revived
our hope. The humility and the tears with which the *Jama'at*
here prayed yesterday was such that if the *Jama'at* in
Lahore, and other places, were also to pray with the same
fervour then perhaps Allah may show mercy. I say only
this to the August Almighty, that I know no one can live
forever, and this man is so dear to You, O Lord, that You
are pleased to call him back to You, but for the sake of
Your Quran extend his life. The new English translation
of the Quran is not complete yet. The scheme to send
books to five thousand libraries is unfinished. So I beseech You, for the sake of Your Quran, Your Promised
Messiah, your Holy Prophet and Your religion, to grant
him more time." (*Paigham Sulh,* 11 October 1950).

After this, his health began to improve. According to medical
advice he had complete bed rest for six weeks, and even after this
he needed much rest for months. During this period he suffered
from some other ailments as well, but on the whole his health was
improving. On 30 October he was permitted to sit on his bed, and
he dictated a message for the *Jama'at* which was published in
Paigham Sulh in the issue dated 8 November 1950 under the
heading: 'The task entrusted to us of spreading the Quran in the

whole world — it grieves me to see that many of us are not taking part in it'.

The message was as follows.

————————————————

" Respected Brothers,
Assalamu alaikum wa rahmatullahi wa barakatuhu

Due to someone's state of health, such as my illness, or when the appointed time comes, death is not something unusual. This is the Divine law that is established in the world. I was taken ill on 17 September. On the 18th it was found that I was dangerously ill, and on the doctor's advice I was confined to bed. Today by the grace of God I have been allowed to sit. During this time there were forty days when everyday I felt that my time had come, as would in fact be for a man nearing eighty years of age. But by the grace of Allah the Most High it appears that I have been given some more time. How long it is, God alone knows. During the time when I was staring death in the face I had but one desire in my heart, and it was also my prayer, that if Allah the Most High wants me to serve the Quran further, He may grant me more time. And He may also grant me the means because I see that in the task entrusted to us of spreading the Quran in the world, though we are doing it, but our progress is exceedingly slow. It grieves me to see that many among us are still not taking part in it, while nothing can be achieved in this world unless a group has an overwhelming urge to do it. Read the history of Islam: it was this overpowering zeal that carried the Divine message to the ends of the world in less than one hundred years, even though there did not exist such means and conveniences at that time as there are for us today. But our hearts lack the urge and fervour that is needed for this task.

While I am lying in bed like a mere body, not knowing how much more time Allah the Most High will grant me, I appeal to you, the dear ones of my *Jama'at,* to create zeal and fervour in your hearts for taking the Quran to the world, such zeal and fervour that is noticed by the world. Hanker not after honour and high position in the world, but try to raise your rank in the estimation of God. To achieve this, ask of God in your prayers during *salat:*

'O God, put in our hearts the same love to spread Your religion and to take Your Quran to the world that You have been creating in the hearts of Your righteous servants before. Your religion and Your Quran are a beauty and a light which has not yet been fully made manifest to the world whose eyes are still too covered to see it. This light has not yet even reached most of the world and there are others who have this light in their hands but their eyes are covered up. O God, remove this covering from my eyes and illuminate my heart with this glare of Your light so that I may enlighten the world with its brightness.'

And not only say this prayer, but along with it make progress in your struggle and striving. My dear ones, remember that the life of this world, whose attraction has made you neglect this light of God, is a mere illusion. Remember that it is God's promise, and it will be fulfilled. I have suffered terribly in the past forty days as never before in my life, but all this time I have been praying: O God, if according to Your will, my time has come then infuse a powerful spirit in my *Jama'at,* and create in it a fervour for Your religion and Your Quran so that Your work does not suffer after I am gone. *Wassalam.*

— *humbly,* Muhammad Ali. "

During this critical illness the entire *Jama'at* offered the most heartfelt prayers for his recovery. Some venerable members wrote letters to Maulana Muhammad Ali's wife, extracts from two of which are given below from *Paigham Sulh,* 22 November 1950:

1. "I was so shocked to learn the news of the illness of Hazrat Maulana sahib that I cannot find the words to express my feelings. Throughout the night I was restless and could not sleep. Prayer is our weapon, and how wonderful must prayer be for such a blessed individual for whom prayers are also being said by the Messenger of God, by the Promised Messiah of God and by the angels of God. If an ordinary sinner joins in such a prayer, his prayer is accepted.

This is the first letter I am writing by my own hand today after two weeks, to express my grief at the Maulana's illness. To show anguish and concern for a sanctified person is a work for earning Divine reward. So I am writing this letter to partake of this free reward. The late Dr. Basharat Ahmad, after recovering from a very serious illness, performed a colossal service to the Movement. The work of writing *Mujaddid-i Azam,* which he did after his recovery, will make his name renowned for all time. It appears as if Allah the Most High intends to have some great religious service performed by Hazrat Amir [Maulana Muhammad Ali].

For fifty years continuously this righteous man has been wielding his pen, day and night, in the defence of Islam. This is no small feat. It is a fact that the Hazrat Maulana has carried to completion the Promised Messiah's mission of the regeneration of the faith. The world's thirst is being quenched by the literature produced by him, and it will continue to be quenched till the time comes when people will be flocking to accept this religion. It is difficult to find another example of the great zeal and passion for the advancement of the Divine religion that Allah the Most High has infused in the Hazrat Maulana. We have not valued him as should have been done, but a time will come when the world will realise his worth.

Faruqui sahib has been bestowed a special grace by Allah, in that the blessed person of Hazrat Amir is at his residence. He has the chance to seek Allah's pleasure as much as he wishes. The spiritual stages that take centuries to traverse can be covered in days. This is the Divine blessing he has been granted, and all of it is because he is auspicious, Godly and a lover of the Holy Quran."

2. "We say prayers in order to accumulate Divine reward for ourselves. These sacred personages are rarely born who do not crave after worldly advancement at any time in their lives because it is not ever-lasting, and they do only that work which God has also acclaimed in the Holy Quran.

... The Hazrat Maulana found love for God from his days as a student, and having turned his back on his career in law, which had a bright future, he accepted the life of an ascetic for almost fifty years. Those from whom God intends to take great service, they are endowed with high qualities in their very nature. ... The doctors forbid him to do any mental work, friends give the same advice, but the difficulty is that such holy men do not want to remain idle. ... Men of God can never rest. Either God places upon them some work, or they themselves embark upon a task requiring them to work hard. It is the most blessed task of all for a man to remain engaged in serving the religion for the sake of God. There is nothing better in the world than for man to work for God, and for God to open up the ways for him and bestow His help upon him.

The passion to spread the Quran is the real nourishment sustaining the Maulana sahib. How can he give it up? In truth, how can these activities adversely affect health? The affairs of the wretched world can certainly have a detrimental effect on the human heart and brain, but the work undertaken by the Hazrat Maulana can only do him good. Each and every member of the *Jama'at* is desperately worried. May Allah the Most High grant him perfect health from Himself."

Addressing the *Jama'at* after recovery — three letters

It was found by medical examination on 15 November that his recovery was progressing satisfactorily, and he was given permission to walk a few steps. Due to weakness he still could not write; nonetheless from his bed he wrote three letters to members of the *Jama'at*. In his first letter he thanked all those who had been praying for him from the depth of their hearts, and wrote:

"I assure them that I also, during my worst condition, was praying for the *Jama'at*. When the severity of the pain was causing me agony, another sigh that was also escaping from my lips spontaneously at that time was for the Messenger and the Book of God, and for those friends who are engaged in the work of taking this Book to the world and making the name of the Messenger renowned in the world. I am certain that just as Allah the Most High has accepted the prayers of my *Jama'at* for me, He will accept my prayers as well." (*Paigham Sulh,* 22 November 1950)

Then he mentioned that when his condition was critical, some friends informed him that Allah had intimated to them glad tidings of the acceptance of their prayers. In the first two days of the illness God had also given good news to Syed Asadullah Shah about his recovery. Maulana Muhammad Ali had himself seen a dream on the first day of his illness, while in terrible agony, that his elder brother Maulvi Aziz Bakhsh was sitting on a prayer mat in the upper storey of his house, bare-headed, his hands held out in prayer, facing east, and was saying heartfelt prayers for his health. Maulana Muhammad Ali interpreted this dream to mean that by the elder brother was meant the *Jama'at,* and facing east during prayer in a dream was an indication of its acceptance. Regarding this he said:

> "I again praise Allah, that He granted the privilege of acceptance to the prayers of my *Jama'at* and saved me from a fatal illness. ... Now I request friends to say another prayer, and hope that God Who accepted the prayers of the *Jama'at* for a useless person like me would certainly accept their prayers for an important purpose."

That "important purpose" was connected with the triumph of Islam. He requested that at least one hundred people should firmly resolve that they would dedicate their prayers for this purpose and let him know their names. They should be so firmly determined in this that even if they were to receive news of his death on the morrow they should not lose their resolve but go on praying for this objective as long as Allah gave them life.

In the second letter, dated 2 December 1950, he mentioned that the work of translating the Quran into various languages was progressing very slowly. The printing of the translations into Tamil, Sindhi and Gurmukhi was not proceeding. He said:

> "Are we becoming lethargic? Have the senior members of the *Jama'at* started to divert their attention from this work?

After being enabled to serve the religion, are we losing that privilege by our own hands? ... Today the condition is that we and our great men are suggesting the closure of this or that mission and the postponing of translations of the Holy Quran. The day this happens is the day when our *Jama'at* will die.[3] ...

As a preliminary to the spiritual exertion of prayer, I would like to make three points. However, I am still very weak. My hand shakes when I write and the doctor has forbidden me to speak to dictate a writing. I am not even allowed to talk at length to friends who visit me. I still have to spend most of the day lying down. As I find myself and my efforts lacking in strength I seek your help."

In this context the first point he made was that unless we have firm faith in the promises of the Quran we cannot develop true passion in our prayers. So we must read the Quran very frequently. The power and glory of its language will strengthen the hearts. You should make a niche in a corner of your house where you can withdraw from the world and its entanglements, and whenever you find time sit there and read the Quran, and say prayers while reading it. He said as follows:

———————

"It is proved from the Holy Prophet's practice that while reciting the Quran when he came to a verse about mercy he would ask for God's mercy and when he came to a verse about punishment he would pray to be spared from it. So when you recite the Quran, wherever Divine mercy is mentioned — and the Quran is full of it on every page — pray that He shower His mercy all over this world, pray particularly for your Muslim brethren, and above all pray for mercy for your *Jama'at* as it is bearing the burden of spreading the Quran in the world at this time. When you come to a mention of those

———————

3. This is a reference to the decision taken in Lahore by the leading members of the Anjuman during his critical illness, when faced with a deficit in the budget of the Anjuman, to close the U.S.A. mission and postpone the translations of the Quran. Maulana Muhammad Ali sent a telegram to halt this decision and suggested other ways of dealing with the deficit.

who received Divine reward, the prophets and the righteous, pray that you are granted all the rewards that Allah bestowed on the earlier righteous ones. Certainly do ask for the very reward and success that Allah bestowed upon the Holy Prophet Muhammad. Where Allah's irresistible power is mentioned, as to how He has ever been making the truth to prevail, then this plea must arise from your heart: 'Today the world is shrouded in darkness in beliefs and deeds, show a sign of Your great power to the world today as before and establish truth in the world'. ... When the magnificence of the Quran is mentioned, or that Allah has sent it as a healing and a mercy, or that this Quran will revive the dead, clear away the hardest obstacles from its path, and reach the corners of the world, stop there and pray: 'O God, today also remove the mountains of difficulties by means of this Quran and provide us the means to take this Quran of Yours to the ends of the earth'. ... When you read about the dead earth coming to life by the rain sent by God, then this prayer should come from your heart: 'O God, shower spiritual rain upon this dead earth, awaken it to life spiritual, and illuminate the hearts of human beings with the light of faith'. ... When you read about the help sent to prophets and the believers, ask for the same help for yourselves because your object also is to exalt the name of God in the world. ... Where mention is made of the past nations who were destroyed and their acts of disobedience, your hearts should shudder with the prayer: 'O God, this Your nation which was raised for the guidance of the whole world, ... save this community of followers of Your Holy Prophet from disobeying Your Holy Prophet and make them bearers of the Quran'.

When those promises of Allah the Most High are mentioned that He will make truth prevail in the world — and remember that in the stories of the earlier prophets as well as in other contexts the Holy Quran is full of this — then this yearning should come from your hearts: 'O God, let the truth be triumphant in this day and age also, destroying falsehood'. And in your state of helplessness this voice should also arise from your heart: 'O God, this is not only my desire, this is Your promise. So fulfil Your promise. ... You sent Your Messenger as a Mercy for the worlds but there are countless nations in the world who are yet deprived of this mercy. You sent Your Quran as a Reminder for the worlds but there are numerous nations whom this message has still not reached. Help us that we may succeed in spreading this Quran in the whole world and showing the beauty of Your Messenger to the world. O God, Your help always comes for certain and will keep coming, but those who should ask for it are lax. Your favours have always been bestowed and will continue to be bestowed, but those who should accept them have become negligent because they are in love with the material world and are desirous of worldly pomp, show and greatness. May You create strength in them'.

The Holy Quran is full of places which can move your hearts to say prayers of this kind. I have only given some examples. I want you to read the Quran daily but not in such a way that its words are merely on your lips and are not entering deep in your hearts. ... The real place of the words of the Quran is not on the lips of people but in their hearts. Read the Quran and understand its meaning. But it has an even higher purpose, that it should enter your hearts. It was revealed to the Holy Prophet's heart: 'For surely He revealed it to your heart' [the Quran, 2:97]. The heart is its proper repository. Read it in such a manner as if it is descending upon your heart. Undoubtedly these are words of Allah the Most High but you can only gain strength from them when they emerge from the depths of your heart."

(*Paigham Sulh*, 6 December 1950)

In his third letter, dated 8 December 1950, he again urged upon members of the *Jama'at* to carry on the spiritual struggle of prayers. For those who could not rise up for *tahajjud* prayer, he advised that they make supplications within their obligatory prayers and read the Quran in solitude from worldly activities, making its words enter their hearts. Addressing every member of the *Jama'at* he drew their attention, besides reciting the Quran, towards memorising certain portions of it, especially those parts where the names and attributes of Allah the Most High and His power and glory are mentioned, and where the Quran speaks of Allah's promises of victory and triumph given to various prophets at times when they were utterly helpless and weak. He said:

> "When you get an opportunity to be alone, and your heart is open to it then lengthen your remembrance of Allah ... but you must bear in mind that the words should not only be on your lips but must reach the depths of your hearts. To achieve this, a hard struggle will be required initially.

The Holy Quran itself contains the command to read it slowly and pausingly, as it says 'and recite the Quran in a leisurely manner' [73:4], because by reading with pauses the words reach the hearts. When a person reads with pauses and tries to make the meaning enter into the heart, then gradually a time comes when those same words first emerge from the heart and then reach the lips. It is this which is the position of nearness to God and of acceptance by Him, that a person utters with his mouth what has arisen in his heart."

(*Paigham Sulh*, 13 December 1950)

Thanks-giving fund

To express joy at Maulana Muhammad Ali's recovery, it was proposed by Mr. Naseer Ahmad Faruqui, on the suggestion of one senior member from Peshawar and one from Karachi, that a thanksgiving fund should be established (*Paigham Sulh*, 29 November 1950). Making this proposal, he said that it was a promise of Allah that "if you are grateful, I will give you more" (the Quran, 14:7). As the Maulana's recovery is a great blessing from Allah for the *Jama'at*, mere verbal thanks are absolutely inadequate. At this juncture, we must open our hearts and sacrifice our most coveted possession, that is material wealth, in the way of Allah, and this fund should be spent as directed by Maulana Muhammad Ali for the propagation of Islam. A large part of the *Jama'at* responded positively to this proposal, and on Maulana Muhammad Ali's directions this fund was spent on sending the Holy Quran and the life of the Holy Prophet Muhammad free or at reduced price to those who could not afford to buy them. Some two thousand copies of the Holy Quran were distributed from this fund.

Return to Lahore

By the end of November 1950 Maulana Muhammad Ali's health had improved sufficiently to allow him to travel back to Lahore. He returned to Lahore on 10 December. According to medical advice, he was still not allowed to move about very much or even to talk at length. So from his bed he used to supervise important administrative affairs and also read the proofs of the English translation of the Quran.

Annual gathering 1950

The annual gathering of December 1950, which was the 37th annual gathering of the Anjuman, was the last one to be held in the life of Maulana Muhammad Ali. He was still under doctors' orders to rest most of the time and was not allowed to make a speech. He came to the venue of the Gathering on the morning of 25 December and sat in a comfortable chair on the stage. The meeting was opened by his written speech which was read by Maulvi Dost Muhammad. The speech opened with a very moving prayer. On Maulana Muhammad Ali's bidding, all the audience stood up holding out their hands in prayer, and kept uttering *Amen* at the prayers. And what were those prayers? Only that the whole world may somehow be enabled to see the beautiful face of Islam, the last message of God the Most High may spread to every corner of the earth, and all of humanity may become followers and devotees of the Holy Prophet Muhammad, may peace and the blessings of Allah be upon him. With every verse of *Sura Fatiha,* he read these heart-felt prayers. Then he said:

> "You and I have worked together for thirty-seven years. However, it is fifty years since our Imam made me give up my worldly occupations to engage in religious service. So praise be to Allah Who enabled me, and gave me the opportunity, to do this work for half a century. Had I achieved the highest position in a worldly profession, I would not have had a modicum of the satisfaction that I have today." (*Paigham Sulh,* 14 February 1951)

He then mentioned the heart-felt desire of the Promised Messiah, as to how it had been fulfilled by the literature we had published. He said:

> "It is more than fifty years today that the Imam of the Age selected me and my late friend Khwaja Kamal-ud-Din. It was proverbially like dust being chosen by an alchemist. Just as other persons benefited from his Divine revealed teaching, so did the two of us. My friend left to meet his Maker in 1932, and I cannot sufficiently express my gratitude for the favours of Allah the Most High upon me in allowing me to serve His religion till now.

Attacks of serious illnesses have been afflicting me since 1934, each attack being worse than the last. It was in 1934 that the doctors for the first time declared one of my illnesses to be fatal, and consequently I hastened the publication of my book *The Religion of Islam*. Then in 1938 when I was in Dalhousie, the medical verdict about me was that I could die at any moment. Again in 1948 a serious illness befell me in Quetta but Allah the Most High with His grace helped me. Now in 1950 there was again no hope left for my survival. But every time God gave me respite He also enabled me to do more work, and it was not only work of writing that I did but the foundations for a great plan like the translations of the Quran, establishing a mission in the U.S.A. and creating an institute for the study and research of the Quran were also laid during the times of these illnesses. I have hope from His threshold that He has again allowed me time for some work, but only God knows if it would be some scholarly work. But when I fell ill, the work I had in mind was to spread that treasure of knowledge in the world which Allah the Most High had enabled me to prepare."

After this he explained that if the first wish of our Imam was to get excellent literature prepared for the nations of the West, his second wish was that these writings, including translations of the Quran, should be spread in the countries of Europe, America and Asia. Although our *Jama'at* had so far distributed free tracts and literature on a vast scale, the best plan in this connection was the one that had just been launched, namely, to send a set of eight books to each of five thousand libraries of the world as a free donation. This work required a total expenditure of 350,000 Rupees, of which almost 150,000 Rupees had already been raised. (This money was raised due to Maulana Muhammad Ali's efforts in Karachi, a large part coming from the general Muslim community outside the Ahmadiyya Movement.) Apart from this, he expressed his wish to hasten the publication of those translations of the Quran which had been completed but not yet printed.

On the second day he attended the afternoon session. A speech written by him was read out, during which he stood up at one point and addressed the congregation for a few minutes. In this speech he mentioned the great hurdles that were overcome in order to carry out the work of the propagation of Islam that had been done so far, and he appealed for the most fervent sacrifices to be made for this religious struggle. He said that the companions of the Holy Prophet were generally not wealthy people but when they were inspired by the love of God they would even deny themselves food in order to spend in the way of God, and as to those who had nothing to give, God has Himself testified about them that they would shed tears at not finding anything to spend in His way. As a result of their sacrifices they became rulers and leaders of the world. He added:

> "Can we show any such miracle of love of God in our hearts? If we can, then shed tears for this cause sometimes and say: O God, Your religion is in trouble. The Quran You sent as a 'Reminder for the nations', so that it should be spread in the whole world, is lying closed in our homes. Far from taking it to others, it does not reach even our own hearts. Grant our hearts the strength that we may follow it ourselves and we may also spread it in the whole world. You sent a Messenger as a 'mercy to the nations', but we are neither following in his footsteps nor making any effort to manifest his true picture to the world. Infuse in our hearts such love for the Holy Prophet Muhammad that we may become among his zealous followers and be intensely devoted to showing his beauty to the world."

Following this, before putting forward some proposals, he said regarding himself:

> "I was convinced of the truth of the Promised Messiah from 1891 when I first heard of his claim. I took the *bai'at* (pledge) in 1897, and this was the *bai'at* that made me visit Qadian, if not once a week, then at least once every two weeks. I used to spend the summer vacations in his company. From 1900 till his death I lived with him. He had entrusted all the administrative affairs to me. I lived in a room in his house. There must be very few people who attained as much company and fellowship of the

Imam of the Age as I did. Since 1914 you people elected me as your *Amir.* You are aware of the work I have done since then, whether good or bad. Today I am not fit enough to stand before you and make a speech. What I have written I have done with a trembling hand. I have not got the power to influence you, but I must draw your attention to one point ..."

(Quoted extracts here are from *Paigham Sulh*, 28 February 1951, containing the second part of this speech. The first part was published in the 21 February 1951 issue.)

He then told the gathering that just as they had prayed for him fervently he now needed them to show the same fervour in making sacrifices. Then he made appeals in very moving words for the following objects: firstly, for regular monthly contributions of one-tenth of one's income; secondly, for donations of ten days of one's income to meet the deficit in the budget; and thirdly, for meeting the expenses of setting up more missions.

Both of these last two speeches of Maulana Muhammad Ali have been published as a pamphlet entitled *Is zamana ka aur her zamana ka sab say bara Islami jihad* ('The greatest Islamic Jihad of this and every other age').

3.8: The last year, 1951, and death

Last letters to members of the *Jama'at*

Immediately after the annual gathering Maulana Muhammad Ali had another minor heart attack, confining him to bed for a few days. When he improved, he again made some addresses to the *Jama'at* through *Paigham Sulh*. In his first letter, published under the title 'A mighty aim and a mighty position', on 14 February 1951, he wrote:

> "After the annual gathering I again suffered a minor attack of illness, and for this reason the doctor advised me to rest in bed for some days. ... Now by the grace of God I am feeling better and want also to give you some good news. ... Arrangements have been completed to distribute a further one thousand copies of the English translation of the Quran to the public, and God willing, this will be achieved at an expense of only 3,000 Rupees from the Thanks-giving Fund. ... At the annual gathering you will have heard another good news, that the annual budget of this small *Jama'at* has now reached almost one million Rupees. ... However, it is a matter of concern that our income fell short of expenditure by 66,000 Rupees."

Then, drawing attention towards the need for more financial sacrifices and propagation efforts, he said:

> "My real aim in drawing attention to this is to turn your minds towards prayer. This is the weapon used by the righteous to reform the hearts. But remember that a prayer not accompanied by effort is not accepted. Along with your efforts and struggle use prayer, and along with your prayer keep up your efforts and struggle. Each of these necessitates the other. Knock on God's door. There is none

who knocked at this door for whom it was not opened. But you cannot knock on it with words of your tongue. You must knock on it with zeal of heart, with the sighs that arise from the heart. Rise up during the night to pray or say prayers during the day. Those who cannot rise during the night should improve the quality of their prayers of the day. ...

The most important question is: what should we be asking for at the door of the Master of masters? As it was our Holy Prophet Muhammad who taught us prayer, we must ask for the same thing for which our Holy Prophet again and again turned to Allah. ... He had no desire to acquire worldly leadership or wealth. The only longing in his heart was for reforming human souls. ... Whether a Muslim learns this point of wisdom today or in the future, it will make him progress towards the high position upon which our Holy Prophet was established. Therein lies the secret of the progress of Islam. It amounts to just this:

> *Namaz* (*salat*) is a supplication.
> It is a petition in the court of the Lord of the Universe.

And the plea is that Allah the Most High may set right the human hearts and spiritually nourish His creatures by means of His Quran and His Prophet Muhammad.

It is true that one aim of prayer is also improvement of your own self, and it is also true that prayer can be said for other purposes as well. However, if you limit your *salat* and supplications to this extent only, and have not that higher purpose before you which the Holy Prophet had in view, then you have not recognised the high rank of the Holy Prophet and are satisfied with a lower aim. If you go with a plea before such a High Authority then ask for something very great ... for He has the power to grant you even what you think is impossible. ... It is God's promise that humanity will be saved. It is God's promise that the whole world will be illuminated with the light of the Quran and the Prophet Muhammad, and Islam shall prevail in the world. What you consider to be impossible, your God says it shall certainly happen. ... Of course, until the same urge is produced in our hearts as was in the heart of the Holy Prophet ... we cannot fulfil the description 'those who are with him' [the Quran, 48:29], nor can we witness the success that Islam has achieved once before.

This is that great favour bestowed upon us by the *Mujaddid* of this century and the Imam of this Age, that by drawing our attention to this exalted purpose he has led us towards a high position ...

Try to make your *salat* like the *salat* of the Holy Prophet Muhammad. ... Go to the mosques to perform prayers in congregation. However, our Holy Prophet has instructed that we should not turn our homes into graves, so some of your prayers should be performed at home. In the mosque you have to rise from your prostration on hearing the Imam's call, but in your *salat* at home fall before Allah with such devotion that you are unable to raise your head."

(*Paigham Sulh,* 14 February 1951)

His other letters are full of the same spirit. In his fourth letter, published in *Paigham Sulh* on 28 March 1951, he writes that arrangements have been made to distribute 2000 copies of the English translation of the Holy Quran to people with money raised for the Thanks-giving Fund. He then added that there was a Divine purpose even in the smallness of our numbers, which was that, in this age also, an example of assistance from God the Most High may be witnessed. Therefore, despite this dearth of human resources, God produced many men who rendered very great services. He said that he was not talking about those elders who had been with us since the time of Hazrat Mirza sahib but those friends who joined us later and are persons of meagre means. Nonetheless, every one of them is doing the work of an entire *Jama'at.* He cited some examples as follows:

"In Assam [Eastern India] our friend Dr. Khadim Rahmani Nuri has done so much work as if we have a mission established there on which we are spending thousands of

Rupees, whereas in fact there is only one man working by himself with the help of God. He even translated the Quran into the Khasi language and also translated many other books and booklets. ... In Iraq, Syed Tasaddaq Husain Qadari has done incomparable work. Only because of him the Ahmadiyya Anjuman Isha'at Islam and its works are well-known in all the Arab countries, and Arabic translations of our books have been spread in Egypt. ... In Siam [Thailand] Ibrahim Quraishi rose with such determination that I was amazed to see his work. ... In Burma we found Dr. Akbar Khan, belonging to the same category of men of meagre means, who translated much literature into Burmese and is now busy in translating the Quran into Burmese. ... By the grace of God we have also found such a person in Istanbul. ... Likewise, Allah the Most High has raised such men in British Guiana [Guyana], Dutch Guiana [Suriname], the Philippines and Trinidad. ... Due to the work of these devoted few people the name of God, His Holy Prophet and His Quran is gaining renown in the world.

I am not mentioning at this time the Anjuman's achievements but only telling you how a few individuals, due to the spirit infused in them by connection with the holy Imam of the Age, have brought about a great change in large populations."

These then were the people with whom he had a heart-felt connection and whom he loved, and they were the examples that he put before the *Jama'at* in these last letters. They all were doing solid work quietly, without asking for financial help from the Anjuman nor desiring any material gain. Mentioning these people, he appealed to members of the *Jama'at* to struggle hard with overwhelming dedication and make sacrifices. After that he wrote:

"At the moment I am busy in this work like a traveller who is to embark on a journey tomorrow but has very little time to make preparations for it. My friends and well-wishers try to stop me, telling me not to work too much. But for me that death would be easier which comes while working. So I beseech my friends to give the same value to my message as to the message of a man who has returned from the next world. ... If you are poor, you should raise your determination for spreading the word of Allah to such a high level that it should shake the heavens. If you have been granted wealth by God, you should make it flow in God's way so profusely as to satisfy the needs of a whole world. ... If you hold a high position in the world, you should try to seek a high status in the court of Allah which would be with you forever. ... My friends, these are the paths worth following, not the ones towards which I see some of my friends starting to take their steps.

It is the favour of God towards me that He bestowed upon me great success. So do not try to make me fail. Every person who is not taking part in this mission according to the instructions of the Promised Messiah, is trying to make me fail. Though he may have ninety-nine pretexts for it, they are insignificant compared to my one plea that this work is for God and His Prophet and His religion. If anyone assists me, he will be helping not me but the religion of God. ... There must be ninety-nine faults in me, but you yourselves decided to disregard and overlook them when you elected me as your *Amir*. So, after having made your affirmations, do not desert me, otherwise you would be like the woman who "unravels her yarn, disintegrating it into pieces, after she has spun it strongly" [the Quran, 16:92]. ... Try to excel one other in good deeds, and do not try to outdo one another in negligence, apathy and fault-finding."

Whereas a large section of the *Jama'at* was devoted to him and made sacrifices according to his instructions, but due to some Divine purpose there were also others to whom this work was not as important as it should have been, and who wanted the *Jama'at* to get involved in matters of secondary importance. In this connection they used to raise objections and criticism against him. In many matters and at meetings of the Anjuman their attitude was very hurtful to him. While a large part of the outside world acknowledged him and appreciated his works, there were some people within who caused him distress. He endured all this for some twenty-two years, but at this age and in this poor state of health these things were bound to have an adverse effect on him.

On 5 April 1951, while he was writing his fifth letter to the *Jama'at*, he had angina pains during the writing and the letter remained unfinished. He had started this letter with the prayer of Moses given in the Quran: "My Lord, expand my breast for me and ease my affair for me and loose the knot from my tongue that they may understand my word" (20:25–28). He said that whatever he wanted to write in this letter he wrote two pages of it and then tore it up because, he thought, who would listen to his exhortations? He wrote:

> "There are some people in the *Jama'at* who do not understand, just as other Muslims do not understand, that the work of the propagation of the word of God is something for which one must put oneself to much sacrifice."

When such people openly called upon the *Jama'at* to other works, the result is that:

> "People think: everyone is beating his own drum, so whom should we follow and whom should we ignore?"

He wanted to stress in this letter also that the *Jama'at* should concentrate exclusively on spreading the word of God. There should be financial sacrifices for this end, as well as prayers at night for it, and this work must not be allowed to suffer because of the emotions of some members. (*Paigham Sulh,* 9 May 1951.)

These, then, were the four or five letters he wrote addressing the *Jama'at* after the annual gathering of 1950 till May 1951 when he went to Karachi, and they well show the state of affairs in the *Jama'at* at the time and the zeal in his own heart.

Meeting delegates to the World Muslim Congress (*Mu'timar al-'Alam al-Islami*) and his fame abroad

A meeting of the World Muslim Congress was held in Karachi in February 1951. After participating in the conference many delegates came to Lahore, and for nearly one week they kept on calling at Maulana Muhammad Ali's residence to meet him, as he was too weak at that time to go out due to illness. The leader of the Turkish delegation, Mr. Omer Riza Dogrul, who was a famous writer as well as a member of the Turkish Parliament, wrote an account of his impressions of his meeting with the Maulana which was published in the May 1952 issue of *The Islamic Review.* Some extracts from it are quoted below:[1]

> "... We had read his writings in Turkey for 30 years with great benefit to ourselves. He enlightened us on many matters, for he had penetrated deeply into the spirit of Islam and understood its aims and objectives, and had set out to explain them to others. ...
>
> On our arrival at the Maulana's house I asked that we should cause him no inconvenience. 'I will go to his room and kiss his hand,' I said. I was promised that my wishes would be fulfilled, and so I waited in the drawing room. After one or two minutes I saw a light shining through the open door; I was irresistibly drawn towards it, and a moment later was embracing Muhammad Ali. His form had really acquired a sort of transparency and translucidity which were not of this world. His hair and beard, which were exceptionally white, surrounded his face like a halo. He was of striking stature. His eyes were pale and dim, and gave the impression that his thoughts were already not of this world. I spoke in order not to tire him; I treated subjects which I knew would interest him, and as I was very well informed about these ideas, he received my remarks with a sympathetic smile. ...
>
> I asked him: 'What are your other occupations?' He replied slowly in a deep voice:
>
> 'I have sworn an oath to send a complete set of my works to all the libraries of the world. I have 5,000 complete sets of my works, for which my friends have collected money in order to send them to all the important

---

1. The extracts quoted here are taken from Mr. Dogrul's original English article as published in *The Islamic Review,* May 1952, pages 17–18.

libraries of the world. Would you kindly give me a few addresses of libraries that would be interested in receiving them?'

I immediately wrote down several addresses, and he gave them to his secretary."

Then Mr. Dogrul writes that as he took his leave Maulana Muhammad Ali stopped him and said to him:

"I beseech you to do all that lies in your power to express the enlightenment of Islam. I am sure that you will never in any way give satisfaction to the fanaticism of the narrow-minded people or even consider supporting the views of the intolerant."

Mr. Dogrul told the Maulana that if anything could keep the Muslims alive it is the interpretation of Islam which was spreading in the world through this *Jama'at*. He informed Maulana Muhammad Ali that many of his books were already translated into the Turkish language and other books would be translated in the near future.

Similarly, delegates from other countries also visited him. The leader of the Ceylon (Sri Lanka) delegation made a special effort to locate Muslim Town in order to come to see Maulana Muhammad Ali, and praised his services and those of the *Jama'at*. He expressed the wish that the translation of the Holy Quran into Tamil may be published soon as this language is spoken by the Muslims of his country as well as a large section of the other population. The Thai delegate, Mr. Ibrahim Quraishi, visited Maulana Muhammad Ali twice and showed him beautifully printed books in the Thai language which were translations of the Maulana's writings. He informed that he was translating the Quran into the Thai language using the Maulana's translations. He was taking the explanation of the meanings of Arabic words from *Bayan-ul-Quran* and the footnotes and commentary from the English translation. Likewise, the Chinese delegate said that translations of the Maulana's books had been published in Chinese.

During those days Maulana Muhammad Ali received a letter from a high Arab official in Egypt by the name of Muhammad

Saeed Ahmad, who was Secretary in the Egyptian Ministry of Railways, Telegrams and Telephones. He asked permission to translate the book *The Religion of Islam* into Arabic, which the Maulana granted with pleasure. A little later, on 27 April 1951, the Egyptian Ambassador to Pakistan, Abdul Wahhab Azzam, who later on became Secretary General of the Arab League, came to see Maulana Muhammad Ali. As on 5 April the Maulana had had another attack of illness and was unable to leave his bed, Abdul Wahhab Azzam was received in the bedroom where they talked at length. He gave the Maulana further details about the proposed Arabic translation of *The Religion of Islam,* and copies of the Maulana's various books were presented to Mr. Azzam.

It is also relevant to mention here that when Liaquat Ali Khan, the Prime Minister of Pakistan, was visiting the U.S.A. in May 1950 he received a telegram from Mr. William Ihrig, Secretary of the Religious Conference of the United Nations in New York. The message was as follows:

> "May I through you express to the people of Pakistan our appreciation for the fine work your countrymen Maulavi Muhammad Ali and the society Ahmadiyya Anjuman Ishaat Islam at Lahore have been doing in bringing to the American people by their Islamic religious publications in English ... a better understanding between Pakistan and the United States ... May I recommend that you induce these highminded persons at Lahore to open a United Nations head quarters branch of their society in the vicinity of New York city either as part of your United Nations delegation or independently. This would enable them to utilize the extensive free local and national and international press and radio and educational forums..." [2]

In this connection, another incident would be of interest. A Turkish woman journalist, Miss Kuterman, correspondent of the famous Turkish newspaper *Ulus,* came to Pakistan in 1950. In Lahore, while attending a gathering of journalists, she began to

---

2. Quoted from the original English text in *The Light,* 24 January 1951, p. 7. See also *Paigham Sulh,* 14 February 1951, p. 8; 20 December 1950, p. 4.

make inquiries about where Maulana Muhammad Ali lived. By coincidence Maulana Yaqub Khan, who was at the time editor of the *Civil and Military Gazette*, was there. He arranged for her an appointment with Maulana Muhammad Ali, who invited her to an afternoon tea. She related to the Maulana that although her mother, who was a religious lady, had arranged for her to learn the Holy Quran, but the Quran remained a closed book for her and she was alienated from religion. Later on, her newspaper posted her to its London office as chief reporter and there by chance she saw a copy of the Maulana's English translation of the Quran. When she read it, it opened her eyes to Islam. Then she read his other books and decided that she would go to Pakistan and kiss the hands of the man who had kindled her interest in the Holy Quran and in religion. She was thankful to God, she said, for receiving that privilege today. Then she kissed his hand and before leaving she requested him emphatically to visit other countries and come to Turkey as well, where Muslims would receive him with great honour.

Similarly, a woman writer from Lebanon, who was also president of the women's association of Lebanon, by the name of Habiba Shaban Bekan, wrote that after reading the Maulana's book *Muhammad and Christ* she kissed it and hugged it again and again, as it had relieved her of the great confusion and perplexity that she had suffered from regarding the issues discussed in the book. This lady got many of his books translated into Arabic and printed in Beirut at her own expense.

A distinguished lady from Lahore, after visiting the U.S.A., related on her return that it was by going abroad that she became fully aware of the honour and respect in which Maulana Muhammad Ali was held. In the U.S.A. she met some new Muslim men and women and when they came to know that she was from Pakistan they asked her with great interest the place in Pakistan she had come from. On hearing the name of Lahore they were thrilled and asked her to tell them about Maulana Muhammad Ali, how he lives and what he does. They told her that they had become Muslims after reading his English translation of the Holy Quran and other books. Similarly, there was a gathering of black Americans who had become Muslims, and they also inquired from her about

Maulana Muhammad Ali and remarked that she was fortunate to live in a city where such a learned, saintly figure was residing.

There are many other events of this kind, which cannot be related to avoid prolonging this book. In brief, the real greatness of the work of Maulana Muhammad Ali is realised from foreign countries (outside Pakistan). In numerous countries there are people who had drunk deep at this fountain whose source was Muhammad Ali. His books have been translated into so many languages that it is difficult to procure a complete record. Books such as *The Religion of Islam, Muhammad the Prophet, The Early Caliphate, The New World Order* and others were even translated into Arabic and acquired great popularity. It is highly remarkable that while Islamic literature (the Holy Quran, Hadith, books on life of the Holy Prophet and Islamic law etc.) already existed in Arabic, as this is of course the original language of Islam, yet books on Islam should be *translated from English into Arabic* whose author is not an Arab, who had himself acquired his knowledge from another non-Arab, and who belonged to a movement which had been widely denounced with condemnations of heresy. This is the most powerful testimony to the personal greatness of that man, and more so, it is evidence of the greatness of his teacher who set him on this path and made him capable of rendering this magnificent service to Islam.

Other work in early 1951 and another attack of illness

Apart from what has been mentioned above, among his other preoccupations during the first four to five months of 1951 there were two other major tasks. One was his personal supervision of the distribution of the sets of books. He was in correspondence with various countries of the world, and addresses of libraries and other similar institutions were being sought, to which these sets were to be despatched. He had taken this task in hand in the beginning of 1950, and till his death, during a period of nearly eighteen months, eight hundred sets had been dispatched to foreign countries. In this connection, new reprint editions of *The Religion of Islam, A Manual of Hadith, Muhammad the Prophet* and *The Early Caliphate* had also been published.

The second task was the proof reading of the revised, fourth edition of the English translation of the Quran. In addition to the staff assigned to read the proofs, he himself would read all of them once and make corrections. In the first three months of 1951, when his health was comparatively better, he would regularly work in his office. Although the morning walk had been given up, he used to take a stroll around the house and would walk to the Muslim Town mosque for the five daily prayers. On the evening of 5 April he was suddenly taken ill, as has been mentioned before, and besides suffering from high temperature and angina his lungs were affected as well. Two famous doctors of Lahore, Colonel Ilahi Bakhsh and Dr. Muhammad Yusuf were treating him. For two days he was given oxygen at home. For some days the temperature kept rising and there was also an attack of influenza. After about ten days the temperature came down and his condition improved. According to medical advice he spent a month in bed. But even in that state he continued to read the proofs of the English translation of the Quran and supervise the distribution of the sets of books.

His last journey to Karachi

At the end of May 1951 his health was much better than before, and as the weather in Lahore was getting hotter he left for Karachi on the morning of 31 May by the 'Pakistan Mail' train service. Photographs were taken on this occasion at Lahore railway station. In Karachi his health improved significantly. His physician, Dr. Paracha, declared after examining him that his heart condition was satisfactory. Gradually he regained his strength and continued his activities in Karachi as previously. Firstly, in connection with the distribution of the sets of books, correspondence with other countries and the despatch of books continued under his supervision. Secondly, he was going through the proofs of the revised, fourth edition of the English translation of the Holy Quran. Thirdly, he was also holding meetings with prominent Muslims of Karachi, ambassadors of Muslim countries based in Karachi (then capital of Pakistan), and other like persons, in order to expand and improve the work of the distribution of the sets of books. On 6 July, the Karachi *Jama'at* held *Eid-ul-Fitr* prayers at the residence of Mr. Naseer Ahmad Faruqui. The *khutba* was delivered by Mr. Faruqui and Maulana Muhammad Ali made a short speech. However, his improving health was dealt a blow by some unpleasant events. Before these are mentioned, it is appropriate to relate some other happenings.

Plan to perform *Hajj*, visit Western countries and Middle East

In the last three or four years Maulana Muhammad Ali had entertained a strong desire to go to perform the Pilgrimage to Makkah and he had made all the arrangements for this. However, as he was continuing the revision of the English translation of the Holy Quran and then its proofs were arriving, if he had gone for the Pilgrimage this work would have been left incomplete. Apart from the *Hajj,* he also planned to visit England and the Middle East, which he had decided to do after meeting ambassadors of Muslim countries. The whole tour was to take six to seven months. He was trying to get the new edition of the Holy Quran printed as soon as possible so that he could be free of anxiety on this account during his visit of these countries. He intended to take with him Shaikh Muhammad Tufail (his assistant and later a missionary of the *Jama'at*). The original plan was to go in April 1950 and first spend a few months at Woking, England. Then he would visit Germany, followed by Turkey and countries of the Middle East, and after performing the *Hajj* he would return back home. But at that time some work still remained to be done on the draft of the new edition of the translation of the Holy Quran and the proofs of the first parts had started to arrive. So he postponed the plans for April 1951. Then in September 1950 in Karachi he had serious heart attacks. After returning to Lahore in December, despite his weak disposition, he stuck to his plan and seats were booked for passage in April. But immediately after the annual gathering of December 1950 when he had a mild attack, the doctors, after examination, strictly forbade him to embark on any long journey. So all the arrangements were cancelled.

Invitation to join Board of Editors of the *Encyclopaedia of Islam*

About the middle of August 1951, Maulana Muhammad Ali received a message, channelled through the government of Pakistan, from the famous orientalist Professor Kraemer of Holland, that he had formed a board of writers for the *Encyclopaedia of Islam*, and had himself proposed the name of Maulana Muhammad Ali to join this group of writers. He expressed the hope that the Maulana, despite his poor health, could join the board in view of the great importance of this work, particularly for Muslims all over the world and generally for everyone else as well. In reply Maulana Muhammad Ali expressed his happy willingness to accept this responsibility and wrote that although due to bad health he was in bed most of the time but he had continued his literary activities and recently had gone through 1400 pages of the proofs of the new edition of the English translation of the Holy Quran and written its preface, so he was willing to take on this additional work. The Maulana also informed the Anjuman of this.

Holy Quran Trust

It had been a long-standing wish of Maulana Muhammad Ali that some permanent arrangement could be made for the publication of translations of the Holy Quran, enabling this work to continue uninterruptedly into the future. His passion and zeal for the propagation of the Quran must have become clearly evident to the readers of this biography and to those who have read his sermons and writings. All those who worked with him and all other members of the *Jama'at* are witness to the fact that the one aim that dominated his mind was to spread the Holy Quran and other Islamic literature in the world on the widest possible scale so that the prophecy of the triumph of Islam could be fulfilled. After 1941 all the campaigns that he placed before the *Jama'at* were connected with producing translations of the Quran, publication of the Quran, and teaching the Quran, the last campaign being the propagation of literature through distributing sets of books. As against this, the difficulty was that the Anjuman had very limited financial means. There was only a small community to support the work of this Anjuman, and it had made unparalleled financial sacrifices. These campaigns that had been undertaken required funds but it often happened that, during financial difficulties, the Anjuman had to transfer funds from one objective to another, and the money collected for a particular cause could not be solely spent on it. As Maulana Muhammad Ali considered the spreading of the Quran in the world to be the primary purpose of the *Jama'at,* he tried several times to raise a reasonable sum of money which would be invested in order to provide a continuous source of income to be spent solely on the propagation of the Quran. He made this attempt for the first time on the occasion of the Silver Jubilee and while launching the plan to do something special for the Jubilee he said: "if that work would not reveal the greatness of the Holy Quran then we would have drifted away from the right path". But afterwards the General Council decided to spend the money collected on the consolidation of the *Jama'at*.

Then in October 1943 he laid before the community a proposal for creating a 'Quran Publication Trust' and outlined it as follows: "Some funds will be donated by the Anjuman for the propagation of Islam and for some we will ask our friends to donate individually. This 100,000 to 200,000 Rupees could be invested in some business, and the resulting income be used to translate the Holy Quran into different languages of the world and publish these translations." On this occasion this proposal was put twice before the General Council of the Anjuman. However, for some reason the name 'Trust' seemed to be a cause of anxiety for the Anjuman, even though the only object of a trust is to dedicate funds for a particular purpose, so that they are not diverted to other ends, creating a permanent source of income for the specified purpose. If that money is left at the general disposal of the Anjuman, then even though it may be earmarked for a specified head of expenditure it could still be diverted to other purposes, and this is what had in fact been happening. By creating a trust, even one subordinate to the Anjuman, this risk can be avoided. On this occasion too the General Council of the Anjuman only agreed to creating a 'Quran Translations Fund'. This was set up in December 1943 and a reasonable sum was raised for it. Work on four translations of the Quran was started during the life of Maulana Muhammad Ali but none was ever published. In 1950 when the Maulana suffered his first serious heart attack and was bed-ridden in Karachi, the leading members of the Anjuman in Lahore decided, in order to meet the deficit in the budget of the Anjuman, to stop the work of translations of the Quran and close the mission in the U.S.A.

There was another factor in the background to the creation of the Holy Quran Trust. Every fair-minded person must have real-ised that the Promised Messiah's wishes regarding the propagation of Islam were fulfilled through the literature produced by Maulana Muhammad Ali during a period of forty to fifty years. However, some leading persons had long been spreading the objection as to why Maulana Muhammad Ali was urging mainly the publication of his own books. As he received royalty on the sale of his books, this meant that there was much scope for the critics to spread misgivings. But it was obvious that if there was a means of intro-ducing Islam to non-Muslims in other countries, especially to Western nations, then it was mainly through the valuable writings of Maulana Muhammad Ali, such as his English translation of the Holy Quran with commentary and books on Hadith, life of the Holy Prophet Muhammad and the teachings of Islam. These wri-tings he had produced specifically for this purpose, and in accord-ance with the wishes and the directions of the Promised Messiah. Hazrat Mirza sahib's wishes had been fulfilled through these books, and he had himself chosen Maulana Muhammad Ali for this task. Also, Maulana Nur-ud-Din had set him on the task of producing English and Urdu translations of the Holy Quran and Hadith and their explanations, for the purpose of the propagation of Islam.

Above all, there was the verdict of the present age testifying that it was this literature that attained the height of success and acclaim in the entire world, brought thousands of people to the right path, and was translated by people of other countries at their own initiative with great eagerness into their own languages, so much so that it was translated into Arabic in Arab countries. In spite of these magnificent, crystal-clear proofs, some persons had misgivings about the propagation of this literature, and conse-quently they refrained from participating in this work in any prac-tical way, which has been referred to in the quotations from the *khutbas* and writings of Maulana Muhammad Ali given above. Not only this, but certain prominent members openly attempted to devalue this precious treasure of literature, as has been mentioned before. This necessarily meant that Maulana Muhammad Ali was compelled to make some arrangements to ensure that, no matter what turn the *Jama'at* may take after his time, this work could continue permanently. This is a dark page in the history of this Anjuman but a biography cannot ignore it.

This was the background to the creation of the Holy Quran Trust. What happened now, in 1951, was as follows. When Maulana Muhammad Ali started the scheme for the distribution of the sets of books, he raised entirely by his own efforts about 150,000 Rupees, much of this being contributed by Muslims outside the *Jama'at*. As all but one of the eight books which constituted the sets to be sent abroad were written by Maulana Muhammad Ali, on which he received royalty, he decided that whatever royalty he received on sets of books purchased through this fund would not be used by him personally. On these books he was due royalty at the rate of one-third ($33 \frac{1}{3}$ %). He deposited this royalty as a bond with the Anjuman in a separate fund called the 'Royalty for Godly Purposes Fund', and instructed the Anjuman that this would be spent on religious purposes as directed by him alone.

Accordingly, from time to time, he spent money from this fund on such purposes at his own discretion, without asking the permission of the Anjuman. He also used it to help some Ahmadis who were in need. But the largest item of expenditure from this fund was the printing of an extra ten thousand copies of the new, fourth edition of the English translation of the Quran which was under print in England. The various editions of the English translation of the Quran before this had amounted to a total of some fifty thousand copies, but as now the literature was to be spread at a faster pace it had been decided that this fourth edition would consist of twenty thousand copies.

Therefore, Dr. Shaikh Muhammad Abdullah, the Imam of the Woking Mosque in England, had made all the arrangements for the printing of twenty thousand copies and paper had been bought as well. However, the Anjuman changed its decision and wanted to print ten thousand copies only. At this, Maulana Muhammad Ali asked the Anjuman to allow him to get another ten thousand copies printed at his own expense, to be paid out of the 'Royalty for Godly Purposes Fund'. These copies would be distributed by him to deserving cases either at reduced price or free and the money received by sale would revert to the 'Royalty for Godly Purposes Fund'. The Anjuman gave its approval, and thus the extra ten thousand copies of the translation were printed out of this fund.

At the end of 1950 and the beginning of 1951 Maulana Muhammad Ali had to face some particularly unpleasant circumstances. This coincided with the time when he had had several heart attacks and his health was very poor. In view of all this background, he decided to form a trust with the remainder of the money in the 'Royalty for Godly Purposes Fund' with the object of the publication of the Quran, and so he named it as the 'Holy Quran Trust'. Besides himself, among the trustees that he appointed there were five persons who were his relations,[3] regarding whom he was sure that they would always run the Trust for the objects that he had laid down. The objects of this Trust were specified by him as follows:

1. To supply the Holy Quran to the deserving, those in search of the truth, and students at reduced price or free.
2. To give scholarships and stipends to persons doing research work on the Quran, other students, and deserving people.

This was subject to two conditions: firstly, that at least 75% of the income is spent on the first aim above, and secondly, that this Trust will work in full co-operation with the Anjuman and respect its decisions as long as the Anjuman observes its obligations as regards payment of royalty.

It must be made clear that the storm of propaganda that was raised, to the effect that this Trust was set up from the funds of the community without the Anjuman's permission, was absolutely false. The funds that were transferred to this Trust came from royalty which, according to the decisions and the practice of the Anjuman and according to the law, was his by right. He had himself devoted it for religious purposes instead of making use of

---

3. All these relations of his were, by the grace of God, staunch Ahmadis who participated prominently in the works of the *Jama'at* and made financial sacrifices. Their 'fault' was that they were his relations, and this was made a basis for objection.

it personally. According to Islamic *Shari'ah* a person can dispose of his money in four ways: give it as a gift, make a will for it, devote it (*waqf*) for some purpose, or leave it to his heirs. The English word for *waqf* is Trust, but this term was presented by the critics as a threat. Khwaja Kamal-ud-Din raised large sums through donations and created a trust with that money. One or two other stalwarts of the *Jama'at* set up trusts using personal funds or left legacies for certain causes without requiring the Anjuman's permission. Similarly, this Trust was also set up with private funds. Any doubt about this is removed by the following writing of Maulana Muhammad Ali which was approved by the Executive Committee of the Anjuman according to its Resolution No. 395, dated 8 December 1950:

> "I should be permitted to have ten thousand further copies printed, over and above the Anjuman's ten thousand copies, at my own expense. The Anjuman would pay only for the first ten thousand copies. All the expenditure incurred by the further ten thousand copies shall be paid by me out of the Royalty for Godly Purposes Fund."

At that time no one objected that this money belonged to the Anjuman and not to the Maulana, but when this fund was transferred into the Trust then this objection was raised.

There remains the question why this fund was not entrusted to the Anjuman for this purpose, and whether the Maulana did not have confidence in the Anjuman? The answer can be found in his following writing:

> "Why did I not entrust this work to the Anjuman? The reason is that the Anjuman, in view of its needs, sometimes spends funds intended for one object on some other object and subsequently it is not returned. Thus last year, during the time of my most serious illness, the Anjuman, after diverting funds earmarked for certain objects towards other purposes, decided to stop the original works instead of considering returning the funds back to those objects. It thus decided to close the U.S.A. mission and stop work on the translations of the Quran. This decision caused me such severe distress as is beyond words. So,

disregarding my critical illness, I wrote letters and sent telegrams to stop this step from being taken.... I presented the proposal to the Anjuman, and at the annual gathering, that the financial problems should be solved not only by calling for special donations but also by the sale of some of the many lands that we had bought only for the purpose of strengthening the Anjuman's financial position, so that our essential work, that of taking the Quran to the world, is kept going."

Soon after the setting up of this Trust, Maulana Muhammad Ali left for Karachi while in a weak state of health.

The creation of this Trust was intolerable to the very people whose attitude was the cause of setting up this Trust in the first place. They misled a large section of the *Jama'at* by warning of imaginary dangers and by spreading groundless suspicions that have been mentioned before. When this came to the attention of the Executive Committee, it was decided to bring it up before the General Council. At this, some persons forthwith considered it necessary to assemble members of the *Jama'at* at Lahore, and these people issued circular letters individually as well as collectively. There also occurred some other events which had a very adverse effect on the health of Maulana Muhammad Ali in Karachi. He was compelled, even in that state of health, to give some response to the letters and circulars that were being spread in the *Jama'at*, and decided to submit the remaining reply at the General Council. During those days he developed breathing problems, had difficulty sleeping, and his health deteriorated. He was treated suitably for all these outward symptoms but after these events his health did not improve.

At the end of September, after some meetings with Shaikh Mian Muhammad in Karachi, Maulana Muhammad Ali came to the conclusion that, as there was a storm of false propaganda raging in the *Jama'at,* and misgivings had been put in the minds of the ordinary members, creating division and disunity, and this state of affairs would remain unchanged no matter how much clarification he issued, therefore he should discontinue the Trust.

So the funds that had been transferred to the Trust were returned into the 'Royalty for Godly Purposes Fund'.

Just for the sake of raising objections even straight-forward matters were twisted. The worst example of this was the objection that in the Trust deed the Maulana had described himself as Hanafi and therefore concealed the fact that he was an Ahmadi. The Trust deed was drawn by a competent attorney of law and according to him it was necessary to write that this Trust was created according to the Hanafi branch of Islamic law (*Hanafi Fiqh*). Everyone knows that the Promised Messiah described himself as a follower of *Hanafi Fiqh* and the Ahmadiyya community follows *Hanafi Fiqh*. To exploit an innocuous legal requirement, in which there was no misrepresentation, in such a cynical manner was deplorable in the extreme. Moreover, this was said regarding the man who was the 'commander' *Mansur* of the army of the Promised Messiah, who for fifty years had dedicated each one of his works to Hazrat Mirza Ghulam Ahmad and mentioned him in the preface of all his major books, and in 1949 in his booklet *Jama'at Qadian aur har Musalman ke liye lamha-i fikria* ('A pause for thought for the Qadian *Jama'at* and for every Muslim') he had shown that his life was a continuation of the life of the Promised Messiah.

This saga ended with the resolution of the General Council passed at the time of the annual gathering following the death of Maulana Muhammad Ali. It was as follows:

> "Resolution No. 51, dated 26–27 December, 1951.
>
> This meeting of the General Council declares it unanimously, in clear and unambiguous words, that the late *Hazrat Amir* (Maulana Muhammad Ali), may the mercy of Allah be upon him, was God-fearing to the highest degree and the qualities of honesty and integrity shone in his person in the most perfect way. He was a great pillar of strength for the Ahmadiyya Movement in this age.
>
> In the last period of his life, some unpleasant events occurred, on which this meeting expresses its regret." [4]

---

4. *Paigham Sulh,* 16 January 1952, p. 6. An earlier resolution was passed

Death of Maulana Muhammad Ali

These unpleasant events had adversely affected the health of Maulana Muhammad Ali. His health had previously improved so much
that his doctors and medical attendants were satisfied with his
condition. He used to walk around the house as usual and was
busy in his work. On the occasion of *Eid* he had even addressed
the Karachi *Jama'at* briefly. However, after these events he began
to be very tired and exhausted. His heart was already weak and
now he developed breathing problems. It was always his habit to
sleep very little, but now that vanished entirely. Even in this
condition he wrote detailed replies to two letters that had been
circulated. But as his detractors had announced that they would
publish ten circulars, and six or seven numbered circulars had
already been issued by them, he wrote at the end of his reply that
he would answer everything before the General Council of the
Anjuman. Those who were issuing these circulars demanded that
the General Council should be called in the middle of August. But
due to the state of his health and the intense heat, it was impossible
for him to travel from Karachi to Lahore for this purpose. So he
intended to call the General Council in October as usual, and had
written a statement in this connection which was finished on 8
October 1951. While in the same condition he had also finally
completed the checking of the proofs of the fourth edition of the
English translation of the Quran.

Mr. Naseer Ahmad Faruqui was having him treated by
specialists in Karachi for his rapid breathing and other problems
that had started but there was no treatment for the sorrow he
had suffered. During the last four or five days of his life he also
developed stomach pains which increased his weakness.

Due to the deterioration in his health, and from some Divine
indications, he had come to know that his end was near, but no
one ever saw the least sign of despair, sorrow or despondency on

in the meeting of the General Council held on 28 October 1951, declaring his
death as "an irreplaceable loss for our community and the whole world of
Islam" and praying that "Allah may enable the *Jama'at* to follow in his footsteps". This resolution was passed with all the members standing out of
respect (*Paigham Sulh,* 31 October 1951, p. 9).

his face. If he ever expressed any anxiety it was about the *Jama'at,* and he expressed it to Mr. Faruqui or one or two other prominent members. During his last days when he felt greatly saddened over the state of affairs of the *Jama'at,* he mentioned to Mr. Faruqui that he had received revelation from God (*ilham*), saying: *yā 'azīm al-martaba* (meaning, 'O highly ranked one'), and upon receiving it he felt, due to his humility, that these words were referring to God. But immediately he received another revelation: *wa yā ḍa'īf al-jaththa* (meaning, 'And O weak-bodied one'). So this second revelation explained that the first revelation was about him. His interpretation was that his body was now so weak that his soul must leave it. His first plan was to go to Lahore on 15 October. When this was mentioned, he said: "But I have seen that I am flying to the heavens in an aircraft".

On the morning of 13 October, he felt a little better. After his morning prayers he had a light breakfast. But shortly afterwards it seemed as if he had made contact with Allah. He turned his attention away from his near and dear ones who were there to look after him. At about 9 a.m. one of his doctors, Colonel Khan, came but the Maulana paid him no attention, even though he always conversed with his doctors and often engaged in some humorous talk with them. As he had been having sleeplessness during the nights, it was assumed that he wanted to sleep. So the doctor gave him a soporific injection, which made him somewhat drowsy. It was in that state that at about 11.30 a.m. on 13 October 1951, corresponding to 10 *Muharram* 1371, the soul of Maulana Muhammad Ali left to meet its Maker — *innā li-llāhi wa innā ilai-hi rāji'ūn* ('We belong to Allah, and to Him do we return'). That day was the tenth of *Muharram.*

The events that followed in Karachi are related in detail in Mr. Faruqui's article at the end of this book (p. 515–520). In brief, in the evening, after the necessary funeral customs for the body of the deceased were completed, the Karachi *Jama'at* said the funeral prayers at the residence of Mr. Faruqui. The coffin started its journey to Lahore by the Pakistan Mail train service at 6.30 p.m. The news of his death was broadcast in the evening and night news bulletins of Radio Pakistan and the same day from All-India Radio and the Asian programme of the Voice of America. As the

Pakistan Mail travelled towards Lahore, at almost every station during the night and the next day people met the train to pay their homage, having heard the news on the radio, and many Ahmadis joined the same train along the way. On the evening of the following day the train arrived at Lahore, where a large crowd of both Ahmadis and non-Ahmadis at the station met the coffin with tearful eyes and carried it from the train. The coffin was first taken, for a short while, to his home in Muslim Town. Then it was taken to Ahmadiyya Buildings. In the mosque at Ahmadiyya Buildings, at exactly the spot from which he had delivered sermons to the *Jama'at* for 37 years, imbued with spiritual content and filled with zeal and passion for the propagation of the Holy Quran, his funeral prayers were led by his elder brother Maulana Aziz Bakhsh. As twenty-four hours had by now passed since the news of his death was announced, it allowed a large number of people not only from Lahore but from other cities as well to attend his funeral prayers. After this, he was buried at about 9.30 p.m. in the Ahmadiyya community plot at the Miani Sahib cemetery. He had left a written will about his place of burial, saying: "I have wished for long that my grave should be at a location where I am lying at the feet of those of my companions who have passed away before me". He was buried according to this instruction.

A will for the *Jama'at*

When Maulana Muhammad Ali had a serious heart attack for the first time in September 1950, he gave Mr. Faruqui some instructions about his funeral. When, on 29 September, his condition worsened greatly and he became certain that he was about to meet his Creator, he called Mr. Faruqui towards him and said something to him in a weak voice, which the latter did not hear the first time. Mr. Faruqui asked him to repeat it, and bringing his ear close to the Maulana's lips he heard him say:

> "Our duty is to spread the Quran in the world, then it will do its own good work."

Later on his health improved and he went to Lahore. The *khutbas* he delivered there have been mentioned before. These words are as his last will and therein lies the secret of the success of the *Jama'at*.

Newspaper reviews and messages at his death

Those who mourned the death of Maulana Muhammad Ali were not only his own family and members of the *Jama'at* but people in many countries throughout the world, even in the farthest corners of the earth which could not be imagined, were also shedding tears for him. The wide scale of the sorrow felt at his death can be judged from the numerous letters of condolence received by his relatives as well as by prominent members of the *Jama'at* from all over the world. Many of these letters were published in the issues of *Paigham Sulh* from October 1951 to January 1952. All those letters would make up a book by themselves. By way of example, some newspaper reviews and letters from Muslims who were not Ahmadis are given below.

Dawn, **leading Pakistan English newspaper, Karachi:**

> "Maulvi Muhammad Ali, whose death occurred in Karachi, probably did more writing on Islamic subjects for almost half a century than any contemporary individual. Immersed in scholarly pursuits and gifted with a researcher's frame of mind, his aims were not academic. He was a missionary who awoke to his calling in life in the environment of the last century when Islam in this subcontinent was a target of concentrated scurrilous attacks from Western missionaries and votaries of a venomous revivalist Hinduism. A man of his academic distinction, in the late nineties, must have overcome a strong temptation in declining to enter Government service — the inevitable goal of education in those days — and choosing a missionary career. The object to which he dedicated his life was the translation of the Holy Quran into English; and he lived long enough after the first edition of his translation and commentary appeared in 1917, to follow it up with many other works. The best among these subsequent works are believed to be his *Muhammad, The Prophet* and *The Religion of Islam.* The former is a biography which pre-eminently serves its purpose; and the latter is almost cyclopaedic in its range of information. As a missionary Maulvi Muhammad Ali had profitably studied the publicity

techniques of European missionaries and his prolific writings reflect his ability to devise a suitable approach to almost every individual section of his readers. Stupendous was the energy that he could put into this task; and as the years grew on him the will-power made up for what was lacking in physical strength. He died working almost till the last. Silent and unassuming as he was, both the man and his works were appropriately reflected in the fact — paradoxical as it might seem — that his writings were better known than the man himself. His death is a real loss. He will be mourned by a wide circle of friends and admirers. We extend our heartfelt sympathy to the bereaved family." [5]

Star, Lahore:

"On October 13, at 11.30 a.m. in Karachi, there passed away from this world a well-known scholar and religious leader — Maulana Muhammad Ali, head of the Ahmadiyya Anjuman Ishaat-i-Islam, Lahore.

Soon after finishing his education, and while still very young, Maulana Muhammad Ali joined the followers of Mirza Ghulam Ahmad of Qadian, and came to the fore as a writer in English on Islam while he edited the *Review of Religions,* a monthly organ of the Ahmadiyya Movement of which the first issue came out in January 1902. The monthly journal, devoted to the comparative study of Religion, did yeoman's service under Maulana Muhammad Ali's editorship by defending Islam against the onslaught of Christian Missionaries and European Orientalists of the old school whose writings were more marked by a virulent prejudice against Islam than by a spirit of honest enquiry and scholarly research.

After the death of the founder of the Ahmadiyya Movement, Mr. Muhammad Ali was assigned the task of

---

5. *Dawn,* Karachi, 16 October 1951, as quoted in *The Light,* 8 November 1951, p. 2.

preparing a translation in English of the Holy Quran; but the work could not be finished in the life-time of Maulvi Noor-ud-Din. Moreover, after the death of Maulvi Noor-ud-Din, a split occurred in the Ahmadiyya Movement over some points of belief and doctrine, as well as general policy to be followed in carrying on the mission of the Movement. Maulana Muhammad Ali was the Head of the section that broke away from Qadian and established itself in Lahore, finally coming to be known as Ahmadiyya Anjuman Ishaat-i-Islam, Lahore.

The translation of the Holy Quran into English, prepared by Maulana Muhammad Ali, was published in 1917, and was at once accepted as a most valuable addition to Islamic literature in English prepared by Muslim scholars and divines themselves, as distinct from what European and American scholars write on the subject, practically always under a deep anti-Islamic bias characteristic of Christian missionaries.

Apart from his translation of the Holy Quran, Maulana Muhammad Ali brought out a translation of *Sahih Bukhari,* and many other books on subjects connected with the superiority of Islam as a religious and social system. By removing him from our midst, death has thus created a vacuum that will long be felt by all interested in the revival of Islam as the most dominant spiritual force in the lives of the Muslim peoples." [6]

Abdullah Battersby (British convert to Islam):

"In the heart of the late Maulana Muhammad Ali, the beloved President of the Ahmadiyya Anjuman Isha'at Islam, there burned that *inextinguishable light* and that tremendous zeal for the Faith of Islam that gave him the power to overcome the frailty and weakness that marked his declining years. In his anxiety for the spread of Islam

---

6. *Star,* Lahore, 20 October 1951, as quoted in *The Light,* 8 November 1951, p. 2.

to the West and his own profound belief in his mission, he surely taxed his strength and, when it was my privilege to meet him, a little less than a year ago, at his Muslim Town home in Lahore, I was struck by the sheer simplicity of this man who had achieved so much in the holy cause of Islam. For him it was indeed a case of 'simple living and high thinking.'...

His immense scholarship and learning easily gave Muhammad Ali a place of pre-eminence among Islamic savants, and no nobler monuments to his memory can be raised than his translation and commentary of the Holy Quran and its companion volume 'The Religion of Islam'.

The renaissance of Islam that is taking place in the West today owes much to the labours of this revered scholar. ...

Nothing seemed able to deter him in the pursuit of this noble ideal. His faith enabled him to live a life of self-abnegation and purity, and one feels that, like Sir Galahad, he could have recited: 'My strength is as the strength of ten because my heart is pure.'

He was a man of culture and a civilized mind, who loved virtue for its own sake, who held a deep faith that Islam shall conquer in the end.

He was prompted from within to sail like a sailor into new seas of thought, to explore the dark channels of Western misunderstanding and to throw the broad gleams of the light of his scholarship along their murky depths. He was inspired by his intense zeal for the Faith to work to the last with haste — the night of life was approaching and his passion to carry out his mission made him impetuous to complete it.

He forgot that time was passing and in his anxiety worked feverishly till eventually God called him to Himself, and there passed from our midst one of the greatest and most beloved scholars of our time." [7]

---

7. *The Light,* 1st January 1952, p. 7.

Maulana Abdul Majid Salik, editor *Inqilab*:

"Maulana Muhammad Ali became a true and staunch Muslim by living in the company of Hazrat Mirza Ghulam Ahmad. Not only that, the greatness of the religion of Islam was so impressed upon his mind and heart that he devoted the whole of his life for its propagation. Every moment in his life was spent in the service of the faith. Besides the English translation of the Holy Quran, he wrote countless books on religious subjects. In my opinion, the best of these is the book *The Religion of Islam,* by studying which an English-knowing person can acquire such detailed knowledge about the religion which even the fully-qualified *maulvis* do not possess.

For the last fifteen years, Maulana Muhammad Ali had been living in Muslim Town, where I also have my residence. So we used to meet often in various gatherings and functions. Despite his religious and pious nature, he was quite informal. He was, no doubt, an Ahmadi, but his relations with other Muslims were extremely sincere and fraternal. One reason was that he was the head of that group of Ahmadis whose beliefs are not intolerant. Secondly, he was by nature peace-loving. He used to give sympathetic support to the campaigns and movements of the Muslims, and did not tolerate *takfir* of them, because he believed that calling Muslims as *kafir* was inconsistent with the work of propagation. He presented the message of Islam not only to India but to the Western world as well. And it is a fact that he possessed the capability of doing so in every way. He was not only a learned man of the religion, but also a high-ranking commentator of the Quran and *mujtahid.* He was an English writer of the highest standard, who well understood the Western mind. He presented Islam to Western-educated people as well as to Westerners themselves in such a style that they could not help becoming convinced of the greatness of this faith. I believe that hundreds of seekers-after-truth in the Western countries became Muslims by reading the writings and books of Maulana Muhammad Ali, and it is as a result of his efforts that today the name of Islam is mentioned with respect in the West, hostility towards Islam having much diminished. The selfless service of Islam, over a long period, will surely be a source of Allah's mercy for Maulana Muhammad Ali, because Allah never wastes the efforts and exertions of the true servants of his faith.

There is no doubt that there was a little difference of belief between him and the general Muslims, but that difference was by no means so serious that the Muslims should ignore his services and fail to appreciate him." [8]

Sidq, Sunni Muslim periodical, Lucknow, India:

"The services which the deceased rendered to Islam with the pen in his long literary life are incomparable and un-paralleled in their place. His pen was the greatest blessing for English readers and also for Urdu readers influenced by Western thought. God alone knows how many people had their faith [in Islam] restored by him, and how many Americans and Europeans seeking guidance found the path to Islam through him. ... The deceased devoted each and every moment of his life to the service of the religion." [9]

Khwaja Hasan Nizami, spiritual leader, Delhi:

"In connection with the work of the propagation of Islam, I had cause to meet the Maulana from the beginning of my life till today. I consider him to be a very great and very successful worker for Islam. May Allah grant him protection, and patience to the bereaved.

I inform my disciples and their leaders in India and Pakistan to hold meetings of reading the *Fatiha* for him. He has rendered so much service to the Quran and Islam that I believe it essential to hold the reading of the *Fatiha* for him." [10]

---

8. *Paigham Sulh,* special issue, 26 December 1951, p. 65.

9. *Sidq,* Lucknow, India, 26 October 1951.

10. *Munadi,* Sept–Oct. 1951; quoted in *Paigham Sulh,* 26 December 1951, p. 65.

Malik Abdul Quyum, Principal, Law College, Lahore:

"*Maut-ul-'ālim, maut-ul-'ālam* — the death of a great scholar (*'ālim*) is tantamount to the death of an entire world (*'ālam*). If this adage applies anywhere truly to a great loss, it applies to the death of Hazrat Maulana Muhammad Ali. It is not easy to find in this age in the whole of Asia, let alone Pakistan, another example of a life like his and of his constant struggle and sacrifice. ... His efforts, day and night, of seventy years have today not only been rewarded by Allah but the place he has attained in the field of the propagation of Islam itself represents a singular achievement. ... Hazrat Khwaja Kamal-ud-Din used to say that Maulana Muhammad Ali is included among those greatest figures in the history of Islam who can, without exaggeration, be called the founders of a new era. This assessment of his life was not based on personal friendship or loyalty, though even that would not be objectionable, but due to his invaluable services to Islam.

In this age, in the world of Islamic writings and literature, his English translation of the Holy Quran and the translation of Bukhari are standard translations and books ...

The late Maulana's life, both physical and spiritual, contains the best possible lesson for Muslims generally and the Muslim youth particularly. He used to rise at 3.00 a.m. and perform *tahajjud* prayers, and after that he was busy with work all day till as late as after the *'isha* prayers, showing the true example of the practice of the righteous Muslim leaders of earliest times. His sincerity, his virtues and his integrity reflected like shining gold on his unblemished character. He is, and will be, counted among those famous Muslims who were born to serve Islam and gave their lives in the same way. He was one of those revered men described in the Quran as: 'These are drawn nigh to Allah, in Gardens of bliss' [56:11–12]." [11]

---

11. *Paigham Sulh,* 26 December 1951, p. 66.

Mr. A.J. Khalil, Advocate, High Court, Maisur:

"He was a true *mujahid* of Islam, who proved to the world
by his work that the pen is mightier than the sword. He
has left behind him such magnificent literature about
Islam and the Holy Prophet, of which he could be justly
proud. The world has not recognised his greatness as it
ought to have done. He was the true, great *mujahid* of this
century. ... I believe that it was the will of God the Most
High that the precincts of the civilized world be adorned
with those pearls of Islamic teachings that have been prepared in the form of the literature he has written on Islam
and the Holy Prophet Muhammad. The English translation of the Holy Quran and the translation of Hadith done
by him would be sufficient in the sight of Allah the Most
High to grant him salvation. ... Such men will rarely be
born till the end of time, and the Muslim people will not
be able to fill the void left by this servant of Islam." [12]

Mr. Bashir Ahmad, Ambassador of Pakistan to Turkey:

"Maulana Muhammad Ali was one of the greatest religious
and spiritual leaders of Pakistan. For a lengthy period in
Lahore he did such work as will make him remembered
always and forever. The English translation and commentary of the Holy Quran, life of the Holy Prophet, the history
of the early caliphate, and his books in English on Islamic
teachings are unique. Even those who differ with him
acknowledge their usefulness. These books are read in all
parts of the world. One year ago Mrs. Muhammad Ali sent
to my wife a few copies of these books in Turkey. The
Turks accepted them as being highly sacred gifts.
A Turkish official who is a friend of mine said to me a few
months ago: However you can, please have me sent the
English translation of the Holy Quran by the Pakistani
author Maulana Muhammad Ali, I am prepared to pay any
price for it.

12. *Ibid.,* p. 66.

The work that Maulana Muhammad Ali has done in freeing the Islamic world of today from doubts and confusion is an achievement of which Pakistan can be justly proud." [13]

Geti Ara *Begum* Bashir Ahmad, wife of Ambassador of Pakistan to Turkey:

"In the 20th century of the Christian era, Maulana Muhammad Ali has tried to take to every corner of the world the message of unity and truth which the Holy Prophet Muhammad delivered to humanity 1300 years ago. He dedicated his life to present to the world the real and true point of view of Islam. Due to his hard work and effort, of night and day, such a magnificent and superb translation of the Holy Quran was completed which is being highly appreciated in all countries. His books on Islam have been acclaimed in many countries. In my two years of stay in Turkey this fact has become clear that the Turkish people have a truly high regard and estimation for the Maulana's services to Islam. His good name is well known among the religious sections of Turkey. His book *The Religion of Islam* is being translated into the Turkish language. ...

We are proud of the fact that in the land of the Punjab, which has produced many famous men, this standard bearer of Islam was born who rendered such magnificent services to Islam from which all the Muslims will derive benefit for centuries. I had correspondence with him from Turkey and received his last letter one month before his death. We had close friendly relations with him for years and I had deep respect for him in my heart." [14]

Maulana Abdul Majid Daryabadi:

"To deny the services of the deceased to Islam is to deny the existence of the sun in broad daylight. In 1930, twenty-one years ago, when I was drowned in the poison of

---

13. *Ibid.,* p. 67.

14. *Ibid.,* p. 67. Geti Ara was daughter of Sir Muhammad Shafi.

agnosticism and rationalism spread by Western ideas, it was the deceased's English translation of the Quran which guided me. Otherwise, only God knows for how much longer I would have been lost, and only God knows for how many people it proved to be the guiding light, as it did for me. Then his writings: the Urdu commentary of the Quran, translation of Bukhari, 'Early Caliphate', Life of the Holy Prophet, 'Islam the Religion of Humanity', 'A Manual of Hadith' — each more useful and excellent than the other — are in existence. ... I had only one occasion of meeting him personally., and that meeting was very amiable. There was an inner light radiating on his face, which is only produced by waking in the night [for prayers] and by spiritual exertions." [15]

Shamsul Ulama Dr. Umar ibn Muhammad Daudpota, Karachi:

"Maulana was a divine of great insight into the teachings of Islam, which he disseminated through his memorable books. His services to Islam and his efforts to make its true value appreciated by both Muslims and non-Muslims will remain an abiding monument to his learning and erudition. We have lost in him one whose compeer can scarcely be found among the so-called Ulema of Pakistan." [16]

Feroz Khan Noon, Pakistani statesman: [17]

1. "I was very sorry to read in the papers of the demise of Maulana Muhammad Ali. Please accept my deepest sympathy. It is a loss which not only I but the whole Muslim world will share with you fully. His works will remain for ever and I do not know of any man who has done so much

---

15. *Ibid.,* p. 67.

16. *The Light,* 8 November 1951, p. 7.

17. Feroz Khan Noon was Governor of East Bengal, Pakistan, at the time of writing these tributes. Later he also served as Prime Minister of Pakistan.

for the revival of Islam ... not even during the last 500 years." [18]

2. "For the present generation of non-Arab Muslims, Islam was a closed book. The late Maulana, by his scholarly translation of the Holy Quran, has opened the door to this sealed treasure, especially for Muslims of the present times. This translation and the other writings of the Maulana have played the most prominent role in the religious, cultural and political revival of the Muslims. Due to this work future generations will always be grateful to him." [19]

Following this page, 436, there is a 4-page photographic section inserted before resuming at page 437.

18. Letter dated 16 October 1951, published in *The Light,* 8 November 1951, p. 7.

19. Message for *Paigham Sulh,* special issue; published in *Paigham Sulh,* 16 January 1952, p. 6.

Last entry in the diary of Maulana Muhammad Ali, in his own handwriting

" 3.3.51

Received a letter from Woking yesterday — containing a copy of a letter from Mr. H. W. Thomas — Abdul Aziz, Camden, New Jersey, U.S.A., dated 29th Jan 51, containing names of eleven persons who had joined Islam — also copy of a report for publication in the Islamic Review containing names of eight persons who joined Islam, and who belong to England and Holland, including one belonging to Australia. Nineteen converts to Islam, the news is no doubt a harbinger of what is yet to come. — *yadkhulūna fī dīni-llāhi afwāj-an.* "

Note: The ending quotation in the above extract is a verse of the Quran, referring to people "entering into the religion of Allah in companies" (110:2).

Photo of prominent founder-members of the Lahore Ahmadiyya Movement, with other staff and workers of the Movement, at the headquarters, Ahmadiyya Buildings, Lahore. Taken in January 1931 on the occasion of the visit of Dr. Abdul Wahab Khan, a leading Muslim scholar of Thailand.

Rows from front to back, and in each row persons from left to right:

Front row, on floor: Dr. Allah Bakhsh, Mr. Rahmat Ali Shah, Mr. Rahmatullah and Mr. Abdul Haque Mahta.

2nd row, on chairs: Dr. Syed Muhammad Husain Shah, Dr. Mirza Yaqub Baig, Maulana Sadr-ud-Din, Maulana Muhammad Ali, Dr. Abdul Wahab Khan of Thailand, Malik Ghulam Muhammad, Dr. Ghulam Muhammad.

3rd row: Mr. Samiullah Khan, Hakim Khuda Bakhsh, Maulana Muhammad Yusuf Garanthi, Syed Ghulam Mustafa Shah, Maulana Yaqub Khan, Hakim Muhammad Hayat, Mr. Abdul Mannan, Sh. Ghulam Muhammad, Ch. Abdul Majid, Master Faqirullah.

4th row: Babu Ch. Manzur Ilahi, Mr. Abdul Ahad, (Unknown), Lal Husain Akhtar, Ch. Fazal Haque, Maulana Abdul Wahab, Mr. Wali Muhammad, Mr. Shukur Din, Mr. Abdul Wajid and Maulana Ahmad.

Some delegates to the World Muslim Congress, 1951, visit Maulana Muhammad Ali at his residence in Lahore

Seated: Major Abdullah Battersby, Maulana Sadr-ud-Din, Mr. Haroon Nahaboo (Mauritius), Maulana Muhammad Ali, Mourad Kiouane (Algiers), Mr. Ibrahim Quraishi (Thailand), Sayyid Asadullah Shah.

Standing: Mumtaz Ahmad Faruqui, Mian Saeed Ahmad, Maulana Yaqub Khan, Ibrahim Blangket (Borneo), Maulana Aftab-ud-Din Ahmad, Masum Chang (China), Maulana Abdul Haq Vidyarthi, Abdur Rahim Jaggoe, Shaikh M. Tufail. *See page 407–409 for this Conference. Apart from delegates, all others are from the Jama'at.*

Part 4

Recollections of Maulana Muhammad Ali

4.1: Home life, qualities, character and habits[1]

Home life

It has already been mentioned that Maulana Muhammad Ali's first marriage was arranged by the Promised Messiah himself in 1901 and that his wife Fatima died in November 1908. Upon her death, the account that the Maulana wrote about the seven years of his married life, and how his wife stood by him in his migration for the sake of religion, has also been quoted earlier (see p. 56–58). Then in 1910, on the instigation of Maulana Nur-ud-Din, he married Dr. Basharat Ahmad's daughter Mehrun Nisa. On 29 April 1910, with a wedding party of only two friends, the Maulana went to Bhera and, after the giving away of the bride, brought her to Qadian. On that occasion he presented his wife with a gift of a beautiful, multicoloured copy of the Holy Quran, in other words the thing he valued and loved most. On 1 May 1946 he wrote the following words on it by his own hand:

> The gift of love I gave, on the occasion of my wedding in late April 1910, to my wife Mehrun Nisa, today on the

---

1. This chapter in *Mujahid-i Kabir* is based largely on the article in *Paigham Sulh,* special issue, 26 December 1951, pages 3–5, 10, by Maulana Muhammad Ali's wife Mehrun Nisa. Here we have added a few more details from that article, including the story of a sceptic who describes observing Maulana Muhammad Ali's *tahajjud* prayer.

36th anniversary of this loving relationship, this note has been written on it in memory. This was the period of my life in which Allah the Most High enabled me to do well the work of serving His Holy Word and made my wife Mehrun Nisa's selfless devotion and love a means to complete the task. — *Allah be praised for it.*

Muhammad Ali, 1st May 1946.

From his first marriage he had one daughter, and from his second marriage he had six daughters and two sons. Atiya, his eldest daughter from his second wife, died after a long illness in 1922 at the age of ten.

All his daughters and his older son got married during his life. His younger son Hamid Farooq was sent to the U.K. in 1948 for higher education and he was there when the Maulana died.

Upon the death of his father Hafiz Fateh-ud-Din in 1913, when the Maulana went to his village, his brothers asked him to be their guardian, which he accepted. He set an example of maintaining family unity, so much so that for fifteen years the land belonging to all the brothers and the sister was managed collectively, and although he owned a part of it he never asked for any share in the produce for himself. On the contrary, he had his nephews come and stay with him, first in Qadian and later on in Lahore, and arranged for their education. He made sure that his sister was given her share of the agricultural land, as required by Islamic law, even though in those days the custom among Muslims was that girls were not given any share of their father's property. After his father's death he respected his elder brother Amir-ud-Din like father. Later on he gave the management of his own lands in the village of Murar entirely to his younger brother Ahmad Ali, and he never asked him to show any accounts. On two occasions when he had a residence built in Dalhousie and one in Lahore, he sold a large part of his estate through his brother. (When the residence in Lahore was being built he also sold land that he had bought for himself in Qadian.) In 1945 when he needed to repay a debt he sold some more land through his brother Ahmad Ali. Whenever he needed money he sold off parts of this land, and with the same proceeds he bought some plots of lands in the outskirts of Lahore which he sold later on to meet much of his needs. Basically he was a member of a family of farmers and took interest in work of the land.

During his stay in Qadian he took a very small salary from the Sadr Anjuman Ahmadiyya Qadian, and after coming to Lahore he had no source of income for five years, and even afterwards his income from royalty on books was not adequate to meet all his needs. However, God blessed this income so much that he maintained a respectable standard of living and built two residences, though some jealous people made even that a basis for objection. In financial matters he was extremely careful, and led always a life of simplicity and economy. He kept a written account of his personal expenses. Likewise, he supervised the financial affairs of the Anjuman with great care, being cognisant of all the expenditure, so much so that if the office made an error in the accounts, as sometimes happened, his cautious and keen eye always detected it immediately.

Domestic life

Maulana Muhammad Ali was a very loving husband and an affectionate father, and right from the start he helped his wife in domestic chores and the bringing up of the children. In the early days he was involved in momentous research work for the English translation of the Quran, having to study many deep and voluminous reference books, commentaries and dictionaries etc. in Arabic and English, which he did at night because of also being busy with works of the *Jama'at*. Nonetheless, despite being absorbed in and concentrating on all this work, he helped his wife in household affairs. When, during his *tahajjud* prayers in the middle of the night, he would sometimes hear a child cry, he would bring the prayer to a close with *taslim* and come and attend to the child as necessary, for example by warming up the milk, and then resume his remembrance of God. He was not only content with providing his wife with a loving home and comforts but also paid full attention to her religious education. She married him at a young age and did not have the chance to complete her education while being with her parents. So he started teaching her the translation of the Holy Quran and the Hadith, and took care to do so regularly.

His every action showed the respect and regard he had for women, in particular for his wife. If his wife could not concentrate on her education due to being busy with the children, he would be somewhat irritated but only go as far as to say jokingly: "It is very difficult to teach your wife; if she does not learn you cannot even punish her". Due to his kindest possible treatment of his mother, sister, wife and daughters, he was a perfect example of the Holy Prophet's teaching: "The best of you is he who treats his family the best".

He always liked to do personal chores himself and would help others with their work. He was extremely co-operative in domestic tasks and did not consider it beneath him to do the most menial job. Whenever they travelled, he did the packing and unpacking of all the household stuff himself. Though there were others available to do the work, even then he was compelled by his hard-working, uncomplicated nature to do it himself. As far as possible he would not trouble the servants.

He would eat whatever was cooked and partook of only one kind of curry dish or pulse dish at one meal. He did not at all like elaborately prepared meals or rich food, and ate only small amounts, but regarded eating fruit as important. Planting fruit trees and vegetables was always his great interest, and when he had a residence built he had a garden planted in it. This was his only hobby, for which he took out some time from his other engagements to spend in caring for the garden. When he had his residence in Dalhousie built, he specially procured plants for apples and other fruits from elsewhere and had them planted. This house was renowned in Dalhousie for its fruit trees. Likewise, he had a small scale garden planted in Lahore also.

As regards clothing, he always dressed very simply but cleanly and tidily. He always wore white as he liked this colour in clothing. Usually he wore a white *kurta* (long shirt) and *pyjama* (Indian style trousers) made of ordinary cloth and would wear a (Western style) coat or an *achkan* (a long coat having buttons in front) according to the weather. On his head would be a *fez* cap or a turban. It was while attired so simply that his personality would make such an inspiring impression on others, which few people can make. His personal cleanliness was of such a high standard that in the days when he was translating the Quran, he was always in a state of *wuzu* (the cleanliness prescribed by Islamic law for saying the regular prayers).

He had a special knack of tending the sick. Whoever was ill, whether child, adult or even servant, he would pay special attention to them. Once his wife was ill and coughed much during the night. So she slept in a separate small room so as not to disturb his sleep as he rose in the early hours to say his *tahajjud* prayer and had only a little time to rest. During the night she woke up and saw him sleeping on the floor in the small space beside her bed. He also woke and asked how she was. She asked him why he was sleeping there, and he replied that it was because if she needed anything he could get it for her.

His daughter Atiya died at the age of ten after a long illness. He nursed her most diligently. He would leave his office again and again to administer medicine, give her food, take her temperature and sit with her to comfort her. During the last days of her illness he used to work during the day as usual and spend almost the entire night nursing her. He would do everything for the sick child himself and never let his wife stay awake at night so that she may be able to look after the other children. Even in these circumstances no one ever saw him lose patience or become irritated. He kept smiling, joking to the children and the family, and working cheerfully.

In old age, when the hard work took its toll even on his strong health, and he would fall ill once or twice a year, during even that time he would be mindful to avoid causing inconvenience to others, and would try to do things himself despite being stopped by others. A year before his death, when due to heart trouble he was bed-ridden for a long time and was not permitted to move about, he would say to his wife that she was suffering on his account. When, on 6 April 1951 in Lahore, he had a heart attack in the evening, the doctor advised that it was not safe to take him to hospital at that time but it was necessary to administer oxygen immediately. So an oxygen cylinder was procured straightaway but due to lack of proper facilities someone was needed to hold the nozzle to his face all the time. During the night he asked for the cylinder to be switched off as people would have to stay awake to administer the oxygen. With great difficulty he was persuaded to agree that people would take turns to sit for no more than two hours each. Though all members of the family loved him very dearly and regarded it as their pleasure to serve him, but he did not want to trouble anyone.

Moral qualities and habits

God the Most High had blessed him not only with physical handsomeness but, much more than that, with beauty of moral qualities and character. The Promised Messiah, who received assurance from Allah that his physical eyesight would never weaken, and the power of whose spiritual sight we cannot even estimate, had written about Maulana Muhammad Ali:

> "During this period in which he has been with me, I have been observing him, both openly and discreetly, to assess his moral character, observance of religion and goodness of behaviour. So, thanks be to God, that I have found him to be a most excellent man as regards religion and good behaviour in all ways. He is unassuming, modest, of a righteous nature, and pious. He is to be envied for many qualities. ... It is obvious that such promising young men possessing these qualities, who are able and honourable, cannot be found by searching." [2]

> "I am sure that my foresight will not go wrong in this, that this young man will make progress in the path of God, and I am sure that by the grace of God he will prove to be so firm in righteousness and love of religion that he will set an example worthy to be followed by his peers." [3]

All the relations of the Maulana, as well as others who had seen him from close quarters (and this includes some persons of

---

2. Announcement dated 9 August 1899, *Majmu'a Ishtiharat,* vol. 3, p. 137, number 206.

3. Announcement dated 4 October 1899, *Majmu'a Ishtiharat,* vol. 3, p. 157–158, number 208.

independent view who observed him with a critical eye), were deeply impressed by his righteousness, high moral qualities and virtues. They held him in the highest esteem from the bottom of their hearts and admired him greatly.

By nature he observed moderation in all matters and hated going to the opposite extremes of too much or too little. Similarly, he greatly detested pomp, ostentation and show. He was simple in his nature and entirely untouched by arrogance or pride, so much so that he disliked wearing a turban with a high crest or sitting at a reserved place in a gathering. His dress was always very simple. He was in the habit of walking fast but never did he swagger. Humility and tolerance were an innate part of his nature, and he never imposed his authority upon others. Due to his kind behaviour everyone sought his pleasure and satisfaction. At home, he was revered and loved by everyone, including children and servants, and they all had confidence in his affection and love.

As his life was free of pretence and flattery, some superficial-minded people, particularly those who like embellishment and enjoy flattery, could misjudge his true nature. But his simplicity and disregard for ceremony usually won hearts at first sight. He would receive dignitaries in his simple everyday attire. If anyone requested to take his photograph, he asked him to take it as he was, without bothering to dress up for it or adopt some special pose for the photograph. He cared not for such frivolities.

Despite being absorbed in his literary engagements, he never showed any displeasure at the arrival of unexpected visitors. In our culture it is uncommon for people to make an appointment to see someone or inform of their coming in advance, and they call at the door whenever they so wish. A person who is involved in writing work can be distracted by the slightest interruption and lose his train of thought. But the Maulana's door was always open, whether for dignitaries or ordinary people, and he welcomed everyone with the same cheerfulness and politeness, listened to them attentively and helped them.

Maulana Muhammad Ali was not a dry religious ascetic. Despite his worship, spiritual exertions and mental efforts of day and night, shouldering great burdens and suffering problems, he was very convivial and affable. In earlier life he was very jovial and was in the habit of telling tasteful jokes and indulging in good humour. Though this diminished later on, he nonetheless retained his good spirits and pleasantness till the last. His cheerfulness and cultured wit and humour was most apparent when he was in the company of his friends. Usually before the congregational prayer, and after it, he would talk to people informally. With some friends he had specially interesting conversation. He used to speak to his friends' children with great love and cheeriness, their conversation showing the depth of his affection for them.

His medical attendants are witness to the fact that even during his long illnesses he never became irritable; on the contrary, he spoke to his visitors in an interesting and witty manner. Once in Lahore, in April 1951, when he was extremely weak after an attack of illness, Colonel Dr. Syed Bashir Husain, son of the late Dr. Syed Muhammad Husain Shah, came to visit him and, after placing his hand on his pulse for a while, said: "Pulse is now fine". The Maulana replied instantly: "You couldn't find my pulse, you are just saying it". The colonel enjoyed this joke about his medical skill, burst out laughing and kissed the Maulana's hand.

He excelled at hospitality and personally attended to the needs of his guests, taking care of their comfort. If his wife was busy he would supervise the making of beds for the guests and made sure that food and drinks were provided for them. Despite his other engagements he would see to the smallest of needs of the guests, and he extended this treatment equally to all, whether rich or poor. In the absence of a servant he would carry food and drink to the guests by his own hands. His wife relates that it so happened many times that guests arrived unexpectedly at meal times and there was not enough cooked food for everyone. He would have all the food sent out to the guests, while he himself would sit in the private rooms of the house and eat plain bread with chutney.

He was in the habit of going for long walks regularly and maintained this practice till the last years of his life. To walk almost three miles in the morning was an integral part of his life and the secret of his good physical health. When he was at hill resorts he walked the same distance in the evenings also. He walked so fast that it was difficult even for most young men to keep pace with him. Later on, when he was weakened by illness, he slowed down his speed. In his early life, he used to walk even 25 to 30 miles on foot when the need arose. When going from Batala to Qadian, if a horse cart was not available at night, it was nothing difficult for him to walk that distance of ten to twelve miles.

As father

Maulana Muhammad Ali was very concerned about his children's education and upbringing, and arranged for his sons as well as his daughters to receive higher education. He also took part, with his wife, in providing them with religious instruction and teaching. He used to teach Arabic and give instruction in the Holy Quran to his children as well as those daughters of Dr. Basharat Ahmad who were still minors. To the very young children, he used to relate the lives of the prophets and events from the life of the Holy Prophet Muhammad in story form at meal times. He urged that children after reaching the age of seven years must be got into the habit of saying prayers regularly. During their summer stays in hill resorts, congregational prayers were held at home, which he made the children join. In Lahore he instructed the children to go to the mosque to join the congregational prayers.

When his elder son Muhammad Ahmad, who had done M.A. in English and Arabic, took up his employment, the Maulana advised him as follows: "Avoid the false allurements of the material world, be regular in prayer, study the Holy Quran and take interest in religious knowledge so that you may at some time be able to serve the religion." This was his advice not only to his son but to every young man of the *Jama'at:* "By all means, earn your own livelihood in the world, but make your aim the service and propagation of Islam, never deviate from truth and honesty, increase your knowledge, and be a source of strength to Islam in one way or another". Maulana Muhammad Ali's earnest desire was always that his sons and daughters should be staunch Muslims and firm and true Ahmadis, and have the urge within their hearts to be of service to Islam.

He was fond of young children. He used to be amused by their childish antics and talked to them jovially. When he lived at Ahmadiyya Buildings his own children were very young. Other relatives used to visit, bringing their own children with them. All these children, playing together, would find their way to his office where the Maulana would be busy, his head bent over the writing desk. Hearing their footsteps he would raise his head and glance at them over his spectacles, smile and talk to them. He would ask them if they wanted anything. Sometimes the children wanted plain paper or ink or wanted to remove stamps from the envelopes in the waste paper basket. He would himself rise and get them what they wanted. He would never scold them or tell them to stop interrupting him. Nor did he ever ask the servants or the children's mothers not to let them come into his office.

So his children never felt that their father was some extra-ordinary, remote figure absorbed in writing monumental books and busy with various commitments. He shared all their joys and problems and took interest in their education and play. It made one wonder what a man he was, from whose mind and pen poured out an invaluable treasure of Islamic knowledge.

During their stay at hill resorts, his family would on occasion go for long walks. If it got dark they would find that he had sent someone after them with a light to help them return, or if it started to rain they would see someone coming to meet them with umb-rellas, whom he would have sent when he saw the gathering clouds. On the insistence of the children of the family, he would accompany them on a day's picnic, joining it with interest. For a long journey he personally arranged for horses or some other form of conveyance. He would always take some work with him and after spending some time enjoying the company of others, he would sit down separately to do his work. At prayer times he would ask a youngster or one of the children to call out the *Azan* and everyone, whether young or old, joined the prayers led by him.

As head of family

Maulana Muhammad Ali was a member of a very large family. All his siblings and those of his wife are Ahmadis, and so are almost all other relatives. He made each and every one of them feel special, each one feeling as if he were the one most loved by the Maulana. He treated rich and poor relations alike. All members of the family were devoted to him. Relatives, both near and distant, loved him and were convinced of his righteousness and kindness towards others. No one had ever seen him lose patience out of anger, shout and scream or make inappropriate or unbecoming remarks. In brief, he was a simply dressed, plain and simple, morally pure, humble, unassuming, smiling, and affectionate personality, who was like a protective shelter for the whole family. They were under the care of a guardian who shouldered all their worries. Whoever had any problems or difficulties would first go to him and he would willingly share their troubles. Never did he tell them that as he was engrossed in concern and worry about the state of the religion of God, they should not burden him with their worldly and personal problems. Everyone believed in the efficacy of his prayers and always turned to him at times of distress. He used to pray for them and help them as far as he was able. In fact, his personality was such that his kindness and attention itself lightened the burdens of others. As to his own sorrows and troubles, he kept them buried in the depths of his heart and never imposed upon others with them.

Love for relations

Throughout his life he provided financial help to a distant female relative of his first wife who was in need. Likewise, he had a relationship of the deepest love and perfect harmony with the family of his second wife. The affection between him and Dr. Basharat Ahmad needs no elaborating. In addition to the family ties between the two of them, the closeness of their religious views strengthened their relationship further. He had great affection for his wife's brother Naseer Ahmad Faruqui due to the latter's righteousness and passion for the propagation of Islam, and he loved him like one of his own children.

As elder of *Jama'at*

His affection and kindness was not reserved for his family only, but he also treated members of the *Jama'at* as his own brothers and children and shared their joys and sorrows. He respected and valued the rich and poor alike, but above all he honoured those people who had a zeal for the propagation of Islam as he did, and who made sacrifices for this cause. There was an Ahmadi named Chaudhry Rahim Bakhsh of Samana (Patiala State) who was very devout but poor and had to labour very hard to provide for his family. His financial sacrifices were so much that he contributed one fourth of his earnings as regular subscription and participated in every fund-raising campaign according to his means. Once at the annual gathering when Maulana Muhammad Ali made an appeal, Chaudhry Rahim Bakhsh as usual handed over all his meagre savings. Mentioning his name, the Maulana said: "Whenever I meet him, I embrace him very tightly, hoping that some of his spirituality may rub off on me".

In the same way he would often mention in his *khutbas* and writings those people who quietly and humbly served the religion, purely in the way of God, and did not seek any high worldly position or greatness. Most members were witness to the fact that the Maulana much appreciated and encouraged such persons for each of their small efforts. However, as the Maulana himself was straightforward, sincere and humble, those who wanted greatness for themselves, and who worked in order to achieve renown, had cause to complain about him.

He loved righteousness and sacrifice, and valued everyone who made progress in this path. He shunned ostentation and show, so he did not indulge in making a gratuitous display of love by clasping children and youngsters to his bosom and embracing them fervently, or other such gimmicks. Like his nature, his love was also sound and solid, and he did not make a shallow display of it but remembered everyone in his *tahajjud* prayers. Another aspect of his love for the *Jama'at* is evident from the fact that he never hesitated to provide references and letters of recommendation on behalf of the poor and needy who were genuinely deservant of them. Besides the impression made by his personality, his recommendations were written with such true sympathy and deep interest that the needy person usually succeeded in achieving his goal.

To sum up, he was a spiritual guide for the *Jama'at* and at the same time a leader concerned about the material welfare of his community. This was the reason why members of the *Jama'at,* except a few, were so deeply devoted to him and why they missed him so much after his death.

One of his great virtues was that he never spoke ill of people behind their backs. There were certain people who caused him a great amount of distress and vexation for a long time, but his close friends have again and again testified that they never heard him speaking ill of such people behind their backs. He would not even mention such matters, and if anyone else raised them, saying that such and such a man had not done good, the Maulana would dismiss it with a smile. If someone caused him excessive distress he would only say: "God knows when my punishment is going to end". When a certain person continued his hurtful behaviour, he said: "He has a strange bent of mind". There was a man about whom the Maulana had a very favourable opinion. He wrote such terribly hurtful letters to the Maulana, again and again, that it cannot be imagined how much pained it caused him. However, the Maulana just said: "Only God knows what he wants from me".

In the meetings of the Anjuman all members could express their views with complete freedom, and some members in the heat of the moment would say something inappropriate, while some would make baseless objections against him. But his great quality was that no matter how hurtful the comments that he had listened to or had read, he would not only never mention it in front of others but behave as if nothing at all had hurt him. He would come home and talk in the same smiling way and take interest in what the women and the children of the house had to say. These are the high moral qualities, adherence to which, throughout one's life, is only possible for the truly godly men.

Strict observance of time schedule and punctuality

Most people used to wonder how, with his multifarious engagements and deep involvement in literary activities, Maulana Muhammad Ali found time to fulfil his worldly and religious duties so well and capably, and how, despite his administrative and management responsibilities and problems, he was able to leave behind such a valuable treasure of literature. The secret was his strict observance of his time schedule and boundless energy for doing work. He never wasted a single minute of the day or night and every task was performed at its appointed time. He was used to sleeping very little and would rise at about 2 a.m. for his *tahajjud* prayers. Usually he had a bath daily. After *fajr* prayer he would go for a long morning walk, and upon his return he would have breakfast. Then, after reading the newspaper for a short while, he would start work in his office, and work continuously till the call was sounded for the *zuhr* prayer. In the later part of his life, after the morning walk and breakfast he would rest for 15 to 20 minutes before starting work. After lunch he would go to the mosque for prayer. Then he would rest for an hour or an hour and a half. Usually at about 3.30 p.m. he would go back to his office. He used to have a cup of tea at the time of the *asr* prayer. In Dalhousie he also went for an evening walk of some two to two and a half miles but in Lahore he only went for the morning walk. Usually people visited him in the evening. After the *maghrib* prayer he used to spend time in the house with the children and have his dinner early. After the *isha* prayer he used to go to bed soon but if he was involved in some important literary activity or other necessary work then he would work at night as well. God blessed his time so much that all the work he did was done to a very high standard.

In his younger days he did not sleep for more than four hours at night. In the winter nights he would also do his writing work before *tahajjud,* from 1 a.m. to about 2.30 a.m., and sometimes after the *isha* prayer. However, in the last three or four years of his life, due to weak health, he had given up working at night at the insistence of the doctors.

In Lahore till 1930 he used to be busy with teaching Quran study classes after the *asr* and *maghrib* prayers. In Dalhousie in the summer, he devoted some time every afternoon to teaching children Arabic and the Holy Quran.

Stamina for work
In addition to time-keeping, his other particular quality was his tremendous stamina for work. Those who have worked with him know how much stamina he had. The young would get tired but

there would be no sign of fatigue in him whatsoever, the main reason for which was his deep interest in his work which he enjoyed doing with full concentration and total attention. Usually he worked at set times, but when he was involved in some important writing he would be so engrossed in his work, devoting so much energy to it, that he would neglect his health. Once when he was in Abbottabad, working on the English translation of the Quran for the first time, he would sit at the desk after the *fajr* prayer and continue without break till the *zuhr* prayer. One day when he got up for *zuhr* prayer, he fainted and fell in the doorway. Dr. Mirza Yaqub Baig and Dr. Basharat Ahmad were also present. They and all others advised him not to work so hard as to put his life in danger, but he paid no particular heed to such advice and never reduced his workload.

The habit of working hard remained with him from his young days till the end. Except in serious illness, he did not care to let minor ailments stop him. Even during serious illnesses, if he felt a little better, he would work lying in bed. In his Friday *Khutba,* on 21 July 1944, mentioning his doing of work, he referred to the writing of Hazrat Mirza Ghulam Ahmad in which he had said:

> "My daily rest is to be busy in my work. In fact, I cannot live without doing the work of revealing the glory of God and of His Prophet and of His Book. I do not care if I am called *kafir*. I perceive the hidden Divine hand helping me. Although, like other human beings, I am a weak mortal but I can see that I get strength from an invisible source."

Then the Promised Messiah added: "I hope God will not let my prayers go to waste".

Mentioning this writing, Maulana Muhammad Ali said:

> "This was written in 1891. These were the objectives of this man of God at the time when the fire of opposition was raging all around him. ... Look at that impregnable fort of faith in God, that when surrounded by fire he is saying that God will fulfil all his aims and hopes. He died in 1908, and though the foundation for the propagation of

Islam in the West had been laid during his lifetime in the form of the journal *Review of Religions*, but the objective of spreading the Holy Quran in English, which had been put in his heart by God, had not yet materialised. Immediately after his death, Allah the Most High put it in the heart of Maulana Nur-ud-Din that the Holy Quran must be translated into English. He and the Anjuman, which was the successor to the Promised Messiah, entrusted this responsibility to a weak person like me. The same hidden Divine hand that the Promised Messiah saw helping him during his life, after his death became my helper in this magnificent task. At that time I was young, lacking in knowledge, but I could see that 'I was getting strength from an invisible hand'. That strength was, in fact, not for me but for that chosen man of God in whose heart this passion first arose, but as I became the instrument to fulfil that aspiration the same Divine hand came to my aid. From that time onwards till today I see that, despite reaching the age of seventy from that young age and being a victim of many illnesses and frailty, whenever I have embarked upon a religious service, a new vigour has been infused in me. I used to take much exercise, walked long distances, and walked very fast. I could walk twenty-five to thirty miles in a day without getting tired. But now if I walk even two miles or so I get exhausted. My body has weakened but whenever I take in hand any work of serving the Quran, instead of getting tired a fresh wave of energy runs through my body. In reality, in the past too it was not my strength but the help of the hidden hand of Allah, and today also it is the help of that hand by which I am enabled to do this work."

(*Paigham Sulh,* 16 August 1944)

It was due to his love for his work and this strength from the invisible source that despite his old age, weakness and various illnesses he continued to work in the same way as he did in his youth. At the age of 72 years he embarked upon the great task of revising the English translation of the Holy Quran and during that time he became seriously ill in Quetta but as soon as his health improved he busied himself in his work as before. If he was advised to rest he would reply that his work was nourishment for his soul, or sometimes he would say that he had very little time left and there was much to be done. In 1950 in Karachi he had a serious heart attack and was bedridden for a time but he did not give up work or his worship. In December, as his health improved, he came back to Lahore and started working regularly in his office. During the next two periods of his illness he continued proof reading the Holy Quran in bed and dictating letters to members of the *Jama'at,* till the work was completed.

Administrative skills

On the one hand he was an embodiment of knowledge and scholarship and a fountain of spiritual verities and blessings, and on the other hand he had perfect skill for administrative affairs. Usually it is observed that while the learned and scholarly are good at writing they have no aptitude for administration nor any interest in it. He was, however, not only the Head of the *Jama'at* but as President of the organisation Allah had bestowed upon him the skills for administrative, office and organisational work. Firstly, he himself worked whole-heartedly, to the full, and he expected the same of those whom he managed. He could not be pleased by empty gestures or superficial actions. Secondly, he was cognisant of the smallest details of all aspects of the Anjuman's office work, knowing every matter fully. The English term *thorough going* can, to some extent, describe this ability of his. Besides a good head for management, God had also endowed him with the analytical ability to penetrate to the heart of any matter.

Style of speech and writing

Some people may think that this leader of the Ahmadiyya *Jama'at* would have caused a great commotion on the stage with his oratory, but his nature was far removed from rousing the audience in this way. He never used flowery language or dramatic bodily gestures in speeches. Before starting his Friday *khutbas* or speeches, he would usually have his hands behind his back. He used to begin speaking in a low voice that gradually increased in volume. His simple but effective words along with solid arguments captured the attention of the audience and penetrated their hearts.

God the Most High had placed such special effect in his simple speeches that is not found in other speakers with their bombastic words and dramatic gestures.

Like his speeches, there was simplicity in his writings as well. Whether in English or Urdu, his writings were free of exaggeration and verbosity, and were effective and meaningful, which appealed in particular to readership in the West. This aspect of his style of writing has been admired by many impartial readers. The treasure of literature he left behind has been appreciated and valued by the world and the popularity it enjoyed in all corners of the world is now a historical fact. Dr. Shaikh Muhammad Abdullah, one of the best and most capable missionaries of the Ahmadiyya Anjuman Isha'at Islam Lahore, who carried out very successful work of the propagation of Islam for nearly 25 years in both the U.K. and Germany, and died in Woking, England, wrote the following about the books of Maulana Muhammad Ali:

> "We are now realising the value and worth of the religious knowledge that the Hazrat Maulana has left behind. Usually it seems, with the passage of time, the writings of even great authors lose their appeal and become out of date but the knowledge produced by the Hazrat Maulana is so unequalled and magnificent that its value is increasing day by day. And this is rightly so, because after all it was the *Sultan-ul-Qalam* ['Master of the Pen', the Promised Messiah] who granted him his own pen. I have been propagating Islam in Europe for twenty years, and very often I am amazed to read the late Maulana's books, as to how a man who had not even been to Europe, the centre of Christianity, has produced so much material for our propagation work. There is no subject on which he has not written, no issue on which he has not shed light and resolved it on the basis of the Quran and Hadith.
>
> His books contain not only a treasure of invaluable knowledge whose scholarly standard is so high that its equal can rarely be found, but by studying it one gains spiritual solace and nourishment. The Hazrat Maulana was not an ordinary scholar but was like a spiritual doctor.

His excellent writings not only showed the right path to non-Muslims, but also Muslims themselves were saved from heresy and deviation and became missionaries of Islam." (*Paigham Sulh,* 15 October 1952, p. 14)

Worship

Maulana Muhammad Ali concentrated profoundly, to the highest degree, when saying his prayers. He gave importance to saying prayers in congregation, of course, but his practice of saying the *tahajjud* prayer, a habit acquired in his youth, was so firm that he did not miss this prayer for the rest of his life. Whether he was travelling or ill, he said his *tahajjud* prayer without fail and always exhorted the *Jama'at* in forceful, passionate words to adhere to this prayer. Even during illness he would wake up at *tahajjud* time and if he could not rise out of bed he would say his prayer sitting or lying in bed. In 1950, when he suffered the most serious heart attacks and the doctors declared it as absolutely essential for him to sleep as much as possible, he still would wake up for the *tahajjud* prayer. In severe pain the doctors had to give him injections to sedate him but even then he would be awake at the time of the *tahajjud* prayer despite the effects of the injection. A Christian nurse who was attending him in those days remarked that he must be a "saint" to worship so much on his sick bed.

His children, near relations staying with him, and travelling companions were all witnesses to the fact that in the later part of the night, in seclusion, he would be falling before God the Most High in prayer. Whenever anyone woke, he or she would hear a melodious, wonderful sound of heart-felt crying and supplicating, which included glorification, praise and sanctification of the Almighty. God alone knows if at that time he was in this world or in another world, but his voice was like that of one who is cut off from this world and all its trappings, and was elsewhere, having lost himself in the Divine Being, and expressing before Him the pain and concern in his heart.[4] This was a picture of what the

---

4. Once a lady guest of Maulana Muhammad Ali's wife, belonging to a family who were well known for their hostility to the Ahmadiyya Movement, stayed for one night in their house when they lived in Ahmadiyya Buildings.

Promised Messiah had expressed in a poetic verse as follows:

> "At this time of affliction [for Islam], we the helpless
> have no remedy,
>
> But to pray in the morning and cry before dawn."

Revelations and communications from God

Maulana Muhammad Ali used to receive Divine revelations and visions but never publicised these. Even to his family he would not mention that he had such experiences, and this was due to his utmost humility. Mr. Naseer Ahmad Faruqui states that he had been in his company for years and was entirely convinced that he was a saint but had never found out whether he had any revelations. At last in 1943 in Bombay he once plucked up the courage and asked him. The Maulana simply smiled and only nodded his head in confirmation. Then Mr. Faruqui asked how he felt at that time. The Maulana replied that he felt as if a great force had taken hold of him and words came upon his tongue involuntarily. Some of his visions and revelations have already been mentioned in this book, and there are some more in Mr. Naseer Ahmad Faruqui's article at the end of this book. The Maulana had written some of his revelations and dreams in a note book which was found after his death. Some extracts from it have also been published.

Before leaving she disclosed to the Maulana's wife that she had stayed there purposely in order to know the real truth, at home, about Maulana Muhammad Ali's reputation for religious observance. She had stood outside the room where he had just started saying his *tahajjud* prayers and observed him through the slightly open door. She related: "He was reciting the Holy Quran with utter humility. I could hear some echo of his voice. He stood for so long that I got tired. At long last he went into *ruku* and was in that posture for a considerable time. Then he went into *sajda* and spent an equally long time in that position. I could not stand any longer, and I found a stool and sat on it. He raised his head from *sajda* at long last and then went into the second *sajda* for a long time. As he had taken more than half an hour in the first *rak'a* of the prayer, I could not wait any further and went back to bed. Some time later I again went to have a look, and saw him still at prayer. Many hours later, when the call for the *fajr* prayer was sounded, he went to the mosque. I am now sure that he is not an ordinary man but a saint of God. I came here with many doubts and ill-feelings [about Ahmadis], but I am leaving after being deeply convinced of his righteousness and greatness."

Love for the Holy Quran

The most prominent and outstanding feature of the life of Maulana Muhammad Ali was his passion for the Quran, which he had inherited from the Promised Messiah and Maulana Nur-ud-Din. The deep desire to spread the Quran in the world kept him restless all the time. In every *khutba* he stressed upon the need to serve the Quran. Behind every campaign and proposal the aim was propagation of the Quran. Whether travelling or staying, whether in good health or ill, he would continue to serve the Quran under all circumstances. God the Most High, by granting his translations and commentaries of the Quran and his other books world-wide acclaim, showed that He values His sincere servants. He used to receive letters from Muslims and non-Muslims from all over the world, saying that they had found the right path after reading his translation of the Quran or some other book. He used to receive requests from abroad asking for his permission to translate his books into other languages and he always granted it happily. Ambassadors of foreign countries and other international visitors used to call on him, some of them kissing his hands out of admiration. Despite open antagonism against the Ahmadiyya Movement in India and Pakistan, many notable dignitaries were among his admirers and they praised him highly, including government ministers and leaders, high ranking officials, businessmen, politicians and religious leaders.

In short, his name had acquired international fame within his own lifetime and his incomparable services to Islam were acknowledged even by his opponents. However, so modest and humble was he that he never exhibited pride or arrogance, nor did he ever make a show of greatness by boasting that high government officials called upon him and acknowledged his services. If he mentioned this, it was by way of rendering thanks to God for this honour, and he always ascribed his work and achievements to the Promised Messiah and the *Jama'at.*

This venerable man saw success with his own eyes but always bowed his head before God in humility. All the time, and under all circumstances, he had but one passion: that somehow the message of the Quran and of Islam must reach every corner of the world.

Today everyone, friend or foe, acknowledges that his life remained dedicated to the cause of Islam and he departed from this world a successful man.

The following was one of Maulana Muhammad Ali's most loved prayers which he always used to say after reciting the *darood* (the *salat-un-nabi*):

> "O Allah! Help him who helps the religion of Muhammad, may peace and the blessings of Allah be upon him, and make us from among such people. O Allah! forsake him who forsakes the religion of Muhammad, may peace and the blessings of Allah be upon him, and make us not from among such people."

Maulana Muhammad Ali delivering khutba in Karachi close to the year 1950.

4.2: Personal Reflections[1]

Impressions and memories of Maulana Muhammad Ali by some of
the scholars, missionaries, workers and other leading figures of the
Lahore Ahmadiyya *Jama'at,* who knew him closely and worked
with him have been collected below.

1. Maulana Abdul Haq Vidyarthi:

"It was from the late Hazrat Maulana that I acquired my interest in the propagation of Islam and the Holy Quran. Although
I had very little opportunity to study from him directly, but mere
encouragement from a teacher suffices for life. And he was a
teacher who had inherited in full measure from the Promised
Messiah the qualities of humility, and respect and appreciation of
friends, as well as the passion to serve Islam. Twice I had occasion to spend summer with him at a hill resort: once in Simla and
once in Dalhousie. People go to hill resorts to enjoy life but what
made the deepest impression upon me was his zeal to serve Islam
and the sound of his fast moving pen with the ticking of the clock.
He would start work punctually and carry on writing and writing.
In those days in Simla he wrote *Sirat Khair-ul-Bashar* and had it
calligraphed for printing. My duty, in addition to other tasks, was
proof-reading with the Maulana. It usually happened that, when
after working all day long we young ones were tired and felt like
going for a pleasant walk in the mountains, we would hear him
call out: Come and let us read the proofs. So untiring was he that,

---

1. In this chapter in the Urdu book *Mujahid-i Kabir* most of the tributes
are taken from articles published in *Paigham Sulh,* special issue, 26 December 1951. For this translation we have added some further tributes from that
issue as well as expanding some of the existing ones. All extracts in this
chapter are taken from that issue, except where indicated otherwise.

459

while we young people would give up, he knew not the meaning of fatigue.

The other thing which made an impression on me was that at that time, while I myself was learning, I also used to teach the Quran to someone. Hazrat Amir [Maulana Muhammad Ali] must have been able to hear me in his room. One day he said to me: 'Your explanation of the Quran is very good and reasonable'. His comments were, I believe, meant to encourage me. A person who is an expert in some field tries to create the same talent in others. On a later occasion too in Muslim Town, he said to me most insistently that I should write my explanations of the Holy Quran, and he further commented that they would be more popular than my book *Muhammad in World Scriptures.* He also offered to get them published.

The second time I went to the hills with him was when I was not in good health. He took me with him to Dalhousie and there he gave me special instructions about my diet. On many occasions he would bring foodstuff to my room and stress that I eat it as it was good for health. My mail came via his address, but never did he call me to come and collect it. He would bring it to me downstairs to my room, saying 'this letter is for you'. This is how he treated his assistants. Even now recalling those days brings tears to my eyes.

Let me also mention something else. In the meetings of the Anjuman, of which I too was a member, every member had freedom of speech. It was not like the subservient court of the *Khalifa* of Qadian. Objections used to be raised and some members would argue with Hazrat Amir and occasionally say something inappropriate. After the meetings, he used to return home to Muslim Town, where I and some other friends met him for prayers in the Muslim Town mosque. He would never mention what happened in the meeting, while it is quite natural for a person who is hurt to talk to others about it. If we ever broached the subject, saying that so and so had acted badly, he would only smile and evade the subject, putting an end to the matter.

I remember there was a time when, in reply to the late Maulana Shibli, a magazine entitled *Al-Nazir* used to be published from Lucknow containing articles against religion and in support of agnosticism. Its objections against the existence of God appeared to be very strong. I presented them to many great *Ulama* but none could give satisfactory replies. There must have been many people who were misguided by those articles. If memory serves me right, they were written by Maulana Abdul Majid Daryabadi who, in those days, used to mock and ridicule God and religion. As he admits, he was agnostic. I would say that he was made agnostic by the translations and commentaries of the Quran which were then commonly studied, and he in turn made other people agnostic. Now the same Maulana Abdul Majid Daryabadi is a translator and preacher of the Quran and lover of Islam. What was this due to? He has himself testified that this change in him was due to the English translation of the Quran by Maulana Muhammad Ali.

The *Masnawi* of Rumi is known as 'the Quran in the Pahlavi language'. Maulana Abdul Majid Salik, former editor of *Inqilab,* himself relates that once Maulana Muhammad Ali asked him for a review of his English translation of the Quran and he replied: If the Holy Quran had been revealed in English, it would have been the translation of Muhammad Ali."

2. Dr. Saeed Ahmad Khan

Dr. Saeed Ahmad Khan[2] was in Stockholm, Sweden, when Maulana Muhammad Ali died. He wrote as follows in an article:

"Such people are rarely born who, when they die, leave a vacuum that cannot be filled, and the shock of their death is felt far and wide. A minor incident made me realise it. In Stockholm there is a very learned Swedish colonel who had read Hazrat Amir's books. When I told him about his death, he was holding something in his hand which he was about to eat. It dropped from his hand and he seemed stunned. His face revealed his inner feelings. Then he rose up and quickly brought an issue of *The Islamic Review* which contained the Maulana's photograph, and talked

2. Dr. Saeed Ahmad Khan was later the third Head of the Ahmadiyya Anjuman Lahore, after Maulana Sadr-ud-Din, from 1981 to 1996.

about him for a long time. There are thousands of such people in the world who share our sorrow.

I was a student in school in Qadian at the age of 13 or 14. I remember that a man, who was a model of humility, used to come to the Nur mosque quietly at times of prayer, say his prayers with full concentration and humility, and leave quietly. Then when the annual gathering came, I heard this quiet man make a speech, appealing to the community for contributions. His words had such power and grandeur, and the gathering listened to him with love and humility, and responded to his appeal. In later years I witnessed such scenes many times but that first time has left a special mark upon me.

On the death of Hazrat Maulana Nur-ud-Din, I had occasion to see with my own eyes in Qadian the strength of faith of this man. The step that he took at that time, along with a handful of his companions who were also men of faith, marks an important juncture in the history of Islam.

From 1915 to 1917 when he came to Abbottabad during the summers, I had much opportunity to see him close at hand. As a result, my devotion to him increased gradually into a love that continued ever to become stronger, never diminishing. Later, when I was a student in Lahore, I often used to go and see him. However, I soon realised that his time was extremely valuable, and wasting it was harmful to the whole Movement. So I exercised restraint, and I noticed that he appreciated it.

During my days as student, I became ill and was on long leave, staying on a hill in my part of the country. Hazrat Amir used to write to me regularly and his letters and prayers gave me much comfort. Once he wrote to me, saying that a certain type of injection, administered to a friend by the civil surgeon of Dalhousie, had greatly helped that patient and he recommended that I should also take those injections. After a few days Dr. Mirza Yaqub Baig sent me a box of those injections by post from Lahore. I wrote him a letter of thanks but he replied saying that I should thank Hazrat Amir because it was he who had asked him to send the injections and had paid for them as well. Such incidents leave a permanent mark on one's heart.

It so happened during 1922–23 that in the hostel of the Medical College, Lahore, there arose a dispute with Hindu students regarding the calling out of the *azan* which a Muslim student used to do. The English principal ordered the *azan* to be stopped. The Muslim students who used to call out the *azan* were inclined to accept this order. I advised them to seek the opinion of Maulana Muhammad Ali on the religious aspect of this question. So some of us students met him in the mosque after *maghrib* prayers and asked for his advice. He told us very firmly that the *azan* could not be stopped and no Muslim could accept an order to stop calling out the *azan*. If you people, he said, show weakness in such a minor matter, what can Islam expect from you? He inspired confidence in us and promised to help us in every way. This made a deep impression on the Muslim students. When we showed firmness we won, and regular *azan* and prayers were instituted in the hostel. It is, in fact, such incidents that make a man's character.

I also had occasion to stay at the house of Maulana Muhammad Ali as his guest. The first time it was at his insistence, but when I saw that this gave me a rare opportunity to benefit from his company, I could not help wanting to stay with him. So on a later occasion I myself requested him that, while in Lahore, I could not bear to be away from him. A guest has an ideal chance to study the life and ways of the host. By my study of him, I found him to be a unique person. His life at home was informal but highly organised. It seemed as if every moment of his life was devoted to a particular purpose. For every task there was an appointed time, and every moment was meant for a particular task.

Once in the Muslim Town mosque at the *fajr* prayer he got hold of me with both hands and took me forcibly to the imam's position to lead the prayer.[3] I was very much embarrassed but could not excuse myself from his order. After the prayer, on our way back home, accompanied by some other friends, the talk turned to recital of the Quran. He related that Maulvi Abdul Karim

---

3. Dr. Saeed Ahmad Khan used to recite the Holy Quran in a beautifully appealing and captivating voice.

used to recite the Quran beautifully. In Qadian [during the time of the Promised Messiah] when he used to lead the morning prayer, an old woman who lived near the mosque used to go to the roof of her house to listen to his recitation. When Maulvi Abdul Karim died and Hazrat Maulana Nur-ud-Din began to lead the prayers, that woman complained about the recitation of the new imam, saying: "He just does it wrongly". After narrating this incident the Maulana laughed heartily and said about himself: "I also 'just do it wrongly' ". Whenever he heard humorous talk from friends he would burst out laughing, but I never heard him speaking ill of anyone, backbiting, carping, being hypocritical or conspiring. If ever there was mention of his opponents, he took their names with respect and honour, as befits a God-fearing believer of the highest order.

Once, when I was ill, I requested him to pray for me. He wrote back saying: "Praying for your health is something I do regularly everyday". Once he told me that while praying for me during prostration he spontaneously uttered the words: "O Allah, grant health to my son Saeed". I said to him: "I had always thought of myself to be your son, so now I am happy that Allah has confirmed it by revelation". I consider his tremendous love for me to be a most precious treasure of my life.

Last year [1950] I was going abroad from Pakistan in the middle of September. After I arrived at Karachi airport, a short while later Maulana Muhammad Ali came along with Mr. Naseer Ahmad Faruqui. They stayed with me for two hours. He talked about the Holy Quran and Islam, and asked me to bring for him from Makkah a copy of the Quran that had been recently printed there, the first time that the Quran had been printed there.

This year [1951] I had to leave Pakistan to go to Europe at the same time of the year. When I met him in Karachi he was recovering from his second attack of illness. I could not think, nor could I accept, that this would be our last meeting. I went to say farewell to him on 13 September before noon. He was seated in a chair, reading some letters. After some talk, he asked me to take with me one set of books and present it to a library. He also asked me to send him addresses of other suitable libraries, and he would arrange to send sets of books to them as well. His conversation reflected his heart-felt urge and the sole purpose of his life, namely, that translations of the Holy Quran and the message of Islam must reach the ends of the earth as soon as possible. I felt that even in that poor state of health the only concern and anxiety dominating his mind was that this work may be left unfinished. When I took my leave, I tried to persuade him not to stand up, but he rose to his feet and said: "This may be our last meeting. How can I say goodbye sitting down?" He then embraced me. It did in fact prove to be our last meeting, as exactly one month later he left us all."

3. Maulana Murtaza Khan Hasan:

"He [Maulana Muhammad Ali] was very mindful of the duty of visiting sick people. He would sit with them for a long time enquiring about their well-being and give them advice about treatment. During my illness and that of my children he visited us many times. There was no formality about these visits. He would leave his residence informally attired in shirt and trousers and come and knock on our door. On one such occasion, when he knocked on the door, I called out from inside the house: "Who is it?" He simply replied: "It's me, Muhammad Ali". This reminds me of an incident of the Promised Messiah. Once at night he went to the room of Maulana Syed Muhammad Ahsan and knocked at the door. When the Maulana asked who it was, the Promised Messiah simply replied: "It's me, Ghulam Ahmad". So the disciple and his mentor had the same nature.

Once there was a burglary at my house and someone informed him. He immediately wrote a letter of sympathy, but I could not answer it promptly. So he wrote again, asking me for details of the loss. He showed such sympathy as if it were his own loss. This sympathy was not confined to words only, and he also provided practical help.

Great men face much opposition. On various occasions some people opposed him but it was his virtue that he would never say anything about his opponents behind their backs. I worked with him for many years, and accompanied him on his travels, but

I never found him trying to question people in order to extract information about others.

He always appreciated every little thing I did. When he gave advice, it was in a wonderfully affectionate way. Once in the Anjuman's office I was given proofs of one of his books to give to him when I returned home to Muslim Town. I put them in my pocket and forgot all about them. Three days thus passed. When he enquired from the office why they had not sent him the proofs, they replied that the proofs were given to Murtaza Khan two or three days ago to take to him. When I met him he smiled and said: 'I have heard a report that you have the proofs. Is it true?' I was so regretful and told him that it was perfectly true. The proofs were in my pocket, so I handed them to him instantly. He said: 'What's the need for such a hurry?' and then laughed heartily.

Once he expressed his pleasure at one of my poems and said: You are both an excellent writer of articles and a good poet as well. I used to write articles for children in the paper [*Paigham Sulh*], which he always admired greatly and used to say that the *Jama'at* should be urged to make sure that children read these articles."

4. Dr. S.M. Abdullah:[4]

"For the first time I came in contact with the late Maulana Muhammad Ali in or about the year 1914 at Lyallpur [now Faisalabad, Pakistan] when I was a boy of about 16 years and he came to deliver a lecture there. I remember very well the title of the subject on which he addressed the audience in Lyallpur, that is 'The Beauties of Islam'. This talk of his impressed me very much and infused in me the zeal for further religious knowledge. Later on I came in constant touch with him during my stay in Lahore as a student at the Punjab University. During my six years stay in Lahore, that is, from the year 1915 to the year 1921, I often used

---

4. Dr. Shaikh Muhammad Abdullah was the Anjuman's Imam and missionary at the Berlin Mosque, Germany, from 1928 to 1939, and at the Mosque in Woking, England, after the war till his death in 1956. This article by him in English was published in *The Light,* 1 January 1952.

to go to the Ahmadiyya Buildings for Friday prayers and heard the learned and soul inspiring sermons of the late Maulana — may his soul rest in peace.

It was during this period that I was attracted to the Ahmadiyya Movement more and more and started reading the original writings of Hazrat Mirza Ghulam Ahmad, the reformer of the 14th century Hijra. In the year 1919 I finally decided to join the Ahmadiyya Movement at the hands of Maulana Muhammad Ali and since then have been more or less in close contact with him. In the year 1921 I visited him in Simla and stayed with him for a week or so, during which I had an opportunity of studying him from closer quarters. His zeal and devotion for the cause of Islam impressed me very much. In the year 1922 I resigned from a Government post and came to Lahore in order to learn more from this great leader and teacher. During the summer recess of the year 1923, when I was a professor at the Islamia College, Lahore, I had the good fortune of spending some two months in his company at Dalhousie and learnt a lot from this great savant and man of learning. I remember very well my attending his learned discourses in the Quran during the month of Ramadan in the year 1924, which added a great deal to my knowledge of the Quran and Hadith.

He was extremely devotional, and especially particular about his late night prayers. I remember that once he travelled from Lahore to Jammu and reached the place very late, and as there were many persons very anxiously and eagerly waiting to see him, some talk continued right up to midnight. In spite of the fatigue of the journey he got up at about 3 o'Clock as it had been his habit for this late night prayer, which showed his devotion and love of prayer. During all these meetings I was infused with a true Islamic spirit which gradually made me drift towards dedicating my life to the service of Islam.

The late Maulana Muhammad Ali led a life of hardship and austerity. He was industrious to the point of endangering his health. He was very regular and methodical in all his habits and works. His unique work and the wonderful literature produced by him will keep his name ever green and infuse a true spirit in the minds of many, who I am sure will devote time and energy for the service of Islam. He wielded his pen for full 50 years and wrote thousands of pages full of Islamic pearls and thereby disseminated the true knowledge of Islam to all the four corners of the world. He was honoured by his admirers by the epithet 'King of the Pen', which title he fully justified by his numerous writings and valuable books on Islam.

Intelligence and hard work very seldom go together but the late Maulana Muhammad Ali was blessed with both. Work to him was his food and as one cannot live without food so he could not live without work. Even during his fatal disease when the doctors insisted upon his abstinence from work he continued the same. He derived all his energy and inspiration from his prayers. The secret of his work, nay, his success, has been due to his sincere regular devotion to prayers, especially the late night prayer which he never missed. May his soul rest in peace."

5. Maulvi Ismatullah

Maulvi Ismatullah related that once he was travelling by train to U.P. (India) with Maulana Muhammad Ali. The second class compartment was too crowded, so when, in the later part of the night, the train stopped at a main station for a long period, Maulana Muhammad Ali disembarked, performed *wudu* at a water tap on the platform, spread his prayer mat on one side and became engrossed in saying his *tahajjud* prayer. He was so absorbed in his prayer that when it was time for the train to depart he was still in prostration. The train whistled and started to crawl. Maulvi Ismatullah was now in a panic, wondering whether to pull the emergency chain to stop the train or not. Suddenly the train halted after a short distance, with loud noises of steam escaping from the engine. Later it was discovered that this was due to bursting of the water gauge. So the train had to wait at the station for quite a long time. In the meantime the Hazrat Maulana finished his prayer and returned to his compartment. Maulvi Ismatullah used to say that people may consider it a stroke of luck that this accident happened by coincidence just at the right moment, but he maintained that God the Most High did not want His beloved servant, who was attending His court, to miss the train and be inconvenienced. This is a matter of one's own perception.

6. Shaikh Muhammad Yusuf Garanthi

In an article about his visit to Mangrol with Maulana Muhammad Ali, he writes:

"It was in 1929 that the Nawab of Mangrol, the late Shaikh Jehangir Mian sahib, wrote to the late Hazrat Amir [Maulana Muhammad Ali] expressing his deep desire to meet him. He was going to Delhi and hoped that the Maulana could come there to meet him. However, the Hazrat Maulana could not go to Delhi while the Nawab was there, and after returning to Mangrol the Nawab again wrote to him, saying that he was greatly desirous of meeting him and the only way was if the Maulana visited Mangrol. Upon this the Hazrat Amir undertook a visit to Mangrol, accompanied by Maulana Sadr-ud-Din, Maulana Ismatullah and myself. ... When we reached the residence of the Nawab he was holding four garlands, and after greeting us, every one of us was made to wear one garland. Then we were taken into the court of the Nawab where every courtier was holding four garlands which they put one on every one of us ...

At night we all went to sleep, each in his own bedroom. As the next day we were to keep fast, there came noise from the servants after midnight as they prepared the meal to be taken before dawn. This noise woke me and I went to Hazrat Amir's room. He was not in his bed. I waited and when he did not come back, I looked for him. He was not in the toilet, not in the bathroom, and the servants did not know where he was. I was standing worried in the hall when I noticed a light coming from the small room at the end of the hall. I peeped through the door and saw him standing praying. There was a high table in front of him, upon which a copy of the Holy Quran was lying open, and he was reading from it. His back was towards me. After a short while he turned the page over and continued reading for a long time and then he stepped back and went in *ruku* and then prostrated for a long time. He got up again, went near the table and started to read the Quran. I said to myself that at least one issue is resolved.[5]

---

5. The "issue resolved" would be whether it is permissible for a person to read from a copy of the Holy Quran during his optional, private prayers.

The next day the Nawab and his heir the late Abdul Khaliq came to meet us and presented some funds, saying: This is a donation for the Anjuman. ... On the last day [after five days' stay] when we were leaving, the Nawab along with his heir and courtiers came to bid us farewell. The Nawab presented to Hazrat Maulana, on a round glass plate covered with a handkerchief, some cash and said: This is for you. This was meant as a personal gift.

On our return Maulvi Ismatullah and I broke journey to visit Ajmer for a day and decided to meet up with the Hazrat Maulana in Sanbhar. When we were leaving the train at Ajmer I borrowed ten Rupees from the Maulana to keep during my journey. When we returned to Lahore I received a note from the Anjuman to return the ten Rupees that I had borrowed into the Anjuman's funds so that a receipt for all the money could be sent to the Nawab. When I went to the Anjuman's office to return the ten Rupees I discovered that the Hazrat Maulana had given the entire sum of the one thousand Rupees, presented to him as a personal gift by the Nawab, to the Anjuman. He had paid the fare of his journey himself, and the personal gift that he received he gave to the Anjuman.

The second time that Hazrat Amir went to Mangrol, I was the only one who accompanied him, apart from a personal servant of his. On this occasion the Nawab gave me some money as a personal gift. Following Hazrat Amir's example, on my return to Lahore I deposited it in the Anjuman's account. When the Maulana came to know of it he had that money repaid to me. This shows that whereas he was Anjuman's well-wisher, he was sympathetic towards its employees as well."

7. Shaikh Muhammad Inam-ul-Haq

He arranged Maulana Muhammad Ali's two visits to Hyderabad Deccan and describes some of his observations during these trips:

"Because of his multifarious responsibilities in the management of the Movement, and being busy with the work of writing and authorship, the late Hazrat Amir did not often have the opportunity to go on trips. He was never able to go outside the Indian subcontinent, and even within the subcontinent he was rarely able to undertake long journeys. This gives particular importance to his two long trips to Hyderabad Deccan. These trips proved useful and fruitful in terms of their results. His personality left a deep impression on the people of Deccan. The first trip was in 1942 and the second in 1946.

On the day of his arrival in 1942, there was a large crowd to welcome him at the railway station. Apart from members and sympathisers of the *Jama'at,* there were also present a large number of religious leaders, dignitaries, professors and other learned persons. He was received most cordially and conveyed to his place of stay with full honours.

His first trip lasted nearly one week. Numerous people were truly delighted at his visit, and the religious and learned circles expressed great happiness. Throughout the day people visited him to exchange views and seek clarification on various issues. He made several speeches. The masses as well as the prominent people of Hyderabad found his knowledge and scholarship to be greater than they expected, and saw him as the greatest servant of Islam of the present age. Some people, breaching the Islamic code on treatment of guests and ignoring the traditions of Hyderabad, started a campaign of opposition, but they met with failure.

Members of the *Jama'at* and other Muslims held numerous functions for him, so much so that many invitations could not be accepted due to lack of time. The greatest achievement was that this visit led to the creation of a regular *Jama'at* in Hyderabad, which remained a large, successful and active organisation until the political change in Hyderabad in 1948. Many people took the *bai'at* to join the Movement formally.

Hardly had a year passed after this first visit that I began to receive demands from all sides to invite Hazrat Amir once again. He promised to come but due to various problems he could not fulfil his promise till 1946. Due to local political troubles at that time, the situation was not calm and peaceful, and arrangements for public meetings and speeches could not be so well made. Despite this, the people of Deccan benefited greatly. There were many speeches, gatherings and functions, and visitors came day and night. He was even requested, in emphatic terms, to visit Hyderabad once or twice every year. He expressed some agreement with this, but due to other engagements, illness, infirmity and the pre-partition disturbances, the late Hazrat Amir could not come again.

Travel is also a test of a man's moral character. In a journey a man cannot maintain artificial morals, and his true self is revealed and exposed. I had the opportunity to spend much of my life in the service of the late Hazrat Amir, and saw and studied him from various angles. During these visits too I made many observations. His virtues, command of knowledge, simplicity, beautiful morals, understanding of matters and depth of thinking, love for Islam and the Quran and devoutness had won the hearts of the people of Hyderabad, so much so that even the opponents and detractors were impressed. Misconceptions about the Ahmadiyya Movement were dispelled on a large scale. Even an old servant and disciple such as myself had many new experiences about the late Hazrat Amir's rare personality.

I have had the chance to meet many prominent men of India and see them closely. I usually find that when they are with people from the upper classes they behave differently from how they meet or address lower and middle class people. I never witnessed such change in Maulana Muhammad Ali's attitude. He spoke and acted in the same manner to the most ordinary of people as he did to those of the upper classes who applauded and praised him.

During these visits I frequently witnessed his spiritual prescience. Apart from his knowledge, experience, intelligence, and understanding of human nature, it was with his spiritual insight also that he was able to judge the opponents' intentions and plans very accurately.

He was always mindful of dignifying his assistants and workers, encouraging them, and introducing them to people high or low. He always introduced them to prominent, honourable visitors in commendable words and would mention their services to religion. He always showed full confidence in his assistants and workers in the presence of others. During his first visit there was a function at which, besides the ministers and chiefs of Deccan, the government minister of religious affairs at that time, Maulvi Abdul Aziz, was also in attendance. I had not been introduced to him before and I requested Maulana Muhammad Ali to introduce me to him as I may need his help in a certain matter. When the minister left the Maulana and was getting into his car, the Maulana took me to him and not only did he introduce me in glowing terms but also told him: "This is one of my men and is close to me, you can have full confidence in him".

During these travels I also noticed that he gave great importance to the opinions of the local workers and allowed them sufficient freedom to organise matters according to their own judgment. During his stay in Deccan he always gave importance to my opinion. He accepted almost all my suggestions regarding local matters, even following my submissions in minor details. One day some chiefs and high officials were to come to see him. Due to his simplicity, he went to the reception room in his shirt. In those days, according to the practice in Hyderabad, it was not considered appropriate to receive visitors without wearing a *sherwani* (long coat). I told him this, and I myself was surprised to see how carefully he bore my advice in mind.

When travelling it is difficult to stick to a time schedule, but the late Hazrat Amir kept it in mind and adhered to it as far as possible. He never wasted any moment. During the second visit he had the manuscript of one of his books with him and whenever he had a few minutes free he revised and corrected it.

He answered the objections of the critics in a pleasant, serious and dignified manner. His replies were given extremely well, in an effective and well-reasoned way. He immediately understood the nature and level of thinking of the critic.

While his death has deprived us distantly-located people of many other wishes, our desire to see this holy personage once again visit Hyderabad and get the privilege of welcoming him will remain forever unfulfilled. But his memory will never fade from the hearts of his admirers in Deccan."

8. Maulana Ahmad Yar, General Secretary, Ahmadiyya Anjuman, Lahore:

"Hazrat Amir Maulana Muhammad Ali, despite being a man of such greatness, was an epitome of humility and modesty. There was not the least trace of haughtiness, arrogance, conceit or vanity in him. He treated all people equally, whether great or small, rich or poor. He loved every person who was a devotee of Islam and a servant of the faith. As secretary of the Anjuman, I had the opportunity to see him close at hand. He was not at all in the habit of backbiting or complaining. Many times people would mention to him that such and such a man says this against you. He would just tell them to pray for that man, that Allah may turn him away from the wrong path and set him upon the right one. He was so mild and gentle that whatever anyone said to him he took it to be true. He was not given to indulging in useless talk, and was always conscious that every moment must be devoted to the service of religion and nothing else. He was so punctual that he can rightly be compared to a clock.

Even during illness he worked for many hours as usual. He went through all the proofs of the English translation of the Quran, while being ill almost all during this time. His eye was so sharp that when, at the end of May 1951, he was about to leave for Karachi, he called for the proofs of the Holy Quran in my presence which had been read once. Even then he located many errors in them. This is why he usually did not have confidence in the work of others, and he was not satisfied unless he checked things himself. Especially in indicating references to sources and in proof reading he was very careful. His pen never stopped. Even in his last days when he was very weak, whenever he was shown any papers he went through them carefully and wrote instructions on them in his own hand.

He treated the Anjuman office staff like his relatives. If anyone was ill, he would go to visit him. If anyone was in financial difficulty, he would make every effort to bring him relief. Sometimes when the Anjuman could not provide financial help to someone, he would help that needy member of staff himself. He felt sympathetic towards every member of the *Jama'at*. If someone was facing problems he would pray for him and then keep on enquiring about his welfare.

He was not formal in the least, nor did he ever talk with an artificial air. When anyone went to see him, the Maulana would immediately ask after his welfare and then be silent. He believed in being to the point."

9. Malik Fazal Ilahi, Manager of the Anjuman's Guest House, Ahmadiyya Buildings, Lahore:

"In 1937 when we came to Lahore for the annual gathering, the delegation from the Jhelum *Jama'at* went to see the Hazrat Maulana. He had been very ill. Besides discussing the affairs of the *Jama'at,* I also said: 'Thanks and praise be to Allah that you have recovered, we were very much worried'. He replied: 'You people should better worry about your faith. Muhammad Ali doesn't matter. If not today, he will go tomorrow. Hundreds of Muhammad Ali's came and went'. We all remained silent out of respect, but his words made a deep impression on our hearts.

Once I had to go to Dalhousie because I needed to get a letter of recommendation from someone through the Hazrat Maulana. There was another person with me, called Muhammad Ismail, who was under a boycott from the Qadiani *Jama'at*. When we arrived in Dalhousie, it was raining and very cold. We were wearing light clothes for warm weather. At long last, enquiring about the way, we reached the Maulana's residence and went directly to the kitchen to sit by the fire and warm ourselves. When the Maulana learnt of this, he sent for us and expressed surprise that in such cold weather we were wearing light clothes. Then he gave us a room to stay. After five minutes he arrived carrying tea in a tray in his own hands and told us to warm ourselves by drinking tea as dinner was to be served later. We were both drinking tea when the Maulana appeared again carrying two blankets and some dry clothes, with a servant following him carrying a hot stove.

Later we all had dinner together. My Qadiani friend was amazed and said afterwards: 'Good God! This is the Head of the *Jama'at* who is entertaining an ordinary person as if he were an important guest. If Mirza Mahmud Ahmad had been in his place, we would have found it well-nigh impossible to be allowed to meet him, let alone that he would bring us tea in person and give us a meal himself.' Afterwards, during conversation, Muhammad Ismail expressed his personal grievances against Mirza Mahmud Ahmad and tried to criticize his character, but Maulana Muhammad Ali stopped him and said that our difference with him is on matters of principles and there is no need for us to indulge in personal matters. The next day he did the work about which we had come to see him.

Once, at an annual gathering, a notice by Maulvi Sanaullah of Amritsar addressed to Maulana Muhammad Ali was distributed, on which it was written:

> As all your *umma* (followers) of Mirza are gathered here today, let us have a decisive debate between you and me. Choose a venue in Lahore. I am also prepared to come to your mosque.

It was signed: Sanaullah of Amritsar, Lion of Punjab, Victor of Qadian, etc. When the Hazrat Maulana started to deliver his speech entitled 'The oneness of God', people were impatiently waiting for his reply to Maulvi Sanaullah's notice. Many Muslims from outside the Movement had come specially for this reason, and they were all waiting to hear what answer he would give to this challenge. While the Maulana was making his speech, a note was handed to him which he put on the table and continued his speech. After ten minutes another note was passed on to him, which he also put on the table. A few minutes later a third note arrived. He then said:

> I was going to give my reply at the end of my speech but people are getting impatient and they wish me to answer now. So listen, brothers, write down my answer and take it to Maulvi Sanaullah. The first point worth noticing is that the Maulvi Sahib says: 'As all your *umma* of Mirza are gathered here today'. In answer, I do not wish to say anything that may detract from his dignity as a great scholar. I leave it to you. Regarding the debate proposed by him, I appoint the Maulvi sahib himself as the arbiter:

let him select for himself any area which is a stronghold of non-Muslims, and let him allocate any such area to us. The two of us can either work in our respective areas or send missionaries to do work. Then after one year we should put forward to the public, at the present venue, reports of our achievements there. This will benefit both sides, even if just one person embraces Islam due to your efforts. The advantage will be that even the loser would not have lost anything, while the other one would be the winner. However, no one is going to gain anything by tit-for-tat replies in a debate. Supporters of each side would claim that its leader prevailed in the debate. Let Maulvi Sanaullah come and give his decision as the arbiter. He must formulate some principle that he works according to. Either he should make people into unbelievers or he should convert people to Islam. Without some principle it is difficult to achieve success.

Hearing this reply, the supporters of Maulvi Sanaullah drifted away, while the answer made a good impression on other people."

10. Mumtaz Ahmad Faruqui:

"I studied at the Talim-ul-Islam High School in Qadian from 1909 to 1914. ... During that time I met or at least saw Hazrat Maulana Muhammad Ali every day. For each one of the daily prayers he went to the Nur mosque and said his prayers slowly, with full concentration and in an attractive manner. Even though he was busy with work on the English translation of the Holy Quran, he still sometimes used to attend the afternoon Quran study class in the Aqsa mosque. I noticed that he spoke little and was serious minded. It was after coming to Lahore that, because of having to give Friday *khutbas* and speeches, he became a great orator and public speaker. In his house three of his nephews lived who were at school. Being children they made mischief and caused damage sometimes, but I never saw the Maulana rebuke or punish any child.

After coming to Lahore I had occasion to stay with him many times. I was at college in those days. Because of the habit of going to bed late I missed the morning prayer in congregation many times. The Maulana was cross with me about this and used to say: "Prayer in congregation has many blessings. What a matter of shame that while that prayer is going on, you are sleeping. You should fear God." Glory be to God, that it so happened once that I fell ill, and the illness used to cause me to wake up in the later part of the night and stay awake till morning. Then I learnt what the Maulana had warned me about. But he also prayed for my health.

I saw the late Maulana becoming angry with people on some matters, but only for a short while. I never heard him backbite his companions and friends. I have not seen anyone so strictly adhere to the order of God: 'and those who restrain their anger and pardon people' [the Quran, 3:134], as did the Maulana.

When Hazrat Amir was taken ill in Quetta, he was suffering badly. Dr. Colonel Ilahi Bakhsh came from Lahore for treating him. The doctor examined him thoroughly and his diagnosis was that the malady was not dangerous and the Maulana would soon be able to return to Lahore. The moment the doctor left the room, I heard the Hazrat Maulana reciting this verse of the Quran: 'Praise be to Allah, Who has removed grief from us. Surely our Lord is Forgiving, Multiplier of rewards, Who out of His grace has made us alight in a house abiding forever; therein toil touches us not, nor does fatigue afflict us therein' [35:34–35]."

11. Shaikh Ghulam Qadir, Ahmadiyya Buildings:

"For fifty years Hazrat Maulana Muhammad Ali made flow rivers of wisdom and knowledge from his pen in the service of Islam but he also had the great virtue that he highly appreciated the smallest contribution of others and encouraged them. I had a long series of articles published in *Paigham Sulh* about the lives of the Companions of the Holy Prophet and the *Tabi'in* [those belonging to the following generation]. The Hazrat Maulana used to praise it highly and once he said to me that when he receives the newspaper he first reads my article and then anything else. All this was due to his appreciation and encouragement, otherwise 'what is mere dust in comparison with a Godly scholar'."

12. Muhammad Karimullah, Editor *Azad Naujawan* (Urdu) and *Thriller* (English):

"At a time when I was flowing like a twig in the stream of the darkness of Christian ideas, this prince of knowledge and wisdom filled my heart with the light of faith. ... Western Christians as well as agnostics are very proud of intellectual reasoning, and this attitude had got into my head as well. I did not accept anything unless I could bring it within my narrow intellect. It had become my habit to distort religious principles and attack them by my line of thinking. However, all this changed and I began to feel that human reason, of which I was so proud, was really a darkness. The light of Divine blessings came and I, a lost traveller, found my destination. I came across *The Teachings of Islam,* the blessed writing of the Promised Messiah translated into English by Hazrat Amir. As a result of reading it, I was saved from sinking in the storm of materialistic reasoning and began to sail in the sea of spirituality. I became desirous of studying other books of this Movement and read *Muhammad and Christ.* This book worked such wonders on me that I could not restrain myself, and bright rays of the sun of truth began shining in my eyes. The enchanting influence of the Cross was broken, and the radiant face of Islam began to create the light of faith.

I came across a copy of *Muhammad The Prophet.* This precious book made me aware of the real glory of the Holy Prophet Muhammad, and both my head and heart bore witness that without doubt he is the model of a perfect human being, like whom no other model for mankind can possibly be found. The Maulana's English translation of the Quran is an ocean of pearls that creates in the heart of its readers the urge for a new life. No fair-minded person, after studying it, can fail to acknowledge that the author of this commentary has written it after receiving special light and guidance from God, and it is a labour that few human beings can perform.

I then considered it essential to read all his other writings. Every person, after reading them, must become utterly convinced of his ability in the literary and religious fields. I do not say this because of being an admirer of his, but all readers acknowledge that his writings show the right path to lost souls. We were dead and this man of God, who found God, breathed the spirit of faith in our dead bodies, bringing us to life. I now have such strong faith that nothing in the world can shake it.

The reason my father wanted to start a magazine was that he was a reader of the *Review of Religions* whose editor was Maulana Muhammad Ali. My father used to say that all the Maulana's articles were of the highest standard. The paper *Azad Naujawan* ('Independent Youngman') was started under the influence of the *Review of Religions.* Hazrat Amir prayed for the success of this paper, and because of his prayer it is still alive till today.

In 1946 I went to Lahore to meet Hazrat Maulana. His captivating speech made me even more enthusiastic, and I was listening to it in complete absorption and wonder. At last, Maulana Abdul Haq Vidyarthi introduced me to him. He met me smilingly and spoke to me pleasantly. After embracing him I felt a new fire of faith in my heart that has not cooled down since. All the misguidance in my soul, darkness in my thoughts and weakness of faith vanished completely. After meeting him in Lahore there was a transformation in me. My concern all the time became the propagation of Islam, and I thought only of Islam during all my daily activities. Before going to Lahore there were many doubts in my mind, but after meeting the Maulana they all disappeared.

After my return, correspondence started between us. Whenever he went out of Lahore, to Dalhousie or Karachi, he let me know of his whereabouts. Till the last he remembered me and wrote to me despite his many engagements. He replied to every letter of mine.

When he heard the news of my father's death, he became very concerned and advised me, in a paternal way, to show patience. He was always delighted to hear news of any success of mine, and prayed for more blessings. This kindness and love was not only limited to me but he loved all my family and asked after their welfare. He used to write to my sisters and ask if their college libraries had Islamic literature; and if a girls' college did not, he would have it sent by the Anjuman.

While Hazrat Amir arranged for translations of the Quran into many languages, one of his last wishes and longings was that the Tamil translation of the Holy Quran be published in his lifetime. The translation was completed but, regrettably, it could not be published in his lifetime.

He asked me again and again about progress on the Tamil translation of the Quran, and kept on instructing me that it should conform to the English translation. I have the manuscript of the Tamil translation — may God enable it to be published soon."

13. Master Muhammad Abdullah, San Francisco, California

"It was 1931, probably August, when I and my wife left Lahore to go to the Fiji Islands. Before departure I was an English teacher in the Muslim High School Baddomalhi, District Sialkot. The man responsible for my migration to Fiji to serve the educational and religious needs of the Muslims of those Islands was the late Babu Manzur Ilahi, Joint-Secretary of the Ahmadiyya Anjuman Isha'at Islam Lahore in those days, who used to be in correspondence with Islamic organisations all over the world as well as with individual Muslims. He received a request through the Anjuman Himayat-i Islam for a teacher and missionary for Fiji.

Whenever any missionaries had previously been sent abroad by the Ahmadiyya Anjuman, a farewell meeting had been held for them, but in my case it so happened that no such meeting was announced. ... We reached the platform at Lahore railway station fifteen minutes before the departure of our train to Bombay, and my wife and our baggage having boarded, I was standing on the platform talking to friends. Suddenly I saw Maulana Muhammad Ali running towards me at great speed. I quickly leapt to greet him, with only five minutes left before the departure of the train. He gripped my hands most firmly and started saying prayers. I could not hear the prayers but I could certainly feel their effects. It seemed as if my hands were connected to an electrical battery and its current was penetrating the fibres of my being. The train whistled and I quickly boarded it. While thanking God for the privilege of feeling the spiritual power of the late Hazrat Amir,

I realised that there was Divine purpose in the farewell meeting not being held for me. Had it been held, there would have been speeches and comments of praise to encourage me, tea and refreshments served for the audience, and a reply address by me. A man attends many such functions in his honour during his life and their effect is only temporary. But the sight of a great man like the late Hazrat Amir running to say farewell to me, reaching the platform just in time, grasping my hands and saying prayers for me, and the effect of those prayers being felt by me there and then — that memory is unforgettable.

I felt that the success I attained [in Fiji] was the result of the prayers of that Godly saint whom the world of Islam knows by the name Maulana Muhammad Ali. ... To him, religion was not limited to the formalities of worship and prayer, but his style of living and his actions were in accordance with the teachings of the Quran and the *Sunna*." (Article entitled 'Last glimpse of Hazrat Amir Maulana Muhammad Ali', *Paigham Sulh,* 1 October 1989, p. 24.)

14. Haji Allah Rakha Mumin, resident, Ahmadiyya Buildings

He related that in Qadian he heard from Sufi Abdur Rahman that one day in 1901 the Promised Messiah told him to clear and clean the place adjacent to the Mubarik mosque, in the lower storey, where the earthen water pots were kept and *wudu* was performed, and to spread a mat there and put a chair and small table. He obeyed the instruction. The next day he saw Maulana Muhammad Ali working in that room. He was surprised at the simplicity of the young man who possessed an M.A. degree and was English educated, and how much he was devoted to the Promised Messiah.

(*Note:* This tiny room was Maulana Muhammad Ali's office from where he wrote those magnificent articles for the *Review of Religions* about which it was alleged by Christian opponents that the Promised Messiah had employed an Englishman to write them.)

15. Ch. Muhammad Abdullah Khan, Muslim Town, Lahore:

"It was 1924 or 1925 that I and some friends, because of the fact that some vociferous young men used to speak out even during the Friday *khutbas* of the Hazrat Maulana, decided to ask him to disallow such a great degree of freedom of expression and to adopt a milder form of the discipline imposed by the Qadiani *khalifa*. But as we lacked the courage to say this to him we agreed to ask Mian Ghulam Rasul Tamim to support our views, as he was a close friend of the Hazrat Maulana and open with him. ... In the company of the Mian sahib we put our point before the Hazrat Maulana. After listening to us, he replied categorically that, as we had left Qadian to save ourselves from just this error, it would be an even more terrible mistake to introduce the same error into the *Jama'at* here. He said moreover: 'Freedom of expression undoubtedly appears to be harmful temporarily, but if it is used with sincerity it brings about progress. If you think that I should become a spiritual despot like the *khalifa* of Qadian, then this is impossible as I don't have duality in my nature.' In the end, we were unable to reply to him and assumed silence."

16. Shahzada Begum, daughter of Khwaja Kamal-ud-Din:

"I am proud that the credit for this sacred work [of the propagation of Islam to the West] goes to these two august men, one of whom, Hazrat Khwaja Kamal-ud-Din, was my father, and the other, Hazrat Maulana Muhammad Ali, was as affectionate towards us as a father. In fact, after the death of Hazrat Khwaja sahib, the protective kindness of the Hazrat Maulana towards us was a source of much benefit to us. Whenever I went to his house, he would usually leave all his work and treat me with affection, and ask after my welfare and the well-being of my children. Today we are deprived of his protection, and only we know of the depth of our grief and sadness. But the good news is that both these eminent men departed from this world after having spent a successful and blameless life, and walked in the ways of the pleasure of God."

17. Maulana Hafiz Sher Mohammad:

"Maulana Muhammad Ali was a very great man. I served under him for ten years, and not even once did I have any cause to complain about him."

(Statement related by Maulana Hafiz Sher Mohammad to Zahid Aziz.)

Gravestone of Maulana Muhammad Ali

4.3: Some impressions of Maulana Muhammad Ali

by Maulana Muhammad Yaqub Khan

The Holy Prophet Muhammad, may peace and the blessings of Allah be upon him, compared his Companions to the shining stars of the sky and said: "My companions are like the stars. Whomsoever of them you follow, you will be guided aright". The Promised Messiah was, in this age, established upon the rank of *fana fir-rasul* (one who entirely effaces his own person in that of the Holy Prophet) and was thus the centre of spreading spiritual light. Those who gathered around him acquired light according to their God-given capabilities.

Maulana Muhammad Ali was among these early pioneers who rose on the horizon of Islam like a huge shining star and shone so brightly as to illuminate both East and West with the rays of the light of Islam. By preserving the events of his life his biographers have fulfilled a great need. Someone should write a collective biography of that spiritual company and that party of the early followers, each one of whom was a shining star in his own right and a living embodiment of the truth of Islam and love for the Quran and the Holy Prophet. Thus the future generations would know who these people were who, after gathering around the man sent by God for this age, became the standard bearers of the second rising of Islam, the revival with which the future of the world is linked and which has already begun. The coming generations could then use the examples of their forebears to kindle the same zeal and fervour in their own hearts.

Privilege of being first in history of Islam

Only those people can fully realise the importance of Maulana Muhammad Ali's services to Islam who visit Western countries and witness with their own eyes the dominance of Christianity on the one hand and the ignorance and suspicion about Islam and the Holy Prophet Muhammad prevailing in those countries on the other. Maulana Muhammad Ali's English translation of the Quran was the first achievement in the history of Islam that started to dispel the darkness in the Western countries and spread the light of Islam from place to place.

Maulana Muhammad Ali's greatest distinction, destined by God for him and which only he was blessed with, was that in the history of Islam he was the first Muslim who conveyed the message of Islam to Western countries in a Western language. The history of Islam produced many conquerors who planted the flag of Islam on a large part of Europe, and this part remained under Muslim rule for centuries. However, it is remarkable that in this period of about a thousand years of Muslim domination in Europe, it did not occur to anyone to translate the Holy Quran, the real source of the message of Islam, into at least one European language and make it available to the Christian population. The result was that while the sword of Islam overpowered the Christian states and powers, we could not conquer their hearts, which was the real mission of Islam.

In the present age, Islam and Christianity again confront one another and a new crusade is in progress between these religions. However, this war is not being fought for land, crown or throne but to conquer the hearts of the people. In this war the sword that can destroy the enemy is the sword of the Quran. It was Maulana Muhammad Ali's good fortune to be destined to prepare the sword of the translation of the Quran for the spiritual conquests of Islam in this new age. Those of us who work in this field know what a tremendous role the scholarly masterpiece of the Maulana has played in changing the hearts of the Westerners. Wherever a copy of this translation reaches, it is as if a missionary of Islam had been sent there. It opens the eyes of the people and makes their hearts perceive that in fact Islam is the only religion that is the voice of human nature.

When the prophecy of the rise of the sun of Islam in the West is fulfilled and people embrace Islam in large numbers, the future historian investigating the causes of this spiritual revolution will certainly give Maulana Muhammad Ali's translation of the Quran the leading place in the list of causes.

Writer

When an outline of the personality of Maulana Muhammad Ali is brought to mind, his second distinction is seen to be his penman-ship. It is difficult to find among his contemporaries another example of one who wielded his pen so profusely, so powerfully, with so much concentration, and for so long in the service of Islam. Recently a man living in Cardiff came to see us in Woking.[1] He is originally from East Pakistan and is not particularly well-educa-ted. He related a dream in which he saw himself sitting in the plain of Arafat. The Holy Prophet Muhammad was also there, and so were Maulana Muhammad Ali and Khwaja Kamal-ud-Din. Maulana Muhammad Ali told him: "Go and write a book on Gog and Magog and *Dajjal* and get it published". He said: "But I am not an educated person". The Maulana replied: "That does not matter, just start writing". Then the Maulana held up to him his right thumb, which was shining brightly and radiating light, and said: "Look, I wrote all my life". What this man saw in the dream is the gist of the Maulana's life, the wielding of the pen in the service of Islam. The rays shining from the Maulana's thumb re-present the light of Islam which is radiating from his books and illuminating the world. That man then did write quite a good-sized book with the help of his British wife and brought it to us for pub-lication, contributing two hundred Pounds towards its printing.

Half a century is no short time that the Maulana devoted to wielding his sword-like pen for the service of Islam. He took up

---

1. This was in 1962 when Maulana Yaqub Khan was director of the Woking Muslim Mission in England. Cardiff is the capital city of Wales in the U.K.

the editorship of the *Review of Religions* in January 1902, and from then till October 1951 he did not lay down his pen until it was actually snatched from him by the hand of the angel of death. For fifty years incessantly, he produced writing upon writing expounding the deep truths of Islam. In the modern age, boards are usually appointed to undertake such monumental works. They have an entire staff of researchers, assistants and secretaries. The Maulana, utterly devoid of any such resources, did so much research single-handedly that it is absolutely astonishing. There is no secretary or assistant. He sits at the table alone, pen in hand. There are piles of reference books lying in front of him: dictionaries, commentaries of the Quran, collections of Hadith, historical works, etc. He looks up every reference himself, consults dictionaries himself, writes the manuscript with his own hand and revises it himself as well. When the proofs come from the press, he reads them himself. This was his daily, regular routine. During the same time, visitors come, affairs of the Anjuman are brought to him, and he puts down his pen to deal with them. As soon as he is free again, he goes back to his pen, his writing and his proof reading.

The dream that the Promised Messiah saw, in which he gave a pen to Maulana Muhammad Ali, was in fact a scene of the *jihad* by the pen that the Maulana was to conduct, shown to Hazrat Mirza sahib. He was shown a sketch of the Maulana's entire coming life, which would be devoted to wielding the pen in the service of Islam.

A busy life

I had the occasion to see the Maulana from close at hand for more or less thirty years. Working in his office, talking to visitors, leaving everything aside at the appointed times of prayer and going to the mosque for prayer in congregation, delivering the *khutba* on Friday, carrying out the functions of President at the meetings of the Anjuman, launching campaigns to further the interests of the Anjuman and making struggles in this regard, supervising the Anjuman's offices, departments, property and finances, making speeches at the annual gatherings and moving for fund raising — all these scenes pass before my eyes like a long film. It is a fact that whatever the Maulana took in hand he brought it success, he gave it life and he made it reach its final goal.

Regard for duty

The Muslim High School had from the beginning been accommodated in rented houses. The Maulana was determined that we should have our own building within our environment in Ahmadiyya Buildings. He himself obtained land for it, raised funds, and had the plans drawn. When the plans were shown to the Department of Education they said that as only four or five months now remained in the school year it would be impossible for these people [Ahmadis] to construct the school building in such a short time. There was a Muslim inspector in the Education Department who was an acquaintance and admirer of the Maulana. He said to the director, who was British: "You don't know these people, when they are resolved to do something no obstacle in their way can prevent them". So the plans were approved and a reasonable grant was sanctioned. The director himself was surprised when, before the end of the school year, the report was received stating that the building was complete. During the construction it was noteworthy that the Maulana used to inspect the work himself once or twice a day. One day when he came, he noticed that a wall that had just been built was bulging slightly in the middle. He questioned the builders most sternly and had the entire wall knocked down and rebuilt. This small incident illustrates his approach to his duties throughout life. As Head of the community he regarded himself as accountable before God to ensure that all work was done with the highest degree of honesty and to the best standard. He could not tolerate any defect or carelessness in it. He showed in his life a practical illustration of the teaching of the Holy Quran: "Surely Allah commands you to make over trusts to those worthy of them" (4:58).

A constructor and builder by nature

Besides the prominent position that his writing work holds in his achievements, I think that there was another of his qualities which is rare — he was by nature a *builder*. Wherever he was, something was being built or constructed. All the time there would be planning for the development of the community, and the planning did not just remain confined to paper but was put into action. As Secretary of the Sadr Anjuman in Qadian, he was the moving spirit behind all the construction done while he was there. The magnificent buildings of the Talim-ul-Islam High School and the adjacent hostel excelled even the college buildings of a city such as Lahore. Next to it was built a large mosque, called Masjid Nur, all the work being done under the direct supervision of the Maulana.

After his migration from Qadian to Lahore, he busied himself in work anew, just as honey bees leave one hive, disperse and gather at another place to build a new hive. Here too it was the Maulana who was the moving spirit behind the raising of a new community. It was around him that the others gathered, who were a mere handful of people. There was not even a table or chair, nor any assets. It was another miraculous spectacle that a new community built from this state of complete deprivation grew so rapidly and began to do such solid work of the service of Islam that, without exaggeration, Ahmadiyya Buildings became a living centre of the revival of Muslim India. Whenever the sensible and knowledgeable sections of the Muslims needed right guidance on any Islamic issue, it was to Ahmadiyya Buildings that their eyes turned.

Made Ahmadiyya Buildings the centre of Islamic thought

Every great leader of the Muslims would come to Ahmadiyya Buildings to meet Maulana Muhammad Ali. Sir Muhammad Iqbal, Sir Fazl-i Husain, Sir Shahab-ud-Din, Sir Muhammad Shafi and Sir Abdul Qadir were considered as the top-most leaders of the Muslims in those days.[2] Every one of them deeply admired Maulana Muhammad Ali and consulted him on all issues facing the Muslims. The leader of the well-known Khilafatist Movement, Maulana Muhammad Ali Jauhar, once came to meet Maulana Muhammad Ali in Ahmadiyya Buildings. He was in his office on the lower floor. Jauhar embraced him immediately upon entering his office and said:

---

2. *Sir* is a title conferred by the British crown upon British subjects. Indians living under British rule of India were also eligible for it.

> "I am benefiting greatly from your name. Wherever I go, inside or outside India, people think I am the Muhammad Ali who has translated the Quran into English, which has become a masterpiece of international renown in the world of learning."

Maulana Jauhar was very candid by nature, and it was his deep admiration for Maulana Muhammad Ali that had drawn him to Ahmadiyya Buildings. This admiration felt by him has also been testified to by Maulana Abdul Majid Daryabadi in his review of Maulana Muhammad Ali's English translation of the Quran.

Long-standing relations with the Quaid-i Azam

The *Quaid-i Azam* Muhammad Ali Jinnah was a visitor to Maulana Muhammad Ali from the days when he was known as plain Mr. Jinnah and was one of the leaders of the Congress party. In those days too he was regarded also as a great leader of Muslim India. Once, when he came to Lahore, Maulana Muhammad Ali gave a tea party in his honour, at which were invited the prominent Muslim figures of Lahore. The party was held in a marquee in the grounds of Islamia College. The Maulana referred, in a brief speech, to the Islamic services of his Anjuman. In those days the Arya Samaj campaign of *shuddi* [to convert Muslims to the Arya Hindu sect] was at its height and the Anjuman had done much work to counteract it. He also explained the beliefs of the Lahore Ahmadiyya *Jama'at* and said that the real purpose of the Ahmadiyya Movement is to serve Islam, while holding itself above sectarianism. This speech had a good effect. Afterwards, when the guests were talking among themselves, Mr. Jinnah took the Maulana to one side and was discussing this topic with him. I was also standing there, listening. Mr. Jinnah praised the work of the Anjuman and expressed regret at the opposition of the prejudiced among the Muslims. The conversation was in English and one sentence, reflecting Mr. Jinnah's informality with the Maulana, still resounds in my ears. In connection with the relations of the general Muslim community with the Ahmadiyya *Jama'at* Mr. Jinnah said:

> "Look here, Muhammad Ali! You should also be tactful. Don't be aggressive in your preachings."

The *Quaid-i Azam* at the Maulana's residence

Much later, when the *Quaid-i Azam* Muhammad Ali Jinnah had taken up the leadership of the Muslims of India in their demand for Pakistan, he came to a tea party at the Maulana's invitation at his residence in Muslim Town. The Maulana had also invited members of the Anjuman. The *Quaid-i Azam* made a short speech in which, while expressing admiration for the Anjuman's services, he mentioned an incident regarding the Anjuman's English weekly organ *The Light*. He said that once during a conversation the Viceroy of India, Lord Linlithgow, had told him that his [Jinnah's] recent statement that democracy [rule purely by majority, with disregard for minorities] was not suitable for India had caused commotion in the country and he did not understand how he could oppose such a wonderful system. The *Quaid-i Azam* said that he told the Viceroy in reply that he would send him a newspaper to read about this. So he sent the Viceroy an issue of *The Light* which contained an article on the topic that parliamentary democracy was not suitable for India. The next day he returned it with a note saying that he understood his position and what he had stated was justified. After relating this incident the *Quaid-i Azam* said:

> "Your Anjuman is doing very fine work. I receive your paper, *The Light*. I am a politician and read this paper for political articles, but along with that I also read religious articles. I keep a file of this paper."

He also said that he received letters from other countries containing enquiries about Islam:

> "Foreigners think that as I am a leader of Muslims they can write to me seeking information about Islam. I pass those letters on to your Anjuman for appropriate answers."

Muslim visitors

Prominent Muslim visitors from abroad coming to Lahore would of necessity visit the Maulana. Once a delegation of three leading *ulama* from the Al-Azhar University of Egypt came on a tour of India and during their stay in Lahore they came to see the Maulana. A lengthy conversation took place about the Ahmadiyya Movement in Arabic. Maulana Ahmad Yar and I were also present.

It was clear from what the *ulama* said that they had high regard for the Maulana's writings, and especially for his English translation of the Quran.

Respect for the Maulana in the Christian world

Non-Muslim religious dignitaries also, when visiting Lahore, would pay a call on the Maulana. Once the famous Dutch orientalist, Dr. Kraemer, while touring Islamic countries, came to Lahore just to meet the Maulana. He spent several hours in conversation with him in the house in Ahmadiyya Buildings and acquired information about the Movement. I was present at this meeting. Later, writing an account of his tour in the famous Christian journal *The Moslem World,* he referred to his meeting with the Maulana and wrote:

> "Their influence is far wider than the number of their adherents would suggest. Their vindication and defence of Islam is accepted by many educated Muslims as the form in which they can remain intellectually loyal to Islam." [3]

From among Christian clergymen, the Reverend L. Bevan Jones, principal of a Christian institution, the Henry Martin School of Islamics, was a frequent visitor to the Maulana. He has mentioned the Maulana in several places in his book *People of the Mosque* and quoted extracts from his writings.

Research on Maulana for Doctorate of Divinity in Rome

The extent to which Christian Missionary circles recognised the greatness of Maulana Muhammad Ali can be judged by the following incident. Last year, a young Pakistani who had been converted to Christianity and had dedicated himself to missionary work, came to us at Woking. He had been sent to Rome's famous Missionary Training College for higher education, and the topic of research that the college had given him, to attain the degree of Doctorate of Divinity, on which he had to write a thesis, was about Maulana Muhammad Ali. This young man had therefore come to Woking

---

3. *The Moslem World,* April 1931, pages 170–171.

from Rome to gather information about the life, personality and writings of the Maulana.

To sum up, the life of the Maulana was like a living and dynamic centre of activity in the world of religion, which impressed and influenced both the Muslim and the non-Muslim worlds. The intellectually high calibre of his thought and the sincerity and integrity of his writing won honour in all circles, despite the fact that he upheld the picture of Islam presented by the Ahmadiyya Movement which embodied certain views that contradicted some of the notions entertained by the Muslim public generally. Likewise, although what he had written about Christianity and other religions demolished their defences, but his style of writing was so unbiased, fair, rational and well-reasoned that it did not offend anyone's feelings. Despite differences of belief, even the adversaries were convinced of the Maulana's scholarship and intellectual integrity.

The Anjuman's financial stability

I have described one of the Maulana's attributes as his ability to construct and build. This ability was not confined only to his religious and scholarly work but comprehended every aspect of life. He laid as much emphasis on developing the financial strength of the Anjuman as on its literary activities. At all times he had some campaign or plan placed before the community which kept alive the spirit of monetary struggle and sacrifice, and God blessed his call with a special efficacy. His manner of speech was entirely devoid of what is known as 'stage acting', and was marked by the same simplicity as his writings. This is the great difference between a rabble rousing, emotional orator and a serious speaker. The former craves for the audience's approbation and plays on their emotions while the latter aims to prepare the people for some solid, constructive work. As a result, the former makes a fleeting impression while the latter leaves a lasting mark. The Maulana's speeches had this quality of permanence. I used to feel, at the annual gatherings, that when he rose up to appeal for funds it seemed as if angels were moving the hearts of the audience. There would scarcely be anyone who would not be impressed, and people would donate generously. His voice was blessed by God with the power of penetrating to the depths of hearts. I remember once that a friend, a famous doctor of Peshawar who was not a member of the *Jama'at,* was so moved by such an appeal that he donated many thousands of Rupees beyond his position.

I was mentioning that the Maulana's abilities were instinctively constructive. Destructiveness was against his very nature. All his efforts were devoted to works of organising the *Jama'at* and its consolidation. It was due to the Maulana's constructive ability that a large estate in Okara was granted to the Anjuman by the government, which strengthened its financial foundations. He acquired a large area of land outside Muslim Town, Lahore, for the Anjuman very cheaply, where a centre could be built in an open locality befitting a Movement of international standing. In Malir near Karachi he acquired a huge area of land at extremely low prices which was later sold by the Anjuman for hundreds of thousands of Rupees. In the Sindh, hundreds of acres of land was also purchased cheaply for the Anjuman. Even from the financial point of view the Maulana performed his duty uniquely in the building up of the *Jama'at.*

Friday *khutbas* (sermons)

I wish particularly to mention the Maulana's Friday *khutbas* because this institution plays an important part in the training and organisation of the community. The Maulana's *khutbas* had the quality of never being stale. Each and every *khutba* was, as it were, a new dish of spiritual food for the congregation. Once, I remember, that the Maulana delivered a long, continuous series of Friday *khutbas* on the *Sura Fatiha.* What amazed us was that there was no repetition. He gave *khutbas* for so many years, yet the listeners never lost interest in the least. This is no easy task. The speaker's knowledge is usually limited and is exhausted in a few addresses. Knowing nothing new, they start repeating the same statements. Then there is no nourishment left in their *khutbas,* and as a result the intellectual and spiritual development of the community comes to a halt. The standard of the Maulana's *khutbas* never dropped. Every Friday people waited for the new, fine and sublime knowledge that was going to come from the Maulana's lips and listened to it attentively. His *khutbas* were of substance. There is a type of speaker who *has to say something* and there is another who *has something to say.* The Maulana's *khutbas* were of the second type, always containing new knowledge. Every week he would prepare, as it were, a new tonic to enliven the community. This feature of his *khutbas* was another of the Maulana's uniquely distinctive qualities, that every *khutba,* in fact every sentence, brought something new. Just as his writings were solid and succinct, devoid of any superfluous words, so also were his addresses comprised of sound knowledge and truths.

I have dwelt upon this in such detail because it is not an ordinary matter to prepare and bring before the community a new, most delicious, spiritual diet every week. Allah had made the Maulana unique in this field as well. Although there were undoubtedly among us many articulate, eloquent and fluent speakers but the effect produced by the simplicity of the words and the manner of expression of the Maulana was incomparable. It cannot be expressed better than in a remark I heard being made by Khwaja Kamal-ud-Din, who said:

> "Usually, whenever a speaker has started to say a few words, I know straightaway what he is going to say next. The whole sketch of his speech is formed in my mind at once and I lose interest. But when *Maulvi* (this was Khwaja Kamal-ud-Din's term of endearment for the Maulana) utters a sentence, I have no idea what he is going to say next. Every new sentence brings forth something new. So I listen attentively from beginning to end."

This was not flattery from a deferential disciple but a tribute from a master of this art himself. The Khwaja sahib was himself an acknowledged, accomplished orator and knew what kind of speech would captivate the hearts of the audience. The beautiful way in which he has commented on the speeches and *khutbas* of Maulana Muhammad Ali, to show that they were full of substance and knowledge, is the Khwaja sahib's own inimitable style. No one could portray better than this the utility of the Maulana's *khutbas.* This also shows the magnanimity of Khwaja Kamal-ud-Din, in that he has so generously acknowledged the high scholarly standard of a companion in the same field of work.

Balanced heart and mind

The Divine will certainly created Maulana Muhammad Ali to perform the special mission of raising aloft the banner of Islam in the
world through his pen in this age of knowledge and reason, and
granted him the nature and disposition suitable for this purpose.
Allah bestowed upon him a heart and mind that were so balanced
that he could be called an embodiment of balance. As regards both
intellectual thinking, which is connected with the human mind,
and emotions, whose source is the heart, Allah had established
him on the path of moderation, steering away from all extremes.
In his daily living, dress, food, relations with others, and in every
other aspect of life his way was that of balance and moderation.
The Holy Quran has drawn a picture of the "servants of the Bene-
ficent God" as being those who walk on the earth in humility, and
when the ignorant address them they respond by saying "Peace",
and when they pass by what is vain they pass with dignity, ignoring it, etc. (25:63–75). The Maulana was a living model of this
picture. Far from talking abusively to anyone, he never even spoke
harshly. In all circumstances he showed an example of dignity
personified.

As President of the Anjuman

As President of the Anjuman he had two distinctive qualities
which were exemplary. The Anjuman is a democratic institution.
Its elections are held every three years by majority of vote, and its
decisions are also taken by majority of vote. From 1914 when the
Anjuman was founded, till 1951 when the Maulana died, he was
throughout this time unanimously offered the offices of Head
(*Amir*) and President by the community. He not only presided
over the meetings of the Anjuman but guided it in all matters,
devoting all his energies to this work. Sometimes members insisted upon having their own way, against his opinion, and the majority decision went against him. The Maulana would here display
the best example of abiding by principle and would accept that
decision without complaint, even while considering it to be not in
the Anjuman's best interest. His leadership and guidance was a
balance between the two ideologies which are at this time being
discussed and debated all over the world in the politics of nations.
His presidency was over a parliamentary type of institution but the

anarchic tendencies of democracy did not arise in it. It had the benefits of unanimity, efficiency and speed that are found in dictatorial institutions, but without the evils of dictatorship. This harmonious union of apparently two opposites was possible only because of his selflessness and godliness. His actions were not motivated by personal gain or quest for power.

An affectionate father

I observed a glimpse of his domestic life in the days when his eldest daughter Atiyya was in the last stages of the pernicious disease of tuberculosis. I was residing in Ahmadiyya Buildings near his house. It happened many times that someone at my home suddenly suffered an attack of illness during the night. I would rush to the Maulana's house in a state of great anxiety. These were long winter nights and it would be the middle of the night. But whenever I would reach the upper storey of his house, at a time of sudden need, I would find him awake, sitting on the floor besides the child's bed, nursing her. Seeing him awake and toiling at night, after being involved in mentally tiring work all day long, would put me to shame for my panic. Even though his daughter was on her death bed and I had gone to him with a relatively minor problem, he would listen to me calmly and attentively and advise me accordingly or help me. Some time later, when at last the child could not survive, his fortitude and composure were remarkable. On the one hand he loved his daughter so much and showed her so much paternal affection that he tended her personally through the nights, but on the other hand when the Divine decree called her back the Maulana's face showed no sign of complaint, and was calm as if nothing had happened.

Ordinary activities

To keep fit the Maulana carefully and regularly followed a set routine. Early in the morning, after the morning prayer and long before sunrise, he would set out for a long walk of several miles. Once a week he would go for an outing. Dr. Mirza Yaqub Baig, who loved the Maulana very much, used to take him out in his car every Wednesday after the *zuhr* prayers some twenty to thirty miles away from Lahore. They would also take me with them. A basket of fruit and guns would be with us, and the Maulana used to take his gun as well. But the hunting was only in name. The real reason was to enjoy being out in the fresh, open air, so that the Maulana would be refreshed to enable him to carry on his mental activities. There was good humour and laughter on these occasions as well. Once, with great effort, I succeeded in getting close to my prey but when I fired the gun I missed the target and the bird flew away. Dr. Mirza Yaqub Baig and the Maulana, who were both watching, burst into laughter. I remarked that it was good that the poor bird's life had been spared. Later on the Maulana used to narrate this incident as a joke and say: "The Khan sahib's hunting is the best way. If he hits the target he is happy that he got his prey. If he misses it he is happy that the animal's life has been spared". During the hunt he would sometimes also walk long distances. Although I was a young man, he had more stamina than I did. Sometimes I had to stop but the Maulana would continue to walk.

In spite of his great scholarship and learning, he was not of a dry nature as most *ulama* are, nor was he lax, idle or comfort-loving as they generally are. He always retained what is called in English the "human touch", and considered himself as just an ordinary person and led such an ordinary style of life. He also enjoyed refined humour, which is a mark of true greatness.

Hazrat Maulana's status

Maulana Muhammad Ali was undoubtedly a great man and the services he rendered to Islam were also monumental. He was the founder and the spirit of the Lahore Ahmadiyya Movement. He had immersed himself so deeply in the Movement that it would be true to say that he personified the Lahore Ahmadiyya Movement and this Movement reflected the person of Maulana Muhammad Ali. To assign him his rightful place in the history of Islam, according to his achievements, is the work of historians in future times. We cannot express our feelings better than in the words of the poet who wrote:

The pitcher of the drink (of knowledge) is now broken,
The one who served us with drink is no more!

4.4: Memories of my beloved

by Naseer Ahmad Faruqui

The late Maulana Muhammad Ali was my brother-in-law, husband of one of my sisters, and because of this close relationship I had much occasion, as would be usually expected, to see him and stay with him. In fact, I had even greater opportunity to be close to him because from 1922 to 1929 I was studying in a college in Lahore and lived right next to Ahmadiyya Buildings. In that time I saw him every day. During the long summer vacation in the college I had the good fortune to stay with him at Dalhousie, where I used to live in his house and was thus in his company day and night. Later on, when I was in government service in Bombay, the Hazrat Maulana paid a visit there twice and stayed at my house. Lastly, fortunately for me, he spent the last three summers of his life with me at my house in Karachi.

Maulana Muhammad Ali's personality, qualities, writings and speeches are so distinguished that in the history of Islam he must be ranked among the most renowned men. You will find details of his services and achievements elsewhere in this book. In this chapter I shall speak only of his personal qualities. While his writings and books exist in print and are spread all over the world, and his speeches have been committed to writing, I wish it were possible to have an equally detailed record of his personal qualities.

Widely respected and loved
Even strangers who met the late Hazrat Maulana were captivated by him. It is no small tribute that there are hundreds of thousands of people who acknowledge his excellent moral qualities, knowledge and learning, and spiritual accomplishments. However, many

men can show a good example of themselves to the general public, but very rare are those who can show such an example in private, in their own home, to those who live with them day and night, making them their wholly devoted admirers. The late Hazrat Maulana fulfilled perfectly the sublime criterion laid down in Hadith that "the best of you is he who is best to his family". His near relations not only held him in the highest possible respect, loved his excellent personal virtues, and regarded him as a very great saint, but they were also entirely devoted to him heart and soul. This is quite remarkable because usually it is among relatives that friction and grievances arise and your relatives are your worst critics.

My late father, Dr. Basharat Ahmad, was himself an outstanding spiritual personage possessing vast knowledge of the Holy Quran, and being Maulana Muhammad Ali's father-in-law he was the Maulana's senior. Nonetheless my father respected the Hazrat Maulana, his son-in-law, as a son respects his father who embodies all virtues. My mother was the same, respecting and revering the Hazrat Maulana as a disciple respects his perfect spiritual guide. Likewise, all near relations did the same.

Extraordinary qualities
In addition to spiritual knowledge, religious learning and moral virtues, he had the unexpected quality of being fully conversant with affairs of the world. He was a specialist in mathematics, had an M.A. degree in English, and had passed his law examination with distinction in the entire province. This, however, had been in his youth. After he spurned all worldly ambitions and dedicated his life to the service of religion, he was engaged day and night for that cause. However, even then he would find time to read newspapers and books to keep abreast of current affairs, so that whenever he expressed his views on world affairs they were knowledgeable and accurate. For this reason, people not only sought his advice in religious and spiritual matters but in worldly affairs as well, and it was mostly sound and correct. God had thus blessed him with both worldly and religious virtues. Although he had no involvement whatsoever in worldly matters, yet he was a well-informed observer of them.

Another extraordinary quality in the late Hazrat Amir was his absolutely strict punctuality and regularity in his work and habits. You could set your watch by him. His times of daily and nightly activities were so fixed and undeviating that he fulfilled all his personal religious and worldly obligations and yet rendered the maximum possible service to Islam. His work in the form of writings and speeches is on such a grand scale that it would have been excusable if he had not been able to fulfil his everyday duties expected of any man. But I observed that he always found as much time as was required to help and care for his relatives, friends and even outsiders. Yet despite this, he would be so busy and engrossed in his writing work as if oblivious of everything else.

During his stays with me in Karachi, when he would rise from his writing table at lunch time, for example, you could tell without looking at the clock that it was five minutes to one because he would always go to perform *wudu* at that time and come to the dining table at 1.00 p.m. After lunch, followed by the *zuhr* prayer, he would rest, and when he would emerge from his room we all knew that it was 3.30 p.m. because after working for half an hour he would come to the table for tea at exactly 4.00 p.m. The part of his time which was under his own control was regulated by him like clockwork. If other people disturbed his schedule, he tolerated it because of his pleasant nature.[1]

His jovial nature

Another of his enviable qualities was that, despite his spiritual exertions and worship, hard work and religious devoutness, he was not at all of a humourless and boring nature, but was always cheerful, laughing and smiling. He used to join his relatives and friends in an informal way and indulge in innocent, good humour.

Once my father was being transferred in the course of his employment from Khanpur to Karnal, and on the way he had to stay in Lahore. There were altogether some twelve to fifteen people in

---

1. This paragraph is added from Mr. Faruqui's article in *Paigham Sulh,* 1 October 1989, p. 13.

the group that was travelling because, in addition to our own family, there were some orphans and widows who lived with us (of whom he was guardian). Due to insufficient space at the Maulana's own home, while most of us stayed with him, some were to stay at the house of Chaudhry Zahur Ahmad, my other brother-in-law. The Maulana informed us of these arrangements in his usual humorous manner, saying: "The old, the children and the sick at my place, the fit and healthy at Chaudhry Zahur Ahmad's"!

Once my father was relating an incident that he was delivering a Friday *khutba* somewhere in severely hot weather. Due to the shady and cool atmosphere inside the mosque, and the constant, soporific pitch of the sound of the sermon, the members of the congregation were lulled to sleep one by one. This left my father standing there, wondering what to do. When he reached this point in the story, the Hazrat Maulana interjected and said: "You should have sat down and dozed off as well"!

My late father loved me very much and this love between father and son was felt by the whole family. The late Maulana would humorously apply the much-used Christian terms "Father", "Son" and "love" to our relationship and then laugh and make all of us laugh as well.

Gentle and mild but courageous

Another of the Maulana's qualities was gentleness and tenderness. In the Holy Quran it says about the Holy Prophet Muhammad:

> "Thus it is by Allah's mercy that you are gentle to them. And had you been rough, hard-hearted, they would certainly have dispersed from around you." (3:159)

This was also what the Hazrat Maulana was like. He was so gentle, kind and forgiving in his treatment of others that it was amazing. On the other hand he was brave and courageous to the highest degree. In Dalhousie his residence 'Darus Salam' was close to my father's house 'Parveen'. Running between these two houses, alongside 'Parveen', was a mountain stream. Higher up there were houses and land belonging to some Hindus. The right approach to their houses was on the other side but to be nearer to the road they wanted to make a path through this stream. On this route the Hindu passers-by used to look into the courtyard and veranda of 'Parveen', violating the privacy of our girls. This dispute eventually went up to the British Deputy Commissioner of the district, Mr. Kennedy. His head clerk was a Hindu who wrote him notes in favour of the Hindus, so Mr. Kennedy took the other party's side. With great difficulty he was persuaded to visit the site and see for himself. He came but treated his visit as a mere formality and started to leave without properly examining the situation or listening to the complaint. My father was not even given a hearing. The Hazrat Maulana was standing there, and as the Deputy Commissioner made to leave, he stepped forward, took hold of Mr. Kennedy by his collar and said to him: "Where are you going? Isn't it your duty to listen to him properly and examine the situation thoroughly?"

Witnessing this scene, my father and all others were utterly dumbfounded — such boldness in the face of a Deputy Commissioner, one who was British and also younger and stronger than the Maulana! To manhandle a government official could itself constitute an offence. Everybody waited to see what would happen next. But by the grace of God, Mr. Kennedy was so over-awed by this that he softened in response. He then listened to the complaint and inspected the area. But after returning to his office he gave his decision against us due to the influence again of his Hindu head clerk. Then the help of God came in the form of the start of the rainy season. The rain water washed away their path, and whenever the Hindus rebuilt it the rain would again wash it away. Ultimately they gave up and started using the longer route.

His forgiveness and forbearance

I know several incidents and many persons, not just one or two examples, where people caused the Hazrat Maulana so much hurt and pain that no other man could have forgiven them. But he forgave all of them and continued to treat them with utmost kindness. I have never seen anyone else doing good in return for evil to such an extent. There was a certain man to whom the Maulana had done many favours since his childhood. He committed a clear error but tried to justify it from the religion and insisted to the Maulana that what he had done conformed with religious teachings.

Although the Maulana was gentle in nature and in speaking, he would never allow truth and falsehood to be confused. He kept on explaining to him politely that religion did not support him. That man became offended and started telling people, and even writing, that the Maulana was an *'ālim bi-'amal* (a learned man only in theory, who fails to act on his principles in practice), who has knowledge of religion but when it came to applying Islamic principles to certain actions he did not follow the religion or his own learning. Hazrat Maulana must naturally have been much aggrieved by these comments but all he wrote to me was: "It is this man's generosity that he at least regards me as learned". I was absolutely amazed.

Similarly, the Hazrat Maulana had an old friend who had great regard for him, but for some reason or other he became displeased with the Maulana (which was not because of any shortcoming in the Maulana's excellent character or conduct). When his son was getting married he invited all his friends to the wedding but pointedly did not invite the Maulana, even though his sons insisted that he should be invited. As soon as the wedding was over, the Maulana visited him at his house one day to offer his congratulations. Instead of being embarrassed he said to him quite boldly: "Maulana, even though my sons much insisted that I invite you to the wedding, but I did not". The Maulana smiled and said: "You did what you thought was right and I did what I thought was right". These are the kind of virtues that are indicated in the saying of the Holy Prophet: "Imbue yourself with the Divine morals".

His prayers

In Dalhousie, the part of the house in the lower storey where I slept was directly under the room in which Maulana Muhammad Ali said his *tahajjud* prayer. I would be sleeping in the deep slumber of youth, but if I woke up during the later part of the night then in the utter silence of the mountains and the deadly hush of the forest where this house was located, I would hear the sound of the Maulana's crying before God coming through the wooden ceiling of my room. I used to wonder as to the overwhelming passion burning in his heart for the propagation of Islam and the difficulties in its way, which made a man who was so content during the day, cheerful and smiling, give up his sleep at night, unable to rest, and cry profusely like a child and plead tearfully like one in great pain. Later, after twenty years had passed and his spirituality had progressed to much higher stages, the Hazrat Maulana spent the summer, during the last couple of years of his life, at my house in Karachi. As during the summer nights it used to feel suffocating indoors, he used to say his *tahajjud* prayers outside on the terrace. My bedroom was on the upper storey and whenever I woke up during the later part of the night I used to catch the sound of him saying his *tahajjud* prayer. Now it had acquired a different form. His crying and pleading was not of an ordinary form now, but of a strange kind. It seemed as if he was in another world, in some other realm, and was chanting like a bird of paradise. What the words were, and what the prayers were, I never understood. But just as a bird calls out melodiously in the garden, similarly this man, unconscious of the world and everything in it, would be praising and glorifying God in a garden of another world, like a beautiful bird.

His physical postures and gestures during prayer were attractive and appealing to look at. The folding of the arms, bowing of the head, the performance of bowing and prostration (*raku'* and *sujud*) etc. were so beautiful, dignified and deeply moving that you wanted to keep on watching him. During the last two years of his life, when he stayed with me, whenever he raised his head from *sajda* (prostration) a light and radiance would be shining upon his countenance, which is what is mentioned in the Holy Quran in the following words: "Their marks are on their faces in consequence of prostration" (48:29).

Passion for service of the Quran

Maulana Muhammad Ali had the utmost love for the Quran and spent his entire life in the service of the Quran. It took him seven years of hard labour to complete the English translation and commentary the first time. I was a small child at that time but my maternal uncle Shaikh Razi-ud-Din Hasan, retired headmaster, told me that he used to see in Qadian that in the Maulana's office there were tables all around loaded with voluminous books in Arabic, English and Persian, such as dictionaries and commentaries of the Quran. While writing, he would be bending over one table or another consulting those books. He said that seeing the room full of so many large books and the Maulana going around them, he used to be amazed at the hard labour and work he was doing. After the English translation, he wrote the valuable and voluminous *Bayan-ul-Quran,* the Urdu commentary in three volumes. In this commentary he has noted all the different meanings of every word and the various explanations of every verse that had previously been given as well as other possible interpretations, and explained the reasons why he prefers the particular interpretation which he has adopted. The great benefit is that people who teach the Quran and its exegetists can find all this treasure of knowledge collected together in one place, and even if they disagree with him they are still indebted to him because it is due to his hard work that all the meanings and explanations have been brought together and they are able to adopt whichever they prefer.

In addition to these, he also wrote brief versions of the commentaries in English and Urdu. In his other books he has also drawn arguments from the Holy Quran to support his explanations. In his articles he has made rivers of knowledge to flow from verses of the Quran. His Friday *khutbas,* addresses at the annual gatherings and other speeches were all based on the Quran. During *tahajjud* and the morning prayers he recited lengthy portions from the Quran. For many years, in Lahore and at mountain resorts in the summer, he taught the Quran from a number of different aspects. At home he would teach the Quran to the women and children. He always himself read and corrected the proofs of the English and Urdu translations and commentaries. On journeys I have myself witnessed that whereas people take other books to read, he always carried a copy of the Holy Quran in his briefcase, reading it when he had free time in the train. In short, he never got tired of reading and teaching the Holy Quran. Even during his final illness, when the doctor administered morphine injections to ease the pain of angina, the influence of the anaesthetic could not make him sleep at the time of his *tahajjud* prayers. He called me in the later part of the night and asked me to read the Quran to him. We did not turn on the light in order to help him to go back to sleep, and I read out the Quran to him by torchlight. In that dim light if I made any mistake in reading, he would correct me even in his semi-conscious state. After finishing my office work in the afternoon, I would visit him and he would ask me to read out from the Holy Quran to him. To sum up, he loved the Quran passionately.

On 29 September 1950 his condition deteriorated greatly. His pulse was failing, so the doctor advised me not to go to the office because his heart could stop at any time. At that time the Hazrat Maulana was unconscious. As soon as he regained some consciousness he called me and told me something. But his voice was so faint that I could not hear what he was saying. Eventually I put my ear near his mouth and heard his very feeble voice. And what was it? He knew his condition was critical, but what was he worried about? His wife or children? His property or money? Some worldly matter? No, what he said was:

> "Our duty is to take the Quran to the world. The Quran will then do its own work."

This was his last will which I conveyed to the *Jama'at* in my speech at the annual gathering after his death, and now I record it in writing.

The Merciful God heard our prayers and he began to improve miraculously. We thought that his recovery took place because our prayers were answered, which would also be a reason. But above that, the reason was that God wanted the new edition of the English translation of the Holy Quran to be completed by his hands. So after his critical condition had passed, for the whole of the next year as the proofs of the new edition kept arriving from England, the Maulana read and corrected them with his trembling hands while lying on his death bed, reclining with the pillow raised. He finished the last proofs only a few days before his death. Hazrat Mirza Ghulam Ahmad had exhorted his community as follows:

> *"O you indifferent, unaware one! gird up your loins to serve the Quran, before the call is sounded that your life is over."*

The Hazrat Maulana had acted on this instruction in a way that is hard to equal.

His love for the Holy Prophet Muhammad was so great that he wrote books both in English and Urdu on the life and teachings of the Holy Prophet, in which he presented his character, personality and magnificent work in the best possible light. Whenever he came across any objection against the Holy Prophet, his family or his companions, he would not rest until he had written a reply to it. During his last days, he saw an obnoxious book by an American author about Hazrat A'ishah. He marked the objectionable passages with his trembling hands and started to write a short book in reply but he did not live to complete it.

While mentioning the rivers of knowledge and wisdom that the Hazrat Maulana made to flow, I recall a dream my father, Dr. Basharat Ahmad, had in the early days when he was working in the Civil Hospital, Campbellpur, from 1914 to 1916, which he recounted to me at the time. It was that in his dream he and I were sitting on the rear facing, back seat of a *tonga*[2] and on the distant horizon there was a man standing who was so tall that while his feet were on the ground his head reached the sky. My father was told (or he thought) that this was Hazrat Data Ganj Bakhsh.[3] He was walking towards us and as he approached us his height was diminishing to human proportions, until when he was close to us we recognised that he was Maulana Muhammad Ali. Seeing him, I said: "Please pray for me". The Hazrat Maulana replied: "I will do so, but you must pray for yourself as well". The interpretation of this dream, as to what it says about the Hazrat Maulana, is that in God's estimation his eminence and greatness is such that his feet are on earth but his head has reached the sky. Renouncing the world and giving up the prospects of a bright worldly future, he had gone to sit at the feet of Hazrat Mirza sahib as an ascetic and then for the rest of his life he stood and remained above worldly concerns, trampling them under foot. His head being in the sky indicates that his thoughts were about spiritually elevated matters and his knowledge was conferred upon him by God. The name of Data Ganj Bakhsh also contains wonderful indications. Just as the

---

2. Horse drawn passenger carriage.

3. A most renowned and revered Muslim saint whose tomb in Lahore is visited from far and wide. His real name was Ali Hujwiri (d. 1071 C.E.).

Data sahib settled in Lahore and was buried here, similarly the Maulana was destined to come and settle in Lahore, do his best work here and be buried in this city. In addition, the words Data Ganj Bakhsh indicate clearly that the Hazrat Maulana is such a *Data* (meaning one who gives generously and liberally) who would give treasures of knowledge to the world. Curiously, it was only a short time after this dream that, in 1917, his long series of writings began to be published, starting with the English translation and commentary of the Holy Quran, and continued till his death.

Incidents showing effect of his literature

I now illustrate by some incidents how God caused the seeds sown by him to spread far and wide all over the world.

1. In Karachi Mr. Yusuf Haroon who, after serving as Chief Minister of the Sindh, later became the Pakistan High Commissioner in Australia, told me that once when he was touring a small town in Australia an Australian came to see him and began conversation in this way: "I heard that you, the High Commissioner of Pakistan, are visiting here so I have come to ask something. In your country there is a city, Lahore, where there is an author called Muhammad Ali who has written a translation and commentary of the Quran. Having read it, I and all my family have become Muslims. Now when I learnt about your arrival, I have come to ask you some questions about Islam." Mr. Haroon told me: "I became worried that he thought every Pakistani would be a scholar of Islam. I had to put him off by a tactful ploy."

2. The visit to Lahore of Miss Kuterman, Chief Reporter at the London office of the famous Turkish newspaper *Ulus,* and her meeting with Maulana Muhammad Ali, has already been mentioned. I was also present on the occasion when she visited the Maulana at his residence and told him how she received guidance from his translation of the Quran and kissed his hands with reverence.

3. Once the Hazrat Maulana came to me in Bombay, not for sightseeing, nor for socializing, but with the aim that dominated his mind, that of making arrangements to send the magnificent

literature that he had produced on Islam to the world. In this connection a meeting was held in the Islam Club Chowpatty under the
chairmanship of Sir Nur Muhammad, attended by the leading
Muslim figures of Bombay. After the Maulana's speech, Sir Karim
Bhai, baronet, rose and said that during the Second World War, he
was living in London when that city was being bombed day and
night. It was a time of great worry and anxiety. In a London club,
an eminent Englishman asked him: "At such a time you are not
looking perturbed or anxious. What is the reason?" Sir Karim said
to him: "I have a book which I read every morning and it gives me
peace of mind." The Englishman asked him to show him that
book. That book was the Hazrat Maulana's English translation of
the Quran. So Sir Karim gave him that translation to read. After a
fortnight the Englishman came back to him and said: "I want to
become a Muslim. What do I need to do?" Sir Karim got him to
recite the *Kalima* to bring him into the fold of Islam.

4. Once in Karachi, Syed Miran Muhammad Shah, who had
been Speaker of the Sindh Assembly for many years and was now
a minister in Sindh, invited me to a tea party. As the Hazrat Maulana was staying with me at that time, I asked the Shah sahib if
I could bring my brother-in-law along, to which he replied: "Do so
by all means". At the party I introduced the Maulana only as my
brother-in-law. After a while Miran Muhammad Shah came to me
and said: "Why didn't you introduce the Maulana properly? You
kept saying he was your brother-in-law, but you didn't say that he
is that famous author and translator. Let me tell you that if his
English translation of the Quran had not reached me by chance
during my college days, I would have become either an atheist or
a Christian". At the same party there was a Muslim from South
India who had been vice-chancellor of Mysore university there.
He also made similar remarks about the Maulana.

5. In New Delhi the prayer centre of the Lahore Ahmadiyya
Jama'at was opposite the Badshahi Mosque and study classes in the
Holy Quran were held there in the evening. Once a stranger came
up the stairs and after the class he said he wanted to say something.
He told us that he was, at that time, a sub-Registrar in U.P. When he
was studying in Aligarh he came into the clutches of a Christian
missionary and was ready to became a Christian. Seeing this, one of

his friends in the student hostel gave him a copy of *Muhammad And Christ,* one of the Maulana's early writings. After reading that book a great change came in his thinking, and in his next meeting with the missionary he started asking him critical questions with the result that the missionary put an end to their meetings. That visitor concluded by saying: "Later on I studied some more of your literature, and today passing by here and seeing your signboard, I came to see you."

Iqbal

Dr. Sir Muhammad Iqbal, who had earlier been a great admirer of the Ahmadiyya Movement and Ahmadis, later became an opponent for some reasons. When he was suffering from his final illness, Maulana Muhammad Ali went to see him despite his opposition to the Ahmadiyya Movement — so magnanimous and generous was the Maulana. During their conversation, Iqbal said:

> "Maulana, please do something for the Muslim youth of today. They are turning away from religion more and more everyday."

The Maulana, referring to Iqbal's poetry and speeches, said:

> "You have done great work for them yourself."

Hearing this, Iqbal wept and said:

> "Maulana, everyone is impressed by my words, but there is no practical effect." [4]

Raising funds

These are only a few examples of the hundreds of such events that have occurred. As to the future, God alone knows how much more success and support He is going to give to the noble aspirations of the man who planted these seeds. This labourer in Allah's cause, like a tiller of the land, cared not for the coldness of the winter or the heat of the summer, nor about his own health or illness, but continued to struggle day and night to plant the seed of

---

4. The Iqbal incident is related by Mr. Faruqui in his article in *Paigham Sulh,* 10–17 October 1979, p. 7.

Islam on as large a scale as possible. He personally made greater financial sacrifices than he could afford, and before making an appeal for funds he used to announce his own contribution first. Because of his appeals, parsimonious people were worried about listening to his speeches and preferred other speakers whose speeches were of high standard but they did not appeal for funds for fear of losing popularity. The Hazrat Maulana also used to appeal to those of his friends and sympathisers who were outside the Movement, though he knew that asking for contributions is to make yourself unpopular.

Although the Maulana was not inclined by nature to mix with the rich and wealthy, nonetheless for the sake of asking for donations for the propagation of Islam he would go and knock on their doors. Once in 1942 he visited the Muslim state of Junagarh. There the Nawab welcomed him and showed him much hospitality and honour but gave nothing in donation. In those days I was stationed in district Thana near Bombay. I wrote to the Maulana requesting him to honour me with a visit as he was so near. He accepted the invitation and when he came he delivered a lecture on the future of Islam to a small group of respected Muslim figures. They were astonished to learn what useful work was being carried out. His speech created such a favourable impression that it would have been easy to raise twenty to twenty-five thousand Rupees. However, a lawyer who was rather emotional stood up and said: "All of us should become Ahmadis". This caused a commotion in the audience and the atmosphere became hostile to some extent. As a result, only ten to eleven thousand Rupees were collected. Even on that the Hazrat Maulana bowed to Allah in gratitude.

In 1945 the Hazrat Maulana came to Bombay and delivered lectures on the imperative need for the propagation of Islam and for financial sacrifices for this cause. These made a very good impact but the anti-Ahmadiyya Muslim clerics, upon learning of his success, started a campaign of opposition through newspapers and meetings. This alienated the Muslim public and the opportunity was lost to lay a magnificent foundation for the work of the propagation of the Quran. Someone else in his place would have been disheartened due to disappointment after such success and would have returned to Lahore to avoid facing the hostility and opposition.

But the Hazrat Maulana on such occasions always showed the courage of a lion and he extended his stay for an indefinite period. Everyday he would go through all the newspapers and immediately reply to the objectionable articles. The President of the *Jami'at-ul-Ulama* of Bombay wrote a letter to the Maulana in which he did not even greet him with *assalamu alaikum* because he regarded the Maulana as a *kafir*. The whole letter was full of offensive and hurtful material, as well as containing threats and ordering him to leave Bombay. Someone like me would have been too angry to reply or would have replied in strong language. But the Hazrat Maulana responded by addressing him courteously. Writing out the complete form of the Islamic greeting *assalamu alaikum wa rahmatullahi wa barakatuhu,* he asked the president what was his verdict now in view of the Quranic order to Muslims "say not to any one who offers you salutation, You are not a believer" (4:94). He also clearly explained his beliefs and mentioned the services to Islam of Hazrat Mirza sahib and the Lahore *Jama'at* and appealed to him. The president did not dare to answer the letter but continued with his opposition through newspapers and speeches. In spite of all this opposition, a considerable amount of donations were received from enlightened Muslims, although not as much as expected.

Later, during his stay in Karachi, the Hazrat Maulana approved and adopted the plan of sending sets of books to the libraries of the world, each set containing the English translation of the Holy Quran, and books such as *Muhammad The Prophet* and *The Religion of Islam*. At the annual gathering of the *Jama'at* that year he appealed for donations for it. Then during his next stay in Karachi he continued his efforts in that direction, which were blessed by God with much success. This has led to the seed of the complete knowledge of Islam being planted all over the world in most of the major libraries. It is Allah Himself Who will enable it to grow and bear fruit — "the most excellent Patron and the most excellent Helper" (the Quran, 8:40).

Once, a saintly member of our *Jama'at* who received communications from Allah, namely, Hazrat Syed Asadullah Shah, had a revelation which he mentioned in a letter to me, saying that he had never had a revelation of such force and severity. This revelation came to him in a dream with such force that he woke up panting and sweating due to its intensity and asking for a drink of cold water despite it being a very cold, wintry night. The revelation was as follows:

Kāna khalīfatu-nā fil-arḍi yuqālu la-hū Muḥammad 'Alī. Huwa lailat-ul-qadri wa ilai-hi marji'u-kum.

which translated is: "There is Our *khalifa* on earth whose name is Muhammad Ali. He is the *lailat-ul-qadr* (meaning that just as heavenly blessings and light descend during *lailat-ul-qadr*, so have they come through this man) and to him you must turn". Along with this revelation, the Shah sahib had other intimations in which the words "four hundred thousand" occurred. I wrote about these revelations to the Hazrat Maulana and added: "I hope that Allah may allow four hundred thousand Rupees to be raised for your scheme of sending books to the libraries of the world". The Hazrat Maulana wrote back saying: "I am praying that the words 'four hundred thousand' refer to the number of people who will join the *Jama'at* and serve Islam on a permanent basis". He used to say: "It is always possible to raise money but what I am concerned about is workers, as they are hard to get."

Death of Maulana Muhammad Ali [5]

During his stay in Karachi in 1950, Maulana Muhammad Ali had a serious heart attack. In spite of being greatly weakened by this, he continued to serve Islam and the Quran as he had ever done all his life. When he came to Karachi the following year, his health was poor. Nonetheless he used to read proofs of the English translation of the Holy Quran most of the time lying in bed. It was at this time that some members of the *Jama'at* caused him much distress. He was already weakened due to heart problems for the past eighteen months or so. He used to say that it was not his illness but those people who had broken his heart. Even in that condition he started to meet this opposition, although we tried to force him to stop because the doctor had strictly instructed that he

---

5. The account in this section has been supplemented by a detailed article Mr. Faruqui published in *Paigham Sulh,* dated 7–14 October 1981.

must avoid such stress and work. At last his strength and stamina gave in and his condition started to deteriorate day by day. During the last two or three days he called me and said: "Inform the *Jama'at* of my condition and request them for prayer. If Allah wills me to live longer then may He relieve me from this distress, and if not then may I drift into the eternal sleep of peace". So I sent a telegram to Lahore.

The third day after this was 13th October 1951, and as it was the 10th of *Muharram* I was at home because it was a public holiday. When we mark his death on 13th October every year, the events and scenes of that day come before my mind's eye like a film. It dawned as a normal day. Although he had grown weak he did not appear to be in any danger, except that when the doctor came and wanted to give him an injection he said (in English): "Doctor, please let me die in peace". The doctor said: "No, please don't talk like that", and gave him his injection and left. The doctor this time did not indicate even indirectly that there was any danger.

At about 11.30 a.m. my wife came to me greatly alarmed and told me to come immediately as the condition of the Hazrat Maulana was very grave. I ran to his room and at that moment he took his last breath, and that holy man had left us forever. Within a short time relatives who could be informed started gathering. It was decided that the body be taken to Lahore that same evening on the Khyber Mail train service which departed at about 6.30 p.m. Some years earlier I had gone through a harsh ordeal in transporting my father's body from Bombay to Lahore, so I was not about to make the same mistakes again.[6] It was already 1 p.m.

---

6. In his article in *Paigham Sulh,* 7–14 October 1981, Mr. Faruqui has at this point recounted in detail that ordeal in transporting the body of his father, Dr. Basharat Ahmad, to Lahore from Bombay by train, where he died in April 1943 while staying with him. He writes:

"Due to inexperience, I had considered it sufficient to reserve a four berth carriage on the Frontier Mail from Bombay to Lahore, not knowing that a coffin was only allowed to be transported in a separate four-wheel carriage, and that such a carriage could never be attached to a Mail train. When we arrived with the coffin at Bombay Central Station, the railway staff only allowed the coffin to be taken in to the platform because it was blocking the

Due to the *Ashurah* holiday, all offices and shops were closed. First of all, arrangements were to be made to take the coffin by Khyber Mail, and that too in the passenger carriage with us. I and the late Hazrat Maulana's elder son Muhammad Ahmad, who was himself in the railways, went to the Divisional Superintendent of Karachi railway who lived near my house. Due to the favour of God upon us, he not only allowed us to take the coffin by Khyber Mail the same day but also to keep it with us in the same carriage, instead of insisting on carrying the coffin in a separate compartment attached to the train. He also telephoned to reserve for us a six-seat compartment, which usually would not have been available at such short notice. In all my life, it had never happened, except rarely, that the apparently impossible became possible in this way. At this occasion the Almighty was showing regard and honour for this holy man whose soul had gone to his Maker but whose body we were planning to take to Lahore that same day.

---

gate, and strictly prohibited it to be taken on board the train. I was asked to obtain permission from Mr. Perry, Deputy General Manager of the Railway, so I ran to phone him but he was not available at home. Meanwhile our relatives and the baggage had gone on board while the coffin was still being prevented from embarkation by the railway staff. As I returned and we argued with the railway staff, the train whistled to leave. I boarded the train with the intention of pulling the emergency stop chain in case the train moved off without the coffin. Suddenly a clerk came running saying that Mr. Perry had granted permission to board the coffin, so we rushed to put it in the carriage. However, the railway staff then demanded that we buy a ticket for it costing over one thousand Rupees. By chance, a friend of mine had sufficient cash, but there being no time to buy it we and the ticket issuer jumped on the train as it moved off and the ticket was bought on board. When we arrived in Lahore the railway staff were astonished and angry to see a coffin emerging from a passenger compartment. They demanded to know who allowed it on board, and I replied: Mr. Perry. They ordered the compartment to be sealed after our disembarkation and telephoned ahead for it to be disinfected when the train reached its destination, Peshawar. I have heard that an enquiry was subsequently conducted into the incident at Bombay railway station to find out which clerk had wrongly stated that Mr. Perry had given permission. That clerk could not be identified. I firmly believe that this was an act of Divine intervention and that God sent someone to deliver us from that intractable predicament for the sake of my father's honour so that his body could complete its final journey with dignity."

After obtaining all these permissions and facilities we returned home and I set Muhammad Ahmad to making telephone calls
to Lahore and other places to convey the news, while I went to
make arrangements for the funeral necessities and the coffin. For
this I decided to seek information from Chaudhry Amjad Khan, an
administrator who had lived in Karachi for long and was familiar
with the city. It was now about 2 p.m. As he had no phone, I had
to go to his residence and this involved crossing Bandar Road.
There I found a huge crowd like a wall in my way. Being the 10th
of *Muharram,* Shia processions mourning the martyrdom of Imam
Husain were passing along that road, which was closed to traffic.
These processions in Karachi are miles long and we had to catch
the train at 6 p.m.! I left my car there and attempted to pass
through the crowd on foot, but the police as well as people in the
crowd angrily tried to stop me, thinking that I was trying to get to
the front for a better view of the processions. Listening to their
abuse and jostled by them, only Allah knows how I managed to
cross the road safely, having passed through the procession in
which swords were being wielded and then through the spectators
on the other side of the road. Then, tired and perspiring, I made
my way through side streets with great difficulty to reach the
building where Chaudhry Amjad Khan lived. His flat was on the
fourth or fifth floor and the lift was out of order. When I finally
reached his flat, breathless and exhausted, I was informed by a
lady inside that he had gone out and would return in the evening.
I cannot put into words the terrible disappointment that I felt
on hearing this. The plan of travelling that evening began to seem
an impossibility.

I now had to return through the same crowd. This time their
abuse and jostling made no impact on me in view of my anguish
that it was almost 3 p.m. now and no arrangements had been made
for preparing the body or procurement of a coffin, while the whole
of Karachi was shut down for the 10th of *Muharram.* Penetrating
through the crowd somehow, I got on to the road but I found it
impossible to pass through the crowd on the other side of the road
to reach my car. I could do nothing but walk along the middle of
Bandar Road, against the flow of the oncoming processions. It was
while I was in that state of utter dejection and sorrow, having no

more strength or energy left, that the mercy of Allah came into action, not for my sake but for that saintly man whose last rites I was unable to perform by myself. Suddenly, right in the middle of the road, there stood before me a police inspector, like an angel sent from above to help me. He recognised me,[7] gave me a salute, and said: "Sir, what are you doing here? Can I be of any help?" I did not know him but obviously he recognised me. It was nothing but Divine assistance that, out of the thousands of police officers in Karachi, I was confronted by one who recognised me. I told him my story and he immediately instructed a police constable to take me to the imam of the 'Police Lines' mosque from whom a shroud, which was kept in reserve, and other necessities could be obtained by giving the reference of the inspector, and then to accompany me to a certain coffin maker who may have a ready-made coffin available. I thanked the inspector from the bottom of my heart. The next worry was that, as the whole city seemed to be out watching the processions on Bandar Road, whether these people would be found at home. Further Divine mercy came to the rescue in that all the funeral necessities were obtained. The coffin maker was also found at home and he had a fine coffin of the right size, which was also airtight and met the railway regulations. Thus it was that a beloved of Allah undertook his last journey according to plan, safely with dignity.

I then returned home and informed that all arrangements were complete and we would be able to leave in the evening. At about 5 p.m. Maulana Abdul Wahhab, his personal assistant for many years, washed the body, we then held the funeral prayers on the lawn of my house and left by Khyber Mail. Without help from Allah, it would have been impossible to make the arrangements on a public holiday so quickly.

The Hazrat Maulana's body, accompanied by his relatives, was brought to Lahore with great dignity on the train, arriving the following evening. It was met by a huge crowd of friends who carried the coffin in their hands. The funeral prayers were held in

7. Mr. Faruqui held, at that time, the high civil service post in Karachi of Chief Secretary in the Government of the Sindh province.

the Ahmadiyya Buildings mosque, led by his elder brother Maulana Aziz Bakhsh, where the late Maulana had delivered Friday *khutbas* for nearly 38 years and said his daily prayers. Then members of the *Jama'at* carried the coffin on their shoulders to the Miani Sahib cemetery, in which the late Maulana had selected his burial spot during his life, and he was laid to rest at nearly 10 p.m.

Spiritual experiences

The Hazrat Maulana was not in the habit of mentioning his spiritual experiences, and due to his humble nature he would rarely mention his visions, revelations and true dreams. The case of the men commissioned by God is different, as they proclaim their experiences and revelations by Divine command. As the Hazrat Maulana held no Divine office he would not himself mention his spiritual experiences out of humility, but if questioned on this matter he would say something.

Once I asked him if he had ever experienced *Lailat-ul-Qadr*. He replied:

> "Yes. Once in Dalhousie I was saying *tahajjud* prayers during the last ten days of Ramadan. When I was reciting *At-tahiyyat* suddenly a very bright light appeared in the window. At first I thought that on the road below some people were passing carrying gas lamps, but then I realized that no one would be out in these backwoods at 3 a.m. Then I looked through the window to see what the light was, and saw that it was illuminating even the trees on the mountain far ahead. That scene disappeared as I watched it. Then it occurred to me that it was the illuminations of *Lailat-ul-Qadr* that Allah had shown me."

Once in Karachi in 1950, again during the last ten days of Ramadan, it was the night of the 29th. During *tahajjud* prayer I found myself deeply engrossed and felt as if my soul was melting away at Allah's threshold. I was in the state that I did not want to rise up from *sajda*. During the pre-dawn meal, where the Hazrat Maulana was also present, I said to him that I thought this night had been the *Lailat-ul-Qadr*. He replied:

> "I think so as well. Last night when I was saying the *'Isha*

prayer, after reciting the *Fatiha* the verse *innā anzalnā-hu fī lailat-il-qadr* came again and again to the tip of my tongue but I recited some other verses. During *tahajjud* just now, when I was reciting the *darood,* suddenly a light spread in front of my eyes. I looked up and saw that the sky and the clouds were illuminated by this light. After a short while this scene disappeared."

Prediction of creation of Pakistan [8]

In 1946 I was Deputy Commissioner of Karachi. The Governor of the Sindh was Sir Francis Mudie, one of the few British who, being fully aware of the machinations of the Hindus, was a great sympathiser of the Muslims and supporter of the Pakistan cause. As I had previously served as his secretary, he used to tell me his inner feelings, especially as he found me to agree with his views. Even after I became Deputy Commissioner of Karachi, he used to have discussions with me in favour of the creation of Pakistan. His support of the Muslims being no secret, the Hindu press used to refer to his name sarcastically, from his initials F.M., as "Fateh Muhammad", and send telegrams against him to the Viceroy Lord Wavell and the Secretary of State for India Lord Pethick-Lawrence. But Sir Francis Mudie, instead of being overawed or intimidated, was undeterred and used to fight these complaints.

A British cabinet mission came to India in 1946, headed by Lord Pethick-Lawrence, to discuss the question of Indian independence, and on their way from London to New Delhi they stayed in Karachi for one night as guests of the Governor of the Sindh. The following morning it was my official duty, as District Magistrate, to be present at Karachi airport for their departure. After they left, the Governor beckoned me to accompany him in his car. As soon as the car moved off, he said to me: "Faruqui, they are not going to give us Pakistan". This appeared to be the final, irrevocable decision of the British government. Naturally, I was filled with sadness and gloom, but due to the confidential nature of this news I could not mention it to anyone. Prayer to God was needed, but

---

8. The account given here has been supplemented by a more detailed article Mr. Faruqui published in *Paigham Sulh* dated 6–13 October 1982.

I myself was far from having closeness to the Almighty. Maulana Muhammad Ali was in Dalhousie at the time, and I knew full well how much his prayers were accepted by God. The matter being confidential, I wrote to him only these lines:

> "The cabinet mission stayed the night in Karachi and proceeded to New Delhi: 'What the eye can see, cannot be brought to the lips; I am in bewilderment as to what the world will become'.[9] Sir, please pray specially for the future and welfare of the Muslims."

The Hazrat Amir replied by return post as follows:

> "I am always praying for the welfare and the religious and worldly success of the Muslims. But on receiving your letter I was praying specially during the night when I heard the voice: *Pakistan Zindabad.*[10] Although there appears to be despondency everywhere, it seems that it has been decided in heaven that Pakistan will come into being. I will continue to pray to God in this matter."

I became satisfied upon hearing this prophecy but my tranquillity soon vanished when the cabinet mission proposed a kind of united India and the Muslim League accepted it and joined the future government to be headed by Nehru. Not only did the dream of Pakistan appeared to come to an end with that, but I became uncertain about the fulfilment of Hazrat Amir's prophecy. However, events changed their course when that plan failed because of the obstacles placed by the Congress party. At last Pakistan came into existence the following year, and towns and cities echoed with the chant *Pakistan Zindabad,* fulfilling the Divine revelation received by that man of faith.

Vision of God
When I went to Lahore from Karachi in December 1950 for the annual gathering, I found the Hazrat Maulana very frail due to his final illness. One day when I visited him in the afternoon, he had just risen from his siesta. I was the only person with him and

---

9. This is a poetic verse quoted by Mr. Faruqui.
10. Meaning: 'Long live Pakistan'.

contrary to his habit he mentioned a spiritual experience without prompting. He said:

> "I have just seen a wonderful vision. I saw that I was an infant and sitting in the lap of a very comely, handsome person. I was made to understand that He was Allah Himself. This person clasped me to his bosom as a mother takes her son to her bosom with love. This expression of love also made me restless so that I unbuttoned his shirt (as if even the shirt did not intervene between them), put my arms around him and clung to him. These words then escaped from my lips: *Allāhumma, anta muḥibbī, fa-j'al-nī min aḥibbā'ik* — O Allah, You love me, so make me from among those who love you." [11]

This lover of God went to His lap to bask in His love. O God, shower Your abundant blessings on the soul of this virtuous, sincere man. As he did good to us and indeed to the whole of humanity, may You reward him in even greater measure. But most of all, kindle in our hearts a spark of the passion that burnt in his heart for the propagation of Islam and the Holy Quran and enable us to follow in his footsteps. May You safeguard and help the *Jama'at* founded by Muhammad Ali which he put to the service of Islam and the Quran so well and successfully for almost forty years. Let the work of the propagation of Islam and the Holy Quran, which Your vicegerent carried out with such toil and labour, thrive and succeed, so that Islam may spread in the world and humanity take refuge in the fold of the Holy Prophet Muhammad, may peace and the blessings of Allah be upon him. O Allah, this world will perish without Your Islam and Your Quran. Come to its rescue. *Amen, O Most Merciful of the Merciful ones!*

---

11. In an article in *Paigham Sulh,* 10–17 October 1979, Mr. Faruqui adds here: "Just then someone else came in. I wanted to relate this vision to him but the Hazrat Maulana stopped me by an indication. However, I do not think there is any harm in relating it after his death."

Appendix 1

List of writings of
Maulana Muhammad Ali

In this Appendix are provided two chronological lists of the books (List I), and tracts, pamphlets and booklets (List II) written in English and Urdu by Maulana Muhammad Ali from 1902 to 1951. These have been reproduced from the original such lists in *Mujahid-i Kabir* after thorough checking and making revisions and additions as found necessary. However, due to the large number of his writings, there may still be some omissions in these lists, and in a few cases a slight inaccuracy in the year of publication.

An asterisk placed after the title of a writing indicates that it has been translated into one or more other languages, including translations of English writings into Urdu and vice versa. Translations have been done into so many languages throughout the world that it is impossible to provide a complete record. The second column shows the year of first publication. The third column indicates the page of this biography on which the publication of that writing is first mentioned (the column being blank if the writing is not mentioned in the biography). If the biography provides further information about a book, other than just mentioning its publication, then the book is also listed in the Index.

Names of the Urdu writings are given here with full transliteration marks for accurate representation, although elsewhere in this book transliteration is not used for simplicity.

I. Books

35. *Al-Masīḥ al-Dajjāl wa Yājūj wa Mājūj* *	1931	p. 196
36. Early Caliphate *	1932	p. 196
37. Muhammad The Prophet, Revised Edition *	1932	p. 196
38. *Maqām-i Ḥadīth,* Revised Edition *	1932	p. 196
39. Introduction to the Study of Hadith *	1932	p. 196
40. The History and Doctrines of the Babi Religion	1933	p. 196
41. Selections from the Holy Quran	1933	p. 196
42. Collection and Arrangement of the Holy Quran *	1934	p. 197
43. The Religion of Islam *	1936	p. 190
44. Introduction to the Study of the Holy Quran *	1936	p. 197
45. Founder of the Ahmadiyya Movement *	1937	p. 197
46. The Muslim Prayer Book *	1939	p. 272
47. *Niyā Niẓām 'Ālam* *	1942	p. 269
48. The New World Order *	1944	p. 269
49. A Manual of Hadith *	1944	p. 270
50. *Al-Muṣliḥ al-Mau'ūd,* Revised Edition	1944	p. 272
51. History of the Prophets	1946	p. 272
52. *Wafāt-i Masīḥ wa Nuzūl-i Masīḥ* [1]	1947	p. 273
53. Living Thoughts of the Prophet Muhammad *	1947	p. 271
54. Prayers of the Holy Quran	1948	p. 272
55. *Zinda Nabī kī Zinda Ta'līm* *	1948	p. 271
56. *Aḥādīth-ul-'amal* *	1948	p. 270
57. *Panjsūra:* Five Chapters of the Holy Quran (text, transliteration, translation)	1948	
58. The Anti-Christ, Gog and Magog	1948	
59. English Translation of the Holy Quran with Arabic text and commentary, Revised Fourth Edition *	1951	p. 367

---

1. This was a re-publication of the 1920 book *'Īsawiyyat kā Ākharī Sahāra.*

II. Tracts, pamphlets and booklets

1.	*Review of Religions,* English and Urdu	1902–1913	p. 28
2.	*Ayk Nihāyat Ḍarūrī I'lān*	1914	p. 102
3.	*Mas'ala Kufr wa Islām*	1914	p. 102
4.	*Mairay 'Aqā'id*	1914	
5.	*Nubūwwat aur Kufr per Ayk Ayk Bāt*	1915	
6.	*Jihād Kabīr*	1915	p. 154
7.	The Ahmadiyya Movement — I. The Founder	1917	p. 171
8.	The Ahmadiyya Movement — II. The Doctrine	1917	p. 171
9.	The Ahmadiyya Movement — III. Prophecy	1917	p. 171
10.	The Ahmadiyya Movement — IV. The Split	1918	p. 171
11.	*Jalsa Sālāna per Tabādala Khiyālāt kai lī'ay Miyān Ṣāḥib ko Da'wat*	1918	p. 184
12.	*Mairī Taḥrīr main Lafẓ Nabī kā Isti'māl*	1918	
13.	*Nabī yā Muḥaddath*	1919	p. 184
14.	*Shanākhat-i Ma'mūrīn*	1919	p. 171
15.	*Khilāfat-i Islāmiyya bi-rū'ay Qur'ān wa Ḥadīth*	1920	p. 171
16.	*Ḍarūrat-i Mujaddidiyya*	1920	p. 171
17.	*Ad'ā-i Nubūwwat*	1921	p. 184
18.	*Inkār-i Nubūwwat aur 1901*	1922	p. 184
19.	*Radd Takfīr Ahl-i Qibla,* 3rd edition² *	1922	p. 173
20.	*Ākharī Nabī* *	1922	p. 184
21.	*Ḥaḍrat Masīḥ Mau'ūd kā Ḥalfī Bayān*	1923	p. 184
22.	*Khwāja Ghulām Farīd of Chachrān wa Ḥaḍrat Mirzā Ghulām Aḥmad*	1923	

---

2. According to the Urdu *Mujahid-i Kabir* this booklet was published in 1922. That was in fact the 3rd edition, as shown by the announcement in *Paigham Sulh* dated 4 October 1922. The 2nd edition had been published in 1920, and the first probably in 1916.

---

3. This is a different, briefer version of the 1918 booklet of the same title.

Appendix 2
About the Authors

 **1. Muhammad Ahmad** (1920–1981) was the principal author of *Mujahid-i Kabir*. As Mr. Naseer Ahmad Faruqui wrote in his Urdu obituary: "The credit for this unique book, which greatly impresses all those who read it, belongs to Muhammad Ahmad. It was he who carried out the underlying research for this writing and did the greater part of the work on it." [1]

After obtaining M.A. in English and Arabic from Government College Lahore, he succeeded in the competitive examination for government service and joined the Indian and then the Pakistan railways as officer, serving from 1945 to 1980, and reaching the highest executive positions in his profession. After retirement he devoted himself entirely to the mission of the Lahore Ahmadiyya *Jama'at,* but fell ill soon after and died in January 1981 while under treatment in London.

Quoted below are extracts from the English obituary in *The Light* by Mr. Naseer Ahmad Faruqui:

"Muhammad Ahmad was by nature shy, sedate and humble. To others, he was gentle, considerate, and helpful. … After an outstanding educational record, with a double M.A. in English and

---

Arabic, he joined the Superior Railway Service. He had an un-blemished record of scrupulous honesty, hard work and conscien-tiousness in the discharge of his official duties. At his funeral, some of his superior Railway officers were present. I heard remarks from them such as 'I had never seen an officer of such integrity and sense of responsibility'; 'He was a perfect gentleman'; 'He never did anything wrong or unworthy'.

He would work late into the evenings or nights, sometimes for his official duties, but sometimes also for his other love — service of Islam and Ahmadiyyat. In the latter cause, his contribution was multifarious but special mention must be made of *Mujahid-i Kabir,* the biography of the late Hazrat Maulana Muhammad Ali. … In compiling this perfect biography of that great man, Muhammad Ahmad must have done months, nay years, of research and exten-sive reading of all the books, journals, letters and other literature having bearing on the period in which his father played such an outstanding role in the religious history of Islam and Ahmadiyyat. The marshalling and arrangement of the relevant material he thus gathered and put into his book could not have been bettered.

Muhammad Ahmad's work in the revision of the seventh edi-tion of the English translation and commentary of the Holy Quran, now under print, was equally painstaking. For that revision, the original spadework done by Dr. Zahid Aziz was the most thorough job I have ever seen. But to collate and give final shape to the suggestions made by Dr. Zahid Aziz and several others, Muhammad Ahmad spent long evenings with me after his office hours. He was known for hard work during office hours too. But he did not seek relaxation and rest, much as he deserved them. For him official duties and after that his labour of love in the service of Islam brooked no relaxation or rest.

He had also completed a new edition of the English transla-tion of the Holy Quran without the Arabic text for more extensive propagation of the Holy Book, being lesser in cost. He had done work, in addition, on the revision of the book *The Religion of Islam,* another world-famous work of his father. He had collected his father's Friday and Eid sermons and letters to his followers which were published in the *Paigham Sulh,* the Urdu weekly of the Lahore Ahmadiyya Jama'at. ... The work of editing and compiling them will be a great service to Islam and Ahmadiyyat, whoever completes the work initiated by Muhammad Ahmad. ...

Muhammad Ahmad was working in the cause of Islam even when he was in Railway service. For that he had to work after office hours and even on holidays. When he was about to retire from Railway service, he got attractive and lucrative offers for other employment. His reply was: 'No, thank you, but I now want to dedicate my life to the whole-time service of Islam and Ahmadiyyat'. ...

Unless illness or absence from the place prevented him, Muhammad Ahmad was regular in attending Friday and Eid congregations, the *Jalsa* (annual gathering of the community) or any other meeting, the Holy Quran *Dars* and the meetings of the Executive Committee of the Anjuman or its General Council meetings. In the last two-named meetings his contribution was always sensible, balanced and sometimes brilliant, reminding us of the times when his late father used to preside over these meetings with enviable wisdom and sublime insight.

It was with some difficulty that Muhammad Ahmad was persuaded to address a Friday congregation and the annual *Jalsa*. His sermon and speech respectively amazed the audience with his knowledge, ability and perfection of presentation, raising hopes that one day he would make outstanding contribution to the intellectual and spiritual leadership of the community. Alas! That was not to be. And that is the most grievous aspect of the great loss the community has suffered in his death." [2]

Mirza Masud Baig, General-Secretary of the Anjuman at the time of Muhammad Ahmad's death, wrote in his Urdu obituary:

"The late Muhammad Ahmad had since 1951, after the death of Maulana Muhammad Ali, been elected as member of the General Council and the Executive Committee of the Anjuman. He attended the meetings regularly and was rarely absent. Soon all

---

2. From *The Light,* 8 March 1981, pages 7–11.

members realized his soundness of opinion, understanding of affairs and support of truth. During this time he rendered honorary service in different areas, especially publications and free distribution. He worked very hard, quietly and speedily.

The heirs of Maulana Muhammad Ali were receiving royalty on his books at ten percent of the sale price. ... Before his second journey to England in mid-January [for medical treatment] Muhammad Ahmad submitted a legal document, on behalf of all the heirs, to the Anjuman stating that from January 1981 they would relinquish royalty, which should remain with the Anjuman in a separate fund to be used for the free distribution of the English translation of the Holy Quran and *The Religion of Islam*. ...

Muhammad Ahmad was an able and scholarly man. The living proof of his accomplished authorship is the magnificent book *Mujahid-i Kabir,* published in 1962, which he wrote while pursuing his career. No one could have written a better biography of Maulana Muhammad Ali, and it is a book that will remain an eternal memorial to his father." [3]

2. Mumtaz Ahmad Faruqui (1899–1978), elder brother of Naseer Ahmad Faruqui, qualified as an Electrical Engineer from the U.S.A. and served in the Indian State Railways from 1927 and then in Pakistan Western Railways from 1947, receiving a distinguished service medal from the Pakistan government. Both during his service and after retirement in 1963, he wrote some books and booklets as well as numerous articles on Islam and the Ahmadiyya Movement. His books include *Anecdotes from the Life of the Prophet Muhammad, Anecdotes from the Life of the Promised Messiah* and *The Crumbling of the Cross*. Besides being a co-author of *Mujahid-i Kabir,* he produced a condensed English translation of this biography in 1966 under the title *Muhammad Ali, the Great Missionary of Islam.* He served the Anjuman in various capacities including Officer Incharge Publications for a time during the 1960s.

---

3. *Paigham Sulh,* 18–25 February 1981, pages 9–10.

Supplement to the Second Edition

In this Supplement, added in the second edition of *A Mighty Striving,* we are providing additional information relating to some of the events covered in the book. This material has not been incorporated within the main body of the book itself as it would have substantially changed the page structure of the first edition, requiring a revision of the page numbers in the index.

1. Comments in *Calcutta Review* (p. 32)

Calcutta Review's claim in its April 1902 issue that Hazrat Mirza sahib was employing an Englishman as editor of the *Review of Religions,* who was using the pseudonym Muhammad Ali, was reproduced in the *Review of Religions* as follows:

> "From the evidence of *English idioms* — peculiarly English, and never used by strangers — it is clear as daylight to anyone that his deliverances in this newly started *Review of Religions* are written or concocted by a European — an Englishman (herein again, curiously enough, reproducing exactly Muhammad and his Syrian Christian "Archangel Gabrael!"). To the European "behind the scenes" we say, remember the old "Archangel Gabriel's" fate! His motive may be good, but he is in a false way, and he can only come to hurt (though it may not be the sudden and compulsory death of his predecessor): let him take heed in time."

(*Review of Religions,* October 1902, p. 390)

2. "Plague incident" (p. 44–46)

This incident was reported at the time in *Badr,* 8-16 May 1904, which gives its date as 4 May. It was also related verbally by Hazrat Mirza sahib in a report in *Badr,* 6 June 1907, p. 2, taken from *Tashhiz-ul-Azhan,* the magazine edited by Mirza Mahmud Ahmad. It is also reported by Mufti Muhammad Sadiq, who was an eye-witness to the incident, in his book *Zikr-i Habib,* p. 123–124. This shows that prominent Qadiani *Jama'at* figures accepted that this sign was evidence that Maulana Muhammad Ali was a faithful follower of the Promised Messiah, and not one who was disobedient.

3. Rules and regulations of Sadr Anjuman Ahmadiyya (p. 52)

Very shortly after Hazrat Mirza Ghulam Ahmad published his Will, *Al-Wasiyyat,* in which he announced the creation of the Sadr Anjuman Ahmadiyya, the rules and regulations of this body and of its Council of Trustees (*majlis-i mu'timidīn*) were published in *Badr,* 16 February and 23 February 1906. The heading was: *Regulations of the Sadr Anjuman Ahmadiyya Qadian, Approved by Hazrat Mirza Ghulam Ahmad, the Promised Messiah.* According to these rules, any change to the composition of the Council of Trustees, by the appointment and removal of members, was to be made by the Promised Messiah during his life, and by the Council itself after his lifetime (and even during his lifetime by his permission). All property and income of the Ahmadiyya Movement was to be owned by the Council of Trustees.

At the end of these regulations, it is stated: "The Promised Messiah appoints the following men as members and office-holders of the Council of Trustees." There then follows the list of members given on p. 52 of this book.

4. Hazrat Maulana Nur-ud-Din's true feelings (p. 95–97)

(i) During his visit to Lahore in June 1912, Maulana Nur-ud-Din saw for the first time the mosque built at Ahmadiyya Buildings. It was reported in the Ahmadiyya community newspaper *Badr*:

> "Hazrat *Khalifat-ul-Masih* [Maulana Nur-ud-Din] stayed at the residence of Dr. Mirza Yaqub Baig, which is situated within its [Ahmadiyya Buildings'] bounds…
>
> After arriving in Lahore, the first thing which pleased Hazrat *Khalifat-ul-Masih* was the Ahmadiyya mosque, built in the middle of Ahmadiyya Buildings. He was the first to enter the mosque. After saying two *nafal* of *salat,* he said many prayers for the founders of the mosque, for their children, and for their future generations. He prayed

so deeply that he said: 'I am sure these prayers of mine have reached the *arsh* of Allah'. We congratulate the *Jama'at* of Lahore on this good fortune. In the construction of this mosque, the entire *Jama'at* of Lahore has participated, each according to his means. However, when it was being built we saw that the man who more than anyone else took pains over its construction and displayed the greatest zeal was our honoured friend Dr. Syed Muhammad Husain Shah. May Allah the Most High reward them all. After his return to Qadian, Hazrat [Maulana Nur-ud-Din] also expressed his pleasure over the mosque in his first talk on the Quran."

(*Badr,* 27 June 1912, p. 3, col. 2)

Here two founding members of the Lahore Ahmadiyya Movement are mentioned, Dr. Mirza Yaqub Baig and Dr. Syed Muhammad Husain Shah, who were, according to the the the Qadiani *Jama'at* propaganda, rebellious against Maulana Nur-ud-Din and whom he was castigating *at this very time.* But the reality is clear from this report, that the Hazrat Maulana was highly pleased with them. His own words from his speech at Ahmadiyya Buildings were reported in the next issue of *Badr* as follows:

"This is the mosque which has pleased my heart very greatly. I have prayed much for its founders and those who assisted in its building, and I am sure that my prayers have reached the threshold of God (*arsh*)."

(*Badr,* 4 July 1912, p. 6, col. 3)

(ii) In 1913, in two of his last Friday *khutbas* that Hazrat Maulana Nur-ud-Din delivered before his death, he defended Khwaja Kamal-ud-Din against the allegations of the supporters of Mirza Mahmud Ahmad. Khwaja Kamal-ud-Din was in Woking (England) at the time, establishing the Woking Muslim Mission.

In the *khutba* delivered on 17 October 1913, Hazrat Maulana Nur-ud-Din said:

"You think ill of others. Khwaja Kamal-ud-Din does not work out of hypocrisy. He works only for Allah. This is my belief about him. Of course, he can make mistakes.

I am happy with his works. There is blessing in them. Those who spread mistrust about him are the hypocrites."

(*Khutbat Nur,* p. 622, from *Al-Fazl,* 22 October 1913. *Khutbat Nur* is available online on the Qadiani *Jama'at* website www.alislam.org)

In the *khutba* delivered on 7 November 1913, Hazrat Maulana Nur-ud-Din said:

"Kamal-ud-Din is a good man. He is doing religious work. If he makes a mistake, [remember that] only God is pure, none besides Him, the only One free from all defects and weaknesses, and possessor of all perfect attributes. He is engaged in a good work. None of you can compete with him. Ignore mistakes, and look at goodness. He calls me his master again and again....

Kamal-ud-Din has not gone there [to England] for personal ends. He has not cared even for his family. Someone wrote that Kamal-ud-Din has shaved his beard [in England]. The other day I saw his photo. The beard is there. I think that even if he had shaved his beard, I would still say about the work for which he has gone there that it is good. If there is some fault, I myself overlook it. There is no one who is free from faults."

(*Khutbat Nur,* p. 631, from *Al-Fazl,* 12 November 1913)

The report of the above *khutba* ends as follows:

"(After this, the *Huzoor* sat down. He felt weak. He then rose and said:) Can any of you do the work which Kamal-ud-Din is doing? If he commits a fault, what does it matter? He is a man who used to earn thousands. I teach the Quran. Many new points of understanding have occurred to me. How can it be known that I did not teach it insincerely? I taught it with sincerity before and do so now as well." (*ibid.,* p. 632)

This report shows that although Hazrat Maulana Nur-ud-Din felt so physically weak that he had to sit down during the *khutba,* yet he rose again merely to continue defending Khwaja Kamal-ud-Din and concluded his *khutba* at that point.

In his final comment, Hazrat Maulana Nur-ud-Din has indicated that just as some people question Khwaja Kamal-ud-Din's sincerity, they might as well question his own sincerity. He has thus placed the proof of Khwaja Kamal-ud-Din's sincerity on an equal level with proof of his own sincerity.

5. Muhammad Ali Jauhar praises English translation of the Quran (p. 159–160)

Besides the quotation from the biography of Muhammad Ali Jauhar (d. 1931) given on pages 159–160, there is a letter by him to Dr. Mirza Yaqub Baig published in *The Islamic Review,* December 1919, written after he and his brother Shaukat Ali received a gift of copies of the English Translation of the Holy Quran from Dr. Mirza Yaqub Baig. The letter not only extols the qualities of the translation but shows the personal affection Jauhar entertained for the Lahore Ahmadiyya leaders Maulana Muhammad Ali, Khwaja Kamal-ud-Din and Dr. Mirza Yaqub Baig.

We quote below extracts from this lengthy letter, which is dated 24 February 1918:

> "I have to commence this letter with profuse apologies for being so late in acknowledging your most precious gifts on Shaukat's behalf and my own. Need I assure you that you could not have sent to us anything more acceptable than the beautiful copies of the Holy Quran rendered into English by my learned and revered namesake, Maulana Mohammad Ali Saheb. I had read the specimen pages in the **Islamic Review,** that welcome reminder of our dear brave Khwaja's mission in Europe, and I was anxiously awaiting the announcement that copies could be had in India, or even in England. When the Indian papers first published the announcement so anxiously and eagerly awaited, I asked Shaukat to write at once to you to send us two copies per V.P.P. He was just about to write to you when on a Friday the two copies, so elegantly printed and bound, reached us. I took them to the Mosque to show them not only to Shaukat, who had just preceded me thither, but also to other Musalmans here, and I can assure you they gave us all a pleasure that nothing could equal.

I would have written to thank you for the rich gift that very day, but, as you had asked me to express my opinion also on this great achievement, I put off even thanking you. ...

I have gone through the Preface, and here and there through some introductory notes prefacing the various chapters and footnotes, and have, of course, glanced through the sectional headings and the index, and greatly admire the general arrangement. As for the English rendering, I am impressed so far as I have read with the simplicity and precision and the adherence to the text which indicate the reverence due to God's own Word from a true believer. ... the great thing is that the great task has been accomplished, and there now exists in at least one European language a rendering of the holy Quran done by a true believer and not by a scoffer, by one who believes every word of the Book to be God's own, every word to be true and full of light, every word consistent with what has gone before and comes after, every word capable of easy interpretation...

Well, I must now take leave of you. If you see Maulvi Mohammad Ali thank him for me as a Moslem who feels proud of his devoted and fruitful labours, and shares with him the privilege of at least the most beloved of names in the entire world. "Bulbul hameen ki qafia-i-gul shawad bas ast."

If you write to my stalwart Khwaja send him my kisses for his shaggy old beard."

(*The Islamic Review,* December 1919, p. 445–449)

6. Tribute by Shaikh Yaqub Ali Turab, editor *Al-Hakam*

Shaikh Yaqub Ali Turab was a leading writer and journalist of the Qadiani *Jama'at*, who started the journal *Al-Hakam* in 1897 which reported the activities of the Ahmadiyya Movement and the talks of Hazrat Mirza sahib. As noted elsewhere in this book, he was a staunch supporter of Mirza Mahmud Ahmad and played a prominent role in opposing Maulana Muhammad Ali and the Lahore Ahmadiyya elders during the events of the Split in the Movement.

At the death of Maulana Muhammad Ali, he wrote the following tribute, which was published in *Paigham Sulh,* 26 December
1951, reproduced from *Al-Hakam,* Karachi, 14 November 1951.

Passing away of Maulana Muhammad Ali:

'Speak well of your dead'

Respected Maulvi Muhammad Ali, President of the Ahmadiyya Anjuman Ishaat Islam Lahore, died in Karachi on
13 October 1951. *Innā li-llāhi wa innā ilai-hi rāji'ūn.*
I personally felt such a shock at the news of the death of
the Maulana as if a dear brother of mine had died. This
feeling is not something imaginary, but a real fact. For
years we grew up under the care of one spiritual father,
and reached adulthood. After the death of the Promised
Messiah, we stayed united around one hand during the first
khilafat. At the beginning of the second *khilafat,* the respected Maulvi sahib separated from us on the grounds of
some differences. This is not the time to discuss the nature
of those differences. He has now passed away, and we too
are travelling on the same road which leads to death. His
affair is now with Allah. Bearing in mind the command of
the Holy Prophet quoted above, I will mention his good
qualities.

Sometimes people use a difference of opinion as the
basis for hostility and animosity. This is not worthy of a
true believer. A true believer never deviates from doing
justice, even to one with whom there is animosity, because
departure from justice is a sin. I have observed and studied
the Maulvi sahib very closely since the year 1897. We
worked together. He entered the Ahmadiyya Movement
with sincerity and true belief. He devoted his life to the
service of the Movement, and earned the approval and
praise of the Promised Messiah. No one can deny what the
Promised Messiah said and wrote about the Maulvi sahib,
and it is because of these sacred words that I have always
held feelings of respect for the deceased. Although I frequently wrote in refutation of some of his views, and wrote
much, Allah knows that there was no spite or malice, and

I never forgot his services. Even though we were, so to speak, at war with him, nonetheless whenever I went to Lahore I would meet all the honoured brethren. We would meet like brothers. Certainly we would debate the differences, but when we would take leave, feelings of love and fraternity would rise up in our hearts, and we could detect the effects of our old connections.

Due to his academic excellence, respected Maulvi Muhammad Ali held a position of distinction throughout his years of study, always attaining the highest marks. And it is also a fact that, even while a student, he was virtuous and righteous. For this reason, he was held in high regard by his teachers and fellow-students. I made his acquaintance when he was appointed to the Islamia College, Lahore, but the real connection began when he joined this Movement. Maulvi Muhammad Ali was born in a village called Murar, in the state of Kapurthala, in an honourable and righteous family of land-owners. His father, Hafiz Fateh Din, was a *hafiz* of the Holy Quran. Another man belonging to this family, Maulvi Muhammad sahib, was a fellow-student of mine in Ludhiana in the school of Maulvi Muhammad Farooq. Eventually, he joined Maulana Nur-ud-Din in Jammu, and once visited Qadian.

So the Maulvi sahib was born in a noble family, and after having attained the highest accomplishment in his education, when he stepped into a worldly career, and looked at the hopes and the promise based on his period of education, he would have risen high in the world had he continued along this path, and reached a distinguished official position. But Allah had willed otherwise for him. He entered the Movement, and the Promised Messiah wished him to serve it. This young man agreed, and he agreed with a truthful heart. Discarding all the hopes and aspirations, for the service of the Movement in obedience to his master he vowed to serve Islam with the pen. And he performed this service till the day of his death. His services, by means of scholarship and by means of the pen, are vast. If Allah please, I shall write in detail about his work.

To have differences with him is a separate matter. It does not mean that I or anyone else should find fault with his work, now that he is no longer in the world. The service he rendered to the Movement in Qadian till 1914 is magnificent, and it is an example to young men to employ their talents with such determination, zeal and sincerity.

At the beginning of the second *khilafat,* he had differences, and went to Lahore, taking a group with him, and started work. Till the end, he remained active in the work, and continued the writing of books which he had earlier begun.

There is no doubt that his writings acquired fame in different countries of the world and in different languages. He gained all this from the Promised Messiah. Our differences with him are at an end. In the Promised Messiah, we were sons of the same father, and now at his death we grieve as we do at the death of a relation.

There were differences among the Companions of the Holy Prophet as well, even leading to war. But the Quran says: "We shall remove whatever of rancour is in their breasts" (15:47). At the end they had clean hearts. May Allah produce the same cleanliness and purity in our hearts. The Maulvi sahib completed the natural span of his life and died. It would have been better if he had lived a while longer, but this was the time of death in the knowledge of Allah. We too shall pass away, and other generations will come and pass away. And in the history of the Movement, there shall remain the mention of the achievements of the respected Maulvi Muhammad Ali sahib.

I express my sympathies to his family with sincerity. I share in their grief. Although I had differences with him, there was love for him in my heart.

Index

see under Mirza Ghulam Ahmad

Azad, Abul Kalam, 111, 199

Aziz Bakhsh, 3, 4, 5, 6, 10, 11, 213–214, 217, 275, 393, 425, 520

Baddomalhi, 202, 481

Badr/Al-Badr, 32, 36, 43, 46, 54, 55, 77, 78, 82, 88, 92–93, 96, 97, 99, 100, 118, 132, 135, 535, 536, 536–537

Baghdad, 247, 269, 358

Baha'i religion, 196, 255

Bahishti Maqbara, 51, 56, 223

Bai'at (Pledge): of HM, 7, 10, 11, 12, 22, 63, 98, 101, 130, 133, 137, 138, 139, 216, 217, 218, 290, 400; after HM, 51, 102, 119, 136, 324; with M. Nur-ud-Din, 98, 136; with M. Mahmud Ahmad, 103–105, 109, 119, 143, 324

Barahin Ahmadiyya, 38, 63, 147, 226

Basharat Ahmad, Dr., 31f., 33, 79, 83, 105, 131, 141, 145, 150f., 157, 176, 239, 245, 269, 391, 437, 445, 447, 451, 501, 509, 516f.–517f.; Quran *dars* of, 200–201, 291–292, 294–295; work after retirement, 201, 207; death and life-sketch of, 290–296; see also *Mujaddid-i Azam*

Bashir Ahmad Minto, 312

Batala, 12, 49, 59, 207, 445

Batalvi, Muhammad Husain, 13, 343

Battersby, Abdullah, 428

Bayan-ul-Quran (see also 'Quran: Urdu translation'), 25, 177, 181, 295, 346, 409, 507; publication of, 165–168, 254; features of, 168–169; modern reviews of, 184–186; condensed edition, 195

Beirut, 411

Berlin, mission and mosque, 178–179, 187, 202, 208–211, 256, 273–274, 466f.; mosque survives war, 274, 312

Bhera, 62, 79, 437

Bhopal, 62, 203; Begum (ruler) of, 84

Bible, 71, 171

Bolus, E.J., 258

Bombay, MA visits, 175, 268, 305–306, 456, 500, 510, 513–514

Books, by MA: scheme of distribution of, 359, 362–363, 371–375, 380–381, 387, 399, 404, 408–409, 412, 413, 418, 464–465, 514; importance of spreading, 359–360, 372–373; objections to, answered, 374, 375–378, 417; translations of in other languages, 269–270, 289, 290f., 405, 409, 411, 412, 434; influence of, 430–431, 433, 435, 436, 454, 457, 486–488, 510–512, 543; see also 'Writings'

Bukhari, 25f., 144, 169, 270, 304, 428; Urdu translation of, see *Fazl-ul-Bari*

Burma, 405

Calcutta, 27, 75, 76

Calcutta Review, 32, 535

Charagh Din, 50, 55, 116

Chaudhry Sir Shahab-ud-Din, 5, 190, 192, 490

Cheema, Muhammad Hasan, 212

China/Chinese Muslims, 289–290, 409

Christianity, 76, 172, 232, 301, 454, 486

Christians, 7, 32, 33, 172, 206, 212, 218, 258, 427, 479, 486, 493

Civil & Military Gazette, 411

Comrade, 159, 161

120; makes himself autocratic over Anjuman, 116, 124–125, 127, 128, 136, 142, 460; transfers Anjuman's income to another body, 129; earlier belief that Holy Prophet was last Prophet, 135; alleges that HM changed his claim to prophet in 1901, 137–139, 183, 331–332, 334, 337–340; fury of against Lahore members, 139, 238, 333; forbids followers from listening to MA, 143–144; attacks MA about Quran translation, 150, 238; claim of to be *Muslih Mau'ud,* 153, 272; alleges 'Ahmad' prophecy applies to HM, 155, 205; wrong beliefs of, 183, 204–205, 220, 234, 323, 325, 332–333; allegations against by own followers, 199, 239; meets MA in Dalhousie, 234; rejects invitations to debate with MA, 236, 325–331; challenged by MA to take oath, 331–333; accused of falsehood by MA, 334–335; invited to *mubahila* by MA, 336–341; does not take oath on beliefs, 341; retracts beliefs at Munir Inquiry, 342–345; see also Qadiani *Jama'at*

Mirza Ghulam Ahmad, Hazrat, the Promised Messiah: MA's acceptance of, 7–12, 400, 427, 541, 542; in Lahore, 6, 10, 50, 58–59, 115–116; letters of to MA, 13–16, 23; stay of MA with, 17, 21, 23, 24, 25, 28, 57, 111, 400–401; opinion of about MA, 27–28, 30–33, 37, 46, 108, 442, 541; and plague incident, 44–46; revelations of about MA, 38–44; gives pen in vision to MA, 39–40, 454, 488; no claim of being

prophet, 10, 131–139, 337, 370; did not change claim in 1901, 137–139, 183–184, 331–332, 334, 337–338, 341; chooses MA for mission, 34–36, 39, 43–44, 50–51, 94, 112, 301, 400, 417; inheritance of for MA, 252, 282, 310, 382, 430, 459; wants Quran translated into English, 35, 38–39, 152, 167, 238, 377, 452; vision fulfilled in Quran translation, 38–39, 147; MA's tribute to about acquiring knowledge from him, 25–26, 167, 168, 279, 367, 369, 372, 376, 398; mission of, to spread Quran, 152–153, 242; wants books written on Islam in English, 35, 190, 238–239, 283, 377, 378, 399, 417; why he formed *Jama'at,* 248–249, 359–360; passion of to propagate Islam and Quran, 10–11, 34–35, 44, 84, 264, 281, 302–304, 310, 372, 399; love of for Quran, 291, 302–303, 306, 385, 457; revelation of about Muslim victory, 249, 384; represented by MA in court cases, 48; makes Anjuman his successor, 51–54, 88, 112, 536; note of, empowering the Anjuman, 52–54, 120, 122, 128; revives true Islamic governance, 85, 99; death of, 58–60, 79, 86, 97, 116, 275; speech of MA after death of, 59–60; meaning of *khalifa* after, 136; did not call other Muslims as *kafir,* 103, 109; doctrine of prophethood of, how and when invented, 131–139; use of word *nabi* for, 132–136, 138, 329–330; and 'Ahmad' prophecy, 155; status exaggerated as with Jesus, 220; MA's book about, 197; and Lahore members, 275–276; and Islamic